THE WHOLE CHILD

NEW TRENDS IN EARLY EDUCATION

THE WHOLE CHILD

NEW TRENDS IN EARLY EDUCATION

JOANNE HENDRICK, Ph.D.

Chairor, Department of Nursery School Education,
Santa Barbara Community College,
Santa Barbara, California

SECOND EDITION

with 76 illustrations

The C. V. Mosby Company

ST. LOUIS • TORONTO • LONDON   1980

Cover photograph by Richard Pierce

The C. V. Mosby Company
11830 Westline Industrial Drive, St. Louis, Missouri 63141

Library of Congress Cataloging in Publication Data

Hendrick, Joanne, 1928-
  The whole child.

  Bibliography: p.
  Includes index.
  1. Education, Preschool. I. Title.
LB1140.2.H44 1980   372.21   79-9135
ISBN 0-8016-2145-3

GW/VH/VH 9 8 7 6 5 4 3 2 1   02/B/228

☐ Preface

The Whole Child is intended to equip beginning teachers of young children with a fundamental point of view and specific skills so they may function effectively with the children in their care. It cites research where it is possible to do so and resorts to common sense and practical experience with children where research does not provide the answers.

This revised edition has moved with the times and includes research that supports the value of preschool education and new information on moral development, exceptionality, and nonsexist education. An entire chapter has been added on helping children cope with crises—including those related to divorce, death, hospitalization of themselves or their families, and child abuse. The chapter on the cognitive self has been amplified, and the one focussing on physical development now contains charts that provide a comprehensive plan for developing the physical abilities of children, as well as material on relaxation techniques and movement education. All chapters include updated research citations and more current References for Further Reading.

The overall philosophy of education expressed in the book remains unchanged, however, since it still does not appear that we have yet reached the point where we have the final answer on how children learn and why they behave as they do. Therefore, the book remains eclectic in terms of learning theory—sometimes recommending behavior modification as an approach and sometimes urging the reader to identify other reasons for behavior and to work toward the mitigation of behaviors that are malign.

The recommendations for curriculum are based on the assumption that children do indeed pass through stages of development—that growth is an orderly, predictable, sequential process, and that a good teacher or parent can help the child grow to his full potential by recognizing these stages and by offering suitable experiences that nurture and challenge him as he develops.

The book is sexist in the sense that it refers to the teacher as ''she.'' I can only beg the reader's indulgence for this flaw, since writing was simply clearer if one sex was consistently ascribed to the teacher and the other used to identify the child. However, I am well aware that teachers and children come in both genders.

Finally, this book assumes that the function of education is to care for the whole child and help him flourish. For this reason, it focuses on five aspects of the child's self rather than stressing various curriculum topics such as science or outdoor play. It is my belief that once the educational needs of these selves are understood, a specific curriculum follows naturally and is relatively simple to generate.

I owe so much to so many people that it is a well nigh impossible task to mention them all. The contribution of students and parents to my point of view and knowledge has been considerable, as have the innumerable things my staff have taught me. In addition, I am forever in the debt of my mother, Alma Green, who not only began some of the first parent education classes in Los Angeles, but also taught me a great deal about young children and their families.

I am also indebted to Sarah Foot and her wonderful Starr King Parent/Child Workshop, which convinced me that my future lay in early childhood education, and to my own children who bore with me with such goodwill while I was learning the real truth about bringing up young people.

As far as the book itself is concerned, I would like to thank Murray Thomas for teaching me, among other things, how to write and John Wilson for convincing me that some things remained to be said and changed in early education. To Chester and Peggy Harris I am forever indebted for a certain realistic attitude toward research, particularly in the area of cognitive development.

My thanks go to Lou Grant and Marilyn Statucki for commenting on the manuscript with such patience and tact. Also, additional thanks to Ms. Donna Dempster of Cornell University and Ms. Ellen Nash of The Ohio State University for their valuable suggestions used in revising this text. I am also grateful to Dorothy Annable for locating count-less books for me and to my typists, Anne Muñoz and Sue Nitsch, for making sense out of an incredible chaos of imaginative typing and illegible scrawls.

Finally, I wish to acknowledge a special debt to Jason Lo'Cicero and Richard Pierce for their sensitive portraits of young children, to Brooks Institute and School of Photography, and to Terry Jones, Head Start Coordinator of Santa Barbara County, who generously granted permission for me to use her collection of Head Start pictures.

Writing a book about early childhood education has been exciting—it has been an interesting task for me to set down what I know about this area. If it is also helpful to beginning teachers and to the children they serve, I will be pleased indeed.

Joanne Hendrick

☐ Contents

PART SEVEN

Working with special situations

PART EIGHT

What lies ahead?

PART ONE

Beginning to teach

Santa Barbara City College Children's Center

1□ What makes a good day for children?

There was a child went forth every day,
And the first object he look'd upon, that object he became,
And that object became part of him for the day or a certain part of the day,
Or for many years or stretching cycles of years.

The early lilacs became part of this child,
And grass and white and red morning-glories, and white and red clover, and
    the song of the phoebe-bird,
And the Third-month lambs and the sow's pink-faint litter, and the mare's foal
    and the cow's calf,
And the noisy brood of the barnyard or by the mire of the pond-side,
And the fish suspending themselves so curiously below there, and the
    beautiful curious liquid,
And the water-plants with their graceful flat heads, all became part of him.

The field-sprouts of Fourth-month and Fifth-month became part of him,
Winter-grain sprouts and those of the light-yellow corn, and the esculent
    roots of the garden,
And the apple-trees cover'd with blossoms and the fruit afterward, and
    wood-berries, and the commonest weeds by the road,
And the old drunkard staggering home from the outhouse of the tavern
    whence he had lately risen,
And the schoolmistress that pass'd on her way to the school,
And the friendly boys that pass'd, and the quarrelsome boys,
And the tidy and fresh-cheek'd girls, and the barefoot negro boy and girl,
And all the changes of city and country wherever he went.

His own parents, he that had father'd him and she that had conceiv'd him in
    her womb and birth'd him,
They gave this child more of themselves than that,
They gave him afterward every day, they became part of him.

The mother at home quietly placing the dishes on the supper-table,
The mother with mild words, clean her cap and gown, a wholesome odor
    falling off her person and clothes as she walks by,
The father, strong, self-sufficient, manly, mean, anger'd, unjust,
The blow, the quick loud word, the tight bargain, the crafty lure,
The family usages, the language, the company, the furniture, the yearning and
    swelling heart,
Affection that will not be gainsay'd, the sense of what is real, the thought if
    after all it should prove unreal,
The doubts of day-time and the doubts of night-time, the curious whether
    and how,

Whether that which appears so is so, or is it all flashes and specks?
Men and women crowding fast in the streets, if they are not flashes and
  specks what are they?
The streets themselves and the façades of houses, and goods in the windows.
Vehicles, teams, the heavy-plank'd wharves, the huge crossing at the ferries,
The village on the highland seen from afar at sunset, the river between,
Shadows, aureola and mist, the light falling on roofs and gables of white or
  brown two miles off,
The schooner near by sleepily dropping down the tide, the little boat
  slack-tow'd astern,
The hurrying tumbling waves, quick-broken crests, slapping,
The strata of color'd clouds, the long bar of maroon-tint away solitary by
  itself, the spread of purity it lies motionless in,
The horizon's edge, the flying sea-crow, the fragrance of salt marsh and shore
  mud,
These became part of that child who went forth every day, and who now
  goes, and will always go forth every day.

WALT WHITMAN
There Was a Child Went Forth (1871)

Teaching preschool children can be one of the best, most deeply satisfying experiences in the world. Children aged 2 to 5 go through fascinating, swiftly accomplished stages of development. They are possessed of vigorous personalities, rich enthusiasm, an astonishing amount of physical energy, and strong wills. With the exception of infancy, there is no other time in human life when so much is learned in so brief a period (Bloom, 1964).

This phenomenal vigor and burgeoning growth present a challenge to the beginning teacher that is at once exhilarating and frightening. The task is a large one: the teacher must attempt to build an educational climate that enhances the children's development and whets their appetites for further learning. The milieu must also nourish and sustain emotional health, encourage physical growth and muscular prowess, foster satisfying social interactions, enhance creativity, develop language skills, and promote the development of mental ability. Moreover, this must all be garbed in an aura of happiness and affection in order to establish that basic feeling of well-being which is essential to successful learning.

With such a large task at hand, it is not surprising

that the beginning teacher may wonder somewhat desperately where to begin and what to do. The following material should help the student gain skills and confidence as well as organize what is known about preschool education into a logical whole so that she may become a relaxed and effective teacher of young children.

No doubt the reader is anxious to press on to discussions of discipline or eating problems or teaching children to share—these are valid concerns of all teachers of preschool children. However, it seems wise to take time first for an overview of whether preschool education is effective and what should go into a good day for young children. What elements should be included when planning the overall curriculum? Once these elements are clearly in mind, we can turn to a consideration of more specific problems and recommendations.

CAN EARLY EDUCATION MAKE A DIFFERENCE?

For more than a decade, research on approaches to early childhood education has sought to investigate the effectiveness of various kinds of programs in changing the behavior and enhancing the development of young children. The results of these investigations have been at times discouraging and at times heartening. On one hand, the Westinghouse Report (Cicerelli, Evans, and Schiller, 1969), the Hawkridge study (Hawkridge, Chalupsky, and Roberts, 1968), and more recently a report by Abt Associates (Stebbins, St. Pierre, Proper, Anderson, and Cerva, 1977) have found little evidence of persistent, across-program change on measures of intellectual ability. In this same tradition, Jencks (1972) challenged the efficacy of education as an antidote to poverty.

On the other hand, work by Bereiter and Englemann (1966), Hodges, McCandless, Spicker, and Craig (1971), Gray and Klaus (1970), Guinagh and Gorden (1976), Karnes, Teska, and Hodgins (1970), Lane, Elzey, and Lewis (1971), and Weikart, Bond, and McNeil (1978) indicates that preschool programs can be effective change agents. Further encouraging results were identified by Horowitz, who concluded, following a comprehensive review of environmental intervention programs in the early 1970s, that preschool intervention programs devised as experimental programs produced "fairly large IQ and achievement gains" (Horowitz and Paden, 1973, p. 391).

Even more exciting, however, is the newer study by Irving Lazar and associates (Consortium on Developmental Continuity: Education Commission of the States, 1977; Lazar, Hubbell, Murray, Rosche, and Royce, 1977), who investigated the persistence of preschool effects. The results of this carefully done follow-up study of a number of experimental infant and preschool programs current in the 1960s are so significant that they merit special review in these pages.

In essence, Lazar asked, "Now that these children are either in their teens or early twenties, what has become of them?" "How have they turned out?" "Did early intervention make a difference in their lives?" In order to acquire answers to these questions, each project traced as many of the experimental and control children as possible, retested them on the Wechsler Intelligence Test and, among many questions, asked *whether they had ever repeated a grade in school or had been placed in a class for educable mentally retarded children* (EMR classroom).

An analysis of the intelligence test material (both current and prior tests) led the investigators to conclude that "although evidence showed that early education can produce significant increases in IQ (over a control group) which lasts for up to three years after the child leaves the program . . . it appears that the effect . . . is probably not permanent" (pp. 19 and 20).

However, the information related to grade retention and/or placement in EMR classrooms was much more encouraging, in part because of its implications for saving public monies (Weikart, 1978), but also in terms of what the findings mean in terms of human happiness.

Even though these data vary considerably between programs (probably because different school districts have different policies on having children repeat grades), they clearly indicate that early education *can* reduce the rate of failure for low-income children,* thereby preventing much humiliation and loss of self-esteem. And if repetition of a grade would likely be humiliating to a youngster, one can only surmise what it might mean to be placed in a classroom for retarded children. Here, once again, the Lazar data provide convincing evidence that early education is worthwhile, since many fewer project children were found to have been placed in such classes. As Lazar points out, "Gordon's project showed 9.4% program children in special education compared to 30.0% control; Gray's 2.8% program to 27.4%; and Weikart's 13.8% program to 27.7% control" (p. 14), and he concludes by commenting, "The cost of teaching a child in special education classes is substantially more than if he or she could perform acceptably in the normal classroom, to say nothing of the trauma to the child of being labeled slow or retarded" (p. 14).

Despite these findings, even as this book goes to press, the argument about program effectiveness

---

*For a more complete interpretation and explanation of this study, the reader should refer to the original reports, which are well worth reading.

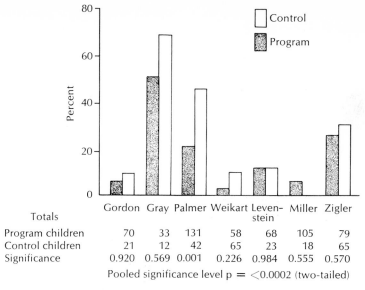

Totals	Gordon	Gray	Palmer	Weikart	Leven-stein	Miller	Zigler
Program children	70	33	131	58	68	105	79
Control children	21	12	42	65	23	18	65
Significance	0.920	0.569	0.001	0.226	0.984	0.555	0.570

Pooled significance level p = <0.0002 (two-tailed)

Percent of program and control children held back a grade.

From Lazar, Hubbell, Murray, Rosche, and Royce: *Summary report: The persistence of preschool effects.* Washington, D.C.: U.S. Dept. of Health, Education, and Welfare, 1977. (OHDS) 78-30129.

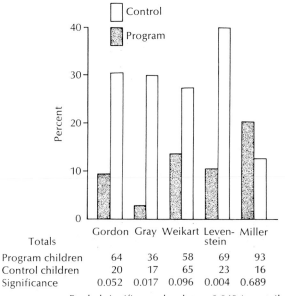

Totals	Gordon	Gray	Weikart	Leven-stein	Miller
Program children	64	36	58	69	93
Control children	20	17	65	23	16
Significance	0.052	0.017	0.096	0.004	0.689

Pooled significance level p = 0.048 (two-tailed)

Percent of program and control children in special education.

From Lazar, Hubbell, Murray, Rosche, and Royce: *Summary report: The persistence of preschool effects.* Washington, D.C.: U.S. Dept. of Health, Education, and Welfare, 1977. (OHDS) 78-30129.

rages on. At present, for example, there is strong debate taking place between the supporters of the Abt Associates' assessment of Project Follow Through (Anderson, St. Pierre, Proper, and Stebbins, 1978) and critics of that report (Hodges, 1978; House, Glass, McLean, and Walker, 1978). (Project Follow Through is the educational program designed to continue gains made in preschool with economically disadvantaged children as they attend elementary school.) Perhaps, as in the happy case of the preschool study, it may ultimately turn out that it is still too early to determine the lasting effects of Project Follow Through—only time and careful research will tell!

WHAT GOES INTO A GOOD DAY FOR CHILDREN?

Whereas one of the statistical strengths of the Lazar study is the fact that the results hold true across a number of programs, one of the questions it leaves unanswered is the tantalizing one of just exactly which ingredients in these programs have what effect upon the children, since examination reveals that programs differ in many respects in their philosophy, teaching techniques, and program content (Brown, 1977; Miller and Dyer, 1975).

The best we can do at present is to rely on somewhat cursory analyses of common program elements, as well as on experience, to identify and select features successful programs have in common. Among such analyses are the ones by Gordon (1970) and Maccoby and Zellner (1970), and it is largely the elements identified by them that are considered in this text; it is left up to the reader to investigate the unique aspects of particular programs listed in the readings at the ends of chapters and references at the end of the book.

GOOD HUMAN RELATIONSHIPS ARE A FUNDAMENTAL INGREDIENT OF A GOOD DAY*

All good preschool programs are built on the foundation of sound human relationships. Warmth

and empathic understanding have been shown to be effective means of influencing young children's positive adjustment to nursery school (Truax and Tatum, 1966), and it is apparent that genuine caring about the children and about other adults in the program is fundamental to success.

In order for warmth and personal contact to flourish, the day must be planned and paced so there are numerous opportunities for person-to-person, one-to-one encounters. In practical terms, this means that groups must be kept small and the ratio of adults to children must be as high as possible. Many occasions must also be provided where the children move freely about, making personal choices and generating individual contacts. Such arrangements permit numerous interludes where informal learning experiences can be enjoyed and where human caring can be expressed. The moments may be as fleeting as a quick hug when the teacher ties a pair of trailing shoelaces or as extended as a serious discussion of where babies come from. It is the quality of individualized, personal caring and the chance to talk together that are significant.

The parent should be included as part of the life of the school*

The day is past when parents were expected to pay their bill but leave their children at the nursery school door. Of course, cooperative schools have long demonstrated the feasibility of including the family in the nursery school experience, but today we can also point to mounting research that confirms that inclusion of the parent in the educational process, whether in home tutoring programs or the nursery school itself, results in longer lasting educational gains for the child (Bronfenbrenner, 1976; Gray and Klaus, 1970; Guinagh and Gordon, 1976; Heber, Garber, Harrington, Hoffman, and Falender, 1972; Lally and Honig, 1977).

Since it is possible to include parents in a variety of welcoming, participating ways (which are discussed in a later chapter), it is only noted here that the value of close interaction between home and school is being increasingly documented by research. Therefore, we should do all we can to make this link a strong one.

---

*Items followed by an asterisk are ones included either on the Maccoby and Zellner (1970) or Gordon (1970) list.

There should be a balance between self-selection and teacher direction—both approaches are valuable*

Value of self-selection. The idea that young children can be trusted to choose educational experiences for themselves that will benefit them goes all the way back in educational theory to Jean Jacques Rousseau and John Dewey, and at present this concept is experiencing a rebirth in England in the British Infant School, as well as continuing its tenure in the majority of American nursery schools.

Philosophical support for the value of self-selection of activities comes from as disparate sources as the self-selection feeding experiments of Clara Davis (1939) and the psychoanalytic theory of Erikson, who speaks of the preschool child's "sudden, violent wish to have a choice" (1950, p. 252). The virtue of self-selection is that it fosters independence and builds within the child responsibility for making his own decisions. It also provides an excellent way to individualize the curriculum because each child is free to pursue his own interests and to suit himself when he is free to choose.

Value of teacher-determined activities. Despite the virtues and attractiveness of the open environment, research indicates that one should not rely entirely on self-selection. At least in programs designed to serve children who come from economically disadvantaged families, it is now evident that planned, structured experiences that are teacher directed are more effective in producing cognitive gains than are programs lacking this characteristic (Bissell, 1973; DiLorenzo and Salter, 1968; Miller and Dyer, 1975). Even though the cognitive self (the part of the child that is concerned with mental activity) is only one aspect of the child's personality, adequate mental development is so closely related to success in school that promising techniques must be taken into consideration when planning a curriculum.

It would be ideal, of course, if all activities were attractive enough that the child would *want* to choose them spontaneously, but there are times when youngsters should participate in learning activities that will enhance their growth even if they are not particularly attracted to them. It isn't fair to let a child graduate from preschool with a degree in trike riding coupled with a deadly inability to put five words together into a coherent sentence.

Good curriculum must be planned with definite objectives in mind*

Evidence is mounting that formulating and carrying out a specific plan for the preschool program is fundamental to success at least when working with economically disadvantaged children (Karnes, 1973b). The value of establishing specific objectives has been convincingly demonstrated in programs having such contrasting philosophies as the Piagetian classrooms of David Weikart (Weikart, Rogers, Adcock, and McClelland, 1971) and the learning drill classrooms of Bereiter and Englemann (1966). A study of Mexican-American preschools (Nedler and Sebera, 1971) presents additional evidence that sequenced, planned learning was effective in their program. In addition, all the Planned Variation Head Start Models required clear definitions of strategies before they could be funded (Klein, 1971).

Yet the value of identifying objectives and formulating plans by which they may be reached is often questioned or ignored by early childhood teachers on the grounds that such planning may deaden creativity, spontaneity, and opportunities for self-selection (Ebel, 1970; Moskovitz, 1973). As Fowler puts it,

[Teachers fear] the formal, didactic and authority centered forms of teaching prominent in education until the development of the nursery school and progressive education movement early in this century (1971, p. 30).

Of course, one would not want the formulation of a plan to result in a return to that style of teaching; but at the same time, the beginning nursery school teacher should realize that a curriculum is not something that can be relied on to develop spontaneously as the day marches along. Days must be planned and overall goals identified and implemented to assure educational success.

Photo by Jason Lo'Cicero, Santa Barbara City College Children's Center.

There are times when the marvelous welling up of an idea or activity does take place, and these teachable moments are to be sought after and treasured— but this does not happen all the time. Nor does reliance on such events assure that every important area will be covered, that necessary goals will be achieved, or that the needs of individual children will be considered. Only planning coupled with evaluation can accomplish these objectives.

A good program should be comprehensive

An aspect of planning that deserves special consideration is that curriculum should be comprehensive in coverage. An easy way to think about this is to picture the child as being composed of a number of selves—the physical self, the emotional self, the social self, the creative self, and the cognitive self. This book is based in part on this division of the child into selves, because experience has shown that various aspects of curriculum fall rather neatly under these headings and that the five selves succeed in covering the personality of the child.

The physical self includes not only large and fine muscle development but also handling routines, since such things as eating, resting, and toileting contribute much to physical comfort and well-being. For the emotional self we consider ways to increase and sustain mental health, to use discipline to foster self-control, to cope with aggression, and to foster self-esteem. Under the heading of the social self are placed ways to build social concern and kindliness, learning to enjoy work, and learning to value the cultures of other people. The creative self covers the areas of self-expression through the use of art materials and creativity as expressed in play and applied in thought. Finally, the cognitive, or intellectual, self is considered in terms of language development, the development of horizontal and vertical curricula, and the development of specific learning abilities. This last self is the newest one to receive intensive consideration and analysis in early childhood education, and much remains to be learned in this area.

Individualization of instruction is important*

Value of suiting curriculum to each individual child. We have already reviewed research that indicates that the teacher will experience greater success if she identifies her educational goals clearly and carries out activities designed to reach these goals. The real art of teaching lies in her ability to clothe these bare-boned goals in the raiment of individual children's interests and pleasures. Fortunately, the small size and intimacy of preschool groups make it possible for teachers to know each youngster well and to plan with particular individuals in mind.

Not only should broad goals be personalized to fit the children's interests, but specific goals should be formulated to suit individual children, since every child is different and learns at his own rate. Prompt assessment of the children's skills is invaluable because it can help the teacher identify specific needs of individual children and plan in accordance with these revealed needs.

A simple test to determine whether curriculum is individualized. There are three questions the teacher can use to determine whether the curriculum she offers is individualized:

1. Can she cite some recent instances where curriculum was based on a child's specific interests?
2. Can she point to examples where a child was deliberately provided with opportunities to learn what evaluations had indicated that he especially needed to know?
3. Can she cite some examples where curriculum plans were changed because a child revealed an unanticipated interest or enthusiasm during the day?

A good program has stability and regularity combined with flexibility

Young children need to know what is likely to happen next during the day. This means that the order of events should be generally predictable. Predictability enables the child to prepare mentally for the next event; it makes compliance with routines more likely and helps children feel secure.

Los Niños Head Start

At the same time, time schedules and routines should not be allowed to dominate the school. (Sometimes this happens because of a strong-minded custodian or cook. I once knew a school where it was necessary for the children to use only half the space from 10:30 until nap time because of the custodian's routine. Sometimes overconformance to time schedules happens because teachers are creatures of habit and simply don't realize that juice and raisins don't have to be served at exactly 9:15.) Rather than sticking right to the clock, it is better to maintain an orderly but elastic schedule, where play periods can be extended when those moments occur when the majority of the children are involved in activities that interest them intensely.

A good program has variety

Children need many different kinds of experiences as well as changes in basic experiences. Research on the effects of stimulus deprivation (Casler, 1968; Dennis, 1960) and of early stimulation (White, B. L., 1968) has highlighted the value of supplying a variety of experiences even for babies, and variety should certainly be incorporated into a program for preschool children.

Many nursery school teachers think of variety of experience in terms of field trips or covering different topics, such as families or baby animals. But another kind of variety that should also be considered is variety in everyday basic learning experiences. What a difference there is between the school that has the same pet rat and bowl of goldfish all year and the school that first raises a rabbit, then borrows a broody hen, and next has two snakes as visitors. Lack of variety is also shown in schools that offer the omnipresent easel as their major "art" experience or others that set out all the blocks at the beginning of the year and leave it at that.

Children should be offered various levels of difficulty in activity materials. If the nursery school combines age levels during the day, so that 3-, 4-, and 5-year-olds play together, it is important to provide materials that are challenging for all the ages within the group. Teachers need to be especially careful to offer materials that are genuinely interesting to the older 4-year-olds and young 5-year-olds. A dearth of stimulating, fresh curricula is the most common cause of posses of children galloping through block areas and housekeeping corners, spreading destruction as they go.

The curriculum should not only offer a variety of levels of difficulty during every day, *it should also become more challenging and move from simple to more complex activities as the year progresses* and the children mature and gain competence. The nursery school curriculum should not look the same in May as it did in September.

Children need changes of pace during the day to avoid monotony and fatigue and to maintain a balance of kinds of experiences for them. The most obvious way to incorporate variation of pace is to plan for it in the overall schedule. For example, a quiet snack can be followed by a dance period.

Additional opportunities to meet individual temperamental requirements of children must also be allowed for. The quieter, less gregarious child needs to have a place available where he can retreat from the herd, and the more active youngster needs the escape hatch of moving about when the group has sat beyond his limit of endurance.

Some kinds of programs appear to have special problems associated with pacing. For example, some compensatory programs attempt to cram so much into such a short time (play time, story time, snack, lunch, special activity time, not to mention visits from the psychologist, field trips, and special visitors) that the day goes by in a headlong rush of children being hurried from one thing to the next without the opportunity to savor any experience richly and fully. At the other extreme, some day-care programs offer a variety of activities and changes of pace during the morning but turn the children loose in the play yard for 3 interminable hours in the afternoon. Such consistent conditions of hurried stress or unalleviated boredom, unless coped with thoughtfully and modified, can ultimately have only a deleterious effect on children.

Photo by Elaine M. Ward

Learning must be based on actual experience and participation

Anyone who has ever taken a young child to the market knows how strong his impulse is to touch and smell and taste everything he encounters. Although occasionally inconvenient, the child's behavior illustrates a fundamental fact of early childhood learning: children learn best if allowed to use all their senses as avenues of learning. Participatory experience is an essential ingredient in preschool education. This means that the curriculum of the nursery school must be based on real experiences with real things rather than limited to the verbal discussions and pictures commonly (though not necessarily ideally) used when teaching older children.

Because educators of young children from Montessori to Bank Street have emphasized the value of real experience as being fundamental to successful education from the turn of the century, and because Piaget has also stressed the importance of participatory experience in the development of intelligence (Hunt, 1961), one might think that this principle need not be reiterated. However, the current influx of word-oriented rather than action-oriented teaching materials on display in the commercial exhibits of most conferences on early childhood and the fact that these materials continue to sell make it evident that this point must be stated very clearly: young children learn best when they can manipulate material, experiment, try things out, and talk about what is happening as it takes place (Torrance, 1970a; Lombard and Stern, 1970). Talking without doing is largely meaningless for a child of tender years.

Play is an indispensable avenue for learning

Another long-held value in early childhood education is an appreciation of play as a facilitator of learning. Although research is still lacking in this area, evidence is beginning to accumulate (Bruner, Jolly, and Silva, 1976; Piaget, 1962; Smilansky, 1968) that lends support to something generations of nursery school teachers have learned through experience. Teachers who have watched young children at play know the intent, purposeful seriousness they bring to this activity. Play is the medium used by children to translate experience into something internally meaningful to them. Piaget (1962) agrees with teachers and maintains that children use it as an important symbolic activity, but it serves many purposes beyond this function. Play clarifies concepts, provides emotional relief, facilitates social development, and creates periods of clearly satisfying delight. Sometimes teachers see its value only as a teacher-controlled, structured experience used to achieve a specific educational end (role playing after visiting the fire station, for example), but it is crucial that there be ample time in the curriculum for self-initiated play. It may well be that further research will show play to be the most significant avenue of learning available to young children.

Nursery school should be pleasureful*

Probably the most significant value a teacher can convey to the children in her care is the conviction that school is satisfying fun. This point has been deliberately left until last in order to give it special emphasis, in case the reader, having waded through the other elements of a good program, has begun to feel bogged down with the sober-sided responsibilities of running a good program for young children.

Not only should the experience be pleasureful for the children, but it should also be a joy for the adults. Young children have their trying moments, but they are also delightful. They see the world in a clear-sighted way that can lend fresh perspective to the eyes of their teacher, and their tendency to live for the present moment is a lesson to us all. Pleasure, enjoyment, humor, and laughter should be very much a part of each nursery school day.

PUTTING THE ELEMENTS TOGETHER
What does a nursery school day look like that combines these basic elements into a coherent whole?

The setting of a good nursery school is established with children in mind: furniture is scaled to the right size; the building has easy access to the yard; and there is a general air of orderly, yet easygoing comfort and beauty that does not put people off because of its newness or perfection. This kind of atmosphere goes a long way toward making parents feel at home and part of the nursery school family.

When it is necessary to form groups, the children are broken into small assemblies. Story hours and snack tables of four or five children and a grownup, for example, should be the rule in order to facilitate conversation and participation. (My staff refers to this as Hendrick's law: "The larger the group, the smaller the learning.") The daily pace is easy enough and the staff unharrassed enough that there are many intimate little opportunities for teachers to talk with the children individually.

There is a reasonably repetitious scheduling of basic experiences planned to provide alternate periods of quiet and active experience. These periods include a morning welcome for each child as he arrives, a snack in the morning and afternoon, and lunch and rest in the middle of the day.

In between these landmark times, many interesting events take place. These are developed with individual and group goals in mind, and they should include, every day, some activity that is creative, another that is messy, something that is new, something that requires the children to think, some carefully varied activities that foster motor development, some opportunity for the children to engage in meaningful work, and many chances to use books, pictures, poetry, and to listen and be listened to. Intertwined among these activities lie all the situations that the teacher must seize and use as they arise to develop social learnings and emotional strengths in the children.

For at least one generous block of time during the morning and afternoon, materials and possibilities are set out, and the child is expected to take the responsibility of selecting for himself what he wants to pursue. During this time, the teacher moves from one place to another as the occasion demands, talking first with one child, helping another group settle a fight, and getting out a piece of equipment for a third. Another part of the day involves more focussed participation but should not be cast in the mold of fifteen children doing the identical thing in one large group at the same time.

If staffing and weather permit, children have access to inside and outdoors as they prefer. Failing this, large muscle activities are available indoors and smaller muscle and more cognitive and creative materials are available outdoors to avoid the "recess" concept so common in elementary school.

This, then, is the overall framework of a sound preschool day. It includes many diverse things and many diverse people. The miracle of a good school is that, somehow, these all go together to produce a good day for both children and staff.

SUMMARY

After more than a decade of research, evidence is accumulating that early intervention in the form of education for young children and their families can make a difference. Moreover, certain elements are emerging that appear to be common to the majority of effective early childhood programs. These include concern for the quality of human relationships, inclusion of the parent as part of the life of the nursery school, a balance of self-selected and teacher-directed activities, the formulation of a well-thought-out plan for the curriculum, and a curriculum that is comprehensive and individualized.

A good nursery school program is basically orderly but also flexible; it provides for variety in experience, levels of difficulty, and pacing; it is based on the principles that learning should be the result of actual experience, that play is a significant mode of learning, and, above all, that nursery school should be a place of joy for both children and staff.

QUESTIONS AND ACTIVITIES

1. *Problem:* Suppose a parent said to you, after touring the school, "My heavens, these nursery school fees are high. Why, my baby-sitter charges less than you do, and she comes to the house and does the ironing while she takes care of little Carolyn. I don't see what costs so much about just taking care of little children!" What would you reply?
2. What are some situations in your own educational background where the learning was primarily by means of language and others where there was an emphasis on experience and participation? Which method did you prefer? What were the advantages and disadvantages of each of these approaches?

3. What guidelines would you suggest to help a teacher determine if she is not providing enough free choices or if there is too much structure in the children's day?
4. As a beginning teacher, how do you feel about the prospect of having parents at school? If a mother is helping at school on the day her youngster has a temper tantrum and refuses to come in to lunch, would it be easier to handle this situation if the mother were not there? Do you agree completely that parents should be welcomed at school? Why or why not?
5. Select a basic activity, such as using tricycles or easel painting, which tends to stay the same throughout the year in many schools, and suggest some variations that would add interest and learning to the activity.

REFERENCES FOR FURTHER READING

Historical Resumés of Early Childhood Education

Kessen, W. *The child.* New York: John Wiley & Sons, Inc., 1965. This lively paperback traces the historical development of ideas about children from William Cadogan to Jean Piaget. It includes selections from many authors as well as comments and explanations by Dr. Kessen.

Snyder, A. *Dauntless women.* Washington, D.C.: Association for Childhood Education International, 1972. Cast in the form of numerous short biographies, this book traces the history of early childhood education through the past 175 years. It is highly readable, funny in spots, and contains delightful illustrations.

Stevens, J. H., and King, E. W. *Administering early childhood education programs.* Boston: Little, Brown and Co., 1976. The first two chapters of *Administering Early Childhood Education Programs* present a concise overview of the history and philosophy of past and current approaches to early childhood education. Chapter 3 is helpful for students who want to know more about the Head Start Planned Variations Study. The authors also provide examples of typical schedules.

Does Preschool Education Make a Difference?

Lazar, I., Hubbell, B. R., Murray, H., Rosche, M., and Royce, J. *Summary report: The persistence of preschool effects: A long-term follow-up of fourteen infant and preschool experiments.* Washington, D.C.: Administration for Children, Youth, and Families, OCD, HEW, 1977. (OHDS) 78-30129. *Everyone* in preschool education should become familiar with this landmark study because it provides such convincing evidence of the value of early education.

Material on Specific Programs

Day, M. S., and Parker, R. K. (Eds.). *The preschool in action: Early childhood programs* (2nd ed.). Boston: Allyn & Bacon, Inc., 1977. *The Preschool in Action* offers the best current overview of a variety of preschool designs recently tried out in the United States.

Human Relationships

Hymes, J. L. *Teaching the child under six* (2nd ed.). Columbus, Ohio: Charles E. Merrill Publishing Co., 1974. This warm, highly readable paperback contains a running discussion of the current "state of the art" in nursery school curriculum and excellent, down-to-earth discussions of what young children are like and what kinds of programs serve them most adequately.

Read, K. H. *The nursery school: Human relationships and learning* (6th ed.). Philadelphia: W. B. Saunders Co., 1976. A classic text that emphasizes interpersonal relationships in relation to nursery school curriculum, this book is a "must" for all early childhood teachers.

Planning and Spontaneity

Fowler, W. On the value of both play and structure in early education. *Young Children,* 1971, *27*(1), 24-36. This article contains a balanced, scholarly discussion of the value of structured and unstructured experience in fostering the development of young children.

Play

Hartley, R. E., Frank, L. K., and Goldenson, R. M. *Understanding children's play.* New York: Columbia University Press, 1952. This is a detailed discussion and analysis of the value of many different play materials for young children. Although an older book, it remains in print because it is of real value to the early childhood teacher.

Putting a Good Program Together

Beyer, E. *Teaching young children.* Indianapolis: The Bobbs-Merrill Co., Inc., 1968. Part One contains a delightful narrative account of what an actual nursery school day is like. The book reads like a novel and yet conveys basic principles and values at the same time; highly recommended.

Crandall, J. M. *Early to learn.* New York: Dodd, Mead & Co. 1974. *Early to Learn* does a first-rate job of capturing the spirit of nursery school education through a comingling of pictures and text; highly recommended.

Schedules

Hildebrand, V. *Introduction to early childhood education* (2nd ed.). New York: Macmillan Publishing Co., Inc. 1976. Two approaches to scheduling that should be helpful to the student who desires specific information in this subject are discussed. Stevens and King (see above) also provide examples of typical schedules.

For the Advanced Student

Bissell, J. S. The cognitive effects of preschool programs for disadvantaged children. In J. L. Frost (Ed.), *Revisiting early childhood education: Readings.* New York: Holt, Rinehart and Winston, Inc., 1973. In Bissell's reexamination and review of several studies of early childhood programs, she concludes that teacher-directed programs based on defined cognitive and language development goals are more effective in producing cognitive gains for preschool children than are programs that lack these characteristics.

Brown, B. *Long-term gains from early intervention: An overview of current research.* Paper presented at the meeting of The American Association for the Advancement of Science, Denver, February, 1977. Washington, D.C.: U.S. Dept. of Health, Education, and Welfare, OCD, 1977. This is an enthusiastic, easy-to-read review of research that also discusses where-we-should-go-from-here.

Caldwell, B. M. What is the optimal learning environment for the young child? *American Journal of Orthopsychiatry,* 1967, *37*(1), 8-21. This is a hard-hitting attack on some assumptions commonly held by child development people and nursery school teachers; stimulating and challenging.

Franklin, M. B., and Biber, B. Psychological perspectives and early childhood education: Some relations between theory and practice. In L. G. Katz (Ed.), *Current topics in early childhood education.* Norwood, N.J.: Ablex Publishing Corporation, 1977. The behavioristic point of view is contrasted with the cognitive-developmental and the developmental-interactive point of view in this valuable article. Helpful for readers who wish to think out more clearly the reasons behind their personal teaching philosophies.

Mann, A. J. *A review of Head Start research since 1969 and an annotated bibliography.* Washington, D.C.: ACYF, OHDS, HEW, 1977. (OHDS) 77-31102. Cast in the form of quick questions and answers at the beginning of the review, this publication moves on to more general synopses of research findings and concludes with an annotated bibliography; emphasis is on positive findings in review section.

Santa Barbara County Head Start

2 □ How to survive in nursery school

SUGGESTIONS AND GUIDELINES FOR THE FIRST WEEKS OF STUDENT TEACHING

Teachers have the chance to make their particular early childhood environment a spot of earth where a young child can live contented, constructive, contributing days.*

The first weeks of teaching are not easy, but they need not be impossible, either. However, it is wise for the student to make allowances for possible stress and not to be disappointed if she feels more tired than usual, or occasionally disheartened, or bewildered. These feelings will become less frequent as time passes and the children, staff, and routine become more familiar. They also diminish as the student gains more skills and confidence. The following material, which contains some basic principles of teaching and getting along in school, should help the student in this process.

CHOOSING A PLACE TO TEACH

The manner by which students are assigned to their practice-teaching schools varies considerably among colleges. Sometimes students are allowed to select their placement from a list of satisfactory schools; sometimes the practice-teaching experience takes place in a demonstration school; and sometimes the student is assigned at the discretion of the supervising teacher.

Regardless of the method of assignment, the student should know there are many kinds of situations in which to work in the field of early childhood education. These can be divided into five main types: the private school, the cooperative, the compensatory program, the day-care center, and the demonstration or laboratory school.

Private schools are so named because they do not depend on public funding for support. They are often half-day programs that tend to offer traditional nursery school curriculum based on the individual needs of the children. The program is likely to stress creativity and social and emotional adjustment. Such schools usually serve middle-class families, and they meet a real need for early childhood education in this portion of the community.

Cooperatives usually have fewer professional teachers and more mothers and fathers participating than private schools do, although they are private in the sense that they, too, do not usually have public funds for support. They offer the special enrichment provided by a high adult-child ratio, and the children who attend them also profit from the abundance of ideas furnished by so many different adults. There have been cooperative nursery schools in the United States for many years (Taylor, 1968), and the movement is flourishing anew on many college campuses where young families are banding together to provide care for their children by this relatively inexpensive method. It is still the case that

---

*From Hymes, J. L. *Early childhood education: an introduction to the profession* (2nd ed.). Washington, D.C.: National Association for the Education of Young Children, 1975, p. 60.

19

many teachers enter the profession by participating in a well run co-op when their children are small, finding that they love to teach and going on to further training in early childhood education.

Head Start, a federally funded program, is the best known of the *compensatory programs,* since it exists on a nationwide basis. Some states also fund additional preschool programs designed to educate children from families of the poor (Education Commission of the States, 1971). Although termed compensatory because they were originally intended to compensate for lacks in the child's home environment, current investigations have found greater strengths in the homes than had previously been noted, and now the programs seek to honor these strengths as well as to compensate for lags in verbal and mental development.

Day-care centers offer day-long child care. They usually serve the children of working mothers, some of whom are fairly wealthy and some of whom are quite poor. Funds for such care are provided both by parents and by state or public agencies. Good day-care programs are delightful and valuable because of the leisurely pace and the extended learning experiences that they provide. Mediocre, custodial day-care services are still a stain on the conscience of some communities and need to be remedied and modified for the welfare of the children (Keyserling, 1972).

Demonstration or *laboratory schools* are typically connected with teacher-training institutions or with research programs. They can be wonderful places for young students to begin their teaching, since they are most likely of all the kinds of schools to be child and *student* centered. Ideally, the student should have teaching opportunities in both laboratory and real-life schools so that she receives a balance of ideal and worldly teaching experiences.

SOME COMFORTING THOUGHTS

Do teachers matter? One of the outstanding characteristics of beginning teachers is the caring and involvement that they bring with them to their work, and it is heartening to remember that these characteristics are important factors in achieving success.

Weikart (Weikart and Lambie, 1970), for example, found that no matter what kind of curricular model was followed (that of Piaget or Bereiter, or a more traditional model), the involvement of the teacher and her implementation of the curriculum was fundamental to the success of the outcome. Another researcher (Katz, 1969) attributed the failure of a program she studied to the fact that the teachers gave lip service to the curriculum but failed to carry it through in practice. Still another study (Scott, 1969) sought to separate successful from less successful head teachers and found that the successful teachers were characterized as being more spontaneous, in better control of the group, reaching their goals more often, showing more positive emotions, and *being more involved* (italics mine).

Even more recently, Pedersen and Faucher (1978) traced the effect of three first-grade teachers on their now adult students and presented intriguing evidence that one particularly loving and forceful teacher had produced more than her share of higher achieving adults.

So, on days when things may not have gone just right, it may be a comfort to remember that involvement and caring are valuable qualities that the student already possesses and brings with her as positive assets to her teaching (Gaylin, 1976; Warren, 1977). It is, of course, an ancient truth that the more one puts into any experience, the more one gets out—and teaching is no exception.

The master teacher is probably ill at ease, too. Sometimes students are so wrapped up in their own shyness that they fail to realize that the teachers they are working with are shy of them as well. They attribute all the awkwardness of the first days on the job to their own insecurities and inexperience. Actually, the master teacher is willing to help, but may also be a little frightened, particularly if she has not had many students before. It will help her help the student if she knows that the student likes her.

One poor experience with a student will not ruin a child's life. Some conscientious new teachers are almost too sensitive to the effect their actions will have on the children. It is true that young children

Santa Barbara County Head Start

are more vulnerable to influences than older children are, and for this reason everyone attempts to do her very best; but the significance of the single traumatic experience has been overrated. It is usually the continuing approach or climate that molds the child. Therefore, the student need not agonize over one mishandled situation on the grounds that she may have scarred the child for life: this is actually a very unlikely result.

Making mistakes can turn a student into a better teacher. Of course, the student will make mistakes, but so will the teachers she works for. Rather than investing a lot of energy in regretting these errors, it is more healthy and productive for the student to learn by analyzing what went wrong and then deciding how to be more effective the next time. It is also helpful to repeat the experience as soon as possible (rather like getting back on a horse and riding again right away after you've fallen off) so that bad memories are supplanted by better ones.

The following excerpts illustrate how one student struggled and succeeded in profiting from her mistakes.

A special project on dance

EVE ATKINSON

I planned to use records for part of the activity and also to have a time when the children could use instruments to make noise to move to. The first day, I planned to have a dance-type session which would deal primarily with the theme for this month, creek life. I got a record which I have known and loved since I was a child (the Grand Canyon Suite) and planned to use that at first, making a creek with our bodies. I felt that this would combine a lot of fun learning with motor coordination and would also be very interesting to the children.

Actual outcome: first day

To start with, the record player was not available. This didn't worry me too much, since I had already planned to have the children use the instruments for music. . . . [The dance session began well, but then] we went on being all the different animals that lived in the creek, but the group slowly got smaller. I think that they began to get disinterested for many reasons, one being the fact that there was no music, and, since I had to move around with them while I played a tambourine, it wasn't adequate. Also, there was another student in the room, but she did not participate or help. I was all the time having to handle other things besides just the dancing. For example, there was one small girl (3 years old) who needed special care, as she has only been here a few days. She wanted me to hold her, and every time I bent down, she jumped on me and wanted to be picked up and cuddled. I gave her as much as I possibly could without losing the group, but it got to be so bad that I had to leave the room to take her to another area where she might be able to get involved, or at least get the attention she needed. When I came back, the group had completely fallen apart. I think that I simply should have asked the other student to take the child elsewhere instead of my leaving.

Conclusions

I'm rather disillusioned about the activity because I had to alter my plans so much during the morning. I feel that if it were better planned, or perhaps if I had planned for a longer time period of different things, or movements and different types of music (lack of the record player was contributing to this problem), that the first group would have held together better. Next time, I certainly would make sure that I was going to be able to have new things ready. . . . Another thing that I think is necessary is to have an adequate person on hand to take care of any problems which I can't solve without taking my attention away from the group.

Second day

This day worked out lovely! I learned an awful lot about how to go about the activity from the previous day. I made sure I had the record player, and I also made sure Clevonease [the head teacher] would come by and see how I was doing, in case I needed any assistance. I planned everything, and had listened to the music enough so that I knew what we might do when the music varied. I decided not to use any instruments, since they were only in the way yesterday. I wanted to use the same theme each day of this session, and also to have basically the same children, so I again concentrated on the creek.

I first set up the lower room with the tables on one side, and also put out a few cognitive activities on one table. (I put these out because on Thursday I found that when the dancing was done I really needed to have something else that the children could get involved in right away.)

Actual outcome: second day

. . . I put the record back on, as I could see that they were all very enthusiastic about doing it again. The music came to the "sinking" part, and I was surprised that they recognized this and said it was time to go into the water. They did many things without my saying much at all. They were anxious to blow the bubbles and did this several times. At the change in the music, the children began to "swim up," and we reached the part where we start back to where we began. They did this completely through to the end.

Conclusions

I learned enough from the first experience so that I planned better for this one. I knew what I needed to do and to have, and I made sure that I followed through with these things. I realized that I had to really guide the children rather than just say, "Now, dance!" They need direction yet enough freedom to be an individual . . . I feel it was an excellent experience for both myself and the children, as it flowed smoothly and the children responded so freely.

Now I realize that one person can control a group if all the children are able to get involved and contribute their ideas and feelings, and therefore it is absolutely necessary to make sure that any activity offers opportunities for the children to do this.

Third day

For my final day with this special project, I thought I would try to expand my activity from the second day, using more children. I knew what to say and how to act, since it worked so well on Friday. Unfortunately, things didn't go as I had thought they were going to. . . .

Actual outcome: third day

I began by going around the school and collecting children. I wanted to include those children that I had been with on the previous day, but it seemed as if most of them were very involved in other activities. Because of this, I simply told them I was going to be dancing in the lower room and that I would really like for them to come and join me after they were through. Anyway, I continued to collect children, and unfortunately I ended up with way too many. This was because I overlooked the fact that I would have children coming in the room to join us a little later. Some of the children who had danced with me before remembered what we had done and told the group about it. Then, one boy took off his shoes (this was the beginning of a catastrophe!), and then another child, and before I knew what was happening, the whole room was full of shoes and children with bare feet. I didn't know whether or not to have them all put their shoes on or whether it was better to simply start the dancing. I chose to do the latter, and for a very short while, this was all right to do. We proceeded to do the dance, waking up and stretching. This went fine until the time when we got up and began to move around. There simply were too many children. They all went to some place in the room and began playing games such as monsters and guns, or playing in the housekeeping corner. The group fell apart, and quite a few children went outside (still without their shoes). I had to fetch them back because it was cold outside and have them put their shoes on. This caused quite a difficulty, since the shoes were all mixed up and were all approximately the same. The children didn't know which were their shoes, and besides that, they simply did not

want to put them on. By this time, the dancing had gotten completely wiped out, and so was I. The children did not want to put on or even find their own shoes. They were playing chase.

My savior was Kathy Wilson [another teacher at the Center]. She came in and saw the mess and offered her help, so I quickly explained the situation, and she right away said very firmly for each child to find his shoes and to put them on right now! I was amazed at how she got them to respond so quickly, since they right away attempted to get their shoes.

After the goers and stayers had been sorted out, we began the dancing again. It went well this time, with the children reacting creatively and enjoying themselves. A couple had danced with me all through this project, and I think this really gave them a sense of accomplishment. . . .

Conclusions

Too many children! I tried to do something which I simply couldn't do alone. With that many children, there has to be another teacher involved with the children, dancing and helping them. I should have left my plans the same as they were for the second day of the project, instead of planning something much beyond my and the children's capabilities. Also, I shouldn't have started the dancing without the children putting on their shoes first. If there was a small number of children or another teacher, then it wouldn't have mattered that the shoes were off, but as it was, the children weren't staying with the activity long enough to complete it and then to put on their shoes. They were leaving in the middle of it, and this wouldn't have mattered if their shoes had been on. Another thing I learned is that if you are going to let them take off their shoes, then make sure their socks get inside the shoes and also that the shoes are not in one pile but in separate areas of the room. . . .

From this experience I think I have learned a great thing—if something works smoothly, it doesn't mean that you have to attempt something twice as involved next time. I realize, too, that when a group gets into such a mess as this one did, the teacher really must speak out to the children so that the children know you mean business. That is why Kathy got the children to obey—they knew she meant put on their shoes, and they knew she was serious. For me, this was an upsetting defeat, and I felt really inadequate at first. Clevonease and I talked about it, and I learned the reason for taking off the shoes was that there had been a dance in-service session at the Center the day before, and everyone had been barefoot. It was as simple as that; the children remembered it and repeated it. The key to the whole thing though, and Clevonease agreed, was just that I had too many children for the number of adults, which was something like one teacher to thirteen children. It should have been limited to four or five, right from the beginning. After I thought about it for a while, I accepted the fact that one learns from mistakes, and I knew I had learned an awful lot, and so I know it wasn't wasted time but actually very valuable.

[I might add that Eve has since gone on to be a very accomplished young teacher.]

BASIC PROFESSIONAL ETHICS

Now that the student is becoming a member of a profession, it will be helpful to know from the beginning some ethical guidelines that are observed by most teachers. In the past few years, concern about ethics has been growing, and there remains considerable debate over which items should be included in a code (Katz, 1977, 1978; Katz and Ward, 1978; Spodek, 1977a; Ward, 1978). Nevertheless, there are some general ethical behaviors on which it seems likely most teachers can agree. Among them are the following.*

When in doubt about the value of a decision, put the child's welfare first. Granted, what is "best" may not always be easy to determine—there will always remain special circumstances where we cannot be certain what is best for his welfare. For example, is it better for a 3-year-old to stay with a loving but emotionally disturbed and disoriented single parent or to place him with a less disturbed but apparently cold and emotionally remote grandmother? But it is also true that much of the time, if the teacher honestly tries to do what is best for the child rather than what is merely convenient or "the rule," she will be on the right ethical track.

Strive to be fair to all the children. The most important guideline to observe is that all children deserve a fair chance and a reasonable amount of con-

_____
*See Appendix A for an example of a proposed code of ethics.

cern from each teacher. Perhaps the student will recall situations in her own school life where a teacher made a scapegoat of some child and picked on him continually, or where another teacher never seemed to notice some of the youngsters. Although nobody intends to have this kind of thing happen, sometimes it does, and teachers should be warned against behaving this way. Every child is important and is entitled to be valued by his teacher.

Keep personal problems private during the day. Teachers should not discuss their personal problems or emotional difficulties with the parents; nor should they discuss them with other teachers while school is in session. Teachers need to leave personal problems at the door as they begin the day, since the time at nursery school rightfully belongs to the children. The discussion of personal matters should take place after the children have gone home.

Show respect for the child. One important way nursery school teachers demonstrate basic respect for others is by refraining from discussing a child in his presence unless he is included directly in the conversation. Sometimes teachers thoughtlessly talk over the children's heads, assuming that the youngsters are unaware of what is being said. But if the student has ever had the experience of eavesdropping while people were discussing her, she will no doubt remember the special potency of that overheard comment. Anything said about a child in his presence needs to be said with him included. Thus it is more desirable to say, "David, I can see you're feeling pretty tired and hungry," than to cock an eyebrow in his direction and remark to another teacher, "Brother, we sure are in a nasty temper today!"

An even more fundamental aspect of respect between teacher and child can best be described as a valuing of the person: the teacher who truly respects and values the child pauses to listen to him with her entire attention whenever this is possible; she remembers that each child is a unique person and relishes him for his differences from his companions, and she allows him to generate ideas of his own rather than subtly teaching him it is better to unquestioningly accept the teacher's ideas as being best.

This kind of respect is, of course, a two-way street. The teacher who holds the child in such respectful regard sets a model for the youngster, who will in time reflect this same fundamental consideration back to her. This process can be accelerated and strengthened if the teacher quietly makes a point of protecting her own rights as well as the children's. She may say something as simple as, "Now, Margaret, I've listened to you; take just a minute and hear what I want to say," or she may make this same point with another child by saying, "You know, my desk is just like your cubby. I don't take your things out of that, and you must never take anything out of my desk, either."

Observe professional discretion. Still another aspect of respect for people is respect for the family's privacy. Family affairs and children's behavior should not be discussed with people outside the school who have no need to know about them: even amusing events should never be told unless the names of the children involved are either not mentioned or are changed. Most communities are smaller worlds than a beginning teacher may realize, and news can travel with astonishing rapidity.

In general, student teachers should be wary of being drawn into discussions with parents about their own or other families' children. This kind of discussion is the teacher's prerogative, and it is a wise student who passes off questions about youngsters by making some pleasant remark and referring the parent to the teacher. Nobody is ever antagonized by a student who does this in a tactful way, but disasters can result from well-meant comments by ill-informed or tactless beginners.

In addition, the student should not discuss with outsiders situations she disapproves of at the school where she works. These remarks have an unpleasant way of returning to the source, and the results can be awkward, to say the least. The principle "if you don't say it, they can't repeat it" is a sound one here. It is better, instead, to talk the problem over in confidence with the college supervisor.

Observe the chain of command. In just about every organization there is a chain of command. It is always wise to avoid going over anyone's head when making a comment or request. Understandably, teachers hate being put in a bad light by a student's talking a problem over with the school director before talking it over with the teacher herself.

A related aspect of this authority structure is being sure to get permission before planning a special event such as a field trip or getting out the hoses after a film on water play. Answers to such requests are generally "yes," but it is always best to check before embarking on a major venture.

SOME RECOMMENDATIONS FOR STARTING OUT

Although not always possible, it helps to find some things out before beginning the first student-teaching day. First, it is helpful to talk with the teacher and determine what time she expects the student to arrive and the kind of clothes she recommends for her school. The question of clothing can be something of a crusade among the young today, but the student-teaching placement is not the place to do battle on the subject. Most schools are pretty reasonable and will recommend sensible clothes. Slacks are frequently worn. An apron with a deep pocket is a decided asset. Besides dressing practically, the student should look as bright and pretty as possible, although many of the children will see her as beautiful no matter what she wears.

Some schools have written guidelines they can give the student to read. Time schedules and lists of rules are also very helpful to review. If the school does not have these things written down, the student should ask the teacher how basic routines such as eating and taking children to the toilet are handled, and she should ask about crucial safety rules and for a brief review of the schedule. If the student can come for a visit when the children aren't there, the teacher will have a better opportunity to take her on a tour of the school. During this visit the student can make a special point of finding out where the children's cubbies are, where sponges and cleanup materials are kept, and where various supplies are stored.

PRACTICAL THINGS TO DO TO INCREASE COMPETENCE

Gain confidence in your ability to control the group. Almost invariably, the first thing students want to discuss is discipline. Since this is the point everyone seems most frightened about, it is recommended that the student begin her preparation for work by reading the chapter on discipline in order to ease her mind and help build her skills in this area. This review of theory will help, but observation and practice are the best way to gain competence in handling children.

Get to know the children as soon as possible. One way to become familiar with each child is to make a list of their names from the sign-in sheet and then jot down a few adjectives or facts to remember about each one. Calling the children by name at every opportunity will help, too. It won't take more than a day or two to become well acquainted.

Develop the proverbial "eyes in the back of the head." One of the most common failings of inexperienced teachers is their tendency to focus on only one child at a time. It is pleasant and much "safer" to sit down and read a favorite book with one or two lovable children and ignore the chaos going on in the block corner. Good nursery school teachers have formed the habit of total awareness. This is true outdoors as well as inside, but to say that the teacher should never plan to settle down with any group would be an exaggeration. Of course, the teacher has to center her attention on

Photo by Elaine M. Ward

specific children from time to time, or there is no satisfaction to the experience for either of them, but she has to keep tuned to the whole room as well. Sometimes such a simple technique as learning to look up frequently will help the student build skills in this area. Another technique is sitting so that the whole room or whole playground can be seen. Many beginning students sit with their backs to half the room—this is simply courting trouble.

Take action in unsafe situations. Since students are sometimes afraid of appearing too restrictive in our liberal nursery school atmosphere, they allow dangerous things to happen because they do not know the rule or school policy about it. The general rule of thumb is that when one is unsure whether the activity is dangerous, it is better to stop it and then check to see what the teacher thinks. Stopping a few activities that are safe is better than letting two children wrestle each other off the top of the slide while the student debates indecisively below. Things will generally look less dangerous to the student as she gains experience and feels less anxious, *but it is always better to be safe than sorry.*

Encourage the growth of independence and competence; avoid overteaching, overhelping, and overtalking. As a general principle, we encourage children in nursery school to do everything they can for themselves. This is different from the behavior of the teacher who sees her role as doing to and doing for children. It takes self-control to wait while John fumbles for the zipper, insight to see how to assist him without taking over, and self-control not to talk too much while he is learning. But building competencies in the children by letting them do things for themselves increases their self-esteem so much that practicing restraint is worth the effort.

Encourage originality of self-expression. One of the most frowned-on things the student can do is make a model of something for the children to copy when she is working with creative materials. It is easy to be trapped into making someone a snake or drawing a man for another youngster, but early childhood teachers dislike providing such models because they limit the child's expression of his own

feelings and ideas. It is better to relish the materials with the children and help them use them for their own purposes.

Keep contacts with the children as quiet and meaningful as possible. Except in a real emergency, the student should walk over to the child to talk with him rather than calling across the room. She should use a low voice and bend down so he can see her face and be less overwhelmed by her size. (An excellent way to find out how big an adult is from a child's point of view is to ask a friend to stand up and teach you something while you remain sitting on the floor. It's enlightening.)

Expect to do menial tasks. No other profession requires the full range of abilities and effort that preschool teaching does. These extend from inspiring children and counseling parents to doing the most menial types of cleanup. Sometimes students do not realize this and so feel imposed upon because they are asked to change a pair of pants or mop the floor or clean the guinea pig, but this kind of work is expected of almost all nursery school teachers as just part of nursery school life. Not only is cleaning up to be expected, but it is also necessary to straighten up continually as the morning progresses. Blocks should be rearranged on shelves and costumes rehung several times a morning to keep the room looking attractive. (Unfortunately, there is no good fairy who will come along and do this.)

Learn from the start to be ingenious about creating equipment and scrounging materials. Nursery schools almost always operate on lean budgets, and every school develops a number of ingenious ways to stretch money and invent equipment. The student can learn a lot from each place she works by picking up these economical ideas from the staff, and she can contribute much by sharing her own ideas about the creative use of materials and new sources of free supplies. She should learn to be on the lookout for so-called waste materials that other businesses throw away; the carpet company's colorful scraps can make handsome additions to the collage box, and rubber tires can be used in fascinating ways to make sturdy play equipment.

Try to be organized. It is very helpful to arrive early on each teaching day so there is time to get everything together in advance for the morning or afternoon. Nothing beats the feeling of security this preparation breeds. Life is also easier if the student checks before going home to find out what will be happening the next time she comes and also to make certain that the supplies she needs are on hand. Advance checking also makes reading up on activities ahead of time possible—a real security enhancer!

It also helps to know the schedule well enough to tell what is going to happen next as well as what time it is likely to happen. This allows time for cleanup and also helps avoid the disappointment of moving into a new activity just as the group is expected to wash up for lunch.

When help is needed, ask for it. People aren't usually critical if a beginner admits she doesn't know something and has the courage to ask, but they are inclined to resent the student who protects herself by appearing to know everything already. When one is unsure of a policy at the school, it never does any harm to say to the child, "I don't know if it's all right to climb on the fence. Let's go check with Miss Clancy, and then we'll both know."

The chance to chat with the master teacher while cleaning up at the end of the morning, or at some other convenient time of day, is an invaluable time to raise problems and ask questions. During the day itself, students often have to "muddle through"—learning by observation and using their own common sense. Nothing disastrous is likely to take place, and teachers are usually too busy to be corralled for more than a sentence or two of explanation while school is in progress.

SOME SPECIAL PROBLEMS

The following problems have come up often enough with students that they deserve discussion. Of course, because each situation is different, recommendations are risky. Nevertheless, the following suggestions may provide solutions that may not have occurred to the student.

What to do if you hate the nursery school to which you are assigned. We have already mentioned that there are several different types of nursery schools and that the same type varies a good deal from school to school. Some schools seem to suit some students, and others fit other students better. Therefore, it is important not to conclude that teaching is not for you just because one placement is less than satisfactory. Maybe a change to another school is the answer to the problem; maybe it isn't. At any rate, the place to begin solving the difficulty is by talking over the reason for the unhappiness with the supervising teacher from the college. This is a more productive as well as a more ethical solution than complaining to a friend.

It is also wise to refrain from making snap judgments about a teacher or placement. The first 2 or 3 weeks in any school will be some of the most stressful weeks of the student's career, and it's essential to realize that some people react to stress by attacking what is frightening them; others shrink up and feel paralyzed or disillusioned. As time passes, the strain will probably lessen, and the school may seem more attractive, a little the way hospital food mysteriously improves as the patient recovers.

What to do if you don't like a child. It's no sin to dislike a child; but it *is* a sin not to admit your dislike, come to terms with it, and try to do something about it. Sometimes what will help most is getting to know him better, since insight often breeds compassion. Sometimes making progress of some sort with him helps. Sometimes figuring out why you dislike him will ease the feeling. With beginning students this can often be traced to the fact that some children challenge adults or put them on the spot. Students who already feel insecure find this behavior particularly trying. Whatever the reason, it is more healthy to risk admitting your dislike to yourself and perhaps to your master teacher if you feel safe with her and then to work toward resolving the problem. Although the suggested remedies may not overcome the dislike completely, they should help. At the very least, it is always possible to be fair and decent to all the children. Probably the liking will come in time.

THE WAY TO YOUR MASTER TEACHER'S HEART

We've already talked about the fact that it takes time to feel at home and to build a friendship with the master teacher. There are four more specific things the student can do that will help generate friendliness. The first is to be prepared to make the small, extra contribution of time and energy *beyond* what is expected. The student who stays the extra 10 minutes on pot luck night to dry the coffee pot is well on her way to becoming a popular member of the staff.

The second thing sounds simple but is often overlooked because new teachers tend to be nervous. It is to *listen* to what the teacher tells you, and do your best to remember it!

The third thing is to offer help before being asked to lend a hand. Some students are so afraid of being pushy or of making mistakes that they never volunteer. But always having to request help gets tiresome for the master teacher, even if the student is willing when asked. It is better to develop an eye for all the little things that must be done and then to do them quietly. Such students are treasured by their master teachers.

Finally, the student should let her enthusiasm show through. The vast majority of nursery school teachers follow their profession because they love it; the rigors of the job and the relatively low pay weed out the others very quickly. The teachers are, therefore, enthusiastic themselves. They're often "born" teachers, and they love teaching students as well as little children. Expressing thanks by being enthusiastic will encourage them to keep on making the extra effort entailed in guiding student teachers.

SUMMARY

The student should grasp three basic principles before beginning to teach in the nursery school: master teachers are human, too; one poor experience won't ruin a child's life; and mistakes can be turned into valuable learning opportunities.

Even beginning students need to observe professional ethics when they are teaching. It is particularly important to respect each child and to preserve the privacy of the families whose children attend the school.

Gaining knowledge of the school's basic routines, schedules, and policies will make the early days of teaching a more comfortable experience for the young teacher. Some practical things to do that will increase the student's competence include gaining confidence in handling discipline situations, getting to know the children, being alert to the whole environment, taking swift action in situations that are dangerous, encouraging the growth of independence and originality of self-expression, making contact with the children as quietly and meaningfully as possible, being organized, and asking for help when needed.

Probably no other time in the life of the nursery school teacher is so exciting, unsettling, and challenging as the first days of student teaching. Teachers are fortunate who manage to retain at least some of this flutter of anticipation throughout their teaching lives.

QUESTIONS AND ACTIVITIES

1. Getting started in the first days of student teaching can be a special challenge, and it is helpful to know yourself and your own reactions well enough to be able to control them. How do you anticipate you will cope with the strangeness and unfamiliarity of the student teaching experience when you are just beginning? Close your eyes and think back to the last two or three occasions when you entered a new group and got acquainted. What was your personal mode of adapting? Did you talk a lot? Clam up? Act extremely helpful? Or . . . ?
2. If you were guiding a young, new teacher, what advice would you give her that might help her through her first days of teaching?
3. Do you believe that master teachers and professors are ever nervous or frightened when dealing with students, or do they seem invulnerable to such difficulties?
4. What are some examples in your own experience with teachers where you felt the teacher genuinely respected the people she was teaching? In these instances what were specific ways you felt this respect was demonstrated? How could these approaches be carried over in your own student teaching?
5. List some effective "dos" and "don'ts" for making friends with young children.

REFERENCES FOR FURTHER READING

Overviews

Hymes, J. L. *Early childhood education: An introduction to the profession* (2nd ed.). Washington, D.C.: National Association for the Education of Young Children, 1975. In conversational style, Dr. Hymes describes services provided by

Head Start, day-care centers, private nursery schools, and so forth, then discusses current problems and needs, and finishes with an enthusiastic statement of the satisfaction inherent in teaching young children.

Tarnay, E. D. *What does the nursery school teacher teach?* Washington, D.C.: National Association for the Education of Young Children, 1965. This pamphlet presents a quick overview of what traditional nursery school education is all about and identifies the underlying educational purpose of nursery school activities. Reprinted many times, it remains one of the best short descriptions of traditional early childhood educational practice.

Books on Specific Kinds of Schools

Beyer, E. *Teaching young children.* Indianapolis: The Bobbs-Merrill Co., Inc., 1968. In a delightful description of a nursery school, Beyer reflects the best of the traditional nursery school values and approaches.

Greenberg, P. *The Devil has slippery shoes: A biased biography of the Child Development Group of Mississippi.* New York: Macmillan Publishing Co., Inc., 1970. The trials and tribulations of the Child Development Group of Mississippi in the early days of Head Start are described; still the best book that has ever been written about Head Start.

Roby, P. *Child care—who cares? Foreign and domestic infant and early childhood development policies.* New York: Basic Books, Inc., Publishers, 1973. This collection of articles about day care touches on many aspects of this subject.

Taylor, K. W. *Parent cooperative nursery schools.* New York: Columbia University Press, 1968. This older book is filled with practical advice on running a cooperative nursery school.

Achieving Meaningful Contact with Children

Ashton-Warner, S. *Teacher.* New York: Bantam Books, Inc., 1965. The author provides a fascinating description of how she, a beginning teacher, came to know the Maori children and how she developed a system of teaching reading based on what was significant in the children's lives.

Helping Children Become Independent

Neill, A. S. *Summerhill.* New York: Hart Publishing Co. Inc., 1960. Although this book describes a progressive English school for older children, it has delighted teachers who teach all ages by its emphasis on trusting the young to act in their own best behalf.

Yardley, A. *Structure in early learning.* New York: Citation Press, 1974. Although this book deals with teaching slightly older children, the attitude and sense of what this English author has to say about teaching children applies to every age; a lovely book!

Sources of Inexpensive Materials

Hodgden, L., Koetter, J., Laforse, B., McCord, S., and Schramm, D. *School before six: a diagnostic approach.* St. Louis: Central Midwestern Regional Educational Laboratory, 1974. This sturdy compendium of suggestions has an appendix entitled "Trash to Treasures," which is a gold mine of suggestions of inexpensive and free supplies and equipment.

Monahan, R. *Free and inexpensive materials for preschool and early childhood* (2nd ed.). Belmont, Calif.: Lear Siegler/Fearon Publishers, 1977. In this invaluable resource are lists of things to send away for, ranging from pamphlets on mental health to educational films and National Dairy Council pictures.

Increasing the Teacher's Self-knowledge

Feldman, B. N. *Jobs/careers serving children and youth.* Los Angeles: Till Press, P.O. Box 27816, Los Angeles, Calif. 90027, 1978. Ever wonder what other kinds of jobs are available for people who want to work with children? This book lists over 400 job possibilities, divided according to level of education one has obtained, including requirements, brief descriptions of duties, and approximate salary ranges.

Jersild, A. *When teachers face themselves.* New York: Teachers College Press, Columbia University, 1955. How to face and cope with emotional problems common to members of the teaching profession is discussed in a matter-of-fact, helpful way.

For the Advanced Student

Combs, A. W. (Chm.) *Perceiving behaving becoming: A new focus for education* (Yearbook, 1962). Washington, D.C.: Association for Supervision and Curriculum Development, National Education Association, 1962. This is a wonderfully readable and inspiring overview of the humanistic approach to education; includes articles by Rogers, Maslow, and Kelley and talks about the positive effects of basing curriculum on an attitude of confidence and trust in the student.

Pedersen, E., Faucher, T. A., with Eaton, W. W. A new perspective on the effects of first-grade teachers on children's subsequent adult status. *Harvard Educational Review,* 1978, *48*(1), 1-31. Anyone who remembers the personal impact of a particularly able and forceful teacher will relish this account of an unconventional research project that links adult success in part with the effect of just such a teacher's influence.

PART TWO

Fostering physical well-being

Los Niños Head Start

3 □ Handling routines in the nursery school

The lunch period should be an occasion for the enjoyment of good food in a social situation. I can remember my first experience as an assistant teacher in an all-day program. Lunch was rolled into the classroom on a wagon. Children (already bibbed) were lying on cots for a pre-lunch rest. Teachers served the plates and summoned the children to the tables. *Everything* on the plate had to be eaten before melba toast chunks were distributed (these were great favorites!) and finally dessert and milk. There was one particularly dismal meal which appeared weekly: a barely poached egg (the white still transparent) sitting on top of some dreary spinach. No one liked it, and one little girl finally refused to eat it. She sat stolidly before the offensive plate, quietly but firmly asserting, "I won't eat it. I hate it. It's not even cooked." The teacher finally removed the plate to the kitchen with the comment that it would be waiting for her after her nap.

After nap, Jill was escorted to the kitchen to be confronted with the cool mess of uncooked egg and spinach. She was told that she could return to the playroom after she had eaten it.

When she returned to the playroom, the teacher asked her if she had eaten her lunch. Jill answered, "Yes, and then I throwed it up." And she had!*

---

*From *Teaching young children* (p. 124), by Evelyn Beyer, copyright © 1968, by Western Publishing Company, Inc., reprinted by permission of The Bobbs-Merrill Company, Inc.

Routines, those omnipresent recurring sequences of behavior, constitute the backbone of the nursery school day and serve as landmarks that divide it into different sections. They typically include the activities of arriving, departing, eating, toileting, and resting.

Adequate handling of routines can foster both emotional and physical health. In recent years teachers have tended to be more aware of the significance of routines in relation to emotional health than aware of the physical significance of good nutrition and adequate rest. But the pasty faces, vulnerability to illness, and low energy levels of many children in compensatory programs now serve to remind us that physical health is vital to well-being and that our young children need these routines to help them build strong bodies as well as stable personalities.

It was surprising to discover that although routines involve a good portion of the day at nursery school and although strong feelings and convictions of what is "right" abound, very little research has been carried out in these areas. What research there is deals with nutrition and the emotional process of attachment and separation rather than with the investigation of alternative ways to handle routines in school. Therefore, the student should understand that the following discussion is based on a consensus of generally followed practice and that the recommendations rest on experience and opinion and are not validated by research.

One other note of caution about routines: if the teacher is unwise enough to go to war with a child on the subject of routines, the child, if he is so inclined, can always win. Thus a child who absolutely won't eat, won't use the toilet, or refuses to go to sleep can win any time he wants to; there is little the teacher can do about it. Fortunately, teachers and children rarely reach this kind of impasse, but it is important to understand that such power struggles can happen and have happened and that the most common way to bring about such a disaster is to reduce oneself to attempting to force a child to comply with any routine absolutely against his will. It just doesn't work.

The best way to prevent conflicts from developing is to realize that children usually find comfort in reasonable routines that contribute to their physical well-being. It also helps if the teacher determines what the most important learnings are to be derived from each routine and then works toward achieving those goals rather than becoming caught up in "winning" for its own sake. For example, it is more important that a child learn to enjoy food and take pleasure in mealtimes than it is that he clear his plate, wait until everyone is served, or not rap his glass on the table. Bearing this primary goal in mind will reduce the amount of criticism and control that may otherwise mar snack and lunch times.

TRANSITIONS INTO ROUTINES

A recent study of several different kinds of nursery schools (Berk, 1976) makes the point that transitions (the time spent in moving from one activity to the next) occupy from 20% to 35% of activity time in nursery school. This surprising statistic certainly emphasizes that transitions are worth thinking about and managing well, so that children can move as smoothly as possible from one thing to the next. It also reminds us how necessary it is to *plan for* enough time when shifting, for instance, from music to lunch, or from lunch to nap so that children are not unnecessarily hassled in the process.

If you find yourself continually nagging and urging the children to hurry through their paces, here are some things you may want to try to make transitions easier for you and them. *It always helps to warn once in advance when a change is in the offing.* It also helps to remember that transitions do not usually present an opportunity for a real choice (the child is supposed to come, not linger in the yard), so it is best not to ask, ''Would you like to come in?'' but to say more definitely, ''In just a minute it's going to be time for lunch, and we will go indoors. What do you suppose we're having today?'' Occasionally, singing a simple song such as ''Here We Go A'Marching'' will also help get children moving in the desired direction.

ROUTINES OF ARRIVAL AND DEPARTURE

It is natural for young children to feel anxious when their mothers leave them at nursery school. This feeling, called *separation anxiety,* appears to be strongest in American children between the ages of 10 to 24 months (Mussen, Conger, and Kagan, 1974). Even beyond this age, however, separation requires time and tactful handling by the staff in order that the child and his mother come to feel comfortable about parting.

Although some research (Schwarz and Wynn, 1971) indicates that many 4-year-olds can adjust rapidly to a school situation without their mothers having to linger, it is not safe to make a blanket rule about this, since there are always individual cases where a child becomes panicky when left behind. This seems to be particularly true for 3-year-olds (Cox and Campbell, 1968) and for retarded children (Kessler, Gridth, and Smith, 1968).

Introducing the child to school gradually

It is common practice and good sense to recommend a visit to nursery school by parent and child for the first day, and then another short stay while the mother leaves briefly, followed by a gradual extension of time as the child's ability to endure separation increases. However, working mothers whose jobs demand that they appear promptly at 8:00, no matter what the nursery school teacher recommends or how hard the child is crying, are not considered in this ideal prescription. If at all possible, special arrangements should be made for such families when their children begin nursery school. A grandmother, father, or aunt might be pressed into service and stay while the child makes friends. Sometimes the mother can bring him by for a visit around lunch time, or the teacher can make a Saturday visit to the home, or the child can come to school with a friend. Any of these arrangements, while not ideal, is preferable to allowing the child to walk in and simply be left in a strange place with strange people for 9 hours on his first day.

Handling outbursts of emotion

It helps to recognize that a child must often deal with three feelings when his mother leaves him (Furman, 1972): grief (the emotion that seems most obvious and logical), fear (also not very surprising), and anger (the emotion that the teacher is least likely to recognize in these circumstances). It is often necessary not only to comfort and reassure the child but also to recognize with him that he feels angry with his mother because she left him at school. I recall one forthright 3-year-old who took real pleasure in biting the mama doll with our toothy rubber hippopotamus as soon as her mother departed. The teacher may also see this angry reaction at being left behind come out at the end of the day when the child insists he wants to stay at school and does not want to go home. If the teacher interprets the true reason for this reaction to his mother, it will help maintain friendly relations all around.

Actually, it is the children who make a forthright fuss as their mothers leave who seem to work through their feelings of loss with the greatest expedition, whereas the child who apparently makes an easy adjustment by becoming instantly involved in activities often becomes downcast a few weeks later as he lowers his defenses; if this happens 3 to 4 weeks after entry to school, the mother is likely to assume something has happened there that makes him want to stay home. The best protection against this conclusion is to explain casually to his mother

before his facade crumbles that the child may show his grief at a later time and that most children feel some sadness and loneliness when left at school.

It is also wise to prepare parents for the fact that children may go through a milder attack of separation anxiety again when they return from vacation. Otherwise, this repeated behavior can discourage parents who underwent a difficult separation experience at the beginning of school. Other unexpected circumstances can also trigger anxiety. Last spring the children in our Center walked to the college cafeteria and met their mothers there for lunch. All went well until it came time to part, and suddenly we had several very unhappy children on our hands. The unusual circumstances had made parting difficult once again for our small charges.

But learning to let go is part of becoming mature. A nice balance of comfort combined with a matter-of-fact expectation that he will feel better soon usually gets the child started on the day. Having something at hand that he especially enjoys will help, too. The teacher must take care that she permits the child to form a relationship with her as a bridge to the other children yet at the same time does not encourage this so much that the youngster droops around longer than necessary or becomes a careerist hand holder.

ROUTINES THAT CENTER AROUND EATING
Importance of adequate nutrition

In these days of plastic foods and casual eating habits, it is important to emphasize the value of good food for young children. Too many schools depend on artificial juices and a cracker for snack supposedly on the grounds that the children are well fed at home, but the underlying reasons for serving this kind of food are that it is convenient and cheap. Yet there is a great wave of studies, such as those by Birch and Gussow (1970), Scrimshaw (1969), and Shneour (1974), that indicate that good nutrition is closely linked to the ability to pay attention and learn (Loehlin, Lindsey, and Spuhler, 1975; U.S. Dept. of HEW, 1976b; Williams, 1978).

Although nutritional problems are most severe

among the poor, it isn't only the children in compensatory programs who are ''orphans of wealth.'' We must also include our more well-to-do youngsters, some of whom subsist on sugared cereals, candy bars, and pop. For this reason, daily dietary requirements are listed in Tables 1 and 2. It is almost impossible to meet these requirements unless the nursery school does its part by supplying fruits, vegetables, milk, and other protein during the day.

The way to achieve good nutrition is to serve wholesome, well-balanced snacks and lunches. Dessert should be fruit in some form and should be regarded as a nutritional component of the meal, not a reward to be bargained for. Variety, particularly

Table 1. The basic four (diet pattern to be used every day in the United States and its nutritive value)*

	Pattern
1. Milk Children: under 9—2 to 3 cups 9 to 12—3 or more cups 13 to 18—4 or more cups Over 18—2 or more cups	Whole, skim, buttermilk, dry, evaporated (to drink or combine with other foods), cheese, ice cream, yogurt 1 eight-oz. cup of milk = 1½ oz or 1½-inch cube cheddar-type cheese 1½ cups cottage cheese 2 cups cream cheese 3 or 4 tablespoons powdered milk† 2 cups ice cream
2. Vegetable-fruit 1 serving citrus or substitute 1 serving dark green or deep yellow vegetable at least every other day 2 servings other fruits or vegetables; potatoes may count as one of these servings	Orange, grapefruit, lemon, lime, tangerine, tomatoes, strawberries, melon, raw cabbage, etc. Adult serving size is ½ to ⅔ cup
3. Meat 2 or more servings	Meat, poultry, fish, eggs and their substitutes of legumes, nuts, lentils Adult serving size is cooked lean meat or fish—2 or more oz‡ or ½ cup diced raw lean meat or fish—3 or more oz eggs—2 medium size legumes—1 cup cooked peanut butter—¼ cup (4 T) nuts—½ cup
4. Cereal-bread 4 or more servings	Whole-grain, enriched or restored: rice, wheat, rye, barley, oats, corn Adult serving is 1 oz (¾ cup) ready-to-eat 1 slice bread (approximately 1 oz) ½ to ¾ cup cooked breakfast cereal, rice, hominy, cornmeal, Italian pasta 1½ oz baked goods has about 1 oz flour

*From Howe, P. S. *Basic nutrition in health and disease* (6th ed.). Philadelphia: W. B. Saunders Co., 1976.
†Amount used depends upon size of granule; follow label instructions.
‡Dividing 1 pound of ground meat into five equal portions would give, when cooked, five servings of approximately 2 ounces. This is due to shrinkage during cooking.
Note: Use other foods as desired to meet calorie needs and to increase palatability. Use water or other beverages: adult—6 to 8 cups, child—4 to 6 cups.

Table 2. Recommended food intake for good nutrition according to food groups and the average size of servings at different age levels*

Food group	Servings per day	Average size of servings					
		1 year	2-3 years	4-5 years	6-9 years	10-12 years	13-15 years
Milk and cheese (1.5 oz cheese = 1 C milk) (C = 1 cup—8 oz or 240 gm)	4	½ C	½-¾ C	¾ C	¾-1 C	1 C	1 C
Meat group (protein foods)	3 or more						
Egg		1	1	1	1	1	1 or more
Lean meat, fish, poultry (liver once a week)		2 T	2 T	4 T	2-3 oz 4-6 T)	3-4 oz	4 oz or more
Peanut butter			1 T	2 T	2-3 T	3 T	3 T
Fruits and vegetables Vitamin C source (citrus fruits, berries, tomato, cabbage, cantaloupe)	At least 4, including: 1 or more (twice as much tomato as citrus)	⅓ C citrus	½ C	½ C	1 medium orange	1 medium orange	1 medium orange
Vitamin A source (green or yellow fruits and vegetables)	1 or more	2 T	3 T	4 T (¼ C)	¼ C	⅓ C	½ C
Other vegetables (potato and legumes, etc.) or	2	2 T	3 T	4 T (¼ C)	⅓ C	½ C	¾ C
Other fruits (apple, banana, etc.)		¼ C	⅓ C	½ C	1 medium	1 medium	1 medium
Cereals (whole-grain or enriched) Bread	At least 4	½ C	1 slice	1½ slices	1-2 slices	2 slices	2 slices
Ready-to-eat cereals		½ oz	¾ oz	1 oz	1 oz	1 oz	1 oz
Cooked cereal (including macaroni, spaghetti, rice, etc.)		¼ C	⅓ C	½ C	½ C	¾ C	1 C or more
Fats and carbohydrates	To meet calorie needs						
Butter, margarine, mayonnaise, oils: 1 T = 100 calories		1 T	1 T	1 T	2 T	2 T	2-4 T

*From Nelson, W. E., Vaughan, V. C. III, and McKay, R. J. *Textbook of pediatrics* (9th ed.). Philadelphia: W. B. Saunders Co. 1969. Prepared in collaboration with Mildred J. Bennett, Ph.D., from "Four Food Groups of the Daily Food Guide," Institute of Home Economics, USDA, and Publication 30, Children's Bureau of the United States Department of Health, Education, and Welfare.

Continued.

Table 2. Recommended food intake for good nutrition according to food groups and the average size of servings at different age levels—cont'd

| Food group | Servings per day | Average size of servings | | | | | |
		1 year	2-3 years	4-5 years	6-9 years	10-12 years	13-15 years
Fats and carbo-hydrates—cont'd Desserts and sweets: 100-calorie portions as follows: ⅓ C pudding or ice cream 2-3" cookies, 1 oz cake, 1⅓ oz pie, 2 T jelly, jam, honey, sugar		1 portion	1½ portions	1½ portions	3 portions	3 portions	3-6 portions

as the year progresses and the children feel at ease, should be a keynote of the food program, and multicultural foods should be regularly included. Snacks should be different every day and can be based on seasonal fruits and vegetables to keep budgets within reason.

The teacher should realize that some children eat more than others do. The quantity consumed is a matter of physiological differences and also a function of how fast the child is growing; appetite is also related to emotional states and needs. All of these factors must be considered when deciding whether a child's nutrition patterns are adequate. As long as he remains healthy and his color is good, there is little need to worry about whether he is eating a lot or a little.

Some basic principles having to do with eating

There is perhaps no area in our social life except the area of sex that has as many restrictions and regulations attached to it as eating does. A class of mine once counted up the rules enforced by their families about mealtimes. We thought of 43 rules within 10 minutes. They ranged from "no dessert until you clear your plate" to "wait until the men are fed before you sit down." We will content ourselves here with enumerating only the principles that

the majority of nursery school teachers have come to feel are important as they have worked with young children.

Eating away from home can be frightening at first. Sometimes teachers underestimate how frightening it can be for children to eat away from home, but this can be the dreaded crisis of the day for new youngsters. They don't know what the teacher will do if they don't eat everything, and they may not recognize some of the food either. For this reason, new children should not be urged to eat, and very familiar food should be served during the first weeks when more of the children are feeling shy. When children enter later in the year, it is ideal to have the mother return before snack or lunch if she can because this helps get the child past that first hump of uncertainty.

Eating should be a pleasure. One way to increase pleasure and minimize misbehavior is to make sure the children aren't kept waiting to be fed. When children are hungry and their blood glucose level is low, they are in poor control of themselves; so food should be ready to be served as the children sit down. If it is placed on a low table or nearby shelf, the teacher can start passing it as soon as everyone has arrived.

Eating together should convey a sense of happy family life to the children. There should be time

Table 3. Sample lunch menus*

MENUS	MONDAY	TUESDAY	WEDNESDAY	THURSDAY	FRIDAY
WEEK I	Oven-baked fish Green beans Carrot sticks Cheese biscuits Milk Fresh pear halves	Beef balls Lima beans Tomato wedges Whole wheat toast strips Milk Stewed prunes	Stewed chicken Buttered noodles Grated carrot- raisin salad Whole-wheat Bread w/ apricot spread Milk Orange slices	Simmered steak Scalloped potatoes English peas Whole wheat muffins Milk Fresh fruit cup	Ground chicken & egg sand- wiches Buttered beets Lettuce pieces & tomato wedges Milk Bananas in gelatin made w/orange juice
WEEK II	Meat loaf Buttered carrots and peas Whole wheat bread and butter Milk Oatmeal muffins	Creamed chicken Buttered rice French green beans Cornbread sticks Milk Seedless grapes	Oven-baked fish Buttered mixed vegetables Whole wheat toast strips Milk Apple wedges	Toasted cheese sandwich Tomato soup Chopped broccoli Milk Cantaloupe slices	Ham Bkd potato w/cheese Celery & carrot sticks Whole wheat toast strips Milk Plain cake with orange sauce
WEEK III	Baked salmon croquettes Scalloped potatoes Okra with tomatoes Whole wheat bread Milk Apple slices	Meat balls with tomato sauce Green beans Enriched bread and butter Milk Banana bread	Cheese cubes Twice-baked potatoes Buttered beets Cooked spinach w/egg slices Milk Vanilla ice cream	Beef stew w/peas, carrots & potatoes French bread pieces Milk Cottage cheese & peach slices	Chicken casserole Buttered broccoli Bran muffins Milk Fresh pineapple & banana slices
WEEK IV	Hard-boiled eggs Green beans with bacon Drop biscuits Milk Orange slices in gelatin	Braised calves liver English peas Perfection salad Whole wheat toast strips Milk Baked apple	Tuna fish sandwiches Lettuce pieces Buttered summer squash Milk Fresh fruit cup	Creamed chicken Buttered spinach Grated carrot- raisin salad Whole wheat bread Milk Applesauce	Beef patty & gravy Peas & potatoes Tomato wedges Milk Sliced bananas in orange juice

*Reprinted, by permission, from "Ideas for Administrators," *The Idea Box,* by the Austin Association for the Education of Young Children. Copyright © 1973, National Association for the Education of Young Children, 1834 Connecticut Avenue, N.W., Washington, DC 20009.

both to eat and to chat. Discipline situations should be avoided whenever possible. It can also be a time to enjoy each other and to help the group by going for seconds, passing food to each other, and cleaning up.

If the food is plain and familiar, and if a lot of it can be eaten with the fingers, the children will eat more. As a general rule, little children are deeply suspicious of casseroles and food soaked in sauces and gravies. They prefer things they can recognize, such as carrot sticks, hamburger, and Jell-O with fruit.

Table 3 shows sample lunch menus. In order to provide more cultural variety, variations on these

Los Niños Head Start

menus might include (1) blackeyed peas with ham, mustard greens, purple plums, corn bread with butter or margarine, and milk or (2) pinto beans with melted cheese, chili peppers with chopped tomato, onion, and lettuce, a flour tortilla, and milk.

Eating should help a child be independent. When I think of the reason we allow children to serve themselves, I remember the little girl who commented that when teachers are cold they make children put their sweaters on. The same thing is true of eating—when teachers are hungry, they serve the children too much; but if food is passed around the table, each child can take what he desires. It is up to him to choose. He knows how hungry he is, and he knows his preferences far better than his teacher does. Then, too, by serving himself he has the opportunity to learn to observe the social rule, "Take some and leave some."

Having sponges close at hand also helps children become independent because they can mop up their own spills. Advertisements to the contrary, it certainly is easier to clean up food from uncarpeted floors, so it is best to eat over linoleum or even outside when possible.

Nursery school is a good place to develop a taste for new foods. Although the quickest way to teach a child to hate a new food is to make him eat it all up, it is desirable to encourage but not force everyone to take a taste of everything that is served. Generally, the teacher can count on the combination of good appetites and enthusiasm to foster venturesomeness, but sometimes a child will refuse to try something new. One teacher of my acquaintance handles these outright refusals by simply remarking, "Well, when you're older, I expect you'll want to try it," and then she changes the subject.

One of the best ways to encourage children to try a new food is to allow them to prepare it. Cooking is a fine learning experience as well as a pleasure for preschoolers. Making vegetable soup, devilling eggs, or baking whole wheat muffins can introduce them to a whole range of taste experiences that they might otherwise shun.

Negative comments on food such as, "It looks like dog pooh pooh!" should be discouraged. A wave of this kind of talk can sweep through a group of 4-year-olds and actually spoil a meal if not controlled. The policy of "You don't have to eat it, but I won't let you spoil it for other people" is a sound one to enforce.

Foods from different ethnic groups should be served at every opportunity. The white middle-class teacher needs to remember that some foods she has eaten all her life can be dishearteningly unfamiliar to the Indian youngster who is accustomed to mutton and sheepherder's bread or to the Mexican-American child whose staple of diet is the tortilla. Cookbooks and family recipes will help, but a cook in the kitchen who comes from a background similar to that of the children's is best of all.

Eating can be a learning experience. Although the most important goal of the eating situation is to furnish nourishment and pleasure, this experience can provide many opportunities for intellectual learnings, too. (MacAfee, Haines, and Young, 1974). The lunch table is a fine place for conversation. Children can be encouraged to talk about their pets, what they did on the weekend, what they like best to eat, and what was fun at school during the morning. The opportunity can also be taken to talk about food, textures, colors, and more factual kinds of information, but some teachers seem to do this to death and forget to stress the more valuable goal of conversational fluency. Eating should first and foremost be fun.

Children with special eating problems

Allergies and other food restrictions. Children who have allergies can have a difficult time in nursery school and so deserve special mention. The allergy that comes up most frequently is the restriction on milk and milk products. When this is the case, the mother should be asked to supply whatever the child requires instead. A simple explanation to the other children that the child's doctor has said he should not drink milk has always been sufficient at our Center. It is wise to be as matter-of-fact as possible in order to avoid making the child feel regretful or persecuted about the restriction.

Sometimes there are other reasons for dietary restrictions. For example, we have had several Black Muslim children and children from vegetarian families in our school, and we always do our best to honor their prohibitions. However, it can be very hard to see a little vegetarian hungrily eyeing the hot dog his neighbor is consuming with gusto. If the problem gets to be too difficult, perhaps the teacher will want to invite the mother to a lunch and ask her what to do about it.

The child who won't eat. Not eating and obesity are luxuries that very few countries in the world can afford, so I suppose we should count our blessings. For most children, soft pedaling the meal situation and allowing a child to skip a meal if he so chooses will gradually solve the problem of not eating. Although it may seem hardhearted, I feel it is a mistake to allow a recalcitrant child to suddenly repent when he realizes that the food is going back to the kitchen. Good food should be set forth; a pleasant opportunity to eat should transpire; and when that time is past, it is past for *everyone* until it is time for snack. This policy should be carried out without vacillation or guilt on the teacher's part. It is up to the child to choose to eat or not eat; it is not the teacher's role to coax, bargain, or wheedle. No one ever starved to death because he missed his lunch.

There are rare occasions when the teacher will come across a youngster who either compulsively insists on eating only a narrowly circumscribed number of foods or who refuses to eat altogether. This behavior is almost always duplicated at home as well. Taking the pressure off and handling mealtimes in a casual manner may not be enough in these special cases, and the condition can be difficult to ameliorate. Under these circumstances, it is important to suggest counseling promptly for the family in order to relieve the situation.

The child who grabs everything. Whereas the noneater is likely to make the teacher anxious, the grabber is likely to make her angry. Some grabbing is due to lack of social experience and consideration of others, and some is due to enthusiasm, hunger, or feelings of emotional deprivation.

The teacher may need to remind the child many times to take some and leave some, as well as recognize his feelings by commenting, ''It looks so good to you that you just feel like taking it all, don't you?'' It is also sound strategy to make sure the hungry one gets a second helping and that he is delegated to go to the kitchen for refills. When he remembers to leave enough for the other children, his thoughtfulness should be commended. When the grabbiness seems to be a symptom of emotional deprivation, it requires a more indirect approach that emphasizes meeting the youngster's emotional needs rather than stressing consideration of others.

PROCESS OF TOILETING
Taking children to the toilet

In general, nursery schools use the same toilet rooms for boys and girls. However, there are always exceptions to this rule, such as some schools who serve mostly Mexican-American youngsters, whose families feel strongly that open toileting violates the modesty of the little girls.

The benefits of toileting together are that the children learn to treat sexual differences quite casually. They will ask or comment about differences from time to time, and this provides golden opportunities to give straightforward, simple explanations. Open toileting has the advantage of reducing the peeking and hidden inspections that may go on otherwise. It promotes a healthier attitude toward sexual differences and therefore should be encouraged.

The majority of children of nursery school age can be expected to go to the toilet when they feel the need, but an occasional child will have to be reminded. Rather than lining everyone up at once and insisting that they use the toilet, it is better to remind children while washing up for lunch or before

nap that they will be more comfortable if they use the toilet first.

It will encourage children to take this responsibility for themselves if their mothers dress them in pants with elastic tops or other easily managed clothing. It is also sound to remark to children that it certainly feels good to go to the toilet, a point of view with which most of them will concur.

Thoughts about flushing. Some children, most commonly between the ages of 2 and 3, are really afraid of sitting on a toilet while it is being flushed (perhaps they fear vanishing down the hole with their product). Therefore, as a general practice, it is wise to wait until the child gets off before asking him to flush the toilet. We have achieved good cooperation by suggesting to the children that it is thoughtful to flush the toilet so that it is fresh for the next person, rather than constantly reminding, ''Don't forget to flush it; go back and flush it.''

Handling mishaps. When children wet themselves or have a bowel movement in their pants, they should be changed without shaming or disgust but without an air of cozy approval, either. Such loss of control often happens when children are new to the school, are overly fatigued, or are coming down with something, as well as when children have not yet acquired the rudiments of control. Many children are humiliated by wet underwear, and the teacher should be sensitive to this and help them change in a quiet place. The inexperienced student may find it helpful to know that it is easier to clean a child who has had a bowel movement if the child helps by bending over during the process.

Theoretically, children should always have a dry pair of pants stowed in their cubby, but actually, these are often not there when needed; so it is necessary to have some extras on hand, with ''nursery school'' written prominently across the seat. It is helpful to have these changes of clothing available in a bureau in the toilet room itself.

Having children toilet trained before admission to school

It has been a common policy among nursery schools in past years to make one of the criteria for

Santa Barbara County Head Start

admission be that the child has been toilet trained. Today, more schools are accepting children in diapers because the age of admission is going down. It is also true that sometimes women need to work and cannot afford to wait until their children are toilet trained before placing them in day care. At one time our Center had six children in diapers, but that was about five too many. It is easier, and may even be vital if the school is minimally staffed, to have the children toilet trained before they are enrolled, even though it is sometimes necessary to enroll children in diapers.

Children with special problems

Once in a while a mother will worry aloud to the teacher that her child "never" has a bowel movement. By this she usually means he doesn't have a bowel movement every day. This may be his natural

Photo by Mike Muckley, Brooks Institute and School of Photography

pattern of defecation, or it may be true constipation. If the child is constipated, it is best to refer the mother to her pediatrician for help.

The same thing goes for a 3- or 4-year old who leaks a little bowel movement in his pants from time to time and refuses to use the toilet. The child is often "clean" at school, but messes his pants frequently at home. The name of this condition is *encopresis,* and it often becomes such a touchy issue between parent and child, and can be so hard to treat, that it requires help from a pediatrician or, more likely, from a competent psychologist.

HANDLING NAP TIMES

If eating in a strange place with unknown people is disturbing to young children, going to sleep under such circumstances can be even more so. Releasing oneself into sleep is, among other things, an act of trust, and it is not surprising that this can be difficult for a young child to allow during his first days at nursery school. Fortunately, there are some things that the teacher can do to make this task easier for him.

Regularize the routine

Keep daily expectations and the order of events the same when approaching the nap period. That is, try to do things the same quiet, steady way every day. One pattern that works well is to send the children one by one as they finish lunch to use the toilet and wash their hands. Then they are expected to settle down on their cots or mats with a book to look at quietly until all the children are ready to begin resting. Next the room is darkened, and the teacher moves about quietly, helping children take their shoes off, find their blankets, stuffed rabbits, and so forth and setting the books aside. This process should be accomplished with quiet affection combined with the clearly projected expectation that the youngster is going to settle down.

When the children are all snuggled in their blankets, some teachers prefer to read a story, while others sing softly or play a quiet record. It helps to have the children spread out as far from each other as possible and to have them lie head to toe; this reduces stimulation and also keeps them from breathing in each other's face. Restless children should be placed in out-of-the-way corners. Teachers need to be quiet and not talk among themselves, and other people must not be allowed to tiptoe in and out.

It takes two teachers to settle a roomful of children, and it may take as long as half an hour or 45 minutes before the whole school goes to sleep. Some children will need their backs rubbed in a monotonous way to soothe them into slumber.

Allow children to get up as they wake up

Usually after about an hour, some of the children will wake up by themselves and begin to stir about. This gradual awakening is convenient because it means that each child can be greeted and helped to dress one by one, and it presents a nice opportunity for friendly, but quiet chats with the teacher. Children are more likely to wake up in a good mood if they are wakened gradually by the activity around them rather than by having the teacher wake them up. They need time to collect themselves and regain awareness before they begin the afternoon activities. It often works well to have a few staff getting children up and the rest of the adults in the play yard, with snack available as the children desire it and some attractive activity also available that the children may select when they feel ready for it.

How long should children sleep?

It is unfair to the parent to allow a child to sleep all afternoon, unless of course, he does not feel well. A sleep of an hour or so is about right for most youngsters, but this does not include the time it takes for them to settle down.

Should all children nap?

All children of nursery school age should be expected to lie down and relax for a while in the middle of the day. The need for sleep itself varies considerably with different children, and this difference needs to be taken into consideration. There will be some youngsters, particularly older children who are approaching kindergarten age, who never go to sleep. They should not be expected to lie stiffly on their mats for 2 hours. Instead, following a reasonable rest period, they should be permitted to go outside and play under the supervision of a staff member. These more mature children often vastly enjoy helping prepare the afternoon snack. It makes them feel important and pays tribute to their more grown-up status.

Occasionally, there will be a child who needs to rest but who is so high strung and active that he disturbs everyone at nap time. Our staff has concluded that it is more satisfactory to take these youngsters out of the nap room and give them something quiet to do in the director's office than to become involved in angry confrontations, which upset all the children as well as frighten the restless one.

A practical note about cots

Storage of cots can be a real problem in some schools. If the floor is not too drafty, folding mats may be used instead of cots. This works well except for children who wet their beds at nap time. Saran-covered cots are better to use with these youngsters so that the urine drips through and doesn't collect in a puddle on the mat. Linoleum floors are, of course, indispensable for those who wet their beds.

SUMMARY

Routines, which consist of arriving and departing, eating, toileting, and resting, are an important part of the nursery school day. If they are well handled, they can contribute both to the physical health and emotional well-being of young children.

Teachers will experience greatest success in

handling routines if they avoid trying to win for the sake of winning, but work instead toward the more worthwhile goals of helping the children become competent, independent people who have healthy attitudes toward their bodily needs and who look forward to eating, toileting, and resting because of the comfort and pleasure associated with these activities.

QUESTIONS AND ACTIVITIES

1. What foods do you particularly dislike? Can you remember the reason for your original dislike? Do you feel you learned anything from that situation which could be transferred to the way you handle eating situations at nursery school?
2. List all the rules you can think of that applied to eating, sleeping, or toileting in your own family as you grew up. After recalling the stated rules, think of some of the deeper, unspoken ones that were also observed.
3. *Problem:* You are the staff teacher who is delegated to greet children at the door every morning, and there is one little boy who always begins to whimper as he comes in the door. At that point the father jollies him along and finally gives him a smack on the bottom, telling him firmly, "Little boys don't cry!" You have learned in your student teaching days that it is important for children to express their feelings. How would you handle this situation?
4. Try an experiment wherein you just tell the children for 3 or 4 days that it is time to come in for snack, and then for the next few days try warning them ahead of time that it will soon be time to come in. Is there any difference in the way they respond?
5. *Problem:* Although you never meant to have things arrive at such an impasse, you have inadvertently made such an issue of a child's going to the toilet that he has become so balky about it that he won't use the toilet anymore but wets his pants instead. At this point, what approach would you try next to solve this difficulty?

REFERENCES FOR FURTHER READING

Handling Routines

Furman, R. A. Experiences in nursery school consultations. In K. R. Baker (Ed.), *Ideas that work with young children.* Washington, D.C.: National Association for the Education of Young Children, 1972. This article is an excellent discussion of separation anxiety and how it was handled in the case of a particular little boy; a shrewd, concise discussion.

Hirsch, E. S. *Transition periods: Stumbling blocks of education.* New York: Early Childhood Education Council of New York City, 1972. *Transition Periods* contains many wise comments and suggestions about making these potentially troublesome times easier for staff and children.

MacAfee, O., Haines, E. W., and Young, B. B. *Cooking and eating with children: A way to learn.* Washington, D.C.: Association for Childhood Education International, 1974. In addition to many recipes practical for use in the classroom,

this booklet contains a thorough analysis of all the learnings possible from cooking and eating.

Provence, S., Naylor, A., and Patterson, J. *The challenge of daycare.* New Haven: Yale University Press, 1977. Chapter 5 of *The Challenge of Daycare* deals with separation in some detail. It discusses adjustment for the child and parents and has some practical suggestions about ways to lessen stress. The discussion centers on children 2 years old and younger, but is of use with older children as well.

Read, K. *The nursery school: Human relationships and learning* (6th ed.). Philadelphia: W. B. Saunders Co., 1976. The chapter entitled "Helping Children in Routine Situations" has a detailed discussion of toileting that will be of particular interest to students devoted to the psychoanalytic point of view.

Wilder, A., Sendak, M., and Engvick, W. *Lullabies and nightsongs.* New York: Harper & Row, Publishers, 1965. This exquisite songbook consists entirely of lullabies. A special treasure, it is beautifully illustrated by Maurice Sendak; nice to use at naptime.

Nutrition

Children's Foundation. *Feed kids. It's the law.* 1028 Connecticut Ave., N.W. Suite 1112, Washington, D.C.: The Children's Foundation, various dates. This is a bimonthly information service that will keep the reader up-to-date on government food programs for children and their families—worth every penny (also available free to those who cannot afford to pay).

Head Start Bureau. *Nutrition education for young children.* Washington, D.C.: Head Start Bureau, Administration for Children, Youth and Families, Office of Child Development, U.S. Dept. of Health, Education, and Welfare, 1976. DHEW Pub. No. (OHDS) 76-31015. This delightful pamphlet covers many ways of teaching children about eating, food, and nutrition. It is very practical and may be obtained from the Superintendent of Documents.

Sunderlin, S., and Wills, B. (Eds.) *Nutrition and intellectual growth in children.* Washington, D.C.: Association for Childhood Education International, 1969. This group of articles summarizes research on the relation of poor nutrition to mental development.

Williams, S. R. *Essentials of nutrition and diet therapy* (2nd ed.). St. Louis: The C. V. Mosby Co., 1978. This book is a well-written, comprehensive introduction to the science of nutrition that contains a lot of practical information, including a chapter on food preferences of various ethnic groups; highly recommended.

Cookbooks

Bowser, P., and Eckstein, J. *A pinch of soul: Fast and fancy soul cookery for today's hostess.* New York: Avon Books, 1970. The book describes itself as containing "delectable dinners from Bread Pudding with Brandy Sauce to Kentucky Burgoo. Super suppers from African Bean Soup to Congo Chicken. All with very little effort, a lot of style and a pinch of soul." The recipes are genuine and very good.

Cooper, T. T., and Ratner, M. *Many hands cooking: An international cookbook for girls and boys.* New York: Thomas T. Crowell Co. in cooperation with the U.S. Committee for UNICEF, 1974, $4.00. It is nice to know there is a delightful cookbook for young children that features recipes from various cultures. It has the added charms of being beautifully illustrated, telling a little about the customs of each country, and rating each recipe according to difficulty.

Ferreira, N. J. *The mother-child cookbook.* Menlo Park, Calif.: Pacific Coast Publishers, 1967. The recipes in this book have been pretested with nursery school children, and the quantities given are sufficient for 16. It is an invaluable volume that divides recipes according to indoor-outdoor, different kinds of skills, and age groups. It also has some ethnic recipes, including Chinese and Portuguese ones.

Piper, M. R. *Sunset Mexican cookbook.* Menlo Park, Calif.: Lane Magazine & Book Co., 1969. The delicious Mexican recipes are written so that Anglos can understand and concoct reasonably authentic Mexican menus.

United States Department of Agriculture. *Food buying guide for child care centers.* Washington, D.C.: U.S. Govt. Printing Office, 1974 (FNS-108). This useful, inexpensive guide has many tables listing size of portions and amount to purchase to serve 25 or 50 children; a helpful reference for cooks and kitchen managers to have on hand.

United States Department of Health, Education, and Welfare. *Quantity recipes for child care centers.* Washington, D.C.: U.S. Govt. Printing Office, 1973b. This recipe card file was designed to provide quantity recipes and other information on preparing meals in children's centers. The easy-to-use file cards offer recipes for main dishes, soups, salads, vegetables, and desserts.

For the Advanced Student

Bakwin, H., and Bakwin, R. M. *Behavior disorders in children* (5th ed.). Philadelphia: W. B. Saunders Co., 1974. This is the classic reference in the field. It lists and discusses innumerable behavior problems, including those associated with eating, toileting, and sleeping, and contains brief discussions of cause, treatment, and suggested further readings in the field.

Kessler, J. W. *Psychopathology of childhood.* Englewood Cliffs, N.J.: Prentice-Hall, Inc., 1966. Written for the serious student who wants to know more about handling special behavior problems, *The Psychopathology of Childhood* has an entire chapter devoted to eating and toileting problems. The book is more detailed than the Bakwins', but not so broad in scope.

Read, M. S. The biological bases: Malnutrition and behavioral development. In I. J. Gordon (Ed.), *Early childhood education: The seventy-first yearbook of the National Society for the Study of Education* (Part II). Chicago: University of Chicago Press, 1972. Read's article provides an overview of the effect of malnutrition on development. Most important, it presents a clear analysis of the effect of severe malnutrition on the development of the brain.

Yarrow, L. J. Separation from parents during early childhood. In M. L. Hoffman and L. W. Hoffman (Eds.), *Review of child development research* (Vol. 1). New York: Russell Sage Foundation, 1964. The chapter by Yarrow analyzes and discusses different kinds of parent-child separations and what is known of the effect of such separation on the development of personality.

Photo by Richard Pierce, Santa Barbara City College Children's Center

4 □ Development of the physical self

Jimmy, for example, was a child of elderly parents. Life in his comfortable home had been filled with listening to music or to stories and quiet play with small blocks or coloring books. When he first came to nursery school, he retreated from the active world in which the children lived. He sat by the victrola, and, if given a choice, would politely refuse to go outside. He didn't care for swinging or climbing or running or jumping—and the children didn't find him fun. After some time the rhythm of swinging seemed to attract him and very slowly he began playing more actively and gaining some motor skills. With skill came confidence and contacts with other children. Jimmy had attended nursery school nearly six months before he could bring himself to try going down the slide. His delight when he succeeded was evident. He used the slide again and again, squealing with joy, calling everyone's attention to his accomplishment. His growth was rapid from this time on. He began to stand up for himself in play. His tenseness diminished and his friendliness increased. He grew more childlike and more of a person in his own right. It had taken him a long time to enjoy the outdoors but when he discovered himself there, he could grow as a child.*

Good food, reasonable toilet procedures, and adequate rest are important factors in maintaining the physical and emotional well-being of young children. Additional factors that affect the physical development of children include health and safety and provision of maximum opportunities for their bodies to grow and develop in the most healthy way.

PROMOTION OF HEALTH AND SAFETY IN THE NURSERY SCHOOL
Basic ways to protect and foster the physical health of children

Beginning teachers who come from middle-class homes sometimes do not realize the necessity for early childhood centers to take the lead in making sure young children have adequate health care.

Many families served by preschool centers have very low incomes but do not understand how to make use of free services available to them through Medicare or other health facilities (Gussow, 1970). Families from the lower middle–income bracket are often even harder pressed to find the money that medical care requires. Both of these groups may need advice from the teacher about how to make use of free or inexpensive community health resources. Even more well-to-do families need to be encouraged to make sure their children have health check-ups and immunizations.

A 1974 survey of 1- to 4-year-olds in the United States revealed that 36.9% had not been vaccinated for polio, 60.6% for mumps, 35.5% for measles, and a shocking 40.2% for rubella (National Council of Organizations for Children and Youth, 1976). The problem with rubella is especially serious, because vulnerable children who become infected may expose their unvaccinated, pregnant mothers to this

*Reprinted by permission from *Let's play outdoors*, by Katherine Read Baker, pp. 9-11. © 1969 by the National Association for the Education of Young Children, 1834 Connecticut Ave., N.W., Washington, D.C. 20009.

disease—a circumstance that often has deadly implications for the fetus, particularly in the first trimester of pregnancy. The student should not be lulled into assuming this situation is improving, since the rate of immunizations actually appears to be declining. For instance, the Public Health Service reports that the number of children aged 5 years and younger who received at least three doses of polio vaccine has declined since 1965, when 74.9% were immunized, to only 62.9% in 1972 (U.S. Department of Health, Education, and Welfare, 1973a).

Physical examinations should be required before the child enrolls. Because the preschool is often the first institution that comes into contact with families of young children in a formal way, it is particularly valuable for each school to require preentry physical examinations. This not only protects the other children in the school but also assures that inoculations are brought up to date and that physical examinations are given to many children who might otherwise slip by without them until entry to kindergarten. Some states already make this part of their licensing regulations for day-care centers and nursery schools; those that do not should be encouraged to add this requirement to their regulations promptly.

The teacher should be prepared to help parents find health care during the year whenever possible. There are a variety of free health services and examinations available in many communities, and the teacher needs to make it her business to become acquainted with each one so that she can refer families who need their help. These services range from university-sponsored speech and hearing clinics to eye examinations paid for by men's fraternal organizations and the special services offered by the Crippled Children's Society. Sometimes arrangements can be made with training schools to supply health services in return for the opportunity to work with young children. Dental hygienists, for example, may be willing to clean the children's teeth in order to obtain experience with preschoolers.

A good way to locate information about such services is to contact the public health nurses in the community. These people are usually gold mines of practical information about sources of assistance.

The teacher should act as a health screener. An alert teacher can often spot problems that have been overlooked by families and even by pediatricians, who, though expert, lack the teacher's opportunity to see the child over an extended period of time. The teacher should particularly watch for children who don't seem to see or hear well, who are very awkward, who seldom talk, or who are unusually apathetic or excessively active. The behavior may be only an idiosyncrasy, or it may require professional help—and the sooner help is sought the better. (See also Chapter 19 for further details on identification of special problems.)

The teacher should make a health check of every child as he arrives at school each day. This serves the purpose of assuring a personal greeting and provides a quick once-over so that a child who is not feeling up to par may be sent home before his parent departs. Although there are some standard things to check for, such as flushed or too pale faces, rashes, and marked lethargy (Vaughn, 1970), the most important symptom to be aware of is any significant change in the child's appearance. Teachers who see the same children every day get to know how they usually look and behave and can often spot such variations promptly and thus avoid exposing other children in school to the condition. (See also Appendix C for a list of common diseases, their symptoms, and incubation periods.)

The teacher must know what to do when a child becomes ill at school. No matter how careful the teacher and conscientious the parent, an occasional child is going to blossom forth with something during the day. Ideally, the child should be sent home immediately, but in practice this can be very difficult to do. Even when parents have been asked to make alternative arrangements for emergency care, these arrangements sometimes fall through, and the school and youngster have to make the best of it. Most schools try to keep children who are ill apart from the rest; usually the office serves this purpose

Photo by John Hutzimarkos, Oaks Parent/Child Workshop

fairly well. The child should have a place to lie down located as close to a bathroom as possible, and he will need to be comforted and reassured so that he does not feel bereft and lonely.

Because sending a child home from school often embarrasses and angers the parent and hurts the child's feelings as well, it is desirable to be firm but gentle when doing this. Sending something home along with the youngster, such as a little play dough or a book, will help him feel less rejected and make his return to school easier when he is feeling better.

General health precautions should be observed consistently by children and staff. Blowing noses on disposable tissue, washing hands before handling food, and not allowing children to share food, cups, or utensils they have had in their mouths are basic precautions that must always be observed. Most schools make it a practice never to administer medi-cation (including aspirin) without the express request of the physician and parent in writing.

It is also important to be aware of the real temperature of the day and to take jackets off indoors and dress the children warmly enough outdoors, but not too warmly. Particularly in the fall, mothers tend to weigh their children down with too much clothing, and the children may be so absorbed in their play that they can be dripping with sweat and not realize it. The teacher needs to remind them about staying comfortable and to help them adjust their clothing to suit the temperature when necessary.

Maintaining the physical safety of the children

The teacher must never forget that the children in her care are not her own and that supervising them carries a special responsibility. All schools should carry insurance, both to protect them against being sued and also to provide accident coverage for the children. In addition, the entire school needs to be checked continually to make sure it is maintained in safe condition. Broken equipment such as tricycles without pedals and wobbly jungle gyms must be removed or repaired promptly. Sticks, particularly with nails in them, should be discarded. Safety precautions such as using swings with canvas seats should be observed. The danger area around swings must be clearly marked, and children should be taught to wait on the bottom step of the slide (which can be painted red to make it easier to identify).

Disinfectants, ant poisons, scouring powders, bleaches, and antiseptics, which are all commonly found in nursery schools, should be kept on high shelves in the kitchen where children are not permitted or, better yet, in locked cabinets.

In Chapter 2 it was suggested that inexperienced teachers stop an activity if it looks dangerous to them rather than permit an accident to happen. One other safety rule has proved to be generally helpful: the teacher should never lift a child onto a piece of play equipment if he cannot manage to get on it by himself (swings are an exception to this rule). Of course, youngsters sometimes climb up on something, feel marooned, and must be helped down; but that is different from lifting them onto the top of the jungle gym or boosting them onto a tippy gangplank before they are really able to cope with these situations.

The concern for safety has to be moderated by the teacher's good sense and self-control. Children must be protected, but they also need the chance to venture and try things out. This venturesomeness is a hallmark of 4-year-olds in particular. Occasional small catastrophes are to be expected, and the teacher should not become so overly protective that she hovers over the children and remonstrates with them constantly to be careful. Instead, she should try to maintain a generally high level of safety combined with the opportunity for the children to experiment with the mild risks that build feelings of competence as they are met and mastered.

HELPING CHILDREN DEVELOP THEIR LARGE AND FINE MUSCLE ABILITIES
Basic principles of development

Before reading about specific ways to foster psychomotor development, the student needs to understand some developmental principles that have important implications for education.

Development occurs in predictable patterns and sequences. Although some investigators are now questioning the concept that chronological age should determine when children are taught various skills (Bruner, 1964; Gagné, 1968; White, 1971), it is still generally agreed that children progress through a predictable sequence of developmental stages (Mussen, Conger, and Kagan, 1974) (Table

Table 4. Age at which a given percentage of children perform locomotor skills*

	25%	50%	75%	90%
Rolls over	2.3 mo	2.8 mo	3.8 mo	4.7 mo
Sits without support	4.8 mo	5.5 mo	6.5 mo	7.8 mo
Walks well	11.3 mo	12.1 mo	13.5 mo	14.3 mo
Kicks ball forward	15 mo	20 mo	22.3 mo	2 yr
Pedals trike	21 mo	23.9 mo	2.8 yr	3 yr
Balances on one foot ten seconds	3 yr	4.5 yr	5 yr	5.9 yr
Hops on one foot	3 yr	3.4 yr	4 yr	4.9 yr
Catches bounced ball	3.5 yr	3.9 yr	4.9 yr	5.5 yr
Heel-to-toe walk	3.3 yr	3.6 yr	4.2 yr	5 yr

*From Arnheim, D. D., and Pestolesi, R. A. *Developing motor behavior in children: A balanced approach to elementary physical education.* St. Louis: The C. V. Mosby Co., 1973.
Selected items from the Denver Developmental Screening Test by permission of William K. Frankenburg, M.D., and Josiah B. Dodds, Ph.D., University of Colorado Medical Center.

4). This is true of both intellectual development (Piaget and Inhelder, 1967) and physical development. Children usually sit before they stand, stand before they walk, and walk before they run (Gesell, Halverson, Thompson, and Ilg, 1940). In addition, specific skills such as running, jumping, and throwing progress through a number of substages of competency before they emerge as mature physical abilities (Wickstrom, 1977).

Teachers need to be able to recognize these stages of development so they can adjust their curriculum offerings to provide a good balance between opportunities for practice in order to consolidate the skill and opportunities for accepting the challenge of a slightly more difficult activity to go on to.

The course of development moves from head to tail. This *cephalocaudal* principle means that children are able to control the region around their head and shoulders before they can control their hands or feet. This is an easy principle to remember if one recalls that babies can sit up and manipulate playthings long before they are able to stand on their feet and walk. Quite simply, children are able to reach, grasp, and use their hands with considerable skill before they are able to master the art of skipping or kicking accurately. The curriculum of the preschool should be planned accordingly.

The course of development moves from large to fine muscle control. Large muscle activities have been identified by Guilford (1958), who factor-analyzed activities from motor proficiency tests as including activities involving static balance, dynamic precision, gross body coordination, and flexibility. Fine muscle activities include such things as finger speed, arm steadiness, arm and hand precision, and finger and hand dexterity. Development from large to fine muscle control means that children gain control over their larger muscles first and then gradually attain control over the finer muscle groups. Thus a child is able to walk long before he is able to construct a tabletop house of tiny plastic bricks.

The educational implications of this developmental principle for early childhood teachers are that preschool children need ample opportunities to use their large muscles in vigorous, energetic, physical play. It can be torment for young children to have to remain confined too long at chairs and tables. However, since the finer muscle, eye-hand skills are also beginning to develop during this period, activities that stimulate the children to practice these skills should also be offered—but not overdone so that excessive demands are made on the children's self-control.

FOSTERING PHYSICAL DEVELOPMENT IN YOUNG CHILDREN
Use of apparatus to promote physical skill

In general, the school should furnish a large assortment of big, sturdy, durable equipment that provides many opportunities for all kinds of physical activity, and it should also provide a teacher who values vigorous large muscle play and who encourages the children to participate freely in this pleasure.

Equipment that is good for crawling through, climbing up, balancing on, and hanging from should be included. The children will need things they can lift, haul, and shove around to test their strength and use to make discoveries about physical properties the equipment possesses. They need things they can use for construction, and they need equipment that provides opportunities for rhythmic activities, such as bouncing and jumping and swinging. In addition, there must be places of generous size for them to carry out the wonderful sensory experiences that involve mud, sand, and water. Finally, they need plenty of space in which to simply move about.

I have been deliberately nonspecific about suggesting particular pieces of large muscle equipment in the hope that talking about the children's activity requirements will encourage the teacher to consider afresh what might be used to meet these needs. However, for those who wish to pursue this question in detail, an excellent publication provides detailed lists of indoor and outdoor equipment and firms that manufacture it: *Selecting Educational Equipment and Materials for Home and School* (Cohen and Hadley, 1976).

Photo by Tim Drake, Santa Barbara City College Children's Center

There currently is an exciting trend toward designing play equipment that is novel, often beautiful, and occasionally cheaper than our more mundane playground furnishings (Lady Allen of Hurtwood, Flekkoy, Sigsgaard, and Skard, 1964; Educational Facilities Laboratory, 1972; Ellison, 1974; Hewes, 1974; Utzinger, 1970).

Equipment need not be expensive to provide sound play value, and several references that give suggestions about how to combine economy with beauty and ingenuity are included at the end of this chapter (Hogan, 1974). It is wise to remember, though, that poorly constructed, cheap equipment can be the poorest kind of economy in the long run.

Children are hard on things, and it doesn't pay to buy or make playthings that are flimsy—better to have a bake sale and raise money for better quality equipment than be stuck with buying two cheap swing sets 2 years in a row.

In general, the more movable and versatile the equipment is, the more stimulating and interesting it will remain for the children. Observation of many schools has convinced me that movable outdoor equipment is one of the things in shortest supply in the play yard; yet it is vital to have plenty of boards, sawhorses, large hollow blocks, ropes, rubber tires, and barrels lest the children feel starved when they cannot complete their more ambitious projects. Schools should budget for more of this kind of equipment every year; there is no such thing as owning too much of it.

Before buying outdoor equipment, however, every teacher should read the discussion by Kritchevsky, Prescott, and Walling (1969) about how to plan and develop play centers that will have maximum attractiveness and play value for young children. Material explaining the English concept of adventure playgrounds should also be investigated (Allen, 1968; Bengtsson, 1972). These wonderfully messy, casual-looking English playgrounds place great emphasis on freedom to try out and explore—the faces of the children in the pictures bear witness to the value of such experience.

Once the equipment has been acquired, it is important to maintain it carefully. Hollow blocks, which are very costly, should be used on grass or outdoor, grass-type carpeting, not on cement or asphalt, where they will splinter badly when knocked down. Wood equipment has to be sanded and varnished every year to keep it smooth, and over a period of time this treatment can make it beautiful as well. Wooden items must be stored under cover at night. Metal items should be stored under cover when possible to avoid rust or oxidation.

Of course, children's vigorous activities do not need to be restricted to the school yard. Children will be delighted with the chance to visit parks with large open spaces where they can run freely and roll down hills. Many communities have wading pools for preschoolers or special play areas set aside for younger children. Even a trike expedition around the block with a pause at an interesting long set of steps can offer challenges that should not be overlooked, particularly in an all-day program.

Role of the teacher in fostering large muscle play

In addition to providing equipment to enhance large muscle play, the teacher can do much to encourage this kind of activity. Probably most important is that she provide enough uninterrupted time for satisfying play to transpire. Children need time to develop their ideas and carry them through, and if they build something, they need time to use it after they build it.

Outdoor play time at nursery school is not treated as teachers often handle recess in the elementary school. Playtime at nursery school requires the active involvement of the teacher with the children. She does not do this by participating as a companion in their play, but by observing and being alert to ways to make the play richer by offering additional equipment or tactfully teaching an intrusive child how to make himself more welcome to the group. Because her function is encouraging play to continue, she tries to be as facilitative yet unobtrusive as possible.

The teacher needs to keep the environment safe, but at the same time she should keep an open mind about the uses to which equipment can be put. If encouraged, children often come up with original or unconventional uses of materials that are not dangerous and that should be welcomed by the teacher because they are so creative and satisfying to the child. For example, one of our Center children recently got together all the beanbags to use as a pillow in the playhouse, and another youngster used the hose to make a worm tunnel in the sandbox. These harmless creative activities are all too easily squelched if the teacher is insensitive to their value or too conventional.

Finally, the teacher should keep on the lookout for children who are at loose ends and involve them in activities before they begin to run wildly and aimlessly about. She needs to be comfortable with a good deal of noise and to welcome the vigorous activity so characteristic of 4-year-olds because they need this opportunity for vigorous assertion and movement in order to develop fully.

SPECIFIC APPROACHES FOR FOSTERING PHYSICAL DEVELOPMENT

There appear to be as many approaches advocated for fostering perceptual-motor skills in older children as there are people who write about this subject (Frostig, 1970; Getman, 1965; Kephart, 1960). However, not as much detailed information is available when the matter of preschool children is discussed. Perhaps this is because most nursery school teachers apparently subscribe to the idea that children's bodies and physical skills will develop adequately if the children are free to run about and do as they wish. Surely, there is much to be said for the value of unrestricted play, but the teacher must also realize that new information is accumulating about how to enhance the physical development and coordination of children and that some of this information applies to preschoolers as well as to their older brothers and sisters.

Techniques for sensory integration (Ayers, 1973; Montgomery and Richter, 1977), for example, are likely to prove a valuable addition to infant and remedial education, and new knowledge of the wide range of perceptual-motor developmental needs should encourage teachers of young children to broaden the kinds of experiences they make available to children both indoors and out. In addition, the more creative approaches to physical development that come under the terms ''movement education'' and ''creative dance'' are worthy of our attention.

Fostering sensory integration and experience

Fostering sensory integration. Sensory integration is one of the most basic aspects of physical development, and there is a lot more to it than just helping children distinguish between rough and smooth, or passing little bottles of different scents around at story time. Everything we learn comes in

by means of our senses, is then interpreted by the brain, and is either translated into action or not as the mind decides. We often think of the senses as being those of vision, hearing (auditory), and touch (tactile), and these are surely important ones for the developing child. But it is also interesting to learn there are additional sensory pathways of great significance—these include the olfactory (smell) and gustatory (taste) senses, and a less familiar one, the kinesthetic sense, which lets us know, from sensations transmitted from nerves in our joints and muscles, what our body is doing and its position in space. Information from these senses is poured into such systems as the proprioceptive and vestibular ones, which then integrate the information and make appropriate reactions possible.

Jean Ayers (1973) maintains that all these senses and systems require stimulation in order to develop adequately and operate effectively together, and that this sensory integration is vital for later sound development. Since sensory integration is a very basic neurological process, *early* stimulation is particularly valuable. Her focus is mainly on providing a series of experiences designed to bring about such integration rather than emphasizing the acquisition of particular skills. Examples of such activities might include stroking a child's body with various textures, having the children roll about inside a carpeted cylinder, or using scooter boards for prone travel (always with a helmet) (Montgomery and Richter, 1977).

Fostering sensory experience. On a more familiar plane, we should also be alert to the truth that cultural restrictions on sensory experience appear to be increasing in number every day. It has been maintained that 80% of everything we learn comes to us through our eyes, but it seems to me that our society encourages use of this one sense far more than is necessary. One has only to watch the deodorant and disinfectant ads on television to become aware of the tremendous emphasis on the desirability of smelling only a few choice fragrances. Children are continually admonished not to touch things, and as they mature, they are also taught not to touch other people except under carefully restricted circumstances. As for tasting, how many times have you heard a mother warn, "Don't put that in your mouth; it's dirty"? The latest victim of the war against the senses appears to be hearing. In self-defense, people seem to be learning to tune out the continual piped-in music of the supermarket and the constant noise of the television set.

The nursery school teacher needs to contend with this narrowing and restricting of the use of the senses by deliberately continuing to utilize all of them as avenues of learning. Children should be encouraged to make comparisons of substances by feeling them and smelling them, as well as by looking at them. Science displays should be explored by handling and manipulation rather than by looking at bulletin board pictures or observing demonstrations carried out by the teacher. Stress should be placed on developing auditory discrimination skills (telling sounds apart) as well as on paying attention to what is said by the teacher. Learning through physical, sensory participation should be an important part of every nursery school day.

In particular, the emotional value of personal physical contact must be understood and appreciated. Ashley Montagu (1971) has reviewed numerous studies that illustrate the beneficial effect of being touched and the relationship of tactile experience to healthy physical and emotional development. He speaks of the "mind of the skin" and comments that although the skin is the largest organ of the body, it remains one of the most ignored. Lawrence Frank (1971) also makes a very good case for the significance of tactile communication.

Young children require the reassurance and comfort of physical affection from teachers. They need to be patted, rocked, held, and hugged from time to time. Cornelia Goldsmith's statement that a teacher's most important equipment is her lap is as true today as when she said it 20 years ago.

Use of perceptual-motor activities to enhance physical development

There are two ways to approach perceptual-motor activities—the first provides opportunities for practice in specific skills, and the second uses physical activity to promote creative thought and self-expression. Both approaches have merit.

Planning for specific perceptual-motor activities. Following the studies conducted by Gesell (Gesell, Halverson, Thompson, and Ilg, 1940), which stressed the role of maturation in relation to development, nursery school teachers have usually been willing to content themselves with supplying an assortment of equipment such as swings and slides, hoping that children will seek out the experiences they need by using this apparatus in a variety of ways. But we now know that perceptual-motor activities can go beyond this sort of thing without requiring children to be regimented and drilled and that we really should offer them a broader selection of physically developmental activities than we formerly did if we wish to enhance the full range of their skills.

The difficulty lies in finding a body of organized knowledge that is comprehensive and whose worth has been validated by thorough research. At present, many of the theoretical frameworks and taxonomies are complex and difficult to apply (Merrill, 1972), or they have been developed for older children (Barsch, 1967), or, as Cratty (1970b), Fleming (1972), and Kirk (1972) point out, their merit has not been adequately substantiated by research. Indeed, some programs make such grandiose claims of success that, as Cratty puts it, "Some parents and educators have embraced various 'systems' with the fervor usually seen only in churches of the more demonstrative religious sects" (1970b, p. 107). It is important, therefore, to caution the teacher of young children to use common sense and avoid being swept off her feet by unusual-sounding activity programs that make extravagant but untested claims.

After considerable review of the literature, I have concluded that a moderate program offering the clearest language combined with a structure easily understood by nursery school teachers and applicable to preschool children is the one utilized by Arnheim and Sinclair in their book, *The Clumsy Child* (1979). They divide motor tasks into the fol-

Photo by Richard Pierce, Santa Barbara City College Children's Center

lowing categories: locomotion, balance, body and space perception, rhythm and temporal awareness, rebound and airborne activities, projectile management, management of daily motor activities (including many "fine muscle" tasks), and tension releasers.

It is relatively simple to think of motor activities in relation to these headings once they have been identified and to make certain that opportunities for *repeated* practice in each of the categories are included in curriculum plans. The trick lies in concocting ways of presenting them that appeal to children. Obstacle courses, or simple want-to-try-this kind of noncompetitive games, or movement activities can all be used effectively—if only the teacher will keep in mind the diversity of action that should be incorporated. Fortunately, the mere challenge of having such possibilities available often provides attraction enough since youngsters are almost irresistibly drawn to physical activities that are just challenging enough without being too difficult. As a matter of fact, if encouraged to experiment, they will often develop the next hardest task for themselves following mastery of its simpler elements.

Table 5 primarily stresses large muscle involvement. Nursery schools, of course, also include many additional "fine muscle" activities, including such tabletop activities as sewing, using pegboards and puzzles, stringing beads, and playing with put-together materials. Also included are block building, which taps stacking and balancing skills, pouring and spooning in their many forms, and manipulating art materials, most particularly pencils, brushes, scissors, and crayons. Woodworking is another more vigorous example of small muscle activity. It takes a good deal of skill to hit a nail with something as small as a hammer head.

THINGS TO REMEMBER WHEN PRESENTING SMALL MUSCLE ACTIVITIES. Offering a range of challenge in levels of difficulty is particularly important in a group of mixed ages, but even in a relatively homogeneous group of 3-year-olds provision must be made for the fact that the level of fine muscle skill, not to mention the amount of emotional con-

trol and ability to concentrate, will vary considerably from child to child. Rather than setting out three or four puzzles of 16 pieces each, it will meet the children's range of abilities better if one or two inset puzzles, and perhaps a 7-, 15-, and 22-piece puzzle, are set out and changed as they become boring.

Sometimes it adds interest to offer two levels of otherwise identical material. Large and small wood beads make an interesting contrast; or occasionally, puzzles that have the same picture but vary in the number of cut pieces can be purchased and made available for use. Children enjoy having access to both levels and like to put into words what it is that makes the materials similar and what it is that makes them different.

Fine muscle activities should be of reasonably short duration. It is difficult for young children to hold still very long, much less sit and concentrate on a fine muscle task that requires considerable self-control. For this reason, several activities should be available at the same time, and children should always be free to get up, move around, and shift to more or less taxing experiences as they feel the need. Quiet periods such as story hours or snack times should not be followed by additional quiet, fine muscle play but by more vigorous large muscle activity.

The teacher should watch out for signs of unusual frustration. I once had a little boy in my nursery school who participated with enthusiasm and happiness in almost everything we did, with one notable exception. Whenever he played with floor blocks, he would work a while and then in a rage send them flying. Yet he was drawn to them as a moth to a flame. His mother and I were baffled; he seemed well adjusted and easygoing, with only this exception. The staff tried building his skills, investigated whether he was happy at home, and watched to see whether other children interfered with his work and made him angry, but we could find no satisfactory answer. Finally one day his mother arrived beaming at school with the following tale. Alan and his father had been looking out the window the week before, and he had said, "Oh, look Papa, see those

Table 5. Categories of physical activities and some suggestions for providing practice of these skills at the preschool level*

Category	Illustrative activities	Comments
Locomotion		
Rolling	Roll over and over, sideways, both directions. Forward roll (somersault).	Nice to have tumbling mats but not essential—rug, grass, or clean floor also works.
Crawling, creeping	Move by placing weight on elbows only, dragging feet. Crawl using arm and leg in unison, on same side of body or use alternating arm/leg crawl.	Works well to give these movements animal names such as "bear walk."
Climbing	Apparatus valuable here—good to incorporate stretching, hanging, and reaching in this activity.	Necessary to be careful of safety.
Walking	Can vary with big, little steps, fast or slow. Encourage movement in different directions.	Good to do walking activities barefoot on contrasting surfaces for sensory input.
Stair climbing	Nice to use this during an excursion unless nursery school has a five- to six-step stairway.	This is an interesting indicator of developmental level: younger children take steps one at a time, drawing second foot up to meet leading foot. Older children alternate feet in this task.
Jumping, hopping, and skipping	Children can jump over lines or very low obstacles, as well as jump down from blocks of various heights.	
	Hopping is difficult for young children; it is a prelude to skipping. Encourage learning to hop on either foot and alternating feet.	Can use animal names here also.
	Skipping often too difficult for nursery school youngsters. Valuable skill to ultimately acquire, since it involves crossing midline in a rhythmical alternating pattern.	Don't encourage running backward—young children often catch feet and trip themselves.
Running and leaping	Nice to find large, grassy area for these kinds of activities; makes a nice field trip.	Often provides emotional relief, too. Gives marvelous feeling of freedom, power, and satisfaction.
Balance		
Static (balance while still)	Balance lying on side. Balance standing on tiptoes. Balance on one foot, then the other, for short periods of time.	
Dynamic (balance while moving)	Use balance beam many ways, or use large hollow blocks as "stepping stones," or walk on lines.	Clatter bridge, if available, is a particularly challenging task; may overwhelm some children.
Balance using an object	Balance beanbags on hands, or back, or head. Work with unbalanced objects—pole with weight on one end, for example.	
Body and space perception	Movement education techniques apply to this category particularly well.	Helps to refer to other people's bodies, too, for example, where is Henry's elbow?

*Based on Arnheim, D. D., and Sinclair, W. A. *The clumsy child* (2nd ed.). St. Louis: The C. V. Mosby Co., 1979.
Note: These activities are only a handful of a great many possibilities. For more extensive material see Arnheim and Sinclair (1979) or Hendrick, 1980.

Table 5. Categories of physical activities and some suggestions for providing practice of these skills at the preschool level—cont'd

Category	Illustrative activities	Comments
Body and space perception—cont'd	How big can you be? How little? Can you make a "sad" face? Can you fit inside this circle? Can you fill up this circle (a very big one)? How much of you can you get in the air at once? Use shadow dancing for effective awareness building.	Listening, imitative actions such as "Simon says" are fun if not carried on too long. Can stress position in space—"over," "under," and so on; tedious if over-done.
Rhythm and temporal awareness	Any moving in time to music or to a rhythmic beat. Can be varied in many ways—fast, slow, or with different rhythmic patterns. Important to keep patterns simple and clear with preschoolers. Remember that many nursery school activities, such as swinging and using rocking horses, also fit this category; fun to add music to these for a change.	Creative dance is the usual medium— "rhythm band" is typical kinder-garten-level activity, which is essen-tially conforming rather than creative. See also material on dancing in Chapter 12.
Rebound and airborne activities	In nursery school these are generally thought of as "bouncing" activities; mattresses, bouncing boards, and large inner tubes offer various levels of difficulty. Swings and hand-over-hand bars are also, in a sense, airborne.	Do not use a trampoline; it requires extraordinarily careful supervision. Many insurance companies abso-lutely refuse to provide insurance for this piece of equipment.
Projectile management Throwing and catching	Throwing and catching usually require teacher participation. Children throw best using rela-tively small objects but catch best using large ones! Can throw objects at target such as wall, or into large box. For catching, older children can use a pitchback net; useful for understanding effect of force in relation to throwing.	Problem is to use objects that move slowly enough and are harmless; Nerf balls, beanbags, large rubber balls, Whiffle balls, and fleece balls meet this requirement. Need lots of beanbags; not much fun to have to run and pick them up every two or three throws.
Kicking	Begin with kicking a "still" ball, then go on to a gently rolling one.	
Striking	Hit balloons with hands and then with paddle. Can hit ball balanced on traffic cone with light plastic bat (Whiffle ball good for this).	Many teachers are nervous about striking activities, but these activities are challenging to children and worth the careful supervision and rule setting they require.
Bouncing	Best with large, rubber ball; use two hands and then progress to one hand; bounce to other children.	
Daily motor activities (fine muscle activities)	Includes many self-help skills such as buttoning and even tooth brushing! Also includes use of almost all self-expressive materials, and use of tools in carpentry and cooking. See discussion on fine muscle activities in text.	Be careful of overfatigue.
Tension releasers	Refer to material in text.	

two kitties!'' But his father had looked and asked ''What two kitties?'' since he could see only one. ''Why, those two little black kitties right over there,'' quoth Al. Shortly thereafter, when his eyes were examined, the answer to his block problem became clear—he was slightly cross-eyed, just enough so that stacking small blocks was a particularly irritating problem for him to solve, and it was this condition that caused him to send them tumbling down when his self-control was exceeded by the difficulty of the task.

This story may help other teachers remember to be alert to activities that seem to provoke consistent frustrations in some children. Such a reaction can often be a symptom of a physical problem that warrants further investigation, since early remediation makes correction more likely.

RELAXATION AND TENSION-RELIEVING ACTIVITIES. Sometimes we do not think of relaxation as being a motor skill—but rather the absence of one—since ''all the child has to do is hold still''! However, the ability to relax and let go can be learned (Jacobson, 1976), and the ever increasing stress of life as people mature in our culture (Selye, 1956) makes acquiring these techniques *invaluable*. Moreover, since day-care centers invariably include naps as part of their routine, knowledge of relaxation techniques is doubly valuable there. Tension, of course, is intimately tied to emotional states as well as to activity level. We all know that children who are emotionally overwrought find it more difficult to relax. It is worth taking extra time and pains with such youngsters to teach them relaxation skills because of the relief they experience when they can let down even a little.

Reducing stimulation from the outside is a good principle to bear in mind. This is often done by darkening the room, playing quiet music, and providing regular, monotonous sensory experience such as rocking or gently rubbing backs.

During movement and dance activities, children should alternate quiet and active activities. They can be encouraged to sense their own bodies and purposefully relax themselves by being floppy dolls or boiled noodles. Relaxation should be contrasted with its opposite state of intense contraction. Even young children can learn to make their bodies stiff and hard and then become limp and soft, thereby applying Jacobson's techniques of progressive relaxation (1938). Stretching, holding the stretch, and then relaxing are also easily understood by children of nursery school age; and they do feel wonderful.

Yawning, breathing slowly, shutting eyes, and lying somewhat apart from other children will make relaxation easier. The attitude of the teacher moving slowly about and talking quietly is a significant influence as well. Sometimes young children are able to use imagery, also, and picture a quiet place they'd like to be. For very young children it is usually necessary to suggest such places—perhaps rocking in his mother's lap, or lying on a water bed, or resting on the grass on a warm, sleepy day.

As we come to understand more about meditation, it is evident that some of these techniques can be used with children also. An interesting example of such an application is *The Centering Book,* which lists many kinds of awareness and relaxation activities, some of which can be adapted for nursery school children (Hendricks and Wills, 1975).

Even more fundamental than these relaxation techniques, however, should be the goal of alleviating whatever is generating tension in the first place. There are numberless reasons why children or adults feel tense—ranging from suppressed anger to shyness or that general feeling of apprehension commonly termed anxiety. Since methods of fostering emotional health are discussed in considerable detail later on, suffice it to say here that perhaps the most basic way to help people become less tense is to enable them to become more competent in as many areas of their lives as possible. This feeling of competency—being in command of oneself and one's life—is a highly effective, long-term antidote for tension.

Using physical activity to promote creative thought and self-expression

Using movement exploration. One of the newer aspects of creative physical education is termed *movement education* (Tillotson, 1970). It is a nice blend of physical activity and problem solving that can be considerable fun for children. It often incorporates the theories of Rudolph Laban (1960). The teacher may ask a youngster, "Is there some way you could get across the rug without using your feet?" and then, "Is there another way you could do that?" Or she might question, "What could you do with a ball with different parts of your feet?" or "Can you hold a ball without using your hands?"

It's obvious how this kind of teaching fosters the development of fluency in ideas, and some research by Torrance (1970b) indicates that where this approach was used with first and second graders in a dance class, they placed significantly higher on tests of creativity than did untrained third graders.

Movement education also contributes to knowing more about the body—being aware of various parts such as elbows or toes and all the things they can do, not only independently, but when used together. According to Joan Tillotson, when thinking about movement education, it is helpful to understand that each action "demands the use of three elements (1) space—straight-line action and indirect bi-plane action; (2) time—fast or slow speed; and (3) force—strong or light effort. Emphasis is also placed on smooth, controlled performance regardless of the movement pattern" (1970, p. 34). I have found that utilizing these kinds of experiences to begin a movement session leads quite naturally into dance. If the problems presented are simple and fun, children soon begin laughing and trying out possibilities with enthusiasm, which has a very desirable, freeing effect.

Using creative dance as a means of self-expression. Dancing can be the freest and most joyful of all large motor activities. For young children dancing usually means moving rhythmically to music in a variety of relatively unstructured ways. The quandary beginning teachers often feel is just how unstructured this should be. It is rarely effective to just put on a record, no matter how appealing, and expect the children to "dance." On the other hand, the teacher who sets out to teach specific patterns, often in the guise of folk dances, surely limits the

creative aspects of this experience. Besides that, the limitation, patterned dances are usually too complicated for young children to learn unless stripped to very simple levels.

What works best is to have an array of records or tapes on hand with which the teacher is very familiar and which provide a selection of moods and tempi. It is important, also, to have several activities thought out in advance to fall back on if something does not "go over" and to plan on participating with the children. Finally, as the session moves along, more and more ideas and movements can be drawn from the children themselves—an approach that makes the activity truly creative and satisfying for them.*

SUMMARY

The promotion of health and safety is vital to the physical well-being of the young child in the nursery school. During the hours he is at school, it is the teacher's responsibility to see that he follows good health practices and to keep the child as safe as possible without nagging at him or being overprotective.

In addition, it is desirable to offer equipment and activities that foster large and fine muscle development. Attaining competence in these physical areas enhances the child's self-esteem and provides opportunities for him to gain social expertise as he develops wholesome feelings of vigor and good health.

Equipment for large muscle activities should be versatile, sturdy, and well maintained. The teacher can encourage active play by tuning in on what is happening and being alert to ways to add to its richness rather than by regarding large muscle playtime as a recess period when she can retreat to the office and have a cigarette.

Fine muscle activity is also valuable to offer at nursery school, but it is important to offer an assortment of levels of difficulty and to be sure that such activities do not continue for too long a time without relief.

---

*Refer to Chapter 12 for more detailed suggestions.

Los Niños Head Start

Increasing knowledge of sensory integration techniques and perceptual-motor development has made it necessary for nursery school teachers to broaden the range of activities offered to young children. At the most basic level, such activities should include experiences intended to stimulate and integrate the various neurological pathways involved in sensory perception as well as the more traditional sensory educational experiences commonly found in nursery schools. On a neurologically more advanced level, teachers should also include activities that provide opportunities for practice in specific perceptual-motor skills as well as providing movement activities that encourage creative thinking and self-expression. By using this comprehensive approach, the teacher can assure herself that physical development of the child is being facilitated to its fullest potential.

QUESTIONS AND ACTIVITIES

1. *Problem:* A little girl has just fallen out of the swing and is brought into the office bleeding heavily from the mouth. Examination reveals that her front tooth is still whole but has cut entirely through her lower lip. As the teacher in charge, how would you handle this emergency? Remember to think about both short- and long-term aspects of the situation.
2. Are there any conditions in the school where you are teaching that are particularly well handled in terms of safety precautions? Are there some possible hazards that warrant attention?
3. Suppose you were beginning a new school and had a budget of $800 for large muscle equipment. In your opinion what would be the most satisfactory way to invest this money? What would you buy and why?
4. Could there be advantages to putting children through a planned series of physical exercises on a regular basis? This might not be calisthenics as such; it might be tumbling or learning ball skills. What might be the disadvantages of this approach to physical education?
5. Many nursery school teachers appear to avoid physical contact with the children. What do you think might be the reasons for this restraint?
6. What are some examples from your own experience where

you are aware that the use of every sense except vision is restricted or curtailed?

REFERENCES FOR FURTHER READING

Health and Safety

American National Red Cross. *Standard first aid and personal safety.* Garden City, N.Y.: Doubleday & Co., Inc., 1973. This valuable reference, which describes how to handle common emergencies, should be available at all nursery schools.

Gussow, J. D. Bodies, brains and poverty: Poor children and the schools. *ERIC-IRCD Bulletin,* 1970, 6(3), 1-20. For a chilling analysis of the effect of poor health on learning, the reader should pursue Gussow's article as well as additional discussions included in the same volume of the *ERIC-IRCD Bulletin.*

Vaughn, G. *Mummy, I don't feel well: A pictorial guide to common childhood illnesses.* London: Berkeley Graphics, 1970. Ever wondered what chicken pox looks like? This book will leave you in no doubt; very useful.

Sequential Physical Development

Cratty, B. J. *Perceptual and motor development in infants and children.* New York: Macmillan Publishing Co., Inc., 1970a. Cratty's work is a more up-to-date reference than Gesell's and also deals with physical development.

Gesell, A., Halverson, H. M., Thompson, H., and Ilg, F. *The first five years of life: A guide to the study of the preschool child.* New York: Harper & Row, Publishers, 1940. This classic reference details step-by-step development of young children in many areas, including various physical skills. Although published almost 40 years ago, it remains the most comprehensive reference in the field.

Wickstrom, R. L. *Fundamental motor patterns* (2nd ed.). Philadelphia: Lea & Febiger, 1977. Wickstrom discusses and illustrates the development of running, jumping, throwing, catching, kicking, and striking skills, beginning with preschool children and extending onward to physical maturity. This is a useful reference for those who are interested in meticulous sequential analyses of these particular skills.

Theories of Perceptual-Motor Development

Gearheart, B. R. *Learning disabilities: Educational strategies* (2nd ed.). St. Louis: The C. V. Mosby Co., 1977. This book has several good chapters that describe the most important schools of thought concerned with perceptual-motor development.

Activities for Physical Development

Arnheim, D. D., and Sinclair, W. A. *The clumsy child: A program of motor therapy* (2nd ed.). St. Louis: The C. V. Mosby Co., 1979. *The Clumsy Child* is a valuable reference not only because of its sensible outline of motor tasks, but also because it describes activities for building motor skills arranged according to age level—the earliest level being ages 3 to 5.

Block, S. D. *Me and I'm great: Physical education for children three through eight.* Minneapolis: Burgess Publishing Co., 1977.

Cochran, N. A., Wilkinson, L. C., and Furlow, J. J. *Learning on the move: An activity guide for pre-school parents and teachers.* Dubuque, Iowa: Kendall/Hunt Publishing Co., 1975. The books by Block and by Cochran and associates provide detailed plans for daily physical activities. They are valuable references primarily because of the multitude of possibilities they suggest.

Montgomery, P., and Richter, E. *Sensorimotor integration for developmentally disabled children: A handbook.* Los Angeles: Western Psychological Services, 1977. For readers interested in pursuing sensory integration techniques in greater detail, this book presents clear descriptions of exercises and their intended purposes.

Robb, M. D., Mushier, C. L., Bogard, D. A., and Blann, M. E. (Eds.). *Foundations and practices in perceptual motor learning—a quest for understanding.* Washington: D.C.: American Association for Health, Physical Education, and Recreation, 1971. In this series of articles, the importance of perceptual-motor learning is discussed, and current concerns and the state of the art are reviewed.

Sinclair, C. B. *Movement of the young child: Ages two to six.* Columbus, Ohio: Charles E. Merrill Publishing Co., 1973. Sinclair's helpful book about movement education focuses on early childhood. Quite practical, it includes a good list of equipment.

Sweeney, R. T. (Ed.). *Selected readings in movement education.* Reading, Mass.: Addison-Wesley Publishing Co., Inc. 1970. This little paperback provides a quick, useful overview of "movement education"; a good get-acquainted book.

Equipment and Buildings

American Alliance for Health, Physical Education, and Recreation. *Choosing and using phonograph records for physical education, recreation, and related activities.* 1201 Sixteenth St., N.W., Washington, D.C. 20036: The Alliance, 1977. All the records in this reference are thoroughly described, priced, and categorized according to age (includes preschool) and purpose.

Cohen, M. D., and Hadley, S. *Selecting educational equipment and materials for home and school.* Washington, D.C.: Association for Childhood Education International, 1976. No teacher should be without this gem of a reference, which includes equipment lists, an annotated directory of manufacturers, and articles on purchasing and equipping schools. Equipment lists prioritize purchases according to essential first-year purchases, second- and third-year additions, and luxury items, and extend from infant centers through upper elementary school. *An indispensible resource* that costs only $3.50.

Educational Facilities Laboratory. *Found: Spaces and equipment for children's centers: A report from the Educational Facilities Laboratory.* New York: Educational Facilities Laboratory, 1972. EFL has turned out a series of excellent publications on school design. This is one of its most practical ones, since it provides many examples of ways to turn unused, unpromising spaces into useful, attractive environments for young children.

Ellison, G. *Play structures: Questions to discuss, designs to consider, directions for construction.* Pasadena: Pacific Oaks College and Children's School, 1974. Many illustrations of noncommercial play structures make this book lively and informative. The stress is on natural and recycled materials; excellent.

Utzinger, R. C. *Some European nursery schools and playgrounds.* New York: Educational Facilities Laboratory and the

Architectural Research Laboratory of the University of Michigan, 1970. In this, as in the Educational Facilities Laboratory work above, one picture is worth a thousand words. Both pamphlets are made up almost entirely of photographs and contain innumerable exciting contemporary ideas for arranging and furnishing nursery schools.

Adventure Playgrounds

Lady Allen of Hurtwood. *Planning for play.* Cambridge, Mass.: The M.I.T. Press, 1968. Lady Allen, a very progressive thinker, was among the first to advocate the development of adventure playgrounds. She describes the purpose of this book as being "to explore some of the ways of keeping alive and sustaining the innate curiosity and natural gaiety of children." It does just that.

Bengtsson, A. (Ed.). *Adventure playgrounds.* New York: Praeger Publishers, Inc., 1972. Crammed with photographs, this publication surveys adventure playgrounds throughout the European community. Pictures are accompanied by an extensive and thorough text, which explains theoretical and practical aspects of how to design, establish and sustain such a playground.

For the Advanced Student

Arnheim, D. D., and Pestolesi, R. A. *Elementary physical education: A developmental approach* (2nd ed.). St. Louis: The C. V. Mosby Co., 1978. Those who would like to acquaint themselves with current approaches to physical education in the elementary school will find this one of the most readable and up-to-date references available.

Cratty, B. J. *Some educational implications of movement.* Seattle: Special Child Publications, 1970b. The author presents a readable, sensible discussion of what is known at present about the effects of movement education upon development; contains many bibliographical references.

Fraiberg, S. *Insights from the blind.* New York: Basic Books, Inc. Publishers, 1977. For an absolutely fascinating account of the effect of the deprivation of one sense (vision) on the development of the infant, the reader should not miss *Insights from the Blind.* The interplay between stimulation by the environment and developmental readiness in the infant is nowhere better documented than in this well-written research report. The book covers 15 years of investigation.

McGraw, M. B. Later development of children specially trained during infancy: Johnny and Jimmy at school age. In R. N. Singer (Ed.), *Readings in motor learning.* Philadelphia: Lea & Febiger, 1972. This famous study of twins investigates the value of stimulating a very young child to engage in activities to the extent of his ability as compared with the value of allowing his twin to develop without deliberate instruction.

Solomon, P., Kubzansky, P. E., Leiderman, P. H., Mendelson, J. H., Trumbull, R., and Wexler, D. *Sensory deprivation.* Cambridge, Mass.: Harvard University Press, 1965. Although this material deals with experiments conducted on adults, the results of sensory deprivation (the deprivation of experiential sensory input) also has serious educational implications for the development of children.

White, B. L. Informal education during the first months of life. In R. D. Hess and R. M. Bear (Eds.), *Early education: Current theory, research, and action.* Chicago: Aldine Publishing Co., 1968. Dr. White's chapter should be read along with McGraw's study because it provides a description of a more contemporary investigation of the effects of early stimulation on the development of the infant.

PART THREE

Nourishing and maintaining emotional health

Photo by Austin Rudneckie, Santa Barbara City College Children's Center

5 □ Fostering mental health in young children

In the evaluation of the dominant moods of any historical period it is important to hold fast to the fact that there are always islands of self-sufficient order—on farms and in castles, in homes, studies, and cloisters—where sensible people manage to live relatively lusty and decent lives: as moral as they must be, as free as they may be, and as masterful as they can be. If we but knew it, this elusive arrangement *is* happiness.*

The valuable contribution early childhood programs can make to fostering mental health has been emphasized in the report of the Joint Commission on the Mental Health of Children (1970), which points out repeatedly that day-care centers, nursery schools, and compensatory programs present outstanding opportunities for carrying out preventive and remedial work in this area.

In an era when at least one in every ten people is destined to spend time in a mental hospital, the importance of such work is clear, and we must give careful consideration to practical things the teacher can do that are likely to foster mental health in the children in her care. For this reason, several chapters of this book are devoted to establishing general therapeutic policies, dealing with crisis situations, handling discipline and aggression, and building self-esteem, because these are all important aspects of developing emotional health. Additional aspects of mental health, covered under the development of the social self, include learning to care for other people, cross-cultural education, and taking pleasure in meaningful work.

*From Erikson, E. *Young man Luther*. New York: W. W. Norton & Co., Inc., 1958.

IMPORTANCE OF DEVELOPING BASIC ATTITUDES OF TRUST, AUTONOMY, AND INITIATIVE IN YOUNG CHILDREN

The most fundamental thing the teacher can do to foster mental health in young children is to provide many opportunities for basic healthy emotional attitudes to develop. Erik Erikson (1959, 1963, 1971) has made a very significant contribution to our understanding of what these basic attitudes are. He hypothesizes that during their life span, individuals pass through a series of stages of emotional development wherein basic attitudes are formed. Early childhood encompasses three of these: the stages of trust versus mistrust, autonomy versus shame and doubt, and initiative versus guilt. Although children in nursery school are likely to be working on the second and third sets of attitudes, it is important to understand the implications of the first set, also, since Erikson theorizes that the resolution of each stage depends in part on the successful accomplishment of the previous one.

In the stage of *trust versus mistrust,* the baby learns (or fails to learn) that other people can be depended on and also that he can depend on himself to elicit needed responses from them. This develop-

69

ment of trust is deeply related to the quality of care that the mother provides and is often reflected in feeding practices, which, if handled in a manner that meets his needs, helps assure the infant that he is valued and important. Although by the time he enters nursery school, the balance between trust or mistrust will have been tipped in favor of one attitude or the other, the need to experience trust and to have it reaffirmed remains with people throughout their lives. This is also true for the other attitudes as they develop.

Therefore, it is vital that the basic climate of the nursery school encourage the establishment of trust between everyone who is part of that community. If the teacher thinks of establishing trust in terms of letting the children know that they can depend on her, it will be fairly easy for her to implement this goal. For example, consistent policies and regularity of events in the program obviously contribute to establishing a trustful climate. Being reasonable also makes it clear to the children that they can depend on the teacher. In addition, if she is sensitive to the individual needs of the children and meets them as they arise, the teacher can confirm the message of their infanthood once again that they are worthy of love and thus further strengthen trust and self-esteem.

In our society the attitudes of *autonomy versus shame and doubt* are formed during the same period in which toilet training takes place. During this time, the child is acquiring the skills of holding on and letting go. This fundamental exercise in self-assertion and control is associated with his drive to become independent and to express this independence by making choices and decisions so often couched in the classic imperatives of the 2-year-old, "No!" "Mine!" and "Me do it!" Erikson maintains that children who are overregulated and deprived of the opportunity to establish independence and autonomy may become oppressed with feelings of shame and self-doubt, which result in losing self-esteem, being defiant, trying to get away with things, and in later life in developing various forms of compulsive behavior.

The desirable way to handle this strong need for choice and self-assertion is to provide an environment at home and nursery school that makes many opportunities available for the child to do for himself and to make decisions. This is the fundamental reason why self-selection is an important principle in curriculum design. At the same time, the teacher must be able to establish decisive control when necessary, since young children often show poor judgment and can be tyrannized by their own willfulness unless the teacher is willing to intervene.

Gradually, as the child develops the ability to act independently, he embarks on building the next set of basic attitudes. Around the age of 4 or 5, he becomes more interested in reaching out to the world around him, in doing things, and in being part of the group. At this stage, he wants to think things up and try them out; he is interested in the effect his actions have on other people (witness his experimentation with profanity and "bad" language); he formulates concepts of appropriate sex roles; he enjoys imaginative play; and he becomes an avid seeker of information about the world around him. This is the stage Erikson has so aptly named *initiative versus guilt.*

In order to feel emotionally satisfied, a child of this age must be allowed to explore, to act, and to do. Nursery schools are generally strong about meeting the children's need to explore and create, but they often underestimate the ability of older 4- and 5-year-olds to participate in making plans and decisions for their group or to attempt challenging projects. Of course, the teacher must make allowance for the fact that 4- and 5-year-olds are better planners and starters than they are finishers. Satisfaction in completing projects is more likely to be part of the developmental stage that follows this one: the stage of industry versus inferiority, which is characteristic of the child during his early years in primary school. But encouraging the ability to initiate plans and take action will enhance the child's feeling of self-worth and creativity as well as his ability to be a self-starter—all highly desirable outcomes necessary for future development and happiness.

HALLMARKS OF AN EMOTIONALLY HEALTHY YOUNG CHILD

To determine whether the child is in good emotional health, the teacher should ask the following questions about him. If she can answer the majority of them affirmatively, chances are good that he is emotionally healthy.

Is the child working on emotional tasks that are appropriate for his age? We have already talked about the fundamental need for planning a curriculum that provides many opportunities for children to exercise their autonomy and initiative. When looking at individual children, the teacher should ask herself if they are taking advantage of these opportunities. She will find that the majority of them are achieving independence, choosing what they want to do, and generating their own ideas with zest and enthusiasm; but there will be a handful of youngsters who need sensitive help to venture forth. This usually involves taking time to build a strong

Los Niños Head Start

foundation of trust between the child and teacher and then helping him advance to increased independence as his confidence grows.

Is the child learning to separate from his family without undue stress and to form an attachment with at least one other adult at nursery school? Considerable space was devoted in the chapter on routines to handling separation anxiety in a constructive way because the ability to separate from significant others and form additional relationships is an important skill. The teacher should realize that most children, particularly shy ones and those who are younger, make friends with a teacher at school before they branch out to make friends with other children. The teacher who is aware that this is a typical pattern can relax and enjoy this process without fretting about the child's dependency, because she has confidence that in time most children will leave her side in favor of being with other youngsters. This bond between teacher and child may not be as evident in socially able 4-year-olds as it is with younger children, but it should exist all the same. If the child has not formed a relationship with some adult after he has been at school for a while, he should be encouraged to do so. Being attached to the teacher makes it more probable that he will use her as a model or come to her for help when it is needed. Affection between teacher and child is also important because it is a fundamental ingredient of good discipline.

At the same time, the teacher has to be sensitive to the quality of the attachment. Oversolicitude for the child's feelings of loneliness or the teacher's own unmet needs for affection can occasionallly create a form of dependency that is undesirable because it restricts the child's venturing out and making friends with his peers. This situation should, of course, be avoided. The teacher must learn to tell the difference between a youngster who genuinely needs the emotional support of a close relationship to begin with, and the one who is using her or is being used by her as an emotional crutch.

Is the child learning to conform to routines at school without undue fuss? Of course, conforming to routines varies with the age of the child and his temperament, and teachers anticipate some balki-

ness and noncompliance as being not only inevitable but healthy. Two-year-olds are particularly likely to be balky and at the same time insist that things can be done the same way every time, and self-assertiveness appears again rather prominently between the ages of 4 and 5. The quality of the behavior seems different though—the assertiveness of twos comes across as being more dogmatic and less logical, whereas the assertiveness of fours seems to be more of a deliberate challenge and trying-out of the other person. However, consistent refusal to conform goes beyond these norms and should be regarded as a warning sign that the child needs help working through this behavior.

Is the child able to involve himself deeply in play? A characteristic of severely disturbed children in mental institutions is that they cannot give themselves up to the experience of satisfying play. Indeed, when they become able to do so, it is encouraging evidence that they are getting ready to be released from the hospital. Being able to play is also very important for more typical children. The child's ability to enjoy participating in play by himself or with other children as he grows older is not only a hallmark of emotional health but contributes to maintaining mental health as well.

Is the child developing the ability to settle down and concentrate? Children may be distractible for a variety of reasons, and no child is able to pay attention under all circumstances. Excitement, boredom, needing to go to the toilet, fatigue, interesting distractions, or not feeling well can all interfere from time to time with any child's ability to concentrate. But occasionally the teacher will come across a child who never seems to settle down: he flits continually from place to place and seems to give only his surface attention to what he is doing. There are a multitude of reasons for this behavior, ranging from poor habits to birth injuries, but a common cause of distractibility is tension or anxiety. Since this behavior can seriously interfere with learning, the teacher should seek to identify the cause and to remedy it as soon as possible.

Is the child unusually withdrawn or aggressive for his age? One of the great advantages teachers have is that by becoming acquainted with hundreds of

Santa Barbara City College Children's Center

children over a period of time, they are able to develop sound norms for behavior that make it relatively easy to identify youngsters who behave in extreme ways. Very withdrawn behavior is more likely to be overlooked than aggressive behavior because it is much less troublesome to the teacher, but she should be aware that either response is a signal from the child that he is emotionally out of balance and needs some extra thought and plans devoted to help him resolve whatever is causing him to cope in that manner.

Does the child have access to the full range of his feelings, and is he learning to deal with them in an age-appropriate way? Some children have already learned by the age of 3 or 4 years to conceal or deny the existence of their feelings rather than to accept and express them in a tolerable way. The nursery school teacher can help children stay in touch with the full repertoire of their emotions by show-

ing them that she, too, has all sorts of feelings and that she understands that children have feelings as well, whether these be anger, sadness, or affection. Healthy children should also begin to learn during the preschool years to express their feelings to the people who have actually caused them and to do this in a way that does not harm themselves or others. Learning to do this successfully takes a long time, but it has its roots in early childhood.

PERSONAL QUALITIES THAT WILL HELP THE TEACHER ESTABLISH A THERAPEUTIC CLIMATE IN THE NURSERY SCHOOL*

The nursery school teacher can utilize her personal qualities as well as more practical techniques

---

*The work in this section owes much to the humanistic philosophy of Carl Rogers and his client-centered approach to psychotherapy.

to foster a therapeutic climate in her nursery school. A *therapeutic climate* consistently allows the active development and maintenance of an atmosphere conducive to mental health. It frees people to develop to their fullest potential as balanced, happy individuals. The personal qualities of a "therapeutic" teacher have a great deal to do with establishing this desirable climate, and for this reason they are discussed below.

Consistency. One way to build a sense of trust between the teacher and the children in her care is for her to behave in ways they can predict and to be consistent about maintaining guidelines and schedules. Thus the children will know what to expect, and will not live in fear of erratic or temperamental responses to what they do. For this reason, emotional stability is a highly desirable trait for teachers of young children to possess. Of course, consistency does not mean that rules must be inflexible, but their enforcement should not depend on the whim of the teacher or the manipulative power of various children.

Reasonableness. Coupled with the steadiness of consistency should go the trait of reasonableness, which I define as "expecting neither too much nor too little from children." One practical way to increase reasonableness is to learn the characteristics of the developmental stages when these are discussed in child development courses. The brief developmental summaries presented in this book are intended to remind the student of general developmental characteristics. Knowledge of these characteristics prevents the inexperienced teacher from setting her standards too high or too low. She does not expect a 2-year-old to have the self-control of a 4-year-old. On the other hand, when a 4-year-old starts making demands more typical of a 2, she knows that he is regressing and that she must search for and alleviate the stresses that are causing his retreat.

Another excellent way to help children (and other adults, also) see that the teacher is reasonable is to really listen when people try to tell you something. I am indebted to one of my students for the following example of what can happen when one "shuts out" such information.

We were in the playhouse corner and Heidi was wearing a coat while doing all her kitchen duties. Jennifer came in and stood beside me and said, "I want that coat!" I was about to see if maybe Heidi was wearing Jennifer's coat when a nearby student teacher said it was Heidi's and that Jennifer had a sweater in her cubby.

"Jennifer, why don't you get your sweater from your cubby?" I suggested.

"But I want *that* coat!" she said, on the verge of tears.

"I can see you want that coat very much, but I can't take it away from Heidi," I said.

"But it's mine; I don't want a sweater."

"Do you have a coat at home that looks like that? Is that why you think it's yours?" I asked.

"Uh-huh. Give it to me!" she demanded (tears still there in the eyes).

"I'm sorry, Jenny, I can see that you're very unhappy not to have your coat, but I can't take Heidi's," I said.

"My mommy said I could have it!"

By now I was finally suspicious, so I checked the coat Heidi was wearing. There, written across the collar, was the name, Jennifer!

Heidi gave up the coat without a fuss, Jenny put it on, I apologized to her, and she went out to play!

The student concludes by commenting, "All I can say is that I would make sure next time of what I was talking about. It taught me, "Look before you leap!" to which I would add the advice, "Take time to listen—you may learn something important."

Courage and strength of character. Particularly when dealing with outbursts of anger, the student will find that courage and the strength of character commonly called fortitude are required to see such outbursts through. Understandably, the embarassment and insecurity of fearing that the scene may not turn out all right make it easy to placate an angry child or, more usually, to allow him to run off or have his way. But the trouble with allowing this to happen is that the child will repeat the behavior and feel contemptuous of the adult who permits it. Therefore, being courageous and seeing a problem through are worth the struggle when coping with the strong emotional reactions that are so common at the nursery school level.

Trustful confidence. Trustful confidence is the faith the teacher feels that the child wants to grow and develop in a healthy way. Interestingly enough, psychoanalysts maintain that this ability to have trust or confidence in the good intentions of other people goes back to the individual's own experiences as an infant, when she found she could or could not generally depend on her environment to be a nurturing one. Be that as it may, contemporary research (Rosenthal and Jacobson, 1968) bears out what many teachers and parents have determined empirically: children respond to what is genuinely expected of them by the people who matter to them. The teacher who optimistically trusts children to act in their own best behalf is likely to obtain this response from most of the children most of the time.

Congruence. The teacher also promotes trustful confidence between herself and the child by being honest with herself and with him about her own feelings. This is what Rogers calls congruence and Patterson (1977) terms genuineness. A congruent person attempts to recognize and accept her own feelings and be truthful about them to other people. Thus a teacher might "level" with one child by saying, "I don't want you to kick me ever again; I feel really angry with you when you do that to me," or with another by saying, "I'm glad to see you today. I've been looking forward to hearing about your new kittens."

However, a note of caution is in order. Rogers advocates revealing such feelings *when it is appropriate to do so.* Children should not be subjected to outbursts of temper or angry attacks by adults in the name of congruence. Uncontrolled outbursts are too disturbing to children, since they know they are relatively helpless and at the mercy of the teacher.

Empathy. Empathy is the ability to feel *as* another person feels, to feel *with* him rather than *for* him. Empathy is valuable not only because it allows the teacher to put herself in the child's place, but also because it helps her identify and clarify for the child how he is feeling. Research supports the value of this quality. A study by Truax and Tatum (1966) has shown that empathic ability combined with the ability to express warmth are effective in fostering positive adjustments to the preschool setting and to peers.

Warmth. Warmth is so important that is deserves special emphasis because its presence has been linked to the development of positive self-concepts in children (Baumrind, 1967; Sears, 1970). The warm teacher lets the children and staff know that she likes them and thinks well of them. Both children and adults flourish in this climate of sincere approval and acceptance. But being warm and accepting does not mean that the teacher just sits around and smiles at the children no matter what they do. There is a difference between expressing warmth and being indulgently permissive, and there are times when the teacher must exert control because a child is unable to. But when she does this for him, she must make it plain that she is taking control because she truly cares for him and not because she wants to obtain power for its own sake or have the satisfaction of winning.

Attaining these qualities

Some of the qualities listed above, such as consistency, fortitude, and reasonableness, can be acquired through practice and experience. The others —empathy, trustful confidence, congruence, and warmth—can often be enhanced by participation in well-run encounter groups or through psychological counseling if they don't seem to "come naturally." Many teachers have found that such experiences have improved both their teaching abilities and their personal relationships.

PRACTICAL THINGS THE TEACHER CAN DO TO HELP YOUNG CHILDREN ACHIEVE HEALTHY EMOTIONAL DEVELOPMENT

Before turning to a discussion of more concrete things the teacher can do to contribute to a therapeutic milieu, the student should remember two principles. One is that young children respond with encouraging quickness to a change in atmosphere or approach. It is possible to quickly bring about positive changes in their feelings and behavior by using appropriate methods.

The other principle has been mentioned before: children are resilient. They bounce back from their own and others' mistakes, and it is unlikely that one imperfect handling of a situation will inflict permanent damage on a child. This is not said to sanction irresponsible actions by the teacher but to reassure her that, when dealing with difficult situations, she should not be unduly hesitant on the grounds she may injure the child. It is the repetition of procedures and the overall quality of the milieu, rather than the single episode, that are likely to enhance or damage.

Develop friendly, close relationships with each family. Nursery school usually marks the occasion in the child's and parents' lives when he leaves their protection for the first time on a regular basis. If the school and family establish a feeling of closeness and a shared interest in the child's welfare, it is easier for him to make this transition, since his world is thereby widened rather than split into two pieces.

Teachers are quick to see the advantage that a friendly, comfortable atmosphere means the family is more likely to seek advice from the school. But another advantage should not be overlooked: the teacher is also in a better position to *accept* advice and suggestions from the parents when a "caring-sharing" atmosphere is established. This two-way respect fosters genuine mutuality and lays the basic foundation for emotional health in the nursery school.

Reduce frustration for the child when possible. Children should not have to spend time waiting for things to happen. Children's needs are immediate, intense, and personal, and the longer they are kept waiting the more irritable they become. Snack should be available as the children sit down, and someone should be outside for supervision as the children are dressed and ready to go out and play. Duplicates of equipment mean that there is generally enough to go around—two or three toy trucks are much more satisfactory than just one. A good assortment of activities must be available so that 3-year-olds are not expected to stack tiny plastic blocks and 5-year-olds do not have to make do with eight-piece puzzles. The day should be planned so that few and moderate demands are made on children at points where they are likely to be tired and hungry.

Of course, the teacher cannot and should not seek to eliminate all frustrating circumstances. Comparative animal studies indicate that a moderate amount of adversity may foster socialization (Elliot and King, 1960; Hess, 1960). But so many interruptions and frustrations happen in even well-run nursery schools (Jackson and Wolfson, 1968) that the elimination of needless sources of frustration makes sense.

Learn to identify and describe the children's feelings to them, and help them express these feelings to the relevant people. In our society we seem to have reached the conclusion that it is dangerous to allow some emotions to be expressed, the assumption being that if they are expressed they will become stronger, but if we ignore them or deny their presence they will vanish. Actually, the opposite of this premise is psychologically true. Blake's poem puts this neatly:

I was angry with my friend,
I told my wrath, my wrath did end.
I was angry with my foe,
I told it not, my wrath did grow.

Negative emotions that are recognized, accepted, and expressed usually fade, but if not expressed they seem to generate pressure that causes the person to relieve them ultimately in a more explosive or veiled, yet hostile way. Moreover, if children are not provided with ways of telling others how they feel, they are almost inevitably driven to *showing* them how they feel by acting the feelings out.

The advantage of helping the child know how he feels is not only that he avoids these overwhelming explosions or complicated emotional displacements but also that he learns that all emotions are acceptable and that, therefore, an important part of himself is acceptable. As he matures, this self-knowledge forms a foundation for learning to express feelings in a way that harms neither himself nor other people.

It takes practice and sensitivity to acquire the skills of describing the child's feelings to him and helping him express them, but research shows that teachers can learn these skills (Reif and Stollak, 1972). There is more to it than just saying to an

Photo by Richard Pierce, Santa Barbara City College Children's Center

angry child, "You're feeling really mad at him, aren't you?" Some examples will help illustrate the technique.

Evelyn says goodbye to her mother and then hangs by the gate, looking after her sadly as she drives away. Her teacher bends down, picks her up, and says, "You look like you wish she'd stay this morning, Evelyn." "I do, I do, I want her to stay—[emphatically] I hate her, that mean old mommy of mine, I hate her, and I wish she'd stay!" "Yeah, I know how it is—you feel sad she's left you, and it makes you mad because you wanted her to stay." "Yes! And I'm never, never going to speak to her again." (They move toward the nursery school room and go inside.) "And I'm just going to feed her turnips and beans for dinner—turnips and beans, turnips and beans, turnips and beans!" But this is said with decreasing venom and increasing humor as she trails off toward the housekeeping corner to embark on her busy day.

In the following example the teacher, working with an older child, encourages him not only to express his feelings but to deal with the person who is causing the unhappiness.

Jonathan arrives at the woodworking bench very excited by the box of new wood he has spied from across the play yard. He reaches for Henry's hammer as it is laid down and is really surprised when Henry snatches it back. The teacher tells Jonathan that all the hammers are in use and he will have to wait. Jonathan stands on one foot and then the other—his hand obviously itching to snatch Henry's hammer. At this point, rather than trying to redirect him to the swings, the teacher says to him, "It's hard to wait, isn't it? I can see how much you want that hammer." "Yes, it is. I wish old Henry'd hurry." "Well, tell him so. Tell him what you want." "Henry, you old son of a bitch. I want that hammer when you're done." (The boys grin at each other.) The teacher suggests, "Why don't you saw some wood while you're waiting?" "Don't mind if I do," says Jonathan.

In the examples above, the teacher doesn't content herself with the simple statement to Evelyn, "You feel angry," or to Jonathan, "You feel im-

patient." Instead, she tries to describe to the child what he feels like doing as well as name the feeling for him if she's fairly sure she can identify it. Describing feelings or intended actions is particularly helpful when working with young children because they understand the statement, "You want her to stay," or "It's hard to wait," better than they grasp the label "angry" or "impatient." In addition, description has the advantage that it stands a better chance of being correct and that it is always better to talk about what a person does rather than what he is.

With a younger child or a less controlled one, the teacher may need to go further and reassure him by saying, "It's okay to want to grab it as long as you don't really do it." Sometimes she will need to go even further than that and actually restrain him, saying, "I can see you want to hit Henry, but I won't let you hurt him. Tell him you feel like taking his hammer." It takes many experiences for a young child to reach the level of the children in our examples, but it can be done.

Also, in the examples above, the teacher neither moralized with Evelyn, "Of course you really love your mother," nor offered an involved interpretation to the children of the reasons behind their behavior. Instead, she concentrated on letting the children know that she understood what they felt, that it was all right to talk about it, and that she would help them draw the line between feeling and acting if they needed that help.

When teaching children to express their feelings, we must teach them gradually to understand the difference between saying how one feels about something (self-report) and telling another person what they are (verbal attack). There's a big difference between allowing a child to attack by shouting, "You selfish pooh pooh pants! You stink! If you don't give me that shovel right now, I'm never going to play with you again!" and teaching him to tell the same child, "I *need* that shovel—I'm dying for it! I can't wait another minute!"

Admittedly, this is a sophisticated concept for little children to grasp. Sad to say, even some adults seem unable to make this distinction. Nevertheless,

Photo by Richard Pierce, Sunrise Montessori School

it is such an extraordinarily valuable emotional and social skill to acquire that teachers should begin to model and teach the rudiments of self-report very early to children. Acquisition of this skill will benefit them all their lives.

There are many additional ways to express feelings through play and through the use of sublimative and expressive materials, which are discussed later on, but the ability to openly acknowledge feelings is the soundest and most fundamental therapeutic skill to use to foster mental health.

Learn to recognize signs of stress and emotional upset in children. Children give many signals besides crying or fussing that indicate emotional stress. Reverting (regressing) to less mature behavior is a very common signal. We are all familiar with the independent 4-year-old who suddenly wants to be babied while recovering from the flu or the child who wets his bed after the baby arrives.

Various nervous habits, such as hair twisting, sighing deeply, nail biting, or thumb sucking, also reveal that the child is under stress. Increased irritability, sometimes to the point of tantrums, is another indicator, as is lethargy or withdrawing from activities. Sometimes children suddenly begin to challenge rules and routines; sometimes they cry a lot; sometimes expressions of tension or stress are more subtle and are conveyed only by a strained look about the eyes or a tightened mouth; sometimes stress is expressed in the more obvious form of excessive activity and running about.

In addition to this knowledge of common symptoms, as the year progresses and she gets to know the children well, the teacher will have the additional advantage of knowing how each child usually behaves. This makes it easier for her to spot changes and identify children who are signalling for special help.

Know what to do for children who are emotionally upset. Emotional upsets have to be handled on a short-term basis and sometimes on a long-term basis as well. (See also Chapter 18.)

SHORT-TERM, EMERGENCY TREATMENT. The first thing to do for a child who is upset to the point of tears is to comfort him. But the manner of comfort will vary from child to child: some youngsters need to be held and rocked, whereas others do best if allowed to reduce themselves to hiccupping silence while the teacher putters about nearby. Children who are using emotional outbursts as a means of controlling the adult's behavior require still a third response—mildly ignoring them until they subside.

No matter why a child is crying hard, it is a waste of energy to try to reason with him until he has calmed down. However, it can help soothe him to repeat something in a quieter and quieter tone of voice so that he gradually quiets himself to hear what is being said. This may be as simple a sentence as, "When you've stopped crying, we'll talk things over," or, "I'm waiting to help you when you've stopped crying." Occasionally, it can also be helpful to remark matter-of-factly if the occasion warrants, "You know, I will keep on holding you, even when you've stopped crying."

As the child calms down, getting a drink of water or washing his face may also soothe him. It's often effective at this point to talk over the difficulty, but sometimes it's better to wait and discuss it in a casual way later in the day to clarify how he felt or why he broke down. Each situation has to be judged in its own context.

Finally, the teacher should either help the child return and resolve the problem in the group, or if she deems it wiser, she should help him get started on another satisfying activity. Activities that are particularly helpful at such times include swinging, water play, or messy activities such as finger painting or clay. Water play generally seems to be the best choice.

LONG-TERM TREATMENT. It is always wise before deciding that an emotional upset represents a serious long-term difficulty to wait and see if the child is coming down with something; incipient illness is a frequent source of loss of emotional control. It is also wise to consider whether an approaching holiday could be causing the disturbance. Christmas and Halloween are notorious tension increasers, and we

Photo by Gene Garrett, Los Niños Head Start

have found in our campus children's center that the weeks before and during college exams are likely to be edgy ones, also. Many episodes of fighting, crying, and other exaggerated responses to minor crises will disappear after such times have passed.

If the symptoms of stress do not subside, it is necessary to find out more about what is causing tension in the child. The behavior may be due to something going on at home or to something going on at school, or to a combination of these things.

One helpful way to locate the cause is to think back to the point when the signs of stress appeared and then to confer with the parent about what else changed in the child's life at about the same time. Perhaps the youngster was moved to another group at nursery school, or his close friend was absent because of chicken pox; perhaps his grandfather died, or his father was away, or houseguests were visiting. Once the cause has been discovered, steps can be taken to help the youngster feel more at ease. Sometimes just recognizing the source helps a lot, without doing anything more.

Other signals of disturbance can be traced to continuing environmental situations. Perhaps discipline policies are erratic at home, or affection is lacking, or the child is excessively fatigued because he watches the late show on television. These are more difficult situations to deal with, but even they can often be successfully resolved by working together with the family.

If the situation is too complicated or difficult to be quickly eased by the teacher's intervention, she must encourage the family to seek counseling from a psychologist or a psychiatrist. The area of guidance and referral is such an extensive one that it cannot be treated in detail here. The reader is invited to pursue the subject further in Chapters 17, 18, and 19.

SUMMARY

The therapeutic nursery school seeks to create as many opportunities as possible for young children to develop their sense of autonomy and initiative in a setting that is reasonable, consistent, trustful, empathic, and warm. Children who are mentally healthy are working on emotional tasks appropriate for their age. They are learning to separate from their families and to conform to school routines without undue stress. They can involve themselves deeply in play, and they are developing the ability to settle down and concentrate. Emotionally healthy children are not excessively withdrawn or aggressive; they have access to the full range of their feelings and are beginning to learn to deal with these feelings in appropriate ways.

The teacher can help the children in her care develop in an emotionally healthy way by forming a good relationship with their families, reducing frustration for them where she can, identifying and describing the children's feelings for them and helping them express these to the relevant people, recognizing the signs of stress that signal that help is needed, and handling emotional problems on a short-term and long-term basis when necessary.

QUESTIONS AND ACTIVITIES

1. What are some matter-of-fact ways to express warmth and liking to young children?
2. Looking back on your own education, give an example of a teacher who had unreasonably high expectations for you as a pupil. What was the effect on your learning?
3. What is the difference between feeling sympathy for someone and feeling empathy for him? Which attitude would be the more desirable one to develop when working with young children? Why?
4. With other members of the class set up some role-playing situations that provide opportunities for "children" to express their feelings, and practice phrasing responses from "teachers" that would help the child identify how he feels and show that the teacher understands him. Practice this a lot!
5. Do you believe it is always wise to be forthright about your own feelings? What limitations might be helpful to remember? On the other hand, can you think of times when it would have been better to take the risk and be more open and frank in your response? What did you do instead of being direct? Do you think that it was a satisfactory solution?
6. What are some examples where you have seen adults ignore, suppress, or mislabel a child's feelings? Could you see how the child was immediately affected by this kind of response? What would you predict might be the long-term effects of a child's experiencing many such responses to his feelings?

REFERENCES FOR FURTHER READING

Overviews

Berman, L. M., and Roderick, J. A. *Feeling, valuing, and the art of growing: Insights into the affective.* Washington, D.C.: Association for Supervision and Curriculum Development, 1977. *Feeling, Valuing and the Art of Growing* is one of the more recent books presenting a philosophical overview of what humanistic education is all about and why educating the emotional side of human beings is as important as educating the cognitive side. It contains many citations for further reading as well as a variety of well-written, persuasive chapters.

Developmental Stages and Emotional Needs of Children

Despert, J. L. *The inner voices of children.* New York: Simon & Schuster, Inc., 1975. The text of this simply written book does a nice job of getting basic points across about the needs of young children, but what is truly remarkable about it are the pictures, which often speak more clearly than words about the values Dr. Despert has selected.

Erikson, E. H. *Childhood and society* (2nd ed.). New York: W. W. Norton & Co., Inc., 1963.

Erikson, E. H. A healthy personality for every child. In R. H. Anderson and H. G. Shane (Eds.), *As the twig is bent: Readings in early childhood education.* Boston: Houghton Mifflin Co., 1971. These publications contain original source material that explains in detail Erikson's concepts of the eight stages of man and the emotional attitudes that are of paramount importance at various stages of development.

Gaylin, W. *Caring.* New York: Alfred A. Knopf, Inc., 1976. Dr. Gaylin emphasizes caring as being one of the positive aspects of human nature often overlooked in psychoanalytic discussions. His tracing of the growth of the ability to care is particularly valuable for teachers and parents of young children to read, since the foundations of caring are established at a very early age in children.

Redl, F., and Wattenberg, W. W. *Mental hygiene in teaching* (2nd ed.). New York: Harcourt Brace Jovanovich, Inc., 1959. Chapter 4 is particularly valuable because it contains a clear-cut description of the mechanisms by which people (including young children) cope with emotional conflicts. It may be the best description ever written on this subject for teachers to use.

Warren, R. M. *Caring: Supporting children's growth.* Washington, D.C.: National Association for the Education of Young People, 1977. This pamphlet, which is filled with wise observations on fostering the emotional health of children, illustrates many aspects of caring related to nursery school education by discussing how to handle such situations as separation and facing harsh realities. It contains good bibliographies for children and adults.

Communicating with Children (and Other People)

Here are a number of excellent books on this subject that should be called to the student's attention.

Ginott, H. *Teacher and child.* New York: Macmillan Publishing Co., Inc., 1972.

Gordon, T. *P.E.T. in action.* New York: Peter H. Wyden Publisher, 1976.

Moustakas, C. E. *The authentic teacher: Sensitivity and awareness in the classroom.* Cambridge, Mass.: Howard A. Doyle, 1966.

Satir, V. *People making.* Palo Alto, Calif.: Science and Behavior Books, Inc., 1975.

Establishing Sound Emotional Relationships

Axline, V. M. *Dibs: In search of self.* Boston: Houghton Mifflin Co., 1964. This highly readable account, based on a case study of an appealing little boy named Dibs, illustrates what goes on in child-centered therapy and gives many examples of how to respond to children by accepting and reflecting their feelings.

Murphy, L. B., and Leeper, E. M. *More than a teacher.* Washington, D.C.: U.S. Dept. of Health, Education, and Welfare, 1970b. This down-to-earth pamphlet, which explains very clearly the value of assuming a "mothering," nurturing role when teaching young children, is filled with everyday examples and useful suggestions.

Rogers, C. R. *On becoming a person.* Boston: Houghton Mifflin Co., 1961. Rogers sets forth his philosophy that desirable emotional relationships between people are facilitated by the presence of warmth, congruence, and empathy. *On Be-*coming a Person is a good book of his to begin with, because it is a collection of articles that can be sampled as the student's tastes and time dictate. The reader may want to go on to Rogers' most recent title, *On Personal Power: Inner Strength and Its Revolutionary Impact.* New York: Delacourt Press, 1977. The chapter by Cecil Patterson in *Feeling, Valuing and the Art of Growing* (Berman and Roderick, 1977) cited in *Overviews* is another good, current discussion of this same point of view.

Descriptions of Mental Health Services

Glasscote, R. M., and Fishman, M. E. *Mental health programs for preschool children: A field study.* Washington, D.C.: Joint Information Service of the American Psychiatric Association and the National Association for Mental Health, 1974. As the title implies, this book surveys seven therapeutic nursery schools scattered throughout the United States. It is an interesting report on the "state of the art" and particularly useful for people looking for special places to study.

Joint Commission on the Mental Health of Children. *Mental health: From infancy through adolescence: Reports of Task Forces I, II, and III, and the committees on education and religion.* New York: Harper & Row, Publishers, 1973. Recommendations for improving the mental health of children are given. The special section on education is particularly good, and the material on the preschool child is also valuable.

Looff, D. H. *Appalachia's children: The challenge of mental health.* Lexington, Ky.: University Press of Kentucky, 1971. The author presents a chatty, anecdotal account of how mental health services were implemented in three counties in Appalachia; interesting reading.

For the Advanced Student

Joint Commission on the Mental Health of Children. *Crisis in child mental health: Challenge for the 1970's.* New York: Harper & Row, Publishers, 1970. The state of mental health and the emotional needs of children at the beginning of the 1970s are assessed. Evaluations and detailed recommendations made to the United States Congress concerning what should be done to improve the quality of mental health for the children of this country are included, and the important role of day-care centers and nursery schools in this area is stressed; surprisingly readable and interesting.

Sigel, I. E., Starr, R., Secrist, A., Jackson, J. P., and Hill, E. Social and emotional development of young children. In J. L. Frost (Ed.), *Revisiting early childhood education: Readings.* New York: Holt, Rinehart and Winston, Inc., 1973. These readings review significant research concerned with social and emotional development; the article cited is particularly valuable because it discusses implications of research for day care at the end of each section.

Goleta Head Start, Santa Barbara

6 □ Helping young children establish self-discipline and self-control

Most arguments about discipline and "permissiveness" miss the point. In the end, the child has to turn either of them into self-discipline. Permissiveness and rigid discipline both shrivel the capacity for self-discipline. Only an increasing freedom within widening limits can resolve it.

MAX LERNER
Santa Barbara News Press, August 20, 1978.

Because discipline worries beginning teachers the most, it is usually the subject they want to discuss first when they begin teaching. Sometimes this is because they fear physical aggression or that the children won't like them, but more frequently they fear losing control of the situation because they don't know what to do next. So when teachers say fervently that they want to discuss "discipline," what they usually have in mind is how to control the children or, as one forthright young student put it, "how to get the kids to do what I want."

TWO BASIC GOALS OF DISCIPLINE

Although "getting the kids to do what I want" is undeniably part of the package, should it be all that is encompassed by the concept of discipline? The teacher should also have in mind the higher goal of instilling inner self-controls in the child in place of teacher-maintained external ones. Therefore, every discipline situation should not only achieve a workable solution to the current crisis (and this will be discussed in the second part of the chapter), but should also seek to interiorize self-control.

ESTABLISHING INNER CONTROLS: EGO STRENGTH AND MORAL DEVELOPMENT
Why does self-control matter?

Self- rather than "other-" control is desirable for a number of reasons: people who can control themselves are trustworthy and responsible. They can be counted on to do the "right" thing whether or not a policeman is standing on the corner watching to see if they run the red light. Because the control is internal, it is more consistent; and, most valuably for mental health, the individual who is "inner-controlled" makes choices in his own behalf. This is the opposite of the neurotic personality who feels powerless, unable to control what happens to himself, and who sees himself as "done to" and in the power of others.

Granted that such internalization is desirable, the question that remains for the nursery school teacher to answer is how she can begin to establish these inner controls in such young children. How can she teach them not only to *know* what is right but to *do* what is right? She must realize that this is a long process taking many years and it rests on the gradual development of ego strength and moral judgment. A strong ego enables the child to control his impulses, and moral judgment (telling right from wrong) enables him to decide which impulses he must control.

Building ego strength

Fraiberg (1977) describes the ego as being the part of the personality that has to do with the executive and cognitive functions of the individual and that also regulates the drives and appetites. Obviously, it is this part of the personality we will want to strengthen in order to make it available to the child to help him control his impulses. One way to do this is to *increase the child's feelings of mastery by giving him many opportunities for making decisions.* However, the choices offered must be appropriate and not too difficult. I recall a 4-year-old who was asked by her divorcing parents to decide which parent she wished to live with—an intolerably difficult choice for a child of that age to make.

On the other hand, the nursery school day abounds with opportunities for decisions well within the ability of most threes and fours to handle. The catch is that *the teacher must be prepared to honor the choice once the child has made the decision.* Such questions as, ''Do you want dessert?'' ''Would you rather fingerpaint or play with the blocks?'' or ''Would you like to pass the napkins today?'' are examples of valid choices because it is all right if the child chooses to refuse. Unfortunately, many teachers use ''Would you like? . . .'' or ''Would you please? . . .'' or ''Okay?'' as a polite camouflage for conveying an order. Thus they inquire, ''Let's get on the bus, okay?'' or ''Would you like to put on your sweater?'' Young children are likely to retort ''No!'' when asked such questions, and then the teacher is really stuck. It is better not to ask, ''Let's get on the bus, okay?'' if the child has to get on the bus anyway, but to try saying, ''The bus is here, and it's time to go home.

Photo by Austin Rudneckie, Santa Barbara City College Children's Center

Where do you want to sit?'' or ''It's cold today. If you want to go out, you will need to put on your sweater.'' In short, honor choices when given, but give no choice when there is no valid opportunity to make one.

It is also important to see to it that the child experiences the consequences of his decisions. Perhaps the reader will recall the example in the chapter on routines where the child who elects to skip snack is not permitted to change his mind at the last minute. As Veatch (1977) suggests, abiding by decisions once they are made teaches youngsters to make responsible choices.

Increase the child's feelings of being a competent, worthwhile person. The feelings of self-esteem generated by competency also make the ego stronger. The child who thinks well of himself because he is competent is in a favorable position to assume command and control of himself because he sees himself as powerful.

Unfortunately, some children are noticed at nursery school only when they do something wrong. This continual negative relationship with the teacher does not enhance their feelings of self-worth. Even the ''worst'' child in school doesn't misbehave all the time. A considerable part of his day is spent in acceptable activities. If his self-esteem and self-mastery are to remain intact, it is vital that he receive credit for his good behavior as well as control for his transgressions.

However, as we shall see in more detail in the chapter devoted to that subject, the most desirable source of self-esteem stems not from the opinion of the teacher, but from the acquisition of competencies. These may range from being able to walk the balance beam to knowing effective strategies for worming one's way into a play group. It doesn't really matter what the competency is, as long as it contributes to the child's perception of himself as being an able person who is in command of himself.

Encouraging moral development: fostering the interiorization of conscience

Another aspect of helping children establish inner controls has to do with the establishment of con-

science and instilling a sense of what is right and wrong. Conscience (sometimes termed the *superego*) can be described as that *inner* voice that tells us what we should or should not do. Theoretical arguments continue over how this voice is instilled (Henderson and Bergan, 1976; Turiel, 1973), but a comprehensive review of research on this subject (Hoffman, 1970) indicates that growth of conscience is facilitated most strongly by the presence of two factors, both of which can be easily utilized by parents and teachers. One of these is the presence of affection and a nurturing relationship between the adult and the child—a condition that should generally pertain in nursery school as well as in the home. This factor was identified as being present in about half the studies reviewed by Hoffman. The second factor that appears to be even more potent, since it was more consistently present in the reported studies, is the use of what is termed ''induction techniques.'' In simple language, this just means giving a child a reason why he should or should not do something. For example, one might say, ''I can't let you hit Ginny with the block—it hurts too much.'' or ''We always flush the toilet so it's fresh for the next person.'' Another more advanced example might be, ''We have to put the candy back —we didn't pay for it. We always have to give the clerk money when we take something. That's how people who work here get money to buy what *they* want.'' Surely such an explanation is preferable to the, ''You're a bad, naughty girl for stealing that candy,'' that is so frequently heard.

Moral development occurs in a number of stages. There is one more fascinating thing about the growth of conscience that the teacher needs to understand. It is that children and adults have very different ways of thinking about what is right and wrong (Turiel, 1973). The work of Damon (1977), Piaget (1932), and Kohlberg (1976) reveals that there are different stages of moral development just as there are stages in the development of reasoning.

Progression from one stage to the next is a result of interplay between cognitive maturation and social experience. Although some research indicates that children who are on the verge of passing on to the next state may be influenced by teaching (Turiel, 1973), in general such growth is thought to be the result of *con*struction by the child rather than direct *in*struction by the teacher. Nor should it be assumed that everyone attains the final level. Some adults remain at Stage 1 or 2, and many at Stage 4 (Kramer, 1968; Krebs and Rosenwald, 1977; Turiel, 1973).

The interesting thing about the stage theory of moral development is that as a result of his moral developmental level the conscience of a child may tell him something is wrong when an adult's conscience tells him the same action is right (Damon, 1977)! Examples of this will be presented later in this chapter. This developmental difference can certainly confuse the teacher if she does not understand how young children view right and wrong and does not make allowances for their differing points of view.

STAGES OF MORAL DEVELOPMENT*

A. *Preconventional level*

Stage 1: Unquestioning obedience based on external power and compulsion. Right or wrong is what is rewarded or punished. Right is "following the rule." Rules are accepted unquestioningly. Child has not "decentered." Moral judgments are based on observable, physical consequences rather than on intentions of person.

Stage 2: Instrumental-relativist orientation. Right or wrong is what instrumentally satisfies own needs and, sometimes, the needs of others. "Back-scratching" kind of reciprocity is understood. One behaves well in order to get what one wants.

B. *Conventional level*

Stage 3: Right behavior is what pleases others. Behavior is often judged by the intention behind it. ("He means well"): good boy/bad boy idea of morals.

Stage 4: Law and order. Right behavior is doing one's duty, showing respect for authority, following rules because they are "right."

*Based on Kohlberg (1976) and Turiel (1973).

C. *Postconventional, autonomous, or principled level*

Stage 5: Social-contract legalistic orientation. Right is a matter of personal values, which have been examined and agreed on by the whole society. Laws are not absolute but subject to modification. The United States Constitution is an example of this level of moral development.

Stage 6: Universal ethical principle orientation. Right is defined by individual conscience in accord with self-chosen, ethical principles of justice, reciprocity and equality of human rights, and respect for dignity of human beings as individual people (Golden Rule is an example of this).

STAGES 1 AND 2: IMPLICATIONS FOR TEACHING. Young children define "right" as being what the rule says. A rule is right because a parent or teacher says it's right. This doesn't mean children necessarily obey the rule, of course, but it does mean that they do not reason and question whether the rule itself is fair or just. I have often been amused, when testing children, to see this fact in operation. Occasionally children will ask me why I'm writing down what they are saying. I've never had a preschooler question me further when I reply that that's what the rule says I'm supposed to do.

Nor do young children make allowances for what someone intended or meant to do. They render judgment only on the observable consequences. (This is similar to their reasoning in the realm of conservation of materials—seeing is believing.) As Piaget points out, children of preschool age conclude that the child who has broken more cups has done a greater wrong than the child who has broken only one, regardless of the reason for the breakage (that is, preschool children reason that the child who breaks several cups while helping his mother should be punished more than the child who breaks a single cup while stealing cookies—older children would, of course, reach a quite different conclusion, based on the fact that stealing itself is "bad," whereas an adult who had advanced to a still higher moral level might decide that the fact the child was starving negated the "sin" of theft because preserving human life is a greater good.

Understanding that young children take results rather than intentions into account may help the teacher comprehend the continuing resentment expressed by a child toward someone who has knocked him down, even after the teacher has explained it was an accident. Despite the teacher's interpretation, it remains difficult for him to grasp the transgressor's harmless intention when he is experiencing the actual result.

Four-year-olds approaching Stage 2 are beginning to understand a very simple form of reciprocity as justice—"I do something for you, and you do something for me." The implication for teaching, and it is borne out by experience, is that this is a practical time to introduce the concept of bargaining as an alternative to simply demanding what one wants. An obvious example of this that I heard recently was a child who bargained, "Well—I'll let you sit in the cradle, but you can't 'waa-waa' all the time!" (A less obvious example occurred when a 5-year-old said to an importuning three, "Well—okay —I'll tell you what—you *can* be the leader, but in *this* gang, leaders always go at the end of the line!")

Finally, both Piaget and Kohlberg emphasize that the young child is centered on himself and that, because of this egocentrism, he has great difficulty imagining himself in the shoes of another. This information has important implications for nursery school teachers who often try to breed empathy and social consciousness by saying, "How would *you* like that if you were *him?* What if *you* were Peter and a little boy threw sand in *your* eyes? How would you feel then?" This kind of reasoning is just too hard for little children to grasp because it's asking them to control themselves and also to picture themselves in another's place. The same lesson can be taught much more effectively by making a simple change in approach, asking, for example, "What if Peter threw sand in *your* eyes? How would you feel then?" or, better yet, "Remember when Patty threw

sand in your eyes? Remember how you felt? Well, Peter feels that way now?" It may not sound like a major difference, but it's much easier for children to understand.

PRACTICAL THINGS TO DO TO MAKE IT EASIER FOR CHILDREN TO BEHAVE IN ACCEPTABLE WAYS

It is evident from the foregoing discussion that establishing ego strength and conscience in young children is a complex and lengthy task that can be only begun in the preschool years. While this is in process, the teacher must be willing to assume control when necessary, always bearing in mind the ultimate goal of helping the child achieve responsibility for himself. There are many practical ways to go about doing this, as well as some things teachers do that make discipline of any kind more difficult.

No one intentionally makes trouble for herself by creating a poor environment; yet so many of the situations listed below happen in nursery schools from time to time that it seems appropriate (as well as being fiendish fun) to begin by pointing them out.

TEN EASY WAYS NOT TO REACH THE BASIC GOALS OF GOOD DISCIPLINE

1. Make the children wait a lot, and expect them to sit quietly while they wait, preferably like little ladies and gentlemen with their hands in their laps and their feet on the floor.
2. Be inconsistent: let the children ride their trikes on the grass on days when you don't feel up to par, but take their trikes away when you're feeling better, because it's against the rules to ride on the grass.
3. Be unreasonable: never make allowances for children who are (1) tired, (2) hungry, (3) coming down with something, or (4) getting over something. It will also help ruin the day to have a great many arbitrary rules that are never explained although rigidly enforced.
4. Decide that the way to let children learn for themselves is never to intervene; pay no at-

tention to the possibility that the younger, smaller children are being bullied and that some older ones are actually learning that "might makes right."

5. Be consistent: always punish the children by doing the same thing to them. For example, no matter what they do, make them sit in the office, or don't let them have dessert at lunch.

6. Give up halfway through a confrontation, and let the child run off. After all, you're not supposed to leave your work station.

7. Lose your temper and yell at the children. This will frighten them into behaving and will make you feel better.

8. Strike a child; pinch him or jerk his arm when no one is looking. This will also frighten him badly, but maybe he'll behave after that.

9. Ignore the problem; just send the troublemaker off to play with the new teacher. It will help her gain experience.

10. Talk too much. Confuse the child: moralize, shame, or embarrass him, or warn him that you're going to tell his mother! This will help him understand the consequences of his actions and set an example of verbal control for him.

When behaviors such as these are singled out, it is clear how undesirable such approaches are; and yet they are more common than one would wish them to be in many schools, probably because they reflect discipline practices many teachers experienced in their homes while growing up. However, if the following principles are put into practice, the need for these more unproductive methods will be reduced.

Besides fostering ego strength and the development of conscience, there are two other fundamental things to do to help children in nursery school behave in acceptable ways and to improve the ease and quality of discipline and control in the group: (1) prevent discipline situations when it is possible to do so and (2) know what to do when a crisis occurs.

Prevent discipline situations when possible

Reward behavior you want to see continued; don't reward behavior you wish to discourage. Children (and adults) repeat behavior from which they obtain satisfaction. This reward doesn't necessarily come in the form of payoffs of chocolate chips or gold stars. Whether teachers realize it or not, they use rewards every time they say "thank you" or "that's a good job," or even when they smile at a child. The value of this technique, which is one form of behavior modification called *positive reinforcement,* has been well proved, (Hilgard and Bower, 1966; Roedell, Slaby, and Robinson, 1976; Walker and Shea, 1976); and there is no doubt that it is an effective way to deal with recurring discipline and behavior problems. Therefore, when undesirable behavior persists, it is a good idea to take a look at what the child is getting out of it. Preventing the payoff can help eliminate the behavior. It is also very effective to note positive actions on the part of the children and to respond to them with pleasure, since this positive reward, combined with the pleasure inherent in successful accomplishment, is a very potent reinforcer.

While on the subject of reinforcement, I want to comment that I agree with Bettye Caldwell (1977) that it is not effective to "extinguish" aggressive behavior in young children by simply ignoring it. In my experience such behavior does not subside when ignored—apparently because children interpret this laissez-faire attitude as permission (Bandura and Walters, 1963). Not only that, one cannot overlook the fact that there are inherent gratifications (payoffs) in attacking other children; these range from simply seizing what is desired to enjoying hitting someone—if you're angry, hitting somebody feels pretty good. For these reasons, it is important to take more assertive action and stop undesirable behavior rather than let it slip past on the ground that it will go away if no attention is paid to it.

When trouble repeats itself, analyze the situation and try changing it rather than nagging at the child. When something happens over and over, in addition to checking up on payoffs, the teacher should also think about changing the situation instead of the child. For example, instead of telling a restless youngster to be quiet all the time, it might be better to let him leave after hearing one story, to ask a volunteer to read to him alone, or even to let him play quietly nearby during story time until he becomes more interested and can be drawn gradually into the group.

Emphasize the positive rather than the negative; always tell the child the correct thing to do. This habit can be formed with a little practice. When using positive directions, rather than saying, "Don't get your feet wet," or "Stay out of that puddle," the teacher says, "Walk around the puddle." She says, "Put the sand in the dump truck," rather than, "Don't throw the sand." This technique is desirable not only because it reduces negative criticism, but also because it directs the child toward something he can do that is acceptable.

Warn ahead of time to make transitions easier. The teacher should anticipate transitions with the children a few minutes before the activity is due to change. She might say, "It's going to be lunch time pretty soon. I wonder what we're going to have?" Or she might warn, "There's just time for one more painting. Then you can help me wash the brushes, and we'll have a story." Warning ahead gives the children time to wind up what they're doing. Sometimes just walking around the yard and commenting here and there that soon it will be time to go in will serve this purpose. It takes the abruptness out of the situation and makes compliance with routines much easier for the children.

Avoid unnecessary constraints. Even in well-run nursery schools, children are constrained from following their own pursuits more often than we may realize. For example, at the University of Chicago Nursery School, Jackson and Wolfson (1968) found that 20 constraining episodes took place every minute of the nursery school day. Although these constraints were not always teacher generated, this study points up the desirability of avoiding them whenever possible in order to reduce the children's

feelings of frustration and increase their feelings of absorbed satisfaction.

Have as few rules as possible, but make the ones you do have stick. Unless the teacher is watchful, rules will grow up like a thicket around each experience. But if situations are reviewed from time to time, unnecessary restrictions can be weeded out.

On the other hand, some rules are genuinely necessary, and their enforcement is desirable not only because research shows that establishing firm limits, coupled with warmth and a simple explanation of the reason behind the rule, enhances the child's self-esteem (Coopersmith, 1967; Sears, Maccoby, and Levin, 1957), but also (as we have seen earlier in the chapter) because it increases his ability to establish inner controls.

The problem is to decide, preferably in advance, which rules are really important. Students, in particular, seem to have trouble in this area—sometimes treating relatively minor infractions such as not saying "please" or "thank you" as though they were major transgressions, while dealing indecisively with more serious misbehavior such as tearing up picture books or running out the front door without an adult in attendance. In general, the most serious infractions of rules are those related to hurting other people, hurting oneself, or destroying another person's property. If a reason isn't easy to come up with, it may be a sign that the rule is not important and could be abandoned.

When supervising children, plan ahead. Try to anticipate the point where the children will become uninterested or the play will fall apart and to have alternatives ready to propose that will help the play continue to flourish. An insightful teacher might think, "Now, if I were he, what would I like to do next with those blocks and cars?" Perhaps it would be getting out the arches or the wood strips to make a garage, or maybe it would be constructing ramps for the cars to run down. Tactfully posing several possibilities to the children will serve to continue play and to lengthen concentration as well as keep the children happily occupied and out of trouble.

Keep the day interesting. To combat idleness, the

nursery school day needs variety—not only variety of pace to avoid the fatigue that leads to misbehavior, but also a variety of things to do to maintain interest and fun and to keep the children busy in productive ways. Accomplishing this requires planning and sensitivity, but it is well worth the investment of effort.

Know what to do when a crisis occurs

Of course, the ideal to work toward even in crisis situations is to teach the children to solve their own problems, since in their adult life they won't always have a teacher present to arbitrate differences. The situations discussed in the following sections, however, are ones where it is evident that the child has to have help to control himself and to be able to take action that is socially acceptable. Even in these situations, the focus should never be on the God-like powers of the teacher to bring about justice, but on development of the child's ability to do this for himself.

When should the teacher step in and control misbehavior? Inexperienced teachers are often unsure of when they should interfere and when they should let children work the situation through between themselves. As I said earlier, the general rule of thumb is that children should not be allowed to hurt other people (either children or grownups), to hurt themselves, or to destroy property. This policy leaves considerable latitude for noninterference, but it also sets a clear line for intervention. An occasional teacher is particularly unsure about whether she should allow children to hit her or kick her as a means of "getting their feelings out." Children should not be allowed to attack adults any more than adults should attack children. Aside from the fact that it hurts and can't help making the teacher angry, permitting such attacks makes the child feel guilty and uncomfortable—he really knows he shouldn't be allowed to do it.

The best way to prevent physical attack if it appears to be imminent is to hoist the child on the hip, with his head forward and his feet stuck out behind. This unglamorous pose, known as the *football carry,* works very well to stave off attack and per-

mit the teacher to carry the child someplace if she has to. Although it is rarely necessary to resort to such measures, it helps to know what to do in a real emergency.

When trouble brews, take action yourself before the child does. Over and over again, I have seen teachers sit on the sidelines and let a situation go from bad to worse until it explodes, and then step in to pick up the pieces. If the situation is one that will have to be stopped at some point, *it is much more effective to step in before trouble starts* rather than a minute after blood has been shed.

Prompt intervention makes it more probable that the teacher can use a rational approach with the children; this is a better environment for teaching any skill. Intervening before the fight occurs also prevents either child from receiving gratification from the attack. For example, stepping in before one child bites another takes preternatural quickness but is vital to do because biting feels so good to the biter that no amount of punishment afterward detracts sufficiently from the satisfying reward of sinking teeth into unresisting flesh.

Keep your own emotions under control. One way children learn attitudes is by observing models (Bandura, Grusec, and Menlove, 1967; Bandura and Menlove, 1968). Teachers need to control their tempers, since by doing so they provide a model of self-control for the children to copy as well as because intense anger frightens children. Also, when discipline situations arise, it is not just one child and the teacher who are involved: every child in the room is likely to be covertly watching what is happening and drawing conclusions from it. Therefore, it is often valuable for the teacher to talk over what happened with various children afterward to help them deal with how they felt about it and to clarify and consolidate what they learned from it.

Sometimes, of course, it is simpler to advocate self-control in the teacher than to achieve it. Self-control is made easier by remembering that one is dealing with a child, by deliberately keeping control of oneself, and by acknowledging the feeling and saying to the child, "Let's wait just a minute until we're both a little calmer. I feel pretty upset about

Los Niños Head Start

what you did.'' The biggest help, though, comes from analyzing scenes and upsets after they have occurred and planning how best to handle them the next time they happen. This experience and analysis builds skills and confidence—and confidence is the great strengthener of self-control. Children sense this assurance in the teacher just the way dogs know who loves or fears them, and children become less challenging and more at ease when they feel the teacher knows how to cope and has every intention of doing so.

Handle disagreements between children fairly. In the chapter on mental health considerable time was spent in explaining how to help children express their feelings verbally. Although this is fairly easy to accomplish when the teacher is dealing with only one child, it is considerably more difficult but just as important when dealing with more than one. When two children are involved, it is a wonderful opportunity to help both of them develop this social skill, and the teacher should urge them to talk things over and to tell each other what they want and how they feel. Telling each other how they feel and knowing these feelings have been heard often mean children are no longer driven to act them out, and the way is opened for compromise.

It is also essential that the teacher avoid being trapped into rendering judgments about situations she hasn't seen. Four-year-olds are particularly prone to tattle about the misdeeds of others. A polite name for this is *prosocial aggression;* it is a natural, if unappealing stage in the development of conscience. Unless the reported activity is truly dangerous, the best course of action in the case of tattling is for the teacher to encourage the child to return with her and settle the matter himself. She should avoid taking sides or the word of one child, because George Washingtons are remarkably scarce in nursery school. When it is a case of who had what first, it may be necessary, if a compromise cannot be reached, to take whatever it is away from both youngsters for a while until they calm down. Remember, it is often the child who is crying the loudest who began the fight, although he may appear to need comforting the most. The only thing to do in situations such as this is be fair and deal with both children in a firm but nonjudgmental way. Impartiality is the keynote.

When a fight boils up, it can also be helpful to call a meeting of the children who are nearby to discuss settling it. The point of such discussions is not to ask the witnesses who was to blame (remember, it takes two to make a fight), but to ask them for ideas and suggestions about how to arbitrate the difficulty. The fighters can often be prevailed upon to listen to what their peers have to suggest, and children often come up with surprisingly practical solutions. Although these tend to be severe (Kohlberg, 1976; Turiel, 1973), it is fine experience for them to think about how to get along together and work out solutions based on real life situations.

When a child has gone so far that he has hurt another youngster, he should be allowed to help remedy the injury. Perhaps he can put on the bandage or hold a cold towel on the bump. This constructive action helps him see the consequences of his act, relieve his guilty feelings, and show concern by doing something tangible. I do not believe children should be asked to say they're sorry. Often they aren't sorry, and even if they are, I fear teaching the lesson that glib apologies make everything all right. Moreover, a replicated study by Irwin and Moore (1971) supports the idea that young children grasp the concept of restitution (doing something to right a ''wrong'') before they understand the true significance of apology, so making restitution is a more developmentally appropriate approach.

Whenever possible, let the punishment fit the crime. Nursery school teachers (and enlightened parents) avoid doling out punishment in its usual forms. Teachers don't spank children, shut them in closets, take away their television privileges, or deny them dessert because they haven't been good. But they do *allow* another form of punishment to happen when it is appropriate. This is simply permitting the child to experience the natural consequences of his behavior. Thus, the child who refuses to come in for snack is permitted to miss the meal; the child who rebelliously tears a page from a book is expected to mend it; and the youngster who pulls all the blocks off the shelf must stay to help put them away. Even young children can see the fairness of a punishment that fits the crime so aptly and appreciate the justice of a consequence that stems logically from the action. It is not necessary to be unpleasant or moralistic when any of these results transpire; it is the teacher's responsibility only to make certain that the child experiences the logical outcome of his behavior.

What to do when children continue to misbehave. Since children do not always stop throwing sand or grabbing tricycles simply because the teacher tells them to or redirects them to another activity, it is necessary to know what to do when a child continues to misbehave. I call the approach I use the five learning steps in discipline: (1) warning the child, (2) removing him, (3) discussing feelings and rules, (4) waiting for him to decide when he is ready to return, and (5) helping him return and be more successful.

1. Warn the child, and redirect him if he will accept such redirection. For example, you might

warn a youngster that if he continues to throw sand, he will lose the privilege of staying in the sandbox; then suggest a couple of interesting things he could do with the sand instead of throwing it. It is important to make the child understand that his behavior is up to him. It is *his* choice; but if he chooses to continue, you will see to it that you carry out your warning.

2. Warn only once. If he persists in doing what he has been told not to do, act calmly and promptly. Remove him and insist that he sit beside you, telling him he has lost the privilege of playing in the sand. This is much more valuable than just letting him run off. Having him sit beside you interrupts what he wants to do, is a mildly unpleasant consequence of his act, and prevents his substituting another activity that is more pleasant.

3. Take time to describe his feeling in an understanding way, but be clear about firmly stating the rule as well as the reason for it. Don't moralize or rub it in too much. Don't talk too much.

4. At step 4, many teachers say something on the order of, "Now you sit here until lunch is ready," thus shifting the responsibility for the child's behavior to their own shoulders instead of putting the child in command of himself. It is better to say, "Now, tell me when you can control yourself, and I will let you go back," or, more specifically, "When you can keep the sand down, tell me, and then you can go back and play." Some children can actually say they are ready, but others will need help from the teacher, who can ask them when they look ready, "Are you ready to go back now?" (Perhaps he nods or just looks ready.) "Good, your eyes tell me you are. What would you like to do for fun there?"

5. Finally, it is important to go with the child and help him be successful when he does go back, so that he has the experience of substituting acceptable for unacceptable behavior. It will probably be necessary to take a few minutes and get him really interested. Be sure to congratulate the child when he has settled down, perhaps saying, "Now, you're doing the right thing. I'm proud of you!"

Occasionally, the teacher will come across a more glib customer who says hastily when removed from the sandbox, "I'll be good, I'll be good!" but then goes right back to throwing sand when he returns. At this point it is necessary to take firmer action. Have him sit beside you until he can think of something acceptable to do, but don't permit him to go back to the sandbox. You might say, "What you did (be explicit) shows me that you haven't decided to do the right thing; so you'll have to come and sit with me until you can think of somewhere else to play. You've lost the privilege of playing in the sandbox for now. Then when he decides, *go with him or alert another teacher so that he does start on something desirable to do.*

Inexperienced teachers sometimes dread these confrontations because they fear that the child will be hostile afterward or actively dislike them for keeping their word and enforcing their authority. However, such confrontations almost invariably build a closer bond between the teacher and the child, who usually seeks her out and makes it evident that he likes her after such encounters.

Most important, notice when children do the right thing, and comment favorably. This entire chapter has been spent talking about preventing or coping with misbehavior. Fortunately, most of the nursery school day does not center around such episodes; many days go smoothly and the children get along happily. When the day is a good one, when the children are obviously making progress, when they mostly talk instead of hit each other, when they share generously and enjoy the opportunities to help each other, let them know that you are pleased with their good behavior. They will share your pleasure in their accomplishments, and this recognition will help perpetuate the growth and self-discipline they have displayed.

SUMMARY

Discipline should be more than just "getting the kids to do what I want." The real goal should be the development of self-controls within the children. This is accomplished, in part, by strengthening the ego and by fostering the beginning of conscience. Two ego-strengthening experiences often used by nursery school teachers are offering appropriate choices to children to give them practice in decision making and helping children feel masterful through attaining competencies.

The growth of conscience is facilitated by the presence of warm, nurturing relationships between child and adult, as well as by the utilization of induction (reason-giving) techniques, but the moral judgments rendered by the conscience are profoundly influenced by the stage of moral reasoning the child has attained. Progress from one stage to the next depends on cognitive maturation combined with social experience. From this interaction the child constructs the next step in moral growth.

There are many undesirable ways to control children, but there are also more desirable approaches, which can be subsumed under the general heading of preventing discipline situations when possible, and knowing what to do when a crisis occurs. When all of these strategies fail and a child continues to misbehave, it is important to take him through all five of the steps in learning self-control: (1) warning him, (2) removing him from the activity while keeping him with the teacher, (3) discussing feelings and rules, (4) waiting for him to make the decision to return to the activity, and (5) helping him return and be more successful. Consistent use of this approach will be effective in helping children gain control of themselves, thus helping them to become socially acceptable human beings.

QUESTIONS AND ACTIVITIES

1. Give three examples of choices you could encourage the children to make for themselves the next time you teach.
2. If you wanted to use an inductive technique, what would you say instead of "Pass the bread," and "It's time to lie down and be quiet"?
3. Have you ever had the experience of deciding, theoretically, how you intended to handle misbehavior, and then found yourself doing something different when the occasion actually came up? How do you account for this discrepancy?
4. What is the difference between moralizing and explaining to a

child the reason why he cannot be allowed to do something? Role play some examples of each approach.
5. *Problem:* A child is throwing sand in the sandbox, and you want him to stop. What should you say to put your statement in positive form rather than telling him what not to do, that is, rather than saying "Don't throw the sand"?
6. Select an activity, such as lunch time, and list every rule, spoken and implicit, that you expect children to observe in this situation. Are there any that could be abandoned? Are there any that are really for the teacher's convenience rather than for the purpose of fostering the children's well-being?
7. Team up with another student and take 15-minute turns for an hour a day, keeping track of how many times you reinforced positive behavior of the children. Then, keep track of how many opportunities for such reinforcement you overlooked.
8. *Problem:* Elaine, who is 4½, is playing at the puzzle table and keeps slipping little pieces of puzzle in her pocket. No one except you sees her doing this. You have already told her twice to keep the puzzles on the table so the pieces won't get lost, but she continues to challenge you by slipping them in her pocket. What should you do next to handle this situation?
9. *Problem:* As you enter the room you see John and David hanging on to a truck, both shouting that they had it first and that they can keep it until they're done with it. How would you cope with this crisis?

REFERENCES FOR FURTHER READING

Setting Limits for Children

Read, K. H. *The nursery school: Human relationships and learning* (6th ed.). Philadelphia: W. B. Saunders Co., 1976. Since it is impossible to touch on every point in every book, reading additional material on a subject as broad as discipline is very helpful. Beginning students should not miss the chapters "Authority and the Setting of Limits" and "Initial Support through Guides to Speech and Action."

Establishing Control of the Group

Murphy, L. B., and Leeper, E. M. *Away from bedlam.* Washington, D.C.: U.S. Dept. of Health, Education, and Welfare, 1970a. Murphy and Leeper's very practical pamphlet discusses in plain terms how to maintain reasonable order and control in a nursery school classroom. It may be obtained from the Superintendent of Documents, Washington, D.C.

Roedell, W. C., Slaby, R. G., and Robinson, H. B. *Social development in young children: A report for teachers.* Washington, D.C.: U.S. Dept. of Health, Education, and Welfare, National Institute of Education, 1976. The chapter Moral Judgment and Good Behavior" contains many valuable behavior management suggestions and also provides an interesting contrast to Piaget and Kohlberg by concentrating on the learning theory point of view.

Stone, J. W. *A guide to discipline* (Rev. ed.). Washington, D.C.: National Association for the Education of Young Children, 1978. This all-too-brief pamphlet is filled with practical advice about how to handle such discipline situations as spitting, biting, and kicking. It contains many examples of things to say that will relieve, control, or prevent tense situations in the nursery school.

Theories and Related Methods of Handling Children

Walker, J. E., and Shea, T. M. *Behavior modification: A practical approach for educators.* St. Louis: The C. V. Mosby Co., 1976. For those who desire a more detailed discussion of behavior modification techniques, the book by Walker and Shea is useful because it is filled with examples and is quite practical in its approach; deals mainly with teaching older children.

Wittes, G., and Radin, N. *Ypsilanti home and school handbooks: Helping your child to learn: The nurturance approach.* San Rafael, Calif.: Dimensions Publishing Co., 1969b. Wittes and Radin provide a well-thought-out, carefully presented explanation of how to help children learn by using an approach based on love, understanding, respect, and mental stimulation. This booklet is an outline of a course developed for parents. It is very clear and contains many examples and group exercises for learning how to apply the suggestions to children.

Wittes, G., and Radin, N. *Ypsilanti home and school handbooks: Helping your child to learn: The reinforcement approach.* San Rafael, Calif.: Dimensions Publishing Co., 1969c. Presented in the same fashion as the booklet described above, this one explains reinforcement theory and outlines how to apply it to modify the behavior of young children. Although there are a great many books that deal with this subject, this is one of the best for beginning teachers because it is short and clear, and it deals with preschool youngsters. In order to obtain a balanced understanding of the values and pitfalls of using behavior modification, I recommend that the student read the article by Lillian Katz, ''Condition with Caution,'' *Young Children,* 1972, *27*(5), in conjunction with it.

Moral Development

Damon, W. *The social world of the child.* San Francisco: Jossey-Bass, Inc., Publishers, 1977. Kohlberg should surely be read for the value of his overall approach to the stage theory of moral development, but teachers of young children will find the work of William Damon even more useful, since his research, which is ingenious, concentrates on children aged 4 to 12. It is interesting material; fun to try out with children in your own group.

Henderson, R. W., and Bergan, J. R. *The cultural context of childhood.* Columbus, Ohio: Charles E. Merrill Publishing Co., 1976. This is a generally excellent book that provides a good overview of theories of moral development and the development of conscience.

Kohlberg, L. The development of children's orientations toward a moral order: Sequence in the development of moral thought. In P. B. Neubauer (Ed.), *The process of child development.* New York: Jason Aronson, Inc., 1976. Here is a lucid explanation of Kohlberg's six-stage theory of moral development that is well written and has good examples of the attitudes characterizing each stage.

Martorella, P. H. Selected early childhood affective learning programs: An analysis of theories, structure, and consistency. *Young Children,* 1975, *30*(4), 289-301. Peter Martorella reviews four commercially available affective programs, including one based on Kohlberg's work. Three of the four begin at the 4-year-old level; all appear to be based exclusively on group discussion of values and situations—a not particularly effective way for young children to learn.

For the Advanced Student

Piaget, J. *The moral judgement of the child.* London: Routledge and Kegan Paul, Ltd., 1932. *The Moral Judgement of the Child* is the hallmark study of moral attitudes that forms the foundation for much of the later work in this area; easier reading than most works by this master.

Risley, T. R., and Baer, D. M. Operant behavior modification: The deliberate development of behavior. In B. M. Caldwell and H. N. Ricciuti (Eds.), *Review of child development research* (Vol. 3). Chicago: University of Chicago Press, 1973.

Sherman, J. A., and Bushell, D. Behavior modification as an educational technique. In F. D. Horowitz (Ed.), *Review of child development research* (Vol. 4). Chicago: University of Chicago Press, 1975. The reader who reviews both these chapters will end up with a complete overview of the theory of behavior modification as well as an in-depth knowledge of the research that supports it.

Turiel, E. Stage transition in moral development. In R. W. Travers (Ed.), *Second handbook of research on teaching.* Chicago: Rand McNally & Co., 1973. This is a scholarly, clear, comprehensive review of research and theory based on Piaget's and Kohlberg's levels of moral development; excellent.

Los Niños Head Start

7 □ Aggression: what to do about it*

It is not sufficient that a child simply be kept from doing damage at a given moment. He must develop standards of conduct that will not require constant policing in order to maintain acceptable kinds of behavior. He must come to possess appropriate internal controls. The kinds of aggression he finally learns to use must be appropriate in form and intensity, and they must be used only under acceptable circumstances.

The necessity for control of both action and learning at the same time leads to some difficulties in training children vis-à-vis aggression, for the consequences of a particular practice may be quite different in its short-term and long-term influences. One can introduce pressures to stop the fussing and whining, but this is only half the problem. Does the child learn to do what his mother wants the next time? What does he learn? How does he behave after the pressure is taken off?†

Now that the general subject of discipline has been discussed, it is time to talk about dealing with aggressive behavior in particular. In this context, aggressive behavior means: "actions that are intended to cause injury or anxiety to others, including hitting, kicking, destroying property, quarreling, derogating others, attacking others verbally and resisting requests" (Mussen, Conger, and Kagan, (1969, p. 370). At the nursery school level we see examples of this kind of behavior manifested when children barge through the room, leaving a bedlam of smashed blocks or ravished housekeeping corners behind them, or when they spend most of their time whooping wildly about being tigers or monsters, or when they deliberately seek to injure other children by destroying what they are doing, teasing them, or physically hurting them.

UNDESIRABLE WAYS TO COPE WITH AGGRESSION

Teachers and parents deal with acting-out behavior in both useful and not-so-useful ways. Some of the more undesirable methods of responding to such behavior follow.

The authoritarian teacher

At one extreme is the teacher who is a tightly controlling authoritarian. She responds to aggression in children as if expressing her own aggressive tendencies, garbed in the disguise of authority and control, were the only way to meet this problem. In forthright cases, schools dominated by such teachers are likely to be riddled with many rules generally determined by what is convenient for the teacher. "Don't run!" "Don't make noise!" "Sit down!" "Line up!" "Be quiet!" "Don't easel paint with your fingers!" "Stay clean!" "Don't splash!" "Take turns!" "Tell him you're sorry!"—and a thousand other tiresome injunctions are typical. Punishments used by such teachers are apt to be se-

*Revised from *Young Children,* 1968, *23*(5), 298-305.
†From Sears, R. R., Maccoby, E., and Levin, H. *Patterns of child rearing.* New York: Harper & Row, Publishers, 1957. P. 230.

Photo by F. Bell, Brooks Institute and School of Photography

vere, occasionally to the point of being emotionally destructive or physically painful.

Sometimes a beleaguered teacher feels that controls of this type are necessary because the classes are too large or too obstreperous for her to cope with any other way. Sometimes she believes that this kind of control is what the parents expect and that she'd better conform to this expectation or the children will be withdrawn from school.

More than likely the real reason for her reaction runs deeper than this and has to do with strong patterns carrying over from her own childhood, when little tolerance and freedom were granted to her by the adults in her life, and she was provided with a very authoritarian model. The frustration, resulting hostility, and covert aggression instilled by this treatment are particularly likely to be rearoused when she is confronted by the challenge of a belligerent 4-year-old. Transgressions are often dealt with by stringent punishments, and contests of will are highly probable if this teacher crosses swords with a genuinely spirited child.

What of the aggressive child who exists in this tightly controlled environment? What is the effect of overcontrol on him? For a few youngsters the bright edge of creative expression is dulled. Some children cannot afford to risk nonconforming (which is the essence of creativity) under these circumstances, and so most of their energy is used up holding onto themselves and "doing the right thing." These children have had their spirits broken. They conform—but at what a price!

There are almost bound to be other defiant young souls who continue to challenge or sneak past such a teacher. Common examples of such underground, continued aggression may range from quietly pulling the fur off the guinea pig to being unable to settle down for stories, or consistently destroying other children's accomplishments at the puzzle table or in the block corner. Other children internalize the angry feelings generated by authoritarian restrictions and become resistant and sullen; still others settle for becoming openly defiant.

In such schools a basic restlessness and tension seems to simmer in the air, and the teacher works harder and harder to hold the line, an exhausting business for all concerned. She tends to operate on the assumption that stronger punishment will result in greater control of aggression, but this is not necessarily true. Evidence from research studies indicates that strong punishment, particularly physical punishment, can actually increase the amount of aggressive behavior (Berkowitz, 1973; Eron, Walder, and Lefkowitz, 1971; Glueck and Glueck, 1950; Sears, Maccoby, and Levin, 1957). This teacher also overlooks the fact that there is a limit to how far she can go to enforce her dicta. What will she do if matters persist in getting out of hand?

The overpermissive teacher

At the other disciplinary extreme is the teacher who feels that "anything goes." Such teachers are often confused about the difference between freedom and license, and they fail to see that true freedom means the child may do as he wishes *only as long as he does not interfere with the rights and freedom of other people*. This extremely permissive teacher is fairly rare in nursery school because the pandemonium that occurs quickly makes parents uneasy. Apparently the results of this kind of mishandling are more obvious to the unprofessional eye than are the results of overcontrol.

In response to overpermissiveness the children may display behavior that is similar to the response for overcontrol. They may destroy other children's accomplishments or unconcernedly take whatever appeals to them. Sometimes they seem driven to tyrannical desperation trying to find out where the limits are and just how far they must go before the teacher at last overcomes her apathy and stirs herself to action. A common example of children's behavior in these circumstances is defiant teasing and baiting of the teacher by being ostentatiously, provocatively "naughty."

What the children really learn in such overpermissive circumstances is that "might makes right." This is a vicious circle, since the aggressor is often rewarded by getting what he wants and so is more likely to behave just as aggressively next time. Indeed, research indicates that attendance at a "permissive" nursery school does increase aggressive behavior (Patterson, Littman, and Bricker, 1967), and additional research by Bandura and Walters (1963) indicates that the presence of a permissive adult generally facilitates the expression of aggression.

The inconsistent teacher

The third undesirable way to deal with aggressive behavior is to be inconsistent. A teacher may be inconsistent because she is unsure that it is really all right to control children, or she may be uncertain about how to control them, or she may be unaware that consistency is important; hence, she deals erratically with out-of-hand behavior sometimes by enforcing a rule when she thinks she can make it stick and sometimes by sighing and letting the child run off or have his own way.

This approach creates deep unease in children and fosters attempts by them to manipulate, challenge, and bargain in order to gain special dispensations. Whining, nagging, wheedling, and implied threats by the youngsters are all likely to be prime ingredients in this environment. For example, a 4-year-old may threaten, "If you don't give me that trike right now, I'll have to cry very, very hard, and then I'll prob'ly throw up, and you will have to tell my mother!"

Inconsistent handling may sound merely weak; however, it may actually be the most undesirable approach of all, since it has been found to increase aggressiveness in the children (Parke and Duer, 1972; Sears, Maccoby, and Levin, 1957). The probable reason for this result is that the reward for aggressive behavior is intermittent rather than continuous, and it has been effectively demonstrated that an intermittent reinforcement schedule is a very powerful means of causing behavior to continue (Duer and Parke, 1970; Parke and Duer, 1972), particularly when there are additional payoffs involved such as having gotten what one wanted by grabbing it.

Conclusion

It is fairly easy to see that the teacher who is overcontrolling (authoritarian) or undercontrolling (extremely permissive) or very inconsistent brings special difficulties upon herself when dealing with aggressive behavior. But it is less easy to determine what constitutes a reasonable balance between aggression and control and to decide how to handle this problem in an effective and healthy way. We want to harness and direct this energy, not abolish it. Teachers often feel confused about how and where to draw the line. They think it is important to relish the burgeoning vitality of young children, and so they want to provide vigorous, free, large muscle play, and plenty of it. But most teachers do not think that large muscle activity should be permitted to be expressed at nursery school as endless, aimless, wild running about or terrorization of the quieter children.

Many teachers can go along with the idea that the child has the right to destroy anything he has made so long as it is his own and not someone else's. However, they also believe that direct aggression in the form of throwing things at people, biting, hitting others with objects in hand, outright insolence, and defiance of basic rules is generally unacceptable.

The problem is how to permit the expression of these feelings in ways that are acceptable at nursery school and in society. The remainder of this chapter provides some basic approaches that will help the teacher solve this problem.

DESIRABLE WAYS TO COPE WITH AGGRESSION
Assess the underlying causes of aggression, and ameliorate them when possible

First, it is helpful to remember that pronounced self-assertiveness is part of the developmental picture for 4-year-old boys and girls. Many boys show evidence of this by attempting feats of daring, being physically aggressive, and swaggering about with an air of braggadocio. Girls are more likely to express it by being bossy or tattling in a busybody way on the wrongdoings of other children. It is important to realize that this rather out-of-hand phase serves a healthy purpose for these youngsters, who are busy finding out who they are by asserting their individuality (it is somewhat like adolescence in this regard).

'Of course, aggression in the form of competitiveness and assertiveness is also sanctioned for adults. For example, there have recently been a flush of books for adults advocating increased *assertiveness: Creative Aggression,* Bach and Goldberg, 1974; *How to Be an Assertive (Not Aggressive) Woman,* Baer, 1976; *When I Say No, I Feel Guilty,* Smith, 1975. Incidentally, it may be helpful for students to read some of these if they are having marked problems asserting themselves with either adults or children. The authors make the point that this form of aggression is basically growth enhancing, since it is really a form of learning to stand up for one's rights. Students should understand that some aggression in children serves this same healthy purpose of self-protection. For this reason, it should be directed and channeled, not crushed or unduly discouraged.

Besides the influence of the developmental stage, native temperament may have a lot to do with the expression of aggression. Some children can stand more frustration than others can without exploding (Block and Martin, 1955). Sex-linked characteristics also affect its expression. Maccoby and Jacklin (1974) summarize many studies indicating that in our culture more direct physical aggression is expressed by boys than by girls, and Feshbach and Feshbach (1972) have reported that girls are more likely to employ indirect means of expressing aggressive feelings; but how much of this behavior is due to biological differences and how much to culturally instilled values has yet to be determined.

In extreme cases of aggression, particularly when it is combined with hyperactivity, the possibility of brain damage should be considered, since lack of impulse control may be indicative of such a condition. In these unusual circumstances medication can produce considerable improvement in such behavior for some acting-out youngsters.

Parental mishandling is the reason most frequently given by teachers as the cause of undue aggression in children; and it is true that rejection, particularly cold, permissive rejection by parents, is associated with aggressive behavior in children (Glueck and Glueck, 1950; McCord, McCord, and Howard, 1961). If this appears to be the case, the teacher should encourage the parents to seek counseling.

It is all too easy for the teacher to slough off her responsibility for aggression in a child by raising her eyebrows and muttering, "He sure must have had a tough morning at home—what do you suppose she did to him this time?" But it is more practical to ask herself how the school environment might also be contributing to the child's belligerent behavior, since this is the only area over which the teacher has any real control. Is she teaching alternative ways of getting what he wants, or is she just stopping his aggressive behavior? How frustrating is the nursery school environment for this child? She must take a look at him and assess how he is relating to the program. At what time of day does he misbehave? With whom? What circumstances bring on an outburst? Does he receive more criticism than positive recognition from the staff? Does he have to sit too long at story hour? Does he consistently arrive hungry and so need an early snack? Is the program geared to tastes of little girls and female teachers and lacking in areas that hold a boy's interests?

Utilize direct control when necessary; then teach the child to find alternative ways to get what he desires

There is nothing quite like the agonizing dread some beginning teachers experience because they fear they will be unable to control one or more children in their group. There's no denying that the problem of gaining confidence in control situations is one of the major hurdles students have to get over in the early days of their teaching. Reading about handling aggression will help to a degree, of course, but the truth is that in order to learn to cope with aggressive children, you have to get in there and cope! It doesn't work to shrink away or to let your master teacher do it for you. Sooner or later, every teacher must be willing to confront children and exercise direct control over them because it is an essential method of coping with children's aggressive behavior.

To recapitulate what was said in the previous chapter, a child must definitely be stopped from hurting another person or destroying property. It is

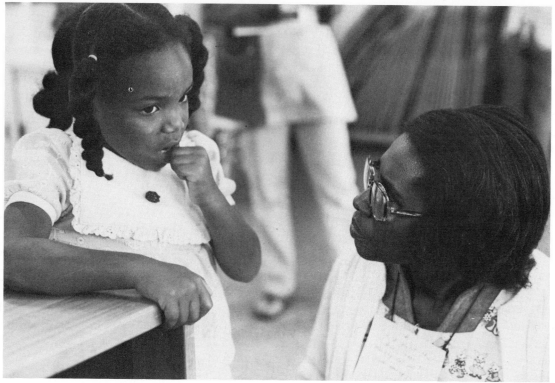

Photo by Richard Pierce, Santa Barbara City College Children's Center

important that the teacher step in *before* the child has experienced the gratification of seizing what he wants or of hurting someone (Sherman and Bushell, 1975). This is particularly true if it is unlikely that the child he has attacked will retaliate. It is also important to intervene promptly because it allows the teacher to act before she is angry herself, and it is highly desirable to present a model of self-control for an aggressive child to imitate (Bandura, 1973).

Once the teacher has put a stop to the undesirable behavior, *it is vital that she teach the aggressor a more acceptable way to achieve his ends*. The first step is to take time with him to recognize his feelings and talk over what it is he wants. This recognition can be phrased as simply as, "I can see that you're dying to grab that trike," or, "I know how much you want to knock over their blocks when they won't let you play." After acknowledging the feel-

ing, the next step is to supply the reason why such behavior is unacceptable. It is best for the child to state this himself if he can. For example, the teacher might ask, "But what is the rule about trikes?" If the child cannot state the reason, the teacher should do this for him. "Remember our rule? The person who has it first can keep it until she's done with it," or "You can knock down the things you build yourself, but you can't knock down other people's buildings unless they say it's all right." The reason provided should be brief and truthful. Moralizing should be avoided; it only antagonizes the child further.

Following the clear statement of the reason for the restraint, the final step is to help the child work out alternative ways of getting what he wants. This teaching of additional social skills is *very* important because it provides the youngster with new ways of coping. Perhaps the aggressor can be encouraged to ask the other child for a turn; sometimes a substitute or similar satisfaction can be provided (perhaps another tricycle can be located); perhaps he can make a bargain ("I'll let you see my sore knee, if you'll let me be the patient"); sometimes a cooperative arrangement can be developed (the child might deliver blocks to the block builders in one of the trucks); sometimes a diversion can be created ("How about using the swing until Marie is done with the wagon?"); and sometimes the child just has to face the reality that he must wait until the other youngster is finished, or he has to accept the fact that he is rejected and find someone else to play with.

Whatever alternative is employed, the teacher should see that the child clearly understands that hurting others is not allowed but that this need not mean he must swallow his anger and knuckle under; instead, there are a variety of both effective and acceptable alternative ways to get what he wants.

Permit reasonable deviations from the rules

Despite the fact that consistency is important and should generally prevail as a policy, there are exceptions to this rule. We have all seen timid children at school and have rejoiced when they finally ventured to shove back and stand up for their rights. It is important for such children to express these aggressive feelings in some form and come out of their shell as a first step; learning control can come later. The teacher simply has to use her knowledge of the children and her good judgment in these matters.

The teacher must also make allowances for children when they are under special stress. For example, her standards should not be unreasonably high at 11:00 in the morning, since lowered blood sugar levels at that time usually mean lowered self-control. This is the time to practice adroit avoidance of confrontations, since children cannot be expected to control themselves very well under such circumstances. The same thing holds true for children who are recovering from illnesses or undergoing family problems. They may require that special allow-ances be made for them until they have regained their emotional balance.

Reduce frustrating circumstances when possible

Although controversy continues over whether aggression is an inherent trait (Lorenz, 1966) or a learned behavior (Bandura, 1973), there is considerable evidence that frustration makes the expression of aggression more likely (Otis and McCandless, 1955; Yarrow, 1948). Thus it makes sense to reduce aggression by reducing frustration where it is possible to do so.

Frustration usually occurs when the child wants something he cannot have, be it the teacher's attention, going outside to play, or the new fire engine. It is not possible to remove all frustrating circumstances from the life of a child, and it would not be desirable to do so anyway, since this would mean that he never has a chance to learn to cope with these feelings. However, there are so many restrictions and frustrations in everyday life that we really do not have to be concerned over the possibility of living in an environment without frustration (Jackson and Wolfson, 1968; Murphy, 1976).

As previously described, the most effective way to reduce frustration is to help the child learn acceptable ways to get what he wants. Another way to reduce frustration is to have a plentiful amount of play equipment available. It is always desirable to have several tricycles, three or four swings, and a number of toy trucks and cars, sandbox shovels, and hammers. Children cannot endure waiting very long, and enough play materials will reduce the agony of anticipation, which if unassuaged can lead to frustration and acting out.

Still another way to reduce frustration is to keep rules to a minimum. The enforcement of the many petty rules cited in the discussion of the authoritarian teacher is one of the quickest ways to build anger in children, because such rules often go hand in hand with unreasonably high expectations of behavior, such as insisting that young children stand in line, sit for extended periods while waiting for something to happen, or never raise their voices.

Finally, two other good frustration preventers, also previously mentioned, are (1) following the policy of warning in advance so that children have the chance to prepare themselves for making a transition to a new activity and (2) providing many opportunities for choices in order to reduce children's feelings of defiance and help them feel that they are masters of their environment.

Provide substitute opportunities for socially acceptable expressions of aggression

The cathartic (emotionally relieving) value of substituting socially acceptable but nonetheless aggressive activities has been questioned in recent years by some researchers who maintain that such activities do not drain off or relieve aggression, but rather reinforce aggressive behavior (Berkowitz, 1973; Feldman, 1975). Their arguments are persuasive, and I can only comment that my own experience and that of other nursery school teachers continue to convince me that offering substitute ways of working off steam does have value, cathartic or not, when working with aggressive children. Such activities are obviously emotionally satisfying to children; they are safe for those around them; and they provide chances to be assertive in a harmless way for youngsters who may be too immature to resist the need to express aggression in some physical form.

These activities are best offered, however, *before* the child reaches the boiling point. It is generally unsatisfactory to march a youngster over to a punching bag after he has hit someone and say, "It's all right to sock this!" By the time this happens, or by the time he gets the boxing gloves on and the fight set up, a lot of the flavor has gone out of the experience. Not only that, it is better to offer acceptable aggressive activities as part of each day, as well as to make sure they are available when the teacher anticipates that the day will be especially tense either for an individual child who is upset or for the entire group (on Halloween, for example). Fortunately, there are a great many activities that will help. Remember, though, that these activities are substitutes for what the child would really prefer to do. When offering someone a substitute experience, be as free with it as possible, and supply plenty of material, plenty of time, and as few restrictions as you can tolerate.

In general, any kind of large muscle activity that does not have to be tightly controlled is valuable. Nursery school teachers tend to buy play equipment that is too small to take the vigorous activity of 4- and 5-year-old children. It is always better to invest a few more dollars and buy sturdy, large equipment that will stand up to hard use rather than to continually nag the children, "Don't shake the jungle gym, you'll break it," or "Not too high now!" Try the following specific suggestions.

Jumping on old mattresses spread out on the grass or jumping off jungle gyms or boxes onto mattresses works off energy harmlessly and satisfies a need to be daring as well.

Swinging is particularly effective, because the rhythm is soothing and because it isolates the child from his companions and calms him at the same time. If the teacher has time to do some friendly pushing, the one-to-one relationship is easing, too.

Trike riding, climbing, and sliding, or, as a matter of fact, anything that works off energy harmlessly helps.

Activities that provide for vigorous use of the hands in an aggressive yet acceptable manner should also be included. If the teacher joins in with gusto from time to time and uses the material herself, the child will often participate with more spirit.

Beanbags are fine to use for this purpose, but rules should be established about where they are to be thrown. A large wall, maybe with a face on it, is best, and the more beanbags the better. It is no fun to have to stop and pick them up after every three throws. Thirty bags are about the right number.

Punching bags have some use, but it is hard for young children to coordinate really satisfying socks with the bag's tendency to rebound.

Inflatable clowns are somewhat useful, but there may be trouble with maintaining them in airtight condition.

Hammering and sawing, and even smashing things, such as old egg cartons, orange crates, or piano cases, are appealing. Very young children can use "knock-out" benches for this same purpose.

Large quantities of dough, (not tiny, unsatisfying dabs) are fine aggression expressers. We restrict the tools the children use with it (such as cookie cutters) and encourage the children to stand at the table so that they can work forcefully, using their hands to pound and squeeze and pinch and punish the dough to their heart's content.

In fingerpainting and other types of smearing techniques such as soap painting, emphasis should be placed on richness of color and lots of gooey paint base, be it liquid starch, wallpaper paste, or homemade, very thick, cooked starch.

Once in a while, a particular child finds relief in tearing and crumpling paper or stomping on crumpled balls of it. Again, large amounts are better than small amounts.

Although cutting up fruits and vegetables requires considerable self-control (by child and teacher), for some children the controlled opportunity to use a knife can be helpful. It's best to start with things such as bananas, which are easy to cut and which don't wobble around. Mashing potatoes is another good outlet.

Noise is a good outlet for expressing aggression. The aggression-expressing possibilities of sheer noise (at least on the days when the teacher doesn't have a headache) should not be overlooked. It is wise to remember that noise has an infectious effect on the entire group and may accelerate activity too much. However, on the many occasions when things are in good order, I am all in favor of noise! Drums are an all-time, satisfying "best" for noise, but pounding on the piano is good, too. Real music and dancing can be added for those who enjoy it. Sitting on top of the slide and kicking heels hard makes a wonderful, satisfying noise. Yelling and playing loudly, and crying—the louder the better—also serve to express feelings harmlessly.

Opportunities for dramatic play can also help the child come to terms with aggressive feelings. Direct participation by dressing up and playing house will let youngsters work through situations that may be troubling them. Anyone who has ever watched an irate young "mama" wallop her "naughty" baby doll will understand the merit of providing this kind of play material as an aggression reliever. Doll house furniture and little dolls are useful, but more so for 4-year-olds than for 3-year-olds.

Sets of fairly large rubber wild animals and hand puppets lend themselves admirably to aggressive play. Interestingly enough, the animal that produces the greatest amount of this play is not the lion or tiger, but the hippopotamus. I have concluded that it is the open mouth and all those teeth that brings this out. It makes me think how angry adults with toothy open mouths must appear to children, particularly since youngsters tend to look up and in!

The best thing for out-of-hand children to play with is water. It is deeply relaxing in any form. Washing doll clothes or plastic cars, playing with soap bubbles, or playing with water in the housekeeping area is beneficial.

Whenever weather permits, the best thing of all is a running hose and lots of sand and mud. This combination has led to some of the calmest, happiest days we have ever had in our school, but pouring and playing with water in tubs or basins can also be satisfying. At home, a warm bath can work miracles.

Finally, encouraging very overactive youngsters to take time out to go to the toilet often simmers things down considerably.

Additional techniques to help reduce the amount of aggressive behavior

So much for the specifics. There are also some general techniques that the teacher may find helpful for handling aggression.

Provide kindly, one-to-one attention for acting-out children. A few minutes consistently invested every day with an aggressive child when he is doing positive things (that is, before he gets into difficulties) often works wonders.

Stopping some activities before they start saves criticism and discipline later. I have learned, for example, to keep an eye out for "angry monster" games or a local variation on the same theme, referred to as "Golden Eagle" by some young friends of mine. When such a game gets too high pitched, the quickest way to bring it under control is to look for the ringleader and get him involved in something else that he particularly likes.

Our staff discourages gun play at our Center. We believe that children can play at better things than killing each other, and it is also true that such play usually leads to overexcited running about. Therefore, when guns are brought to school, they are stored in the cubbies until it is time for the children to go home.

Be on the lookout for combinations of personalities that are currently poisonous, and do what you can to dilute them. Children who egg each other into trouble should not snack together or rest near each other, and other friendships for both children should be encouraged.

Finally, plan, plan, plan! Plan to provide interesting activities that children really like, and plan the daily program with specific children in mind. ("John is coming today, I'd better get out the hammers and saws.") The program must not make undue demands on their self-control and should include acceptable outlets for their energy. As a general principle, consistent opportunities that allow children to achieve mastery and competence in acceptable areas should be provided. Every time a youngster can do something well, whether it's building blocks, doing helpful, meaningful work, creating a painting, or learning to pump on the swing, his aggression has been channeled into accomplishing something constructive.

SUMMARY

Aggressive behavior is defined in this chapter as action that is intended to cause injury or anxiety to others. This kind of behavior needs careful handling and guidance in the nursery school so that children are not forced to suppress such feelings completely, but learn instead to channel these impulses into socially acceptable activities.

Three approaches to coping with aggression in young children are particularly undesirable, since they are all likely to increase aggressive responses from them. These include authoritarian, overper-

missive, and inconsistent methods of dealing with such behavior.

On the more positive side, several approaches for working with acting-out children are effective in reducing and channeling such behavior. Among these are assessing the underlying causes of aggression and ameliorating them when possible, utilizing direct control when necessary, and teaching the child to find alternative ways to obtain his desires. In addition, permitting reasonable deviations from the rules in special cases and reducing frustrating circumstances when possible are helpful. Finally, substituting socially acceptable opportunities for expressing aggression can relieve the child's feelings without jeopardizing the safety and happiness of those around him.

The teacher who applies these principles when handling aggressive behavior will reduce tension within the child and herself by preventing aggressive feelings from building up and will also help the child remain happier, more open, and more ready to welcome life with enthusiasm.

QUESTIONS AND ACTIVITIES

1. Everyone seems to have different "breaking points" in tolerating aggression. For example, one person sees red if a child is insolent, whereas another finds it more difficult to put up with a child who is cruel to animals or who deliberately hurts another child. Compare notes among the people in class about what they feel constitutes acceptable ways to express aggression and where their breaking points are.
2. Some reasons why a teacher might be too authoritarian are suggested in this book. What are some reasons that might lie behind the behavior of the teacher who is too permissive?
3. Keep an eye out during the coming week, and observe and briefly record several situations where children or staff members appeared to be angry. Note what each individual did about this feeling. If the teacher was working with a child, what did she do to help the youngster recognize and express his feelings in an acceptable way?
4. Are there any "discipline" situations in your school that seem to recur? For example, are the children always being told not to tap their glasses on the table while waiting for lunch? Suggest several ways the situation could be changed instead of continuing to "teach the children to behave."

REFERENCES FOR FURTHER READING

Introductory Overviews

McCandless, B. R., and Evans, E. D. *Children and youth: Psychosocial development.* Hinsdale, Ill.: Dryden Press, 1973. The chapter entitled "Areas of Psychosocial Conflict" contains a succinct but good overview on the subject of aggression, including a review of the effects of television on aggressive behavior. It concludes with some helpful recommendations about ways to reduce the expression of aggression.

Sears, R. R., Maccoby, E. E., and Levin, H. *Patterns of child rearing*. New York: Harper and Row, Publishers, 1957. This material is based on a research study, but the discussion ranges beyond the usual narrow description of results and presents a penetrating analysis of aggression and its probable antecedents; readable and clear.

Practical Advice about Dealing with the Aggressive Child

Beyer, E. *Teaching young children*. New York: The Bobbs-Merrill Co., Inc., 1968. Evelyn Beyer uses a realistic, anecdotal approach to describe an overly aggressive and an overly withdrawn child. These chapters contain many practical recommendations for managing both kinds of behavior.

Caldwell, B. M. Aggression and hostility in young children. *Young Children,* 1977, *32*(2) 4-13. A thoughtful, excellent discussion of the most important elements to bear in mind when dealing with aggressive children.

Croft, D. *Be honest with yourself: A self-evaluation handbook for early childhood education teachers*. Belmont, Calif.: Wadsworth Publishing Company, Inc., 1976. Part of working well with young children has to do with knowing yourself—how you are likely to react to situations and why. *Be Honest with Yourself* provides many opportunities for learning more about yourself by describing "critical incidents" and then asking the reader to reply with her most likely response. These incidents also provide good takeoff points for discussion.

Feldman, R. Teaching self-control and self-expression via play. In S. Coopersmith (Ed.), *Developing motivation in young children*. San Francisco: Albion Publishing Company, 1975. This is about the best discussion of handling the aggressive preschool child I have found. It combines up-to-date research with sound practical recommendations on implementation.

Karnes, M. B., and Strong, P. S. *Nurturing leadership talent in early childhood*. Urbana, Ill.: Publications Office, Institute for Child Behavior and Development, University of Illinois, 1978. This unusual pamphlet provides some practical suggestions for harnessing the kind of behavior often viewed as being "aggressive" and turning it into more positive channels.

Read, K. *The nursery school: Human relationships and learning* (6th ed.). Philadelphia: W. B. Saunders Co., 1976. Another good discussion of hostility and aggression is contained in Chapter 17. Katherine Read discusses probable causes of aggression and makes recommendations for accepting and handling hostile feelings. Chapter 17 should be read in conjunction with Chapter 18, "Authority and the Setting of Limits." The tone of the book is somewhat Freudian.

Redl, F. *When we deal with children*. New York: The Free Press, 1966.

Redl, F., and Wineman, D. *Children who hate*. New York: The Free Press, 1951.

Redl, F., and Wineman, D. *Controls from within*. New York: The Free Press, 1952. All three of these books are indispensable for understanding the causes of aggression and the means of handling it. Drs. Redl and Wineman know a great deal on both a theoretical and a practical level about working with angry, acting-out children; highly recommended.

For the Advanced Student

Bandura, A. *Aggression: A social learning analysis*. Englewood Cliffs, N.J.: Prentice Hall, Inc., 1973. The author favors the utilization of behavior modification techniques to reduce aggressive behavior; an important reference in this field.

Berkowitz, L. Control of aggression. In B. M. Caldwell and H. N. Ricciuti (Eds.), *Review of Child Development Research* (Vol. 3). Chicago: University of Chicago Press, 1973. In addition to reading Risley and Baer (1973), and Sherman and Bushell (1975) cited in the Advanced References in the previous chapter, everyone with an interest in the research "why" that lies behind the pedagogical "do's and don'ts" should read Berkowitz on aggression.

Photo by Jason Lo'Cicero

8 □ Developing self-esteem in young children

Children cannot be fooled by empty praise and condescending encouragement.*

Feeling oneself to be a person who has something worthwhile to contribute to the life around him is an important aspect of being mentally healthy. It is the kind of feeling I have in mind when describing an individual who possesses self-esteem. A person who feels this way about himself is able to venture out into the world, work toward attaining what he hopes for, and welcome life with pleasureful anticipation.

On the other hand, individuals who suffer from low self-esteem fit, to varying degrees, the following description.

Persons who seek psychological and psychiatric help frequently acknowledge that they suffer from feelings of inadequacy and unworthiness (Wylie, 1961). They tend to perceive themselves as helpless and inferior (Rogers and Dymond, 1954), have difficulty in either giving or receiving love (Fromm, 1939), and tend to feel isolated and alone (Coopersmith, 1967). They are likely to feel guilty, ashamed, or depressed, and to derogate their own potential and accomplishments (Coopersmith, 1967). . . . Furthermore, the anxious child's tendency to derogate himself tends to generalize and affect his image of his bodily integrity and adequacy as well (Ruebush, 1960; Walsh, 1956). A negative self-concept appears to promote defensiveness in the child's reactions to himself and others (Riley, 1966; Ruebush, 1960).*

It is apparent then, that a good self-concept and self-esteem are highly desirable qualities to foster in young children, since no one wants children to suffer from the feelings described in the paragraph above. What teachers and parents need to understand more clearly is how to help children generate good feelings about themselves that are based on reality.

RELATIONSHIP OF SELF-ESTEEM TO SELF-CONCEPT

Self-esteem and self-concept are very closely related to each other. Self-concept refers to an individual's idea of who he is. His feelings of self-esteem result from his reaction to what he judges himself to be and to his anticipation of being accepted or rejected (Dinkmeyer, 1965). Thus a youngster who is well coordinated, who is sought after by his playmates, and who gets along well with his teacher will probably see himself as adequate and will possess good feelings of self-esteem, whereas an overweight high school girl suffering from a poor complexion and few friends may come

---

*From Erikson, E. *Childhood and society* (2nd ed.). New York: W. W. Norton & Co., Inc., 1963. P. 235.

*From Mussen, P. H., Conger, J. J., and Kagan J. *Child development and personality*. New York: Harper & Row, Publishers, 1969, p. 489.

to think of herself as being unattractive and un-lovable and as a result will hold herself in low esteem.

SOURCES OF SELF-ESTEEM

Although individuals should ultimately develop internal resources for generating self-esteem, in the early stages of growth the child's feelings of self-esteem come from the people around him. Parents are very significant influences (Baumrind, 1972; Coopersmith, 1967; Samuels, 1977). As children move out into the larger world, the opinions of other adults, such as teachers, become important, too, as do the opinions of their peers. That society also has an impact is evident from studies indicating that many people of minority groups possess lower self-esteem than other nonminorities do (Dworkin, 1965; Zirkel, 1971). Because the unhappy effects of persistent prejudice on the self-image and self-esteem of minority children cannot be overestimated, an entire chapter is devoted to a discussion of ways to sustain or improve the self-image of such youngsters (Chapter 10).

Since there are so many powerful factors that influence the development of self-esteem, teachers should not believe that they can completely alter the way a child sees himself. However, the numerous research studies cited by Coopersmith (1975) and Samuels (1977) support the idea that teachers can establish policies in their classrooms that will help build a child's self-esteem, and they can meticulously avoid employing practices that are likely to have destructive side effects.

COMMON SCHOOL PRACTICES LIKELY TO REDUCE FEELINGS OF SELF-ESTEEM
Using comparison and competition to motivate good behavior

Competitiveness reaches a peak in children around the age of 4 to 5 years (Stott and Ball, 1957), and it is all too easy for the teacher to use this fact to obtain quick results by asking, "I wonder who can get his coat on quickest today?" or by commenting, "See how carefully Shirley is putting her blocks away? Why can't you do it like that?"

The trouble with motivating behavior by drawing such comparisons and setting up competitive situations is that only a few children "win" under this system. Even the child who turns out to be "best" and whose self-esteem has presumably been enhanced pays an unfortunate price, since he has obtained his self-esteem at the expense of the other children's well-being and may have earned their dislike in the process.

A more desirable way to use comparison is by invoking it in relation to the child's own past performance. This can be a true source of satisfaction for him when the teacher says, "My goodness, John, you're learning to pump better and better every time you try!" or, "Remember the way you used to bite people? You haven't done that in a long time now. I'm proud of you!"

Overhelping and overprotecting children

A teacher may unintentionally lower a child's self-esteem by doing too much for him. Thus she rushes in to carry the bucket of water so that it won't slop, or without thinking she puts all the shoes and socks on the children following nap. Helping in these ways has the virtue of saving time and assuring that the job will be done properly as well as keeping the teacher busy. But it is much more desirable to wait and let the child do things for himself, since this allows him to experience the triumph of independence that such achievement brings.

Judging children in their hearing

Children often develop ideas of who they are from hearing what other people say about them. Sometimes this happens in direct form, as when the teacher says impatiently, "Come along now; you're always so slow," or asks, "How can you be so selfish?" Other children are also prone to deliver pronouncements such as, "You pig! You never share anything," or "Hazel is a pooh-pooh pants, Hazel is a pooh-pooh pants!" Labels such as these tend to stick; enough of them plastered on a child can convince him that he is neither liked nor worth much, so he might as well not try. This is one of the reasons why teaching children to use self-report rather than verbal attack is so important. Verbal attacks are very destructive to other people's self-esteem.

Sometimes negative evaluations are not delivered directly to the child but are said over his head to someone else instead. ''My, aren't we in a terrible temper today!'' ''I see she's having a hard day again!'' ''There's no point asking *him*—he always holds on like grim death!'' Somehow, overheard comments have a special, painful power to compel belief. The teacher should avoid making them not only for this reason but also because they may hurt a child's feelings and can strengthen a negative self-image. On a more subtle level, talking over a child's head implies that he is not important enough to be included directly in the conversation.

POSITIVE METHODS OF ENHANCING SELF-ESTEEM
Unconditional positive regard

The most effective way to help a child build a basic feeling of self-esteem is, unfortunately, also the most elusive for some teachers to achieve: it is the ability to feel and project what Carl Rogers terms unconditional positive regard. This kind of fundamental acceptance and approval of each child is not contingent upon his meeting the teacher's expectations of what he should be but simply depends on his being alive, being a child, and being in her group. A good test of being accepting or not is to become aware of what one is usually thinking about when looking at the children. Ask yourself, ''Am I taking time to enjoy the children, or am I more likely to look at each one with a critical eye—noting mainly what behavior should be improved?'' If you catch yourself habitually noting only what should be changed, this is a sign you are losing sight of half the pleasure of teaching, which is to appreciate the children and enjoy who they are right now, at this particular moment in time—no strings attached.

This ability to be uncritical implies a kind of faith in the way the child will turn out, which subtly makes him aware that the teacher has confidence

he will grow in sound directions. There is no substitute for these underlying feelings of trust and confidence in the child. Some teachers are fortunate enough to have developed optimism about people as a result of their own trust-building childhood experiences, some gain it from long experience with children themselves, and some acquire it by means of psychotherapeutic treatment, which helps restore their own confidence as well as their faith in others.

Acceptance of the child as he is also includes accepting his right to be different from the teacher and from the other children. Here again, ethnic and cultural differences come particularly to mind (Chapter 10). A teacher can make a significant contribution to increasing the self-esteem of minority children by unconditionally valuing them herself and by using herself as a model to influence the attitude of the other children and their families.

Honest recognition and praise

Rewarding a child with praise is usually the first way teachers think of to build self-esteem. Unfortunately, sometimes praise is the *only* method they think of. Actually, it is only one of several ways to enhance a child's feelings of self-worth.

It almost goes without saying that such praise must be sincere and merited in order to be effective. Seligman is right when he says, ''A sense of worth, mastery, or self-esteem cannot be bestowed. It can only be earned. If it is given away, it ceases to be worth having, and it ceases to contribute to individual dignity'' (1975, p. 159). Teachers who use praise continually as a means of reinforcing behavior often dole it out in such a mechanical way that it comes to have almost no meaning at all. On the other hand, some teachers hardly ever take time to comment favorably on what a child has done. They seem to feel that praise weakens character and that individuals should do things simply because it is right to do them; but praise that is merited should be given freely—honest recognition is sweet indeed.

Teachers should also encourage the children to take pleasure in each other's accomplishments. This requires a certain generosity of spirit among them that probably stems from the inner assurance that each child knows he will be recognized for his abilities from time to time. It's all too easy to allow such situations to deteriorate into ones where the teacher says, "Oh, look, children—look what Johnny did! Isn't that nice?" and the children, like a little Greek chorus, dutifully agree. This is surely different from the honest appreciation freely given that I have in mind. At this point I'm not certain how to teach this generosity other than by modelling the behavior for the children, and showing approval of them when *they* show approval. It's really the reflection of a very fundamental attitude or climate that the teacher establishes throughout the classroom rather than a specific strategy.

It is also important to appreciate the effort of children when they have not been successful. They particularly need encouragement at this point, since the reward inherent in successful accomplishment has not been realized. The teacher can say, "I see how hard you've worked at that," or, "I'm proud of you; you really tried," or, "It takes a while to learn to do that. You've really stuck with it; pretty soon you'll learn how."

Respect

Respecting the child is such a high-minded phrase that examples of behavior must be provided in order to see how respect can be implemented in the nursery school. One basic way to show respect is to abide by the child's decision when he has been given a valid choice (also see Chapter 6). When a teacher does this, she is really saying, "What you want is important. I have confidence that you know yourself better than I do, and I count on you to choose what will enhance your existence most." Children also feel respected when the teacher asks their opinion and listens carefully to their replies. Even little children can answer "Do you think we should . . ." kinds of questions.

Another way to show respect and thus sustain the child's self-esteem is to avoid humiliating a child in front of other people. It is best to carry out discipline measures as unobtrusively as possible. Be-

littling a child's behavior at any time is, of course, fundamentally disrespectful as well as destructive of self-esteem.

A third valuable way to show respect is to pay the child the compliment of explaining the reason behind the rule. Coopersmith (1967), who carried out an extensive study of children possessing high self-esteem, found that parents of such youngsters were firm in their control of them but also took time to explain the reason for their actions. Such reasoning confers respect because it assumes that the child is important enough to be entitled to an explanation and intelligent enough to comprehend it.

Finally, we must never lose sight of the fact that children are intensely aware of how the teacher feels about their families. The teacher who truly respects and values the child's family shows this each day in the way she welcomes them to the classroom, by the way she avoids making derogatory remarks about them, and by the way she really listens to family members when they have something to tell her.

Helping the child achieve competence

The practices enumerated thus far are external sources of a child's self-esteem. Although all of them are sound in that they will help build positive self-pictures for children, they have one weakness in common: they all depend on the good will of another person for implementation. Yet the ultimate goal should be the internalization of esteem in order that the individual will not remain permanently dependent on others to supply his feelings of self-worth.

Robert White (1968, 1972) has suggested that the drive toward competence is a powerfully motivating agent in people's lives. He defines competence as "effectiveness in dealing with the environment." This effectiveness builds a child's self-esteem by helping him feel masterful; thus competence is worth enhancing in young children. Fortunately, there are many opportunities to do this in the nursery school.

The teacher can help a child develop inner sources of self-esteem by fostering this competence, and each morning she should ask herself, "How can I help each child be successful today?" Once a child is able to do something well, whether is it practicing diplomacy in the housekeeping corner or using the brace and bit, he has gained a small portion of confidence in himself that does not require the plaudits of others to sustain it.

Allowing children to experience mastery by making their own choices and by being as independent as possible are two ways to encourage competence that have already been discussed. Coupled with allowing children to do things for themselves goes the establishment of reasonable standards of achievement. For instance, a teacher who wishes to build self-esteem in a newly generous little girl appreciates her helpfulness when she volunteers to pass the snack and overlooks the fact that she has served herself first, just as she thanks the child who has stuffed his boots away in his cubby and refrains from telling him to fix them so the toes point out.

The teacher can also provide many different ways for children to experience success. Sheer variety of activities is important here, since one child may excel at assembling puzzles, whereas another's forte may be hanging by her heels on the jungle gym. It is important, also, not to be too hidebound when selecting curriculum activities, since a youngster may possess a special skill not usually thought of as suitable for nursery school but one that, when well used, can confer distinction on him and enrich the lives of the other children. Our Center, for example, had a child attending who loved to embroider. She knew several stitches, and two or three of the older children relished learning them from her, although "everyone knows" that embroidery is too difficult for preschool children to carry out successfully.

The recent interest in nonsexist education has emphasized the value of building cross-sex competencies of various kinds. It is still the case that girls often grow up unable to use power saws or drills or lacking even rudimentary understanding of the combustion engine, and boys are sometimes described as limited in their ability to express emotion. Most women (and many men) have only to re-

call the last time they dealt with a garage mechanic to realize the sense of inferiority such incompetency produces. Methods of remedying these deficiencies are discussed at greater length in the chapter on social competency, so it will only be noted here that broader and more various educational experiences for both sexes should be encouraged.

Creative activities offer excellent opportunities for experiencing competence, since there is so much latitude for individual abilities and differences in these areas. It feels good to make something that is attractive; and if the materials and colors provided by the nursery school teacher are harmonious, most things made by the children will have a satisfying outcome and thus enhance the children's feelings of self-esteem.

It is also worthwhile to provide opportunities that are challenging but not excessively difficult in order to give the children the chance to test themselves against difficulties. The derring-do of 4-year-olds is a prime example of this desire to make things a little bit harder every time they attempt them. (The reader may recall learning the game of jacks and its steady progression from "Rolling Down Broadway" to the more difficult game "Around the World" and finally on to "Eggs in a Basket" and "Shooting Star.") In general, children should always be allowed to attempt more difficult feats as they think of them unless it is evident that they have not anticipated any serious dangers that may be involved.

Something else students sometimes forget is that it takes practice to acquire a new skill. I have seen students offer an activity once and assume that would be sufficient opportunity for the children to learn how to do it. Whether it be using the Irish Mail or cutting around a circle or playing "Lotto," other things being equal, repeated practice increases competency, so it's important to provide chances for children to do something more than once if you want them to become skillful.

In addition to competence in activities and motor skills, interpersonal competence is of great importance. The child who feels that he can get along with others, that he is liked by them, and that he generally manages to have his needs met is likely to feel pretty adequate. The following chapter presents a more detailed discussion of how to help children gain skill and competence in interpersonal relationships.

SUMMARY

The nursery school teacher who wishes to increase feelings of self-esteem in the children in her care has at her disposal many ways of accomplishing this. However, practices such as using comparison and competition, being overprotective, and judging children in their hearing should be avoided, since they tend to lower self-esteem.

Esteem-building practices that should be made part of the daily life of the nursery school include the expression of unconditional positive regard, the provision of recognition and praise when warranted, and the expression of genuine respect for every child.

Finally, the attainment of competence should be valued in the nursery school. The more opportunities the child has to acquire instrumental and interpersonal skills, the more likely he is to acquire an inner conviction of his own ability to cope. This inner conviction of basic competence is, in the long run, the most satisfactory builder of self-esteem.

QUESTIONS AND ACTIVITIES

1. Pick a nursery school or family life situation (perhaps a trip to the market) for role playing, and include in it as many possible ways you can think of to deflate and lower the self-esteem of the ''children'' who are involved.
2. Select a youngster in your school who seems to suffer from low self-esteem. As far as you can tell, what are some principal reasons for this self-image? What could you do to modify it in a more positive direction?
3. Many activities, even for college students, center on externalized sources of self-esteem. Grades are a prime example of external input. What college-related policies appear likely to produce internalized sources of positive self-esteem?
4. This chapter questions the value of using competition to motivate behavior, since competition reduces feelings of self-esteem. Is this necessarily true in all cases? Are there times when competition is both satisfying and desirable?
5. Listen to yourself for several days while you are working with the children. Every day put ten pennies in your pocket, and whenever you hear yourself talking about a child in front of him, transfer a penny to your other pocket. Can you go an entire day without shifting any pennies?
6. Imagine that a new rule has been passed at your school: you may not praise a child for anything during the day, and yet you must increase his self-esteem substantially. How would you go about doing this?
7. Go down your roster, and try to identify opportunities during the past week where each child had the chance to gain competence in some activity. Did each youngster have a chance to accomplish this in some manner?

REFERENCES FOR FURTHER READING

Overviews

Briggs, D. C. *Your child's self-esteem: The key to his life.* Garden City, N. Y.: Doubleday & Co., Inc., 1970. This book, which deals with building self-esteem in children and its influence on the entire life of the child, is written primarily with parents in mind but can also be helpful reading for the teacher.

McCandless, B. R., and Evans, E. D. *Children and youth: Psychosocial development.* Hinsdale, Ill.: Dryden Press, 1973. The chapter on ''The Development of the Self'' presents a good overview, including developmental trends and conceptual and philosophical problems involved in studying this concept, and closes with a discussion of some educational implications.

Samuels, S. *Enhancing self-concept in early childhood: Theory and practice.* New York: Human Sciences Press, 1977. This valuable book contains several chapters reviewing research on self-concept as it relates to sex role, race, social class, the effect of teachers, and so on. It also discusses classroom strategies for improving self-image. In addition it contains several good, annotated lists of children's books dealing with such topics as ethnic books, family relationships, and separation.

Zimbardo, P. G. *Shyness.* Menlo Park, Calif.: Addison-Wesley Publishing Co., 1977. Many children and adults react to stress with undue shyness. This readable book provides insight and practical advice on how to deal with this agonizing feeling so closely related to poor self-esteem.

Development of Competence

White, R. W. *The enterprise of living: Growth and organization in personality.* New York: Holt, Rinehart and Winston, Inc., 1972. The chapter on competence, which discusses its importance in relation to development, traces its growth through various stages, and talks about why the concept is significant, is excellent. The entire book is first-rate reading.

Factors that Contribute to Poor Self-esteem

Baumrind, D. Socialization and instrumental competence in young children. In W. W. Hartup (Ed.), *The young child: Reviews of research* (Vol. 2). Washington, D.C.: National Association for the Education of Young Children, 1972. The effect of society's expectations on the self-concepts of little girls is discussed, and how girls are socialized to become instrumentally incompetent is described. A good bibliography is included.

Kirkhart, R., and Kirkhart, E. The bruised self: Mending in the early years. In K. Yamamoto (Ed.), *The child and his image: Self-concept in the early years.* Boston: Houghton Mifflin Co., 1972. This chapter is helpful primarily because of its review of practices that are likely to reduce self-esteem in young children.

Porter, J. D. R. *Black child, white child: The development of racial attitudes*. Garden City, N.Y.: Doubleday & Co., Inc., 1970. This book has two good chapters on the development of racial self-concepts and on the development of self-esteem among black children. Following this, the implications of the specific research reported in the book are discussed, and recommendations are included for improving the self-image of black children. This book is particularly worthwhile for the nursery school teacher because it concentrates on preschool children.

For the Advanced Student

Coopersmith, S. *The antecedents of self-esteem*. San Francisco: W. H. Freeman and Co., Publishers, 1967. Coopersmith recounts a classic study that sought to identify the factors within the family that influence self-esteem either positively or negatively.

Coopersmith, S. Building self-esteem in the classroom. In S. Coopersmith (Ed.), *Developing motivation in young children*. San Francisco: Albion Publishing Co., 1975. Here, the author discusses fundamental aspects of increasing self-esteem and supports his recommendations with various research studies. Incidentally, the entire book, which deals with the affective aspects of education, is well worth reading.

White, R. W. Motivation reconsidered: The concept of competence. In M. Almy (Ed.), *Early childhood play: Selected readings related to cognition and motivation*. New York: Simon & Schuster, Inc., 1968. In this classic the author reviews various theoretical approaches concerned with the nature of motivation and then proposes that certain behaviors are motivated by the need to achieve competence; good, scholarly reading.

Zirkel, P. A. Self-concept and the disadvantage of ethnic group membership and mixture. *Review of Educational Research*, 1971, *41*(3), 211-226. Many research articles having to do with the relationship of self-esteem to membership in various ethnic groups are reviewed. The author concludes that the relationship is still unclear because of the variation in methodological approaches.

PART FOUR

Fostering social development

Photo by Jason Lo'Cicero, La Mesa Preschool, Santa Barbara

9 □ Developing social competence in young children

This point was brought home to me by the comments of a distinguished Soviet psychologist, an expert on development during the preschool years. He had been observing in an American day-care center for children of working mothers. The center was conducted under university auspices and reflected modern outlooks and methods in early childhood education. It was therefore with some concern that I noted how upset my colleague was on his return.

"I wouldn't have believed it," he said, "if I hadn't seen it with my own eyes. There were four children sitting at a table, just as in our nurseries. But each was doing something different. What's more, I watched them for a whole ten minutes, and not once did any child help another one. They didn't even talk to each other. Each was busy in his own activity. You really are a nation of individualists."*

Early childhood is a time that can be rich in social learnings; it is a dynamic period characterized by many beginnings but few completely attained learnings in the development of social skills and interactions. Although the home is profoundly influential in this area, nursery school teachers can also make a valuable contribution to social development. Before pursuing important social goals for the young children in her care, however, the teacher should review the developmental trends and theories of social growth discussed below, in order for her to know what social behavior to expect from the children.

DEVELOPMENTAL TRENDS IN SOCIAL GROWTH

We know that as children grow older the amount of social play increases between them (Rubin, 1977)

and that they develop more friends as they move from infancy to kindergarten. They also tend increasingly to select friends who are of the same sex (Hagman, 1933). As they grow older, the number of quarrels between children decreases, but the length of the altercations increases (Dawe, 1934), as does the number of social contacts (Maudry and Nekula, 1939). Feelings of rivalry and competition begin to develop and appear to be at an intense level between the ages of 4 and 6 (Greenberg, 1932), although this behavior varies considerably from child to child. Generous behavior tends to increase with age and has been shown to occur even at the preschool level (Hartup and Coates, 1967). Role taking (the ability to put oneself in another's place) also increases as a child becomes older (Flavell, 1966).

Tables 6 and 7 summarize some of the many additional social behaviors that are characteristic of children at various ages.

In addition to these developmental trends, one of

---

*From Bronfenbrenner, U. Preface. In H. Chauncey (Ed.), *Soviet preschool education* (Vol. 2: Teacher's commentary). New York: Holt, Rinehart and Winston, Inc., 1969. P. 5.

Table 6. Progress indicators of social development, first 3 years*

Behavior item	Age expected
	(Weeks)
Responds to smiling and talking	6
Knows mother	12
Shows marked interest in father	14
Is sober with strangers	16
Withdraws from strangers	32
Responds to "bye-bye"	40
Responds to inhibitory words	52
Plays pat-a-cake	52
Waves "bye-bye"	52
	(Years, months)
Is no longer shy toward strangers	1-3
Enjoys imitation of adult activities (smoking, etc.)	1-3
Is interested in and treats another child like an object rather than a person	1-6
Plays alone	1-6
Brings things (slippers, etc.) to adult (father)	1-6
Shows beginning of concept of private ownership	1-9
Wishes to participate in household activities	1-9
Has much interest in and watches other children	2
Begins parallel play	2
Is dependent and passive in relation to adults	2
Is shy toward strangers	2
Is not sociable; lacks social interest	2-3
Is ritualistic in behavior	2-6
Is imperious, domineering	2-6
Begins to resist adult influence; wants to be independent	2-6
Is self-assertive; difficult to handle	2-6
Is in conflict with children of own age	2-6
Refuses to share toys; ignores requests	2-6
Begins to accept suggestions	3
Has "we" feeling with mother	3
Likes to relive babyhood	3
Is independent of mother at nursery school	3
Tends to establish social contacts with adults	3
Shows imitative, "me, too" tendency	3
Begins strong friendships with peer associates, with discrimination against others in group	3-6

*Abridged from L. H. Stott. *The longitudinal study of individual development*. Detroit: Merrill-Palmer School, 1955.

Piaget's concepts concerning social and intellectual development has considerable relevance for understanding the social behavior of young children. Piaget (1926) maintains that children in the preoperational stage of development, which includes the nursery school years, are primarily egocentric. That is, they see the world from their own point of view and experience considerable difficulty putting themselves in others' places. The teacher should understand that this self-centeredness is typical and is not due to "selfishness" or reprehensible callousness. Rather, this unabashed self-interest is a developmental stage, and during the time the child is in nursery school, he is only just beginning to learn to decenter, to see the world from another's vantage point, and to care about how other people feel. The nursery school can facilitate this trend in many ways, particularly if the teacher understands the pro-

Table 7. Progress indicators of social development, ages 4 through 10*

Behavior item	Age expected (years)
Is assertive, boastful	4
Has definite preference for peer mates	4
Tries to gain attention; shows off	4
Tends to be obedient, cooperative; desires to please	5
Seeks approval; avoids disapproval of adults	5
Shows preference for children of his own age	5
Shows protective, mothering attitude toward younger sibling	5
Is sensitive to parents' and others' moods, facial expressions	6
Has strong desire to be with father and do things together (especially true of boys)	6
Insists on being "first" in everything with peers	6
Bosses, teases younger siblings	6
Has rich capacity to "pretend" in social play	6
Shows compliance in family relations	7
Desires to be "good"	7
Begins to discriminate between sexes	7
Forms close friendships with one of the same sex; the age of "bosom pals"	8
Sex cleavage is definite; girls giggle, whisper; boys wrestle, "roughhouse"	9
The age of "clubs"	9
Sex differences are pronounced: girls show more poise, more folk wisdom, more interest in family, marriage, etc., and in their own personal appearance	10

*Abridged from L. H. Stott, *The longitudinal study of individual development.* Detroit: Merrill-Palmer School, 1955.

cesses by which children become socialized and makes use of these principles in her teaching.

How do children become socialized?

Although opinion remains divided about how children become socialized (Parke, 1972a), it appears that children learn to become like other people and to get along with them as a result of identifying with and imitating them and also by being reinforced for desirable social behaviors.

Considerable evidence indicates that children learn by observing grownups and other children and that, particularly if the person is nurturing and is powerful, they will seek to be like the model and imitate his behavior (Bandura, 1977; Bandura and Huston, 1961; Mischel and Grusec, 1966). There is also some evidence that indicates that children are more likely to be influenced by behavioral models than by moral preachments (Bryan, 1970; Rosenhan, 1972), so it behooves the teacher to model the behavior she wishes to encourage rather than just talk about it or, worse yet, preach something she does not practice.

There is also considerable evidence that children learn socially acceptable responses as a result of reinforcement either by adults (Allen, Hart, Buell, Harris, and Wolf, 1964; Horowitz, 1967) or by peers (Patterson, Littman, and Bricker, 1967). This can be either negative reinforcement in the form of punishment that may suppress behavior (Parke, 1972b), or positive reinforcement in the form of recognition, praise, or other responses and satisfactions that come from without or within themselves. In addition, a study by Thompson (1944) shows that teachers can facilitate the development of some specific social behaviors by assuming an active, guiding role.

Implications for teaching. We can conclude from these findings that the teacher needs to do more than sit idly by while the children grow and develop: she should assume a role based on active teaching. Since one way children acquire social behaviors is by identifying with models and imitating their behavior, obviously the teacher should provide a good example. In addition, the relationship between her and the child should be based on mutual liking (Bandura and Huston, 1961; Damon, 1977; Mussen and Parker, 1965) and warmth (Yarrow, Scott, and Waxler, 1973).

Because young boys may tend to imitate male models more readily than they do female ones, it is also desirable to include male teachers and volunteers in the nursery school whenever possible.

Since children learn as a result of positive reinforcement, the teacher needs to be sure that children receive satisfaction from acting in socially desirable ways. Sometimes this reinforcement will be in the form of a pleasant comment or expression of affection from herself, but a more desirable approach is for the teacher to point out to the child that it feels good to help other people so that the pleasure stems from this inherent reward rather than from a calculated external one.

However, the teacher should not view social learning as taking place mainly between adults and children. Most social learning takes place between child and child in play situations (Grief, 1977). As Hartup puts it, "Children learn many things through rough-and-tumble activity that would not be possible in adult-child relations" (1977, p. 5). This, then, furnishes us with yet another reason for including ample opportunities for interactive play, since play provides the richest opportunities of the nursery school day for social learning to occur.

SUGGESTIONS FOR TEACHING APPROPRIATE SOCIAL SKILLS

When young children want something, be it attention, assistance, or possession of an article, their need is *immediate, intense, and personal*. Their reactions, therefore, to having to wait or to consider the rights of others can be very strong, and it takes patient teaching backed by fortitude to develop in children the ability to wait a little, to control their feelings to a degree, and to consider the rights and desires of others when necessary. All of these skills are central to the process of getting along in a social world. If the teacher remembers to take into account the strength of these immediate, intense, and personal needs as she reads about more specific social learnings, she will gain an added appreciation for the magnitude of the child's task in learning to become a socialized human being.

There are, of course, many more social goals than the seven listed below, but these seven goals have been selected because they are frequently listed by teachers of young children in the United States as being important and as having real social value.

Goal I: Help children learn to be generous and able to share equipment, experiences, and people with others

Although much of the research on social development dates back to the 1930s, there is new interest in identifying effective ways to foster what is sometimes called *prosocial behavior* or *altruism*, and generosity is one of the most investigated areas. This research has indicated that when affection from the teacher is combined with verbal comments about what is happening, the greatest number of charitable responses is produced in children (Midlarsky and Bryan, 1967). Modelling generosity also increases this behavior (Rosenhan, 1972), and paternal nurturing facilitates generosity in boys of nursery school age (Rutherford and Mussen, 1968). Thus we again find support for the recommendation that teaching a prosocial behavior is accomplished most effectively by a teacher who sets a good example and expresses affection while at the same time clarifying what is happening by discussing it with the children.

Help children learn to share equipment. Teaching a specific aspect of generosity such as sharing (a social skill of real concern in nursery school) requires something more than nurturing and setting a good example. It requires carrying through clear-cut policies that are directed toward building the generous impulse within the child rather than relying on externally enforced generosity supervised by the teacher. As one of my students put it, "I want him to share from his heart, not because I make him do it."

Many teachers try to teach sharing by regulating turn taking. ("You can have it for 2 minutes, then he can have it for 2 minutes.") They seem to interpret sharing as meaning that the child has to hand over anything he is using almost as soon as another child says he wants it. Teachers who enforce taking turns on this basis find they are constantly required to monitor and referee the turn-taking themselves. This is not only tiresome but puts the locus of control and decision outside the child rather than within him, and it means that a child may not be permitted to have enough of an experience to be filled up and truly satisfied by it. This builds a kind of watchful hunger and avarice, which should be avoided.

Rather than struggling to institute the policelike control of the previous procedure, the teacher can establish a climate of generosity by making sure that the child has enough of most experiences. Therefore, she does not limit him to two paintings or allow him to ride the trike around the course only three times because another child is waiting. Instead, she follows the rule that the child may keep what he has or do what he is doing until he has had enough of it. This means that children don't have to be calculating and defensive about hanging on to things; and it makes settling arguments easier, because it is relatively simple to base decisions on who was using it first and then to state the rule, "Whoever had it first may keep it until he's done with it."

Once assured that his own rights and desires will be protected, it becomes much easier for a child to share. When another child is waiting, the teacher can point this out, perhaps saying, "John, when you're done with the swing would you remember to tell Helen? She'd like a turn when you're through." The final step in this process is recognizing when he *does* remember to tell Helen that he is done by commending him and pointing out, "Look how pleased Helen is that you remembered. She's really smiling at you. I guess you're her friend!"

It helps in such situations to have enough equipment available that children do not have to wait and wait. Several easels are better than one, and feeling free to improvise in order to meet peak demands will help, too. For example, if painting is suddenly very popular, setting out paint tables might help, or giving children cans of water and old brushes to paint the fence could satisfy their need and reduce waiting.

Help children learn to share the teacher. Children not only have to learn to share equipment, they also have to learn to share their teacher and her attention with other children. Again, the best model is the generous one, where each gets what he needs rather than each getting an identical, metered amount. This may mean that only one child is rocked while several others play nearby in the block corner rather than every child being rocked a little. As long as each child receives comfort when he needs it, the teacher doesn't have to worry about whether she is being "fair." She can explain to the children that different people get different special things according to what they need, and then, to remind them that this policy applies to everyone, she can cite examples of times when they had special attention.

Some individual satisfactions have to be put off, since it is not possible for one child to monopolize the teacher's attention throughout lunch or story time. To handle such demands the teacher might say, "You know, lunch is for everyone to talk together, but I can see you really want to talk to just me. I promise we'll have time for that while I'm getting you ready for nap."

Goal II: Help children develop empathy

Being able to understand what another person is feeling or why he acts as he does is a valuable social skill. As Flavell says:

Making good inferences about what is going on inside these objects (i.e., other people) permits us some measure of understanding, prediction, and control in our daily interactions with them (Flavell, Botkin, Fry, Wright, and Jarvis, 1968, p. v).

Piaget (1926) has long maintained that young children are egocentric and are unable to put themselves in the place of another. But recent research (Borke, 1971; Flavell, 1966, 1973; Hetherington and McIntyre, 1975), as well as the experience of many nursery school teachers, indicates that this egocentrism is not an all-or-nothing condition. As children grow from 2 to 5, they become increasingly able to assume roles (Flavell, 1966, 1973). They can also, with training, become more sensitive to other people's feelings and to the effect their actions have on these feelings.

Encourage role playing. There are several things the teacher can do to increase the awareness of how it feels to be someone else. One of the most obvious of these is to provide many opportunities for dramatic and imaginative play involving role taking about what people do. Most nursery schools maintain housekeeping corners, which facilitate the role playing of family life so dear to 3- and 4-year-olds. We have seen that as children reach 4 and 5 years of age, their interest in the world around them increases and extends beyond the family and the school. For these youngsters, enriched role opportunities can be offered with accessories for doctors and nurses, bus drivers, nursery school teachers, or anyone else who is familiar to the children. For example, we have a fine time in our children's center with chefs' hats and coats since our cook, whom the children adore, always wears such garments when serving lunch. The costumes need not be complete. Indeed, it seems wise to leave something to exercise the children's imaginations; but hats are particularly fun, and it is good to have a variety of them representing different characters.

Help the child understand how the other person feels. Teaching children how other people *feel* in addition to what they *do* is more difficult but not impossible. One virtue of encouraging children to tell each other what they want or how they feel is that in addition to relieving the speaker's feelings, it informs the other child about someone else's emotions and desires. The other important reason for doing this, according to Piaget, is that children are freed of egocentrism by experiencing interactions with other people. The hypothesis is that both social conflict and discussion facilitate cognitive growth and an accompanying ability to put the self in another's place (Piaget, 1926; Smedslund, 1966).

The teacher can increase empathy for another's feelings by explaining how a child is feeling in terms that are personal to the observing child, relating the feeling to one that he has also experienced. For example:

Henry, who has just caught his finger in the door, is crying bitterly as the teacher holds him and comforts him. Frankie comes in and stands watching silently, his thumb in his mouth. He looks interested and worried, and as the teacher pats Henry on his back, she explains to Frankie, "Henry hurt his finger in the door. Remember when I rocked on your toe with the rocking chair?" Frankie nods. "Well, his finger feels like that." "It hurt," says Frankie. "It hurt a lot. But we put cold water on it and that made it stop. Let's put his finger in cold water." The teacher says, "That's a great idea! Henry, Frankie is telling you something." Frankie says, "Come on, Hennie, we'll put your finger in water—that will help." And off they go.

Here, the teacher related Henry's feelings directly to what Frankie already knew from his own experience. This helped make the feeling real to him and also encouraged him to use this insight to provide practical comfort for his friend.

Goal III: Help the child learn that it feels good to help others

I agree with the Russian's implication at the beginning of this chapter that American children are not encouraged to help their friends as much as they might be. Providing opportunities for children to experience the satisfaction and pleasure that come from helping someone else appears to be a sound way to generate willingness to take prosocial action. Sometimes helping others takes the form of comforting another child; sometimes it is as simple as passing the cups at snack; and sometimes it is as sophisticated as thinking of an excursion everyone will enjoy (Moore, 1977).

Children should be *encouraged and expected* to help each other. The teacher should emphasize that helping other people is a worthwhile, important thing to do. Here are some simple examples fur-

Photo by Elaine M. Ward

nished by student teachers* of how this can be clearly and consistently taught in the nursery school when teachers are sensitive to teaching these values.

This episode took place in the hollow block area with some cardboard blocks that have foam packing glued to their insides. Janelle, Timothy, and Jenny were all climbing around on them.

Timothy: "Watch, I can climb out of here by myself." He proceeds to do so.

Me: "Boy, Timothy, you sure can. I wonder if it's just as easy to climb in?"

Timothy: "Yeah, I can. I got to put my leg over first." He climbs in the box, accidentally putting his foot on Janelle's shoulder.

Janelle: "Watch out, Timothy!"

Me: "Woops! He accidentally hit your shoulder, huh?"

Janelle: "Yeah. Watch me hide in this corner." She does so, and almost gets stuck between the layers of foam. She finally gets herself out. "I almost got stuck!"

Me: "Yeah, you finally slipped your way out."

Jenny: (who has crammed herself in more firmly, shrieks) "Help me, teacher. I can't get outta here!"

Me: "Uh oh! Now Jenny's stuck in there. (Jenny continues to twist and struggle.) Janelle, do you remember how you got out?"

Janelle: "Yeah! Here, Jenny. I'll help you." With Janelle pulling and Jenny pushing, Jenny manages to get out.

Me: "Good, you guys! She sure needed you, Janelle!"

Jenny: "Yeah, I was stuck! I woulda spent the night in there!" (She laughs.)

Or sometimes helping takes the form of one youngster teaching another something.

Roe (aged 4 years, 8 months) is washing and drying some toy animals when Yvonne (aged 2 years, 3 months) walks up, takes up the other towel, and wants to play. Roe takes the towel away from Yvonne and looks at me.

---

*My thanks to Mary Kashmar, Lauren Davis, Sandi Coe, and the children for the following episodes.

Roe: "Will *you* dry?"

Me: "Yvonne looks like she really wants to play. Why don't you ask her to dry them for you?"

Roe is agreeable to the suggestion.

Roe: "Yvonne, will you dry?" (Yvonne nods her head "Yes." She begins to dry but is having difficulty.)

Roe: (snatching the towel away impatiently) "She's too slow. *You* dry."

Me: "I think you should give Yvonne a chance. Maybe you can show her how to do it."

Roe: "Here, Yvonne, do it this way."

Yvonne catches on quickly and squeals with delight.

Roe: "Wow, now she's waiting for me. I better hurry up."

Me: "You girls work well together. Thanks, Roe."

Soon all the toys are washed and dried.

Or it takes the form of both comfort and help.

At the swings two children were playing and unhooked the seats from the chains. Anathea (playing in the cornmeal) looked over and saw this. "They broke it!" she cried! She seemed really upset by it.

Earon reached over and patted her on the back, saying, "It didn't break," and went on playing. Then he repeated this about three more times. "It didn't break, Anathea; it didn't break."

I said, "You're right, Earon, but can you tell Anathea what happened?"

"They didn't break it—they just took it off of there. See?" (He goes over and hooks them up.) Anathea smiled at him, and they both went back to playing in the cornmeal.

Note that it is necessary to handle these situations carefully in order to avoid the undesirable effect of comparing children with each other. For example, rather than saying, "Why don't you do it the way Alan does—he's a big boy," it is better to say, "Alan just learned how to zip his coat. Why don't you ask him to show you how it goes together?" Children are often generous about teaching such skills to each other as long as it doesn't take so much time that they lose patience.

Goal IV: Teach children that everyone at nursery school has rights and that these rights are respected by all

I made the point earlier that children have individual needs and that the teacher should not hesitate to meet these on an individual basis; that is, she should not interpret fairness as meaning that everyone gets exactly the same thing. But children do, in general, have to conform to the same rules. This impartiality of rule enforcement will help children gradually understand that everyone is respected as having equal rights.

Teach children that rules apply to everyone. A good example of this may be seen in handling sharing problems. At the beginning of the year there always seems to be one or two children who seize possession rather than asking and waiting for turns. Of course, the teacher often has to restrain such a youngster from doing this. It is particularly important with this kind of child that she also watch carefully and almost ostentatiously protect the seizer's rights when someone tries to take his trike away, so that he sees that everyone, *himself as well as others,* has his rights of possession protected. This is a very effective way to teach fairness and to help the child see what the rule is and that it applies to every child. The message is, "You may not intrude on their rights, and they may not intrude on yours, either." As the year progresses and the child learns to know and apply these rules himself, he will become increasingly able to enforce them without the teacher's help and thus be able to stand more securely on his own socially.

Teach respect for others' rights by honoring personal privacy. Children enjoy bringing things from home; it's a cheerful link between their families and the school. Since these items are their personal possessions, it should be their choice whether to share them or not. Even the teacher should ask, "May I see it?" before she reaches out to handle a personal possession.

When he does not choose to share something, the child should put it in his cubby. Keeping his possessions there provides an opportunity to teach privacy and personal rights if the rule is enforced that a child may go only in his own cubby, never in anyone else's without permission. Of course, there will be many transgressions of this rule, but the children will learn to honor this policy over a year's time, just as they will learn to stay out of the teacher's desk and out of the staff rest room if these rules are insisted on.

Goal V: Emphasize the value of cooperation and compromise rather than stressing competition and winning

Competition and winning over others is so much a part of American life that it hardly seems necessary to emphasize them in nursery school, and yet many teachers do so because appealing to children's competitive instincts is such an easy way to get them to do what teachers want. It is particularly easy to employ competition as a manipulative device with older nursery school children. Research shows that rivalry increases around the age of 5 years (Stott and Ball, 1957) and competition rather than cooperation is the favored response among American children of elementary school age (Bryan, 1975); thus, using competition to manipulate behavior plays right into a developmental characteristic of the child.

The teacher is using this method when she makes such statements as "Oh, look how well Johnny's picking up the blocks; I bet you can't pick up as many as he can," or "It's time for lunch, children. Whoever gets to the bathroom first can sit by me. Now remember, no running!" Such techniques reward children for triumphing over other children and neglect the chance to teach them the pleasure of accomplishing things together.

Model cooperation yourself. One effective way for the teacher to substitute cooperation for competition is to model it by helping the children herself. Thus when it is time to put away the blocks, the teacher warns in advance and then says, "It's time to put the blocks away. Come on, let's all pitch in. I guess I'll begin by picking up the biggest ones. Henry, would you like to drive the truck over here so we can load it up?" He may refuse, of course,

Photo by Elaine M. Ward

but after a pause, he'll probably join in if the teacher continues to work with the group to complete the task, meanwhile thanking those who are helping.

Teach the art of compromise. Being able to compromise is another basic part of learning to cooperate. Four-year-olds love to strike bargains and are often able to appreciate the fact that everyone has gained some of what he wants when a fair bargain or agreement is reached. The following episode, which occurred at our children's center, is a good example of this.

Jimmy has been pulling some blocks around the play area in the wagon. Finally, tiring of this, he asks the teacher to pull him instead. Just at this moment Alan arrives and wants the wagon. This is too much for Jimmy who, dog-in-the-manger style, suddenly decides he wants to pull it after all. He says, "No, Alan! You can't have it! I'm using the wagon. I'm not done. I want to pull it! Get off!" "My gosh, Jimmy!" says the teacher. "Weren't you just saying you wanted a ride? Here's your chance. Weren't you just asking for someone to pull you?" She pauses to let this sink in. "Maybe if you let Alan have a turn pulling the wagon, he would give you the ride you want." She turns to Alan. "Would you do that, Alan?" She turns to Jimmy, "Would that be okay with you, Jimmy?"

Thus the teacher helped the boys strike a bargain whereby both got what they wanted.

As the children become more socially experienced, the teacher could encourage the boys to think the situation through for themselves rather than intervening so directly herself. Perhaps she might say at that point, "Jimmy, Alan is telling you he really wants to use the wagon, too. Isn't there some way you can both get something good out of this?" If the boys can't conceive of any solution, then she can go on to the more obvious approach outlined above.

Teach children to work together. The teacher should also be on the lookout for opportunities where it takes two children (or more) to accomplish what they want. Perhaps one youngster has to pull on the handle while the other shoves the wagon of sand from behind, or one must steady the juicer while the other squeezes. When these circumstances arise, encourage the children to help each other, rather than hurrying too quickly to help them yourself.

There are also a few pieces of play equipment that require cooperation for success, and a point should be made to acquire these. Double rocking horses, for example, just won't work if the children don't cooperate and coordinate their efforts; neither will tire swings that are hung horizontally. Some kinds of jump ropes also need at least two people participating for success, as does playing catch.

Goal VI: Help children discover the pleasures of friendship

Children become more and more interested in having friends as they grow older. By age 5 they are likely to spend more than half their playtime with other children (Valentine, 1956), and friendship bonds between particular children are generally much stronger at this age than they are in younger children (Green, 1933). By second grade it is almost intolerable to be without a friend. Ways of demonstrating friendship have recently been shown to pass through a number of developmental stages (Youniss, 1975)—moving from a 6-year-old's interpretation of showing friendship by means of sharing toys and material items through the stage of playing together as a primary indication and going on to showing friendship by offering psychological assistance, such as giving comfort when needed.

Friendship depends on many variables, including similarity of age, sex, and sociability, as well as the less readily analyzable qualities of personal attractiveness (Young and Cooper, 1944). There also appears to be considerable variation in the capacity and need for close friendships at the preschool age.

It sometimes seems that the only friendships nursery school teachers are aware of are the ones they try to break up between older boys who egg each other on into trouble. Yet there are many desirable relationships, which should be noted and nurtured in the preschool.

Facilitate friendliness by using reinforcement to reduce isolated behavior. Social interaction between

Santa Barbara City College Children's Center

children can be increased by the judicious use of reinforcement. This is a particularly helpful technique to employ with shy, isolated children (Allen, Hart, Buell, Harris, and Wolf, 1964). Using this approach, the teacher provides some kind of social dividend whenever the child approaches a group or interacts with them, but withholds such recognition when the child withdraws and plays by himself. (It is hoped that over a period of time the pleasure the youngster finds in being part of the group will replace this more calculated reward.) Note that this approach is just the opposite of the pattern that often occurs in nursery school where the teacher tends to "try to draw the child out" when he retires from the group, thereby rewarding with attention the very behavior she wishes to extinguish.

Increase the social skills of disliked children. Another way to foster friendships and cordial social relationships among children is to teach less likable youngsters social skills that make them more acceptable to the other children. For example, a child who has learned to ask for what he wants is generally more welcome than one who rushes in and grabs whatever appeals to him.

This can sometimes be best accomplished on a one-to-one basis where children are "coached" by the teacher in more successful ways to behave. Sometimes, for example, it really clarifies things if the teacher simply points out, "You know, when you knock their blocks down, they don't like you. It makes Hank and Charley really mad, and then they won't let you play. Why don't you try building something near them next time? Then maybe they'll gradually let you join them and be your friends."

Particularly with 4-year-olds it would be interesting to determine if very simple small group discussions of what works and what doesn't might also help children learn techniques that foster friendly relations. It would, of course, be important not to single out specific personalities during these discussions as being either "good" or "bad" examples.

Asher, Oden, and Gottman (1977) report two fascinating studies on the effect of teaching social skills by means of modelling (Evers and Schwartz, 1973; O'Connor, 1972), where a film demonstrating successful methods of entering a group was shown to young children. Observation of their behavior following this film revealed marked and continued improvement in their utilization of these strategies. Although such films are not readily available to most nursery schools, other ways of presenting models can be developed easily. I recently observed two teachers acting out such situations in brief, simple skits for their 4-year-olds at group time.* The children were delighted and readily talked over the skits afterwards. Again, it is important to avoid the temptation to parody specific personalities in the group.

Pair children together. Pairing children together sometimes helps them make friends. Coming to school in a car pool or going home from school to play together can cement a friendship, as can doing a number of jobs together or sharing an interest in common. In the long run, though, it is up to the child to form the friendship; all the teacher can do is make such possibilities available to him.

Goal VII: Help children determine and develop behavior that is appropriate to their sex

The problem of establishing sexual identity. Teachers need to be aware that, during the years of early childhood, children are developing many concepts having to do with sexual identity. This is both a fascinating and touchy subject at present, since stereotypes of what constitutes "appropriate" sex roles for human beings are undergoing change in some segments of our society. (This is not solely the result of the recent Women's Movement. It is interesting to note that as long ago as 1961, research showed that some traditionally sex-linked pastimes and games were becoming more acceptable to children of both sexes. In 1961 Sutton-Smith and Rosenberg compared four studies of games selected by children from 1896 to 1959 and found an increasing similarity between the sexes in game preference. This change seemed primarily due to a shift in play preferences among the girls, who have grad-

---

*I am grateful to Sharon Brownette of the Santa Barbara Preschool Program for sharing this idea.

ually come to participate more frequently in such activities as swimming, playing tag, and flying kites.)

In a recent comprehensive review of what is known of psychological differences between the sexes, Maccoby and Jacklin (1974) list a number of beliefs about such differences that have *not* been supported by research and investigation. These include the beliefs that (1) girls are more "social" than boys; (2) girls are more "suggestible" than boys; (3) girls have lower self-esteem; (4) girls are better at rote learning and simple repetitive tasks, boys at tasks that require higher-level cognitive processing and the inhibition of previously learned responses; (5) boys are more "analytic"; (6) girls are more affected by heredity, boys by environment; (7) girls lack achievement motivation; and (8) girls are auditory, boys visual.

On the other hand, Maccoby and Jacklin also identify four psychosexual differences that are fairly well substantiated by research. These are that (1) girls have greater verbal ability than boys, particularly beyond the age of 11 years; (2) boys excel in visual-spatial ability, again a finding more consistently present in adolescence and adulthood than in childhood; (3) boys excel in mathematical ability, true particularly from age 12 or 13 on upward; and finally, (4) males are more aggressive, both physically and verbally. The authors comment that "this difference [i.e. more pronounced aggressive behavior] has been observed in all cultures in which the relevant behavior has been observed . . . and that this sex difference is found as early as social play begins—at age 2 or 2½'' (p. 352).

In terms of physiological differences, in addition to primary sexual ones, boys eventually become larger and stronger than girls, boys have a higher activity level and, in the early childhood years, girls have about a 12-month lead over boys in general physiological maturation (Korner, 1977; Lee and Gropper, 1974).

Other recent research, which supports these findings, indicates that some differences in behavior between males and females are evident even during the first year of life (Goldberg and Lewis, 1969; Hutt, 1976; Moss, 1967). How much of this behavior is due to the subtly pervasive influence of culture and how much is the result of psychological or physiological predisposition is impossible to say at this time. The real issue is, as Lee and Gropper point out, ". . . not whether genetic differences exist, but what we make of them" (1974, p. 377).

The questions for the teacher who is living in an era of changing sexual values and roles are: "How do I respond to this possible shift in values and role descriptions? Is it in the best interest of the children to let my personal convictions radically affect what I teach in the classroom? Does the restructuring of the male/female concept mean I must avoid all social definitions of what constitutes masculinity and femininity as we think of them at the present time?"

It seems too risky to advocate that sexual roles be abandoned altogether (even if this were possible, which it more than likely is not). Children need to have clear ideas of who they are and of how to behave in ways that will be accepted by other people. In our society these are so closely linked to the sex of the individual that attempting to scrap all such teaching might result in unanticipated and undesirable side effects related to possibly serious confusions about self-image.

But this does not mean that the teacher should do nothing different about teaching sexual roles and establishing sexual identities for the children; it does mean that she should be thoughtful, careful, and not destructive about what she plans to do and that she should have a clear grasp of the difference between a nonsexist curriculum and one that attempts to deny or destroy a child's deep, basic valuing of his own sexuality.

Valuing one's own sexuality. At the nursery school level there are two approaches to helping children value their sexuality that are important to discuss. The first has to do with teaching simple physiological facts that place a positive value on each sex. Open toileting has long been the rule in most nursery schools because, when boys and girls use the same toilets, secrecy about sexual differences and toilet practices is avoided. This policy also generates opportunities for the teacher to supply answers to things young children wonder about, such as explaining why boys urinate standing up whereas girls sit down. The teacher makes simple statements about these matters: "Yes, boys and girls are made differently. Boys have penises, and so they stand up to urinate. Girls have vulvas, and so they sit down." If little girls still want to know why they can't stand up, the teacher can invite them to try it—there's no substitute for learning by experience! Casualness and answering questions actually asked, rather than ones that the teacher is nervously afraid the children will ask, should be the order of the day.

Differences in the mother's and father's functions should be handled the same way—simply, and by answering the child's question; and the value of each parent's role should be explained. The father starts the child growing within the mother; mothers have babies and sometimes nurse them from their breasts; then mothers and fathers work together to care for the baby afterwards.

It is necessary to think about the child's home situation when discussing such matters. So many children in day care now come from single-parent homes that this has to be gently taken into account so that the child does not feel "different" or peculiar because he has only one parent. And yet, it is these very children who may be least experienced with mother-father roles and who need most help in understanding the ideal mutuality of the parenting relationship. It takes a combination of sensitivity and matter-of-factness without sentimentality or pity to deal with this problem successfully.

Questions about sex at the nursery school level are not likely to be too difficult to answer. They are usually as simple as, "Can I have a baby when I grow up?" "Where does the baby come out?" "Doesn't the father get to do anything?" The reader may wish to refer to the references for further readings at the end of this chapter for a list of books that will give detailed advice on how to answer individual queries.

Finally, the use of correct terms and language should be part of teaching about physiological facts. It is just as easy to say penis as wee-wee, and the use of the correct word takes away the aura of unspeakable secrecy about sexual differences and helps make such knowledge a forthright part of the child's life.

The second approach to helping children value their own sexuality has to do with encouraging the boys' feelings of maleness and meeting their needs for role models in the nursery school. Although it is difficult to talk about this without having it misinterpreted as advocating sexist practices, experience has taught me that it is necessary to remind women teachers to provide young boys with many experiences that fit their needs. At least in our current society, boys are more physically active (Davis and Slobadian, 1967) and aggressive than girls; but women teachers tend to suppress this vigor and energy, since it is contrary to the teacher's own behavior patterns and also makes running a nursery school more difficult. Boys especially need opportunities for vigorous physical activity. They must have room to climb and wrestle. Their play requires large, sturdy equipment, plenty of space, and a teacher who genuinely welcomes such activity, rather than regarding it as a threat to her ability to control the children.

Not only must boys be supplied with enough room to move and to let off steam, but they must also have the chance to form relationships with men who can serve as models for them. In an age when divorce is increasing and many unmarried women are electing to raise their children rather than surrender them for adoption, many children in day-care centers come from single-parent, mother-centered homes. The effect on the boy's developing sense of masculinity of these mother-centered, father-absent homes is at present uncertain. Herzog and Sudia, after an extensive review of research, sum up current findings when they say, "The findings reviewed do not provide clear-cut and conclusive answers to . . . questions about the sturdiness of the masculine identity of fatherless boys as compared with that of boys in two-parent homes" (1973, p. 184). However, common sense cannot help encouraging one to believe that the presence of a father facilitates sex role development (although there is also evidence that boys can develop normally without it). For this reason, nursery schools should do all they can to provide consistent contacts for boys with men who care about children. Girls, too, benefit from such experience, since it is probable that it also helps them develop concepts of masculinity and femininity.

Incidentally, one of the continuing and unfortunate examples of sexism in our society is the fact that very few men are employed as nursery school teachers (Greenberg, 1977; Lee and Wolinsky, 1973). This is due in part to the perception of such work as requiring the nurturing qualities commonly attributed to females rather than to males, but it is also due to the low salary schedules still tolerated by women nursery school teachers. (These low salaries are, of course, an additional illustration of sexist employment practices as well as an indication of the low priority early education has in the financial commitments of many families.) Until this problem can be remedied at a more fundamental level, we will continue to need to use ingenuity in thinking of ways to include men as participants in the nursery school day. High school and college men can often be employed as aides, and occasionally, warmhearted fathers will volunteer to come regularly and spend time with the children. All of these contacts, though admittedly not as satisfactory as a father's presence, will help both boys and girls formulate their concepts of what it means to be a man or woman in our society and, ideally, will help boys and girls grow up to be sturdy, attractive men and women themselves.

Providing a nonsexist curriculum. Are boys really better than girls at solving mechanical problems? Are girls really better than boys at nurturing and comforting others? We don't know; and yet a lot of socialization involves reacting to such possibilities as though they were true and structuring curriculum and behavioral expectations so that, in fact, they become true. Teachers should be wary of limiting children's potential by operating on assumptions that may be inaccurate. Some of the girls are, no doubt, just as clever at inserting a cotter pin in the wagon axle as boys are, and some of the boys may be

Photo by Jason Lo'Cicero

easily as sensitive to people's feelings as are the girls, if only they are given opportunities to explore and demonstrate these abilities and qualities.

Nursery school teachers should present an open curriculum that provides opportunities for both sexes to participate in all learning activities rather than restrict children to obsolete sex-role expectations. Teachers should work to develop wider competence and equal privileges for both sexes rather than seek to obliterate differences between them. Preschools are often the last chance children have to try out materials and activities that are contemptuously labeled in elementary school as "girl stuff" or "unfeminine." Surely activities such as woodworking should be freely available to girls, just as opportunities to enjoy dressing up or sewing should be available for boys. The chance to experience a full range of roles enriches the knowledge of each sex, does not produce sexual perverts, and, ideally, deepens understanding and empathy for the opposite sex.

Barbara Sprung and the Women's Action Alliance have produced a first-rate book replete with examples of how nursery school curriculum can be presented so that all areas, whether it be blocks or the housekeeping corner, will attract both boys and girls (1975). It is, of course, important not only to offer wider opportunities to girls, but also to offer them to boys. For example, opportunities for additional male roles should be included in homemaking such as scaled-to-comfortable-size men's clothing for workmen of various kinds, and these garments should be freely available for use by both sexes (Cuffaro, 1975), and boys should be encouraged to join in formerly female-dominated activities, such as cooking and caring for children.

All teachers should take a closer look at the materials they offer for educational activities. Since this book was first published, a few more nonsexist, multiracial materials in the way of puzzles and lotto games have become available if one searches diligently enough through catalogs. The companies of which I am most aware at present who have made a real effort to produce them include Milton-Bradley, Instructo, and the Judy Company. Things to be on the lookout for are puzzles, simple tabletop activities, flannel board figures, and records. However, because these materials are rarely sufficient for the needs of the nursery school, teachers should also expect to make many of their own items; the book by Sprung contains fairly detailed directions on how to do this.

Children's books are also worthy of inspection for the values they present, which we, in turn, accept unquestioningly. A study by Saario, Jacklin, and Tittle (1973) points out the many undesirable aspects of sex role stereotyping that occur in early readers and testing materials, and Mitchell (1973) mentions that books about boys outnumbered books about girls three to one in the list of Newberry prize-winners up to 1969. This finding was recently confirmed in an analysis of the 32 favorite picture books used in nursery schools. (Vukelich, McCarty, and Nanis, 1976). In these books, males were main characters in three times as many of the books as females were, and the only occupations besides homemaker depicted by women characters were saleswoman and nun! Two publications that include lists of nonsexist books appropriate for preschool children are the ones by Rausher and Young (1974) and Sprung (1975). The Women's Action Alliance* is also a rich resource for information on nonsexist materials.

More basic, however, than all the nonsexist curriculum in the world is the need to sensitize men and women to the negative consequences of unconsciously biased sexist teaching. What happens to the self-esteem of little boys who are criticized by female teachers for their high-energy, aggressive response to life? What effect does the constant use of such words as mail*man,* fire*man,* and police*man* have on little girls and their anticipation of future occupations?

We have, indeed, a long way to go in raising our awareness and understanding of the underlying prejudices such behavior reveals before we can offer truly nonsexist education.

SUMMARY

Social competence develops at a rapid rate during the years of early childhood. Children become socialized partly as a result of identifying with and emulating models they admire and partly as a consequence of reinforcement that encourages or suppresses various kinds of social behavior.

Although children begin to attain many social skills during this period, seven were selected in this chapter as being particularly important: learning to be generous, developing empathy, understanding that everyone at nursery school has rights that must be respected, learning that it feels good to help other people, discovering the value of cooperation and compromise rather than stressing competition, discovering the joys of friendship, and determining and developing behavior that is appropriate to the sex of the child.

*Women's Action Alliance, 370 Lexington Ave., New York, N.Y. 10017.

QUESTIONS AND ACTIVITIES

1. *Problem:* You are working as a teacher in a cooperative nursery school. One of the new mothers is supervising the trike area and is firmly telling each child that he can ride his trike around the track three times and then must give a turn to the next child who is standing in line (there are several children standing there already, making plaintive noises about wanting turns). What would you do to handle this situation on both a short- and long-term basis?

2. In this chapter the comment was made that sex roles seem to be changing in the United States. Do you think that, if teachers make a point of offering nursery school children of both sexes equal experiences and equal privileges, this policy is likely to result in the loss of sexual identity for the children?

3. During the next week, watch for situations in which a child could be helped to understand another person's feelings or point of view. Using the situations you observed, discuss possible ways that genuine feeling for another person could have been developed from these situations.

4. Analyze the books in your nursery school: Are there ones that present both boys and girls as effective, active people? Are there ones that appear to perpetuate stereotypes of little girl and little boy behavior? Are these necessarily undesirable?

5. *Problem:* You are working in a school that serves many single-parent families where mothers have primary care of the children. Many of the children, therefore, have relatively little experience with men. Suggest some practical plans that would help alleviate this deficit for the children you care for.

6. How much do *you* know about effective ways of entering a group? Make a list in class of strategies adults and/or children can employ for successful entrée.

7. Do you think it's true that some activity areas in nursery school attract boys and others girls? Keep a tally on this for various areas such as housekeeping, blocks, carpentry, and art. If the results show a disproportion, that is, more of one sex than the other involving themselves, should the teacher attempt to bring about a different balance—or should the children be allowed to continue to select freely as they prefer?

REFERENCES FOR FURTHER READING

Overviews

Damon, W. *The social world of the child.* San Francisco: Jossey-Bass, Inc., Publishers, 1977. This lively, interesting work combines reviews of research with descriptions of the author's own considerable contributions in the realm of social behavior as it relates to moral development in young children.

Murphy, L. B., and Leeper, E. M. *From ''I'' to ''we.''* Washington, D.C.: U.S. Dept. of Health, Education, and Welfare, Office of Child Development, Bureau of Child Development Services, 1974. (OCD) 74-1033. Another in the "Caring for Children" series, this pamphlet discusses in clear, simple terms such things as sharing, waiting, and becoming competent and makes practical recommendations on how to help children become more socially able.

Roedell, W. C., Slaby, R. G., and Robinson, H. B. *Social development in young children.* Washington, D.C.: National Institute of Education, U.S. Dept. of Health, Education, and Welfare, 1976. Still another useful, inexpensive analysis of how to help children acquire social skills, this uses numerous citations of research to back up the recommendations.

Rosenhan, D. Prosocial behavior in children. In W. W. Hartup (Ed.), *The young child: Reviews of research* (Vol. 2). Washington, D.C.: National Association for the Education of Young Children, 1972. This review provides a concise summary of research on prosocial behavior in children. It is a good place to begin for a student who is interested in learning how such research is conducted.

Sharing and Respecting the Rights of Others

Nicolaysen, M. Dominion in children's play: Its meaning and management. In K. R. Baker (Ed.), *Ideas that work with young children.* Washington, D.C.: National Association for the Education of Young Children, 1972. The value of permitting children to establish territories for their own use while playing is discussed, and several practical examples of how individual and group needs may be harmonized are included.

Role Playing

Bender, J. Have you ever thought of a prop box? In K. R. Baker (Ed.), *Ideas that work with young children.* Washington, D.C.: National Association for the Education of Young Children, 1972. This article is brief but rich in ideas and suggestions for extending role playing to people in the community who are familiar to nursery school children.

Nonsexist Education

Cohen, M. D. (Ed.). *Growing free: Ways to help children overcome sex-role stereotypes.* Washington, D.C.: Association for Childhood Education International, 1976. This pamphlet provides a good, quick overview of the significance of nonsexist education, suggests some materials, and presents a little research as well.

Greenberg, M. The male early childhood teacher; An appraisal. *Young Children,* 1977, *32,* 34-38. The author makes a persuasive case for including male teachers in the nursery school and also discusses significant reasons why there are so few males in this profession.

Sprung, B. *Non-sexist education for young children: A practical guide.* New York: Citation Press, 1975. This paperback contains a wealth of practical ideas for conducting a nonsexist nursery school using five curriculum topics as examples; the best reference in the field.

Teaching Children about Sexual Differences

Arnstein, H. S. *What to tell your child: About birth, illness, death, divorce, and other family crises.* New York: Condor Publishing Co., 1978. This is a practical compendium of advice suitable for parents and teachers too. It covers the topics as listed and updates a previous version done originally in collaboration with the Child Study Association of America.

Strain, F. B. *New patterns in sex teaching.* New York: Appleton-Century-Crofts, 1940. This old but invaluable reference is a special help for teachers who are worrying about what to reply to such questions as, "But how does the baby get inside?" and "Why are the dogs fighting?" Chapter 10 gives many examples of exactly what to say.

Some Recommended Books about Sex for 3- to 6-Year-Olds

The following list is provided through the courtesy of the Department of Home Economics, California State University, Long Beach, Calif.

Andry, A. C., and Scheep, S. *How babies are made.* New York: Time-Life Books, 1968.

Evans, E. K. *The beginning of life: How babies are born.* New York: Crowell-Collier Press, 1969.

Gruenberg, S. M. *The wonderful story of how you were born.* Garden City, N.Y.: Doubleday & Co., Inc., 1970.

Hegeler, S. *Peter and Caroline: A child asks about childbirth and sex.* New York: Abelard-Schuman Ltd., 1957. (Translated from the Danish.)

Hodges, B. W. *How babies are born: The story of birth for children.* New York: Essandess Special Editions, 1967.

Scheffield, M., and Bewley, S. *Where do babies come from?* New York: Alfred A. Knopf, Inc., 1972.

Schima, M., and Bolian, P. *The magic of life.* Englewood Cliffs, N.J.: Prentice-Hall, Inc., 1970.

For the Advanced Student

Bandura, A. *Social learning theory.* Englewood Cliffs, N.J.: Prentice-Hall, Inc., 1977. *Social Learning Theory* assembles all of Bandura's ideas on this subject in one place at one time and makes a good case for the importance of modelling as a means of acquiring behavior.

Bryan, J. H. Children's cooperation and helping behaviors. In E. M. Hetherington (Ed.), *Review of Child Development Research* (vol. 5). Chicago: University of Chicago Press, 1975. For those readers desiring a comprehensive overview of the subject, this work by Bryan is recent and thorough in discussing research related to cooperation, empathy, and helping behavior.

Hoppe, R. A., Milton, G. A., and Simmel, E. C. *Early experiences and the process of socialization.* New York: Academic Press, Inc., 1970. This excellent collection of papers, which discusses the process of socialization from a number of theoretical points of view, has a particularly interesting report of a study by Harvey and Felknor on parent-child relations and their influence on conceptual functioning.

Howard, N. K. *Sex differences and sex role development in young children: An abstract bibliography.* Urbana, Ill.: College of Education, University of Illinois, 1975. This reference briefly describes the subject of each study but lists no findings; a good starting point for further research.

Lee, P. C., and Gropper, N. B. Sex role, culture and educational practice. *Harvard Educational Review,* 1974, *44,* 369-410. In my opinion, this is the most interesting, best-written discussion of the relationship of culture to the development of the sex role. It reviews research, raises questions, and discusses implications for education; highly recommended reading for everyone.

Maccoby, E., and Jacklin, C. N. *The psychology of sex differences.* Stanford: Stanford University Press, 1974. This valuable, sensible book documents recent research on the psychology of sex differences and identifies what is and is not at present substantiated by research. Containing an extensive annotated bibliography, this is a landmark book for those interested in this field.

Margolin, E. *Sociocultural elements in early childhood education.* New York: Macmillan Publishing Co., Inc., 1974. In this thoughtful book, Margolin attempts to blend what is known of socialization theory with curriculum development for young children.

Los Niños Head Start

10 □ Cross-cultural education in the nursery school

I hear the train a'comin,
A comin' round the curve
She's using all her steam and brakes
And straining every nerve.

Get on board, little children,
Get on board, little children,
Get on board, little children,
There's room for many-a-more.

The fare is cheap and all can go
The rich and poor are there.
No second class aboard this train,
No difference in the fare!

Get on board, little children,
Get on board, little children—
Get on board, little children!
There's room for many-a-more!*

One of the most exciting possibilities in day-care and Head Start type programs is the opportunity they present for incorporating cross-cultural education into the curriculum. The broad selection of people served by these centers does indeed provide us with a wonderful opportunity to help make the second verse of this old gospel tune come true, but in order to bring this about, the teacher must have a clear understanding of how to reach these goals.

DO YOUNG CHILDREN NOTICE ETHNIC DIFFERENCES?

Is nursery school too early to begin learning about ethnic differences? Would it perhaps be better to leave well enough alone and not risk making children self-conscious about ethnic differences and similarities when they are so young? Although some teachers might still prefer to answer ''yes'' to these questions, research on the perception of differences in skin color shows that children as young as age 3 respond to the skin color of blacks and Mexican Americans (Landreth and Johnson, 1953; Morland, 1972; Rohrer, 1977; Werner and Evans, 1971). Beuf (1977) has reported that this is also true for preschool-age Native American youngsters of Southwestern and Plains tribes. Moreover, the number of these differentiating responses increases markedly from age 3 to 5. Fortunately, the perception of difference at this early age does not necessarily result in rejection. In one nursery school study, Stevenson and Stevenson (1960) found that Southern white children continued to play with black youngsters even though they perceived a color difference between the groups. But sometime during this period or a little later, negative reaction to color evidently begins to form. In their study of white children in elementary school, Miel and Kiester (1967) found that out of 237 children surveyed, 187 preferred to play with white children, 31 with black, 15 with both, and 2 said they didn't want to play with either. It is evident from these findings that it is during the years of early childhood that children are beginning to note ethnic differences, just as they are noting sexual differences and differences in occupations. Therefore, if we wish to combat the formation of prejudice, we must conclude that early childhood is the time to start.

*A particularly well-sung version of this gospel tune is available on the record *Songs of My People* with Paul Robeson. An RCA, Red Seal re-release, LM-3292.

141

TWO APPROACHES TO CROSS-CULTURAL EDUCATION

Two approaches to cross-cultural education, particularly when combined, are effective in fighting prejudice. First, the teacher must seek to honor each child for his cultural and ethnic uniqueness. This positive valuing has a profound effect on increasing his self-esteem, which is vital to maintaining good mental health. Such acceptance and honoring of diversity, sometimes termed *teaching cultural pluralism,* helps children learn that different does not mean inferior.

Second, the teacher can fight prejudice by teaching the children that everyone has similar bodily and psychological needs, which can be satisfied if people work together in a cooperative way. This approach is sound because it fosters a feeling of belonging to a group, and belongingness reduces the sense of isolation and alienation that burdens many minority people (Lystad, 1969).

Although an adequate cross-cultural program should be centered around both of these important social learnings, the emphasis in this chapter is primarily on multiethnic pluralistic education, because this appears to be the place where teachers need the most help.

RECOGNIZING AND HONORING CULTURAL DIFFERENCES
Importance of sensitivity

The policy of recognizing cultural differences and honoring them used to be the exception rather than the rule in public schools. Readers may recall the books used in their own elementary school days wherein pink and white children visited Grandpa's farm and pulled their puppy around in a shiny new wagon. Now the trend is in the other direction, and we are finally able to purchase at least a few books and learning materials that have true relevance to family life in a variety of cultures.

Although this trend is good, the student must also realize that teaching about differences must be done with sensitivity. In their extensive study of children's views of foreign peoples, Lambert and Kline-

berg (1972) question the desirability of teaching that emphasizes that foreign people are different or peculiar. The desirability of emphasizing differences should also be questioned when teaching about friends and neighbors. We do not want young children to deduce from our presentations of varying cultural strengths and values that a child should be set apart because of variation in custom or behavior. It would defeat the entire purpose of cross-cultural education if we generated experiences where people felt that they were being used or as though they were being mounted on the head of a pin and examined.

Instead, the basic learning should be that everyone is worthwhile and that each child brings with him from his family special things that enrich the group and that are fun to share. In other words, we hope to teach that each child is special, not that each child is peculiar.

Relate cross-cultural learnings to the here and now

Just as other learnings are linked to reality, cross-cultural learnings should be linked to present experiences in which the children are actually involved. A study by Estvan (1966) provides support for the value of basing learning experiences on familiar things. He found that children who came from urban environments indicated they generally preferred the pictures that had to do with urban things, since these pertained to items with which they were acquainted. This study reminds us that nursery school teachers should base cultural teachings on real experience with children and families in the nursery school rather than on concepts of "our friends in foreign lands" or "Marie, the little Swiss goatherd." I don't know what leads otherwise sensible teachers to lose their heads and retreat to quaint pictures of little Dutch girls when they begin to talk about people of different cultures. Perhaps it is a way of avoiding coming to grips with the reality of our current life, where a fresh emphasis on the integrity of various minority cultures has, in some cases, frightened the white middle class. But frightened or not, the time is past when white teachers can afford to live with their heads in the sand. It is time to learn how to welcome cultural pluralism in the classroom.

Since it is impossible to discuss each ethnic or cultural group in detail in a single chapter, I have included many references at the end of the chapter for more extended reading and used examples from as many individual cultures as possible in the text. There is, of course, no one set of culture-based learning experiences that is universally appropriate to all nursery school programs, because each group of children has its own ethnically and socially unique composition.

Provide many opportunities for children to participate in cross-cultural experiences

There are a variety of ways to honor cultural differences at nursery school. Some are obvious, others more subtle.

The past 10 years has witnessed the publication of many stories about black, Indian, Mexican-American, and Asian children; resource lists for these are included at the end of this chapter. Records and pictures are also in better supply now, although some schools appear to be unaware of their availability. But it is not necessary to depend on commercial sources. Children often know rhymes and songs from their families, and the teacher can learn these with the parents' coaching and then help youngsters teach them to the group. Most homes have popular records or tape decks, but this is a resource frequently ignored by teachers who deem the music vulgar. However, many of the children's homes are saturated with blues or hard rock, and using such music in school can draw children into movement and dance who spurn less colorful songs about little duckies waddling around the fish pond.

Reaching the child by using his dominant language is even more important. Someone must be available in every nursery school room who can understand what the child has to say and who can make friends with him in his own language. Even

such simple courtesies as learning to pronounce the child's name as his family does rather than anglicizing it can make a difference. The subject of teaching English as a second language and the use of black English is discussed more fully in Chapter 15. I pause here only to emphasize that a bicultural or multicultural program is a farce if we deny the child the right to speak his native tongue or dialect. To be truly effective, cross-cultural programs must honor language as well as traditions.

Serving familiar food is another excellent way to honor particular backgrounds and to help children feel at home. Sometimes a shy child who appears to be a poor eater is actually just overwhelmed by the strangeness of the food served to him. Food in some day-care centers still seems to be planned with the best of nutritional intentions but with total disregard of local food patterns and customs. This situation can be remedied by asking parents for suggestions about appropriate food, by using recipes from ethnic cookbooks (see the references following Chapter 3), and by employing a cook who comes from a culture similar to that of the majority of the children. Children can also be encouraged to bring recipes from home that they can cook at school, or mothers or grandmothers may have time to come and participate in this way. As the children feel more at ease, it can also be fun to branch out and visit local markets and delicatessens that specialize in various ethnic foods. For example, even in a community as small as my own, we have a Chinese market, several Mexican-American tortilla factories, and a German and a Greek delicatessen. (Delicatessens are particularly good to visit because the food is ready, and it smells good and looks attractive.)

Holidays and other special occasions are also good times for children to share various customs. I recall one event in our group when a young boy lit Hanukkah candles and explained their purpose and the custom of gift giving very clearly. (It was specially fortunate that he was able to do this because he had recently experienced a severe burn, and the prestige of lighting the candles helped him over-

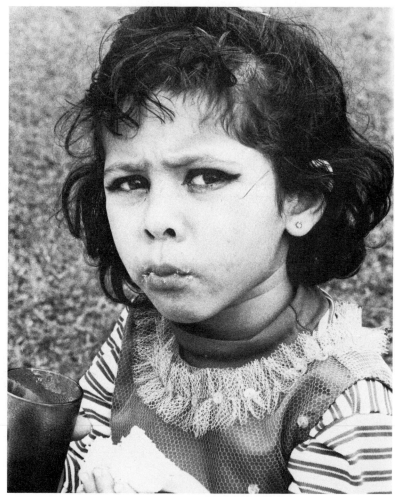

Los Niños Head Start

come his fear of fire as well as add enrichment to the life of our group.)

The backgrounds of each child may be savored by the group in many additional ways. Dress-up clothes that reflect the occupations of various parents or national costumes, when they can be spared, contribute much to the life of the school. Stories brought from home, dolls that are both ethnically accurate and attractive, and pictures that are integrated are also good choices. Such cross-cultural materials should be available consistently rather than presented as isolated units. Dolls, pictures, books, and music from many cultures should be deliberately, though apparently casually, woven into the fabric of every nursery school day.

It is, of course, also necessary to take a continuing, close look at the materials, particularly books, that are offered to the children to make certain they are not teaching undesirable attitudes. Just as we are making the effort to become sensitive to sexist books that perpetuate certain role models as acceptable for girls or boys, so must we also become more sensitive to racist themes and roles. Appendix D offers some helpful guidelines to follow when selecting books for young children to help us guard against both sexism and racism.

What worries me about listing such ideas as the ones above is that so many teachers seem to think this is all there is to multicultural education, whereas it is actually only the beginning (Arenas, 1978). We must realize that the basic purpose of providing multicultural experiences is *not* to teach the children facts about Puerto Rico or Japan, or to prove to the community that the teacher is not prejudiced. *The purpose of multicultural curriculum is to attach positive feelings to multicultural experiences so that each child will feel included and valued, and will also feel friendly and respectful toward people from other ethnic and cultural groups.*

When you get right down to it, all the multiethnic pictures and recipes and books in the world won't make much difference if the teacher, in her heart, cannot appreciate the strong points of each child and his family, and help the other children appreciate them also.

Continually work to overcome middle-class prejudices

Extent of teacher prejudice. Nobody wants to be prejudiced, but evidently almost all of us are. Some of the most recent evidence that these feelings show through in relations between teachers and students is provided in a survey of 429 junior and senior high school classrooms. The survey revealed there were substantial disparities in the way teachers behaved toward Anglo-American and Mexican-American students. Teachers gave significantly less praise and encouragement to Mexican Americans, accepted and used their ideas less often, gave them fewer positive responses, asked them fewer questions, and indulged in fewer instances of noncriticizing talk with them (United States Commission on Civil Rights, 1973).

Different people, of course, are prejudiced against different things. Some teachers who are not concerned about skin color or ethnic background may find they have real difficulty accepting the life styles of some families they serve. They may feel ill at ease with long-haired students or uncomfortable with vegetarians, or they may disapprove of how welfare recipients spend their money.

The problem for the teacher is that it is difficult to genuinely accept and not wish to change the attitudes of someone who has different values. Most teachers either consciously or unconsciously intend that families and children will move over to the teacher's side of the value scale and never consider whether they themselves might change and grow in the direction of the families. Thus teachers are likely to use the term culturally deprived to describe children who, though deprived of middle-class Anglo culture, actually possess a rich culture of their own.

A splendid example of this one-direction expectation is provided in an article on educating non-whites in South Africa (Ireland, 1972). The author quotes the staff as asserting that the purpose of sending Bantu children to nursery school is to teach them to conform to the ways of the white world: "The staffs of the two prototype nursery schools in Johannesburg . . . have developed a dynamic curriculum with the specific aim of making each child completely at home with every facet of white culture" (p. 487).

Shouldn't there be more to nursery school than this? But we do not have to look as far away as Africa to find examples of this approach. It is still quite common, though not as openly expressed, in many American nursery schools.

Suggestions for controlling and overcoming the expression of prejudice. Prejudice and other emotional reactions become deeply ingrained in people. There are no real answers yet about how to overcome these feelings, although prevention is no doubt the soundest long-term solution. But at the very least, the teacher can make sure she practices some mental hygiene rules, such as these suggestions quoted by Kenneth Clark.*

1. As a beginning, find ways to become acquainted with at least one person or family of each racial and cultural group in your community.
2. Extend common courtesies and titles of address to persons of all groups, regardless of sinful community customs, regardless of their position, and regardless of however strange it may seem at first.
3. Learn the difference between paternalism (that is, loving down, loving in "their place") and true . . . respect of one human being for another.
4. Keep a close check on your thoughts and feelings. Watch out for any tendency to blame whole groups of people for what individuals do.
5. When you hear rumors that reflect on any group, demand proof. Do not repeat lies.
6. Never use hateful terms that slur any group. Show disapproval when others use them.
7. Do not tell stories, however funny, that reflect on any group. Do not laugh at them.
8. As a present or future employee, welcome new workers without regard to race or creed. Make very sure the boss does not refuse to hire people of some group because he imagines you would resent

it. If you are seeking a new job, inquire among organizations where no such distinctions are made.
9. Request a policy of non-discrimination where you spend your money. (Remember, business firms may discriminate in employment and in serving customers because they imagine this pleases you. Make sure they know that it does not.)
10. Where there is a choice, take your patronage where there is the most democracy in every way. And let the proprietor know why.
11. . . . When going with interracial groups to public places, always assume that you will be served. Many places will say "no" if you ask in advance, but will serve you when you come. It is good education for them to know you assume that they will serve you.
12. Watch out for the term "restricted." It generally means discrimination against someone.

Acquisition of knowledge about different ethnic groups and cultures can also foster understanding and acceptance and help the teacher overcome her own cultural deprivation. For example, the teacher who understands that Navajo good manners require children to keep their eyes cast down when speaking with a respected elder does not keep insisting that these youngsters look her in the eye when they have something to say. Nor does the teacher visiting the home of an Italian family refuse the glass of wine often offered as a welcome. It can be extraordinarily instructive to live for even a month on the amount of money allotted by the welfare department. Although some aspects of doing this are admittedly synthetic, finding out the ways people make do and manage to get by can increase the teacher's respect for their ingenuity as well as her understanding of their feelings of rage and helplessness. Finally, learning the language of the families and nerving oneself to use it forms the best cultural bridge of all, since the use of their language says to the families, "I'm really trying to meet you half way."

Ethnic studies programs offer a wealth of information on particular cultures, and teachers should take such courses whenever they can. It will not only broaden their horizons but may also teach them

---

*From Clark, K. B. *Prejudice and your child.* (2nd ed.) Boston: Beacon Press, 1963. P. 107.

how to avoid offending those whom they really want to help. Even just reading about the characteristics of various ethnic groups can help build appreciation and sensitivity to variations in cultural style.

It is encouraging to know that attitudes can and do change. For example, despite reports of "white backlash," the most recent report on a long-term study of attitudes toward integration carried out by the National Opinion Research Center indicates that attitudes of whites toward blacks have gradually become more liberal during the past decade and a half. Although this trend has been particularly apparent in the age group born after 1924, changes in the direction of increased acceptance have also been identified in the older population. Apparently attitudes are changing for the better, albeit slowly (Taylor, Sheatsley, and Greeley, 1978).

Show respect for people of differing ethnic origins by employing them as teachers

Cross-cultural learning in the nursery school must be based on real experiences with real people. This means, for example, that when we talk about how to emphasize that black people are effective human beings, it is just not satisfactory at the nursery school level to use the historical examples recommended in many black curriculum guides. Historical figures are so remote and intangible that they do not mean much to preschoolers.

A much more effective way of teaching young children that people of all ethnic backgrounds are important is to employ them in positions of power. Many schools have reached the point where they employ black and brown people as aides. But this is far from enough. Children are quick to sense the power structure of the school, and they need to see people of all colors employed in the most respected positions as teachers and directors.

Unfortunately, Asian, Mexican, Indian, and black nursery school teachers are still relatively rare. Nursery school associations can and should help remedy this deficiency by encouraging their local colleges to recruit heavily among ethnic groups other than Anglo, and they can also help by offering scholarships to sustain such students through college. Even a modest book scholarship may mean the difference for some young people between going to junior college or working in the dime store.

Increase the number and variety of children in the nursery school who come from various ethnic and cultural groups

As I commented earlier, day nurseries and compensatory groups are luckier in the assortment of children who come naturally to their doors than are middle-class schools. Such multiethnic contacts can introduce children at an early age to the values of an integrated society. It can teach the basic fact that James's face is not dirty because it is brown and can couple this learning with the fact that James is fun to play with because he's the best block builder in the school.

Suggestions for recruiting children for middle-class nursery schools. In *The Shortchanged Children of Suburbia* Miel and Kiester (1967) comment on the "extraordinary effort [that] was required to bring about any encounter between a child of the suburbs and persons different from himself. . . . He is largely insulated from any chance introduction to a life different from his own" (p. 3). Since this is clearly an undesirable situation, many middle-class schools are trying to achieve a better ethnic balance through recruitment. The teacher should realize, however, that families understandably resent being used as tokens or being included only because of their color or poverty. The slightest trace of condescension or patronage will give offense, and it requires tact and genuine warmth to achieve participation by all.

Middle-class schools may do best when recruiting if they find three or four mothers who can come at the same time and therefore lend each other moral support. The fact that some states now allow their welfare departments to purchase child care from any licensed nursery school also makes recruitment easier. Sometimes the children of foreign students can be sought out and included.

Of course, the closer the school is to the children

it serves, the more likely it is that families will participate. Why should a black mother trek her child half way across town for the dubious privilege of placing him in an all-white nursery school? It is hardly reasonable to accuse blacks of being stand-offish under such circumstances; yet I have heard this conclusion drawn when such an invitation was refused.

Another way to increase ethnic representation is to do tradeabouts. Several nursery schools in our local community who have been unhappy about their ethnic sterility now make a practice of exchanging groups of children with day-care centers every week. This provides variety in social contacts and curriculum for all the children and has proved profitable and refreshing for everyone. Remember a "one-shot" experience does not allow enough time for children to become friends. The contacts must be frequent and regular.

Suggestions for recruiting children for schools who serve low-income families. Although most programs that have been operating for a while find they have more children available than they have facilities to serve, new schools may still need to recruit. One way to find children is to contact families whose children are already enrolled in the elementary school or to contact the welfare department for suggestions. In the early days of Head Start we even went door to door, introducing ourselves and making friends and spreading information about the new schools that would be available. In some areas posting invitations and notices in Spanish and English in such places as markets and laundromats helps get word about the school around and says to the community that their ethnic background is being taken into consideration.

Mothers and children who have had a happy experience are the best recruiters of all. Over a period of time, this word of mouth will make or break the school.

Involve and honor all parents when they visit the nursery school

I recommended earlier that teachers should seek to acquaint themselves with various cultures by reading, taking courses, learning the language, and so forth, but I want to emphasize here that the most vigorous and lively source of ethnic learning is right on the school's doorstep—namely, the families themselves. In the long run, cooperative sharing of themselves and their skills will teach the teacher and the children the most about the personal strengths of family members. As a matter of fact, I don't see how one could conduct a multiethnic classroom without drawing on these resources.

Successful communication is vital. The teacher who is unafraid of parents and who genuinely likes them will communicate this without saying anything at all; there is really no substitute for this underlying attitude of good will and concern for the children. All parents appreciate the teacher who has the child's welfare genuinely at heart, and this mutual interest in the child is the best base on which to build a solid teacher-parent relationship. Since listening is also more important than talking, the teacher should cultivate this ability in herself.

Other matter-of-fact things about communication can help when speaking with the foreign born. A friend of mine to whom English is a foreign language suggests that teachers speak somewhat slowly but without condescension when talking with parents who are learning English. It is also very helpful to go to the trouble of having a translator handy when necessary. This may be another adult, but sometimes it can even be a 4- or 5-year-old who is bilingual. Notices sent home stand a much better chance of being read if they are written in the language of the home. Both languages should be printed side by side to avoid the implication that one is first and thus better than the other. Best of all is the teacher who is working to master the second language herself and who attempts to use the language of the family. The reaction to this is not criticism but, typically, an amused, kindly helpfulness from the families, who are obviously pleased at such efforts.

Welcome parent volunteers. The problem with making mothers feel at ease and glad to participate in the nursery school program is that they are always a little out of their element in the beginning. I have often thought that it would be fair to require the teacher to visit and help out in the families' homes on a turnabout basis. If this were possible, it would certainly help the teacher gain a better insight into how it feels to step into a strange situation where the possibility of making a fool of herself is quite likely.

Over and over I have witnessed teachers using mothers only to wipe off tables or to help in the kitchen, or letting them simply stand around, smiling a lot, but knowing in their hearts their time is being wasted. Mothers may prefer simple occupations in the beginning because these are familiar, not threatening, and because they do not want to make waves or antagonize the teacher. However, keeping them at such tasks is fundamentally denigrating, teaches the children that parents are not important at school, and deprives the children of the unique contribution such visitors can make if properly encouraged. For example, instead of setting up the tables for lunch, a mother might share a book with the children she has kept from her own childhood or bring pictures of her family's latest trip to Mexico, or help the children make her child's favorite recipe. Sometimes mothers are willing to bring their baby for a visit and even let the children help bathe him—this presents a specially nice opportunity to teach about the universal similarities of human beings.

Remember that the fundamental purpose of providing these experiences is to create emotionally positive situations for the children and the adults who are involved. For this reason, the teacher should concentrate on doing everything possible to help visitors feel comfortable and successful. It takes considerable planning but the results are worth it.

Although it is not fair to put parents on the spot and ask them to control a group of children they don't know, it can be genuine fun and very helpful to have parent volunteers come along on field trips where everyone can be together and where everyone takes some responsibility. Families who are poor may lack such opportunities to get out and do things, and field trips can be a refreshing change

for mothers who are homebound otherwise. On trips where toddlers would be a burden, we have, from time to time, worked out arrangements whereby two mothers take over the little ones while others come on the trip, and then switch off childcare for the next trip.

Families can often provide ideas for excursions, too. The children at our Center greatly enjoyed a visit to a communal organic garden one spring, and they also loved a trip to a father's fishing boat.

Make visitors welcome for meals. One of the wisest policies of the Head Start program has been their welcoming, open attitude at meal times. I cannot recall working in a Head Start center where people were not spontaneously invited to share meals with the children, and it is true that breaking bread binds people together in basic friendliness. If possible, this is a good policy for all schools to follow. When finances cannot support this drain, visitors can order lunch a day in advance and pay a nominal fee to defray the cost.

Trust and use parent expertise on the advisory board. All programs receiving federal funds are required to have advisory boards that must have at least 50% parent representation to be legal. But many schools use such boards as rubber stamps and present parents with programs and plans literally for approval rather than for consideration and modification—a policy that certainly does not make parents feel welcome or respected. A much better way to make plans is to trust the parents. It is unlikely that they will suggest activities or policies that are detrimental to the children; and when differences arise, they can usually be settled by open discussion, which educates everyone.

The teacher who seeks out parents' suggestions because she values their practical experience with their children will find that this approach reduces the parents' feelings of defensiveness when the teacher happens to be better educated or better paid. If meetings are held during times when child care is available, more board members are likely to attend. Attendance also increases when parent suggestions are actually used and when parents are thanked sincerely for coming.

EMPHASIZING THE SIMILARITIES AS WELL AS VALUING THE UNIQUENESS OF PEOPLE

Children not only need to have their cultural uniqueness welcomed and valued, they also need to learn that all people have many things in common and that they are alike in some fundamental ways.

Teach the commonality of biological and psychological needs

One way to teach the similarities of all people is to emphasize the commonality of biological and psychological needs. Thus, when talking about the children's favorite food or what they traditionally eat for various holidays, the teacher can remind them that no matter what we like to eat best, everyone gets hungry and everyone likes to eat something. Or she can point out at the right moment that it feels good to everybody to stretch and yawn or to snuggle down in something warm and cozy.

The same principle can be taught in relation to emotions: everyone feels mad sometimes, everyone wants to belong to somebody, most people want to have friends, and most children feel a little lost when their mothers leave them at school.

In addition, the teacher can draw the children's attention to the fact that people often use individual, unique ways to reach a goal that most people enjoy. For example, Josie's father plays the guitar, while Heather's mother uses the zither; but they both use these different instruments for the pleasure of making music and singing together with the children.

Help families look beyond various differences to focus on common goods and goals

The effective cross-cultural nursery schools described by Mary Lane and her colleagues (1971) have demonstrated that families of considerable diversity can learn to appreciate differences and at the same time find goals in common that cause them to band together to make a positive impact on their neighborhoods.

Nursery schools of various types can provide op-portunities for friendships to form and for people to thrive. Cooperatives are famous for doing this, of course, but it can also be accomplished in other groups. Advisory boards can take the lead in draw-ing families into projects that focus on the children and benefit everyone. This activity can take the form of a potluck dinner, with slides of what the children have been doing at nursery school; it can be a series of discussions on topics chosen by the parents; it can be a work day combined with a picnic lunch where everyone pitches in to clean and paint and tidy up. (There's nothing like scrubbing a kitchen floor together to generate a common bond.) It makes little difference what is chosen, as long as it results in the realization of a common goal and creates op-portunities for everyone to be together in a mean-ingful, friendly way.

Keep working toward the basic goals of socialization that teach children to consider the rights and needs of everyone

Finally, the teacher should remember that work-ing toward the goals of socialization discussed in Chapter 9 will also help children learn that every-one is respected and treated fairly at nursery school. The social goals that are most important to empha-size in relation to cross-cultural education are de-veloping empathy for how other people feel, learn-ing that everyone has rights that are respected by all, and gaining skill in cooperating rather than achiev-ing satisfaction by competing and winning over others. If these social skills are fostered, living in the group will be a good experience for all the chil-dren, and a healthy foundation will be laid for a more truly integrated society in the future.

SUMMARY

Since children as young as the age of 3 differenti-ate between people of differing skin colors, it is im-portant to begin a program of cross-cultural educa-tion at the nursery school level so that they learn that different does not mean inferior. This cross-cultural program should emphasize two main points: (1) each child brings with him a unique ethnic and cultural background that should be honored by the teacher as being a valuable contribution to the life of the group; and (2) everyone has similar bodily and psychological needs that can be satisfied if people work together to meet them in a cooperative way.

Schools who incorporate a cross-cultural emphasis in their programs can help the child learn to value both the differences and similarities of their friends and teachers as being positive strengths; this valuing is the essence of cross-cultural education.

QUESTIONS

1. Have you been with a young child when he commented on differences in skin color or other differences related to ethnic group membership? What did he say, and what would be an effective way to reply to his comments or questions?
2. Do you feel it might be confusing or contradictory to teach children that people are alike and different at the same time?
3. You are a middle-class, white, well-meaning teacher, and you have just gotten a job working with a Head Start group where the children are predominantly first-generation Puerto Ricans. What will you do to make these children feel truly welcome? How can you utilize the rich cultural traditions of this minority group in your classroom? Suppose that you could not serve Puerto Rican food, use their native dances, or read books to the children about Puerto Rican children. What might be other valuable, though more subtle, ways to honor the cultural uniqueness of these youngsters? Are there ways you might change to match the groups you are serving more closely? Would changing yourself mean that you are losing your own cultural heritage?
4. *Problem:* A delegation of parents calls on you and says they want to discuss the racist policies of your school. In particular, they question the fact that all the teachers are white, and all the aides are minority people. They have called a meeting for this evening and invite you to attend. What would be a desirable way to deal with this situation? Be sure to consider short-term and long-term possibilities.
5. It is the beginning of the year, and there are many new parents in your group whom you hope to involve in participation. List some things you plan to do that will foster this participation. Also list some policies that would subtly discourage parents from wanting to come and be part of the life of the school.
6. Do you ever wonder if perhaps you are unconsciously behaving in a prejudiced way by paying more attention to children from certain ethnic groups and less to members of other groups? One way to check up on yourself is to ask a trusted colleague to keep track for various time periods of your contacts with the children over a week or more. All it takes is a list of the children's names and putting a check by each one for each contact made. If you wish to refine this strategy, plus and minus checks can be used depending on the kind of encounter, whether it's disciplinary, showing positive interest, and so on. (A word of encouragement—this behavior is fairly easy to correct once the teacher is aware of it.)
7. Could some of Kenneth Clark's mental hygiene rules for overcoming prejudice apply also to sexism? Which ones apply most directly in your opinion? Can you produce examples where sexism has been expressed at the college level? At the preschool level?

REFERENCES FOR FURTHER READING

The One Best Reference!

Schmidt, V. E., and McNeill, E. *Cultural awareness: A resource bibliography.* Washington, D.C.: National Association for the Education of Young People, 1978. Just as I was embarking on the revision of this chapter, this veritable treasure trove of a reference arrived. It includes books for adults and children, as well as other resources including films, records, posters, and periodicals. The children's books are identified according to age group. This publication does the job I could never hope to do because it can devote an entire book to the subject—by all means, acquire this resource. About $5.00.

General Discussions on Implementing Cultural Pluralism

Arenas, S. Bilingual/bicultural programs for preschool children. *Children Today,* 1978, 7(4), 2-6. The reader will find this article by Soledad Arenas, who is Director of Head Start Strategy for Spanish-speaking children, filled with helpful, specific suggestions for honoring cultural diversity.

Banks, J. A. *Teaching strategies for ethnic studies.* Boston: Allyn & Bacon, Inc., 1975. James Banks has written a valuable basic text, useful for all teachers because it begins each chapter with a concise summary of the history of each major ethnic group during the time they have lived in the United States (Native Americans, European Americans, Afro-Americans, Mexican Americans, Asian Americans, Puerto Rican Americans, Cuban Americans, and Native Hawaiians). Unfortunately for our purposes, the curriculum suggested begins at elementary school level, but this is still a valuable book that is well known in the field.

Clark, C., and Rush, S. *How to get along with black people: A handbook for white folks *and some black folks, too.* New York: The Third Press, 1972. This book has excellent down-to-earth advice on how to act like a decent human being and avoid offending people in general and blacks in particular.

Forbes, J. *The education of the culturally different: A multicultural approach.* Washington, D.C.: U.S. Government Printing Office, 1968. Jack Forbes questions the usual meanings of "disadvantaged" and "deprivation." He also provides an excellent general discussion of what a multicultural education should include; a classic in this field.

Granger, R. C., and Young, J. C. (Eds.). *Demythologizing the inner city child.* Washington, D.C.: National Association for the Education of Young People, 1976. This book is valuable because it discusses teaching and learning from the point of view of the effect of social class as well as ethnic background, although the emphasis is mainly on black youngsters. Particularly strong are the chapters by Rubin, illustrating how a teacher can base teaching on the children's interests and responses, and the beginning chapters by Schmitz (on the philosophical position of W. E. B. Du Bois), Irvine, and Hilliard.

Hovey, E. *Ethnicity and early education.* Urbana, Ill.: Educational Research Information Center Clearinghouse on Early Childhood Education, University of Illinois, 1975. *Ethnicity and Early Education* presents a quick overview of the better-known literature concerned with the question of ethnicity and its relationship to self-concept, schools and teachers, social class, and so forth.

Stone, J. C., and DeNevi, D. P. (Eds.). *Teaching multicultural populations: Five heritages*. New York: Van Nostrand Reinhold Co., 1971. The editors cover black, Puerto Rican, Mexican-American, Indian, and Asian cultures, discuss various characteristics of each group, and make practical educational recommendations. An extensive bibliography is included.

Impact of Discrimination and Fear

Coles, R. *Children of crisis: A study of courage and fear*. New York: Dell Publishing Co., Inc., 1967. This thorough, sensitive study by a psychiatrist on the effect of integration on the people of the South is a fascinating account based on interviews with all kinds of people. Dr. Coles seeks to present both sides of the integration question fully and fairly.

Hill, R. B. *The strengths of black families*. New York: Emerson Hall Publishers, Inc., 1971. In this refreshing reminder that adverse circumstances can sometimes build power and strength as well as destroy, five strengths possessed by many black families are identified: adaptability of family roles, strong kinship bonds, strong work orientation, strong religious orientation, and strong achievement orientation.

Holt, J. *How children fail*. New York: Dell Publishing Co., Inc., 1964. Holt perceptively analyzes what goes on between teacher and student in many classrooms. Although not cast in terms of working with cultural differences, Holt's comments call to mind in a painful way the Civil Rights Commission report on the treatment of Mexican-American students.

Descriptions of Curricula for Various Ethnic Groups

Note that the following list is *only a sample* of what is available—by all means refer to the Schmidt and McNeill reference for a more in-depth range of references.

Black Children

Spodek, B., Andrews, P., Lee, M., Riley, J., and White, D. *A black curriculum for early childhood education: Teaching units* (Rev. ed.). Urbana, Ill.: University of Illinois, 1976. Although this guide is for elementary school children, it contains numerous resources that would be appropriate to use for nursery school children. The guide is based on educational goals and objectives and also outlines teaching procedures and materials for attaining the goals.

Native American Children

Clark, A. N. *Journey to the people*. New York: The Viking Press, Inc., 1969. Mrs. Clark gives an inspiring description of her work among the Indians of the Southwest. There is a good deal of love and no condescension in this account of how she came to understand and accept the culture of the Indian children she spent a lifetime teaching. Nursery school teachers may also recognize Mrs. Clark as the author of *Tia Maria's Garden* and *The Secret of the Andes*.

Mexican-American Children

Castillo, M. S., and Cruz, J., Jr. Special competencies for teachers of preschool Chicano children: Rationale, content,

and assessment process. *Young Children*, 1974, **30**(6), 341-347. In this article Castillo and Cruz point out that cultural orientation does make a difference in learning style, and they single out some differences in styles and values between Anglo- and Mexican-American children. Following that, they show how a competency-based program for teachers in training could help them understand and "fit" the learning style of the Mexican-American child more satisfactorily.

Spanish Dame Bilingual Bicultural Project. *The daily curriculum guide: A preschool program for the Spanish-speaking child*. Austin, Tex.: Dissemination and Assessment Center for Bilingual Education, 1975. Although designed primarily for paraprofessionals working with families at home, these materials can also be adpated for use in other programs. There is a series of books available at reasonable cost from The Dissemination Center, 7703 N. Lamar, Austin, Tex. 78752.

United States Commission on Civil Rights. *Toward quality education for Mexican Americans* (Report 6: Mexican American education study). Washington, D.C.: U.S. Commission on Civil Rights, 1974. This publication deals with the educational needs of all Mexican-American students and makes practical suggestions on how to improve the education with which they are provided.

Asian-American Children

I'm sorry to say I could not locate an age-appropriate curriculum guide for the numerous and diverse group of young children represented by this category. Teachers may find the following books helpful, however.

Inui, L., and Odo, F. *Asian American experience: Syllabus reader*. Long Beach, Calif.: Asian Studies Department, California State University at Long Beach, 1974. This publication provides cultural information about a variety of people including Filipino, Korean, Chinese, Japanese, and peoples of the Western Pacific.

U.S. Dept. of Health, Education, and Welfare. *Tips on the care and adjustment of Vietnamese and other Asian children in the United States*. Washington, D.C.: U.S. Dept. Health, Education, and Welfare, Office of Human Development/Office of Child Development, Children's Bureau, 1975. DHEW Publication No. (OHD) 75-72. Although this little booklet does not deal with curriculum *per se*, I have included it because it provides quick, succinct information about our newest group of young immigrants, which is almost unobtainable elsewhere.

Nursery School Level Curriculum Guides Containing Suggestions for Multicultural Educational Units

Christy, K. *Multi-cultural resource book for teachers of young children*. La Habra, Calif.: The Impact Co., 1974.

McNeill, E., Allen, J., and Schmidt, V. *Cultural awareness for young children at the Learning Tree*. Dallas: The Learning Tree, 1975. There is a real need and place for publications of this sort, but I do wish to reiterate that *providing these kinds of environmental embellishments and activities should constitute only the beginning of true multicultural learning*. The real purpose of multicultural curriculum is to attach positive feelings to multicultural experiences so that each child feels included and valued, and friendly and respectful toward people from other ethnic and cultural groups—we must not settle for the trappings of culture.

Cross-cultural Education

Lane, M. B., Elzey, F. F., and Lewis, M. S. *Nurseries in cross-cultural education: Final report*. Washington, D.C.: National Institutes of Mental Health, 1971. This report describes the intent of the cross-cultural program that served black, Oriental, and white families in San Francisco. It explains how its humanistic values were implemented in the curriculum and conveys a sense of the struggles and triumphs of the families and staff while the project was in operation. It reads more like a novel than a final report; highly recommended.

Parent Involvement

Miller, B. L., and Wilmshurst, A. L. *Parents and volunteers in the classroom: A handbook for teachers*. San Francisco: R and E Research Associates, Inc., 1975. A reality-based attractive addition to the literature on parent participation, this book covers a range of opportunities, always stressing the positive approach. It includes material on parent education programs, how to make volunteers comfortable, how to suit the adult to the job, and so forth; strongly recommended.

Pavloff, G., and Wilson, G. *Adult involvement in child development for staff and parents*. Atlanta: Humanics Associates, 1972. Developed primarily for Head Start programs, the Pavloff-Wilson book is clear, concise, and so direct that it sometimes seems almost arbitrary in tone. It is based on extensive experience with staff and Head Start families, and it concentrates on parent meetings, advisory committees, and so forth rather than saying much about participation in the classroom *per se;* it provides a good balance to the Miller and Wilmshurst book discussed above.

Bibliographies of Books and Records

I strongly suggest you contact the Council on Interracial Books for Children, 1841 Broadway, New York, N.Y. 10023 in order to keep up to date on nonracist, nonsexist books. Write for their publications lists, subscription service, and so forth.

Cross-Cultural Family Center. *A multi-cultural curriculum for today's young children: An outgrowth of a cross-cultural nursery school*. San Francisco: The Center, 1969. This brief summary of the Lane-Elzey-Lewis report listed above identifies the basic purposes of Nurseries for Inter-Cultural Education and describes ways that these were translated into life in the nursery school. It is valuable to own because it contains an excellent list of cross-cultural records and books ranging from Hebrew and Japanese to African and Indian.

Day Care and Child Development Council of America. *Multi-ethnic reading and audiovisual material for young children: annotated bibliography*. Washington, D.C.: The Council, 1972. Pub. No. 101. This is a good resource because it lists references on Native American as well as Mexican and black youngsters, although some of the books are for older children. About fifteen books in each category are listed.

Griffin, L. *Multi-ethnic books for young children: Annotated bibliography for parents and teachers*. Washington, D.C.: National Association for the Education of Young Children, no date. This bibliography lists an exceptionally good assortment of books about children ranging from Jewish to Asian and also includes a section on Southern and Appalachian youngsters. Books are identified by age of child and cultural background and are annotated.

Latimer, B. I. (Ed.). *Starting out right: Choosing books about black people for young children, pre-school through third grade*. Wisconsin Department of Public Instruction, 1972. Reprinted, Washington, D.C.: Day Care and Child Development Council of America, 1972. The editor first discusses criteria for selecting books for black children and then, in an annotated bibliography, gives a series of frank appraisals of children's books, rating their weaknesses as well as their strengths; very enlightening.

Sources for Ethnic Records

Although space does not allow me to list all the record supply houses that make a point of carrying ethnic records, I include two of the best companies for the benefit of the novice teacher.

Bowmar, 622 Rodier Drive, Glendale, Calif. 91202

Folkways Records, 43 West 61st St., New York, N.Y. 10023

For the Advanced Student

Beuf, A. H. *Red children in white America*. Philadelphia: University of Pennsylvania Press, 1977. I have included this book particularly because it contains the first study done on racial attitudes ever conducted with Native American children from Southwest and Plains tribes. It's really interesting reading.

Gordon, I. J. *Parent involvement in compensatory education*. Urbana, Ill.: Educational Research Information Center Clearinghouse on Early Childhood Education, no date. Research on the effect of family and culture on the developing child is reviewed, and then a variety of research-based programs that have parent involvement as their goal are summarized. A lot of information is packed into a rather small book.

Henderson, R. W., and Bergan, J. R. *The cultural context of childhood*. Columbus, Ohio: Charles E. Merrill Publishing Co., 1976. This has become just about my favorite child development text because the authors make such a consistent and unusual effort to report research about children from a variety of cultures.

Moskovitz, S. *Cross-cultural early education and day care: A bibliography*. Urbana, Ill.: Educational Resource Information Center Clearinghouse on Early Childhood Education, University of Illinois, 1975. Rather than single out one or two books on early education abroad, it makes more sense to draw the attention of the reader to this growing body of literature by citing this excellent bibliography, which covers education in such diverse countries as Columbia, China, India, Israel, and many more!

Stent, M. D., Hazard, W. R., and Revlin, H. N. *Cultural pluralism in education: Mandate for change*. New York: Appleton-Century-Crofts, 1973. This reference contains a series of articles about inculcating the concept and practice of cultural pluralism in the American public school. In their thoughtful discussions, the authors often make general recommendations and suggestions that apply to implementing almost any culture in a classroom.

Taylor, D. G., Sheatsley, P. B., and Greeley, A. M. Attitudes toward racial integration. *Scientific American*, 1978, *238*(6), 42-49. This article is one of a long-term series going back to 1956 that traces the changing attitudes of white Americans toward blacks.

Los Niños Head Start

11 □ The pleasures of meaningful work*

To give and give up, to do for others, is testament to ourselves of our worth and strength. To deny the young the privilege of service is to deny them the pride of maturity.†

Does the idea of young children performing meaningful work sound ridiculous, impossible, or even repugnant? Apparently it does to many nursery school teachers because it is an area rarely considered in textbooks on early childhood education‡ (Spodek, 1977), even though we know it is vitally important for adults to have good feelings about their work. In *Childhood and Society* (1963) Erikson quotes Freud, when asked the question, "What should a normal person be able to do well?" as replying, "To love and to work." Maslow also supports the value of work in his comment: "This business of self-actualization via a commitment to an important job and to worthwhile work could also be said, then, to be the path to human happiness" (1965, p. 5).

But is early childhood too soon to begin laying the foundation for enjoying work? Pleasure in work cannot be expected to suddenly appear full blown as the child attains adulthood; at some point in human development it must begin to be nurtured and encouraged. Since work is such a fundamental part of our culture, teachers should start with children as young as age 3 or 4 to establish a wholesome conviction that work is rewarding and that it can be a significant way of giving meaning and satisfaction to life.

TEACHING CHILDREN TO DISLIKE WORK

We all know of people who face the working day as though it were a deadening burden, an oppression to be struggled through; this is nothing short of tragic. What happened to these people that caused them to feel like that? Some of our work-burdened adult friends must have been subjected to very negative training about work as they grew up. Let us picture what such a negative teaching model might be, bearing in mind that this model may exist at home as well as at school.

Suppose we begin by asking, "How do you teach a 3- or 4-year-old child that work is to be loathed, shirked, and put off as long as possible?" For people who have such an aim in mind, the following commandments should be followed faithfully to teach children to hate work—and what better time to begin than in the early, formative years?

1. Select the chores you dislike most yourself, such as picking up every one of the small blocks, and insist that each time a child uses such equipment he pick it all up immediately as soon as he has finished. Never offer to help him with such jobs, because this will make him too dependent on you. Bright children catch on to this quickly: "Oh, no! Let's not get those out, we'll just have to put them all away!"

*Adapted from *Young Children*, September 1967, *22*(6), 373-380.
†From Gaylin, W. *Caring*. New York: Alfred A. Knopf, Inc., 1976. Page 36.
‡Montessori is a rare, welcome exception to this statement.

2. Be sure that all work is tedious and drawn out. Also insist that the child finish every task he begins on the grounds that this will teach him to be diligent.

3. Be sure that everyone always works at the same time because this is fair.

4. Provide no variety to the work; keep it dull. Expect each child to repeat the same portion to perfection, over and over, because repetition is valuable habit training and preparation for later life, where a lot of things will be boring anyway.

5. Never allow enough time, and remind the child constantly that he should hurry. This will encourage him to stick to business.

6. Expect a great deal, and be very critical of any work a child attempts. This will teach him that high standards are important.

7. Tell the child exactly how to do the work; be rigid; be demanding; watch closely so that he doesn't make any mistakes, and be quick to call his attention to all errors so that he will learn to do it the ''right'' way. This will prevent him from forming bad habits.

8. Compare his achievements with the other children's; draw his attention to where he has failed and how he could do better by copying them. This will help him appreciate other children's strong points.

9. If a child does express interest in doing some helpful job, accept his help with condescending indulgence rather than with thanks and respect. After all, he's only a child.

10. Above all, act abused yourself. Talk to the other adults about how tired you are, how much work everything is, and grumble over the unfairness of it all. Be careful to do this in front of the children because it will teach them to appreciate you more and to look forward to becoming a grown-up working person.

TEACHING THE POSITIVE VALUES OF WORK

What if we want the children in our care to relish work, to find deep rewards in accomplishment, and to anticipate each day with at least a mild pleasure because of the interest their jobs hold for them? Then we must not fall into the trap of assuming that work should consist only of doing what we don't like or don't want to do. We must be wary of thinking that work for young children can never be more than helping out in routine tidying up, and we must stop assuming, even tacitly, that the only work children are capable of is the routine, lengthy, repetitive kind of chore usually disliked by both teachers and children.

In place of such negative attitudes we must substitute an appreciation of the potential that meaningful work holds for young children's development and understand the kinds of work that they are likely to find satisfying.

Work allows the child to experience the pleasure of accomplishment linked with helping other people. One of the most important values of work is that it provides children with the opportunity to experience achievement, which possesses obvious social value, since doing a job often results in accomplishing a task and helping other people at the same time. Thus the 4-year-old who has washed the dishes after making cookies or who has sawed off the sharp corners of the woodworking table experiences not only the glow of satisfaction that comes from honest labor but also feels good because he has contributed to the welfare of the group, particularly if the teacher points this out to him and remembers to say ''thank you.''

Work increases the reality of role playing. Another pleasure inherent in work grows out of young children's passion for imitating adults. When Joel repairs the seat of the rowboat ''just the way my daddy would,'' he gains insight into what it is like to be a man. Perhaps he thinks, ''This is the way grown-ups do things. I am just a little boy, but one day I, too, will be doing things like this all the time, and it's good to do them.''

Role playing need not stop at the ''family'' level. In the past few years interest in career education has increased for children of all ages (Budke, Bettis, and Beasley, 1972; Leifer and Lesser, 1976). Although information of career awareness and attitudes for children of preschool age remains very scanty, one trend is apparent. Leifer and Lesser cite two studies that reveal that even as early as preschool, girls show a more restricted number of career choices than boys (Kirchner and Vondracek, 1973). Girls saw themselves as parents, teachers, and nurses, whereas boys chose a wider range of occupations including such things as doctor, police officer, and firefighter. This finding was further supported by Beuf's study (1974), which showed that the vast majority of preschool children chose sex-stereotyped jobs for themselves. In addition, the study found that "all the girls could suggest occupations they might hold if they were boys, while many of the boys could not imagine what jobs they might hold if they were girls." The report of a conversation with one preschooler illustrates the boy's perplexity:

He put his hands to his head and sighed. "A girl?" he asked. "A girl? Oh if I were a girl I'd have to grow up to be nothing" (Leifer and Lesser, 1976, p. 18).

If the teacher wishes to conduct a nonsexist, nonracist classroom, the implications of these findings on career awareness are obvious—even at the nursery school level we should surely make a point of widening both boys' and girls' ideas of job possibilities that are becoming available for both men and women of all ethnic backgrounds.

Using work as a means of experiencing many careers can be done successfully even with very young

Photo by Mark Lohman, The Oaks Parent/Child Workshop

children. I am thinking of such possibilities as helping the visiting nurse unpack tongue depressors and assemble the examination light, or raking up leaves for the gardener, or helping the delivery person store the milk cartons in the refrigerator. This kind of education takes considerable cooperation, briefing, and patience by the adults involved but can be very effective from time to time.

In addition, various work roles can be investigated by taking the children on field trips particularly to places where their parents work. It is also helpful having visitors come to school to show children what they do. A special effort should be made to include people in nontraditional occupations and to make certain that people from a variety of ethnic groups are included. Parents and grandparents are wonderful resources for occupations—not only because of the variety of jobs they do themselves, but also because of their acquaintance in the community with other people whom they can prevail on to visit the school. It is always a good idea to talk with these visitors in advance, explain carefully the kinds of things the children will understand and encourage them to wear their work clothes and bring their tools —otherwise, visitors tend to talk too long at too advanced a level.

Work is an ego strengthener. The experience of success in work can strengthen the ego and build self-esteem. Every time a child accomplishes something tangible and sees the results turn out reasonably well, his image of himself as being a capable person is strengthened. This is particularly valuable for very retiring or very aggressive children.

At school one year our staff had a boy who had been rejected from kindergarten. At the age of 5 he was already convinced that he was helpless, worthless, and a menace, and he expressed this self-despair in the kindergarten room by throwing scissors, destroying other children's achievements, and refusing to try anything himself. When he joined us at nursery school, we all held our breath. Although the teachers worked on the problem from a number of angles, what appeared to do the most direct good for him was the staff's thinking of some specific simple jobs he could do to help them. I recall that the first one of these was smashing, and I mean *smashing,* an old piano box we no longer needed. It was a real help to us and a genuine relief and achievement for him. His self-image was rebuilt largely through this avenue of productive work. We're still using a beautiful tree in our insect cage that he made for us.

There is something to be said, too, for the value of work in reducing guilt feelings. I would much rather help a child ''fix'' something he has broken, clean up after a spill, or apply a Band-Aid to someone he has hurt than settle for, ''Say you're sorry!'' It is valuable not only because a child should experience the actual consequence of his action through repairing the result, but also because it is a good way for him to learn that doing something ''wrong'' is not the end of the world and that one can often make amends.

INCORPORATING MEANINGFUL WORK INTO THE NURSERY SCHOOL

Now that the reasons have been reviewed why work can be beneficial for nursery school children, the question remains, ''Just what kinds of jobs can young children do?'' The following list constitutes some of the activities I have seen them participate in that were both productive and pleasureful. Most teachers will be able to supply many more examples from their own schools.

Washing dishes after cooking with them

Loading sand in a small wheelbarrow, carting it to the swing area, and shoveling it under the swings after a rainy day

Planting and weeding the garden

Fertilizing and watering the garden

Cutting flowers and arranging them

Cleaning the aquarium

Setting up the rabbit cage for a new baby rabbit

Feeding and cleaning the rabbit (which reminds me of one 3-year-old who looked at the rabbit droppings and informed me, soberly, ''Dem's not raisins!'')

Mixing paint

Washing the fingerpainting tables

Cutting up fruits and vegetables for snacks

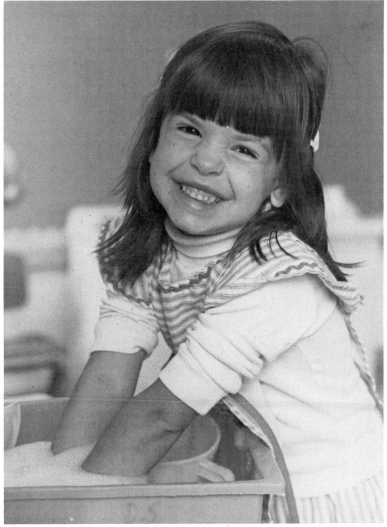

Photo by Elaine M. Ward

Helping set up the snack baskets

Fetching juice for the snack table

Doing all kinds of cooking (making butter, uncooked fondant, soup, biscuits, cranberry-orange relish; using a grinder is a special joy because children can carry out the work of assembling it as well as using it)

Carrying simple messages such as, "Mrs. Coffman needs some more clothespins"

Sanding and waxing blocks and then stapling different grades of sandpaper to them to make music blocks for our music corner

Sawing square corners off the tables to make them safer

Puttying up the holes in the much drilled-on woodworking table

Filling the holes in the edges of a new shelf with putty

Dyeing egg shells and crushing them for collage material

Nailing the seat more firmly into the boat when it works loose

Hammering nails back into the benches so that clothing is no longer snagged on them

Taking down bulletin board displays and helping put up new ones

Hosing off the sandy sidewalk

Mopping the housekeeping corner when the water play runs deep

Oiling tricycles when they begin to squeak

Using the flatbed ride-'em truck to load up and deliver the baskets of sand toys to the sand pile

Washing easel brushes (a favorite)

These chores, which adults regard as rather run-of-the-mill, were all performed with interest and enthusiasm by the children. Their pleasure did not come mainly from satisfaction with the finished job. Children are more fortunate than that in their approach to work. They love the process as much as the product and do not drive relentlessly toward the single-minded attainment of the goal; their satisfaction is spread throughout the experience. It would be ideal if this were also true for more adults in their own working lives.

Handling the experience of failure. It may also be illuminating to talk about some of our failures as well as our successes, because, of course, some work projects do not turn out well.

The second year of the garden was one of these occasions. We gave the children some excellent shovels and talked about seeds, flowers, and worms, and they started to dig with a will—and quit almost as promptly. We couldn't get any enthusiasm going for the garden: the earth was packed too hard. We had assumed that since it had been dug up the previous season that would be sufficient, but it wasn't. The job was too difficult and took too much strength. However, after we spaded it up, the children returned with a gleam in their eyes and dug deeply and well until they pronounced the time ripe for planting.

On another occasion we needed the large hollow blocks sanded lightly before revarnishing them.

"Aha!" thought the adults, "This isn't hard work, and it will be a real help." But the children tried it and wandered away. The job was too tedious and dull. We gave up on that one and did it ourselves. The adult goals of saving money and preserving the blocks motivated us, but the children couldn't have cared less.

We had only partial success with another task: the tricycles needed to be painted, and we had to remove the dirt and grease (from all that lubricating by the children) so that fresh paint would stick. The children enjoyed scrubbing with stiff brushes and soapy water, but our standards were pickier than theirs so that we teachers had to really scrub to finish the job to our satisfaction.

Once we tried to bake and decorate cookies all in one day (at least we had the sense not to attempt to roll and cut cookies). This was too extensive a task, and working under too much pressure made us all cranky. Now we buy sugar cookies and content ourselves with decorating them at school, or we bake them and eat them plain.

These less successful experiences raise the problem of how to handle failure. In the cases above, where the teachers failed, we admitted honestly to the children that things hadn't worked out as well as we had hoped and promised we would try to work out something better next time. Then we analyzed what was wrong and changed what we could.

Sometimes, too, we ask children why they didn't like a project. They will often go right to the heart of the matter and tell you, "It's no fun," "It's too hard," "I don't want to," or from the more sophisticated 4-year-olds, "My mother doesn't want me to do that today."

When a child tries and fails, there's no point and possibly real harm in pretending he has done something well when he hasn't. Maybe he can't tie that shoelace or get the nail in straight. Honest recognition is still possible, and reassurance is also highly desirable in these situations. The teacher can say, "You're really trying, Nancy. One of these days you're going to get that knack," or "Thank you. I can see you really want to help, and I appreciate it," or "You're working hard. Can I help you?"

Suggestions and conclusions about planning work opportunities so they remain appealing

One basic suggestion for keeping work attractive is that *jobs should be short* or capable of being broken down into short portions. When we made the sand-music blocks, some of the children enjoyed putting the wax on the blocks, but an older crowd was attracted by the use of the stapler and did that part of the job.

Except in the late spring when the teacher may deliberately plan projects that take 2 days to finish (such as painting and shellacking something), tasks should be finished in 1 day. Part of the pleasure of the music blocks was that we made and used them in the music corner the same morning. Young children need the immediate reward and satisfaction of seeing something through promptly.

Reasonable expectations by the teacher are very important. The goal should basically be pleasure in process and accomplishment, not perfection in performance. If a job is too hard or the child must be too meticulous, much of the joy in working that we hope to foster falls by the wayside. Work must be adjusted to the reality of the child's ability and to what he wants to do. A good way to find out what they like to do is to listen for the times children volunteer and take them up on their offers of help. Even if the tub of water is too heavy to carry by themselves, they can turn on the faucet and help carry the tub, with the teacher's hand on the handle, too.

Children need real tools to do work. They should not be given miserable little dime store imitations. Sometimes tools are best if scaled to size. For example, clamming shovels, which are strong but shorthandled, are superior to the longer variety. Sometimes regular, adult-sized tools are necessary and surprisingly easy for the children to manipulate. Stout hammers and well-sharpened saws, real C-clamps, and a standard-sized vegetable grinder are all worthwhile investments. Dull tinny tools build frustration and encourage children to give up in disgust.

In many cases the child should have the privilege of selection and the right of rejection in choosing jobs. In this respect, schools are luckier than families because, with so many children available, chances are good that almost every task will appeal to someone. Since some chores attract particular children and some draw others, a perceptive teacher should try to think of specific things that are likely to be attractive for each individual.

In general, three kinds of materials attract all children and can be successfully incorporated when planning work experiences. These can be stated very simply by the following axioms:

Anything involving food is fun.

Anything involving earth is fun.

Anything involving water is the *most* fun!

Most work requires supervision. Almost all jobs require some supervision by the teacher. This is perhaps one reason children aren't allowed to do more work at home as well as at school (until they are too old to want to do it, of course). Adults often feel it is easier on a short-term basis to do it themselves than to allow the time and exercise the patience it takes to let the child make the effort. The other common reason children aren't allowed to help more is that adults underestimate their abilities. But think what such consistent underestimation does to the child's self-concept!

The teacher's own attitude toward work is significant. The teacher's attitude toward work can influence the way the child feels about it, since children acquire attitudes from models whom they care about. The teacher who willingly lends a hand if the job is onerous (picking up blocks again comes to mind) is setting a pattern for a future young mother who may one day offer her help with equal generosity to her own child. The teacher who enjoys her own job is helping convey the idea that work can be pleasureful as well as challenging. Finally, the teacher who expresses a genuine attitude of respect for the child's work helps him build good attitudes toward it even more directly. If she reveres his power of concentration and refrains from interrupting him while he is working, if she values his suggestions about how to accomplish the task, and if she is quick to acknowledge his achievements, the child's pleasure in this kind of activity will be deepened, and he will be more likely to participate in working again when opportunity arises.

SUMMARY

Although we would never wish to emphasize work in the nursery school to the extent that it minimizes the significance of play, work is a valuable experience to offer young children because it allows them to enjoy the pleasure of accomplishment linked with helping other people, it builds reality into role playing, it promotes an expanded awareness of job opportunities, it strengthens the ego, and it enhances self-esteem.

Many different jobs at nursery school, ranging from preparing the snack to making simple repairs, are both interesting and not too difficult for children to perform. The children's pleasure in these tasks can be increased if the teacher keeps them reasonably short and easy, provides tools that are effective, allows children to select jobs that they prefer to do, and maintains a healthy attitude toward work herself.

QUESTIONS

1. What is it about work that causes many people to think of it as a difficult, tiresome activity to avoided if possible?
2. In your opinion, would it be practical to rely on children to volunteer to help with work spontaneously when the opportunity comes up, or is it fairer to have a list of jobs that must be done each day and have the children assigned to different ones at different times?
3. If you happen to be someone who feels that work is enjoyable, can you account for how you came to feel this way about it?
4. Why do you think real work is an appetizing activity to young children?
5. Do you feel children should be paid for doing chores around the house, or should they be expected to do them because they are contributing members of the family unit?
6. Watch during this coming week for opportunities for children to participate in new kinds of work experiences that they have not tried before. Be prepared to assess what made these experiences successful or unsuccessful.

REFERENCES FOR FURTHER READING

Overviews

Neff, W. S. *Work and human behavior.* New York: Atherton Press, 1968. In this interesting, readable book Neff discusses the topic of work in terms of its being a human and social problem, in terms of the individual, and in terms of related counseling problems. The chapter titled "The Components of the Work Personality" is particularly helpful because it traces the theoretical development of this part of personality from early childhood to maturity.

White, R. W. *The enterprise of living: Growth and organization in personality.* New York: Holt, Rinehart and Winston, Inc., 1972. Although it deals with the adolescent and young adult, White's chapter on "Finding an Occupation" should be read by teachers of young children to fill in their knowledge of early forces that influence the occupational choices of older individuals.

Work in Relation to Young Children

Leifer, A. D., and Lesser, G. S. *The development of career awareness in young children: NIE papers in education and work* (No. 1). Washington, D.C.: U.S. Dept. of Health, Education, and Welfare, National Institute of Education, 1976. This rare pamphlet reviews what is known of career perceptions among young children, including preschoolers, and then goes on to discuss current TV programs, such as Sesame Street and Captain Kangaroo, that carry an occupational component. It concludes with a review of school-related educational models that deal with the subject of career education, but most of that material applies to children of elementary school age.

Montessori, M. *The discovery of the child.* Translated by M. J. Costelloe. Notre Dame, Ind.: Fides Publishers, 1967. *The practical life activities* recommended by Dr. Montessori in this and other books describing her curriculum remain one of the rare discussions of work that can be successfully performed by young children.

Teaching Responsibility

Although the subject of work as such is infrequently discussed in relation to children of preschool age, some recommendations concerning "chores" and home tasks can be gleaned under the topic of "responsibility." The following references are written with family life in mind, but the principles should also be applied at school.

Foster, C. J. *Developing responsibility in children.* Chicago: Science Research Associates Inc., 1953.

Neisser, E. G. *Your child's sense of responsibility.* New York: Public Affairs Pamphlets, 1956. Pamphlet No. 254.

Young Children and Money

Alexander, A. M. *The money world of your preschooler.* East Lansing, Mich.: Cooperative Extension Science, Michigan State University, 1967. Money as it relates to the preschool child is a rare topic indeed and worth listing here because of money's relationship to work. Alexander gives a sensible, brief discussion of how understanding the uses of money can be part of teaching preschool children to get along in society.

For the Advanced Student

de Grazia, S. *Of time, work, and leisure.* New York: The Twentieth Century Fund, 1962. The author raises the question of what lies beyond the performance of work and discusses problems involved in the use of free time and contrasts it with the productive use of leisure to enhance human existence; excellent reading.

PART FIVE

Enhancing creativity

Santa Barbara City College Children's Center

12 □ Fostering creativity by means of self-expressive materials

If a man does not keep pace with his companions, perhaps it is because he hears a different drummer. Let him step to the music which he hears, however measured or far away.

HENRY DAVID THOREAU
Walden (1854)

Nursery school teachers have long valued creativity and sought to enhance it by fostering self-expression in the young children they care for. In the past we teachers have been particularly successful in presenting expressive materials and activities such as paint, clay, and dance in a manner that fosters unique personal responses from the children. But today we are coming to realize that artistic creativeness represents only one facet of creative endeavor and that there are additional aspects of creativity in play and in divergence and originality of thought, which should be encouraged more fully. For this reason, the discussion of creativity in this book does not stop with the presentation of expressive materials but extends, in two additional chapters, to play and to the fostering of originality in thought.

DEFINITION OF CREATIVITY

Defining creativity where young children are concerned is rather difficult, since the commonly accepted definitions include not only the requirement that the idea or product be novel but that it be related to reality and stand the test of being worthwhile, too. However, a definition by Smith suits our needs well, since it fits young children's creative abilities more aptly: creativity is the process of "sinking down taps into our past experiences and

putting these selected experiences together into new patterns, new ideas or new products'' (1966, p. 43), and in a more recent book, Rollo May also describes it as "the process of bringing something new into being'' (1975, p. 39).

This "putting prior experiences together into something new'' is a good description of what we hope young children will be able to do when they use self-expressive materials, play imaginatively, solve problems, or generate new ideas. It stresses originality and doesn't emphasize the quality of evaluation, which is less applicable to very young children, although even they can be encouraged to try out ideas, thereby going through reality testing and evaluation in an informal way.

The student should also understand that creativity is not limited to a few gifted Rembrandts and Einsteins; nor is it necessarily associated with high intelligence. The work of Getzels and Jackson (1962), Wallach and Kogan (1965), and Ward (1968) has demonstrated that high scores on creativity tests do not correlate strongly with high scores on academic tests of achievement or with high scores on standard measures of intelligence. In addition, a study by Margolin (1968) indicates that teachers who deliberately foster uniqueness and originality of response in creative activities can actually increase the

165

variety and diversity of such responses in young children.

These findings imply that we do not have to wait for that specially gifted child to come along in order for creative behavior to take place in our groups. The ability to generate original ideas and to produce satisfying, freshly conceived products resides in many children; and since such behavior can be increased by appropriate responses from the teacher, it is worthwhile for her to learn how to do this.

IMPORTANCE OF CREATIVITY

The experience of being involved in creative activity satisfies people in ways that nothing else can, and the ability to be creative appears not only to reflect but to foster emotional health. First, the act of creation enhances the child's feelings of self-esteem and self-worth. (The reader can test the validity of this statement by recalling the last time she produced something original—perhaps something as simple as a Christmas decoration or making a set of book shelves—and then recalling how she felt when it was accomplished.) There is something about creating a unique product or idea that leaves people feeling good about themselves.

Besides enhancing self-esteem, creative experiences offer opportunities to express emotions and to come to terms with them (DiLeo, 1970). Since they have this strong affective component, they provide a balance for the emphasis on intellectual development, which may overwhelm the rest of the program unless it is carefully managed.

Finally, creative activities offer an excellent opportunity to individualize teaching. Materials and activities that depend on open-ended replies permit uniqueness and diversity to flourish and allow each child to be himself rather than require him to conform to closed-system, authority-centered learning.

STAGES OF DEVELOPMENT

One of the peak periods for creative self-expression in our culture occurs between the ages of 4 and 6. This stage correlates well with Erikson's developmental stage for this age, which he identifies as the stage of initiative versus guilt (Gowan, 1972).

Erikson's stage is characterized by reaching out, exploring, and experimenting and also reflects an increase in creative behavior, which is partially characterized by this same kind of activity.

As is true in other areas, children pass through general stages of development in the use of creative materials (Smart and Smart, 1972). First, *they explore the material itself* and investigate its properties. Two- and three-year-olds, for instance, spend many satisfactory hours in what appears to be mainly manipulation and exploration of paints and brushes or in relishing the mixing of play dough, and they employ all their senses to do this. Who has not seen such a youngster meticulously painting her hands up to the elbow or beheld another squeezing the sponge in the paint bucket or a third looking thoughtfully into the distance as he licks the back of the clay spoon?

Once the qualities of the material have been explored and some skill has been gained in its manipulation, the child is likely to move on to what is called the *nonrepresentational stage*. Paintings at this stage, for example, seem to have more design and intention behind them, but the content is not readily recognizable by anyone but the painter. Since painting at this stage is not always done with the intention of depicting something in particular, the teacher must beware of asking "What is it?" lest such a question unintentionally put the child on a spot.

Ultimately, the youngster reaches the pictorial or *representational stage,* where he quite deliberately sets out to reproduce or create something. He may paint a picture of himself or the sun in the sky or depict a fascinating event such as the toilet overflowing or going trick-or-treating. Some children attain this stage of representational art in nursery school, but many children develop this ability during their year in kindergarten.

Implications for nursery school teachers

One implication to be drawn from these sequential stages of development is that teachers should permit children countless opportunities to experience and explore expressive materials, because this learning is fundamental to the creative experience.

The full knowledge gained through such exploration extends the ways a child may use the material, thereby enriching his creative opportunities; and the freedom to explore is also likely to keep alive his interest and openness to the medium.

The second developmental implication is that, when using expressive materials, young children should not be expected to produce a finished product. Some 4-year-olds will do this, of course; but since many will not, the expectation of some sort of recognizable result is not a reasonable creative goal to set for children in their early years.

GENERAL RECOMMENDATIONS ABOUT CREATIVITY

It is hoped that the reader will apply to all three chapters on creativity the general comments made here on fostering the child's creativity with self-expressive materials.

Be aware of the value of nonconforming behavior and of "unattractive" personality characteristics

Paul Torrance (1962) has frequently emphasized that the kind of behavior teachers identify as desirable in children does not always coincide with characteristics associated with the creative personality. For instance, the teacher who thinks she values uniqueness may find when a youngster has spilled his milk because he tried the original method of holding the cup with his teeth, that she doesn't like creative exploration as much as she thought she did.

Not only can this lack of conformity be inconvenient, but the teacher should also realize that some creative individuals possess character traits that she may not care for. Torrance cites 84 characteristics that differentiate the more creative person from the less creative one. (For a sample of these, see Table 8.) Some of the less attractive qualities include stubbornness, finding fault with things, appearing haughty and self-satisfied, and being discontented— qualities often disliked by teachers. Yet it is easy to see how stubbornness might be a valuable quality to possess when carrying through a new idea, or

how finding fault and being discontented could result in questioning and analyzing a situation before coming up with suggestions for improving it. In all fairness, we must admit that we don't know at present if some of these less attractive attitudes lie at the root of creativity or if some of them are only the result of squelching and mishandling by teachers, peers, and families as the child matures. On the other hand, Torrance also found that creative children possessed many likable qualities, such as determination, curiosity, intuition, a willingness to take risks, a preference for complex ideas, and a sense of humor.

The purpose of pointing out these possible problems of living with creative children is not to discourage the teacher from fostering such behavior but to enlighten her so that she will not subtly reject or discourage creative responses because she fails to recognize the positive side of such apparently undesirable behavior. Ideally, her understanding will result in increased acceptance and valuing of creative endeavor. Acceptance is vitally important because it will encourage children to develop these abilities further and because it will help balance the rejection and isolation to which people who dare to be different are often subjected. As long as we have creative youngsters in our care, we can help guard against rejection by recognizing and supporting originality in thought and deed.

Cultivate three teaching skills in yourself

Each creative area requires a specific teaching skill for its facilitation. The cultivation of these skills is discussed at greater length in the appropriate chapter, but they are listed here to provide the reader with a quick overview.

In fostering creativity by means of expressive materials, the teacher should make ample materials freely available and cultivate her ability to stand back and let the child explore and utilize them as his impulses and feelings require. When seeking to facilitate play, the teacher needs to be able to move with the children's imaginative ideas and respond to them by providing materials and support that keeps the play ongoing and creative. When developing

Table 8. Contrast of the characteristics of highly creative persons and the values and characteristics of our society*

> From studies that were done to distinguish highly creative persons from less creative persons, the following list of characteristics of highly creative persons was compiled.† From what you know about our society and of what most people in our culture value, contrast the characteristics of highly creative persons with the characteristics our society values highly.

Characteristics of highly creative persons†	Characteristics and values of our society‡
1. Accepts disorder	1. Disapproves of disorder; demands neatness, tidiness, regularity
2. Adventurous	2. Security
3. Strong affection	3. Indifference; views overt expressions of affection as weaknesses
4. Altruistic	4. Self-centeredness; benevolence thought of as "corny"; any help offered is material rather than moral
5. Awareness of others	5. Noninterference; fears involvement
6. Always baffled by something	6. Unquestioning acceptance
7. Attracted to disorder	7. Rejects disorder
8. Attracted to mysterious	8. Comfortable with and desirous of the known, the concrete facts, the unambiguous
9. Attempts difficult jobs (sometimes too difficult)	9. Desire for the average, the golden mean; undertakes easy, practical, feasible tasks
10. Bashful outwardly	10. Outgoing, extroverted personality
11. Constructive in criticism	11. Criticism interpreted as personal insult; destructive criticism of others to improve one's own status
12. Courageous	12. Spiritlessness, shyness, and timidity viewed as safe personality characteristics
13. Deep and conscientious in convictions	13. Shallow and superficial convictions
14. Defies conventions of courtesy	14. Stresses social etiquette
15. Defies conventions of health	15. Stresses healthy living habits
16. Desires to excel	16. Desires status quo
17. Determination	17. Vacillation, skepticism, distrust
18. Differentiated value-hierarchy	18. Profession of rigid, conventional values
19. Discontented	19. Contentment, satisfaction, tranquility
20. Disturbs organization	20. Adheres to organization
21. Dominant (not in power sense)	21. Dominant (in power sense)
22. Emotional	22. Suppression of emotions
23. Emotionally sensitive	23. Emotionally apathetic, evasion of "involvement"
24. Energetic	24. Passivity, procrastination, lethargy
25. A fault-finder	25. A praise and compliment-giver; flattery
26. Doesn't fear being thought "different"	26. Feels need to be like and do as the crowd
27. Feels whole parade is out of step	27. Falls in and tries to keep in step with parade
28. Full of curiosity	28. Nonchalance, unconcern, "who cares!"

*From Brown, M., and Plihal, J. *Evaluation materials for use in teaching child development.* Minneapolis, Minn.: Burgess Publishing Co., 1966. Pp. 155-158. (NOTE: Since space does not permit inclusion of the entire list, only the first third is included here.)
†E. Paul Torrance, *Guiding creative talent.* © 1962. Reprinted by permission of Prentice-Hall, Inc., Englewood Cliffs, New Jersey.
‡This is the column students construct. Some examples of society's characteristics and values are here given.

original thinking, the teacher must reinforce the children's production of ideas by recognizing their value and by learning to ask questions that encourage the development of their thoughts.

Do your best to maintain an emotionally healthy climate in your nursery school room

In the chapters on emotional health, handling routines, and discipline, considerable time was spent discussing ways to keep the nursery school environment reasonable, consistent, and secure so that children will feel emotionally at ease. Such a stable, predictable climate is valuable for many reasons, but one of the outstanding ones is that it forms a sound base for the generation of creative activity, which in turn contributes to the development of emotional health. Children who feel secure are more likely to venture forth, try new experiences, and express themselves in creative ways than are children who are using up their energy by worrying or being frightened or anxious.

In addition, some research supports the idea that highly structured classrooms where preschool children are continually the focus of adult control and adult-designated activities appear to reduce the amount of imaginative play (Huston-Stein, Freidrich-Cofer, and Susman, 1977) and curiosity and inventiveness (Miller and Dyer, 1975). These findings provide yet another reason nursery school teachers who wish to foster these creative traits should make certain there is an open structure to the program that provides many opportunities for children to think for themselves and to make choices and decisions within reasonable limits.

USE OF SELF-EXPRESSIVE MATERIALS TO FOSTER THE CREATIVE SELF

Expressive materials include such diverse media as painting, collage, dough and clay, woodworking, sewing, and dance. Although the materials themselves are different, some basic principles apply to all of them. (Suggested guidelines for use of specific materials are included later in the chapter.)

Value of using free-form materials

The most valuable quality that expressive materials have in common is that there is no one right thing to do with them or one right way to use them; so, in a real sense, these materials are failure-proof for the child. As long as the child observes a few basic rules, such as keeping the sand down and seeing that the dough stays on the table and off the floor, there is no way he can make a mistake with them. For this reason alone, such materials are an invaluable addition to the curriculum.

There are additional reasons why expressive materials are indispensable. Psychologists and experienced teachers agree that these experiences provide many opportunities for children to express their feelings and come to terms with them. It can be fascinating to watch the development of a shy child who may begin fingerpainting by using only the middle of his paper and then see him gradually come to fill his paper with rich colors and swooping strokes of joy as he gains confidence during his months at nursery school. Since each child is free to do as he wishes, these materials also represent the ultimate in individualized curriculum. The youngster can express who he is and what he is as something within him urges him to do; he is able to suit the material to himself in an intensely personal way.

In addition, many values associated with creative materials lie in the social, sensory, and intellectual spheres. Children who are working side by side often develop a spirit of camaraderie. Using creative materials provides numerous opportunities for rich sensory input in that dough feels sticky and then firm; fingerpainting feels cool, gushy, and slippery; dance makes the child aware of his body as he moves in response to the music. Finally, the amount of factual information children acquire about the substances they are using contributes to their intellectual growth: red and yellow mixed together creates orange; some woods are easier to saw through than others; two smaller blocks equal one large one.

Although these social, sensory, and intellectual learnings are worthwhile, I still regard them as being like the frosting on the cake. The primary values of using expressive materials remain in the affective

Photo by Richard Pierce, Santa Barbara City College Children's Center

sphere. Expressive materials are fundamentally useful because they foster creativity, build self-esteem, and provide a safe, failure-proof experience. Most important, they can be the source of open-ended opportunities for the child to be himself and for him to express and work through his individual feelings.

Practical ways to encourage the creative aspect of self-expressive materials

Interfere as little as possible. As I mentioned earlier, the most significant skill the teacher can cultivate in presenting self-expressive materials is her ability to stand back and let the child explore them as his impulses and feelings require. This does not mean that children should be allowed to experiment with scissors by cutting the doll's hair off or that they should be permitted to smear clay all over the nursery school chairs to "get their feelings out." It is as true here as in other nursery school situations that the teacher does not allow the child to damage property or to do things that may hurt himself or someone else.

However, although inexperienced teachers occasionally allow destructive things to happen in the name of freedom, experience has taught me that the reverse circumstance is more likely to occur. Many teachers unthinkingly limit and control the use of expressive materials more than is necessary. Thus they may refuse to permit a child to use the indoor blocks on the table "because we always use them on the floor," or they may insist he use only one paint brush at a time despite the fact that using two at once makes such interesting lines and patterns. These ideas are essentially harmless ones and should be encouraged because of their originality.

Never provide a model for the children to copy. A copy is not an original. When I was a little girl in kindergarten, the "creative" experiences that were offered consisted mainly of making things just the way the teacher did. I particularly recall sewing around the edges of paper plates to make letter holders and cutting out paper flowers to glue on sticks. I suppose that what was creative about these activities was that we got to pick which flowers to cut out, and, as I remember, we could choose any color of yarn to sew with. Whatever educational merit such activities possess, creativity is not among them. Yet some nursery schools persist in offering such experiences in the name of creativity. If the teacher really wishes to foster originality and the child's self-expression rather than her own, she will avoid models and will merely set the materials out and let the children go to it for themselves.

Sometimes a child will attempt to lure the teacher into drawing something for him to copy by pleading, "Draw me a house" or "Draw me a man so I can color him." Rather than complying, the wise teacher meets this request by recognizing the child's deeper request, which is for a one-to-one relationship; so she meets this need by talking with him, meanwhile encouraging him to make the picture himself.

Understand and respect the child's developmental level. We spoke at the beginning of the chapter of the stages through which children's drawings pass as they become more mature. I am also including here a developmental chart (Table 9) calling attention to the usual age at which children are able to copy various shapes, because some teachers do not understand that the ability to do this rests at least in part on maturation and so struggle endlessly to teach children at too early an age to draw such shapes as squares and triangles when everyone's energies could surely be better expended teaching and learning more important things.

Understand that it is the process not the product that matters most to the young child. We live in such a work-oriented, product-centered culture that sometimes we lose sight of the simple pleasure of doing something for its own sake. For young children, however, getting there is more than half the fun. They savor the process and live for the moment. Therefore, it is important not to hurry them toward finishing something or to overstress the final result. They *will* love to take their creations home, of course, and all such items should be carefully labeled and put in their cubbies so that this is possible, but the primary emphasis should remain on doing.

Allow plenty of time and opportunity for the child

Table 9. Drawing and writing movements*

Age (In years-months)	Behavior
0.1-1	Accidental and imitative scribbling
1-1.6	Refinement of scribbles, vertical and horizontal lines, multiple line drawing, scribbling over visual stimuli.
2-3	Multiple loop drawing, spiral, crude circles. Simple diagrams evolve from scribblings by the end of the second year.
3	Figure reproduction to visually presented figures, circles, and crosses.
4	Laboriously reproduces squares, may attempt triangles but with little success.
4.6-5	Forms appear in combinations of two or more. Crude pictures appear (house, human form, sun). Can draw fair squares, crude rectangles, and good circles, but has difficulty with triangles and diamonds.
6-7	Ability to draw geometric figures matures. By seven can draw good circles, squares, rectangles, triangles, and fair diamonds.

*From Cratty, B. J., and Martin, M. M., *Perceptual-motor efficiency in children: the measurement and improvement of movement attributes.* Philadelphia: Lea & Febiger, 1969.

to use the materials so that his experience is truly satisfying. In the discussion about sharing I made the point that it is important for each child to have enough of an experience in order that he be truly satisfied before he gives his place up to someone else. This is particularly true when using expressive materials. One painting or one collage is just not enough. Children need the chance to work themselves into the experience and to develop their feelings and ideas as they go along. For this reason it is important to schedule long enough time periods to allow for many children to move in and out of the expressive experience as their needs dictate. For real satisfaction this opportunity needs to be available for an hour or an hour and a half at a time.

Learn how to make comments that enhance the child's creative productivity. Making effective comments as the child creates will encourage him to continue and to involve himself ever more deeply in the activity. But it can be risky as well as embarrassing to be trapped into commenting on what the child is making either by trying to guess what it is or by asking him to name it. As mentioned previously, children often do not deliberately set out to represent anything in particular, and, even if they do intend a representation, it may defy recognition by anyone else. An additional drawback to requesting that creations be labeled is that it places emphasis on the product rather than on the creative, dynamic aspect of the experience.

It is more enhancing to comment on the pleasure the child is feeling as he works or to ask him if he would like to tell you about it. These remarks show him that you are interested in and care for him, but they avoid the taint of passing judgment on the quality of what he has made or of emphasizing that the end is better than the means (Sparling and Sparling, 1973).

Grant the child who is dubious the right to refuse. Children benefit from the opportunity to stand and watch before they plunge into an activity more vigorously. Three-year-olds do a lot of this standing around, but older children who are shy or new to school may behave this way, too. This is a valid way to learn, and the teacher should respect the child who copes with new experiences in this manner. Usually, after a few days he will want to try whatever it is he has been watching so intently.

A few children are extraordinarily concerned about getting painty or sticky. These youngsters are usually reassured if the teacher talks with the mother in their hearing and asks the mother to tell them that using paint and glue is all right at school. It can also help if "clean" materials, such as soap paint-

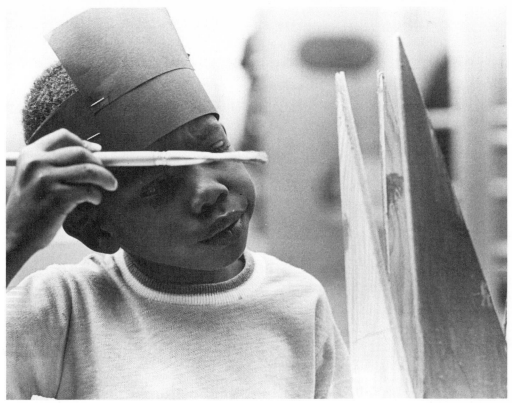

Los Niños Head Start

ing or snow, are offered as beginning messy activities. It should be made clear to such youngsters that there is water instantly available should they feel the need to wash their hands and that the apron will protect themselves and their clothes from undue contamination.

Some comments on expressive materials themselves. It is important to provide enough of whatever the children are using. There is nothing sadder than children making do with skimpy little fistfuls of dough when they need large, satisfying mounds to punch and squeeze. The same thing holds true for collage materials, woodworking, and painting. Children need plenty of material to work with, as well as the chance to make as many things as they wish.

Providing enough material for the children means

that the teacher must develop her scrounging and pack rat instincts to the ultimate degree. Not only must she ferret out sources of free materials, but she must also find time and energy to pick them up regularly and produce a place to store them until they are needed. Parents can be very helpful in collecting materials if the teacher takes the time to show them examples of what she needs. There are many sources of such materials in any community (Appendix E is included to inspire the beginner).

Variety in materials is also crucial. Creative activity should not be limited to easel painting and paper collage. The reader will find examples of variations suggested at the end of each materials outline; but I want to caution the reader to be quite clear that there is a difference between the use of self-expressive materials and many ''craft-type'' projects advocated for preschool children, even when these materials do not require making something just like the model. Day-care centers are particularly likely to be seduced by such crafts because of the need to provide variety and stimulation for the children in order to keep their interest. Unfortunately, the emphasis with these items is usually on learning to manipulate the material and on how clever the teacher was to think of doing it. The attraction for the teacher of sheer novelty tends to obscure the tendency of such crafts to (1) be inappropriate to the age and skills of the children, (2) to require excessive teacher direction and control, and (3) to fail to allow for adequate emotional self-expression.

It's difficult to see what real benefits children gain from string painting, for example. The string is dipped in paint and then placed between a folded piece of paper and pulled out. The results are fortuitous, and although the colors may be pretty this activity is not likely to be satisfying to the child unless he manages to turn the process into finger painting—which frequent observation proves to be the common outcome unless the teacher prevents it! Fortunately, there are several very good references currently available that list innumerable and appropriate ways to present basic materials that also keep in sight the fundamental values of self-expression (Bos, 1978; Cherry, 1972; Pitcher, Lasher, Feinberg and Braun, 1979).

Finally, creative materials that will be used together should be selected with an eye to beauty. For instance, rather than simply setting out a hodgepodge, the teacher should choose collage materials that contrast interestingly and attractively in texture and color. Pieces of orange onion bags could be offered along with bits of dark cork, white Styrofoam, beige burlap, and dry seed pods; a black or bright yellow mat would be a good choice as a collage base for these items. Fingerpainting colors that make a beautiful third color should be selected. For example, magenta and yellow combine to form a gorgeous shade of orange, but purple and yellow turn out dull gray.

PRESENTATION OF SPECIFIC MATERIALS

I have selected only the more common materials for the outlines in the following pages, but the reader can find additional suggestions in the references at the end of the chapter. I hope that these ideas will not be followed as gospel but will serve to inspire the teacher to develop and carry out her own and the children's creative ideas.

The suggestions for presentation of various materials in this and the following chapter have been written as individual, self-contained units so they may be abstracted and posted in various areas about the school should this be desired. For this reason, I hope the reader will forgive a certain repetition in the descriptions of setting out and cleaning up.

Easel painting*

Easel painting is perhaps the one form of artistic endeavor offered by all nursery schools, and it is an outstanding example of a creative material that is intensely satisfying to young children. In the fall, particularly with younger children and with newcomers, it is wise to begin with the basic experience of a few colors, one size of paint brush, and the standard, *large-sized* paper; but as the year progresses and the children's skills increase, many interesting variations and degrees of complexity can be offered that will sustain interest and enhance the experience of easel painting for the more sophisticated young artists.

When looking at paintings or other expressive products, one can be tempted to play psychologist and read various interpretations into the children's work. Although it is perfectly all right to encourage a child to tell you about what he has painted if he wishes to do so, the interpretation of children's painting should be left to experts. Correct interpretation depends on a knowledge of the order in which the paintings were produced, knowledge of the availability of colors, access to the case history,

---

*I am indebted to the staff and students of the Santa Barbara City College Children's Center for their help in formulating the following outlines.

and a complete record of comments made by the child while the work was in progress. In addition, young children often overpaint, restructuring paintings two or three times as they work; this increases the likelihood of misinterpretation. Since all this information is required for understanding, it is easy to see why even professional psychologists may differ considerably about interpretations of such material, and it makes sense that teachers who have only a modicum of training in such matters should be very circumspect about ascribing psychological meanings to children's art.

A. Preparation

1. Decide where to put the easels for the day. Painting is easiest to clean up if done outside, but in bad weather the easels can and should be moved indoors.

2. Assemble the equipment. This will include easels, easel clips, aprons, paint containers, brushes, large paper, paint, and a felt marker. You will also need clothespins, drying racks or a line, a sink and towels or a bucket and towels, and a sponge.

3. Check the paint to make sure it is rich and bright, not watery and thin. Decide, possibly with the children's help, on what colors to offer.

B. Procedure

1. If time permits, invite one or two children to help you mix the paint. (Sometimes this is done a day in advance, but it is always good to invite a child to help—mixing paint is interesting and educational.) Begin by shaking a generous quantity of powdered paint into the mixing container. Next, add water a little at a time, stirring constantly just as one does when making flour and water thickening for gravy. The paint should look rich and bright; it should not be a thin, watery-looking gruel. If the paint was mixed the day before, be sure it is thoroughly stirred before pouring so that all the pigment is mixed back into the water. A dash of liquid detergent added to each container seems to help paint wash out of clothing more easily.

2. Several pieces of easel paper may be put up at one time—doing this makes getting a new sheet ready for use much faster.

3. Put just a small quantity of paint in each easel container. The paint may have to be replaced more frequently, but frequent replacement means the paint stays brighter, and small amounts mean less waste when it is spilled.

4. If necessary, invite children to come and paint, and help them put on the aprons. Use *plastic* aprons to protect clothes, and remember to roll up sleeves firmly.

5. Write the child's name and the date on the back right-hand corner.

6. If it is windy, use additional easel clips at the bottom edges of the paper.

7. Encourage children to remember to replace brushes in the same color paint and to do their color mixing on the paper. Older fours can learn to rinse brushes in between times.

8. Children may use their hands in the painting as long as they keep them off other children.

9. Hang pictures on drying racks, chain link fence, or clothesline.

10. Children should wash hands *before* removing their aprons. Use an outdoor sink or bucket for hand washing if possible. If children must wash in the bathroom, be sure to alert a nearby teacher to keep track of what is going on. Sometimes children also enjoy sponging off their aprons—if this is the case, rejoice!

C. Cleanup

1. Encourage children to help clean up. Washing paint brushes is usually a richly enjoyed experience. Store brushes bristle end up to dry.

2. Put clean, unused paint back into the storage bottles, and ruthlessly discard spoiled, discolored paint.

3. Replace all equipment in the correct storage places.
4. Roll and store dry paintings in the children's cubbies; the paintings should go home every day.

Suggested variations. Offer a wide variety of colors, and ask children to select those they prefer; use a different size or shape of paper or one with a different texture, such as corrugated cardboard or "oatmeal" paper. You may want the children to experiment by learning how to mix a new color from the ones you have presented. Try using the same color paint on the same color paper, or several shades of just one color. Different sizes of brushes, or different kinds of bristles in the same color paint make a nice contrast. You might want to try painting to music, painting woodworking, painting the fence with water, using watercolors, having several children paint on one large sheet to make a mural, or painting on a flat surface instead of an easel. Printing and stamping, using paint and sponges, can also be an interesting although not extraordinarily successful experiment to try. Cookie cutters are really more effective for stamping.

Fingerpainting

Fingerpainting is one of the most tension-relieving and delicious creative experiences available in nursery school. The brilliance of the colors and the general gushiness that characterizes successful participation make it both appealing and relaxing. It is particularly valuable because it is so messy, beautiful, and free, and because it is a direct sensory experience for the children. It should be offered several times a week.

A. Preparation
1. Decide what kind of fingerpainting you will offer. There are many satisfying variations available (Stangl, 1975).
2. Fingerpainting should look rich and bright. This means that plenty of paint and starch must be used.
3. Assemble all equipment before you start. Once begun, this activity is so beloved by

children that the teacher will find it difficult to obtain even a moment to fetch something she has forgotten. Needed equipment will include *oil cloth* or *plastic* aprons (paint soaks right through old shirts if a child leans against the table—and most of them do), fingerpaint paper, a felt pen for names, starch, tempera paint (it is possible to buy ready-mixed fingerpaint, but this is likely to cost more), plastic-covered tables, something to hang the paintings on, clothespins, buckets of soapy water, sponges, and towels.
4. When weather permits, set up outside; cleanup is infinitely easier there.

B. Procedure
1. Fingerpainting is more successful when children stand up. Standing enables them to use their large arm muscles more freely, reach the entire paper without straining, and really see what they are doing.
2. Roll up sleeves and take coats or sweaters off. Even liberal mothers may balk at a child coated with fingerpaint from head to toe. Put on aprons.
3. Allow each child to do as many paintings as he wishes, and let him return for as many as he desires.
4. Fingerpaint is usually mixed right on the paper as the child works. Pour about 3 or 4 tablespoons of liquid starch on the paper. Shake powdered paint onto the starch. Ask children to tell you which colors they want, but don't let them shake it themselves; they often waste it.
5. Offer one, two, or three colors of tempera placed on different paper areas so that the children can combine them. Unless you have some special purpose in mind, pick colors that combine to make an attractive additional color.
6. Hang up finished paintings. Offer the child a chance to make another one.
7. Show children how to rub their hands with the sponges in the bucket *before* they remove

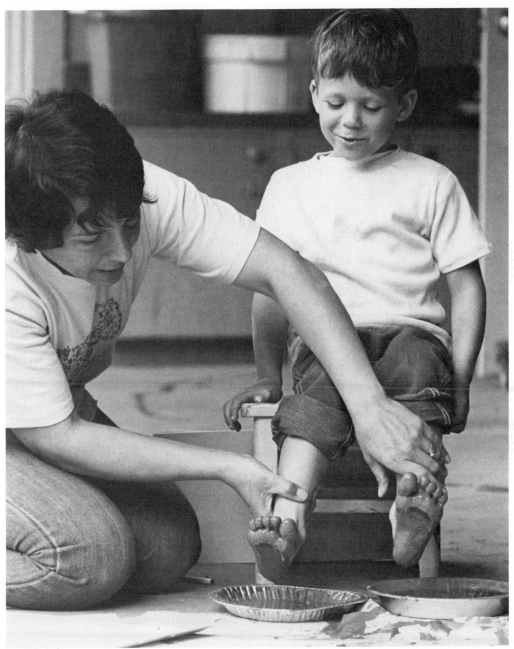

Photo by Mark Lohman, The Oaks Parent/Child Workshop

their aprons. (Many children will spend additional time squeezing the colored soapy bucket water through the sponge—another fine sensory experience.)

8. If the day is windy or the room drafty, sponging the table lightly with water before putting the paper down will keep it from blowing away.

C. Cleanup

1. Invite some children to help clean up. (The use of soapy water and sponges will attract helpers.) Wash off table, aprons, and so forth. Be sure to wash the edges of tables.

2. Return all supplies to correct storage places.

3. Roll up dried paintings and place in ·cubbies.

Suggested variations. Children may paint directly on the table, using a whipped soap flake mixture, either white or tinted with food coloring. (For some reason, Lux flakes, not granulated Lux, work best. Ivory Snow is also successful. Remember, the children will enjoy helping beat this up. Adding some vinegar to the wash water will make cleanup easier.) They may also fingerpaint directly on the table and take prints of their painting by pressing a piece of newsprint down on it. These prints are often stunning. Painting can be done on textured papers, or different recipes can be used for variation in texture. Using cooked cornstarch in place of the liquid variety is always interesting because different thicknesses can be concocted, and it is also more economical.

CORN STARCH FINGERPAINT

Dissolve ½ cup cornstarch in 1 cup of cold water and pour mixture into 3 cups boiling water; stir constantly until shiny and translucent. Allow to cool and use as fingerpaint base, or ladle into jars and stir in tempera or food coloring.

If a thicker mixture is desired, be sure to add glycerine to reduce stickiness. Adding a little glycerine or talcum powder makes painting particularly slick. Scents such as oil of cloves may be used to add fragrance. Starch bases can be refrigerated and then offered as a contrast to warmed starch—perhaps one kind for each hand.

Collage and assemblage

Collage is particularly useful because it fosters an appreciation of the way different materials look when arranged together, thereby emphasizing the elements of design and composition. If offered as recommended below, it also provides opportunities for deliberating over selections and making choices and provides many exposures to a wide variety of materials, which may range from cotton balls to shells and wood shavings. Also included might be bright bits of ribbon and yarn, coarse netting, sponge, tin foil, corks, and packing materials. Collage or assemblage lends itself nicely to carrying out nursery school themes or other matters of interest to the children. Using natural materials in this kind of work adds potential beauty and interest to the activity. For example, shells, seaweed, and sand are nice to use as collage ingredients after a trip to the beach. The teacher should remember that the intent is not to have the child make a picture of where he has been or copy what the teacher has made; the intent is to encourage the appreciation of contrast in texture and color and to foster pleasure in creating a design based on these differences.

A. Preparation

1. Plan what materials to use, both background mats and collage substances. Remember that anything may be used as a base; it should not be paper plates, which are generally too small to be satisfactory. Cardboard, construction paper, or large pieces of bark are ideal. Select materials for contrast, variety, and beauty. Choose ones that will be esthetically pleasing when used together.

2. Plan to use *two* tables for collage: a work table covered with newspaper and a "choosing table" from which the children will make their selections. If you set the materials out on colored paper or in attractive containers, they will be more appealing and also easier to keep sorted and neat.

3. If the collage items are heavy, use undiluted

white glue, such as Elmer's, which may be purchased by the gallon for economy. If light items, such as feathers, fabrics, or paper, are used, dilute the glue with starch or water.

4. Offer scissors or clippers to encourage children to modify the shape of materials to suit themselves.

5. Assemble aprons, glue brushes, white glue and containers, felt tip pens, aprons, and collage materials.

B. Procedure

1. Give each child an apron. Roll up sleeves.

2. Encourage the child to take a collage tray and go to the choosing table. Gradually teach children to think about their choices: would that be interesting to use? How would this feel? What would go well with what?

3. On returning to the work table, give each child a brush and glue container (with very little glue in it at a time; children need to learn that glue is not paint), or allow the child to dip each item lightly in a saucer of glue.

4. Collage takes patience and perseverance. Many younger children will spend only a little time at it, but most older children will spend 15 to 20 minutes or longer if deeply interested.

5. Unless monitored carefully, it is easy for the choosing table to become an unsorted mess of rumpled materials. Keep it neat and good looking in order to facilitate judging and selection by the children.

6. Collages have to dry flat. Glue takes a long time to dry, so select a drying place that will be out of the way.

C. Cleanup

1. Children may help wash glue brushes; warm water will make this easier.

2. Return undiluted glue to the bottle and diluted glue to the thinned-glue container. Remember to wipe off the neck of the bottle!

3. Wipe off furniture that has glue on it.

4. Put dried collages in cubbies.

Suggested variations. Almost anything can be used as collage material, and it is pitiful to limit it to cutouts from magazines. This is one area where the good scrounger is in her element. Carpet scraps, pumpkin seeds, buttons, fur, and textured papers are all attractive ingredients. The experience can be varied by using different mats and bases: large pieces of old bark, heavy cardboard, or pieces of wood too hard to saw make interesting foundations. Food coloring can be used to tint the glue, or tempera can be added if a stronger, brighter-colored glue base is desired. The variety can be endless and the satisfaction great!

Dough and clay

Dough and clay are alike because they both offer opportunities to be creative while using a three-dimensional medium. They also provide particularly satisfying opportunities to release aggression harmlessly by hitting, punching, and squeezing. In addition, these materials allow the child to enjoy smearing and general messiness, activities that many psychologists value because they feel it provides a sublimated substitute for handling feces. (Whether or not the reader agrees with this theory or is repelled by it, she will certainly find, if she listens, that children often do talk with relish of ''pooh pooh'' while they work with this kind of material.) For all these reasons, *dough and clay should usually be presented without cookie cutters, rolling pins, or other clutter,* since these accessories detract from the more desirable virtues of thumping and whacking as well as from making original creations.

Besides these general benefits, mixing play dough helps the child learn about the transformation of materials and changes in texture. It also provides opportunities to learn facts about measuring and blending.

A. Preparation

1. Cover tables with oil cloth for quick cleanup later on. Keeping a special piece of oil cloth just for clay saves work, since it can be dried, shaken off, and put away for another day without wiping. Masonite boards or plastic-topped boards can also be used very handily.

2. Assemble materials: clay or dough, aprons,

Photo by Sheri Calhoun, Peninsula Montessori School

oil cloth, clean-up buckets, and towels. (Do not allow children to wash their hands in the sink; this is the quickest way to clog the plumbing.) If mixing dough, assemble ingredients and equipment according to the requirements of the recipe. Offer small pans of water for moistening hands only if children are using clay.

B. Procedure
  1. Put on aprons, and help children roll up sleeves.
  2. Give each child a *large* lump of clay or dough. It is important to offer plenty.
  3. Use the materials to foster children's imagination and creativity: clay and dough often generate a lot of playful talk among the children. Avoid making models, such as ashtrays, for them to copy. Emphasize squeezing, rolling, and patting.
  4. Supervise the children's hand washing before removing their aprons.
  5. Clay and dough products are usually not saved but are just returned to the storage container.
  6. Mixing play dough
     a. Always plan this event so the children can participate in making the dough, because this is an additional valuable learning experience and great fun.
     b. Talk about the procedure while it is going on. Ask them, ''What's happening? What do you see? How does it taste? How has it changed? How does it feel?''
     c. When mixing dough, make at least two batches at once in two separate dishpans. This avoids overcrowding and jostling among the children.

C. Cleanup
  1. Cleanup from these activities takes quite a while, so begin early enough that the children have time to help, too.
  2. Sponge off aprons and anything else that needs it.
  3. Replace leftover ingredients in containers. Clay goes in tightly sealed containers. Make

a depression in each large ball of clay with your thumb, and fill with water—this is an old potter's trick that will keep clay moist until used again. Dough should be stored in the refrigerator.
  4. Flush the buckets of water down the toilet to avoid clogging drains.

Suggested variations. Allow the dough or clay objects made by the children to harden, and then paint and shellac them, or dip painted clay objects in melted paraffin to give a ''finish.'' Occasionally use dough and clay with accessories such as dull knives for smoothing or cookie cutters and rolling pins. Offer chilled play dough as a contrast to the room temperature variety. Cookies and bread recipes are also dough experiences. Vary the dough experience by changing the recipe. The following are two of the best.

PLAY DOUGH

3 cups flour	6 tablespoons salad oil
¼ cup salt	Add water until right consistency is reached

Powdered tempera may be added in with the flour, or food coloring may be added to finished dough. This dough may be kept in the refrigerator in a plastic bag or covered container for approximately 2 weeks.

CLOUD DOUGH

6 cups flour	1 cup oil

Mix flour and some tempera together; then add oil. Add enough oil to make dough soft and pliable. This dough is very soft and elastic and is different from regular play dough. It can be used with ease by 2-year-olds as well as by 4- and 5-year-olds. Keep in a covered container or plastic bag in the refrigerator. *This dough is greasy and will spot floors and carpets, so it is best used outdoors or supervised very carefully inside.*

Woodworking

Woodworking is a challenging and satisfying experience that should be available to the children at least two or three times every week. It requires unceasing supervision from the teacher, not so much because of possible hammered fingers or minor cuts

Photo by Mark Lohman, The Oaks Parent/Child Workshop

from the saw, but because an occasional child may impulsively throw a hammer and injure someone. Although rare, this can happen in the twinkling of an eye, and the teacher must be alert so that she steps in before this occurs. *Never leave a carpentry table unsupervised.* The teacher can alleviate frustration by assisting children who are having difficulty getting the nail started or the groove made for the saw.

It is essential that the school purchase good-quality tools for the children to use. Tinny little hammers and toy saws are worthless. Adult tools, such as short plumber's saws, regular hammers (not tack hammers, because their heads are too small), and braces and bits can all be used satisfactorily by boys and girls. Two real vises that can be fastened securely at either end of the woodworking table are essential to hold wood while the children saw through it. A sturdy, indestructible table is a necessity.

One of woodworking's best qualities is the opportunity it offers for doing real work. Children can assist in fixing things while using tools or can make a variety of simple items that *they have thought up.* These often include airplanes, boats, or just pieces of wood hammered together.

I particularly like offering carpentry because it is so easy to increase the challenge and difficulty of the experience as the year moves along. Children can begin with simple hammering, go on to using the saw, and finally enjoy the brace and bit. During the year they can learn many kinds of tool-related skills, and they can learn how to select the right tool for the right job. Carpentry is also an excellent way to develop eye-hand coordination. (But beware of the canny youngster who says, "Now, you hold the nail while I hit it.")

Finally, woodworking is a splendid way to harness intense energy and to sublimate anger. Hammering and sawing in particular are very effective relievers of feelings.

A. Preparation
   1. Check the wood supply in advance. You may need to visit a cabinet or frame shop or a con-struction site to ask for free scraps if your supply is low. Teach yourself to tell hard from soft woods. Plywood and hard woods are good for gluing but are usually too frustrating for children to use in woodworking.
   2. Decide whether to use any accessories, such as spools or bottle caps, for added interest.
   3. Assemble wood, tools, supplies, and a pencil for labeling products.
   4. Arrange tools and materials so that they are easy for children to reach. Make the arrangement attractive. Encourage children to select what they need and to replace what they don't use. Keep rearranging if the area becomes disorganized.
B. Procedure
   1. Decide how many children you will be able to supervise at one time. For safety's sake you will probably need to limit yourself to three or four children at once. Encourage each child to work on separate sides of the table to spread them out.
   2. Help children when necessary; teach them to treat tools with respect and to use them safely.
   3. Be alert to interaction between children. Self-control at this age is not highly developed; intervene swiftly when necessary.
   4. Be sure to encourage children who persevere in particularly difficult tasks, such as sawing through a large board or making a nail go all the way through two pieces of wood.
   5. Remember to label finished products.
C. Cleanup
   1. Replace tools and wood scraps in correct storage area.
   2. Put each child's work in his cubby.

Suggested variations. Allow the children to take the brace and bit and the vise to pieces to find out how they work. Have a number of various-sized bits available for making different-sized holes, and purchase dowels that will fit these holes. Furnish different accessories for variety: bottle caps and jar lids make nice wheels or decorations. String or roving cotton twisted among the nails is interesting. Unusual wood scraps that come from cabinet shops are nice. Wood gluing in place of nailing appeals to some youngsters and is a quicker form of wood construction. Many children enjoy going on to paint whatever they have made; this works well if done under another teacher's supervision at a separate table. Children will enjoy using a wide array of nails, ranging from flat, broad-headed roofing nails to tiny little finishing nails, which for some reason they often like to hammer in all around the edge of boards. Sandpaper is occasionally interesting, particularly if there are several grades of it available for comparison. An occasional child will also enjoy measuring and sawing to fit, although this activity is more typical of older children. Very young children will do best if soft plasterboard or even large pieces of Styrofoam packing are offered rather than wood.

Sewing

Sewing is not often offered in nursery school, and yet it is interesting to some children, boys as well as girls. Besides the obvious value of developing eye-hand coordination, it also offers good opportunities to experiment and to be creative. Occasionally it can be an opportunity for accomplishing meaningful work and can also provide a chance to experience the satisfaction of role playing a "motherly" activity.

A. Preparation
1. Choose a loosely woven fabric as the material for sewing. Thick or heavy fabric will be too difficult for the children to get the needle through.
2. Assemble the equipment: yarn or thick cotton string, fabric, large, dull embroidery needles, scissors, and embroidery hoops. Offer a choice of different colors of yarn and materials if possible. Make sure the scissors will really cut the fabric.
3. You might prethread some needles in advance. It helps to knot the thread onto the needle if it constantly slips out, providing the material is coarse enough, or to use double

threads knotted together at the ends to prevent them from pulling out of the needle.

B. Procedure
1. Choose a fairly small group of children to work with—four or five children at a time.
2. Be prepared for stuck fingers, some frustration, and a lot of requests for help, especially the first few times. Some children are disappointed with their technique, but don't end up sewing for them because they want it to look a certain way. Encourage them to do it their own way, and be pleased with their experiments.
3. Embroidery hoops help a lot, although children tend to sew over the edges of them. Rather than constantly criticizing this tendency, you can have them snip the yarn later for an interesting fringed effect. Children will also gradually learn to sew in and out rather than up and over as they become acquainted with the material, but it takes a while to acquire this concept.
4. Safety pin the child's name to his work.

C. Cleanup
1. Put the sewing materials away; never leave needles lying about.
2. Place finished work in cubbies.

Suggested variations. You may want to try sewing on Styrofoam meat trays or sewing through plastic vegetable baskets; these have the advantage of being stiff and light to hold. An occasional very adept 4- or 5-year-old will enjoy sewing top and side seams on simple doll clothes. Sometimes children enjoy sewing very large buttons to material. Children may enjoy appliqueing cutouts loosely to burlap to create wall decorations for home or school. An old variation to sewing, which is fun but not really creative, is the punched cardboard sewing cards, and laces enjoyed by youngsters since the turn of the century.

Dancing and creative movement

Dancing has great potential for self-expression because it stimulates the child's imagination and offers many opportunities for emotional release. Moving to music can involve the child's entire body and draw satisfying expressions of emotion and pleasure from him that other creative experiences cannot tap.

There seem to be two extremes in presenting dance experiences that are not creative. In one, the teacher conceives the dance entirely beforehand and then puts the children through the paces. This is, of course, simply providing a model for the children to copy. At the other extreme, the teacher puts on some music and sits passively by while she expects the children to generate the entire experience for themselves. Children usually require more stimulation than this from the teacher in order to get a dance experience going. Beginning teachers often feel self-conscious about participating, but dancing with the children is essential for success. Taking a couple of modern dance classes at college frequently helps students feel more at ease with this medium.

A. Preparation

1. Reread the student's analysis and recommendations about her dance experience, which are given in Chapter 2, and the suggestions for relaxation and movement exploration in Chapter 4.

2. Decide what kind of music to use, and familiarize yourself with its possibilities.

   a. It is ideal to have available a pianist who can improvise as the teacher and children request, but this is not essential. Records or percussion instruments are also satisfactory.

   b. Familiarize yourself fully with records that are available. Choose two or three that offer a good range of rhythms and emotional expression.

   c. Don't overlook the possibilities offered by popular music. It has the virtues of being familiar and rhythmic, and it offers a wide variety of emotional moods as well.

3. Clear the largest room available of chairs, tables, and so forth.

4. Arrange to avoid interruptions. It is fatal to the experience for the teacher to answer the phone or to stop and settle a fight on the playground.

B. Procedure

1. Avoid having other activities going on in the room at the same time, although some children will need to putter around the edges, watching before they join in. Accomplished teachers often feel comfortable having children drift in and out of the group, but beginners may find that a more secluded atmosphere where children may leave as they desire but where newcomers may not intrude is helpful. Don't try to have all the children in school participate at once.

2. *The most important skill to develop in dance is the ability to be sensitive to individual responses and ideas as the children generate them and to encourage these as they come along.*

3. It is necessary for the teacher to move freely along with the children. Sometimes it helps to ask other adults to stay away while you are leading a dance activity to avoid self-consciousness. Sometimes a teacher feels more secure with two adults present.

4. It is good to have in mind a general plan that contains some ideas about ways to begin and also things to try that will vary the activity. Always have more activities in mind than you could possibly use. It's better to be safe than sorry, but remember to use the children's suggestions whenever possible. It is essential to offer relaxing experiences and to alternate vigorous with more quiet ones to avoid overstimulation and chaos. Children enjoy showing all the ways they can think of to be kittens or the ways they can get across the floor on their tummies, or, as they become more practiced and at ease, ways of moving as the music makes them feel.

C. Cleanup

1. Warn the children, as the end nears, that the time is drawing to a close.

2. At the end, involve the group in some kind of quiet response to the music so that they have themselves under reasonable control as they leave the room.
3. Help them put on their shoes and socks if these have been taken off.
4. Return the room to its usual order.

Suggested variations. Accessories add a great deal to dancing and are helpful materials to use to get dance started. Scarves, long streamers, and balloons help focus the child's awareness away from himself and so reduce his self-consciousness at the beginning. Ethnic dance materials offer a rich resource for dance and creative movement. Folk dance records and other rhythmic songs and melodies are delightful resources to draw on. Using percussion instruments can also vary the experience. Dancing outdoors often attracts children who shun this activity in a more enclosed setting. Remember to include dance activities that appeal to boys as well as to girls. Moving like submarines, airplanes, seals, or bears helps take the stigma out of dance for boys, who may have already decided dancing is "sissy."

Using rhythm instruments

There are other ways to respond to music besides dancing, and participating with rhythm instruments is one of them. This activity is both somewhat creative and somewhat an exercise in conformity,

Los Niños Head Start

since children may respond imaginatively and individually with their instruments while doing something together at the same time. Basically, participating in a musical experience will introduce children to the pleasures and delights of sound, rhythms, and melodies. If well handled, it should also teach children to care for instruments as objects of beauty and value and should help them learn to listen to music and respond in a discriminating way.

A. Preparation
  1. Familiarize yourself with the music you will present. Listen to the records or practice on the instrument you intend to use yourself.
  2. Select the instruments for the children to use.
  3. Plan to start with a small group of children and a small number of instruments at first. You can always add more things later when you know how many children you can comfortably supervise.

B. Procedure
  1. Instruments are not toys and to prevent abuse must be supervised when used. It will help if you plan in advance details such as where the children will put them when they are finished and how they will get another instrument. Decide on a reasonable procedure that will allow you to relax and not worry about the possibility of a child stepping through a tambourine that was left on the floor.
  2. Insist on these few basic guidelines: Drums and tambourines are to be hit with the hand only. (Drum heads do not stand up under steady pounding from sticks. Hit the rhythm sticks together if stick hitting is desired.) Allow one maraca to a child. Maracas crack easily when hit together.
  3. Be prepared to get right into the music with the children and become involved. Your enthusiasm will communicate itself and make the experience special.

C. Cleanup
  1. Warn ahead.
  2. Put records back, and return instruments to their area, arranging them so they look attractive and orderly.

Suggested variations. Improvisations with musical instruments are a delight. Children can be encouraged to use them as the music makes them feel —to play soft or loud, fast or slow, together, or a few at a time. They can also make some simple instruments of their own, such as sand blocks and shakers (Hunter and Judson, 1977). Moving to music while using instruments (typically, marching) can also be a satisfying way of integrating this experience into a larger activity.

SUMMARY

Nursery school teachers have always valued the creative part of the child's self and have sought to enhance its development by fostering the use of self-expressive materials. Today we also seek to foster creativity in additional ways, which include generating creative play and encouraging originality of thought. In order to accomplish these goals, there are three teaching skills the teacher should cultivate in herself. When presenting self-expressive materials, she must cultivate her ability to stand back and let the child explore and utilize them as his impulses and feelings require. When seeking to facilitate play, she must learn to move with the children's imaginative ideas and support them. When working to develop originality in thought, she must be able to recognize the value of the children's ideas and to ask questions that will encourage further development of ideas.

Creativity is particularly valuable because it increases the child's feelings of self-esteem, facilitates self-expression and the expression of emotion, provides a vital balance for the cognitive part of the program, and helps the nursery school teacher individualize her curriculum.

The teacher can foster creativity by understanding and accepting the creative child and by maintaining in her group an environment that helps children feel secure. When presenting self-expressive materials for the children's use, she should avoid making models for them to copy, emphasize the process rather than the product, allow plenty of time and opportunity for the child to use the material, learn to make enhancing comments, and give reluctant children the right to refuse to participate. But the most important thing for her to do is to make the materials freely available and to stand back and let the child explore them as his impulses dictate.

QUESTIONS

1. If copying a model is really inhibiting to the development of creative self-expression, why do you think so many teachers persist in having children copy projects "just the way the teacher made it"?
2. Do you think of yourself as being artistic, or are you the sort of person who "can't even hold a paint brush right side up"? What attitudes in your previous teachers do you feel contributed to your feelings of confidence or lack of confidence in this area?
3. *Problem:* Chester, who is 3 years old, is still new at school and has been watching the fingerpainting with considerable interest. At last he engages himself in this activity, only to discover to his horror that the purple paint has soaked right through his cotton smock onto his tee shirt. He is very concerned about this, particularly when the teacher is unable to wash all the paint out of the shirt, and his mother is genuinely angry when she picks him up that afternoon. How would you cope with this situation?
4. *Problem:* Irene is painting at the easel and gradually begins to spread paint off the paper onto the easel itself, then to paint her hands and arms up to the elbows, and then to flick drops of paint onto a neighboring child and his painting. Should the teacher intervene and control any or all of this behavior, or should it be allowed to continue?
5. The variations of self-expressive activities listed at the end of the chapter represent only a few of numerous possibilities. What other activities have people in the class witnessed that could be added to these lists?

REFERENCES FOR FURTHER READING

General Subject of Creativity

Brittain, W. L. *Creativity, art and the young child.* New York: Macmillan Publishing Co., Inc., 1979. This *excellent* book discusses some recent research findings on the creative use of art materials by preschool children and then makes recommendations based on these findings for presenting such creative materials in the nursery school classroom. It is profusely illustrated and well written; highly recommended.

Kellogg, R. *Analyzing children's art.* Palo Alto, Calif.: National Press Books, 1969. The author stresses the universality of certain themes in children's art, sets forth a developmental theory, and provides hundreds of examples of how children use art to express themselves.

Maynard, F. *Guiding your child to a more creative life.* Garden City, N.Y.: Doubleday & Co., Inc., 1973. This is an excellent book suitable for parents and teachers. It contains good discussions of play, creativity, and the use of self-expressive materials. It also contains lists of children's books and records tastefully selected.

Robertson, S. M. *Rosegarden and Labyrinth: A study in art education.* London: Routledge and Kegan Paul, Ltd., 1963. This book has everything and nothing to do with the subject of making creative experiences available to young children since it only discusses working with older ones. Still, it conveys the author's own excitement and thrill of discovery as she taught "art" in such an inspiring way that all teachers can derive great benefit from reading it.

Torrance, E. P. *Creativity.* Belmont, Calif.: Fearon Publishers, 1969. Almost all books that deal with the general subject of creativity ignore the preschool level. This small volume by Torrance deserves special mention, not only because Dr. Torrance is a primary researcher in the field but also because it is based on research and theory as they relate to early childhood. Torrance first reviews what research exists and then lists suggestions about how teachers and parents may foster creativity in very young children.

Presentation of Expressive Materials

Bos, B. *Please don't move the muffin tins: A hands-off guide to art for the young child.* Carmichael, Calif.: the burton gallery, 1978. Nicely illustrated, *Don't Move the Muffin Tins* has many practical suggestions, including a discussion of "traps" or pitfalls, on the presentation of basic expressive materials. It draws a nice distinction between "crafts" and "art."

Cherry, C. *Creative art for the developing child: A teacher's handbook for early childhood education.* Belmont, Calif.: Fearon Publishers, 1972. Another very practical book filled with suggestions for presenting *appropriate,* self-expressive activities to preschool children.

Graham, A. *Foxtails, ferns and fish scales: A handbook of art and nature projects.* New York: Four Winds Press, 1976. "Foxtails" is a good resource of how-to crafts for a teacher who wishes to emphasize natural materials—it makes a good resource of ideas for Christmas presents and so forth; crafty rather than self-expressive in tone.

Pitcher, E. G., Lasher, M. G., Feinburg, S. G., and Braun, L. A. *Helping young children learn* (3rd ed.). Columbus, Ohio: Charles E. Merrill Publishing Co., 1979. The authors cover the majority of creative experiences and deal with other aspects of curriculum as well. This is primarily a how-to book that is filled with practical, factual information and curriculum ideas based on brief discussions of theory. It has a good bibliography at the end of each chapter and an excellent list of children's books.

Fingerpainting

Stangl, M. J. *Finger painting is fun.* Camarillo, Calif.: Educational Techniques, Inc., 1975. This short book is of particular value because it presents this subject in detail and includes many suggestions for variations.

Woodworking

Moffitt, M. W. *Woodworking for children.* New York: Early Childhood Education Council of New York, no date. There is straight talk here for teachers who may not know much about woodworking. Moffitt actually explains how to use various tools and what to do about such problems as bent nails and splitting wood. The booklet is intensely practical and should be owned and used by every teacher.

Music and Dance

Buttolph, E. G. *Music without the piano*. New York: Early Childhood Education Council of New York, 1968. This short pamphlet is filled with suggestions about how to present music using simple instruments and the children's ideas.

Cherry, C. *Creative movement for the developing child: A nursery school handbook for non-musicians* (Rev. ed.). Belmont, Calif.: Fearon Publishers, 1971. Clare Cherry bases her approach to dance on creative movement. The material is simply presented, and all the suggested activities can be accompanied by familiar tunes and improvised words, which are included in the text.

Dimondstein, G. *Children dance in the classroom*. New York: Macmillan Publishing Co. Inc., 1971. For readers who wish a satisfying, full treatment of the subject, *Children Dance* is an excellent book. It not only has resource lists of records and suggested reading, but also contains good, solid discussions complete with suggestions for presentation; highly recommended.

Fleming, G. A. (Ed.). *Children's dance*. Washington D.C.: American Alliance for Health, Physical Education, and Recreation, 1973. This is a rich, useful resource; highly recommended.

Hunter, I. I., and Judson, M. *Simple folk instruments to make and play*. New York: Simon & Schuster, Inc., 1977. *Simple Folk Instruments* is a useful, carefully illustrated book that contains a great many possible ethnic instruments that would be fairly easy for teachers to make for the children to use during music and dance experiences.

Stecher, M. B., and McElheny, H. *Joy and learning through music and movement improvisation*. New York: Threshold Division, Macmillan Publishing Co., Inc., 1972. This book really concentrates on nursery school age children and their movement needs. It is a sensible book that talks about the use of instruments and singing as well as dancing.

For the Advanced Student

Arasteh, A. R., and Arasteh, J. D. *Creativity in human development: An interpretive and annotated bibliography*. New York: Schenkman Publishing Co., 1976. Research in the field of creativity, at least as far as young children are concerned, seems to be in the doldrums. Arasteh presents a comprehensive review of what has been done to study creativity and related processes in the young child in Chapter 1 of this book.

Arieti, S. *Creativity: The magic synthesis*. New York: Basic Books, Inc., Publishers, 1976.

May, R. *The courage to create*. New York: W. W. Norton & Co., Inc., 1975. Both written by psychiatrists, the Arieti and May books will be of interest to students who wish to consider the psychological philosophy that lies behind the generation of creativity.

Torrance, E. P. *Guiding creative talent*. Englewood Cliffs, N.J.: Prentice-Hall, Inc., 1962. Dr. Torrance has written many helpful books, but this is one of the best for early childhood teachers because it contains a chapter on development and another on maintaining creativity. In addition, it has a good chapter on sustaining relationships with people who have creative talent.

Los Niños Head Start

13 □ Fostering creativity in play

If life's problems are solved satisfactorily during the years when imagination predominates, then a residue of imaginative activity and a resource of initiative remain, to enliven, sparkle, inspire, and push throughout the rest of life. Such a person will get fresh ideas and will not be afraid to experiment with them. Even though he has attained objectivity, his thinking and feeling will be so flexible that he will be able to take off on flights of his imagination. Both creativity and true recreation have their roots in imaginative play.*

Play is the way a child learns what no one can teach him.†

In recent years considerable material has been written on a theoretical level about the value or purpose of play (Almy, 1968; Bruner, Jolly, and Sylva, 1976; Herron and Sutton-Smith, 1971). Despite the fact that the purposes ascribed to it appear to vary in accordance with the background of the person proposing the theory, we should rejoice that interest is once again increasing in this important subject. It is evident to most people who work with young children that play is serious business to them and that the opportunity to play freely is vital to their healthy development (Butler, Gotts, and Quisenberry, 1978; Curry and Arnaud, 1971; Frank, 1968); yet in the past few years, when the emphasis in early childhood has tended to be on developing more structured ways of fostering intellectual gains (Becker, 1977; Bereiter and Englemann, 1966), the value of play has often been understressed or overlooked. Now, although there is much disagreement about defining basic purposes, at least the subject is once again attracting interest—a step that is definitely in the right direction.

It is difficult to say why some educators have undervalued play from time to time. Perhaps it goes back to our Puritan ethic, which is suspicious of pleasure and self-enjoyment. Unfortunately, as people advance through our educational system, they seem to conclude that any activity that generates delight cannot result in real learning—in order to learn, one must suffer. But play is a pleasureful, absorbing activity indulged in for its own sake. The live-for-the-moment aspect of it, combined with the fact that play arises spontaneously from within the child and is not teacher determined, lends an air of frivolity to it that may lead work-oriented persons to assume it is not worthwhile. In addition, this uniqueness and spontaneity have made it difficult to categorize and examine in a scientific way. It is only in recent years that work by such people as Sutton-Smith (1967) and Smilansky (1968) has demonstrated the feasibility of more precise investigation of play.

PURPOSES OF PLAY

A variety of reasons why play is valuable for young children are given here because nursery school teachers must be prepared to defend and ex-

---

*From Smart, M. S., and Smart, R. C. *Child development and relationships* (2nd ed.). New York: copyright © 1972, Macmillan Publishing Co., Inc. P. 281.
†Hartley, R. E. Play, the essential ingredient. *Childhood Education*, November, 1971, as quoted in P. M. Markun. *Play: children's business: And a guide to play materials*, Washington, D.C.: Association for Childhood Education International, 1974.

plain the worthwhile character of this activity to people who still attack it as being a trivial waste of time, which they contend would be better spent "really learning something."

Play fosters physical development

Play fulfills a wide variety of purposes in the life of the child (Bruner, Jolly, and Sylva, 1976; Hartley, Frank, and Goldenson, 1952). On a very simple level, it promotes the development of sensorimotor skills. Children spend hours perfecting such abilities and increasing the level of difficulty to make the task ever more challenging. Anyone who has lived with a 1-year-old will recall the tireless persistence with which he pursues the acquisition of basic physical skills. In older children we often think of this repetitive physical activity as the central aspect of play, since it is evident on playgrounds where we see children swinging, climbing, or playing ball with fervor; but actually physical motor development represents only one purpose that play fulfills.

Play fosters intellectual development

Piaget (1962) maintains that imaginative play is one of the purest forms of symbolic thought available to the young child, and its use permits the child to assimilate reality in terms of his own interests and prior knowledge of the world. Thus it is evident that imaginative, symbolic play contributes strongly to the child's intellectual development. Indeed, some investigators maintain that symbolic play is a necessary precursor of the development of language (Edmonds, 1976; Greenfield, Smith, and Laufer, 1976).

Play also offers opportunities for the child to acquire information that lays the foundation for additional learning. For example, through manipulating blocks he learns the concept of equivalence (two small blocks equal one larger one), or through playing with water he acquires knowledge of volume, which leads ultimately to developing the concept of reversibility (Moffitt and Omwake, no date).

The work of Smilansky (1968) has offered additional support for the importance of play in rela-

tion to mental development. She points out that sociodramatic play develops the child's ability to abstract essential qualities of a social role and also to generalize role concepts to a greater degree.

Play enhances social development

In addition, there is a strong social component to certain kinds of play (Fein and Clarke-Stewart, 1973; Garvey, 1977; Krasner, 1975). Here again, the methodological analysis provided by Smilansky is helpful. She speaks of dramatic and sociodramatic play, differentiating between the two partially on the basis of the number of children involved in the activity. Dramatic play involves imitation and may be carried on alone, but the more advanced sociodramatic play entails verbal communication and interaction with two or more people, as well as imitative role playing, make-believe in regard to objects, actions, and situations, and persistence in the play over a period of time.

Sociodramatic play also helps the child learn to put himself in another's place (Bruner, 1975; El'Konin, 1969; Kohlberg, 1969), thereby fostering the growth of empathy and consideration of others. It helps him define social roles: he learns by experiment what it is like to be the baby or the mother or the doctor or nurse. And it provides countless opportunities for acquiring social skills: how to enter a group and be accepted by them, how to balance power and bargain with other children so that everyone gets satisfaction from the play, and how to work out the social give and take that is the key to successful group interaction.

Play contains rich emotional values

The emotional value of play has been better accepted and understood than the intellectual or social value, since therapists have long employed play as a medium for the expression and relief of feelings (Axline, 1969; Schaefer, 1976; Wolfgang, 1977). Children may be observed almost any place in the nursery school expressing their feelings about doctors by administering shots with relish or their jealousy of a new baby by walloping a doll, but play is not necessarily limited to the expression of negative feelings. The same doll that only a moment previously was being punished may next be seen being lulled and crooned to sleep in the rocking chair.

Eveline Omwake cites an additional emotional value of play (Moffitt and Omwake, no date). She points out that play offers "relief from the pressure to behave in unchildlike ways." In our society so much is expected of children, and the emphasis on arranged learning can be so intense that play becomes indispensable as a balance to pressures to conform to adult standards that may otherwise become intolerable.

Finally, play offers the child an opportunity to achieve mastery of his environment. When he plays, he is in command. He establishes the conditions of the experience by using his imagination, and he exercises his powers of choice and decision as the play progresses. The attendant opportunities for pretended and actual mastery foster the growth of ego strength in young children.

Play develops the creative aspect of the child's personality

Play, which arises from within, expresses the child's personal, unique response to the environment. It is inherently a self-expressive activity that draws richly on the child's powers of imagination. Since imaginative play is also likely to contain elements of novelty, the creative aspect of this activity is readily apparent. The freedom to experiment creatively with behavior in the low-risk situations typical of play is one of the virtues of it mentioned by Jerome Bruner (1974), who points out that play provides a situation where the consequences of one's actions are minimized and where there are many opportunities to try out combinations of behavior that under other circumstances could never be attempted. In addition, Sutton-Smith points out that play increases the child's repertoire of responses. Divergent thinking is characterized by the ability to produce more than one answer, and it is evident that play provides opportunities to develop alternative ways of reacting to similar situations (Sutton-Smith, 1971). For example, when the chil-

dren pretend that a fierce dog is breaking into their house, some may respond by screaming in mock terror, others by rushing to shut the door, and still others by attacking the "dog" or throwing water on him. The work of Lieberman (1968) provides added indications that playfulness and divergent thinking are related—though which comes first remains to be determined.

Another researcher interested in "pretend play" is Catherine Garvey. She points out various ways children signal to each other that they are embarking on "pretend" or have stopped pretending. These include *negation* ("Well, you're just Jon. You can't be a monster while we eat lunch"), *enactment of a role* (crying affectedly like a baby, for example), or *stating the role or transformation that is taking place* ("This is the operating table—lie down, baby, so I can cut you up!") (Garvey, 1977; Krasner, 1975).

In young children creative play is expressed primarily in two ways: through the unusual use of familiar materials and equipment (Chapter 12) and through role playing and imaginative play.

Conclusion

No matter what value the theoretician perceives in play, the fact remains that it is common to all cultures and that it is the lifeblood of childhood. Thus Russians may offer hollow blocks while reasoning that their size promotes cooperation, whereas Americans may offer them on the grounds that their cumbersome qualities develop feelings of mastery. But the children continue to use blocks with satisfaction regardless of adult rationalizations, just as they continue to play house on the windswept tundra of the North and in the Wendy corners of the British Infant School.

DEVELOPMENTAL STAGES OF PLAY

As is true in so many other areas, children's play progresses through a series of stages. The most frequently used theoretical model divides play into four of these. Although names used to describe them vary from author to author, there is general rough agreement about the ingredients of each stage.

According to researchers (Butler, Gotts, and Quisenberry, 1978; Rubin, 1977; Smilansky, 1968), play begins at the *functional* level (simple, repetitive sensorimotor activities such as playing with toes), moves on to *constructive* play (the creative use of play materials which may or may not contain a theme), develops next into *dramatic* play (including interactive, sociodramatic play involving more than one child), and finally proceeds to the stage of *games with rules.*

It is the two middle levels of play, *constructive* and *dramatic,* that are of most interest to nursery school teachers. According to Butler, Gotts, and Quisenberry, constructive play is most frequently seen in children aged 2 to 4 years. And it is characterized by children learning the uses of simple or manageable play materials and then employing them to satisfy their own purposes. For example, a child might learn how to string beads and then make a necklace for himself. Dramatic play increases in frequency as children mature, and the golden age of sociodramatic role playing develops between ages 4 and 7, although we see the beginnings of this play in much younger children. It is at this level that we see children assigning roles ranging from ''teacher'' to ''baby'' to ''dog biter'' to themselves and others around them.

Apparently, progression from one stage to the next depends not only on inherent developmental processes but may also be influenced by the kinds of experience the youngster has had or has lacked. Investigations by Smilansky (1968), Rubin (1977), and Feitelson and Ross (1973), for example, report that the play of children from economically disadvantaged families may not be as advanced as that of children of the same age who come from middle-income families. This information is not included for the purpose of denigrating such youngsters, but is intended to point out to the preschool teacher that children in Head Start Centers, for instance, may need special help in developing play skills in order to reach their true developmental potential. Some suggestions for accomplishing this are included later on in this chapter.

Implications for education

Early studies of play (Parten, 1932, 1933) encouraged the notion that children progressed from solitary through parallel play (play beside but not with another child) and then progressed to social play. While acknowledging that solitary play happens more frequently with younger children, more recent research (Rubin, 1977) also provides evidence that there are varying levels of sophistication in solitary play. That is, while some of that kind of play takes place at the sensorimotor level, some of it, as anyone can attest who has watched a 4-year-old playing alone with a doll house, utilizes a great deal of imaginative language, role assigning, and story telling at a more mature, dramatic play level. Therefore, the teacher should not assume that solitary play by older preschoolers is generally regressive and undesirable. It is particularly important to recognize the value of such individual playful preoccupation in day-care centers where children are almost relentlessly in contact with other people all day long. Children need the opportunities to think and develop their ideas through play by themselves as well as while in the company of other children. Of course, if solitary play continues too long or is the only kind of play indulged in by a 4-year-old, it should be cause for concern, but some of this less social play is to be expected and even encouraged for most children attending nursery school.

Although nursery school teachers are likely to see sensorimotor, constructive, and dramatic play, they will rarely come across the final stage, games with rules, because this kind of play is the prerogative of older children. The nursery school teacher should realize that organized games are developmentally inappropriate as well as uncreative for young children. Activities such as relay races, dodge ball, and ''Duck, Duck, Goose'' are loved by second and third graders but do not belong in nursery school.

While hoping to foster originality and imagination in young children's play, we must realize that not every idea generated by the children will be new no matter how supportive and encouraging the atmosphere of the school. Children's inspirations will be like flashes—touches here and there, embedded in a foundation of previously played activities. There will always be a lot of "old" mixed in with a little "new."

Finally, the teacher should be prepared for the somewhat chaotic quality of creative play, since it is impossible to organize inspiration before it happens. But this "chaos" can be very productive, and the teacher can maintain reasonable order by picking up unused materials and returning them to their place and by seeing that the play does not deteriorate into aimless running about.

FACTORS LIKELY TO FACILITATE CREATIVE PLAY

There are many things the teacher can do to encourage the creative aspects of play.

The teacher avoids dominating the play

As is true with self-expressive materials, the teacher does her best to avoid dominating the play experience but seeks instead to foster the child's ability to express himself in his own unique way. Such a teacher helps children base their play on their own inspirations because she is convinced they can be trusted to play productively without undue intervention and manipulation by her.

Some teachers are so eager to use play as a medium for teaching that they cannot resist overmanipulating it in order to provide a "good learning experience." For example, I recently visited a teacher who had taken the children to the fire station for a visit. The next day, overwhelmed by the temptation to use play as a teaching device, she set out all the hats, hoses, ladders, and pedal trucks she could muster, and, as the children walked in the door, she pounced on them, announcing, "Boys and girls, I have the most wonderful idea. Remember when we went to the fire station yesterday? Well, why don't we play that here today? Jon, you can be the chief. Now, who wants to hold the hose? . . ."

Children may learn a good deal about fire en-

gines this way, and if this is the real purpose, very well. However, the spontaneous, creative quality of the play will be greatly reduced by the teacher's using this approach. It is generally better to wait until the children express an interest and then ask them how you can help and what they need.

On the other hand, there are other circumstances where the teacher must assume a more direct, intervening role since, as mentioned earlier, some children come to nursery school with very poorly developed play skills. Smilansky (1968) and more recently, Butler, Gotts, and Quisenberry (1978) advocate deliberate intervention by the teacher in play situations with these unskilled youngsters in order to help them develop more adequate sociodramatic play.

This approach is well described in *Play as Development* when the authors advise that "you become an active participant in the play by making suggestions, comments, demonstrating activities or using other means relevant to the situation" (Butler, Gotts, and Quisenberry, 1978, p. 68). However, this can be very tricky advice to give a beginning teacher, since many beginners have great difficulty maintaining the subtle blend of authority and playfulness required to sustain this role. Instead, they either overmanage and overwhelm the children or reduce themselves to "being a pal"—approaches that are not at all what those authors had in mind. It is vital to remember that even when teaching children with special educational needs, *the purpose is not to dominate but to stimulate* play, and the teacher should make interventions accordingly—stepping in only when necessary and withdrawing whenever possible.

The teacher encourages divergence of ideas

As in creative thought, the teacher seeks to remain open to originality of ideas in the children's play and to do all she can to reinforce their production of imaginative ideas by giving them the satisfaction of trying the ideas out. For this reason, she does not overrestrict the children's use of equipment, and she allows them to use familiar equipment in original and unusual ways. She also keeps play materials accessible so they are instantly available when the children require them.

The teacher casts herself in the role of assistant to the child

Fostering creative play demands that the teacher add another skill to her repertoire: the ability to move with the child's play and support it as it develops. This does not mean that she plays with the children as their peer, any more than she sits on the sidelines being thankful that the children are busy and not in trouble. Rather, the teacher who is skilled in generating creative play senses what will enhance the play, and she thinks constantly of what she might offer to sustain or extend it should this become necessary. This kind of teacher casts herself in the role of supportive assistant to the child; she imagines herself inside his skin and sees the child's play from his point of view. This gives her an empathic understanding, which enables her to serve his play needs well. Sometimes she expresses this insight by as simple a thing as going to the shed and getting out a variety of ropes, chains, and hooks for a construction project. Sometimes it is evident on a more subtle level as she quietly decides to delay snack in order that the play may build to a satisfying climax.

Some of this empathic ability may go back to remembering what it was like to be a child oneself, and some of it may be related to opening oneself to sensing the child and taking time to "hear" him. It is a skill well worth cultivating because it makes possible the perception of the child's play in terms of what he intends. This enables the teacher to nurture the play by sensitively offering the right help at the right moment.

Putting the child in command of the play situation is not only valuable because it fosters his creative ability. It is also fundamentally worthwhile because it strengthens his feelings of mastery. When the teacher becomes his assistant and helper and defers to his judgment, the child is freed to determine what will happen next in his play. He exercises his ability to make choices and decisions. As mentioned previously, Erikson maintains that becoming autonomous and taking the initiative are fundamental tasks of early childhood. Creative play presents one of the best opportunities available for developing these strengths.

A rich background of actual life experience is fundamental to developing creative play

Children build on the foundation of real experience in their play. The more solid and rich the background of experience that children accumulate, the more various the play will become. Field trips, holidays, and experiences with many ethnic groups, as well as things brought into the school in the way of science experiments, books, and visitors, will increase the base of experience upon which they can build their play. There is no substitute for this background. In addition, play is thought to serve the function of clarifying and integrating such experiences (Piaget, 1962) as the child gains a greater understanding of reality through his recapitulation of it in make-believe.

Equipment plays an important role in facilitating play

The teacher should buy equipment that encourages the use of imagination. The kinds of equipment the teacher provides have a considerable influence on the play that results. The teacher should be wary of buying equipment that can be used only in specific ways, because it restricts the use of imagination. Boards, blocks, and ladders, for example, lend themselves to a hundred possibilities, but a plywood train tends to be used mostly as a plywood train. The teacher should ask herself, "How many ways could the children use this?" If she can think of three or four rather different possibilities, it is a good indication that the children will use their imaginations to think of many more.

However, there is also a place for more lifelike materials in imaginative play. Dolls, costumes, and little rubber animals generate a lot of very satisfactory "pretend" situations because they induce the child to play through experiences and ideas about

Photo by Sandy Drake, Santa Barbara City College Children's Center

life. But, although these projective materials have acknowledged value, the teacher should be wary of the tendency to purchase countless imitations of adult items. There is no need to furnish the doll corner down to the last toaster and fake banana. The children will conjure these up from their imaginations if they are allowed to do so.

The teacher should select a wide variety of basic kinds of equipment. There need to be good range and balance to the sorts of equipment that are selected, also. This means that careful attention must be paid to all areas of curriculum—both indoors and outdoors. For example, puzzles should be chosen not only with a varying number of pieces in mind, but also in terms of different kinds of puzzles—have they informative pictures in the frame behind the pieces?—or are they printed on both sides to make them more complicated?—or are they the three-dimensional kind? And outdoor, wheeled equipment should not be limited to only trikes and wagons. Instead, it should include scooters, an ''Irish Mail,'' and a wheelbarrow.

Although equipment does and should vary from school to school, it is also helpful to refer to basic lists from time to time. Two of the best may be found in *Selecting Educational Equipment and Materials for Home and School* (Cohen and Hadley, 1976) and in *Selecting Equipment for Head Start Classrooms* (Office of Economic Opportunity, no date). The Cohen and Hadley reference is particularly useful for new centers because their lists set priorities for purchases according to essential first-year items, suggest second- and third-year additions, and extend from infant through upper elementary levels.

The teacher should change equipment frequently. Changing accessories in the basic play areas such as the housekeeping area and the block corner will attract different children, keep life fresh and interesting for them, and encourage them to play creatively. Adding boys' clothes or an old razor (minus the blade, of course) or bringing the guinea pig for a visit might break the monotony in the housekeeping corner. Using trains, rubber animals, doll house furniture, or the cubical counting blocks could provide variety in the block area. Moving play equipment to a new location is another fine way to vary play and foster creativity. Boys, for example, are more likely to play house if the stove and refrigerator are out on the grass or if the house is made of hollow blocks for a change. Different locations attract different customers.

The teacher should store equipment in convenient, easy-to-reach places. Besides purchasing equipment that will stimulate imagination and changing it to keep the play fresh and interesting, the teacher must also arrange adequate storage for these materials. This is often the place nursery schools scrimp, but good storage will keep equipment available and save the teacher's sanity as well. Storage can actually make or break a play situation; so it is well worth the time, effort, and money involved to solve this problem adequately. Material should be conveniently arranged so that it can be reached easily, and, of course, it should be returned to the same place after use to expedite locating it the next time it is needed. Labeled shelves, racks, hooks, and storage closets that are large enough all help. In addition, storage should be located close at hand so the teacher may continue to provide supervision while she is getting something out that the children have requested.

Play areas should be attractive

The general appearance and presentation of the play areas will inspire (or discourage) children to play there. All areas should be set up at the beginning of the day in a fresh, appealing way. New touches should be added here and there to spark interest and avoid dull repetition.

Play is also better encouraged if materials are not allowed to degenerate into a shambles during playtime. No one wants to wade through a welter of costumes on the floor or build in a chaos of blocks dumped and abandoned in that corner. Attractiveness fosters attraction, and the teacher is the person who bears the primary responsibility for creating and maintaining appealing play areas.

A final thought

One last reminder: children need plenty of freedom, time, and materials if they are to become maximally involved in imaginative play. They need the freedom to move from one activity to another as their tastes dictate; they need uninterrupted time to build a play situation through to its satisfying completion; and they need enough materials to furnish a challenge and supply a feeling of sufficiency. Making these resources available is a good way to say to a child in tangible terms that there is enough of what he needs in the world and that he need not scheme and plot to get his fair share.

SPECIFIC ACTIVITIES TO ENCOURAGE CREATIVITY IN PLAY
Water play*

Water play is one of the freest, finest play opportunities we can offer children. Although inexperi-

---

*I am indebted to the staff and students at the Santa Barbara Community College Children's Center for their assistance in developing the outlines on the following pages.

enced teachers often dread it because they fear that the children may become too wild or overstimulated, the opposite of this behavior is usually the case. Water play is absorbing and soothing; children will stay with it a long time and come away refreshed and relaxed if it is well presented. It is also valuable because it offers children many opportunities to work through conflicts resulting from the demands of toilet training (there is no better present for a newly trained 2-year-old than a sprinkling can), it provides relief from pressures and tensions, and it stimulates social play. Sometimes children will play companionably with others while using water, although they remain isolated the rest of the day.

Activities such as pouring and measuring help develop eye-hand coordination. Children also acquire intellectual concepts having to do with estimating quantity (how much will the cup really hold?), with conservation (but it looks like more in the tall bot-

Los Niños Head Start

tle!), and with physical properties of water (what became of the water when we poured it on the hot sidewalk?). At the end of this chapter a particularly good pamphlet is included in the references, *Mud, Sand and Water,* which makes useful supplementary reading on this subject.

Water play should be offered several times a week to provide maximum satisfaction for the children. In winter, a large indoor bathroom with a drain in the floor is an invaluable asset. Water can be offered in deep dishpans or sinks, but is best offered in larger containers, such as galvanized laundry tubs, concrete-mixing tubs made of plastic, or even wading pools. At the Center we offer it at floor level when we can because this keeps the children's clothes drier.

A. Preparation
  1. Decide what kind of water play you want to offer and what kind of water you wish to use (soapy, colored, clear, hot or cold).
  2. Assemble additional equipment and accessories for play.
  3. Be sure to include oil cloth or plastic aprons, deep containers for the water, sponges, and towels.

B. Procedure
  1. Make any rules or guidelines clear to the children before they begin. Children cannot be allowed to run around in soaked shoes or clothes when it is cold. It is better to explain the temperature of the day and also the limits of the experience before someone impulsively gets drenched.
  2. The children will enjoy helping fill the tubs and setting out the equipment.
  3. Put on aprons and roll sleeves up as far as possible. *Remove shoes* and do what you can to minimize the problem of getting wet, but be prepared for the fact that considerable dampness is the inevitable accompaniment of water play.
  4. Expect some incidental splashing, but control deliberate splashing unless the weather is warm. You may give a splasher a second chance; but if he or she persists, then the

privilege of participating must be surrendered for a while.
  5. While the children are playing, talk about pouring, measuring, or whatever you have planned as the focus of the activity with the children.
  6. Listen carefully to the children's comments and ideas, and change and provide equipment accordingly.

C. Cleanup
  1. Children may help bail out water tubs or tip them over on the grass at the end of the play.
  2. If rags are at hand, many children like to help dry buckets and toys.
  3. Replace all equipment in proper storage areas.
  4. Wipe aprons and change wet clothes.

Suggested variations. Too many schools limit this kind of play to hand washing or dabbling in the sink. Although these activities are certainly better than not having water available at all, they stop far short of what children really require for this experience. Many variations can be employed for a change, although basic water play always remains a favorite. Running water from the hose is a fine thing to offer, though it is, of course, a warm weather activity. Water can be used in conjunction with the sandbox or mud pit with real pleasure—apartments and manicured suburban gardens deprive children of the opportunity to play with such concoctions.

In addition, water can be offered to use in sinking, floating, pouring, and quantifying experiments. Unbreakable bottles and containers, as well as various sizes of sieves and funnels, can be saved for this purpose. Ice is a fascinating variation to offer; or washing activities with dolls, doll clothes, nursery school furniture, cars, or tricycles can be presented. Scrubbing vegetables, watering the garden, and washing dishes should not be overlooked as additional variations, which have the added appeal of participating in meaningful work. Making a variety of pipes and joints available for assembling and using with water is fascinating to children and teaches them some valuable concepts about cause and effect. Adding sponges, soap, or a little color will also change the appeal of the water and create additional interest.

Mud and sand

Mud and sand have wonderful messy, unstructured qualities that make them among the most popular creative play materials in nursery school. They offer rich tactile sensory experiences and provide emotional relief as well: messing and slopping through water and sand or mud is relaxing and is thought by some psychologists to provide relief from the stringent toilet training demands of our society. These materials also facilitate a lot of social interaction. Older children play imaginatively and cooperatively with each other while digging tunnels, constructing roads, and carrying on "bake-offs"; but sand and mud are also very rewarding for younger children to use, and they often settle down to this activity in a particularly absorbed and satisfied way. In short, the chance to mix, stir, pour, measure, mold, and squish sand and mud are indispensible components of the nursery school curriculum.

Since this experience is often restricted at home, it is particularly important to offer it consistently at nursery school, where it can be planned in advance and where it is relatively easy to clean up. It is good planning to locate the sandbox as far from the nursery school door as possible, in the hope that some of the sand will shake off clothes on the way inside, and it is also sound to check pants cuffs when the play has been especially vigorous, to reduce the likelihood of dumping the whole sandbox on the carpet. The sandbox should have a wide border around it so that children may sit on it and stay warm and dry when the weather is chilly. A waterproof chest beside it will make storage of commonly used equipment easier; plastic laundry baskets also make good equipment containers because they allow the sand to fall through.

Mud is different from sand, and the nursery school should provide chances for the children to play in both these materials. A mud hole and the opportunity to dig deep pits and trudge around in mud is very interesting to children, so a place in the yard should be set aside for this purpose. (If the holes are very deep, it will be necessary to fence them off for safety's sake.) Children will dig astonishingly deep pits if given room, good tools, time and opportunity, and the satisfaction of doing this work is plain to see on their faces.

A. Preparation

1. Consider various possibilities for sand and mud play in terms of the weather and time available. If the day is warm, water is a valuable addition to this experience.

2. Make sure the sand is at least damp so that it holds its form well when patted and molded. It may be necessary to sprinkle it a little.

3. In hot weather, if the area is not shaded, set up paper beach umbrellas to provide cool oases for the play.

4. In cold weather, encourage the children to sit on the edge of the sandbox to keep knees and seats of pants warm and dry.

5. Have some sandbox accessories set out as the children arrive, but be alert to special requests and ideas from the children; it is excellent policy to change equipment according to their expressed needs.

B. Procedure

1. Stay nearby and keep a careful eye on what is happening. Children will occasionally throw sand and will need to be controlled from time to time. Shovel users need lots of space and must learn to be careful of other people's toes and noses.

2. Think of additional ideas you might suggest to continue the play if the children's interest lags.

3. If the day is warm and water is being used freely, have the children roll up their pants and take their shoes off.

4. Encourage children to keep the sand in the box and mud in the pit so it will be there for play next time.

5. If sturdy shovels are being used for digging, make sure there is plenty of space between children and that they have shoes on so that shovel edges will not cut their feet.

6. Foster the use of imagination and language

Photo by Elaine M. Ward

whenever possible by playfully chatting with the children about what they are doing.

C. Cleanup

1. Warn the children that it will soon be time to finish their play.
2. Solicit their help in gathering up the play equipment and putting it away.
3. If the day is warm, hose off the area to get rid of the sand and mud, or sweep up the extra sand and return it to the box.
4. Help the children brush each other off, and shake out cuffs of pants and sweaters.
5. Put away accessories that will not be used during the next play period.

Suggested variations. It's a shame to leave the same old buckets and shovels in the sandbox day after day when there are so many interesting variations that may be employed. All kinds of baking and cooking utensils make excellent substitutes and may be readily and cheaply acquired at rummage sales. Toy trucks and cars are nice to add, too, particularly if they are wood or very sturdy plastic, since metal ones rust and deteriorate alarmingly fast if used outside. Sturdy tools of various kinds are also good to use. (Remember that, when digging large holes, children need real shovels or clamming shovels—often sold in "surplus" or sporting goods stores—just as they need real hammers and saws at the woodworking table.)

Adding water to sand and mud is the best accessory of all. It can be offered in deep galvanized washtubs or buckets or as running water from hoses (having two hoses available at once will considerably reduce fighting and competition). Many children will enjoy having temporary low tables, constructed from sawhorses and planks, added to the sandbox. Such tables are particularly helpful to provide when the weather is cold and children shouldn't get chilled.

Substitutes for sand and water may be offered when the real thing is unavailable. Cornmeal is good for pouring and measuring, and may be presented in deep tubs or a sand table indoors, but the reader should realize that cornmeal makes floors slippery. Some schools also use rice or dried peas as a substitute.

Gardening is another useful variation of digging and working with mud. Since digging is the best, most involving part of gardening from the children's point of view, several weeks of this experience should be offered to the children before seeds are planted.

Creative dramatic play

Creative dramatic play such as dress-up and housekeeping is usually very social and imaginative in nature. It almost always involves more than one child at a time and contains a lot of role assigning and role assuming ("Now, you be the mother and I'll be . . ."). Three-year-olds tend to play a simple version of "house," but four-year-olds love to embellish the premises with dogs, milkmen, naughty boys, and interesting domestic catastrophes. All of these activities develop the use of language, since the children will discuss and describe among themselves what is happening ("Let's get the babies and pretend they've been in that mud again!"). Teachers should encourage this use of imaginative language whenever possible.

Costumes can enhance the play, but having unstructured materials available that may be used in many ways is even more desirable because it helps the children be inventive and use their imaginations. Thus a scarf may become a hat, an apron, a blanket, or even a child's wished-for long hair.

A. Preparation

1. Be attuned to the interests of the children. Has something happened in the life of the group that could be played through? Perhaps a child has had her tonsils out or the children went to see a car being lubricated. Have a few props available that may enhance this play if it develops.
2. Think back to yesterday's play: could it be drawn over and continued with satisfaction today? Is there a little something extra that might be added to sustain interest?
3. Arrange materials attractively. If costumes

Los Niños Head Start

are offered, hang them neatly in view, or set out play accessories in an appealing way. Make sure the clothing is clean and not torn and that buttons and fastenings are in place.

4. Hold one or two possibilities in reserve to offer in case play begins to lag (perhaps an old piece of rope to hitch the wagon to the trike in case the boys decide to lubricate a trailer truck).

B. Procedure

1. Sit quietly nearby, or, while working in the general area, keep an eye on the role-playing activity.

2. Stay alert; step in with a facilitating suggestion before the play deteriorates into a hassle, but be prepared for the children to refuse your idea if they wish.

3. The teacher's role is facilitation of the play, but not participation as a peer. However, sometimes it is necessary to be more involved at first and then withdraw gradually.

4. Be sensitive to the children's needs as they materialize. It is better to supply helpful equipment on the spot as requested rather than tell the children you will "get it tomorrow; it's put away now."

5. Remember that too obvious an interest in the play or amused comments to other adults will make the children ill at ease and self-conscious, thereby destroying some of their pleasure in the activity.

6. Tidy up unobtrusively whenever possible in order to keep the area attractive. (This advice should not be construed as advocating compulsive neatness but is intended to encourage the teacher to pick constumes up off the floor and return unused, scattered equipment to the appropriate play area.)

C. Cleanup

1. Warn the children in advance that it is almost time for the play to draw to a close.

2. Encourage them to restore order and to take satisfaction in arranging the materials for the next time. This is also a good time to chat with them about what they did and what fun they had.

3. Remove any torn, soiled, or broken materials for repair, or discard them.

4. Put away accessories you do not intend to use during the next play period.

Suggested variations. Some teachers enjoy assembling play kits for the children. This is all right as long as the teacher resists the tendency to supply every little thing or to offer such specific equipment that there is no room left for developing a creative use for a familiar material. It is essential to vary dress-up clothes and housekeeping accessories regularly. Using different hats and costumes, different pans, empty food packages or a milk bottle holder and bottles can kindle new interest. Dress-up clothes for both sexes should be provided. Hats, vests, and old firemen's jackets and boots will find favor with boys, but both sexes should be encouraged to try all kinds of garments. Ethnic costumes are a nice variation, too, and often enhance the image of the child who lends them, but be sure these are not valuable, treasured mementoes. Doctor play is always popular, partly because it represents thinly veiled concerns about sexual differences and partly because it offers invaluable chances for children to play out their fear of doctors, shots, and being hurt. The teacher should be available for interpretation and control when such play takes place.

Blocks

Blocks are one of the timeless, classic play materials that have withstood the many comings and goings of ideologies and theories of early childhood education ranging from Froebel's "gifts" to the big hollow blocks designed by Patty Hill. No matter what theory of learning is espoused by which educator, children have continued to play with blocks with concentrated devotion.

Infants begin to stack objects (a very primitive block-building skill) almost as soon as they are able to sit up, and children continue to use blocks with satisfaction throughout elementary school years if given this opportunity. Blocks provide endless op-

Photo by Sandy Drake, Santa Barbara City College Children's Center

portunities for the development of emerging perceptual-motor skills. Stacking, reaching, grasping, lifting, shoving, carrying, and balancing are only a few of the countless motor skills practiced in block play.

Possibilities for emotional satisfactions abound as well. What teacher has not seen a shy child build himself a corral and seek safety within it, or a pent-up child send blocks toppling down, or two little girls construct block houses and establish families firmly within their confines?

Blocks lend themselves readily to achieving large effects quickly, thereby building ego-expanding structures of considerable height and large dimensions, which help the child feel strong and masterful, as well as providing opportunities for him to be creative.

Blocks are also strong in their contribution to learning the intellectual operations basic to Piagetian theory. They offer many opportunities for the child to grasp the principle that operations are reversible (when a tower falls, it returns to a prior form). They may be used to demonstrate conservation (four blocks can be piled into a variety of shapes and yet retain their quality of "fourness"), and they provide additional opportunities to demonstrate the principle of transitivity (four short blocks equal two longer ones, which in turn equal one very long one).

Finally, blocks foster the development of creative play. By nature, they are unstructured and may be used to build anything that suits the child's fancy. Older children enjoy planning such structures in advance, but younger ones will content themselves with the experience of stacking and balancing for its own sake and perhaps assign a useful function to the construction at a later point in the building.

A. Preparation
   1. Make sure the blocks are well sorted and neatly arranged.
   2. Try to include accessories that are related to current curriculum interests; for example, it may stimulate play to offer some boats after a visit to the harbor.
   3. Recall what the children were interested in the previous day when they played with blocks, and be sure to have these materials

(and a possible embellishment) readily available should they be called for again.
   4. Be sensitive to the expressed interests and requests of the children as they draw near the blocks; *the best accessory is the one they request.*
   5. Children may be attracted if the teacher builds some small, interesting structure to begin with (the old principle of the nest egg under the chicken); but this creation should be offered as a stimulus, not as a model intended for emulation.
   6. Avoid setting out every accessory the school owns. This usually results in a clutter, which ultimately discourages participation.
   7. Outdoors, a good supply of large hollow blocks should be set out to begin with. Children should be encouraged to get out the rest as needed. There is no point in owning a beautiful supply of outdoor blocks if they remain unused in the shed.
B. Procedure
   1. Settle yourself nearby on a low chair. The teacher's presence is one of the best incentives to block play.
   2. Teach the children to select blocks and carry them somewhat away from the shelves or storage shed so that everyone can easily reach more of them as building continues.
   3. Be an interested observer of the children's block play, but be ready to redirect children or offer suggestions to extend the activity according to their interests should the need arise. Avoid taking over the play; make sure it remains the children's activity.
   4. Remember that children need time to play with their block structures after they have built them. Children appreciate having the privilege of leaving such things up during nap or overnight if it is possible to arrange this.
   5. Remember to stress that block buildings belong to the children who did the work. Children may knock down their own structures but may not destroy the work of other chil-

Los Niños Head Start

dren unless they have the owner's consent. Dumping all the blocks onto the floor and running off or throwing blocks should be prevented. Children who sweep blocks off the shelves need to stay and help pick them up.

6. Drawing diagrams of the children's constructions from time to time increases the child's interest and satisfaction in this activity. If a carbon copy is made, one copy can go home and the other be retained in the child's folder as part of his developmental record. Be sure to date it and note the child's companions and comments.

7. Mathematical relationships such as equality and seriated relationships should be casually drawn to the children's attention as the occasion warrants.

8. Tidy up as needed to keep the play area attractive and to make room for further building.

C. Cleanup

1. Some teachers discourage the use of blocks because they dislike picking them up, but this problem can be somewhat alleviated by encouraging children to help, too. However, it is not desirable to enforce the rule, "You have to put away every block you got out before you leave the block corner." Since many children won't participate under these conditions, enforcement of this rule can spoil play. The teacher will obtain the best cooperation from the children if she pitches in with them and everyone puts the blocks away together at the end of the morning.

2. Always neatly categorize blocks when putting them away, and shelve them with the *long side in view* so their size is readily apparent. *Never store blocks by dumping them into a bin or tub;* it is impossible for children to find needed sizes in such a welter, and it knocks corners off the blocks as well.

3. Return extra accessories to the block closet, and arrange the remaining ones so they make attractive, colorful accents in the room.

Suggested variations. Accessories that may be offered to stimulate block play are legion. Since blocks are usually neutral in tone, the touches of color lent by accessories add beauty as well as stimulation to the play. Doll house furniture and rug samples, small rubber animals, and miniature people are all successful accoutrements. Variations in blocks themselves, such as gothic arches, flat "roofing" blocks, spools, and cubical counting blocks, add embellishment. Not all the blocks should be offered all the time: it is sound to save the arches, switches, or triangular blocks and ramps and offer them as interesting variations when the more common varieties begin to pall. The Skaneateles train is an incomparable block accessory; tracks and additional cars should be purchased every year, since it seems to be impossible to own enough of these materials. It is also fun to build pens for the rats and guinea pigs with blocks, although this requires careful supervision from the teacher for the animal's protection. Cars, trucks, derricks, boats, and airplanes are also delightful to use with block materials.

Outside, the addition of boards, sawhorses, ladders, and old bedspreads and parachutes will extend large block play in a very satisfactory way. Large, sturdy boxes and cement pipes are additional accessories that make good combination units with blocks, and wagons and wheelbarrows are handy for carting blocks about and delivering them to many locations in the yard.

It is also fascinating to combine large and small blocks indoors. Older children often enjoy using the small blocks as trimming on large block constructions, and some very creative and interesting structures can result from this merging of materials.

SUMMARY

Play serves many valuable purposes in the life of the child. It provides occasions for intense practice of sensorimotor skills; the symbolic nature of imaginative play fosters development of the intellect and generates increased understanding of events; play facilitates role playing and develops social skills; it furnishes opportunities to work through emotional problems and to experience the relief of acting like a child instead of an adult; and it provides many occasions for the child to be creative by using his imagination and his ability to think in divergent ways.

The teacher who wishes to foster the creative aspects of play will avoid dominating it and will encourage children to make original use of materials. She will purchase, plan, and arrange equipment so that creativity will be enhanced. But above all, the teacher who wishes to foster creativity in play will cast herself in the role of assistant to the child, seeking to move with and support his play as it develops and to serve his play needs to the best of her ability.

QUESTIONS AND ACTIVITIES

1. *Problem:* Suppose a parent comes to you, after touring the school, and says dubiously, "Well, it looks nice enough here, and I can see the children are happy; but don't they ever learn anything? Don't they ever do anything but play around here?" How would you reply?
2. Take time to make a brief record of the play of several children during the coming week. Can you find evidence in these observations that play is used symbolically by children to translate experience into a deeper understanding of events? Did you find evidence that children employ play to express emotions and work these through? Did you observe any instances where the children generated new, divergent solutions to problems by trying them out in play?
3. What is the difference between overcontrolling play and acting in a supportive, fostering role that encourages it to develop in greater depth? Role play the same play situation, demonstrating differences between these two approaches.
4. *Problem:* It is winter time, and you live in a northern city. The children play outdoors at your school, but water play cannot be offered outside for most of the year, because it is too cold. Identify several ways it could be offered on a regular basis indoors.
5. Survey the play yard of your school. List the different play units around which activity occurs. Are there some that appear to generate more imaginative activities than others? Identify what properties these units possess in common. How are they alike?
6. Put all the housekeeping equipment away for a change, and offer only hollow blocks in its place and some props, such as pots and pans and dolls. Observe what happens to the children's play under these circumstances.

REFERENCES FOR FURTHER READING

General References

Almy, M. Spontaneous play: An avenue for intellectal development. *Young Children,* 1967, *22,* 265-277. Almy discusses the place of structured and spontaneous play in the nursery school and makes a very good case for the significance and value of fostering spontaneity.

Curry, N. E., and Arnaud, S. (Eds.) *Play: The child strives toward self-realization.* Washington, D.C.: National Association for the Education of Young Children, 1971. This is a good, basic pamphlet that contains several papers on the value of play—its use in dealing with stress, the role of the adult in facilitating the activity, and a discussion of current issues related to this subject.

Millar, S. *The psychology of play.* Baltimore: Penguin Books Inc., 1968. Millar begins his thoughtful discussion of play with a review of historical theories, next discusses the play of animals, and then covers the functions of play. He draws interesting comparisons of play between a variety of cultures and presents a good, though brief, discussion of the uses of play therapy.

Smart, M. S., and Smart, R. C. *Child development and relationships* (2nd ed.). New York: Macmillan Publishing Co., Inc., 1972. Chapter 7 has a solid discussion of play and imagination that is well worth reading. The authors also talk about other creative activities, such as expressive materials and creative storytelling.

Specific Values of Play

Axline, V. *Play therapy* (Rev. ed.). New York: Ballantine Books, Inc., 1969. In this thoughtfully written, practical text, Axline describes how play is used as a therapeutic technique.

Hartley, R. E., Frank, L. K., and Goldenson, R. M. *Understanding children's play.* New York: Columbia University Press, 1952. This old but invaluable book discusses the virtues of specific play materials and what each contributes to the healthy development of young children. Of particular interest here are the chapters on dramatic play; but blocks, water play, clay, and graphic materials are also discussed in detail.

Moffitt, M., and Omwake, E. *The intellectual content of play.* New York: New York State Association for the Education of Young Children, no date. These two articles contain a sound analysis and defense of play as it relates to the intellectual development of young children; worth reading.

Schaefer, C. (Ed.). *The therapeutic use of children's play.* New York: Jason Aronson, Inc., 1976. The collection of articles contained in this book does an excellent job of covering the emotional values of play and also presents descriptions of how play is utilized in various forms of therapy.

Practical Advice on Generating Play

Cherry, C. *Creative play for the developing child: Early lifehood education through play.* Belmont, Calif.: Fearon Publishers, 1976. Another one of Mrs. Cherry's sound books on curriculum, this particular volume deals with play in the broadest sense of the word and includes discussions of gross and fine motor activities, science experiences, and so forth; dramatic play is also discussed.

Wittes, G., and Radin, N. *Ypsilanti home and school handbooks: Helping your child to learn: The learning through play approach.* San Rafael, Calif. Dimensions Publishing Co., 1969a. Wittes and Radin present a series of lessons, designed for a parent group but applicable also to nursery school, which are intended to teach mothers how to foster and generate play at home. The authors are particularly strong on discussing the purpose of offering play activities and in making practical suggestions about what to do—very down-to-earth. They advocate a strong leadership role for the adult.

Specific Activities and How to Present Them

Hill, D. M. *Mud, sand and water.* Washington, D.C.: National Association for the Education of Young Children, 1977. A newly rewritten version of an old favorite, *Water, Sand and Mud,* that is now out of print, this useful analysis emphasizes the virtues of using these materials for play and learning. It also contains lists of suggested equipment.

Hirsch, E. S. (Ed.). *The block book.* Washington, D.C.: National Association for the Education of Young Children, 1974. *The Block Book* is the most comprehensive discussion of block play presently available. Published by NAEYC, it does an outstanding job of covering this subject in a helpful, thoroughgoing manner.

Johnson, H. M. *The art of block building.* New York: Bank Street College of Education, 1933. Johnson gives an excellent description of block play, which includes a list of suggested blocks, and a description of developmental stages of block building, accompanied by many illustrations of the children's constructions. This is the classic publication in the field and, although first published in 1933, remains in print because of its excellence.

Matterson, E. M. *Play and playthings for the preschool child.* Baltimore: Penguin Books Inc., 1965. This is a first-rate but unpretentious little paperback from England, which is filled with practical suggestions, pictures, and discussions of various play materials and how to present them; has a nice emphasis on how to make things yourself.

For the Advanced Student

Almy, M. *Early childhood play: Selected readings related to cognition and motivation.* New York: Simon & Schuster, Inc., 1968. This collection of papers includes materials by Erikson, Frank, Almy, and Sutton-Smith. The article by Lawrence Frank, ''Play in Personality Development,'' is particularly valuable and hard to find elsewhere.

Berman, L. M. Curriculum leadership: That all may feel, value, and grow. In L. M. Berman and J. A. Roderick (Eds.), *Feeling, valuing, and the art of growing: Insights into the affective.* Washington, D.C.: Association for Supervision and Curriculum Development, 1977. Despite the title of this chapter, it is primarily a tribute to the value of play and the playful approach in the lives of grownups. This is good, thoughtful reading.

Bruner, J. S., Jolly, A., and Sylva, K. (Eds.). *Play: Its role in development and evolution.* New York: Basic Books, Inc., Publishers, 1976. This landmark book contains a fascinating assortment of articles on play written by such diverse people as Jane Goodall, L. S. Vygotsky, and Erik Erikson. These remind us that human beings are not the only animals who utilize play to foster development. An interesting book to sample or to read all the way through.

Butler, A. L., Gotts, E. E., and Quisenberry, N. L. *Play as development*. Columbus, Ohio: Charles E. Merrill Publishing Co., 1978. In my opinion, *Play as Development* is the best recent book on this subject because there's such a satisfying mix of research and common sense in it. It is a basic book that should be read and used by every teacher of young children.

Corrado, J., and Reed, J. *Play—with a difference*. New York: The Play Schools Association, 1970. This is a report of the staff training program carried out by the Play Schools Association, 1970 at Letchworth Village. It is a heartening and fascinating description of how profoundly retarded individuals were encouraged to involve themselves with simple play materials and of the difference this made to their happiness and personal growth.

Ebbick, F. N. Learning through play in other cultures. *Childhood Education*, 1971, *48*, 2. Ebbick provides an interesting cross-cultural discussion of play and the way it is viewed by people of differing cultural backgrounds.

Herron, R. E., and Sutton-Smith, B. *Child's play*. New York: John Wiley & Sons, Inc., 1971. This is the most comprehensive book on the theory of play thus far available. *Child's Play* analyzes theoretical approaches having to do with play in terms of its normative, ecological, psychoanalytic, comparative, cognitive, and developmental aspects.

Piaget, J. *Play, dreams and imitation in childhood*. New York: W. W. Norton & Co., Inc., 1962. In his classic description Piaget discusses how children assimilate knowledge of the world around them by means of imitation and the use of symbolic play; rather difficult but interesting reading.

Smilansky, S. *The effects of sociodramatic play on disadvantaged children*. New York: John Wiley & Sons, Inc., 1968. This book represents a breakthrough in methods of studying play. Smilansky describes the way she and the project teachers sought to increase the ability of the children to play on the sociodramatic level by improving the play techniques of the children; interesting work.

Carpinteria Head Start

14 □ Fostering creativity in thought

What happens to children's curiosity and resourcefulness later in their childhood? Why do so few continue to have their own wonderful ideas? I think part of the answer is that intellectual breakthroughs come to be less and less valued. Either they are dismissed as being trivial . . . or else they are discouraged as being unacceptable — like discovering how it feels to wear shoes on the wrong feet, or asking questions that are socially embarrassing, or destroying something to see what it's like inside. The effect is to discourage children from exploring their own ideas and to make them feel that they have no important ideas of their own, only silly or evil ones.*

Smith's definition of creativity as "the process of sinking down taps into our past experiences and putting these selected experiences together into new patterns, new ideas or new products" (1966, p. 4) applies to thought as well as to play and the use of expressive materials. The ability to put prior experiences together to form new ideas is crucial in developing creative thinking, although building on past knowledge can produce unexpected results sometimes. I recall hearing of two young friends who were eating lunch together when the following dialogue took place.

Henry: "Well, you know, Andrew, I'm black! I'm black all over — from my head right down to inside my shoes!"

There is a pause while this information is digested in silence by his friend, Andrew.

Henry continues, "But that's *okay!* Cuz my Mother says, 'Black is beautiful!'"

Andrew continues to eye Henry speculatively while Henry somewhat complacently spoons up his Jell-O. There is silence around the table.

"Well," says Andrew, putting down his spoon and looking thoughtfully at Henry, "I guess being black's okay, all right — it's okay with *me* — but you know, Henry, if you wuz green, you could hide in the trees!"

Using prior information as Andrew did to produce new solutions is just one kind of creative thinking. Children are also thinking creatively when they produce more than one answer to a question, or conceive of new uses for familiar materials, or generate uniquely descriptive language and self-expressive stories. In order to do these things they need a wealth of experience to draw upon, and they need the help and expertise of the teacher to encourage them.

Although nursery school teachers have long maintained that the development of creative thinking in children is desirable, in recent years the work of J. P. Guilford has drawn fresh attention to the value of thinking that emphasizes a many-answers approach. Guilford terms this ability *divergent thinking* and contrasts it with *convergent thinking*. He maintains that the critical difference between these mental operations is that in convergent thinking the kind of response is completely specified (that is, there is only one correct answer), whereas in diver-

*From Duckworth, E. The having of wonderful ideas. In M. Schwebel and J. Raph (Eds.), *Piaget in the classroom*. P. 265. New York: © 1973 by Basic Books, Inc., Publishers.

gent thinking more than one solution or answer is possible (1967).

Convergent thinking is elicited by such questions as, "What color is this? Can you tell me the name of this shape? What must we always do before we cross the street?" There is nothing wrong with this kind of mental activity; children need to have a variety of commonly known facts at their fingertips. But teaching that stops at the fact-asking level fails to develop the creative aspect of the child's mental ability. Children who are trained like robots to produce facts when the right button is pushed are unlikely to grow up to produce the new ideas desperately needed in science, medicine, and human relationships.

Unfortunately, most teaching is still geared to convergent, one-answer learning. Zimmerman and Bergan (1971) found that even as early as first grade there was what they termed "an inordinate emphasis placed on factual knowledge questions." They reported that only about 2% of the questions asked by first-grade teachers were structured to draw forth divergent replies. But just because this has been true of teaching in the past does not mean it must continue. The following examples of ways to generate creativity in thought may encourage teachers to produce more divergent thinking in the children in their groups. Doing this is fun; it is interesting; and it can be exciting for both children and teachers when it is presented in the right manner. All it takes is practice.

THINGS TO REMEMBER ABOUT CREATIVE THINKING
The number of original ideas can be increased if the teacher recognizes their value and responds to them in a positive way

It is easy to go on doing things the same old way or to establish a set of procedures that have become so sanctified by custom that no one considers deviating from the established formula. But an open-minded teacher who keeps on the lookout for spontaneous ideas and suggestions will find she can frequently go along with variations in approach and changes in procedure when they are suggested

by the children. The teacher who is willing to let the children put their ideas into practice offers strong positive reinforcement for this behavior, which will nourish creative talent in the children, and she will find herself blessed with ever more interesting, fresh contributions from the youngsters in her group.

For example, I remember the time we offered a cooking project that involved slicing bananas for Jell-O. The inexperienced young student in charge felt she could watch only two children working with paring knives at once and therefore sensibly limited the activity to two children at a time. A third little boy hung around and watched, badly wanting to have a chance with the bananas; but the student truthfully explained she was so new that she felt she just couldn't supervise more than two knives at once. Then he said to her, "I tell you what—I could use one of the scissors for the bananas. I know how to do that. I *never* cut myself with scissors." She immediately saw the value of his suggestion and let him snip up as many pieces as he liked.

Another independently minded 2½-year-old was going through a streak of wanting to get into the swing by herself. Since she was short and the swing was high, she struggled and wriggled, doggedly refusing assistance. Finally, she rushed away and returned with a large hollow block, which she put under the swing and used successfully as a mounting block.

Asking thought-provoking questions will help children generate creative ideas

Although a few youngsters may continue to solve problems and create interesting stories without outside help, the teacher generally needs to take an active role in stimulating creative thought. The most effective way to do this is by asking the child questions that help him think up his own answers.

Sorting out fact and thought questions. We have already noted that all questions are not alike. Some simply require the child to tell the teacher something he has learned. These questions can usually be spotted because they (1) request information ("Do you make cookies in the oven or in the broiler?''), or (2) request labeling or naming (''Let's see, I have some things in this bag, and I wonder if you can tell me what they are.''), or (3) request the child to recall something from memory (''How about telling us what happened when you went to the pet store? Did you buy rabbit food?''). All of these questions are ''closed,'' or convergent, questions since they anticipate simple, correct-answer replies.

Questions that are likely to draw forth creative, divergent ideas are phrased like these: ''What could you do about it? How could we fix it? I wonder if there's another way. How else could you do that? What else could we use? What's your opinion?'' These kinds of questions place the burden of thinking up possibilities and solutions on the child. They emphasize process and problem solving and leave room for many suggestions and answers.

Waiting for answers and asking only a few questions. Even when the question is well phrased, something additional is required. After asking the child a question, *the teacher needs to pause and wait,* looking at the child in an expectant but relaxed way. Many teachers ask excellent questions but then plunge right ahead and answer them themselves; perhaps they are afraid of silence or of the child's failing. But children, like adults, need time to collect their thoughts and formulate their replies. Pausing allows them to do this.

Another thing to beware of is asking too many questions. The plaintive little song by Hap Palmer puts this neatly when he inquires:

Questions, questions, askin' me endlessly
How many more must I answer today?
Questions, questions, don't drive me crazy, please,
How much more can I say?*

In our zeal to help children think we must remember that most young children are not highly verbal, and they do not enjoy long, drawn-out intellectual dialogues. To prevent questions from becoming burdensome, it is best to weave them into general dis-

cussions while the actual experience is going on, as well as to provide all possible opportunities for children to promptly put their suggestions into practice.

Stimulating the inquiry process by helping children figure out answers for themselves. To develop creative thinking, the teacher must also learn to deal sensitively with questions the children ask her. And, of course, they ask questions endlessly. Teachers have to learn that it is *not* their primary function to provide answers. Of course, children are entitled to information when they cannot figure things out for themselves, but often a child can satisfy his curiosity by providing his own answer if the teacher does not rush in and furnish the fact immediately. This is another instance where she needs to pause and think before replying.

Thus when a child asks, ''What do rabbits eat,'' the teacher does not immediately reply, ''Oh, rabbits eat lots of things—carrots, alfalfa pellets, lettuce, and clover.'' Instead, the teacher who wishes the child to investigate for himself and generate his own answers might say, ''Well, I guess they eat a lot of things. What do *you* think they eat?'' One of our Center children replied to this by saying, ''Well, they eat those green things in the bowl, I know that! And I think maybe they eat those little black things in the cage, too.'' The student refrained from explaining what those little black things were, but asked, instead, if he could think of anything else the bunny might also eat. He listed pellets (both green and black), meat, oranges, and lettuce. Then she asked him if he could think of some way to find out if the rabbit really would eat them all. They decided to put the things he suggested in the cage and watch and see which ones the rabbit ate—an experiment that proved to be quite interesting to all the children. When the ''black things'' remained untouched in their bowl, this led to further speculations and experiments.

The moral of this tale is that *it is always better to answer a question with a question, if possible.* Answering a child's questions by supplying a fact deadens his ability to produce his own answer. It deprives him of the chance to think for himself (Duckworth, 1973).

---

*From ''Feelin' Free,'' a record by Hap Palmer made for Educational Activities, Freeport, New York. AR 516. (There are also some nice creative questions on this same record.)

Ideas that turn out to be unsuccessful are also a valuable learning experience

Of course, creative ideas and experiments don't always work; and adults, who have a much better grasp of cause and effect as well as more experience than children have, can often foresee problems and difficulties associated with ideas produced by young thinkers. But, if the situation is reasonably safe, the children should be allowed to try out their ideas even if the adult knows they won't work. Children are entitled to the right to fail as well as to the right to succeed. The sensitive teacher will be very matter-of-fact and low-keyed about such ineffective trials. She might say, "I'm sorry that didn't work out just right, but I'm proud of you for trying it," or, simply, "I can see you're really disgusted. Can I help?" or, "Well, it was worth trying—otherwise how would we know it doesn't work?

Children can learn a lot from experiencing failures, just as they learn from successes. Sometimes they can modify the idea and make success more likely next time. More important than that, they can learn to cope with the experience of failure if they undergo it in a generous, noncritical atmosphere.

Language should be used along with more tangible means of trying out ideas

Although there are perils in overintellectualizing the role of question asking, language is of genuine importance in the development of ideas. Language is a great facilitator of thought, and language and cognition are closely linked (Lewis, 1963). Therefore, it is vital to couple talk with experience and to discuss what the children learned when the experience is completed; but conversation must not be allowed to take the place of actual involvement with real things.

EXAMPLES OF CREATIVE MENTAL ACTIVITIES AND SUGGESTIONS ABOUT HOW TO ENHANCE THEM
Encourage the child or the group to produce more than one answer

In divergent thinking, as opposed to convergent thinking, more than one correct answer is possible.

Teachers need to learn how to encourage children to propose more than one possible solution to a problem.

Making sure the child's ideas are not criticized will help generate many answers, whereas negative reinforcement will make sensitive children clam up and refuse to take the risk of confiding a second thought. If the goal is to encourage children to mention their ideas, it makes simple good sense to welcome the suggestions and ask for more rather than to submit each one to instant critical appraisal.

In addition, as mentioned before, questions such as, "What else could you do?" or "Is there another way?" will stimulate many suggestions from the children. For example, Aline and Franklin, both 4-year-olds are trying to get the rat cage open to feed him. As they work, the teacher jokes with them a little and asks them, "I wonder what we'd do if the gate were really stuck and we *couldn't* get it open. How could we feed rat then?" "We could poke it through the lines [bars]," says Franklin. "Sure we could—that's a good idea, Franklin—but let's suppose we couldn't get it through the bars; what then?" "We could teach him to reach out," says Franklin. "Yes, he likes to reach; but if he couldn't do that, what then?" There is a long silence while the children consider. "But he *can*," answers practical Franklin. "But let's imagine, just pretend for fun, that he can't. Could we feed him another way, or would he just get hungry?" Suddenly Aline brightens visibly and says, "We could slide the tray out and feed him from the cellar!" (She means from underneath.) "Yes, we could," says the teacher. "My goodness, Franklin, you and Aline sure have a lot of ideas. I guess we'll be able to feed rat after all," and the children laugh with her.

This kind of elementary brainstorming can be done quite successfully with preschool children in a playful way. It encourages them to see that questions can have a number of right answers and to develop the habit of looking for more than one solution to a problem.

Sometimes with older 4- and 5-year-olds this approach can be presented as a guessing game during lunch or group time. A problem can be postu-

Photo by Mark Lohman, The Oaks Parent/Child Workshop

lated such as, "What if we didn't have any blankets at nap; how could we keep warm?" Then all kinds of possibilities can be suggested. (One of our little boys said, "Grow fur.") Four-year-olds often delight in thinking up nonsense solutions whose funniness adds delight to this process and exercises their sense of humor as well.

"Just suppose" questions are also fun and help stimulate imaginative replies. For example one might ask the children to just suppose:

Your mother changed places with your daddy for one day—what would they do?

Your legs grew so long that you were taller than anyone else in this room . . .

Plants could talk to you . . .

You had to go to the store and buy all the food for your family to eat for breakfast, lunch, and dinner . . .*

Permit the child to explore new ways to use equipment, and provide opportunities to try out unconventional ideas

Dealing with questions for which there is more than one right answer is just one example of creative thinking. Children can also be encouraged to develop creative thought by allowing them to use equipment in fresh and unconventional ways. When they do this, they are carrying out what Guilford terms *transformations*. They are looking at a familiar thing in a new way and perceiving new possibilities in it. This is a fine way to develop originality.

Sometimes such uses can be quite ingenious. An acquaintance told me an interesting instance of such an unconventional idea. His little boy was going through the stage of flipping light switches on, something he could just manage to do by standing on tiptoe and shoving up on the switch. The trouble was that he was too short to pull the switch down again, so his father always had to walk over and turn the light off for him. This went on for several days; and finally, as he said, "I reached my limit—I'd had it. He flipped the switch, and I was just too tired to get up and turn it off. I was really mad.

So I said to him, "All right Joey, I've warned you, and you did it anyway. Now *you* think up some way to turn it off, and you do it before I count to ten. No! you can't drag that chair over there; that scratches the floor.' And so," he continued, "I began to count: one, two, three, four. Well, he just stood there for a minute and looked at the light and looked at me. Then he ran over to me and took my steel measuring tape out of my pocket and hurried over to the switch. He extended the tape up to reach it, hooked the little metal lip over the switch, and pulled it down. I gotta hand it to that kid! Don't you think that was smart? After all, he's only 3!"

The incident above is a particularly felicitous example of using familiar equipment in an original way, but teachers can have this kind of original thinking happen at nursery school, too, if they do not overrestrict children and equipment. Many things children want to try out are unconventional but not seriously dangerous. I have seen various children try the following things, which, though unusual, were reasonably safe.

1. A child turned a dump truck upside down and pushed it along, making train noises.
2. Another one extended the slide by hooking a board to the end of it. Then, finding that it slid off and dumped him on his bottom, he talked his crony into bracing it at the end to keep it from slipping.
3. Another youngster used the half-moon plywood blocks to make a cradle for her doll.

None of these ideas worked perfectly or were world shakingly different, but all of them had two cardinal advantages: they were original ideas that came from within the children, and they required a generous amount of imagination to make them be completely satisfactory.

And from another culture come these delightful examples collected by Ruth Spar and Oralie McAfee.

On the Navajo reservation when I was little I tended my grandfather's sheep. I would search out areas where I could find soft clay. I would shape figures of men and women and sheep with the clay. I would find sand and press it in my hand and shape it into a small hogan. I

---

*From the Newsletter of the Arrowhead Section of the California Association for the Education of Young Children, January 1978.

pushed my finger into the side to make a door and stuck a small twig in the top to make a chimney. The clay figures of the sheep went in a small twig corral near the hogan, and the people would fit into the hogan.

There were many different colors of sandstone near our home. I spent hours pulverizing the sand and layering it in soft colors in an old canning jar.

We made corncob dolls. The ear of corn was the doll, the silk was the hair, and the leaves were draped around the corn as clothes.

We would fill the small milk-cartons our older brothers and sisters brought home from school with mud mixed with dried straw to make adobe brick. We built doll-houses with roofs of small tree twigs or branches.

We played a lot with mud and water, constructing roads, ditches, rivers and canals.

We molded mud-pies in empty flat cans.*

Foster the development of imaginative, self-expressive storytelling

As we saw in the chapter on creative play, children often play out situations that are developed from their past experience but that are not literal representations of events as they actually occurred. This part fact/part fantasy condition is also true when young children are encouraged to tell stories. In order for the teacher to know what to expect in the stories of children of various ages, it is helpful if she understands their developmental trends.

Pitcher and Prelinger (1963) have studied over 300 stories told by children aged 2 to about 6 years. They found that as the children matured, their stories included an increasing utilization and mastery of space, a less clear differentiation of main characters from other characters but an increasing complexity of such characters, more happenings that affect the characters, and a significant increase in the use of fantasy and imagination. Therefore, when pursuing creative stories with nursery school children, the teacher should be prepared for consider-

able literalness in stories by younger children and a greater use of fantasy and imagination by older ones. But, since the stories are personal descriptions and reflections of the children's feelings and perceptions, they may also be considered self-expressive and hence creative.

The following two examples of dictated stories are both factual and quite expressive of feelings.

The doctor and the nurse

MARICE

When I got the cast off we used an electric saw, and I had something on my ears. The saw was very sharp and looked just like the sun.

The thing I had on my ears was round. I couldn't hear the electric saw, but the other doctors could. It played music very loud, as loud as the saw.

The doctor held my hand because he didn't think I could walk by myself. He's not a very good doctor, and I don't like him, either—the first doctor I'm talking about.

The nurse clipped the cast off. She went out after that. I needed my privacy anyways.

My house story

ANGELIQUE

This first page will be about my dog. His name is Toulouse. Sometimes I can't play with him, because he goes to dog school. At dog school somebody makes him fetch sticks and makes him beg. Then he comes home, and he shows me what he has learned. I also have a cat. His name is Goya, named after a painter. We always name our animals after painters.

Now about my grandmother and grandfather. My grandmother goes to Weight Watchers. They weigh her there without her shoes on.

Now about my grandfather. He drives a car. It's a red Datsun wagon pickup.

My house is white with a white picket fence. My grandma, grandpa, mommy, and me all live in the house.

My grandfather went to the hospital the day before yesterday. He had his operation yesterday. I don't like to have him in the hospital. He's not here to read me a bed-time story.

I miss him.

These stories mattered a lot to the children who wrote them. At that time, the teachers were using little handmade books for recording the stories so that the children were free to illustrate them if they

---

*McAfee, O. To make or buy. In M. D. Cohen and S. Hadley (Eds.), *Selecting educational equipment and materials for home and school*. Washington, D.C.: Association for Childhood Education International, 1976, p. 27. Reprinted by permission of Oralie McAfee and the Association for Childhood Education International, 3615 Wisconsin Avenue, N.W., Washington, D.C. Copyright © 1976 by the Association.

wished. This provided an additional way to work off their feelings and be creative. But it is not necessary to make storytelling that elaborate an occasion. Taking the story down as the child dictates it often provides sufficient encouragement for the young storyteller. Evelyn Pitcher collected her stories by waiting until a child was either sitting quietly by himself or playing alone and then by saying, "Tell me a story. What would your story be about?" This is a good way to get started. Of course, children sometimes don't want to participate. In this case the teacher just says, "Well, I expect you'll want to do it another time. I'll ask you then."

As with other creative materials, the teacher should scrupulously avoid suggesting what the story should be about or what might happen next. But it does encourage the creator to ask, "Then what happened? Then what did she do?" or "Do you want to tell me anything else?" These questions will help sweep the child along into the narrative.

Creative stories can also be stimulated by providing hand puppets or flannel board materials, which can be set out for the children to use as they feel the need or used at group time for this purpose. Rubber dolls and toy animals offer another medium for imaginative stories and play. Creative stories can also be stimulated by providing pictures, which may be used as starting points for discussion.

SUMMARY

Creativity does not have to be limited to the use of self-expressive materials such as paint and clay or to creative play. It also includes the realm of creative thought.

The teacher can do three specific things to enhance creative mental ability in young children: she can (1) encourage the child to produce more than one solution to a problem, (2) permit him to explore new ways to use equipment and try out unconventional ideas, and (3) foster his ability to create imaginative, self-expressive stories.

It is particularly important that the teacher reinforce such activities by responding to them positively and that she form the habit of asking questions that encourage original and various replies.

QUESTIONS AND ACTIVITIES

1. The next time you have to solve some sort of problem, take a few minutes and just for fun list all the ways, both silly and practical, that the problem might be solved. Try not to evaluate the merit of the ideas as you produce them, but just play around with many possibilities. Then evaluate them. Is there a fresh one included that might be a good, new, though perhaps unconventional way to solve the situation?
2. *Problem:* You have in your room a little boy about 3 years old who asks a lot of questions. For example, he may ask, "Why are we going in now?" When dutifully provided with the reasons, he then asks, "But why do we have to do that?" When answered, he asks, "But why?" If you were his teacher, do you think this type of inquiry should be encouraged? How would you handle it?
3. Select a learning experience based on a scientific subject (ants, for instance), and make up a list of questions on this subject that will require convergent answers. Now modify the questions so they will encourage creative thought and divergent replies instead. Can you determine the basic differences between the way these kinds of questions are phrased?
4. Isn't it a waste of time to let children try things out that obviously won't work? Might it not be better just to lead a discussion with them about the proposed solutions rather than going to all the trouble of actually trying something out, only to experience failure?
5. Observe the children during the next week, and report back to the class the unconventional ways you say them using equipment. What role did imagination play in their activities? How practical were their substitutions and solutions? How satisfying?
6. Make up blank paper "books," and invite the children to dictate stories to you on any relevant subject. Many youngsters will relish adding illustrations to these tales if encouraged to do so.

REFERENCES FOR FURTHER READING

Learning to Ask Productive Questions and Generate Creative Ideas

Duckworth, E. The having of wonderful ideas. In M. Schwebel and J. Raph (Eds.), *Piaget in the classroom.* New York: Basic Books Inc., Publishers, 1973. Duckworth makes it clear that having wonderful ideas comes from being allowed to figure things out for oneself—not from "discovering" the correct answer the teacher has in mind.

Estvan, F. J. Teaching the very young: Procedures for developing inquiry skills. In R. H. Anderson and H. G. Shane (Eds.), *As the twig is bent: Readings in early childhood education.* Boston: Houghton Mifflin Co., 1971. In my research, I came across only one discussion of inquiry training that was suitable for very young children. It is this brief article by Estvan, which discusses how the teacher should go about asking questions to guide the child through the inquiry process.

Karnes, M. B., and Strong, P. S. *Nurturing creative talent in early childhood.* Urbana, Ill.: Publications Office, Institute for Child Behavior and Development, University of Illinois, 1978. This is an unusual pamphlet that deals with ways of generating creativity in the thought of young children. It contains practical suggestions, focussing mainly on fantasy, story telling, and encouraging originality and fluency of ideas.

Further Information about Guilford's Ideas

Meeker, M. N. *The Structure of Intellect: Its interpretation and uses*. Columbus, Ohio: Charles E. Merrill Publishing Co., 1969. Although the advanced student should read the original source, the newcomer may prefer to read a book written for teachers in which Guilford's Structure of Intellect is discussed in simple terms and in which many examples of how this material may be applied to teaching are provided.

Examples of Children's Creativity in Thought

Chukovsky, K. *From two to five*. Translated by M. Morton. Berkeley: University of California Press, 1968. This classic work by the well-known Russian author Chukovsky captures the excitement and genius of children as they learn to use language. The chapter "The Tireless Explorer" is rich with examples of the way children use language to question and reason.

De Bono, E. *The dog exercising machine*. New York: Simon & Schuster, Inc., 1970. This is one of my favorites. Replete with illustrations of a great many dog-exercising machines conceived by children of various ages, this amusing book provides a good example of divergent solutions to a single problem.

For the Advanced Student

De Bono, E. *Lateral thinking: Creativity step by step*. New York: Harper & Row, Publishers, 1970. This perceptive, leisurely book written for teachers is intended to assist them in fostering creative thinking in the classroom.

Guilford, J. P. *The nature of human intelligence*. New York: McGraw-Hill Book Co., 1967. This is the basic reference in the field, in which Guilford describes all 120 components of the Structure of Intellect. It is technical and somewhat difficult, but also quite interesting to read.

Pitcher, E. G., and Prelinger, E. *Children tell stories: An analysis of fantasy*. New York: International Universities Press, 1963. The authors make an interesting attempt to analyze the content of young children's stories and to interpret their fantasies in terms of Erikson's theory of psychological development. The book abounds with examples of stories by children ages 2.3 to 5.10 years.

Watson, J. D. *The double helix: Being a personal account of the discovery of the structure of DNA*. New York: Atheneum Publishers, 1968. This is a readable account of how two young men solved the riddle of the chemical construction of deoxyribonucleic acid. All the excitement, disappointments, satisfaction, intuition, and tenacity associated with this supremely difficult kind of creative effort comes through clearly in this book. Watson and Crick were about 25 years old when they won the Nobel Prize for their discovery.

PART SIX

Developing language skills and mental ability

Photo by Jason Lo'Cicero

15 □ Fostering the development of language skills

It is easy for us as teachers to admit that we need to know more about mathematics. But, because we all talk, we assume that we're experts on language. The trouble is that the knowledge about language we require as teachers is one level beyond using it ourselves, no matter how richly we may do so. We need to know about language. And then we have to plan how to use that knowledge in the classroom.*

Language is not an abstraction of the learn'd nor of dictionary-makers, but it is something arising out of the works, deeds, ties, joys, affections, tastes of long generations of humanity, and has its bases broad and low, close to the ground.†

In the past few years we have become increasingly aware of the value of developing language skills in early childhood, and almost without exception the newer, research-based schools have included a language component in their curriculum. This emphasis is the result of research findings that indicate that a close relationship exists between language competence and cognitive development (Bruner, 1978; Edmonds, 1976; Lichtenberg and Norton, 1970), that differences exist between the speech of middle- and lower-class children (Bernstein, 1960; Bruck and Tucker, 1974; Deutsch, Katz, and Jensen, 1968; Labov, 1970; Shriner, 1971), and that children acquire most of their language skills, though not most of their vocabulary, by age 4 or 5 at the latest (McCarthy, 1954; Menyuk, 1963). As preschoolers pass the age of 3, ego-enhancing boasting statements show an abrupt increase, and children begin to use more joining and collaborative statements as well as simply talking

more with their peers. Also, around age 4 and 5, children go on to even more highly socialized speech then this—speech that takes the needs of the listener more into account. For example, fours and fives use more "because" sentences that give the listener reasons or explanations for their behavior (Schachter, Kirshner, Klips, Friedricks, and Sanders, 1974).

Whether one sees language as being separate from thought, as does Piaget (Piaget and Inhelder, 1969), or as ineluctably bound together, as theorized by Luria (Beiswenger, 1968), there is still general agreement that the development of language abilities goes hand in hand with the development of mental ability (Lewis, 1963). For this reason, we devote considerable attention to methods of fostering language development as we study the child's intellectual self.

Petty and Starkey (1967) have defined language as a learned, arbitrary, structured system of sounds and sequences of sounds that includes a system of socially shared meanings. But this is a bare-boned definition indeed to the preschool teacher, who must

---

*From Cazden, C. B. *Child language and education.* New York: Holt, Rinehart and Winston, Inc., 1972.
†Attributed to Walt Whitman.

225

come to grips with the problem of how to foster language development to maximize the child's potential for both comprehension and expression. In order to bring this about, she must understand how the ability to use language is acquired and how it develops; above all, she must determine what she can do in the nursery school to foster its growth.

HOW LANGUAGE IS ACQUIRED

Knowledge about language acquisition is increasing rapidly, and it behooves nursery school teachers to know as much as possible about the process so they may apply this knowledge when teaching language skills. At the present time, we have considerable information on what happens and when it happens. But since we still do not understand completely how it happens, it is necessary to employ several theories that are, at best, only partial explanations of the process.

Role of imitation and modelling

Brown and Bellugi (1964) present a clear-cut discussion of some processes by which children acquire speech. According to them, imitation is one primary means of speech acquisition. In their study of two children nicknamed Adam and Eve, they present evidence that some of the very early sentences used by the children were obviously imitations of the mother's speech. But imitation works in two directions. The investigators also found that much of the maternal speech consisted of imitation and expansion of the infant's speech—the mother preserving the infant's word order but adding auxiliary words. For example, when Eve said, "Mommy sandwich," the mother replied, "Mommy'll have a sandwich." This building directly on what the child knows is enough to gladden the heart of any educator.

More recently, Bandura (1977) has championed the value of learning language by means of imitation, which he terms "modelling" or "observational learning." Work by Hamilton and Stewart (1977) has also demonstrated that children in preschools add to their vocabulary by copying the language of other children—a fact that is not news to

any nursery school teacher who has seen a whirlwind of profanity sweep through the 4-year-olds in her school! However, the de Villiers (1978) point out that children appear to imitate selectively, not indiscriminately, and there is more to learning language than just parrotlike imitation. As they put it, children *do* imitate, but also, somehow, extract rules for putting language together from what they hear. It is his mastering of these rules for constructing language that ultimately enables the child to formulate "novel" sentences, that is, sentences he has never heard spoken.

Role of reinforcement

But the question remains: What causes children to imitate their mothers or to imitate other people who are important to them? Perhaps the most satisfactory explanation can be found in learning theory, which is based on the principle that people tend to repeat acts from which they gain satisfaction. Children probably imitate because their imitation is rewarded with maternal pleasure and warmth as well as with getting other things they want.

Thus the process of language acquisition begins with imitation, perhaps first by the mother, who stimulates the infant to repeat his random vocalizations. When his repetition is reinforced in turn by maternal pleasure, the baby persists in the behavior: this process finally results in verbal labels becoming attached to important things in the environment, such as "mama," "bye-bye," and "baw" (bottle). After a number of these labels have been acquired, the child gradually pairs them together (Braine, 1963) and then begins to place them in sequences.

Contributions of linguistics

From the practical point of view of the nursery school teacher, the most valuable contribution of linguistics so far is the information it is providing on the order in which various grammatical structures develop in the speech of children. Although linguistic theory is too advanced and complicated a subject to be presented in detail here, two examples of the kinds of information this science is produc-

ing may help the beginning student gain an appreciation of the importance of this approach. For a more extensive treatment of linguistics, the reader is referred to the de Villiers' book, *Language Acquisition* (1978).

One early example of applied linguistics is the study by Paula Menyuk (1963), who used the grammatical theory developed by Noam Chomsky, a linguistic theorist in transformational grammar, to study the language of young children. She studied 3- and 6-year-olds and found that there were very few examples of restricted children's grammar at this level. Surprisingly, most of the children's speech was similar to that of adults, and the children had gained a remarkable proficiency in structuring language correctly even by age 3. This is important information for the nursery school teacher to possess, since it implies that we need to stress the development of language function skills earlier than age 4—the point at which many preschool compensatory programs now begin. Obviously, if grammatical structure has been largely acquired by this time, we should be building language skills in children between 18 months and 3½ years old to be maximally effective.

In another study, Courtney Cazden (1970) also used transformational grammar to analyze the way children learn to pose questions. Briefly, she found that children first form questions by using inflection. Following that, questions become the "yes-no" kind, which depend on interchanging only two phrases. For example, "The boy can drive a car" would change to "Can the boy drive a car?" Next, children learn to perform a more difficult transformation, the "wh" question—"When can the boy drive a car?"—which involves two transformations. The next step involves forming negative questions: "Won't he be able to drive the car?" Finally comes the use of tag questions: "It's all right if he drives the car, isn't it?"

As more of these studies become available, it will become possible to outline sequential steps for many forms of grammatical structures. Then, following an analysis of a child's present level of ability, the teacher will be able to refer to these "maps" and

know what next step should be selected for him and to plan her teaching accordingly.

Contributions of sociolinguistics

Some researchers are becoming increasingly dissatisfied with the emphasis on the significance of grammatical structure in the development of speech and are stressing the interactional importance of the social and developmental aspects of language acquisition (Bloom, 1975; Bruner, 1975; Clark, 1973; Halliday, 1975).

They point out that the child can say the same thing (that is, the grammatical structure can be identical), and yet mean quite different things depending on the *social context* (the circumstances) in which he says it. For instance, a 1½-year-old may say "Mine!" very emphatically, meaning "Give it to me right now!" or "I won't let you have it!" or even "At last I've got it!"

Another growing edge in language acquisition is the interest in the interrelationship and interdependency between language and stages of mental development. Edmonds (1976) and Sinclair (1971), for example, maintain that children cannot generate their first words until they have attained the Piagetian stage of object permanence. Young children must be aware that an object has a separate, independent existence before they are able to use language, and, conveniently, language then enables them to represent these objects even when they are absent.

Finally, Jerome Bruner has been engaged in observing mothers and children, and he emphasizes the importance of interactive communication between them as a primary influence on how babies learn to talk (1975, 1978). He speaks with admiration of the sensitive "fine tuning" of the mother to the abilities and developmental level of the child. Bruner points out that learning to carry on a conversation between mother and baby is probably the earliest form of turn taking learned by youngsters, and he also takes the position that children learn to talk not primarily because they are "reinforced" for this behavior but "in order to get things done with words" (1978, p. 49).

Conclusion

And so the debate on how the miracle of language comes about continues—with, it seems, an ever-widening range of things that affect its acquisition being considered. It is an exciting, fast-growing area of study and research that is particularly interesting because it has attracted the attention of people from a variety of academic disciplines who, by their diversity of approaches, have greatly increased the richness of our understanding.

One asks at this point, have we reached the place where these studies offer sufficient explanations of how language is acquired? Surely the foregoing explanations are sensible and useful as far as they go, but the fact remains that although we are in the process of acquiring linguistic maps, and although we are fairly certain that imitation and reinforcement play an important role in the acquisition of these forms, and although we acknowledge that context and development and social interaction are important influences, we still cannot explain the fundamental magic of what happens in the child's mind that enables him to substitute symbol for object and to assemble these symbols into sentences he has never heard. As Bruner says, "Learning a native language is an accomplishment within the grasp of any toddler, yet discovering how children do it has eluded generations of philosophers!'' (1978, p. 42)

DEVELOPMENTAL MILESTONES

In addition to understanding that grammatical structure develops according to predictable rules, the teacher should become acquainted with additional developmental milestones so that she can identify children who show marked developmental lags and also so that she may have a clear idea of what is reasonable to aim for when establishing goals for language development. The teacher may find Table 10, developed by Mary Wooton Masland for the National Institute of Neurological Diseases and Stroke (1969), quite helpful; but she should remember that the checkpoints represent averages, and children who are developing well may often be either above or behind the suggested time listed.

The lag should be considered serious enough to warrant concern if the child is more than a year behind on a particular measure.

Another quick rule of thumb for checking language development is sentence length, still thought to be one of the best indicators of verbal maturity. In general, sentence length increases as the child grows older. McCarthy (1954) lists the following pattern.

Sentence of 1 word	18 months
Sentences of 2 to 3 words	30 months
Complete sentences averaging about 4 words	40 months
Sentences averaging 5 words	78 months

When assessing language competence, the teachers in our Center have also found it helpful to determine whether English or some other language, typically Spanish, is the child's dominant language and also to determine whether he appears to possess what I term "the habit of verbalness.'' For whatever reason, be it temperament, age, level of intelligence, cultural pattern, or socioeconomic status, it is evident to our Center teachers that some children use language to meet their needs more frequently than others do. We always try to note this behavior and to use the techniques described in the following section to encourage less verbally oriented children to increase their language abilities while attending the Center.

METHODS USED FOR INCREASING LANGUAGE COMPETENCE IN YOUNG CHILDREN

As one might expect, methods of teaching language skills are closely linked to the philosophy of the teachers involved, and at present there is much controversy about how nursery school teachers should teach language. Approaches range from Moore and Anderson's talking typewriter (1968) and Bereiter's (1969) emphasis on drill and rote learning to using finger plays that stress the development of English sounds for Mexican-American chil-

Table 10. Milestones in the development of language ability in young children*

Average age	Question	Average behavior
3-6 months	What does he do when you talk to him?	He awakens or quiets to the sound of his mother's voice.
	Does he react to your voice even when he cannot see you?	He typically turns eyes and head in the direction of the source of sound.
7-10 months	When he can't *see* what is happening, what does he do when he hears familiar footsteps . . . the dog barking . . . the telephone ringing . . . candy paper rattling . . . someone's voice . . . his own name?	He turns his head and shoulders toward familiar sounds, even when he cannot see what is happening. Such sounds do not have to be loud to cause him to respond.
11-15 months	Can he point to or find familiar objects or people when he is asked to? *Example:* "Where is Jimmy?" "Find the ball."	He shows his understanding of some words by appropriate behavior; for example, he points to or looks at familiar objects or people, on request.
	Does he respond differently to different sounds?	He jabbers in response to a human voice, is apt to cry when there is thunder, or may frown when he is scolded.
	Does he enjoy listening to some sounds and imitating them?	Imitation indicates that he can hear the sounds and match them with his own sound production.
1½ years	Can he point to parts of his body when you ask him to? *Example:* "Show me your eyes." "Show me your nose."	Some children begin to identify parts of the body. He should be able to show his nose or eyes.
	How many understandable words does he use— words you are sure *really* mean something?	He should be using a few single words. They are not complete or pronounced perfectly but are clearly meaningful.
2 years	Can he follow simple verbal commands when you are careful not to give him any help, such as looking at the object or pointing in the right direction? *Example:* "Johnny, get your hat and give it to Daddy." "Debby, bring me your ball."	He should be able to follow a few simple commands without visual clues.
	Does he enjoy being read to? Does he point out pictures of familiar objects in a book when asked to? *Example:* "Show me the baby." "Where's the rabbit?"	Most two-year-olds enjoy being "read to" and shown simple pictures in a book or magazine, and will point out pictures when you ask them to.
	Does he use the names of familiar people and things such as *Mommy, milk, ball,* and *hat*?	He should be using a variety of everyday words heard in his home and neighborhood.
	What does he call himself?	He refers to himself by name.

*From National Institute of Neurological Diseases and Stroke. *Learning to talk: Speech, hearing and language problems in the pre-school child.* Washington, D.C.: U.S. Dept. of Health, Education, and Welfare, 1969.

Table 10. Milestones in the development of language ability in young children —cont'd

Average age	Question	Average behavior
2 years —cont'd	Is he beginning to show interest in the sound of radio or TV commercials? Is he putting a few words together to make little "sentences"? *Example:* "Go bye-bye car." "Milk all gone."	Many two-year-olds do show such interest, by word or action. These "sentences" are not usually complete or grammatically correct.
2½ years	Does he know a few rhymes or songs? Does he enjoy hearing them? What does he do when the ice cream man's bell rings, out of his sight, or when a car door or house door closes at a time when someone in the family usually comes home?	Many children can say or sing short rhymes or songs and enjoy listening to records or to mother singing. If a child has good hearing, and these are events that bring him pleasure, he usually reacts to the sound by running to look or telling someone what he hears.
3 years	Can he show that he understands the meaning of some words besides the names of things? *Example:* "Make the car go." "Give me your ball." "Put the block in your pocket." "Find the big doll." Can he find you when you call him from another room? Does he sometimes use complete sentences?	He should be able to understand and use some simple verbs, pronouns, prepositions, and adjectives, such as *go, me, in,* and *big.* He should be able to locate the source of a sound. He should be using complete sentences some of the time.
4 years	Can he tell about events that have happened recently? Can he carry out two directions, one after the other? *Example:* "Bobby, find Susie and tell her dinner's ready."	He should be able to give a connected account of some recent experiences. He should be able to carry out a sequence of two simple directions.
5 years	Do neighbors and others outside the family understand most of what he says? Can he carry on a conversation with other children or familiar grownups? Does he begin a sentence with "I" instead of "me"; "he" instead of "him"? Is his grammar almost as good as his parents'?	His speech should be intelligible, although some sounds may still be mispronounced. Most children of this age can carry on a conversation if the vocabulary is within their experience. He should use some pronouns correctly. Most of the time, it should match the patterns of grammar used by the adults of his family and neighborhood.

dren (Forrester, 1969). The works by Bereiter (1969), Carter, (1969), Forrester (1969), Hodges, McCandless, Spicker, and Craig (1971), and Kraft, Fuschillo, and Herzog (1968) provide examples of kinds of nursery school programs that present a wide variety of approaches to the teaching of language.

It is not within the scope of this book to go into detail about these individual programs. In summary, all the programs of the authors listed above had the effect of significantly increasing IQ scores and scores on the Illinois Test of Psycholinguistic Abilities or the Peabody Picture Vocabulary Test. The great diversity of these programs makes it evident that a variety of approaches can succeed in teaching language to children.

I prefer an approach that seeks to develop fluency and the child's ability to use language to verbalize concepts and express thought. This approach, characterized by Bartlett (1972) as being based on instructional dialogue, is illustrated by curricula developed by Lavatelli (1970a, 1973b). Bank Street College (1968), Weikart (1971), and many others. These programs have the advantage of providing a framework for the teacher so that she knows what she should teach next; yet they also allow enough scope that the child, as well as the adult, is free to initiate conversation.

There are some basic principles that the beginning teacher should seek to apply, however, no matter what program she decides to espouse. They are fundamental to the success of any more particularized language program the school may elect to use.

SEVEN BASIC WAYS TO FOSTER LANGUAGE DEVELOPMENT
I. Listen to the children

Many adults, particularly women and most particularly nervous women teachers, are so busy talking themselves that they drown the children out. But children learn to talk by being heard. Paying attention to what they say and listening both to the surface content and to the message underneath offer the most valuable inducements to children to continue making the effort to communicate.

Of course, it isn't always easy to understand what they have to say. If a comment is unintelligible, it is all right to ask a child to repeat it; and, if the message is still unclear, it may be necessary to admit this and say, "I'm sorry, I just can't tell what you're saying. Could you show me what you mean?" At least this is honest communication and shows children that the teacher is really interested and is trying.

II. Give the children something real to talk about

Children's talk should be based on solid, real, lived-through experience. Sometimes inexperienced teachers want to begin at the other end and set up group experiences wherein the children are supposed to discuss planting seeds or thinking about what will sink and float before they have been exposed to the experience itself. This means they are expected to use words that have few actual associations for them and to talk about something vague and relatively meaningless. No wonder their attention wanders! It is much more satisfactory to provide the opportunity to live through the experience and to talk about what is happening while it is going on as well as after it has been completed. At this point the child can really associate "sink" with "things that go down" and "sprout" with the pale green tip that poked its nose out of the bean.

Note, also, that talk and questioning are advocated as an accompaniment to experience. In former years, some nursery school teachers seemed to assume that mere exposure to interesting materials in the presence of a warm adult would automatically produce growth in language and mental ability. The work of Blank and Solomon (1968, 1969) has shown that unfocused attention in a rich environment is *not* enough. Children develop language best when required to use words to express concepts and thoughts about what is happening, has happened, or will happen; it is this kind of activity that produces the greatest gains.

III. Encourage conversation and dialogue

There is much more to language development than teaching the child to name colors or objects on demand, although learning the names of things and building vocabulary is of value, too. More important than the acquisition of words is using them to express ideas, and building conversational skills is fundamental to this ability.

In order to develop such interchanges the teacher has to relax and stop seeing her role as one of instructor and admonisher. *Always supplying a fact or rendering an opinion in reply to a child's comment kills conversation very quickly.* Cazden quotes a perfect example of this. As she points out, the more frequent the prohibition in an adult's talk, the less the children reply.

Tape plays
Teacher: Oh, you tease, Tom, what are you telling Winston?
Tom: I tellin' him my brother Gary a bad bad boy.
Teacher: O, now that ain't nice.

After an analysis and discussion on this tape recording, the same teacher returns to the child, and the following conversation ensues.

Teacher: Tom, what was you tellin' Winston this mornin' when you playin' with the ball?
Tom: I tole him Gary my brother.
Teacher: You like Gary?
Tom: Yeah, I lahk him, but he bad.
Teacher: Why's dat?
Tom: 'Cus he walked up and set with his friend when they was singin' 'bout Jesus and the preacher was preachin'.
Teacher: Who whipped him?
Tom: Daddy—he tuk him outside and whupped him with a red belt.
Teacher: Did Gary cry?
Tom: Oh, yeah, he got tears in his eyes. Mama wiped his eyes with a rag when he come back in. Then he popped his fingers. That boy can't *never* be quiet.*

The example brings out another important point to remember when building conversation. *The teacher should seek to prolong the interchange whenever she can.* Tossing the conversational ball back and forth is a very sound way to build fluency and also to establish the habit of verbalness.

---

*Adapted from Greenberg, P. *The Devil has slippery shoes*. New York: Macmillan Publishing Co., Inc. Copyright © 1970 by Polly Greenberg.

The value of the one-to-one situation cannot be overestimated in this regard. It isn't necessary to put this off and wait for a special moment; indeed, this is impossible to do if the teacher wants to talk specially with every child every day. Instead of waiting, the teacher can seize many little interludes to generate friendly talk between herself and a child or between two children. One of the teachers in our Center maintains that some of her best opportunities for such chatting occur while she is helping children go to the toilet; another capitalizes on brief moments while putting on shoes and greeting children as they arrive at school.

The teacher should monitor herself regularly to make certain that she is not talking mainly to the most verbal children, since at least one research study shows that teachers talk most to children who are the best talkers to start with (Monaghan, 1974). Some youngsters have a knack for striking up conversations with adults, whereas others do not. It is the children who lack this ability who are often overlooked and who, therefore, receive the least practice in an area where they need it the most. If the teacher will make a checklist of the children's names and review it faithfully, she will be able to recall which youngsters she has talked with and which she has not and then make a particular effort to include the ones who have been passed over in conversation.

Besides these one-to-one conversations, there are two classic larger group opportunities that occur each day in the nursery school where it is particularly possible to generate conversation: at the snack or lunch table and during story time.

Developing conversation at mealtimes
Gone are the days when children were expected to be seen and not heard at meals or when they had to clear their plates before they were allowed to talk. There are several practical ways the teacher can encourage conversation during meals.

Keep lunch and snack groups as small as possible. It is worthwhile to keep the mealtime groups down to five or six children if possible. Anyone who has ever sat at a banquet table knows how difficult it is to get conversation going under such circumstances, and yet an occasional nursery school persists in seating twelve or fifteen children all around one table. This kills interchange (as well as making supervision difficult).

Adults *do* need to plan their activities so that they are free to sit with the children during meals. Surprisingly often when I have visited day-care centers at mealtime I have seen staff roaming restlessly around, passing food, running back and forth to the kitchen, or leaning on counters, arms folded, simply waiting passively for the children to eat but not being part of the group at all. Good advance planning on food delivery should make it possible for staff to sit with the children, and a clearer understanding of the potential educational value of such participation should make them willing to do so. Sitting with the children fosters the feeling of family time that young children need and also encourages the relaxed chatting that makes mealtime a pleasure.

On the other hand, it is wise to avoid putting two adults together at one table. The temptation to carry on a grown-up conversation over the heads of the children is too great when two adults eat lunch together. It is better to add more tables when more adults are present, thereby seizing this golden opportunity to reduce group size and making it more likely that individual children will join in the talk.

Think of good conversation starters. Such questions as, "Did you see anything good on TV last night?" "What would you like for Christmas?" or, "How's that kitty of yours?" will lead the children into talking about things that really interest them and that they can all share together. It is also fun to talk about brothers and sisters, new clothes, birthdays, or what they did over the weekend. In addition, their memories can be developed by asking them if they can remember what they had for lunch yesterday or what they saw on the way to school.

It takes tact to ensure that one ardent talker doesn't monopolize the conversation under these circumstances, and the teacher may need to make a deliberate effort to draw all the children into the discussion lest someone be consistently drowned out; but in the space of the half hour or so that lunch requires, there is really ample opportunity for everyone to converse.

Some teachers don't seem to realize that it is also desirable to generate talk *between children* rather than making themselves the center of attention all the time. Fostering social interaction between children is an important way to encourage fluency. One way to encourage this is to provide conversational "openers" for children who might otherwise sit silent throughout the meal. The teacher might say, "Wait 'til you hear what Lori did yesterday," or, "You know, Jamie has a rabbit, too—Jamie, did you tell me he was just a baby one?" It can also be helpful to deliberately direct the children's attention to one another. "Hank, did you hear what Amos said? He's really telling you something interesting about the wheel on his trike," or, "You know, Mary, I don't think Frank has heard about your chicken yet."

Don't let the children get by with pointing to food they wish to have passed or with saying "I want that!" Conversation as such is highly desirable to develop at the lunch table, but mealtime also provides many opportunities to build the children's vocabulary and concepts. All too often teachers permit pointing and saying "give me" to pass for language. This is just not enough. Children, particularly children from low-income families, need to acquire commonly used vocabulary, and mealtime is a very effective place to teach this. It is easy for the teacher to make sure that the child says the real name of the food he is requesting and then give it to him promptly—there's no quicker way to teach him that talking pays off!

If the child doesn't know the word, the teacher can say, "This red stuff is called Jell-O. Now you can tell *me*." When he does, she should give it to him right away and tell him, "Good for you! You said the real name." Sometimes, however, the child refuses to reply. It is best to pass over such a response lightly without making a major issue of it, perhaps saying, "Well, maybe you'll be old enough to tell me it's Jell-O next time."

Mealtimes are also good opportunities to teach certain concepts. For example, the teacher might start by talking about the food: "What are we having today? Did any of you look in the kitchen to see what dessert is?" She might then go on to ask,

Photo by Elaine M. Ward

''What does this meat taste like? Is it hard or soft? Hot or cold? Tough or tender? Can you think of anything else that's like that?''

A word of warning is in order here. Mealtimes should remain basically social occasions where verbal fluency and fun are the keynote, not opportunities for continuous boring inquisitions. Vocabulary and concept building should not be allowed to dominate the occasion, and such a delightful event as lunch should never be permitted to degenerate into a mechanical drill where the talk centers on naming each food and discussing where it came from.

Developing conversation during story time

We know that reading aloud to children can be a very effective way to encourage verbalization. In his classic study Irwin (1960) reported that when mothers of lower-class children read aloud to their youngsters (aged 17 to 30 months) 15 minutes a day, the children's vocalization rate increased phenomenally.

In order to obtain maximum benefit from the story time, children should not be lumped together all in one large group any more than they should sit banquet fashion at lunch. Such large groups almost always produce behavior problems because of lack of involvement and inattention, which means that the assistant teacher spends her time admonishing some children, patting others on the back, and holding still another restless nonparticipant on her lap. It is much better to split the group in half so that each staff member reads to a small number of children. Under these circumstances there can be a better balance between reading and conversation, and the children will pay closer attention and develop their language skills more quickly and richly.

It helps a lot to select books that the children genuinely enjoy. Unfortunately, the world abounds in

Photo by Elaine M. Ward

dull books designed to improve children's minds but not lift their spirits. These can spoil a story hour. However, there are also some interesting books, such as *Curious George* (Rey, 1941), *The Circus Baby* (Petersham and Petersham, 1950), *Whistle for Willie* (Keats, 1964), and *Dear Garbage Man* (Zion, 1957). The teacher who selects stories like these will enjoy them right along with the children, and they will arouse much comment and discussion from everyone. When a book is dull and the children are not interested, it is not necessary to read grimly through to its end; it is better to simply set it aside and go on to a more attractive choice.

Remember, there are many additional language-inducing and language-building activities that can also be incorporated into story time. These include fingerplays, flannel board stories, the use of hand puppets, poetry (which I believe should be included every day), songs, and storytelling rather than only reading. (Several references in these specialized areas are included at the end of this chapter.) Repetition of songs, poetry, and fingerplays will not dull the children's pleasure in them. Actually, it takes several repetitions on several days for the children to learn such items well enough that they can join in freely.

IV. Use questions to generate and develop language

Ask questions that require more than one-word answers. In Chapter 14 I mentioned the desirability of asking questions that are open-ended so that more than one reply is possible. It is also desirable for the teacher to avoid asking questions that require only single-word answers, such as, "How many bunnies are there on this page?" or "What color is this?" If the teacher wants to lead the children into discussion, it is more productive for her to frame questions so the children will need to use several sentences in reply. For example, when reading she might ask before turning the page, "Gosh! What do you think will happen next?" or, "Well, he certainly *is* in trouble now. If you were George, what would *you* do?"

When replying to a child's question or state-ment, elaborate. After the work of Brown and Bellugi (1964) revealed that parents spend a good deal of their time reconstructing and expanding the restricted sentences used by their small children, some teachers concluded that this technique of expansion would naturally be the most effective way to teach enriched language to all young children. Thus when a child commented, "Train, bye-bye," the teacher would dutifully reply, "Yes, the train is going bye-bye." It now appears that this technique may be most effective with children about 18 months to 3 years old, but Cazden's work (1965) with developing vocabulary seems to indicate that expansion is not as effective as providing enriching replies when working with 4-year-olds. This would mean that rather than replying "Yes, the train goes bye-bye," the teacher would respond to an "older" child by saying, "Yes, the engine is pulling the train out of the station. Good-bye, train. Goodbye, people." This kind of enrichment is superior to simple expansion in fostering language progress.

V. Provide auditory training for the children

Sometimes teachers forget that children have to be able to hear differences in sounds and words before they can produce them accurately. In addition to building fluency, conversation, vocabulary, and concepts, the teacher must plan daily opportunities for the children to develop their ability to listen carefully and discriminate between sounds.

In general, the nursery school curriculum has been very weak in this area. Perhaps this is because teachers shun drill and practice exercises for preschool children and do not realize that such activities don't have to be presented as drill. There are many simple activities, such as matching the sounds of shakers, some of which have been filled with sand, some with beans, and some with rice; shutting eyes and opening them when a particular sound is heard; listening for words left out of familiar nursery rhymes; or having the children signal when they hear sentences that don't make sense, such as "When I went to the market, I bought a camelope," a game that appeals strongly to 4-year-olds.

Most speech correction texts (Van Riper, 1978, for example) contain many suggestions for such activities that may be adapted for nursery school age children. Auditory discrimination skills are important, and practice on them should be consistently incorporated into the curriculum at the preschool level. For a list of suggested activities, the reader may refer to Appendix F.

VI. When necessary, seek professional assistance promptly

Every once in a while, a teacher will come across a child who speaks rarely, if at all, or one who has a pronounced speech problem of some description. These disabilities are discussed in more detail at the end of this chapter, but I want to emphasize here, as a basic principle, that it is important to seek professional help for these children promptly. Too often, both teacher and parent let the year pass by, hoping the child will somehow outgrow his difficulty. Although this does happen occasionally, it is generally wiser to refer such youngsters for professional help after 2 or 3 months at most. *Children who have pronounced developmental lags or other speech disorders and who do not show signs of improvement by that time generally need consultation from a qualified speech therapist or psychologist, and a gentle referral is definitely in order.*

VII. Become acquainted with research-based language development programs, and draw on these for resource materials

The need for utilizing packaged programs varies a good deal in relation to the requirements of the children in the school and the sophistication, philosophy, and background of the staff who teach there. There is nothing reprehensible in taking the advice of experts on such an important matter as language development, but it is worthwhile to take a close look at the philosophy and coverage of such programs rather than just buying the glossiest one that is advertised by mail. We are fortunate that a summary of many different language development programs is now available (Bartlett, 1972); the teacher should read it over carefully before making up her mind about which program to choose.

LANGUAGE AND DIALECTICAL DIFFERENCES
Which language should the teacher encourage?

In the chapter on cross-cultural education a good deal of time was spent discussing ways to honor the cultural background that the child brings with him from his home. Although there is no finer way to do this than by welcoming and encouraging him to use his native language or dialect at nursery school, teachers are often torn in two directions on this question. On one hand, they want to make the child welcome and facilitate his learning in every possible way. This makes the use of his dominant language essential. On the other hand, the teacher can't help looking ahead and knowing that, as schools function today, each youngster will soon move on to elementary school, where he will have to speak standard English, the dominant language of the middle-class world.

It is quite a dilemma. Somehow, the teacher who provides the first school experience for such children must stand with a foot on either side of the stream. To be truly effective, she should be bilingual herself, as well as knowledgeable about dialectical differences that exist between herself and the children in her care. Failing this, she should at least see that the assistant teacher possesses these strengths.

It is also vital for the teacher who forms this bridge to acquaint herself with recent research which indicates that black children who come from city ghettoes speak a form of nonstandard English, whose value, before the work of Labov (1970), went largely unassessed and unappreciated. For example, white teachers often bemoan the lack of language skills of their black students and yet are in total ignorance of verbal games such as "the dozens," which are played on street corners and depend on the ability to concoct elaborate and very funny insults—obviously a language-based skill of a very high order. Moreover, middle-class teachers are often unable to grasp even the most common form of argot that is used by the black families they serve (Cazden, 1966). This ignorance causes them to look down on the verbal abilities of the children. However, there is now a rapidly growing body of literature on the subject of black English; and as our understanding about this dialect grows, it is becoming evident that its grammar has definite rules and that there is real sophistication to its structure (Bambara, 1973; Labov, 1970; Smith, 1973a, 1973b). Indeed, some theorists are already asserting that the variation in language that exists between social classes or ethnic groups may ultimately turn out to be more a question of difference than defect or deficit (Cole and Bruner, 1972; Hill, 1977).

The best recommendation appears to be that the teacher should respect the black child's dialect just as she respects the Mexican or Puerto Rican child's Spanish, yet, while doing this, also make it possible for him to learn standard English because many black parents as well as teachers agree it is a valuable tool for the child to possess (Cazden, 1972). It is to be hoped that the child has the opportunity to learn this English in an atmosphere that values and appreciates his already present linguistic strengths rather than in one that smacks of condescension and noblesse oblige.

At present, the effects of learning two languages at once remain difficult to assess, since most research studies about bilingualism are confounded by the presence of additional variables such as poverty. Therefore, we don't know whether bilingual children who lag behind their monolingual peers do so because they are bilingual, because they come from families of the poor, or because of other reasons yet to be identified (Fishman, 1977).

Common sense, however, argues against the folly of insisting that children try to learn important new concepts in a language they are only beginning to acquire. Imagine having to learn geometry by means of first-year French, which you are learning simultaneously—that's the stuff nightmares are made of. Yet we are, in essence, often expecting this degree of expertise from a young bilingual child when we teach him "all the important things" only in his second language (Arenas, 1978; Gonzalez-Mena, 1976), and we continue to do this despite reports of studies such as the one by Collison (1974), which demonstrated that Ghanian school children (after 6 years of English language instruction) operated at a lower conceptual level when using English than when using their dominant language.

Probably the best we can do at present, since children are expected to speak English in grade school, is follow the bilingual model wherein children are taught concepts first in their dominant language and then in English. This approach has been shown to be successful in a number of studies involving concept training or learning to read (Macnamara, 1966; Nedler and Sebera, 1971; Orata, 1953) and has been effective with children speaking a variety of languages and ranging in cultural background from Mexican American to Irish. Children who are coming to school for the first time are undergoing a complicated enough set of adjustments without the teacher's expecting them to function entirely in a new language at the same time.

Make it clear to the families that you value the child's native language and cultural background

In the following discussion I use Spanish for the sake of brevity, but Navajo, French, Japanese, or any other language could be used to make the same points.

The most important thing for children to learn about school is that it is a place where they feel welcome and comfortable. Including songs and stories in Spanish, multiethnic pictures, and observing Mexican customs honors the family by using the language and customs of the home at school. Asking children for the Spanish equivalents of English words will help clarify that there are two languages and, if done with respect and enthusiasm, points up the fact that the Spanish-speaking child has a special ability and skill.

It is also valuable to form close bonds of mutual concern with the parents of the children (Arenas, 1978). Not all parents want their children to continue to learn in Spanish. This attitude varies a good deal from family to family, and the teacher should discuss this subject with them, help them weigh the pros and cons, and respect their preferences in every way she can. Most families are realistic about the value of learning English and are almost too eager to have their children gain this skill. It may even be necessary to explain why Spanish is being included as a major component in the curriculum. Other families, more rare in number, will welcome the bicultural emphasis to such an extent that they may be reluctant to include English at all.

Sometimes school values in language development run counter to deep-seated cultural values in the home. For example, it may be necessary to explain to parents the positive relationship between language competence and the maximum development of intelligence. Such explanations may encourage families to overcome their traditional view that children should be seen and not heard, and the parents may make greater efforts to encourage their children to talk more at home.

Sometimes, of course, it is the teacher rather than the family who needs to make the cultural adjustment. Some teachers, for instance, in their eagerness to promote verbalness in the children fall into the habit of allowing them to interrupt adult conversations whenever they please. This is frowned on in Mexican-American homes, and in such cases the teacher would do well to change her policy and encourage participation by the children while seeing to it that they continue to observe the basic good manners taught by their own culture.

When teaching bilingual children, do not attribute all verbal, expressive, and comprehension difficulties to bilingualism

Many children who come to nursery school speaking only a little English are quite fluent in their mother tongue, and for them the transition to English is not too difficult. *It is very important to distinguish between these youngsters and those who do not talk very much in either language.* These non-talkers are the ones who need all the help they can get in developing the habit of verbalness. For such youngsters the goal is to increase fluency and participation in whichever language they feel more at ease; teaching English to them is of secondary importance to gaining fluency and the habit of talking.

Further suggestions about teaching English

As I have said before, at the present time children need to learn English while in nursery school to help prepare them for the later grades. The following suggestions are intended to guide the teacher in this task. However, basic concept learning should take place first in the dominant language to facilitate the acquisition of ideas.

Speak simply and use both languages. In the beginning it works best to say something first using the child's dominant language and then repeat the message in English. After a time, as the children become more at ease and familiar with hearing the language, it will gradually be possible to speak the English sentence first, pause to give the child a chance to grasp what is being said, and then repeat it in Spanish if necessary. For the sake of clarity and good usage of both languages, it is wise to avoid a polyglot approach where words from both languages are used and mixed up in the same sentence.

Demonstrate what you mean in order to increase comprehension and retention. As in any other subject area, young children learn best when they are involved in real experiences. For this reason, it is better to build vocabulary about rabbits while playing with them or to pick up a paint brush and demonstrate what you have in mind while asking, "Would you like to paint?"

Reinforce and encourage the use of English. Be alert and respond quickly to the child's attempts to use the newer language. He is bound to feel self-conscious about using it at first, and responding to him promptly without making a big fuss about it will encourage him to continue. It is also helpful to try to have all the children talk and play together. In some schools English and Spanish speakers divide themselves along language lines; this deprives both groups of valuable learning opportunities.

It is particularly important when we work with bilingual children to keep track of each youngster and make certain he is being talked with each day. All too often the shyly smiling, well-mannered minority child is passed over in discussions at lunch and story time to avoid embarrassing him by putting him on the spot, so the child remains shy and ill at ease in the second language. Of course, it is vital not to humiliate shy children in front of the group, but they must not be left out, either. The solution is to use a checklist to assure coverage and to generate daily, quiet chats on a one-to-one basis to ensure that every child is learning English as the year moves along.

Remember to continue using Spanish throughout the year. Finally, be sure that, just because the children are gaining facility in English, Spanish is not abandoned at school. It is always a temptation to let this happen, particularly if the teacher is not a native Spanish speaker; but a teacher who truly honors both cultures will continue to make use of both languages throughout the year. Many truly bilingual classrooms now consistently alternate days of the two languages throughout the year.

CHILDREN WHO HAVE SPECIAL DISABILITIES OF SPEECH AND HEARING

Children with several kinds of speech and hearing disabilities are seen quite commonly in the nursery school classroom. Indeed, the teacher may find that she is the first person to be aware that the child has a speech problem, since the mother may be too accustomed to it to notice or too inexperienced to identify it as deviating markedly from normal speech. The four problems the teacher is most likely to come across in nursery school are articulation disorders, delayed speech, children who are hard of hearing, and children who stutter.

With all these conditions, if the difficulty is pronounced or continues without positive change for 2 or 3 months after the child enters nursery school, the teacher should talk the problem over with the parents and refer them to the most appropriate resource in their community. Colleges and universities often maintain speech and hearing clinics that are free to the public because they are used to train speech clinicians. Children's hospitals often have speech clinicians on their staffs, and public schools almost always have a speech therapist available who will be glad to suggest appropriate referrals for speech therapy if the teacher and family are unacquainted with these resources.

Children with disorders of articulation

The teacher's problem with articulation disorders is deciding which ones are serious and which should be overlooked. In order to make this decision, the most important thing the teacher must know is that children do not acquire accuracy in pronouncing certain sounds until they are in the first or second grade. At the nursery school level, therefore, there will be many distortions, substitutions, and omissions that can be treated with a combination of auditory training and benign neglect. *However, re-*

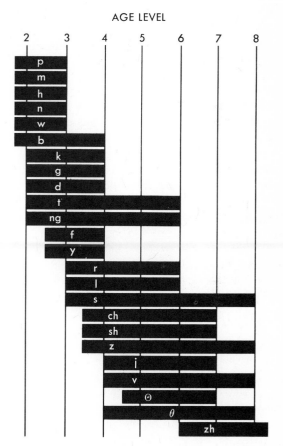

Average age estimates and upper age limits of customary consonant production.
The solid bar corresponding to each sound starts at the median age of customary articulation; it stops at an age level at which 90% of all children are customarily producing the sound. (From Sander, E. K. When are speech sounds learned? *Journal of Speech and Hearing Disorders*, Feb. 1972, *37*(1), 62.)

ferral is warranted when the child's speech is generally unintelligible and the child is older than 3 or 3½, since it is likely that he will need special help from a professionally trained clinician to learn to speak more plainly. The only unfortunate outcome of such a referral is that the therapist might decide the child does not need special help after all, and this can be mildly embarrassing to the teacher, but it is better that she take this risk if the child's speech seems seriously impaired than let him continue to practice poor speech habits until he reaches kindergarten.

Besides knowing when to refer and when to overlook the articulation disorder, the teacher should realize that there is a lot more to correcting an articulation problem than just reminding the child, "Don't say 'wed' say 'red'." Speech therapists usually proceed by (1) working with the child to help him hear the error and tell it apart from other sounds, (2) eliminating the cause of the disorder if possible (for example, encouraging the parents to raise their speech standards at home so that the child no longer gets by with infantile speech patterns), (3) teaching him to make the correct sound by itself, and (4) finally incorporating it into familiar words (Van Riper, 1978). The nursery school teacher can assist this process by providing regular auditory training and by avoiding spot corrections of the "Don't say 'wed'" variety; that kind of nagging is rarely successful.

Children with delayed speech

Although articulation disorders are encountered with greater frequency, the teacher is more likely to notice the child who does not talk or who talks very little. Such youngsters are often referred to nursery schools by pediatricians and in certain cases can be helped very effectively by the nursery school teacher.

Causes of delayed speech. Causes of delayed speech are myriad and range from the child's being hard of hearing to having a neuromuscular disorder such as cerebral palsy. Low intelligence is another common cause of delayed speech, and negativism or extreme shyness also takes its toll.

Lack of sufficient environmental stimulation or low parental expectations may also mean that a child has not developed to his full verbal potential.

In such cases the teacher needs to take a keen, continuing look at the child to try and determine what lies behind the lack of speech. Making a home visit can help ascertain whether he just does not talk at school or whether his nonverbal behavior is consistent in all situations.

It is often difficult or impossible to spot the cause of lags in speech development. Contrary to general opinion, children who are slow learners do not necessarily look different from their peers. I have known several instances where mildly or even moderately retarded youngsters were denied help and appropriate teaching because the cardinal symptom of delayed speech went unquestioned by an inexperienced teacher because the child "looked normal." The services of a competent psychologist can be enlisted to identify the slow learner if the child is referred to him. Neuromuscular disorders do not always manifest themselves in obvious ways, either; so when such a condition appears to be a likely possibility, a referral to the child's pediatrician is a sound approach to take.

Children who restrict themselves from talking because they are overwhelmed by the newness of school or who do not talk because they appear to have been deprived of sufficient speech stimulation at home are the ones with the brightest prognosis. In these cases, the teacher can gently draw them forth and elicit more speech by responding positively to their venturings. Many of these children will make a heartening gain in fluency during the year or two they spend at nursery school if the methods described in the previous section on developing language skills are applied to them.

Children with disorders of hearing

Another useful way the teacher can help the children in her care is to be on the lookout for those who do not hear well. This is a surprisingly common disorder, and yet it often goes by unnoticed. One year, for example, the teachers in our Center discovered that three children out of a group of forty-five showed a significant hearing loss when tested by the school nurse. Fortunately, the hearing of all three improved greatly following tonsillectomies and adenoidectomies.

A child with the following behaviors or conditions should alert the teacher to the possibility that he may be hard of hearing.

The teacher should be on the lookout for:

1. The child who does not talk
2. The child who watches you intently but often "just doesn't seem to understand"
3. The child who does not respond or turn around when the teacher speaks to him in a normal tone of voice from behind him
4. The child who consistently pays little attention during the story hour or who always wants to sit right up in front of the teacher
5. The child whose speech is indistinct and difficult to understand—most particularly if high-frequency sounds such as "f" and "s" are missing from his speech
6. The child who talks more softly or loudly than most of the children
7. The child whose attention you have to catch by touching him on the shoulder
8. The child who often asks you to repeat sentences for him or says "Huh?" a lot
9. The child who has a perpetual cold, runny nose, frequent earaches, or who usually breathes through his mouth
10. The child who consistently ignores you unless you get right down and look him in the eye as you talk to him
11. Any child who has recently recovered from measles, meningitis, scarlet fever, or from a severe head injury

Such youngsters are prime candidates for audiometric testing. Of course, it is also true that children talk indistinctly, want to sit close to the teacher, or fail to pay attention for reasons other than hearing loss; but particularly if more than one of these symptoms describes his usual behavior, the possibility of a hearing deficit would be worth investigating. Referrals may be made to an otolaryngologist (a doctor who treats ear and throat disorders) or to the child's pediatrician, who will send him to the best place to receive help.

Hearing losses can result from many causes. Sometimes the loss can be remedied through surgery; but if the loss is permanent, continued professional guidance will be necessary. Although hearing aids do not alleviate all forms of deafness, they can be effective in many cases, and hearing aids combined with speech therapy and auditory training are helpful for many children suffering from loss of hearing.

Children who stutter

Although we do know that an easy, unselfconscious form of repetitive speech is often observed in children of nursery school age, we do not yet understand why this should be the case. This first stage of repetitive speech differs markedly from the strained, emotion-laden hesitancies and repetitions of the confirmed stutterer and is more than likely liable to vanish if teachers and family don't react to it with concern and tension.

The nursery school teacher can play a very effective role in helping parents deal with their concern over this potential problem. First, she should encourage them to relax and not to direct attention to the behavior. This includes *not* saying to the child, "Now, just slow down; I'll wait 'til you're ready," or "Don't talk so fast," or "Your ideas just get ahead of your tongue; take it easy." The teacher should also reassure the family by explaining that this behavior is common in young children who are undergoing the stress of learning to talk. The goal here is to encourage parents to relax so that the child will not become concerned about his speech.

Since stuttering seems to increase when the child is undergoing stress, it is also wise to find out if something is currently making life harder for him and to mitigate the situation whenever possible. Examples of stressful events could include a visit from a critical grandparent, parents taking final examinations, moving to a new home, the arrival of a new baby, holding the child to unreasonably high standards of behavior, a death or divorce in the family, or generally weakening situations, such as continued poor health or consistently late bedtimes (Travis, 1971). Tension-relieving activities can be provided at school to tide a child over these rough spots. Dramatic play, water play, and various forms of sublimated aggressive activities may help him feel easier and reduce his tensions and attendant stuttering.

As with other speech disorders, it is also necessary to have some rule of thumb for referral when working with a child who stutters. At the nursery school level, it seems wise to refer the family for further help if they appear to be reacting very strongly to the behavior and are unable to control their signs of concern or if they seem incapable of reducing the tension-generating situations without outside help. Sometimes psychological counseling is the answer, and sometimes the matter is best handled by a speech clinician.

SUMMARY

The development of language skills in preschool children has become of cardinal interest to nursery school teachers as evidence mounts that linguistic competence and mental ability go hand in hand.

Children appear to acquire language in part through the process of imitation and in part by means of reinforcement. The science of linguistics is also providing the teacher with valuable maps of the order in which linguistic structures are acquired. At the present time, however, we still cannot provide an adequate explanation of how children learn to form novel sentences. This remains one of the tantalizing mysteries of human development. But we do know that the growth of language occurs in a predictable, orderly sequence.

The nursery school teacher can do many things to facilitate children's language acquisition: (1) she listens carefully to what children have to say; (2) she provides a meaningful base of experience to talk about; (3) she fosters the growth of language by using one-to-one encounters and lunch and story times to develop conversation; (4) she uses questions to generate and develop language; (5) she extends rather than just expands her replies to the children's questions; (6) she provides consistent practice in auditory training; (7) she seeks profes-

sional help for children who require it; and (8) she acquaints herself with research-based speech development programs and draws on these resources when they match her philosophy and educational goals.

In this chapter the question of bilingualism in the nursery school was also discussed, and some suggestions were included about teaching English as a second language. Finally, four common disorders of speech and hearing were identified: disorders of articulation, delayed speech, deficient hearing, and stuttering. Recommendations were made for classroom treatment and remediation of these disorders, and suggestions for referral were included.

QUESTIONS AND ACTIVITIES

1. Identify some factors in the school where you teach that encourage the development of conversation between children and adults: What are some things that discourage conversation between them?
2. List some additional conversation starters you have found useful in getting young children involved in talking with the teacher or with other children.
3. Role play a story hour where the teacher seems to do everything possible to prevent the children from talking.
4. For the sake of variety and in order to extend your language-building skills with the children, resolve not to use books at all during group or story time for a month! What will you offer instead that will enhance the language abilities of the children?
5. *Problem:* A mother calls and says her pediatrician has suggested that she place Silas in nursery school because he has been a little slow in learning to talk. As you become acquainted with Silas, it does appear to you that his speech is slow to develop. He is 3 years old and still communicates mainly by grunting, nodding his head, or pointing when he wants something. List some possible reasons why his speech might be developing so slowly. How would you go about determining which cause is the most likely one? Propose a course of action that would be most appropriate for each probable cause.
6. Do you feel that teachers have the right to change something as personal to the child as his dialect or dominant language? Under what circumstances do you think doing this is warranted or unwarranted?
7. Do you advocate setting up schools that use only the child's native tongue or dialect? What would be the strong point of doing this? What might be the drawbacks to doing this?

REFERENCES FOR FURTHER READING

Overviews

Cazden, C. B. *Language in early childhood education.* Washington, D.C.: National Association for the Education of Young Children, 1972. This book contains a series of valuable articles that provide an overview of oral language education in the nursery school. Although scholarly and based on research studies, it is both readable and practical in tone and is an excellent place to begin a more detailed study of language as used by young children.

Development of Language

de Villiers, J. G., and de Villiers, P. A. *Language acquisition.* Cambridge, Mass.: Harvard University Press, 1978. *Language Acquisition* is so well written that it is difficult to put down if the reader is at all interested in this topic! Based on descriptions and conclusions of important research studies, it provides a balanced presentation of this complex, fascinating subject.

National Institute of Neurological Diseases and Stroke. *Learning to talk: Speech, hearing and language problems in the preschool child.* Washington, D.C.: U.S. Dept. of Health, Education, and Welfare, 1969. This is an elementary but sound pamphlet written primarily for parents to help them identify children who may have hearing or communication problems. It has clear explanations of the basic mechanisms of speech, gives standards of appropriate expectations for speech behavior for young children, and then goes on to discuss hearing and speech problems in nontechnical language. The pamphlet contains one of the best informal discussions of the development of speech presently available.

Specific Recommendations

Bartlett, E. J. Selecting preschool language programs. In C. B. Cazden (Ed.), *Language in early childhood education.* Washington, D.C.: National Association for the Education of Young Children, 1972. Bartlett surveys and summarizes various language development programs and creates order out of a welter of information; an indispensable reference.

Engel, R. C. *Language motivating experiences for young children.* Van Nuys, Calif.: DFA Publishers, 1968. Engel offers many suggestions for activities, ranging from shining shoes to taking walks around the school. Since suggestions of what to talk about are always included, this book is helpful for beginning teachers who may feel at a loss for conversational topics.

Karnes, M. B. *Helping young children develop language skills: A book of activities* (2nd ed.). Washington, D.C.: Council for Exceptional Children, 1973. This is another book of activities that employ language to develop thought. Activities are classified under such headings as "Verbal Expressive Abilities," "Verbal Associations," and "Auditory Memory." The book is strongly teacher centered.

Pasamanick, J. *Talk about: An early childhood language development resource* (Book 1 and 2). Great Neck, N.Y.: Center for Media Development, 1976. (Box 203, Little Neck, N.Y. 11363) This is a developmentally sequenced resource book containing all kinds of language experience–related activities. Using a nice multiethnic approach, it covers language, arts and crafts, food, ethnic games, songs, and outdoor play.

Weiss, C. E., and Lillywhite, H. S. *Communicative disorders: A handbook for prevention and early intervention.* St. Louis: The C. V. Mosby Co., 1976. The chapter entitled "101 Ways to Help Children Learn to Talk" contains exactly that—many helpful, basic ideas about how to increase fluency in children. This is a valuable resource on which to be able to draw.

Bibliographies of Books for Young Children

Bauer, C. F. *Handbook for storytellers.* Chicago: American Library Association, 1977.

Association for Childhood Education International. *Bibliography: Books for Children.* Washington, D.C.: The Association, 1977.

Pitcher, E. G., Lasher, M. G., Feinburg, S. G., and Braun, L. A. *Helping young children learn* (2nd ed.). Columbus, Ohio: Charles E. Merrill Publishing Co., 1974.

The three books listed above provide a good assortment of references on this subject. The reader should also consult references in Chapter 10. "Cross-cultural Education," for further resources.

Fingerplays

Glazer, T. *Eye winker tom tinker chin chopper; Fifty musical fingerplays.* Garden City, N.Y.: Doubleday & Co., Inc., 1973. Tom Glazer has gotten together a nicely presented collection of very familiar fingerplay songs mingled with familiar folk songs, all scored for piano and autoharp and accompanied with fingerplay directions.

Grayson, M. *Let's do fingerplays.* Washington, D.C.: Robert B. Luce, Inc., 1962. This collection is particularly useful because it is indexed by first line and by topic.

Flannel Boards

Anderson, P. S. *Story telling with the flannel board; Book one.* Minneapolis: T. S. Denision & Co., Inc., 1963. This book contains both stories and poems and plentiful patterns for flannel board use.

Music

Bayless, K. M., and Ramsey, M. E. *Music: A way of life for the young child.* St. Louis: The C. V. Mosby Co., 1978. One of the newest books in the field, *Music: A Way of Life* may be the most satisfactory single resource on music for nursery school teachers to possess, since it combines a sensible, wide-ranging text with *very simple* arrangements scored for piano and autoharp, lists of records for dancing and singing, and simple instructions for playing the autoharp.

Landek, B. *Songs to grow on: A collection of American folksongs for children.* New York: William Sloane Associate, Inc., 1950. This collection of folksongs has been around a long time, but its value is testified to by the fact that it is still widely used and still in print.

Seeger, R. C. *American folk songs for children.* Garden City, N.Y.: Doubleday & Co., Inc., 1948 (still in print). What better way is there to acquaint children with the richly diverse cultural heritage of the United States than by teaching them American folk songs? Another classic that is a must for every nursery school library.

Quality Records of Children's Songs*

Birds, Beasts, Bugs and Little Fishes. Pete Seeger. Scholastic Records, 906 Sylvan Ave. Englewood Cliffs, N.J. 107632. A classic in the field, sung with real style.

Come for to Sing, POS 1033. Pathways of Sound, 102 Mt. Auburn St., Cambridge, Mass. First-class presentation of American folk songs by a number of artists.

---

*Please note this is just a handful of the quality records presently available for young children.

Rhythms of Childhood with Ella Jenkins, SC 7653. Distributed by Scholastic Records, address above. Excellent, tasteful, multicultural collection of songs categorized according to birds, water, dance rhythms, Africa, and so forth.

You'll Sing a Song and I'll Sing a Song, Ella Jenkins, FC 7664. Distributed by Scholastic Records, address above. Another first-rate record that features responsive singing and once again utilizes music from many cultures.

Songs for Children with Special Needs, Vol. I and II B 118 LP. Bowmar Records, 622 Rodier Dr., Glendale, Calif., 91201. These songs are simple and sung slowly enough that children can really learn them. Incidentally, Vol. I has "Happy Birthday" and "Jingle Bells." Very good records to use with all young children.

Spin, Spider, Spin AR 551 Marcia Berman and Patty Zeitlin. Educational Activities, Freeport, N.Y., 11520. The good taste and interesting subject matter of this record are characteristic of these artists, who have had extensive experience teaching preschool youngsters.

Poetry

To date, I have not found one or two books of collected poetry that are appropriate for young children and that rise above the level of triteness—the collection of poetry used by our Center has, therefore, been accumulated from many sources ranging from Aldis and Livingston to Farjeon and Stevenson. When I find a poem I like I type it out and mount it on heavy cardstock, index it according to subject, and file it so that it is instantly available when needed.

Storytelling

There are several books on telling stories available, but limitations on space permit me to mention only two of the best.

Bauer, C. F. *Handbook for storytellers.* Chicago: American Library Association, 1977. I chose this book because it is so comprehensive and filled with good ideas and tasteful selections of literature—it even includes a little music, suggestions for films, some fingerplays, and, of course, lists of books; *highly recommended.*

Schimmel, N. *Just enough to make a story: A sourcebook for storytelling.* Berkeley, Calif.: Sisters' Choice Press, 1978. A cheerful inventive book, this discussion contains some original stories as well as much practical advice about how to share stories with children.

Language Acquisition

Bruner, J. S. Learning the mother tongue. *Human Nature,* 1978, *1*(9), 42-49. Bruner traces the beginnings of language back beyond the "first word" to the interchanges between mother and infant; well-written, delightful reading.

Cazden, C. B. *Child language and education.* New York: Holt, Rinehart and Winston, Inc., 1972. The student who wishes to learn more about the theoretical structure of language and how it develops will profit from reading this book. It presents research in clear, readable form; a valuable reference.

Cole, M., and Bruner, J. S. Preliminaries to a theory of cultural differences. In I. J. Gordon (Ed.), *Early childhood education: The seventy-first yearbook of the National Society for the Study of Education* (Part 2). Chicago: University of Chicago Press, 1972. Cole and Bruner present a thoughtful analysis of the "deficit" hypothesis as compared with the "difference" hypothesis discussed in relation to mental and linguistic ability. They examine the question of what constitutes genuine competence in terms of the individual's own culture.

Edmonds, M. H. New directions in theories of language acquisition. *Harvard Educational Review,* 1976 *46*(2), 175-198. A good example of the current dissatisfaction with the limitations of the "nativist" linguistic explanations of language acquisition is provided by this article, which stresses the importance of meaning in language and also presents research that links language development to Piagetian stages of cognitive development.

Bilingual and Multidialectical Education

Hughes, M. M., and Sanchez, G. I. *Learning a new language.* Washington, D.C.: Association for Childhood Education International, 1957. This pamphlet was published far ahead of its time; its statements about bilingual children still ring true; a classic worth reading.

Labov, W. The logic of nonstandard English. In F. Williams (Ed.), *Language and poverty.* Chicago: Markham Publishing Co., 1970. Labov provides a spirited analysis and defense of the strengths and values of the language used by children from urban ghetto areas. He makes a strong, documented attack on the theory that such youngsters are suffering from verbal deprivation. He attacks Bereiter and Jensen in particular. This chapter should be read by every person who works with children who come from families of the poor.

LaFontaine, H., Persky, B., and Golubchick, L. H. *Bilingual education.* Wayne, N.J.: Avery Publishing Group, Inc., 1978. This wide-ranging overview contains many interesting articles and is a good, up-to-date way to begin an acquaintance with this field of special study.

Mackey, W. F., and Andersson, T. (Eds.). *Bilingualism in early childhood.* Rowley, Mass.: Newbury House, Publishers, 1977. Though recently published, this book is actually a compilation of papers delivered in 1972. Nevertheless, its comprehensive nature serves to remind us that the domain of bilingualism extends far beyond the problems of Spanish-speaking children; a useful book.

Williams, F., Hopper, R., and Natalico, D. S. *The sounds of children.* Englewood Cliffs, N.J.: Prentice-Hall, Inc., 1977. Williams and coauthors also cover language development and theory; particularly outstanding is the discussion of Black and Hispanic English. Although a relatively inexpensive book, it includes three records that illustrate points in the discussion.

Disorders of Speech and Hearing

Travis, L. E. *Handbook of speech pathology and audiology.* New York: Appleton-Century-Crofts, 1971. This hefty compendium of articles by many authoritative authors covers the entire field of speech and hearing disorders; it includes discussions of etiology (cause) and therapy; a comprehensive reference.

Van Riper, C. *Speech correction: Principles and methods* (6th ed.). Englewood Cliffs, N.J.: Prentice-Hall, Inc., 1978. This classic text is filled with countless suggestions of activities that may be used to correct a wide variety of speech problems. It is a practical book written with the beginning speech clinician in mind, but it is one that also makes a useful reference for teachers who wish to build language skills in children.

For the Advanced Student

Bloom, L. Language development review. In F. D. Horowitz (Ed.), E. M. Hetherington, S. Scarr-Salapatek, and G. M. Siegel (Assoc. Eds.), *Review of child development research* (Vol. 4). Chicago: University of Chicago Press, 1975. This review provides a basic, scholarly review of the status of research in this area that reveals its difficulties and the "hair splitting" that is going on, as well as summarizing findings.

Brown, R. *A first language: The early stages.* Cambridge, Mass.: Harvard University Press, 1973. Brown gives a highly technical description of the way very young children acquire speech using the principles of transformational grammar.

ERIC/ECE. *Bilingual education for children: An abstract bibliography.* Urbana, Ill.: ERIC Clearinghouse on Early Childhood Education, University of Illinois, 1975. Bibliographies are helpful because of the entré they provide into various subject areas—this one is particularly helpful because it lists prior bibliographies and current studies.

Fishman, J. A. Bilingual education: A perspective. *IRCD Bulletin.* 1977, *12*(2), 1-12. *Bilingual Education* provides a description of four approaches to such education as well as analyzing the values of these approaches.

Krasner, W. *Children's play and social speech: An NIMH program report.* Rockville, Md.: Public Health Service, National Institute of Mental Health, Alcohol, Drug Abuse and Mental Health Administration, 1975. Stock no. 017-124-00593-2. Krasner explains sociolinguist Catharine Garvey's studies of the relationship of language to social play. This is interesting work that, once again, indicates the significance of play in the development of the young child.

Teitelbaum, H. T., and Hiller, R. J. Bilingual education: The legal mandate. *Harvard Educational Review,* 1977, *47*(2), 138-170. This review not only examines the legal decisions that pertain to bilingual education but also analyzes the most frequent objections raised by school districts against providing these services, and interprets the implications of court decisions in terms of these objections. It raises cogent points about the difficulty of following prescriptions for desegregation and providing for bilingual education at the same time.

Los Niños Head Start

16 ☐ Developing the cognitive-analytical aspects of the child's self

I sincerely believe that for the child, and for the parent seeking to guide
him, it is not half so important to know as to feel. If facts are the seeds that later
produce knowledge and wisdom, then the emotions and the impressions
of the senses are the fertile soil in which the seeds must grow. The years of early
childhood are the time to prepare the soil. Once the emotions have been
aroused—a sense of the beautiful, the excitement of the new and the
unknown, a feeling of sympathy, pity, admiration or love—then we wish for
knowledge about the object of our emotional response. Once found, it has
lasting meaning. It is more important to pave the way for the child to
want to know than to put him on a diet of facts he is not ready to assimilate.*

I have left the analytical thinking and reasoning aspect of the child's self until last for several reasons. For one thing, this kind of learning prospers best when the child is physically healthy, emotionally stable, and socially competent, so it was logical to discuss these aspects first. Creativity was discussed following that, not only because it is an educational value highly esteemed by early childhood teachers, but also because it deserves special emphasis since it is such an important element of mental development.

Indeed, the idea that intuitive, creative, synthesizing thought is as valuable as analytical thought has gained increasing respectability in recent years, thanks to the work of such neuropsychologists as Robert Ornstein (1977, 1978) and Philip Lee (1976), who have been studying the differing cognitive styles or ways of knowing of the left and right sides (hemispheres) of the brain. (According to their findings, the left hemisphere specializes in dealing with things that occur in sequence—such as logical,

analytical reasoning and language-based activities—whereas the right hemisphere deals more with all-at-once, non-language–based perceptions often described as intuitive, insightful ways of knowing.) Their work has helped emphasize that both ways of knowing, though different, are valuable. This is a point with which I heartily concur, and before continuing I wish to remind readers that although this chapter deals primarily with ''left brain'' functions, considerable attention has already been devoted to ''right brain'' functions in the chapters on creativity.

The other reason I left the discussion of the cognitive-analytical self until last is that working with the cognitive aspect of the child's self seems to bring out the worst in some teachers. By putting this chapter toward the end of the book, I hope that readers have absorbed enough of its basic philosophy to be armed against the tendency to reduce intellectual learning to a series of isolated activities and drills or to assume that the fundamental intent in developing cognitive-analytical ability should be acceleration of the child to the point of precocity.

Rather than focussing intellectual learning on academic exercises or struggling to push adequate-

---

*From Carson, R. *The sense of wonder*. New York: Harper & Row, Publishers, 1956.

ly developing children beyond their peers, the true goal of cognitive development is to give each youngster ample opportunity to achieve levels that are reasonable for his age and commensurate with his ability. In my opinion, this is best accomplished by providing a balanced program that keeps children in contact with their feelings, encourages original ideas and problem solving, fosters the use of language, and provides practice in certain reasoning and thinking skills. Such opportunities are helpful for all children, but they are vital for children from our lower economic groups who tend to lag behind middle-class children in this area.

SELECTING VALUES AND PRIORITIES IN THE COGNITIVE REALM

In order to help all children realize their true potential, teachers have to get their values straight on what they want to emphasize in the area of cognitive development (and many nursery school teachers are very confused about this). Getting these values straight requires careful thinking about priorities (what it is important for children to learn); and, once decisions about this have been made, it also requires clear understanding of how to offer instruction that will honor these priorities and will foster the development of certain fundamental mental abilities.

As you rank priorities, it is most helpful to consider them in terms of their relative merit. For example, is it more important that the child experience joy and verve when learning or that he learn to sit quietly and not interrupt the teacher? Is it more significant that he speak fluently and spontaneously, or that he speak standard English? Is it more valuable to know the names of the colors or be able to figure out how to capture a runaway duckling?

It is not that any of the values listed above are reprehensible or should not receive attention when the teacher plans her cognitive curriculum; it *is* a question of deciding which goals should receive *primary* emphasis, because the teacher who elects to foster joy and verve is likely to employ a different teaching style from one who feels that quietly paying attention is vital to classroom success.

Thus we must begin by asking ourselves what are the most important things we want children to learn in the cognitive sphere, which goals should have first priority (Spodek, 1977b). Then we can go on to consider some additional points that are significant but secondary in value to those discussed below.

Priority I: Maintain the child's sense of wonder and curiosity

As nursery school teachers know, most children come to school wondering about many things. They want to know where the water goes when the toilet flushes, why the dog died, and what makes their stomach gurgle. The age of 4 is particularly appealing in this respect. Four-year-olds are able to look beyond the horizons of their close personal relationships and are ready to inquire about the larger world. As anyone who has read the Lois Lenski books, such as *Cowboy Small* or *The Little Fire Engine,* to them will attest, 4-year-olds are avid gatherers of facts and are interested in everything. For this reason it is a delight to build a cognitive curriculum for them. But 3-year-olds are seeking and questioning also. They are more concerned with the manipulation of materials and with finding out what everyday things and people close to them are like. This kind of investigation, although different in focus from that of the 4-year-olds, may also be utilized to make a rich contribution to mental development.

The most obvious way to maintain the children's sense of curiosity is by encouraging them to continue to ask questions and helping them find out the answers. But underlying the teacher's willingness to encourage investigation lies something deeper: her ability to support the child's drive toward venturing and independence—to capitalize, in other words, on their passing through the stage of autonomy described by Erikson (1963). Autonomy and the willingness to venture flourishes best in a climate where there is a balance of reasonableness, choice, protection, spontaneity, moderate control, and challenge. Given both security and encouragement, the child feels he has a firm base from which to explore when the impulse moves him to do so.

Sometimes rather than sustaining and encouraging curiosity, the teacher finds it necessary to awak-

Photo by Elaine M. Ward

en it. This is best done gently by presenting materials that are fascinating and by modelling curiosity and wonder as well. Asking simple questions about cause and effect or wondering together what will happen next often captures the interest of unawakened children and starts them observing, wondering, and thinking for themselves. Thus the teacher might discuss with the children whether the mother rat will do anything to get ready for her babies now that she is growing so fat and full of them, or she might ask the children whether they think it would be better to keep the ice in the sun or shade until time to make the ice cream. Given this kind of encouragement, children who have not done so will soon begin to question and wonder for themselves, and then the teacher can encourage them and lead them on to further investigation and thinking.

Priority II: Let cognitive learning be a source of genuine pleasure

If we agree with the behaviorists that people tend to repeat activity that is rewarded in some way, it follows that we should do everything in our power to attach pleasure to cognitive learning. We want children to want to think and learn, and they are more likely to continue to do so if they experience pleasure while they are involved in learning (Wilson, Robeck, and Michael, 1969). Therefore, the second most important priority that we should consider when planning a cognitive curriculum is presenting it so that it is a genuine source of pleasure to the child. This can be accomplished in a number of ways.

Sustain interest by making curriculum content relevant. In these days of "relevant curriculum" it has become almost a truism to say that a good curriculum for any age is based on the student's interests and that it teaches him what he wants to know. A curriculum that does not accomplish this goal breeds disinterested, dissatisfied learners, no matter how old they are. Yet even nursery school teachers often lay out a year's curriculum in advance formulated, at best, on knowledge of what other children in previous years have cared about. Thus a schedule will show that in September the school will be building experiences around the family, in December on holidays, and in the spring on baby animals. Although this approach has a certain value, the danger of such extremely long-range planning is that the teacher may become so tied to it that she is unable to respond to the interests of the children who are now in her nursery school room, thereby deadening some of their pleasure and motivation for learning. This does not mean that the curriculum will be completely unpredictable; it does mean that the subject matter should be drawn from the current interests of the group.

The teacher's responsibility is to use the children's interest in two ways: she supplies the children with information and vocabulary about subjects that matter to them, and she also employs the material as a medium for teaching a number of basic skills she feels they need to acquire. For example, almost any topic of interest to children, whether it be animal homes or changes in the weather, can be used to provide interesting facts, to foster proficiency in language, and to develop such thinking and reasoning skills as grouping, ordering, or learning about simple cause-and-effect relationships.

Keep it challenging. Although keeping the curriculum relevant to the child's expressed and discovered interests is the best way to help sustain his pleasure in learning, there are other ways to keep the experience satisfying and pleasureful for him. One way is by creating learning opportunities that are challenging but not so difficult that they are beyond the child's grasp. This does not mean that the child should be continually confronted with a fresh array of facts about fire engines as soon as he has finished investigating how animals eat. Rather, it means that the teacher understands how to move the curriculum from easy to more difficult as the year progresses so that the bright little 4-year-olds in her class are not bored by too much repetition at the same ability level all year. It also means that the teacher knows what level of learning can reasonably be expected at various developmental stages so that she expects neither too much nor too little.

Keep it real. Cognitive learning should be based on actual experience (Piaget and Inhelder, 1969), a point I shall not belabor further, since I have discussed it a number of times in earlier chapters.

Keep it brief and unstressful. Thinking is hard work. The episodes should be brief enough that the children do not feel strained from working too long. It is always better to stop before stress and boredom set in, since stopping at the right moment makes it more likely that the child will want to return the next time.

The teacher must learn to recognize common signs of stress in children because these behaviors are an indication that it is past time to stop or that the activity needs to be modified to a more attractive and appropriate level. Common signs of stress include thumb sucking, wiggling, inattention, restlessness, hair twisting, constantly trying to change the subject, asking to leave or just departing, picking fights, and creating disturbances.

Enjoy the experience with the children. The final way to sustain the child's pleasure in learning is to enjoy it with him. Cognitive learning does not have to be a sober-sided, no-nonsense business. It is a fine place for one-to-one experiences that include humor and fun when the teacher enjoys the activity along with the children. The teacher who is able to share her joy in learning with the youngsters in her care makes a valuable contribution to their satisfaction.

Priority III: Bind cognitive learning to affective experience whenever possible

Other emotions in addition to pleasure are bound to be involved in cognitive learning, since such learning does not take place in an emotional vacuum. For this reason the curriculum outline at the end of this chapter begins with suggestions for developing affective and social components because feelings and social experience should be a fundamental part of cognitive learning. Good education recognizes, accepts, and deals with feelings as they arise; it does not ignore them or push them aside until later because now it is time to learn about baby animals or study the weather. The same principle holds true for social skills. Many opportunities for understanding and getting along with others will arise during experiences that are primarily intellectual—these moments should be capitalized on as they occur.

Priority IV: Accompany cognitive learning with language whenever possible

The word *accompany* is crucial here because language should be part of rather than precede cognitive learning. One of the most common errors of beginning teachers seems to be that they forget this principle when they approach cognitive development, and the first thing they do is begin a new experience with a formal discussion. As noted in the chapter on creative thought, a discussion about growing things is largely worthless for children who need to have experience with real beans and earth and water and sunlight before they can talk meaningfully about how plants develop.

On the other hand, mere experience has also been shown to be insufficient (Blank and Solomon, 1968, 1969). The teacher plays a vital role in concept and mental development because it is she who blends language with experience, adding a word that the children cannot supply themselves or asking a thought-provoking question that leads them to think something through more clearly. It is this deliberate interweaving that enriches the meaning of both experience and language for young children and increases the likelihood of mental activity and development.

Priority V: Develop concept formation abilities in addition to teaching facts and names for things

As a study of the questions asked by teachers substantiates (Zimmerman and Bergan, 1971), even in the early grades many teachers still see their role as that of fact provider and extractor. But with factual knowledge increasing at a phenomenal rate, it appears that learning time is better spent on developing underlying concept formation abilities and processes for dealing with facts rather than emphasizing mainly facts themselves.

In the past the problem with developing these abilities in children was that teachers felt unsure of what the processes involved. Since they were uncertain, they tended to teach colors and names of shapes because they knew that at least children could pass certain tests if they possessed this particular information. Thanks to such men as Piaget and Guilford, however, we are now beginning to have a more adequate grasp of what some of these concept formation skills are; therefore, the task of building a cognitive curriculum is not as difficult or mysterious as we once surmised.

CONSTRUCTION OF A COGNITIVE-ANALYTICAL CURRICULUM

Developing a cognitive curriculum that meets the priorities discussed above requires a great deal of flexibility and open-mindedness on the part of the teacher. Because of this, inexperienced teachers sometimes assume that flexibility also means that planning is either unnecessary or undesirable. Actually, the reverse is true. Implementing these priorities requires that the teacher have a clear idea not only of her goals but of how to reach them as well. Planning, then, is crucial to success. The remainder of this chapter provides a model plan showing how nursery school teachers can use both facts and thinking skills to develop the mental abilities of their children.

Three steps in the construction of a cognitive curriculum must be considered and included if the model is to be maximally effective. The first is the utilization of spontaneous contributions and interests that come from the children. This provides the foundation on which the curriculum is built. The second is the horizontal expansion of their interest through the provision of additional information and experience, and the third is the development of a vertical curriculum that provides opportunities for the practice of certain concept formation abilities (thinking skills) that we believe underlie later intellectual competence.

Step I: Identifying what interests the children and choosing that topic as a focus for the curriculum

The best way to find out what the children are interested in is to observe their play. They may be very interested in trucks and tunnels and cars out in the sandbox, or they may be on a baking spree in the same area. Or perhaps one of the boys has had a high fever and lost some of his hair, and the children are concerned and interested in hair as a result, or perhaps a subdivision is being built next door to the school, or maybe several mothers are expecting babies. These are the kinds of interests that are quite directly revealed in the dramatic play of children (remember, dramatic play happens all over the school, not just in the housekeeping corner), and it is this sort of topic with its rich relevance to the children's lives that is best chosen for expansion in curriculum. The advantages are numerous: the curriculum will surely be related to the children's interests; using the children's ideas enhances their feeling of being valued; such a topic almost always

includes the home in some way; and, for all these reasons, the children are almost bound to enjoy it. (Remember what we said about the value of making learning pleasureful?)

The children's interests are also wonderful sources for those quick spontaneous learning situations that arise each day. The teacher who quickly fits a caterpillar poem to a fuzzy visitor or produces the hospital kit for a potential tonsil patient increases her own pleasure in teaching as well as the satisfaction of the children in being at school.

The only real problem with spontaneity is that excessive reliance on spur-of-the-moment curriculum may result in the children's gaining only small pepperings of factual knowledge on a multitude of subjects but lacking an overall sense of integration and direction in what they learn. In addition, it may mean that some valuable opportunities for practice of more specific conceptual abilities are not provided, since the fortuitous nature of these curriculum "happenings" makes advance planning impossible, and improvisation in vertical curriculum development is difficult for all but the most experienced teacher.

Step II: Developing the horizontal part of the curriculum

Once a genuine interest of the children has been identified, it is time to advance to Step II curriculum, and most nursery school teachers are good at developing this level. Step II curriculum typically involves teaching interesting facts to children and is also likely to involve reading books, setting out interesting displays, singing songs, taking field trips, and having many experience-based learning opportunities centered on a particular topic. I call this "horizontal" curriculum because it seems to me to spread out flatly into widening circles of information and participation from the basic interest areas. Rather the way dropping a stone into a quiet pool creates ripples of water moving outward from it, a "focus" in curriculum provides the energy for waves of interest to spread out from it in various directions while remaining centered about the subject at the same time.

Thus, if children are studying birds, many dif-

Photo by Elaine M. Ward

ferent experiences involving every avenue of the senses are provided. These might include hatching out a chicken, making suet bird feeders, bringing in old nests to examine, eating hard-boiled eggs, raising a baby duck, keeping parakeets, or visiting an aviary—the list of possibilities is endless. The experiences are typically accompanied by language that identifies and labels different aspects of the ex-

perience. For example, the children may learn a number of words, such as *feathers, wings, hatch, droppings, sea gulls,* and *robins.* Many schools also add books, songs, pictures, and poetry, which widen the experience and, happily, encourage the use of symbolic representation as well.

This horizontal curriculum, therefore, provides the children with an excellent opportunity for reality-based experiences about what birds are actually like. This kind of learning is indispensable, as anyone who has ever felt the underside of a setting hen knows. Words alone can never equal the adventure of slipping a hand between the eggs and the warm softness of that irritable chicken.

Additional advantages to this broadening development of subject matter include the fact that the teacher can select the next experience in accordance with the children's interest as it develops from the previous one. For example, she might go on to investigating things that fly by visiting the airport, building kites, and blowing up balloons with some youngsters, or by visiting the mynah bird at the zoo and inviting a parrot to school for other children who have become interested in how birds talk. Thus a horizontal curriculum is relevant to the real interests of the children (unless the teacher becomes carried away with her own interests and enthusiasm and loses sight of their concerns), is based on actual experience, results in the acquisition of facts and information, can be used to develop language ability, and is also satisfying to the teacher, because it draws on her own creative powers to present experiences that are attractive, integrated, and various.

With all these strong values, it is easy to understand why many nursery school teachers stop at this point and do not go on to the third step of curriculum construction, which has to do with fostering less familiar conceptual abilities. But children need more than the opportunity to acquire the rich experience and vocabulary that horizontal curriculum provides; they also need the chance to do some thinking. For this reason, the third aspect of curriculum development should not be overlooked.

Step III: Developing the vertical part of the curriculum

The third step in curriculum development is termed *vertical* because it builds on the tangible, indispensable, concrete experiences provided by the horizontal curriculum of Step II and uses those facts and experiences as a means of practicing thinking skills. At this level, the subject matter is just the medium through which the skills are taught—it becomes the means to an intellectual end.

For example,* one of the more useful mental abilities for young children to develop is the ability to sort groups according to a common property. This is the earliest form of classification and an important precursor to mathematics and other reasoning skills. In order to provide practice in this, the teacher might give the children little models of birds and other animals to sort, or older preschoolers could be asked in a playful, riddlelike way, to begin to define what a bird is and what it isn't. "Are kites birds? Oh, they aren't! How do you know? Well, then, what about airplanes—are they birds?" Or if she wanted the children to practice temporal sequencing (the order in which events occur in time) she might use pictures taken while the nursery school chicks hatched and ask the children to tell the story of what happened while arranging these in order; or she could help the children understand cause and effect by comparing a raw egg with a poached one and then encouraging them to propose and test out possible reasons for the hardening.

In all of these examples, the subject matter (birds, chicks, and eggs) is really used as the means of providing practice in thinking and reasoning skills rather than just for the purpose of teaching facts about them. Unfortunately, many nursery school teachers do not understand the value of this kind of instruction and settle for teaching only Step II information. This is regrettable, because facts can change and the amount of available information is growing by such astronomical leaps and bounds that none of us can keep up. Besides that, many children from low-income homes do not receive exposure to this kind of mental activity at home. For all these reasons, it is really valuable for the teacher to provide children with opportunities to develop mental abilities to *deal* with the facts, rather than just stuffing them full of information.

The inclusion of Step III learning at the preschool level is not difficult once it is understood, but it does require careful planning by the teacher, and this rests in turn on a clear knowledge of what she is doing and what conceptual skills she is seeking to

---

*Ways of presenting such materials are discussed in much greater detail later in the chapter; these examples are only for the purpose of illustration.

enhance. It also requires that she participate actively with the children, since it is not only necessary to develop learning materials but also essential to talk with the children while they are using the materials and to ask them questions that encourage them to think. As Kamii so aptly puts it, "The art is to ask the right question at the right time so the learner can build his own knowledge" (1973, p. 203). Children of nursery school age need this assistance in order to focus clearly on the task at hand.

Summary

There are, then, three steps in building a cognitive curriculum for preschool children. The first and very vital step is to choose subjects that are of particular interest to the children being taught. The second step, the development of horizontal curriculum, deals with expanding the child's informational horizon, increasing his labelling vocabulary, and so forth; and the third step, the development of vertical curriculum, uses the materials and experience also used in Step II but for a different purpose. The purpose of Step III curriculum is to provide opportunities for children to practice and develop such mental abilities as basic grouping and classification skills, the concept of temporal ordering, and the ability to reason about cause and effect.

A well-rounded cognitive curriculum requires that the teacher appreciate and include all three of these curriculum steps when she plans her educational program.

FURTHER COMMENTS ON THE DEVELOPMENT OF A VERTICAL CURRICULUM

Since the vertical step in curriculum construction is the most poorly understood of the three, the remainder of this chapter concentrates on this aspect. However, the reader should bear in mind that, although important, the following material is only the final one of three steps in such planning and that the first two steps are also important.

As I have indicated from time to time, teachers who have yearned to teach more than the names of colors or go beyond teaching such limited concepts as "The ball is *on* the table" versus "The ball is *under* the table" have had considerable difficulty identifying just what mental abilities they should select when working with young children. Fortunately, in the past few years some of this problem has been resolved by the work of Jean Piaget and J. P. Guilford. Both of these men, working from quite different points of view and with different methods of research, have provided us with information on what some of these mental abilities might be. It is for this reason that, before proceeding to more specific discussions of these abilities, I will discuss their ideas.

Contributions of Jean Piaget

Although it is not within the scope of this book to attempt a comprehensive summary of his work, any discussion of the thought processes of young children must begin with at least a brief review of the work of Jean Piaget, since he has devoted a lifetime to studying the mental development and characteristics of young children (Piaget, 1926, 1930, 1950, 1962, 1963, 1965; Piaget and Inhelder, 1967, 1969).

Although Piaget has been criticized on such grounds as inconsistency of theory, obscure terminology, and poor scientific rigor, there is little doubt that despite these weaknesses he has made many significant contributions to our understanding of the growth of children's mental abilities. Among these contributions is the idea that mental development is a dynamic process that results from the interaction of the child with his environment and that it is also the product of interaction among maturation, experience, socialization, and equilibration. Although his own areas of investigation have been primarily in the cognitive realm, Piaget maintains that affective, social, and cognitive components go hand in hand (Piaget and Inhelder, 1969). Since these components are interdependent, it is evident that a school where good mental health policies are practiced and where sound social learning is encouraged will also be one where mental growth is more likely to occur (Kamii, 1972).

Piaget sees growth as progressing in an orderly manner through a series of predictable, observable stages (Table 11). He has demonstrated that children's thought processes differ in kind from those of adults in certain characteristic ways at particular points. For example, in the preoperational stage, which is typical of most children attending nursery school, youngsters are likely to be deceived by appearance and believe that a taller jar contains more water than a squat jar does, even though they have previously seen that the quantity of water in both containers is equal. At this stage, also, children may have difficulty shifting objects into more than one kind of category (sorting according to size and then to color, for example), taking two attributes into account at once (sorting large pink circles and pink squares, small blue circles and blue squares into separate categories), or arranging a long series of graduated cylinders in regularly ascending order. Adults, however, no longer have difficulty grasping these concepts.

Piaget also believes that certain mental abilities underlie the logical thought processes characteristic of older children and adults. According to Kamii (1972) these primary abilities include classification (which I refer to as *grouping,* since true Piagetian classification applies to children of elementary school age), seriation (ordering things according to their relative dimensions), structuring of time and space (which is, in part, a form of temporal ordering), social knowledge (knowledge of accepted conventional ways to behave), and representation (using a symbol to represent an actual object or activity). He maintains that children use language and play to represent reality. For this reason he emphasizes the value of play and extols it as a basic avenue through which children learn. Finally, he stresses the importance of actual manipulation of materials and concrete experience as a medium of learning, particular-

Table 11. Summary of the Piaget model

Basic stages	Behavior commonly associated with the stage
Sensorimotor stage (0-2 years) Understanding the present and real	Composed of six substages that move from reflex to intentional activity involving cause-effect behavior Involves direct interactions with the environment
Preoperational stage (2-7 years) Symbolic representation of the present and real Preparation for understanding concrete operations	Child uses signifiers: mental images, imitation, symbolic play, drawing, language Understands verbal communication Believes what he sees—is "locked into" the perceptual world Sees things from his own point of view and only one way at a time ("centering") Thinking is *not* reversible Busy laying foundations for understanding concrete operations stage, which involves grasping concepts of conservation, transitivity, classification, seriation, and reversibility
Concrete operational stage (7-11 years) Organization of concrete operations	Has probably acquired the following concepts: conservation, reversibility, transitivity, seriation, and classification; that is, now believes that length, mass, weight, and number remain constant; understands relational terms such as "larger than" and "smaller than"; is able to arrange items in order from greatest amount to least amount; can group things according to more than one principle
Formal operational stage (11-15 years) Hypothesis making Testing the possible	Age of abstract thinking Able to consider alternative possibilities and solutions Can consider "fanciful," hypothetical possibilities as a basis for theoretical problem solving

ly for preschool children (Piaget, 1962), and he emphasizes the value of discussions between children as a mode of learning.

Many of Piaget's ideas are bound to sound both familiar and comfortable to the contemporary student, since a good deal of what he has been saying for 50 years has been practiced in nursery schools during the same period and is similar in part to the philosophy of John Dewey and Maria Montessori. For a variety of reasons, however, his work passed largely unnoticed in the United States until the 1960s, and it is only in the past few years that it has been deliberately implemented in the classroom by such investigators as Almy (Almy, Chittenden, and Miller, 1966), Kamii (1972, 1973, 1975), Lavatelli (1970), and Weikart (Weikart, Rogers, Adcock, and McClelland, 1971).

At present, it appears that in addition to his general theoretical ideas, his identification of significant cognitive concepts and the steps and means by which they develop may be the most helpful contribution he has made to our understanding of the cognitive self. It is this understanding that makes possible the generation of a curriculum for stimulating the growth of cognitive abilities.

Contributions of J. P. Guilford

Another classification of mental abilities is less well known to nursery school teachers but is also helpful to use when building curriculum, since it includes descriptions of additional mental abilities. This is the Structure of Intellect developed by J. P. Guilford (1967; Guilford and Hoepfner, 1971). It can be visualized as a three-dimensional cube that represents 120 abilities divided into three primary categories: operations, contents, and products. Each ability consists of one item taken from each of these categories. (See Appendix G for a more detailed explanation.)

Although the language that describes the mental abilities is somewhat difficult for a novice to grasp, the serious student should make the effort to become

Model of the Structure of Intellect.
From Guilford, J. P. *The nature of human intelligence.*
New York, © 1967, McGraw-Hill, Inc. Used with permission of McGraw-Hill, Inc.

acquainted with the Structure of Intellect (SOI) model in addition to Piagetian theory because the SOI enumerates and defines many more abilities than Piaget's theories do. For example, one large area of the SOI is concerned with divergent thinking and with transformations—concepts that were discussed at length in the chapter on fostering creativity in thought. Another emphasis of the SOI lies in the area of memory, which plays a significant role in the thinking processes expected of children in elementary and high school.

Since Guilford's work on mental ability is based primarily on research carried out with young adults, evidence is not always available that similar abilities exist in very young children. Nor does Guilford discuss the steps by which such abilities develop. However, the particular SOI abilities selected for discussion in the following pages have been shown to be present in tests that were carried out with preschool children and analyzed in terms of Guilford's theory (Orpet and Meyers, 1966; Sitkei and Meyers, 1969; Stott and Ball, 1965); so we are on fairly firm ground as far as these particular conceptual skills are concerned.

Why choose these particular concept formation abilities?

Although there are numerous differences between the theoretical approaches of Guilford and Piaget, which need not concern us here, an examination of their work reveals the existence of some conceptual abilities identified by them both. These include *grouping* (Piaget, grouping and classification; Guilford, cognition and evaluation of semantic and figural classes), *ordering* (Piaget, seriation; Guilford, cognition and evaluation of semantic and figural systems), *perception of common relationships between items* (Piaget, one-to-one correspondence; Guilford, cognition and evaluation of figural and semantic relations), and *cause and effect* (Piaget, causality; Guilford, cognition and evaluation of figural and semantic implications). In addition to these concepts, the following sections also include a discussion of the Piagetian principle of *conservation*. *Matching of identical items* is also discussed

(Guilford, cognition and evaluation of figural and semantic units).

All these abilities are selected because it appears likely that they will provide valuable foundations for the construction of later mental skills needed by children in elementary school. Piaget argues that the gradual development of such abilities underlies progression from the preoperational stage to that of concrete operations wherein children become capable of more advanced logicomathematical reasoning. Since this idea and vocabulary are difficult for novices to grasp without very extensive explanations, it may be simpler to point out some more ordinary ways these skills provide valuable foundations for later successful functioning. For example, matching (being able to tell whether things are the same or different) is an important prerequisite for being able to read—if you can't tell the difference between "d" and "b" how can you tell the difference between "dog" and "bog"? Grouping (identifying the common property of several nonidentical items) underlies the concept of class inclusion that is necessary for understanding set theory, and is also an essential element of such sciences as botany where classification is very important. Seriation (arranging things in regular, graduated order) gives real meaning to enumeration. Finally, common relations (the ability to identify pairs of items associated together) help children learn to draw analogies. This fascinating ability to move from one known relationship to a second by perceiving parallels in the two sets involves transferring ideas, and making such new linkages is surely an element in creative thought.

I want to stress once again, however, that the purpose of including the following material on developing mental skills is not to foster precocity in young children. It is included because experience has taught me that hardly any nursery school teachers possess a framework that identifies significant mental abilities or explains how to go about fostering these skills in young children. Although teachers may use a few lotto games that give practice in matching or grouping, or talk from time to time about the order in which something has happened, offering these activities seems to be haphazard and fortuitous rather than part of a deliberate, coordinated plan. This *may* be all right for middle-class children who seem to absorb these skills through their pores, but it is unforgivable for the large group of preschool youngsters who, though possessing other strengths, apparently lack experience with these aspects of learning in their daily lives. Quite literally, teachers need to get their own heads together on the subject of cognitive development so that they can systematically and regularly provide opportunities for practice of these mental abilities at a developmentally appropriate level. (Incidentally, all the activities suggested in the following sections have been used over and over with preschool age children in our Center as well as by students in other nursery schools, so we know they are not too difficult.*) It is my hope that regular exposure to these kinds of activities will furnish all children with beginning thinking and reasoning skills that will stand them in good stead as they move on to the next stage of intellectual development.

CONCEPT FORMATION ABILITIES THAT SHOULD BE INCLUDED IN A VERTICAL CURRICULUM

Grouping

I use the word *grouping* here in place of *classification* to remind the reader that we are discussing an elementary form of the more sophisticated skill described by Piaget (1965) wherein older children can form hierarchical classes and/or classify items according to a number of properties at the same time. Preschool children perform at a simpler level than classification, but 4- and 5-year-olds in particular are able to sort objects or pictures into categories that are meaningful to them. Such activities range from placing doll house furniture into rooms according to their function (kitchen equipment in the kitchen, for example) to sorting shells according to

Photo by Jason Lo'Cicero
Santa Barbara City College Children's Center

whether they are clams or mussels or pectins, rough or smooth, large or small. Teachers encourage categorizing every time they ask children "Are airplanes birds? Why not?" or say "Show me all the buttons that belong together." In these instances the child is being asked to determine what it is that various items have in common—to determine the common property that defines the class—and then he is usually expected to decide whether an additional item also possesses this property and can be included.

In essence, there are three ways to present such material. First, the child can be confronted with an assembled group and asked to choose additional things to add to it (perhaps it is pictures of clothing such as a sweater, dress, and shirt, and the additional pictures might be a doll, a pair of pants, and an ice cream cone). Second, he can be presented with an assembled group and asked to remove items that do not belong. ("Everyone who isn't wearing a

---

*For a more detailed discussion of research projects dealing with teaching some of these abilities see Hendrick (1973) or Safford (1978). The research of Meeker, Sexton, and Richardson (1970) also contains many specific examples of teaching strategies, although these focus on elementary age children.

plaid shirt, sit down.'') Finally, he can be given a melange of articles or pictures and asked to sort them according to whatever criteria *he establishes*. This third kind of presentation permits more divergent thinking than the first two do and has the additional advantage of making regrouping according to different criteria more feasible.

Four-year-olds are rarely able to put their reasons for forming such groups into words at the beginning of the learning experience, although they can indicate by the sorting activity itself that they do perceive common properties. At our Center we have found that many of them gradually learn to explain why particular items go together as they practice throughout the year (Hendrick, 1973). Thus a child who is inarticulate in the fall may by spring put a toy frog, turtle, and salamander together and be able to tell us that he did this because they all like water.

Even though many children will at first be unable to put the reason for grouping particular things together into words, the category may be obvious to the onlooker. If a child is unable to formulate a reply after he has assembled a group, the teacher can help by saying, ''Hmmm, it looks to me as though you are putting all of the red ones here and the blue ones here. Is that what you're doing?'' This assists the child in translating his actions into words.

It is wise to encourage the child to determine the categories for himself whenever possible. If the teacher hands him a box of little animals and tells the child to ''pick out all the red ones'' or to ''pick out all the ones we saw at the zoo,'' she has done most of the thinking for him before he goes to work. But if she says, ''Show me which ones you think belong together,'' and follows this with, ''Why do they go together,'' he must do more of the thinking for himself. This is quite different from and more valuable than expecting the child to ''discover'' the category that the teacher has thought up.

Of course, it isn't necessary to limit ''grouping'' activities to small muscle experiences. Every time children are asked to show how many different ways they can run or to choose what equipment they need to play house with in the sandbox, they are essentially thinking of things that fit a particular category or class just as they are determining categories when the teacher asks them, ''Do you think the wheelbarrow should be kept with the wagons and scooters or with the garden equipment?'' Additional practice is also provided by asking older fours and young fives to select three or four children from the group who are wearing something similar—boots, perhaps, or plaid clothing—and then have the rest of the children guess what it is they have in common.

Piaget has noted that younger children will change categories as they sort. This is a natural phenomenon and does not mean they are unintelligent. Maturation combined with opportunities to practice and talk about grouping will help the children learn to maintain consistent criteria.

Occasionally teachers become confused and attempt to teach grouping by using identical items for this purpose. Although being able to pick out things that are exactly the same and to tell them apart from those that are different is a useful prereading skill, it is not grouping; it is simple matching. *In order to teach grouping it is necessary to use materials that possess common properties but are not identical.*

The easiest form of grouping is sorting that requires simple responses to a prominent sensory quality such as color (Lavatelli, 1970a, b). Some children at nursery school will need to begin at this level, but this is only the beginning. The task may be made more difficult by asking the children to think of a way the materials can be regrouped, by using more complex materials, by increasing the emphasis on verbalization, or by asking them to group materials according to several properties at the same time. There are several examples of grouping activities included in the curriculum outline at the end of this chapter, and the reader may wish to refer to them in order to see how such experiences can be worked into the ongoing nursery school curriculum.

Ordering

Ordering means arranging objects or events in logical order. The two kinds of ordering that appear to be most useful are arranging a variety of items according to a graduated scale (spatial or-

Photo by Richard Pierce, Santa Barbara City College Children's Center

dering; Piaget's *seriation*) and arranging events as they occur in time (temporal ordering). The basic question that the child must be able to answer when dealing with either of these concepts is ''What comes next?''

There are many interesting activities that require a child to answer this question and to infer the logical order of either a spatial or temporal series. For example, almost any kind of item that comes in graduated sizes may be used for the purpose of teaching spatial, or seriated, ordering: various sizes of bolts and nuts, sets of measuring cups or spoons, nested mixing bowls, and empty tin cans of assorted sizes. There are also many commercial materials made for the purpose of practicing seriation. Montessori cylinders are excellent for this purpose, and an examination of equipment catalogs will reveal many additional possibilities, ranging from nesting blocks to flannel board materials. Hardwood blocks, of course, present classic opportunities for becoming acquainted with the relationship between their varying lengths as well as for studying the regular relationships of equivalency that occur in block construction, since blocks may vary in length but generally are of the same width and depth.

I also favor including variations on seriation that teach gradations in quality. Grades of sandpaper can be provided so that children have opportunities to arrange them in order from rough to smooth; flavors can be provided that range from sweet to sour; and tone bells can be arranged from high to low. Large muscle experiences that will draw the children's attention to graduated sizes might include having the children arrange themselves from shortest to tallest. (This can be fun to do if everyone lies down side by side and their height is marked on a big roll of paper and then the same paper is used again later in the year to measure their growth.) Or they can be given a set of four or five boxes and allowed to throw beanbags into them when they have been arranged correctly.

The easiest kinds of seriation problems are ones where the youngster is asked to choose which items should be added to a chain of two or three in order

to continue an upward or downward trend (Siegel, 1972). Preschool children manage well using three, four, and even five and six items at a time as they become more experienced. Very young children often grasp this principle best if it is presented in terms of, ''This is the daddy, and this is the mother, and now show me what comes next.'' The activity may be made more difficult by increasing the number of objects to be arranged, and even more difficult by asking the child to arrange a series and then giving him one or two items that must be inserted somewhere in the middle to make the series more complete. Finally, the challenge can be increased even more by asking the child to arrange two sets of objects in corresponding order or, more difficult yet, in contrasting order, for example, going from low to high for one set and high to low on a parallel set. This is *very* difficult! Nuts and bolts make particularly nice items to use for this purpose, as do padlocks with various sized keys and paper dolls with appropriately sized clothing.

Recalling or anticipating the order of events as they occur in time is called temporal ordering. A child can be asked to recount the order in which he got up that morning: ''First you got up, and then you went to the bathroom, and then . . .'' Flannel board stories are another fine way to help children visualize the order in which things happen, and some social occasions also make excellent topics for discussion and pictures. Birthday parties, for example, often run quite true to form: first the guests arrive, then the birthday child opens his presents, and so forth. Recipes, also, can be set out with the ingredients arranged in the order in which they will be needed. Many of these orderly events can be played through as well as discussed—recapitulation through play is a most valuable way to rehearse the order in which events take place. Growth sequences based on human, plant, and animal development fit in here very naturally as a topic for study, as does the excellent series of sequenced puzzles that are generally available.

Although even 2-year-olds are keenly aware of the order in which daily events occur and are sticklers for maintaining that order, as many a mother will attest, older preschoolers need continuing practice with this concept. The level of difficulty for these more sophisticated children can be increased by adding more episodes to each event, asking the child to arrange a series of pictures and then to interpolate additional ones after the series has been formulated, asking him to arrange the events in reverse, or asking a child to consider what might happen if something occurred out of order (''What if you got in the bathtub and then took your clothes off?'' To which one child replied, ''Nothing—as long as I don't turn the water on!'') Asking children to plan an activity step-by-step in advance also provides practice in temporal ordering—I recall doing some very serious planning with one group about how to proceed with giving my springer spaniel a bath—all went well until Lady shook herself vigorously—''We didn't plan on that!'' said one 4-year-old, looking with disgust at his dripping clothes.

Conserving

Perhaps no mental ability has come under more investigation in recent years than the ability to conserve quantity (Reese and Lipsitt, 1970). When a child possesses this ability, he is able to recognize that the amount of the substance remains the same despite changes in its appearance. When he is too young to be able to conserve (typically in our culture before age 6 or 7), the child is deceived by appearances into reasoning that the quantity has increased or decreased because a change in shape has made the material look like more or less. For instance, two glasses of water that have been judged equivalent will then be judged unequal when one is poured into a squat, low dish and another into a tall, thin cylinder, and the two are compared again; or two balls of clay previously demonstrated to be the same amount will be judged different in quantity when one has been mashed flat or divided into many little balls.

Considerable interest has centered on the question of whether children can be taught this skill before

the time they would typically acquire it, but the findings have been mixed and appear to be affected by a number of factors. For example, Inhelder (1968) reports that the amount children improve in their ability to conserve is always related to their prior level of development, and Bruner (1966) reports that modifying the way materials are presented affects the children's answers to conservation problems. The age of acquisition of most conservation skills has also been shown to vary according to culture. Reporting on a survey of cross-cultural studies, Ashton (1975), for example, concluded that ''acquisition of most conservation skills is delayed in non-Western cultures'' (1975, p. 481). Following a review of the literature, Reese and Lipsitt (1970) conclude that it is still too early to make any general statements about how teachable this Piagetian task may be. Generally, it appears that children who are on the verge of comprehending conservation may be pushed on to the next step in this process if they receive adequate instruction. The value of doing this, of course remains open to debate.

Acceleration, however, is less important than making sure the child has ample opportunity to develop richly and fully at every level as he passes through it. This opportunity is particularly significant for children who come from lower socioeconomic levels, since evidence is mounting that such youngsters often lag behind their middle-class peers in developing such abilities (Almy, Chittenden, and Miller, 1966; Golden, Bridger, and Martare, 1974; Sigel and McBane, 1967) and that additional experience and opportunities to practice may help them catch up.

Therefore, the nursery school teacher should see to it that the children in her group have many occasions to try out and experiment with the results of pouring liquids back and forth into various-shaped containers in order to learn that shape does not alter quantity. Blocks present outstanding opportunities to demonstrate conservation of mass, since it is relatively simple to see that a tower of four contains the same number of units as does a two-by-two stack. Clay and dough also lend themselves well to teaching this concept. In short, any material, whether liquid or solid, that can be divided and put together again may be used to investigate the principle of conservation.

It is also worthwhile to provide opportunities for measuring in order to demonstrate equality or inequality. Scales are useful in this regard, and yardsticks and measuring tapes are also valuable. Or children can create their own units of measure, using cutouts of feet or paper clips or Popsicle sticks. However, the teacher must realize that despite these aids, children who are unable to grasp the principle of conservation will continue to insist that what their eyes tell them to be true *is* true.

The teacher's role in this area lies in providing many opportunities for the children to manipulate materials and experiment with changing their forms and with returning them to their prior state (reversing the reaction). In addition to supplying experiences, she should make a point of talking with the children and drawing their attention to the unchanging nature of quantity as they manipulate the materials. This is also an excellent time to build related vocabulary, such as *more than, less than,* and *equal to.* Finally, besides talking with the children herself, the teacher should foster discussion and ''argument'' among the children about the nature of conservation, since research (Murray, 1972; Smedslund, 1966) supports Piaget's (1926) contention that such interaction between children will help them decenter and also help them reach correct conclusions.

It is unlikely that children of prekindergarten age will do more than begin to grasp the principle of conservation, but it may be of interest to know how problems could be increased in difficulty should they do so. Conservation problems can be made more difficult by making the contrasts in form more extreme; that is, by making the cylinder taller and thinner or the balls of clay more numerous. (This principle is easy to remember if the reader recalls that even adults can be seduced into believing that tall, thin cereal boxes are a better buy than thick, squat ones of the same weight.) The more pronounced the apparent contrast is between the two quantities, the more likely it is that the child will be misled by appearance and forget that the quantity is actually equal.

Perceiving common relations

The basic skill required in developing this concept is the ability to identify and pair items that are usually associated together but are *not* identical. The activity of perceiving common relations is similar to grouping because it depends on the identification of a common property or bond; it differs from grouping because it involves *pairing* such items rather than working with larger numbers of them. It is useful to cultivate because it probably forms the basis for the later understanding and formulation of analogies (ring is to finger as belt is to—waist, buckle, or sash?). Since these combinations are usually culturally based (salt and pepper, shoes and socks, hat and head), it is important to know the home backgrounds of the children in order to develop pairs that are likely to be familiar to them.

Opposites can also be included in this activity, since there is also a true relationship between them. Thus, hot can be contrasted with cold, up with down, and thick with thin.

We have found that 3- and 4-year-olds enjoy practicing this conceptual task a great deal. It has the kind of appeal that riddles generally have, and the children relish pairing up an assortment of items that are either presented all together in a box or in more gamelike form where several items are set out and their related members are drawn out of a bag one by one. There are some commercial materials on the market that are useful for this purpose, such as two-piece puzzles linking animals with their homes or occupations with appropriate tools. It is also helpful to acquire many pairs of real objects or models of them that belong together and to keep a reserve of these handy to be brought out from time to time for the fun of it.

When the teacher is working with these combinations, it is usually effective for her to ask the child to pick out the thing that *goes most closely* with a selected item or that *belongs best* with it. This is language that the children understand and that is clear enough for them to be able to follow the directions.

Perceiving common relations may be made more difficult by including less familiar combinations, by increasing the number of choices, or by setting up true analogies in which the child has to ascertain the quality common to both pairs of items.

Matching

Matching is the ability to perceive that two items are identical, and it depends on the child's grasping the concept of sameness and differentness. At our Center we have found that this is one of the easier concepts for young children to acquire. Even 2- and 3-year-olds will work at this occupation with interest and diligence if the materials are attractive and not too detailed.

Many commercial materials are available that may be used to provide practice in matching. These range from simple, obvious pictures with few details to quite elaborate discrimination tasks that contain a great deal of detail and very subtle differences. Lotto and bingo games are probably the most prevalent examples of such materials. But matching should not be limited to these kinds of activities. Younger children can grasp this concept by matching buttons (a perennial favorite), matching animal stamps or Christmas stickers, or playing simple picture dominoes. Fabric swatches and wallpaper samples are fun to use for this purpose, too, and can be surprisingly difficult. Incidentally, putting blocks back so that all of one kind go in the same place is a matching *not* grouping exercise, because the blocks are identical.

Matching experiences need not be limited to the sense of vision, of course. Children will also enjoy matching by touch (for texture and thickness), by hearing (duplicating simple sounds, rhythms, or

Photo by Richard Pierce, Santa Barbara City College Children's Center

melodies), or by taste and smell (it is interesting to cut up a variety of white fruits and vegetables, for instance, and ask the children to taste bits of them and find the ones that are the same). Imitation can also be thought of as an attempt to match actions; shadow or mirror dancing, follow-the-leader, and Simon-says may be employed for this purpose. Large muscle activities may be further incorporated by setting out two or three pictures and choosing a youngster to walk over to match one of them with the picture in his hand. (He then has the privilege of picking the next child to do this.) Children who are proficient at pumping may be asked if they can match the arc of their swings with that of the child beside them.

When asking children to complete a match, the teacher should use sentences such as "Show me the one that matches" or "Find me one that's just the same" rather than, "Show me two that are just alike," since an occasional child is misled by the term *alike* and will blithely select something to show the teacher, saying, "Here, I like this one best!" Once he has acquired this verbal misconception of what the teacher means, it can be difficult to get him to change his mind; so talking about *same* rather than *alike* is the more effective choice of language.

As the child becomes more skilled, matching tasks may be increased in difficulty by making the matches more complex and difficult to analyze. This is usually accomplished by increasing the number of details that must be inspected in each picture and also by increasing the number of items to be compared. Ultimately, the material shifts from depending on pictorially meaningful content to more symbolic form; this leads, finally, to using the symbols of the alphabet and numbers.

Understanding the relationship between simple cause and effect

Although it takes children a long time to develop clear ideas of physical causality (Piaget, 1930), they can begin to acquire this concept while attending nursery school. Indeed, good discipline often depends on teaching exactly this kind of relationship between action and outcome, since letting the pun-

ishment fit the crime usually results in allowing the child to experience the logical consequence of his behavior. Thus the child who pulls all the blocks off the shelf is expected to help restack them, and the youngster who dumps his milk on the table must get the sponge and wipe it up himself.

In addition to understanding cause and effect in terms of the social consequences, 4-year-olds can often handle cause-related questions that are phrased, "What would happen if . . . ?" (Kamii, 1972) or "What do you think made [something happen]?" These questions are sound to use because they do not require the child to apply or explain scientific principles that lie beyond his ken, but depend instead on what he can see happen with his own eyes or on what he can deduce from his own experience.

Some examples of successful questions are:
1. What will happen if we add some sugar to the dough?
2. What will happen to your shoes if you go out in the rain without your boots on?
3. How come John dropped the hot pan so quickly?
4. What made the kittens mew when mama cat got up?
5. What made the egg get hard?

Finding the answers to these questions can be accomplished by setting up simple experiments to identify the most probable cause. These experiments enable the children to try out suggested causes, compare results, and then draw conclusions about the most likely reason for something's happening, thereby introducing them to the scientific method.

For example, in order to determine what makes plants grow, the children might think of possibilities such as roots, water, and sunshine and then think of ways they could find out if their ideas are correct—they might think of cutting the roots off a marigold and putting it in earth and comparing this with a rooted one, or putting one plant in the dark and another in the sun, while watering both. Or they might try growing plants with and without water. Of course, doing experiments like this may involve

Photo by Gene Garrett, Los Niños Head Start

wasting and breaking or destroying some things, but the teacher really can't allow a misguided idea of thrift to stand in the way of letting the children figure something out. Four-year-olds in particular enjoy carrying out this kind of investigation, although they will need help figuring out how to set up the experiment. Remember that it is much more valuable for the children to propose possibilities, make predictions, and try them out than for the teacher to guide them to thinking of possibilities she has thought up already.

Teaching about simple cause-and-effect relations presents one of the most interesting educational opportunities available to the nursery school teacher, and both natural history and physical science offer rich possibilities that can be used for this purpose. For this reason, several references on science for young children are listed at the end of this chapter.

Of course, cause-and-effect experiences needn't be elaborate, full-blown experiments. Here is a partial list of simple cause-and-effect experiences recently identified by students in the Cognitive Development Class*: using a squirt gun, flashlight, or garlic press (with dough or clay); blowing soap bubbles; turning on a light; blowing up a balloon and pricking it with a pin; using all sorts of wind-up toys such as hopping frogs, little cars, and paddle boats; using grinders and graters; scales (weighing heavy and light things for contrast); listening to children's hearts after they've been sitting, walking, or running; using a bank made like a dog house—when a penny goes in the front, the dog comes out and grabs the money; turning a kaleidoscope; striking a match; mixing paint to obtain different colors; pushing a button to make the clown move; and stretching rubber bands between various nails on

---

*My thanks to the Class of 1978 Nursery School majors of Santa Barbara City College.

St. Andrew's Nursery School

a board—different tensions producing different pitched sounds.

Any of these experiences can generate good learning opportunities if the teacher encourages the children to explain in very simple terms to each other what made the action happen, and/or to do some predicting in advance.

PROVISION OF OPPORTUNITIES FOR PRACTICING CONCEPT FORMATION SKILLS
Develop needed materials

There are two ways to obtain materials to use for teaching these concept formation tasks. The easiest, most expensive, and most obvious way is to rely on commercially developed tabletop activities. There are many such materials available, particularly in the area of matching and seriation. The trouble with them is that they often do not relate closely to curriculum topics, and they generally use only pictures as the medium of instruction. (Montessori materials are a welcome exception to this trend.)

The second way to introduce opportunities for this kind of concept development is to embed them directly in the curriculum. This is likely to be more work for the teacher, who will have to develop materials for the children's use, but it is also more satisfying because it gives her a chance to be creative and to utilize a much wider variety of materials and activities. Best of all, teacher-developed experiences mean that vertical activities can be directly related to and coordinated with the subjects that have interested the children. It is not difficult to generate such ideas; the outline that follows this section provides an example of how this can be done using the subject of water. Interested readers would also gain a good deal from studying *The Cognitively Oriented Curriculum* (Weikart, Rogers, Adcock, and McClelland, 1971).

Although the curriculum-embedded approach is generally to be preferred, the more specifically designed tabletop activities have the advantage of being readily available and convenient and can be self-selected and monitored by the children. The danger that must be guarded against is offering only boxed activities for concept development. This results in too narrow and dull a presentation to be fully effective.

Provide consistent opportunities for practice

It is necessary to provide repeated opportunities for experience and practice (Hendrick, 1973). One or two chances to practice grouping, matching, or ordering are not sufficient. To understand these concepts fully, children need to practice them consistently, using many materials and moving from simpler to more difficult activities as their skills increase.

Above all, make certain the activities are fun

Every year the students in my college classes devise and construct a great many activities to stimulate mental development, and every year I am struck by the attractiveness of these materials—indeed, if children are passing the door, it's all we can do to shoo them out while we are discussing what the teachers have made. Teachers seem to have a much better basic grasp of how to devise appealing materials than most manufacturers do. The activities are so colorful, and they reflect a real familiarity with what young children really care about.

Pleasure is also increased for the children when the activities are at the right developmental level—the satisfaction of meeting the challenge of an activity that is just a little bit but not too much harder than what the child has already mastered is obviously gratifying. Throughout the previous discus-

sion, suggestions have been included showing how the levels of difficulty of various abilities can be increased, so strategies will only be summarized here that might be used with any of the abilities to increase the challenge. These include adding more choices, asking if there is another way to do it, asking the children to put what they are doing into words, utilizing a different sensory mode in place of vision (such as using only touch, or only hearing), using memory, asking children to tell you something in reverse order, or using items that are less familiar. A word of caution—we have had children in the Center, usually 5-year-olds, who enjoyed being challenged in all these ways; however, the key word here is *enjoyed*. The purpose is not to make things so difficult that children sweat and struggle over them. The foregoing list is included merely to provide an idea of possibilities to go on to.

Another caution I want to add is the undesirability of resorting to competition and comparison to generate ''fun.'' Setting up activities with the aim of seeing who can do something quickest or ''best'' takes a lot of fun out of it for the losers. It is fairly easy to substitute something like suspense in place of competition in order to sustain interest. Suspense strategies can be as simple as having children pull things out of a mystery bag and then decide where they should go, or asking them to choose from one hand or the other when the teacher holds two things behind her back.

Here are some additional activities that one student developed for matching ''games'' that were fun for the children.*

Instead of choosing a cognitive game from the Center, I decided to make an original one. The idea is based on a game my Grandmother used to give me to play. She would take the buttons from her button box and ask me to ''help'' her by sorting them into the compartments of her sewing tray. I was always so proud that I had been able to ''help.''

My cognitive game is simple to make. You simply cut an egg carton in half (either plastic or

*Activities courtesy Mary Anderson, Class of 1979.

cardboard). The six cups are used as the compartments, and the lid (with the cut end closed with a strip of cardboard and tape) is the tray that holds the assortment to be sorted. For my game I have chosen a kitchen assortment of shapes and sizes of macaronis and spaghetties. These objects can be dyed with a little food coloring if color is desired. For younger children you might glue one of each thing in the bottom of each cup; for the older children this is not necessary. I have made six of these for group time. Each child receives his own individual game to work on by sorting the items into the cups.

Then to make it more fun, the teacher can use it as a group game. She can put several of each item into a "feely" box and have each child put his hand in and pick up one item and identify it in the box before he pulls it out. He can identify it by picking up a matching item from his own tray to show they are the same.

Another fun way to play this game, which the older children like especially, is to have them do the sorting with their eyes closed. Simply tell them which item they are to sort out from the others in their tray and have them do it by feel only.

Another way to use this game is to have a child choose one of the items (by turning his back) and to enclose it in his fist and pass it into the fist of the next child. That child then tries to identify it without looking (by choosing an identical item from his tray).

This cognitive game is simple to make and costs nothing. It develops the mental skill of matching as well as giving practice in haptic shape identification and can also be used for size ordering (as when the teacher asks "Which is the largest?" or "Which is the smallest macaroni?"). It can also be used to help develop receptive skills such as listening and comprehending what directions were given and following through on these, and it helps develop fine muscle control and eye-hand coordination.

SAMPLE OUTLINE FOR DEVELOPING A UNIT OF COGNITIVE CURRICULUM

The difficulty with offering an outline of curriculum is that it may give the impression that the teacher planned it all beforehand and then simply dished it out to the children. This should never be the case. A curriculum must stem from the children's interests as these develop. The teacher capitalizes on these interests to provide (1) opportunities for emotional and social learnings, (2) information and vocabulary that she feels would be valuable for the child to possess, and (3) opportunities to practice various concept formation tasks.

A cognitive curriculum based on water*

This focus was selected because most of the children in the nursery school where Mrs. Weiler was teaching were living in a town that was water conscious because of a drought. The children seemed quite concerned about conserving water, and would report running taps, or water running on the pavement from sprinklers. She also chose this topic because the children all loved to play with water, and she felt this subject would give them pleasurable experiences as well as provide worthwhile subject matter. (I chose it because there are other well-done curriculum suggestions on this topic [Glockner, Shapira, and Spencer, 1976; Hill, 1977], and I thought it would be of interest to use it to illustrate a less traditional approach to thinking about the educational values of water.)

The curriculum was developed to fit 3½- and 4-year-old children. The group consisted of 15 children, the ethnic makeup happened to be two Finnish youngsters, four Japanese children, and nine Anglos. They all come from low- or middle-income families.

I. Affective learning possibilities
   A. Learnings that will foster emotional health
      1. We will offer lots of water play. The sensory experience, the release of tensions, and the relaxing quality of such play foster emotional health.
      2. We will be doing some planting and watering, and the children will give wa-

---

*I am indebted to Joan Weiler, Class of 1978, for most of the following outline.

ter to the animals at the school. The development of responsibility and self-esteem during these activities will also foster emotional health.

B. Learnings that will foster social development

1. We will be caring for our plants (garden) together, and learning that plants need water. This, ideally, will foster social development as the children work together. We will also do some cleaning jobs together using water, such as washing dishes or doll clothes, or, perhaps, washing a dog. Such tasks of meaningful work, done together, enhance social development.

2. We will be doing some sand and mud construction. This often leads to social interaction. (This semester, for example, the children often worked together to build extensive waterways leading to an "ocean.") We will also be utilizing lengths of plastic pipe and connectors (hoses, gutters, and joints). These kinds of things elicit cooperation since children need to help each other join pipes, make plans, and so forth.

C. Learnings that foster cross-cultural understanding

1. Since we want to emphasize that all people of all cultures use water, we will ask our families to share any containers they may have from other cultures that could be used to carry water (I already know of a gourd dipper from Africa, a Hopi pot, and a brass pot from India). These should be unbreakable if possible or used only at group time if breakable.

2. We will talk about how different peoples of various cultures use water for bathing, and we have been invited to bathe at the home of one of our Japanese families who have an authentic Japanese-style bathroom. Next we will invite the par-

ents of our Finnish children to come along on another day when we try out the sauna available under special arrangement with our YMCA and finally we will partake of the outdoor "hot tub" owned by a third Santa Barbara family.

II. Step II learnings—horizontal curriculum (those that primarily teach facts and increase labelling vocabulary*)

A. Living things need water to survive (fact). Children will be able to explain what happens when living things are deprived of water (objective).

1. We will have two identical plants in pots and observe what happens when one is watered and one is not.

2. We will read *The Water We Drink* (Bloome, E., 1971) to explore people's need for water.

3. Those children who wish to may try going an entire morning without drinking anything.

B. Water always runs downhill (fact). Children will be able to show this is true by citing examples where they have tested out this statement and found it was accurate (objective).

1. Encourage the children to try to pour something up instead of down!

2. Ask them to suggest ways to make the water go up (such as turning the hose on harder or lifting cupfuls of water up on a ledge). What happens if the water is not contained in some way after it goes up?

C. Water can assume different forms or states (fact). Children will be able to name several of these forms and describe what they are like (objective).

1. Children will visit the local "ice house"

---

*Please note that in the remainder of this outline, capital letters identify the goals or educational objectives and numerals identify some activities that could be used to help children reach these goals.

and bring back a large cake of ice and observe what becomes of it when left out overnight.

2. Children will watch a pan of water boil and see steam condense on a lid held over it. (NOTE: *great care must be taken with this activity—steam burns badly and doesn't look hot; this is one activity children may only watch!*)

III. Step III learnings—vertical curriculum

A. Grouping. The child will be able to identify the common properties that define a group and to discriminate between what does and does not belong to the group.

1. Make a grouping game of pictures of things that are wet (fish in a bowl, rain, mud puddles) and dry (basket of dry, clean clothes, dry grass, and so on) and use it for lotto and sorting activities.

2. After water play, set out several storage baskets and ask the children which kinds of equipment should be sorted together (possibly sieves in one, things that hold water in a second, or . . . ?)

B. Seriation. The child will be able to arrange things according to a graduated change in size or condition.

1. Carrying water to the garden, have four or five buckets with varying amounts of water in them—make a game of carrying them to the garden in the order of their fullness.

2. Using several identical sponges, ask children if they can squeeze them so they range from very soggy to almost dry.

C. Temporal ordering. The child can arrange events according to the order they occur in time. Because of the children's interest in conservation it seemed worthwhile to teach them at least the rudiments of the water cycle. To make this more real I will draw on what they have learned about evaporation from the steam experiment, and about how water always runs downhill, and we will also read several stories, such as *Raindrop Splash* (Tresselt, 1969), *A Drop of Water* (Rosenfeld, 1970), and look at the beautiful pictures in *Paddle to the Sea* (Holling, no date), so they will have a grasp of how water falls from the sky, flows to the sea, and evaporates to the sky once more.

1. Picture cards of the stages of the water cycle can be arranged on the flannel board—perhaps leaving out one step and asking the children to tell what's missing or putting up two or three cards in order and asking them to pick out and put up the one that comes next.

2. Sing "There's a Hole in the Bucket, Dear Liza." This is an old folk song setting up a whole sequence of happenings involving a leaking bucket.

D. Common relations. The child can indicate which nonidentical objects are most closely related, that is, which belong together as a pair.

1. Offer a tabletop game of pictures of things that go together that have to do with water (faucet and water drop, soap and towel, goldfish and bowl, rain and an umbrella, and so forth.)

2. Draw attention to wilted and nonwilted plants—ask which ones need water.

E. Piagetian conservation. The child will be able to explain that the quantity remains the same although the appearance may change. As previously discussed, we would not anticipate that children of nursery school age could do this. Nevertheless, they need many opportunities to experiment with pouring and comparison, since this helps lay the foundation for later understanding.

1. Present many opportunities for water play utilizing a good assortment of different-sized containers—occasionally an older child even enjoys referring to the

lines on measuring cups and looking at what happens when equal amounts of water are measured and then poured into different-shaped containers.

2. Young children are also interested in the fact that one can reverse states when using water: changing water into ice and back into water.

F. Matching. The child will be able to identify two items that are identical (exactly the same) or different.

1. Using clear containers of all the same size (glass, though perilous, is really best for this purpose if meticulously supervised), fill a number of pairs of jars with the same amounts of water (varying the amounts for different pairs), and ask the child to put together the ones that are the same. Ask them if there are other ways they could tell they were the same (or different). They might want to strike them with spoons to show they make the same sound, or make some kind of measuring device to compare heights, or . . . ?)

2. Set out eye droppers and little plastic bottles, and ask children if they can use them to fill bottles to equal heights.

3. Fill one cup with crushed ice and another equally full of water—will the cups still be filled to the same level when the ice melts?

G. Cause and effect. The child is able to associate a particular action with a specific result. In our case the children were especially interested in the effects of wasted water or having no water (conservation, but, of course, not conservation in the Piagetian sense of the term). When this curriculum was actually used, they decided that wasting water caused the shortage.

1. The children talked over how we could use less water at nursery school and decided we should use fewer faucets. To

remind us all not to use them they tied rags around their handles.

2. They also, on their own initiative, decided that using a running hose for water play caused too much waste and confined themselves to using tubs instead.

3. There are, of course, many other cause/effect relationships related to the subject of water that could be explored, ranging from finding out what makes ice melt to what makes a toy waterwheel turn around or what causes the earth to erode.

QUESTIONS AND ACTIVITIES

1. What are some of the pros and cons of stressing intellectual development at the preschool level? Can you suggest a model for such learning that you feel would have undesirable side effects?

2. Do you agree that pleasure should be the inevitable accompaniment to learning? Can you think of occasions where this has been true of your educational experience and cases where it has not been true? Analyze the circumstances that made the learning pleasureful or burdensome.

3. Might it be possible that nursery school teachers are depriving children of the right to learn the things that would help them succeed best in elementary school when we stress play, creativity, and mental health rather than emphasizing prereading skills such as learning the alphabet and counting? What might be the case for placing greater emphasis on academic learning at the preschool level?

4. After viewing the Stendler-Karplus films on classification and conservation, try out some of the Piagetian tasks demonstrated in the films with children ranging in age from 3 to 8. Do your experiments bear out Piaget's contention that children pass through various stages of development in thinking? Try rewording what you say to the children. Does this make any difference in their response?

5. Pick up on a current interest of the children in your group, and make an outline, based on the examples at the end of the chapter, that utilizes affective and cognitive learning and incorporates both horizontal and vertical curriculum.

6. Concoct activities that fit the various mental abilities, such as ordering and grouping, and try them out with the children. Then add variations to the activities that make them easier or more difficult in order to suit the needs of individual children in the group. Set aside some shelves in your school where these materials can be accumulated.

7. Once you have acquired a fundamental understanding of these mental abilities, keep a record of ways you have been able to add spontaneous practice of them to your curriculum as the day develops, and discuss these activities with your curriculum class.

8. Turn back to the picture of the boy and rooster at the begin-

ning of this chapter. Which mental ability might he be using as the chicken pecks him?

REFERENCES FOR FURTHER READING

Building Desirable Attitudes toward Learning

Ashton-Warner, S. *Teacher*. New York: Bantam Books, Inc., 1965. Sylvia Ashton-Warner gives an exciting description of the way she approached teaching and learning and made these activities truly relevant to the lives of her young Maori students.

Carson, R. *The sense of wonder*. New York: Harper & Row, Publishers, 1956. This is a beautifully written account concerned with generating a sense of wonder in young children. The outstanding illustrations in this volume, combined with the excellent text, make it a classic of natural history.

Jackson, N. E., Robinson, H. B., and Dale, P. S. *Cognitive development in young children*. Washington, D.C.: National Institute of Education, U.S. Dept. of Health, Education, and Welfare, 1976. In a relatively brief booklet, *Cognitive Development* relates recent research on various aspects of this subject to educational practices in early childhood classrooms. It is very clear and backs up every recommendation with a number of citations; highly recommended.

Understanding Piaget and Guilford

Since both Piaget and Guilford can be difficult reading for the uninitiated, it is best to begin with descriptive overviews of their work.

Beard, R. *An outline of Piaget's developmental psychology for students and teachers*. New York: The New American Library Inc., 1972. This is a brief, well-written summary of Piaget's major concepts presented in chronological order from infancy through adolescence; excellent, clear, unpretentious handling of potentially obscure material.

Brearley, M., and Hitchfield, E. *A guide to reading Piaget*. New York: Schocken Books Inc., 1966. Brearley and Hitchfield present Piagetian concepts according to topics such as moral development, number, and measurement. They include many samples of quotations from Piaget's own writing, which convey the flavor and style of his investigations.

Charles, C. M. *Teacher's petit Piaget*. Belmont, Calif.: Fearon Publishers, 1974. This is about as plain and simple as you can get and still talk about Piagetian theory at all—it is a good place for the absolute beginner to begin!

Formanek, R., and Gurian, A. *Charting intellectual development: A practical guide to Piagetian tasks*. Springfield, Ill.: Charles C Thomas, Publisher, 1976. *Charting Intellectual Development* provides very clear descriptions of how to present various Piagetian tasks in order to determine the developmental level of the child.

Lavatelli, C. S. *Piaget's theory applied to an early childhood curriculum*. Boston: American Science and Engineering, Inc., 1970. Lavatelli demonstrates how Piaget's findings can be translated into classroom policies and curriculum. She reviews the steps by which important concepts such as classification and seriation develop and provides examples of curricula that would be appropriate for working with these concepts.

Meeker, M. N. *The Structure of Intellect: Its interpretation and uses*. Columbus, Ohio: Charles E. Merrill Publishing Co., 1969. This book is written with teachers in mind, and in it Meeker defines and explains the various Structure of Intellect categories, identifies tests for each cell, and gives many suggestions for a curriculum intended to fit the categories. Although written for use with older children, it is possible to modify some of the suggestions and use them with preschool children.

Relationship of Language and Thought

Lewis, M. M. *Language, thought, and personality*. New York: Basic Books, Inc., Publishers, 1963. Chapter 10, "Language and Concrete Thinking," contains a good analysis of the relation of language to cognitive development cast in terms of Piagetian theory. It is nice to read because it describes the Piagetian concepts and discusses research on language related to these concepts.

"Left and Right Brain Psychology"

Ornstein, R. The split and whole brain. *Human Nature*, 1978, *1*(5), 76-83. This is an up-to-date, well-written explanation of the "split brain" theory and of some of the research that lends credibility to it. For a fuller treatment of this subject, Ornstein's book, *The Psychology of Consciousness* (2nd ed.), New York: Harcourt-Brace Jovanovich, Inc., 1977, is highly recommended.

Suggestions for Curriculum and Activities for Developing Various Mental Concepts

Cratty, B. J. *Intelligence in action: Physical activities for enhancing intellectual abilities*. Englewood Cliffs, N.J. Prentice-Hall, Inc., 1973. The suggestions included in this book are helpful because they remind us that cognitive learning can and should be implemented by use of large muscle skills as well as by means of more typically intellectual activities.

Kamii, C., and DeVries, R. *Piaget, children and number*. Washington, D.C.: National Association for the Education of Young Children, 1976. For those interested in beginning arithmetic skills, this pamphlet offers many examples of activities that demonstrate how to apply Piagetian theory when teaching elementary number concepts.

Marzollo, J., and Lloyd, J. *Learning through play*. New York: Harper & Row, Publishers, 1972. Written in nontechnical language, *Learning Through Play* suggests many activities intended to provide practice in various abilities. It is notable because the activities are interesting, and each one is accompanied by a specific explanation of its intended purpose; delightfully illustrated; suitable for teachers and parents.

Meeker, M. N., Sexton, K., and Richardson, M. O. *SOI abilities workbook*. Los Angeles: Loyola-Marymount University, 1970. This workbook lists innumerable activities fitting the Guilford cells. It is primarily appropriate for older children but still useful because it suggests ideas that could be translated into activities suitable for younger children.

Sharp, E. *Thinking is child's play*. New York: E. P. Dutton & Co., Inc., 1969. This simple, yet well-done book begins with a brief outline of Piaget's philosophy and then describes various games to be used for the purpose of providing experience in classifying, seriating, and so forth; contains many useful ideas.

Weikart, D., Rogers, L., Adcock, C., and McClelland, D. *The cognitively oriented curriculum: A framework for preschool teachers*. Washington, D.C.: National Association for the Education of Young Children, 1971. The authors describe a model of a Piagetian nursery school, discuss the philosophy and management of the school as a whole, and then provide sample days that illustrate the way Piagetian concepts can be integrated into ongoing curriculum; an invaluable resource for nursery school teachers.

Specific Resources for Teaching Science

Carmichael, V. *Science experiences for young children*. Los Angeles: Southern California Association for the Education of Young Children, 1969. This book contains a wealth of suggestions for teaching science to very young children. Exceptionally good lists of additional references, including books and movies, follow each chapter.

Harlan, J. D. *Science experiences for the early childhood years*. Columbus, Ohio: Charles E. Merrill Publishing Co., 1976. I recommend this book as being a particularly rich source of additional curriculum-related ideas, including music, fingerplays, lists of children's books, creative ideas, and even some examples of third-step curriculum labeled ''thinking games.'' This is a valuable book to own.

Holt, B.-G. *Science with young children*. Washington, D.C.: National Association for the Education of Young Children, 1977. Rather than utilizing a cookbook method of how to teach science, Bess-Gene Holt's book concentrates on a broader approach that emphasizes strategies and enthusiasm; this book bubbles!

Neuman, D. Sciencing for young children. In K. R. Baker (Ed.), *Ideas that work with young children*. Washington, D.C.: National Association for the Education of Young Children, 1972. This is a clear-cut discussion of how to plan a curriculum that is based on science. It provides some good examples of suitable materials, but the article is most helpful because of the theoretical framework that it describes. Neuman stresses the importance of process rather than fact learning.

For the Advanced Student

Refer also to the references at the end of the book for a list of publications by Piaget and Guilford.

ERIC. *Cerebral dominance and its psychological and educational implications: An ERIC abstract bibliography*. Urbana, Ill.: Educational Resource Information Center/Early Childhood Education, University of Illinois, 1978. For those intrigued by the concept of left brain/right brain functioning, this bibliography will prove useful, since it covers everything from handedness to creativity.

Evans, E. *Contemporary influences in early childhood education*. New York: Holt, Rinehart and Winston, Inc., 1971. Evans presents a solid review of the pros and cons of Piagetian theory. This work should be read with attention, since it discusses weaknesses and raises issues as well as describing the theory itself.

Flavell, J. H. *The developmental psychology of Jean Piaget*. Princeton, N.J.: Van Nostrand Reinhold Co., 1963. In this classic work Flavell reviews and interprets the bulk of Piaget's writing; still an important reference for any serious student of Piaget.

Gruber, H. E., and Vonèche, J. J. (Eds.). *The essential Piaget*. London: Routledge and Kegan Paul, Ltd., 1977. This is an anthology of most of the more important contributions of Piaget. It's convenient to have these all in one place; selections are preceded by brief introductory explanations.

Sagan, C. *The dragons of Eden: Speculations on the evolution of human intelligence*. New York: Random House, Inc., 1977. It's a pleasure to recommend such a lively ''best-seller'' that is so full of information and interesting ideas about the human brain; well worth reading; available in paperback.

Sigel, I. E. The Piagetian system and the world of education. In D. Elkind and J. H. Flavell (Eds.), *Studies in cognitive development*. New York: Oxford University Press, 1969. Sigel provides a thoughtful discussion of the implications of Piagetian theory for teachers and raises a nice point about the often unappreciated value of using divergent thought in relation to developing classification skills.

Sigel, I. E., and Hooper, F. H. (Eds.). *Logical thinking in children: Research based on Piaget's theory*. New York: Holt, Rinehart and Winston, Inc., 1968. Research that explores various aspects of Piaget's theory can make almost as interesting reading as Piaget's original ingenious investigations. Sigel and Hooper present the findings from many such projects conveniently gathered together in one place for the benefit of the student; an important, basic reference for the serious student.

PART SEVEN

Working with special situations

Photo by Richard Pierce, Santa Barbara City College Children's Center

17 □ What mothers need*

Before this enlightened point of view came into practice, parents were usually treated as people to be endured or to be taught. In those days, parents' meetings were strictly "telling" occasions. Parents were either told what they should do or not do, or were told what the teachers did and why it was right. The implication was "if you did the same, you would have no problems." They were told what toys to buy, what books to read. It seems quite likely that such practices succeeded admirably in increasing their sense of inadequacy.†

No matter how dedicated and meticulous we are about establishing a good life for the child at school, nursery school teachers must never forget that the most significant part of the environment of the young child lies outside the school. Quite wholesomely and rightly, there is a much more profound influence in the child's life—his home, his family, and, most particularly, his mother. Because this is true, it makes good sense, if we hope to establish the best total environment for the child, to include his mother and family as an important part of the nursery school experience.

This is a desirable policy to follow because the child's anxiety over leaving his home will be lessened if he senses that there is a strong bond between his home and the school. It is also desirable because the teacher may be able to offer the mother meaningful help about everyday problems of child rearing as well as gain the opportunity to learn much from the mother about her youngster and how to get along with him.

*Adapted from Hendrick, J. *Young Children,* 1970, *25,* 109-114.
†From *Teaching young children* (p. 160), by Evelyn Beyer, copyright © 1968, by Western Publishing Company, Inc., reprinted by permission of The Bobbs-Merrill Company, Inc.

PROBLEMS THAT INTERFERE WITH GOOD COMMUNICATION

Despite the important advantages in keeping communication open, many mothers and teachers do not get along comfortably together.

The teacher may dread the mother's criticisms ("Why does Harry have paint on his shirt again?") or feel financially at her mercy because a displeased parent may yank her child out of nursery school. Moreover, the teacher may blame the mother for the child's shortcomings; this is bound to interfere with a good relationship between them.

The mother also feels vulnerable to criticism. After all, her child, who is an extension of herself, is on view. First-time mothers particularly can be quite frightened of the teacher's opinion, and all mothers yearn to know that the teacher likes their child and that he is doing well. The relationship is doubly touchy because the mother may be seeking validation of her own worth as a person by ascertaining that the teacher approves of her offspring. She is ready to believe the teacher (and also to feel threatened and angry) if blame is implied.

The mother may also fear that if she speaks frankly and mentions something she doesn't like about the school or about what her child is doing there, she will antagonize the teacher. She worries about the possibility of reprisals on the child when she is not there. This is comparable to the parent who fears complaining to hospital personnel lest they discriminate against her child. The fact that most professional people are more mature than this may not affect the parent's innate caution in this matter.

Besides being vulnerable to criticism and wishing to protect her child, the mother may dread being displaced by the teacher in the child's affections. Separation involves mixed feelings for her. On one hand, she deeply wants to wean her child: she is tired of changing his pants and tying his shoes and never going anywhere alone. But, at the same time, something inside her resents having the teacher take over. To add to her confusion, the mother may also be struggling with guilty feelings over the relief she feels at being able to parcel Agatha out for a few days a week. Surely, if she were a ''good mother,'' she wouldn't feel so elated at the thought of going shopping by herself! So she worries about what the teacher would think of her if the teacher only knew.

For both mother and teacher there remain all the past experiences and previous relationships with other teachers and mothers that set the tone of what each expects of the other. In addition to pleasant memories, there are emotionally powerful ones of the principal's office, staying after school, authoritarian teachers and militant, unreasonable parents that lie at the back of consciousness and plague parents and teachers during their initial contacts. It's no wonder then, with all these things conspiring to build walls between families and teachers, that we must invest some effort and understanding if we wish to establish a more rewarding relationship between the adults who are so important in the life of the young child.

SUGGESTIONS FOR ESTABLISHING A GOOD RELATIONSHIP BETWEEN MOTHER AND TEACHER

Surely there must be some way to establish a bond that leads to problem solving rather than to defense building. The question is, how can the teacher go about doing this?

Probably the most essential ingredient in a more satisfactory relationship between teacher and mother is that the teacher have the child's welfare truly at heart and that she be genuinely concerned about him. My experience has been that when the mother believes this to be true—which means, of course, that it has to *be* true and not just something the teacher *wishes* were true—when the mother really senses the teacher's good will, she will forgive the teacher her inadvertent transgressions, and the relationship will warm up as trust develops.

Genuine concern and caring can be expressed in a variety of ways. Faithful caretaking is one way. The teacher takes pains to see that everything the child has made is valued by being put in his cubby for him to take home, his belongings are kept track of, his nose is wiped when it needs it, and, although he may not be the pristinely clean youngster at the end of the day that he was upon arrival, he is tidied up and has had his face washed before his mother picks him up. The teacher also shows that she cares by carefully enforcing the health and safety regulations and by planning a curriculum that is interesting, various, and suited to the needs of individual children.

Another way for the teacher to show concern is by expressing genuine interest in each child to his parent. For example, it is always sound practice to comment to the mother on something her youngster has enjoyed that day. It may be the friendly statement that ''Helen really loves our new bunny; she fed him and watched him half the morning,'' or it might be, ''I think Jerry is making friends with our new boy, Todd; they spent a lot of time with the trains in the block corner today.'' These comments assure the parent that the child has had attention from the teacher and that she is aware of him as an individual rather than as just one of the troop.

Still another kind of caring can be indicated on a more subtle level by letting the mother know that the teacher is on the child's side *but not on the child's side as opposed to the mother's.* Occasionally teachers fall into the fantasy of thinking, ''If only I could take that child home with me for a

Brooks Institute and School of Photography

week and give him a steady, loving environment . . . '' Sometimes a child will say in a rush of affection, ''Oh, I wish *you* were my mother!'' In order to avoid an emotionally confusing and difficult situation for the child, it is important that the teacher clarify her role. She can handle this by gently replying, ''We *are* having fun, and I like you, too; but, of course, you already have a mother—I'm not your mother, I'm your *teacher*. I take care of you at school, and your mother takes care of you at home.'' This avoids rivalry and makes a friendly alliance between mother and teacher more likely.

It is also difficult to be on the mother's side if the teacher blames the parent for all the child's problems. This disapproval, even if unspoken, cannot help being sensed by the mother. In any situation where I feel critical of a parent, I have found it helpful to remember what Beth Leonhard recommends: ''Ask yourself, if *I* were that mother, with that set of problems and that background, could I do any better with that child?''*

Another thing to remember is that, as any mother of more than one child knows, children are born with different temperaments. No matter what parents do, children are different to start with and remain so, no matter what the environment. Therefore, it is ridiculous to hold the parent accountable for all the child's shortcomings.

Thus we see that the teacher can put the mother at ease by letting her know that she is concerned about the child, that she is on both the child's and mother's side, and that she does not feel that everything the child does is the mother's fault. After all, mothers are not ogres—they also want what is best for their children. A sense of common, shared concern is worth working for, because once the mother feels its existence, she is freer to work with the teacher in the child's behalf.

Working with mothers in a positive way requires that the teacher be accessible in two senses of the word. First, she must be accessible because she cares about the child; second, she must be physically

---

*Leonhard, B. Keynote address. Paper presented at the TAEYC Workshop, September 1963, Santa Barbara, California.

available when the mother is around the school. In some schools, availability can be hard to come by. The teacher may be occupied with setting up as the children arrive and able to give the parent only a passing word, or at the end of the day she may be so harrassed that she hasn't time or energy to talk.

It is possible, however, to arrange the schedule so that whoever handles counseling does gate duty the first and last 15 minutes of the day or during peak arrival and departure times. If she is free from other responsibilities at that time, she can see each parent for countless casual meetings and can build relationships of friendliness and trust more easily. The sheer informality of this encounter robs it of a good deal of threat. Chatting right by the gate, the mother knows that she can hasten away if the conversation takes too threatening a turn. In addition, she is likely to see the teacher in a variety of moods and predicaments, which will increase the teacher's humanity.

This repeated, consistent contact is far superior to relying solely on the more formal and frightening ''conference'' which may occur once or twice a semester. After a comfortable, everyday relationship is well established, than an occasional conference with a longer uninterrupted opportunity to talk can be used to better advantage.

COUNSELING WITH PARENTS

Once lines of communication are open, the question remains, what do we do then?

When people talk together, many levels of relating can exist between them. During the year all these levels can be used by nursery school teachers, depending on the situation.

The simplest level is a rather impersonal one where the teacher may say to the parent, ''This is what we did in school today,'' or ''He's coming along very well.'' On this level, at least the mother knows that the teacher wants her to know what's happening at school. Most new relationships have to start about here.

On another level the teacher acts as the supportive information provider and general comforter. In this guise she interprets the child's behavior to the mother on the basis of her extensive experience with other children. For example, the simple information that many 4-year-olds relish ''disgraceful'' language can be a great relief to a mother who is secretly tormented by the worry that she suddenly has a pervert on her hands.

At yet another level the mother-teacher relationship has more of a counseling flavor to it. This is guidance, but not guidance in the sense that the teacher tells the mother what to do. Guidance means that the teacher works with the mother in terms of conscious motivation and behavior to help her discover what may be causing various behavior problems in the child and to help her figure out how to cope with them.

My impression is that teachers who have had special training are more likely to have the aplomb to attempt this third level. However, all teachers could increase their skills, do no harm and probably considerable good by offering themselves in a guidance role to parents in need of help—especially if they concentrate on listening rather than prescribing. The truth is that even when parents ask for help, they usually know the answer already. They are simply having difficulty applying it.

Excluding the occasional special situation where more professional help is required, what mothers need in order to work out a difficulty is the chance to talk out how they feel and evaluate whether a tentative solution is right for them and their unique child. Tremendous comfort comes to a distressed mother when she is given the opportunity to air a problem with someone who can listen attentively and who is not too shaken by the confession that Ethel and Mary have been sitting behind the back fence doing you know what! Allowing her to express her feelings of shame, or occasionally even anguish, over her child's behavior is a positive good to offer a mother in a counseling situation.

It is also true that teachers who have known literally hundreds of youngsters do have a broader background of experience than most parents. It seems only right to pool this knowledge with the mother's, as long as the teacher's alternatives are offered in such a way that the mother feels free to accept or reject them. The parent will be able to use the

teacher's range of knowledge most easily if the teacher points out to her that no matter how much she knows in general about children, she will *never* know as much about the individual child as the mother does.

Instead of providing instant answers to all problems posed by parents, the teacher will find it more useful to ask questions instead, such as ''Why don't you tell me what you've tried already?'' or, ''What are your thoughts about what to do next?'' When a mother comes to say that her child has begun ''misbehaving'' in some new way (perhaps he is fighting a great deal with his sister or has begun having nightmares), the best question to ask is ''I wonder if you could tell me what else happened about the same time?'' The typical response is, ''Well, nothing much. Let me see, now, I guess that was about the time my in-laws came to visit, and, oh yes, his little dog was run over, and . . .'' By this means the mother gains useful insight into what has upset her child and usually can formulate a plan about what she might do to help him get on an even keel again.

Another cornerstone of good counseling is patience. It seems to be human nature that we want instant results, but change often takes a very long time. I used to despair when I made a suggestion that the parent ignored. I was most concerned on the occasions when I referred the family to a specialist, and the parent declined to act on the referral. My implicit assumption was that if the family didn't do it then, they never would. Happily, I have found this to be a false assumption. To be sure, parents may not be ready this year to face the problem of Jeffrey's temper tantrums and hyperactivity, but they have at least heard that the possibility of a problem exists, and the next professional person who approaches them may have greater success because the ground has been prepared.

Nowadays I am more wary of the mother who agrees completely and instantly with my suggestions. Usually there isn't very much movement in these cases. The chance to think out, backtrack, consider various solutions, and take time to get used to an idea is indispensable in a guidance situation.

LIMITS TO GUIDANCE WORK

We must also recognize that there are some behavior and developmental problems that are beyond the teacher's ability to handle. It is vital to be clear about where to draw the line and how far to go in guidance work. My rule of thumb is, "When in doubt, refer." If the situation looks serious or does not respond to matter-of-fact remedies, it is time to suggest a specialist. In general, it is too risky and takes more advanced training than a typical nursery school teacher possesses to draw implications and offer interpretations to mothers about deeper, more compelx reasons for behavior. Fortunately, there are highly trained, skilled specialists on whom we can rely to solve serious problems, so let's leave Oedipus and his troublesome kin to our psychiatric cohorts.

SUMMARY

Sensible caution and referral to an expert is advisable under some circumstances, but teachers can offer a lot of help and work in many ways with parents to bring about a happier life for their children. In order to do this, it is first necessary to overcome various problems that make communication between parents and teachers difficult. One of the most effective things a teacher can do is make it plain to the parent that she has the welfare of the child at heart and that she wants to join with the mother to help the child. She can also take care to be available when the mother wants to talk, and she can provide the opportunity for many easy-going, casual contacts.

Once the lines of communication are open, the teacher can offer help by serving as a friendly listener who assists the parent in assessing the nature of the difficulty and in proposing alternatives until she finds the one best suited for her and her child. Teachers who assume this guidance function offer mothers what they need the most—an accepting attitude, an open ear, and a warm heart.

QUESTIONS AND ACTIVITIES

1. Have the class split into groups of two. One person in each pair should select a problem or difficulty to discuss while the other person listens. The only restriction on the listener is that, before making any other reply, she must first restate in her own words what she hears the speaker saying; that is, her primary task is to be open to the feelings and import of the communication. Then shift roles and have the speaker practice this sort of listening and responding.

2. Select children in your group who appear to require special diagnostic help of some description. List the reasons for your conclusion that they need help. With another student, practice how you might broach the subject of referral with the family. It is helpful to practice this with a "parent" who is resistant, one who is overly agreeable, and one who is obviously upset about your suggestion.

3. If you have children of your own, have you ever been summoned to school to discuss a problem? How did you feel about being asked to come in and do this?

REFERENCES FOR FURTHER READING

Beyer, E. *Teaching young children.* New York: The Bobbs-Merrill Co., Inc., 1968. Beyer's chapter on working with parents traces the development of the concept of mutuality of concern as it has replaced the older idea of the teacher as a didactic parent instructor. It does a good job of describing the overall climate that should be established between teacher and parent and includes matter-of-fact suggestions for achieving it.

Bromberg, S. L. A beginning teacher works with parents. In K. R. Baker (Ed.), *Ideas that work with young children.* Washington D.C.: National Association for the Education of Young Children, 1972. Bromberg presents a candid, comforting, and informative discussion of the successes and failures of an inexperienced teacher learning to work with parents.

Frank, T., and Gordetsky, S. Child-focused mental health consultation in settings for young children. *Young Children,* 1976, *31*(5), 339-344. Frank and Gordetsky describe a model wherein everyone pools their knowledge together for the child's benefit. My own experience supports their position that this approach is of great value.

Gotkin, L. G. The telephone call: The direct line from teacher to family. In K. R. Baker (Ed.), *Ideas that work with young children.* Washington, D.C.: National Association for the Education of Young Children, 1972. Gotkin advocates use of the telephone as an additional way to reach parents quickly and directly.

Hildebrand, V. *Introduction to early childhood education* (2nd ed.). New York: Macmillan Publishing Co., Inc., 1976. Hildebrand provides an overview that contains many practical suggestions of different ways to link family and school together more effectively.

Markun, P. M. *Parenting.* Washington, D.C.: Association for Childhood Education International, 1973. This excellent pamphlet considers parenting in its many guises. It contains several strong articles in it; among the best are the one on Mexican-American parents and the one on the problems of the parent who is divorced.

Read, K. H. *The nursery school: Human relationships and learning* (6th ed.). Philadelphia: W. B. Saunders Co., 1976. The chapter entitled "Teachers and Parents Work Together" has a good discussion of the feelings parents may bring with them to the nursery school experience.

Schulman, E. D. *Intervention in human services* (2nd ed.). St. Louis: The C. V. Mosby Co., 1978. For a thoroughgoing, sensible book on interviewing, this publication is hard to beat. It contains innumerable examples of actual counselling situations taking place for a variety of purposes.

Taylor, K. W. *Parent cooperative nursery schools*. New York: Teachers College Press, Columbia University, 1968. This classic discussion of teacher-parent interaction remains one of the best in the field. Taylor talks about real life problems the teacher may experience when working with parents and proposes helpful ways to work these through in the framework of a cooperative nursery school.

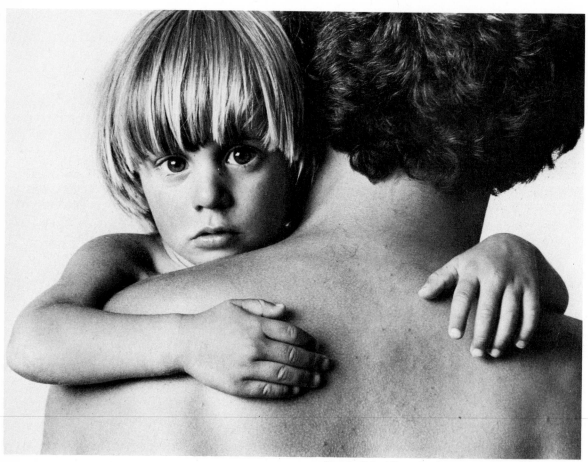

Photo by Richard Pierce, Brooks Institute and School of Photography

18 □ Tender topics*

HELPING CHILDREN MASTER EMOTIONAL CRISES

I, a stranger and afraid
In a world I never made.

A. E. HOUSMAN
Last Poems, XII, 1922

Young children are as subject to stress and strain when a crisis strikes their families as the adults are, but this may be difficult for the family to recognize. They often hope that if nothing is said, the child will be unaware of the problem, or they may be so overwhelmed by the crisis that they have little emotional reserve available to help their children through their troubles at the same time. But children are keen sensors of emotional climates, and they are aware of telephone conversations, comments by neighbors, and so forth. As Furman says:

Children are so observant of and sensitive to their parents' moods and nuances of behavior that, in our experience, it is impossible to spare them from knowing or to deceive them about the true nature of events (1974, p. 18).

Indeed, the secrecy and avoidance often practiced by families when crises occur may serve only to deepen the child's anxiety (*Cancer Care,* 1977). It is far better, then, to reduce this misery where we can by facing facts squarely and providing as much stability as possible than to worsen the problem by failing to deal with it.

Moreover, the experience of crisis is not always

undesirable in itself. If well handled, a crisis may actually strengthen character. This is the theme of the popular volume, *Passages* (Sheehy, 1976), wherein the author maintains that crisis is a predictable, "normal" part of human experience and even contends that it *must* occur in order for adults to achieve identity and a truly personal point of view. An older book, *Cradles of Eminence,* also validates the positive side of turmoil and unhappiness. In this book the Goertzels studied the childhoods of 400 men and women who had achieved fame of one sort or another and found that the vast majority of these people had experienced trauma or unhappiness while growing up. Among several findings they report:

Three fourths of the children [in the study] are troubled —by poverty; by a broken home; by rejecting, over-possessive, estranged, or dominating parents; by financial ups and downs; by physical handicaps; or by parental dissatisfaction over the children's school failures or vocational choices (1962, p. 272).

And yet all of these people had gone on to achieve eminence in some form as adults—often in fields associated with creativity.

So, while perusing the following material, the reader should remember that there can be a positive side to difficult experiences and that at least some people tested in crucibles of stress come through

---

*I am indebted to Donna Dempster of California State University at Long Beach for suggesting that a chapter on Tender Topics be included in the revised edition of *The Whole Child*.

stronger and more able to cope with future problems. Needless to say, this is not always the case. Little children seem particularly vulnerable to potential disaster, in part because they lack experience and in part because they are relatively powerless and helpless (Seligman, 1975). If they are lucky, they *do* have adults who can help them through these difficult times, and because nursery school teachers occasionally have such opportunities, the following material is included.

WHAT CONSTITUTES A CRISIS?

We usually think of a crisis as being something sudden, and surely death or illness or a trip to the emergency room falls in this category. Other crises are of longer duration—the mental illness of a parent, a divorce, a new baby, physical abuse, moving to a new neighborhood, or even adjusting to nursery school all constitute crises of a more prolonged nature.

All such events are likely to produce marked changes in the life of the child. They also occur far more commonly than one would wish. For example, one study estimates that one child in twenty experiences the death of a loved one by age 5 (Kliman, 1968), and divorce now affects one in every five families in the United States (National Council of Organizations for Children and Youth, 1976).

Fortunately, some of the effects of these events can be mitigated if families and teachers know where to turn and what to do. It is my hope that the following material will be useful in this regard. *However, because of the nature and gravity of the crises presented, the reader should understand that this chapter represents only the barest minimum of information and that it is intended only as a starting point, not as a comprehensive guide.*

SOME GENERAL PRINCIPLES

There is no other time in life when the parent is more important to the child than during a time of crisis (Kelly and Wallerstein, 1977). Teachers, psychologists, social workers, and sometimes even police may also offer meaningful aid, but the family is the most significant influence; for this reason, the fundamental goal of the teacher should be to support the family as well as she can. There are a number of ways to accomplish this.

Things to do for the family

Make certain the parents understand that it is better to include the child in the situation than to exclude him. Particularly in matters of death, serious parental illness, or job loss, adults may attempt to shield children from what is happening but, as mentioned before, children always know when something is wrong. Parents may not realize how frightened this can make youngsters if they are left to fantasize about the nature of the trouble or the reason for it. It is the primeval "fear of the unknown." To remedy this, the teacher should encourage the family to explain in simple terms *but not gory detail* the nature of the emergency.

The same recommendation applies to expressing feelings—children should be allowed to participate in feelings of concern or grief rather than be excluded. Again, I would caution that this principle should be followed within reason. The point to get across to the family is that it's all right for children to understand that grownups sometimes feel sad or frightened or upset—as long as this is mingled with steady assurances from family members that life will continue and that the child will be taken care of.

Try not to overreact, no matter what the parent tells you. The teacher can be of little help if she allows herself to become as upset as the parents are over a crisis, though I cannot deny that crises such as suicide or the rape of a 4-year-old are deeply shocking to everyone. However, if the teacher can present a model of relative calmness as well as concern, she can influence the parent to behave in the same manner; and by providing information on what will help the child, she can encourage the institution of rational steps in dealing with the situation.

The teacher should also guard herself against being overcome with pity for a youngster or their parents, because pity is not beneficial for the family either. I recall one situation where a little boy, returning to school after his mother died, was greeted by a teacher who threw her arms around him and burst into tears, saying, "Oh, you poor child! Whatever will you and your poor papa do now?" This unfortunate response overwhelmed the boy and froze him into an inexpressive state from which it was very difficult to retrieve him. One would think an adult would have more sense, but crises do strange things to people.

Of course, pity is not always so obvious. It may manifest itself in the more subtle forms of overindulgence or spoiling, and this is equally undesirable. Pity is a weakening experience for the person who is its object. It encourages feelings of despair, self-pity, and helplessness (Seligman, 1975)—the exact opposites of competency. It is far better to substitute compassionate understanding and to express quiet confidence that, although the family and child feel bad right now, you are certain they are ultimately going to come through the experience all right and that you are there to do whatever you can to help them.

Do not violate the privacy of the family. Particularly when something sensational has happened, whether it be a car accident or a home burning to the ground, it can be tempting to participate in the tragedy by gossiping about it with other parents. It's impossible to avoid discussion of such events entirely when they are common knowledge in the community, but care should be taken to keep private details private. For one thing, any parents who hear the teacher repeat such personal details are bound to conclude that the teacher will gossip about their personal affairs also, and, for another, behaving this way is a breach of professional ethics.

Offer yourself as a resource. Being a good listener is one way to do this (see Chapter 17, "What Mothers Need"), as long as the parent doesn't come to feel that you are mostly interested in the sensational aspects of the crisis or that you can't wait for her to stop talking so you can offer advice. Remember, also, that sometimes families do not want any help, and this desire must be respected, too.

Sometimes, after the emergency aspect has subsided, parents find it helpful if the teacher has a good reference book to lend them, such as Anna Wolf's little book *Helping Your Child Understand Death*

(1973) or Atkin's and Rubin's *Part-time Father* (1976). If the nursery school has a reserve of at least a few such basic books on hand, they can be instantly available when needed. (A few books of this kind are suggested at the end of this chapter.)

Finally, the teacher can also be a resource for referral to other supporting agencies. This ticklish matter is discussed in greater detail in Chapter 19, "Working with Exceptional Children," so I will only comment here that it is necessary to be careful of offering referral resources too hastily lest the family interpret this as wanting to get rid of them and their uncomfortable problem. On the other hand, crises that result from a sudden deep shock or trauma, such as being in a severe automobile accident, experiencing rape, or witnessing a murder or suicide, require immediate psychiatric attention.

Things to do for the child

*Don't ignore the situation by pretending it hasn't happened.** It takes a sensitive teacher to achieve a matter-of-fact facing of a crisis with a child without overdoing it or rubbing it in. Nor should the teacher imply that everything is fine and dandy and that getting over the disaster will be easy or that everything will be just like it was before. It's better to admit that it's not a happy time, while making the point that it's not the end of the world, either.

It helps to be alert to clues that the child wants to talk about his feelings or that he has the problem on his mind. Sometimes this occurs long after the event in question. For example, one of the children in our Center suffered a serious burn on her arm that caused her a good deal of misery. She didn't come to terms with it completely at that time. Several months later, she happened to be part of a group of youngsters who went on a field trip to inspect the skeleton in the biology department. She was very quiet while she surveyed the bones, and slipping her hand into the teacher's on the way home, she whispered to her, "But what happened to his skin?" To

---

*For further discussion of coping with emotional disturbance in children refer to Chapter 19, "Working with Exceptional Children." Indications of disturbance are discussed in Chapter 5, "Fostering Mental Health in Young Children."

Photo by Elaine M. Ward

which the teacher responded, ''Are you wondering if it got burned off?''—and all of Amy's concerns about skin and injuries came tumbling forth.

But it's best if the situation can be dealt with while it's happening. If the child is unable to bring the problem up, the teacher can provide play experiences for working the event through, can include a book on the subject at story time, or can mention the problem casually herself when the opportunity for a quiet, private interlude presents itself. Sometimes this can be done tactfully by saying, ''I remember when I was little and had my tonsils out—I didn't know what was going to happen in the hospital. I wondered if my Mother would stay. And if . . . [include a shrewd guess about what is troubling the particular child]. I wonder if you are wondering about that, too.''

The focus of such discussions should be on what the child thinks and what he is worried about. Reassurance and explanation have their place in talking problems over with little children, but they are not nearly so helpful as listening and encouraging the youngster to express his worries through talk and, most valuably, through play.

Provide play opportunities to express and clarify feelings about the crisis, and try to be on hand to help the child interpret them. Imaginative play is a very satisfactory way for children to resolve their feelings about crises. Some kinds of play, such as hospital play, benefit children most if special equipment is provided. This might include a set of crutches, something that can stand in for shot needles (we use turkey basters for this purpose), aprons, surgical gowns, and masks.

Hand puppets, little rubber dolls and doll house furniture, and a housekeeping corner well equipped with dolls and other paraphernalia of family life also provide a good setting for expressing concerns related to the family situation.

A watchful teacher can be aware of the turn the play is taking and help a troubled child ease his feelings. She might, for example, remain close enough to a housekeeping group to comment quietly to a 3-year-old pounding on a baby doll, ''Gosh! You really want to show that baby he makes you mad!

You want him to stop bothering you and crying so much. That's okay—it's okay to feel that way. You can pretend anything you want. Of course we can't do that to the real baby even when we feel that way, but we *pretend* anything we want. We can *feel* what we wish, but we must control what we do.

Play opportunities that permit the sublimated expression of feelings are also valuable (see Chapter 7, ''Aggression: What to Do about It''). Some materials are especially good as aggression relievers—dough and fingerpaint that can be pounded and squished, and simple hammering come to mind—and some are more relaxing and tension relieving—waterplay and swinging, for example. In general, unstructured materials that make few demands for performance are the most effective ones to use for such purposes.

Absolve the child from guilt. Young children are not good reasoners about cause and effect. Piaget has provided us with many examples where they have reasoned that effect was the cause. (For instance, a child may see trees bending in the wind and conclude that trees bending make the wind blow!) Piaget also teaches us that young children are self-centered and see things mainly in relation to themselves. And, finally, we know that children are prone to magical thinking, tending to believe that the wish has the same power as the act.

If we think about the implications of these developmental facts, it becomes easier to understand why children often conclude that they are the cause of the family's disaster—something usually so far from the actual truth it may not even occur to adults that the child is blaming himself for the trouble and feeling guilty and unhappy as a result. Rita Warren in her excellent pamphlet, *Caring,* suggests that the teacher can offer comfort in this kind of situation by helping the child separate adult from child business. For example, she suggests that the teacher might say:

When your parents fight, that is very hard for you and sometimes makes you cry. But grown-ups' fighting is really grown-up business. Even if they are fighting about you, it is because they are mad at each other and not because of you or anything you did (1977, p. 22).

Another way to help the child is to maintain as stable and dependable an atmosphere as possible for him while he is at nursery school. This means that the child is expected to adhere to regular routines, and that, in general, the same rules are applied to his conduct as are usually applied. It doesn't mean that allowances aren't made—they must be. The teacher needs to be extra understanding and tolerant if the youngster can't eat or is particularly irritable or has trouble falling asleep or cries a lot. However, keeping the routines and rules steady means that at least part of the child's world has not changed, and this offers substantial comfort to a child whose home world is in turmoil.

Help the child know what to expect. Sometimes families know in advance that a crisis is approaching, since they can generally anticipate such events as having a new baby, routine surgery, or moving to a new city. Here it is important not to build up unrealistic ideas of what such a change entails. The new baby will *not* be a wonderful little playmate for the preschooler as soon as he arrives, and ice cream is *not* going to taste wonderful after a tonsillectomy!

It is not necessary to be negative about changes and build undue apprehension. It just helps to talk over what will happen in advance to reduce the element of the unexpected. This is particularly true if the teacher and family talk to the youngster in terms of the plans being made for him—how his pet cat will get to the new house and where the family will have dinner on the day of the move. It's this kind of simple detail that children find reassuring and that adults sometimes forget to tell them, since they already know the answers or consider them unimportant.

INFORMATION ABOUT SPECIFIC CRISES
Adjusting to nursery school and dealing with the parent who picks the child up late

In Chapter 3, "Handling Routines," I have already discussed helping the child adjust to nursery school, but it should at least be pointed out here also that coming to school can represent such a change in the child's life that it may be a real crisis from his point of view. Particularly if the adjust-

ment is a difficult one, we should not underestimate the anguish he is experiencing when separated from his mother, and we should do all we can to alleviate it.

Another part of attending nursery school that can be a crisis to a child is a late pickup by his parent. I have known children to fly into a panic over this if it is not handled well by the teacher, so a few suggestions are in order. First of all, be careful to reassure the child that his parent *will* come and that you will stay with him until he does. It also is reassuring to say that you know there are some good reasons why he or she is delayed (and avoid speculating within the child's hearing over what various disasters may have befallen the parent along the way). Second, locate an alternative person to come as soon as possible. Part of the entry record for each child should be a list of the telephone numbers of at least three people to be contacted in case the child becomes ill during the day or when the parent is late. However, don't let the child stand beside you as you dial number after number, getting no response! *No child should ever be released to any adult who is not on the parent's list.*

Third, hold your temper and don't make the child pay for the parent's sins. It's really hard at the end of a long day for a teacher to wait and maybe miss her bus, but it's not the child's fault his parent is tardy. In some schools where parents are consistently inconsiderate, policies are established of charging extra for overtime care or not allowing the child to attend the next day, but these penalties are best avoided if possible because they breed ill will. It is usually sufficient to explain, when tempers have cooled, why the teacher prefers to leave on time and to ask the parent to be more considerate in the future.

Arrival of a new baby

Parents are often quite skillful about preparing a youngster for a new baby during the 9-month wait, yet once the infant has arrived somehow assume the preschooler will be delighted and certainly not jealous! But the reality of the mother going to the hospital, possibly having someone unfamiliar taking over meanwhile, and then seeing his world changed by the homecoming of the baby himself with all his demands on the parents' time and energy can turn out to be an unpleasant surprise to a preschooler. Then, too, sometimes children who weather this initial stress with equanimity become upset later on when the baby begins to crawl around and get into their things.

Some simple remedies the teacher can apply to help alleviate these feelings of intrusion and jealousy are not to dwell on how wonderful it is to have a new baby in the family and to provide plenty of opportunities for the preschooler to act like a baby if he wants to. I recall one youngster who derived deep satisfaction from sitting in my office being rocked and fed a bottle occasionally—he especially liked being burped!

It also helps to be realistic about the situation—point out the things the baby *can't* do, as well as all the obvious privileges and attention accruing to him. Help the other child find satisfaction in his own abilities and competencies that are related to being more mature, and make it clear that he will retain this advantage for a long time to come. After all, he will always be the older child.

Finally, if jealousy is interpreted to the parents as *the fear of being left out,* it may enable them to stop deploring it and make plans that show the child he is definitely included. These can be as simple as reading to him by himself for a little while before bedtime, or making a special time of going to the market while the baby remains at home. When the baby begins to crawl, it's only fair to provide a safe place for the older child's belongings. Sometimes older children appreciate having one of those stretchy gates across their doors that they can hook to keep the baby out. (It's an interesting fact of human nature that the more protection of the child's rights the parent provides, the less protective the child will feel driven to be.)

Hospitalization

Preparation in advance. When surgery or other treatment can be anticipated in advance, there is time for home and nursery school to help the child grasp what will happen, and he is entitled to this information—after all, it is his body that will, in a sense, be violated (Haller, 1967). There are several good books for children about doctors and hospitals, and a recent bibliography of such books is described in the References for Further Reading. Hospital play and discussion of the forthcoming hospitalization will also help—not only to reassure the child himself but also to comfort his playmates. In these discussions I have found that using the word ''fix'' is helpful—saying the doctor is going to fix a bad leg or the infected tonsils seems to be a concept that children can grasp and that they find comforting. Haller comments that using hospital masks in dramatic play is of special value, since such masks are often one of the more frightening aspects of hospitalization. (Remember how upsetting masks are to some children at Halloween?)

Some hospitals permit children to visit first. This possibility should be suggested to the parents, even if it means they must ask the doctor to make special arrangements. (I will never forget the relief of one of my own children, aged 6, when she went for such a visit and discovered there would be a television set in her room, something it had not occurred to me to mention. Since she wasn't allowed to watch TV during the day at home, this was indeed a selling point for the hospital!)

While the child is recovering and out of school, it is important to consider the feelings of his playmates as well as the youngster himself and to provide something they can do for their friend. Children often have very good ideas about this, such as baking something special or making a card with all their handprints on it.

Once again, upon the child's return, more hospital play is definitely of value. This enables the child to work out his feelings and clarify them and helps inform the other children of what went on as well. Incidentally, the mastery role of being doctor or nurse as well as that of victim is particularly satisfying to children who are struggling to overcome their feelings of angry helplessness generated while under treatment—and giving shots to someone else is best of all.

Information for parents. Parents should be encouraged to stay with their children as much of the time as possible while their youngsters are hospitalized. Many hospitals today maintain open visiting privileges with no time limits for parents, but a few still do not. It is worthwhile to become acquainted with the policies of various hospitals in your area so you can inform parents about these in advance. Older fours and fives can also maintain contact with their families, particularly siblings, by talking with them on the phone, and this should be encouraged.

Parents are usually cowed by hospitals and apprehensive of antagonizing staff. They don't know their rights, and they are also likely to be upset and worried. A chat beforehand can alleviate some of their concerns and enable them to insist on what is best for their particular child. Moreover, they should be reassured that it is desirable for children to express their feelings. Indeed, it is the quiet, passive child

conforming unquestioningly to hospital routine who arouses the greatest concern among psychological consultants (Bergmann and Freud, 1965; Bowlby, 1952; Haller and others, 1967). Children should not be admonished, ''Don't cry,'' or lied to, ''This will just sting a little,'' or threatened, ''You do it, or I'm going to go home!'' It is truly surprising that parents sometimes expect more of their children in these difficult and especially trying situations than they normally would dream of expecting at home!

They may also need to be prepared for the fact that children sometimes reject their mothers when they finally return home (Heinicke and Westheimer, 1965). This can come as a painful shock to families unless they have been prepared with an explanation of the reasons for the hostility. It is thought to really be an expression of the child's anger at being separated from his parents, particularly the mother,—so, in a way, the hostility expressed by the child is a kind of compliment to the

Photo by Elaine M. Ward

family for the strength of their emotional bonds— but it can be a confusing compliment if misunderstood.

The emergency room

One of the most trying crises for young children to experience is a visit to the emergency room. This is because no advance preparation is possible, the parents are maximally upset, time is short, and the reason for being there is generally serious and painful. It will come as no news to experienced parent-readers of these pages to learn that accidents are most likely to occur between 3:00 and 11:00 PM and that twice as many boys as girls require emergency care (Resnick and Hergenroeder, 1975).

One can make a very good parents' night out of offering a discussion of what to do in the emergency room to buffer the child from the worst shocks. Recommendations for parents include (1) staying with the child as much as possible, (2) staying as calm as possible, (3) explaining very simply to the child what is going to happen next so he is not taken completely by surprise when a doctor suddenly materializes with a shot needle, and (4) modelling fortitude by explaining, with assurance, that it may not feel good, but the doctor has to do whatever he or she is doing because it will help the child get well.

Hospitalization of parents

A rare series of three studies reported by Rice, Ekdahl, and Miller (1971) reveals that emotional problems are likely to result for children whenever a parent is hospitalized for any length of time, whether it be for physical or mental illness. The impact of mental illness, particularly illness of the mother, causes the most marked difficulties. At least half the children studied gave evidence of such disturbance. This is due to several factors. There is the unhappiness and disorganization that typically precede confinement in a mental institution as well as the fact that families usually have no time to prepare children for the hospitalization. Child abuse may have taken place before hospitalization, and incarceration of the mother makes it more probable that the child will have to be cared for outside his home

—often thereby losing the security of his familiar school and friends as well.

Of course, the nursery school plays only one part in solving the overall problems of families involved in such difficulties, but it can be a significant one if the provision of child care means the child can stay within the home and that he is provided with a stable, understanding environment while at school. The general recommendations given at the beginning of this chapter capsulize what will help these children; here are three additional suggestions.

1. In such circumstances, the children's center should make a special effort to coordinate its services with those of other agencies and be prepared to report undue distress to the social worker or psychologist along with a request for help.

2. Little children are often particularly distressed over the unpredictability of the disturbed parent's behavior. Because of the possibility that angry encounters took place between parent and child or that a depressed parent may have been unreachable by the child, it is of great importance to explain in simple terms to the youngster that he was not the reason his mommy went to the hospital.

3. Finally, it is still true that many, perhaps the majority, of people regard mental illness as a shameful stigma, and being near former mental patients fills them with unease. The nursery school teacher who can master this apprehension by behaving naturally with recovered patients offers a gift of acceptance much appreciated by the family.

Helping children through divorce

Research indicates that in 1974 more than 15% of all children under the age of 6 lived in single-parent families headed by women—a number totalling 2,800,000 children. This is due chiefly to the sharp rise in divorce rates; the reader may recall that, in the same time period, one in every five marriages ended in divorce (National Council of Organizations for Children and Youth, 1976). Yet, despite the number of preschool children so affected, little research concerning this age group and divorce is reported (Kelly and Wallerstein, 1977).

Occasionally the teacher is aware in advance that families are having marital difficulties, but the announcement of an impending divorce often takes her as much by surprise as it does the child in her nursery school room. There are a few things to remember when this happens.

For one, try not to take sides. This is difficult not to do, in part because blame-assigning by friends and acquaintances seems to be part of the cultural pattern of divorce, and in part because the parent who confides in the teacher tends, understandably, to present the other parent in a bad light. Something else the teacher should remember is to invite each parent to make appointments with her when it is time for parent/child conferences. All too often, the father is ignored by the school following a divorce, and yet the majority of men remain deeply concerned for their children and greatly appreciate being included. Third, be prepared for the fact that the child himself is likely to exhibit irritability, regression, confusion, and anxiety during and after the divorce (Wallerstein and Kelly, 1976).

Still another difficulty that may be encountered by the nursery school is related to custody. Occasionally nursery school staff are subpoenaed to testify in custody altercations. This is usually the case when one parent wishes to prove neglect by the other one. Here, written records of attendance, written reports of parent conferences, and observational records of the child are valuable to have available for citation.

Potential custody problems constitute an additional reason for requiring written, signed lists of individuals to whom children may be released when the parent is not picking the youngster up from school. Refusing release can create temporary inconvenience and bad feeling, but the school is legally responsible for the child while not in his parent's care. This explanation will usually appease irritated would-be helpers, and enforcement of the rule may protect the child from "parentnapping."

Both parents, should, of course, be welcome visitors at school—although once or twice I have found it necessary to make it clear they are welcome just as long as the occasion remains a happy one for the youngster and is not used by either parent to generate an upsetting scene.

Explaining the divorce to the child. In a rare discussion of a research project concerned with divorce and its effect on preschoolers, Kelly and Wallerstein (1977) emphasize that this situation is better handled by the family than by the mental health worker. I suppose that this recommendation holds true for the nursery school teacher, too. They comment that many of the preschoolers seen in the project had been given *no explanation at all* of the reasons for the divorce and that they felt confused and guilty about what had happened to their families. The moral to this is so obvious that it is not necessary to comment. Kelly and Wallerstein also point out that it is important for families to investigate the children's fantasies about the divorce (what they imagine has happened or will happen) so that various misapprehensions can be corrected.

However, divorce is not always perceived as being unfortunate, even by young children. Youngsters are often well aware that their parents are unhappy and may experience real relief when the final separation takes place. Indeed, two studies indicate that children from frankly broken homes generally do better than those from intact but unhappy households (Landis, 1960; Nye, 1957).

Evelyn Pitcher (1969) recommends that the child be provided with simple explanations of what has happened, and she suggests that parents should explain, "Your father and I don't want to be married anymore. We aren't going to live together anymore," which is preferable to saying "Your father and I don't love each other anymore." This is because loving is not necessarily related to marriage in the child's mind. He is loved also, and yet he is not married. If loving can stop, perhaps he, too, is in jeopardy.

If parents are advised to avoid degrading the other parent in the child's hearing, the youngster will be less distressed (Kliman, 1968). Children are usually feeling pain enough over divided loyalties anyway, and being party to the denigration of the other parent only complicates their emotional problems further. It is also of great value to explain to the child which parent he will be living with and reassure him that he will (ideally) have many regular opportunities to be with the other parent as well.

Divorce frequently means a move, often from a house to an apartment. In the child's eyes, this may mean the loss of a beloved pet, a change of friends, and sometimes even a change of schools. His mother may be leaving him for a full-time job for the first time, too. No wonder Grollman (1969) likens the experience of divorce to death for young children, since so many often painful adjustments must transpire.

Building sensitivity to single-parent families within the school. The nursery school teacher needs to be especially sensitive to single-parent children at school, not only because they may be unhappy or exhibit various kinds of emotional distress, but also because so many activities in nursery school typically revolve around family life. The contemporary teacher needs to broaden her cultural awareness to include the many patterns of single parenting that now exist, and she must divest herself of the tacit assumption that most of the children in her school undoubtedly come from intact families. At least in day care, this is not likely to be true—our own Center, for example, is composed almost entirely of single-parent families.

The teacher may also need to divest herself of ingrained prejudices against divorce and divorced people. There is not necessarily anything "wrong" with people who are no longer married or perhaps never have been. Indeed, many single parents, men and women, should be admired for the extraordinary manner in which they have held their families together and continued to care for them. As Herzog and Sudia put it in their comprehensive review of research on fatherless homes, "To focus only on problems and weaknesses [of fatherless homes] is to distort the picture and obscure some clues to ways of building on strengths" (1973, p. 202). It is kinder, also, if the teacher learns to speak of "single-parent families" rather than speaking of children from "broken homes."

In terms of curriculum, Mother's and Father's Day can take on a peculiar significance for single-parent children, as can vacations. Unless the teacher is careful, some children will be routinely expected to make gifts for parents they rarely or never see. Rather than have this happen, it's better to be well acquainted with the youngster's living arrangements. It may well be that he would prefer to make something for a grandparent or his babysitter or his mother's boyfriend.

The teacher should take care in selecting books, also, so that all kinds of family structures are represented. It's as unfortunate for some children to be continually confronted with the stories of the happy, intact family going on a picnic as it was for black children of the last generation to be exposed only to "Dick and Jane." A list of such books is included in the Bernstein (1976) reference at the end of this chapter.

Research on the relation of father absence to the establishment of adequate male and female role concepts remains inconclusive according to Herzog and Sudia (1973), but it is probably an especially good idea to employ male teachers in the nursery school, particularly when divorce makes it likely that children will be deprived of male companionship outside the school. Surely it is more desirable for children of both sexes to have some regular opportunities to relate to men rather than be raised during their preschool years entirely by women.

Helping children understand death

Although death remains a taboo subject for many people, the increasing frequency of publications and discussion about it (there is even a *Journal of Thanatology* devoted solely to this topic) provides evidence that at least a few people are no longer pretending that death does not exist. And, even though we might prefer to deny it, we must face the fact that death is a part of life for young children as well as for their elders. Kliman, for instance, estimates that by kindergarten age, one of every twenty children has experienced the death of a parent (1968). Of course, children are also exposed to the deaths of grandparents, other family members, friends, and beloved animals, not to mention the continual accounts of death and murder reported endlessly on television. For these reasons, it is necessary to learn how to help children cope with this subject, even though we may be barely learning to talk about it ourselves.

What can the teacher do? It is heartening to learn that in the area of death education, there *is* something the nursery school teacher can do that can be of real assistance to young children. Kliman terms this "psychological immunization" and describes it as helping children acquire at least a modicum of "mastery in advance." By this he means that it is helpful if the subject of death is included matter-of-factly as part of the curriculum of the nursery school in order to desensitize children by providing both information and mild experiences with it before a more emotionally laden death occurs. This can be accomplished in many ways.* Perhaps the most effective of them is based on the death of animals at nursery school. This should include talking about how the animals have changed and what will become of them, as well as helping children carry out the simple burials that are of such intense interest to them at that age. Books and discussions are also helpful, and some nursery schools even advocate visiting cemeteries, which are, after all, quite beautiful places.

Helping the child and the family when death occurs. Dr. Kliman also points out that teachers and other nonmedical personnel, such as clergymen, are more likely to be asked for help when a death occurs than doctors are, probably because the families feel less hostile toward such people than they do toward the medical profession following bereavement. For this reason, the teacher should be well prepared with some down-to-earth suggestions for helping the children, with some resources for further information, and with knowledge of possible referral sources should this be requested.

Once again, I must repeat that the fact of a death should not be avoided by telling a child that his fa-

*For a more complete discussion of teaching about death in the curriculum, please refer to Hendrick, J. *Total Learning*, St. Louis: The C. V. Mosby Co., 1980, Chapter 4, "Teaching Children to Understand and Value Life.

ther has gone away on a long trip or that grandma will come back in the spring. This principle must be reiterated because studies reveal such statements are *particularly prevalent* when families deal with death and preschool children (Furman, 1974). Children need to be allowed to participate in the family's grief, because it strengthens their feelings of belonging instead of feeling isolated, and it helps them express their own sadness, too.

As time passes, they should be encouraged to reminisce about the absent parent (Furman, 1974; Kliman, 1968; Wolf, 1973). All too often once the initial crisis has passed, families and teachers hesitate to reawaken memories, but recall actually helps ventilate feelings so that the emotional wound can heal cleanly. It also helps the child retain his identification with and feelings of affection for his parent. Family stories about "Do you remember when . . . ?" photographs, and even movies have been found to be helpful.

Reliving old memories is also the second of three stages of mourning. The first one is the acceptance of loss; the second is remembering the past; and the third is substitution of a new relationship.

Parents can do a better job if they also understand that the emotion of grief for children (and for adults as well) is not composed only of sadness. There is also a component of anger (Bowlby, 1969; Kübler-Ross, 1969; Wolfenstein, 1969). Just as children feel a mixture of grief and anger when left at nursery school, so do they also experience, to a much stronger degree, these same feelings when a parent abandons them in death. It's doubly important to understand this, because young children often connect this anger back to some angry interlude before death and conclude they have caused the parent to die (just as they may believe this about divorce). They then may reason that the death is a punishment for their misbehavior—truly a terrible burden of guilt for a child to bear (Bernstein, 1977).

To counteract this, simple reasons for the death must be given ("Your father didn't want to leave us, but he was so sick the medicine couldn't help any more"), combined with reassurances that the surviving parent and child are not likely to die for a long time yet. Children should also be told that the surviving parent is going to go right on taking care of them, and be reminded that there is also Grandma, Grandpa, and Aunty Margaret, all of whom love him and care for him. The presence of siblings can provide an additional source of strength and family feeling, particularly among children who are older. The anger should be acknowledged by mentioning its presence and its naturalness. Statements such as "I guess you feel mad your Dad died and left us. . . . I see you feel like socking things a lot. . . . We know he could't help dying, but it's hard to take sometimes, isn't it?" usually relieve some of the hostile impulses.

Adults must also be cautioned against likening death to sleep. We surely don't want anxious children to guard themselves against sleep because they fear death may come while they are sleeping. A second, less obvious reason for this recommendation has to do with the way preschool children are thought to perceive death. They view death as being a temporary condition, one from which the person can be revived (Kastenbaum, 1967; Kübler-Ross, 1969; Nagy, 1959). Speaking of death as sleep only encourages this misunderstanding. But most fundamentally, the reason for not equating death and sleep is that it is dishonest. Why speak euphemistically of "sleep" and "slumber rooms" when what we mean is "death" and "a visiting room where people can view the body"? Why not face facts?

Finally, student teachers often ask me what to do about religious beliefs and children in relation to death. In general, writers on this subject maintain that talking about religion tends to be confusing to young children and should not be stressed when death occurs (Kliman, 1968; Plank, 1968). Surely, it is not the teacher's place to do this, anyway, although she may find it helpful to be conversant with the points of view of the major religions. Grollman's book, *Explaining Death to Children* (1967) is a good source of information on this subject.

The question really raised by students, however, is what to do about statements by children with which they cannot agree. For example, a child may say, "My mommy says my puppy went to heaven, and now the angels are singing over him. Someday I'll see him up there," or, "You know what? My Grandmother has it all fixed so she'll be froze solid when she dies—then she can come alive again when she wants to."

Actually, it isn't necessary to agree or disagree with such statements. All one has to do is show that you respect the family's teaching by listening, and then either ask the child what he thinks, or say something that responds to the feelings, such as "I can see you really miss him," and "You'd like to see your puppy again," or at least say something noncommittal, such as, "So that's what your Grandma is planning."

Child abuse, neglect, and sexual molestation

Child abuse constitutes one of the most terrible crises of childhood. The occurrence of such attacks is fundamentally repugnant to most people, and for a long time the subject went virtually ignored and uninvestigated. As late as 1962, statistics only began to accumulate when Kempe initiated the first survey on the subject (1962). Almost 20 years later we still lack accurate data. Recent estimates of physical abuse range from a low estimate of 8.8 cases per 1,000 children to a high of 13.4 per 1,000 (Nagi, 1975).

Neglect is also a serious problem (Polansky, Hally, and Polansky, 1976), as is psychological abuse (Martin, 1976). Unfortunately, data remain very thin in these areas, although the effects of such adversive experiences are undoubtedly serious for children. At the present time, most of the activity centers on prevention of physical attack. Perhaps this is because physical abuse is particularly horrifying, since it may result in the death of the child; and perhaps it is also because, though still tough to prove in court, physical abuse is somewhat easier to substantiate than is psychological abuse (Kent, 1977) or neglect.

Kempe and Helfer (1972) maintain that the majority of physical abuse cases occur during the preschool years. This may be because very young children are unable to retaliate or tell others of their peril, or it may be due in part to other reasons discussed later in this chapter. Although many of these cases occur in infancy and toddlerhood, children of nursery and early elementary school age are not immune. It is for this reason that we teachers of young children must learn to identify possible cases of abuse and understand what to do and *what not to do* when our suspicions are aroused (Education Commission of the States, 1977b).

Nursery school teachers, in particular, need special advice about how to handle such problems, not only because they are more likely than most teachers to note evidence, since they undress children for naps or toiletting. They also need help because most nursery schools operate autonomously without benefit of advice from school nurses, principals, social workers, and so on.

What to do when abuse is suspected. The teacher who discovers evidence of abuse is likely to feel very upset about it. She may find it hard to believe that that nice Johnson family could do a thing like that and thus deny it, or be so frightened for the child's safety that she does not think clearly and therefore acts too impulsively. For this reason, before going any further with this discussion, *I want to emphasize that handling such cases requires skill and delicacy.* The first approach made to the parents is thought to be crucial in successful management of the case (Helfer and Kempe, 1974), and the consequences of unsuccessful management may be so serious that we cannot risk jeopardizing such chances by acting in an ill-considered way. *Therefore, the teacher must not suddenly plunge into the problem by accusing the parents or even reveal her suspicions by questioning them or the child too closely.* Instead, if she suspects a case of abuse, she should contact whatever agency or individual in her community has the responsibility for handling such cases and report it. *She should ask these people for advice and do what they tell her to, to the best of her ability.*

How to find help. The agency the teacher should seek out is whatever agency in her community is responsible for children's protective services. These agencies go by different names in different parts of the country: "Department of Social Services," "Social Rehabilitation Service," "Bureau of Children and Family Services," and so forth. Directories of such services also exist (see References for Further Reading), but it may be impossible to locate such a directory quickly if needed in an emergency. Still another way to locate protective services is to ask the public health nurse whom to call. If no such agency exists, as is sometimes the case in small or rural communities, a mental health clinic, a child psychologist or psychiatrist, or a knowledgeable pediatrician should be asked for help.

Action should be prompt. Because abusers often repeat their behavior, prompt action is advisable; yet teachers sometimes hesitate to get involved. The teacher should realize that all states now have mandatory reporting laws and that many of these specifically identify teachers as among these people *required* to report cases where abuse is suspected (National Center for Child Abuse, 1975a). Even where teachers are not specifically mentioned, the law is generally on the side of anyone reporting such a case "in good faith" (Paulsen, 1974). Besides the necessity of conforming to the law, *reporting such cases is an ethical and moral responsibility that the teacher must not overlook.*

A publication by The National Center on Child Abuse suggests the following guidelines concerning referrals.

You should be aware of the official policy and specific reporting procedures of your school system, and should know your legal obligations and the protections from civil and criminal liability specified in your state's reporting law. (All states provide immunity for mandated, good-faith reports.)

Although you should be familiar with your state's legal definition of abuse and neglect, you are not required to make legal distinctions in order to report. Definitions should serve as guides. If you suspect that a child is abused or neglected, you should report. The teacher's value lies in noticing conditions that indicate a child's welfare may be in jeopardy.

Be concerned about the rights of the child—the rights to life, food, shelter, clothing, and security. But also be aware of the parents' rights—particularly their rights to be treated with respect and to be given needed help and support.

Bear in mind that reporting does not stigmatize a parent as ''evil.'' The report is the start of a rehabilitative process that seeks to protect the child and help the family as a whole.

A report signifies only the suspicion of abuse or neglect. Teachers' reports are seldom unfounded. At the very least, they tend to indicate a need for help and support to the family.

If you report a borderline case in good faith, do not feel guilty or upset if it is dismissed as unfounded upon investigation. Some marginal cases are found to be valid.

Don't put off making a report until the end of the school year. Teachers sometimes live with their suspicions until they suddenly fear for the child's safety during the summer months. A delayed report may mean a delay in needed help for the child and the family. Moreover, by reporting late in the school year, you remove yourself as a continued support to both the child protective agency and the reported family.

If you remove yourself from a case of suspected abuse or neglect by passing it on to superiors, you deprive child protective services of one of their most competent sources of information. For example, a teacher who tells a CPS worker that the child is especially upset on Mondays directs the worker to investigate conditions in the home on weekends. Few persons other than teachers are able to provide this kind of information. Your guideline should be to resolve any question in favor of the child. When in doubt, report. Even if you, as a teacher, have no immunity from liability and prosecution under state law, the fact that your report is made in good faith will free, you from liability and prosecution (1975b, pp. 70-71).

What to look for. Many of us are so inexperienced in identifying the results of abuse that it is necessary to include the following information, which has been extrapolated primarily from the work of Kempe and Helfer (Helfer and Kempe, 1974; Kempe and Helfer, 1972) as well as from my own experience.

The teacher should be alert for evidence of bruises, particularly a combination of old and fresh ones, or of burns such as cigarette burns. These are likely to occur in relatively concealed places, often on the small of the back or the buttocks. Red weals or strap marks should also arouse suspicion, as most certainly should a black eye (although children also suffer black eyes for a multitude of other reasons) or swollen ears. One author cautions that the soles of the feet should be checked, also, since this is a ''popular location'' (Weston, 1974, p. 64). If a child arrives at school smelling of alcohol or under the influence of drugs, this is also evidence of abuse —and this *does* happen.

A more general reason for concern exists when the parent's voluntary account of the accident does not match the kind or extent of the injury. The usual excuse for bruises is falling down stairs or out of a crib or bed (Weston, 1974), but common sense often tells the teacher that such an event could not possibly have caused the series of diagonal welts across the child's bottom. Still another cause for suspicion of abuse or at least neglect occurs when the child is subject to repeated injuries. The laughing comment by a mother that she ''guesses her child is just accident-prone'' should not be repeatedly accepted by the teacher, particularly when the level of the child's physical coordination at school does not support this parental conclusion.

Literature on the emotional symptomatology of these children describes their behavior as generally either very passive or very aggressive (Holmes and Kagel, 1977; Mirandy, 1976). Mirandy, reporting on the first 19 preschoolers admitted to Circle House Playschool (a center for abused young children), comments that most of them were very passive and inhibited, and she describes their behavior during their first months in school as

. . . overly compliant, anxious to please, seeking out permission before initiating any new action. They were quite hypervigilant to the total environment of the preschool. None of the children demonstrated any separation anxiety in leaving mother and they were indiscriminately and often physically affectionate with adult strangers. They were oblivious to peer interaction. There was often a hollow smile on a child's face and a complete void of emotions. . . . All lacked true joy. The children rarely expressed anger or pain, they had a poor sense of safety, frequently injuring themselves. Crying was either *highly* infrequent or continual. . . . Most abused children appeared compulsively neat. . . . Play was often noncreative and use of materials highly repetitive, the majority of such children appear to be lacking basic play skills. . . . Most have poor expressive language skills. . . .

It is crucial to stress that most of these traits, such as neatness, perseverance, quietness, compliance and politeness are valued in the "normal" child and that if the teacher is not aware of the abused child's special needs, these traits may be further reinforced. An abused child has the ability to initially blend in too well and slip by unnoticed (1976, pp. 217 and 218).*

Finally, there are some commonsense indications of possible abuse to which the teacher should be sensitive. Children who startle easily and cringe or duck if the teacher moves suddenly may be revealing the fact they are often struck at home. Then, too, it is sometimes evident in conversations with parents that they expect too much or are too dependent on their children, or that they know, themselves, they get too angry and "do things they shouldn't" or "wish they hadn't." Such statements are really cries for help and should not be brushed aside on the grounds that everyone feels like that sometimes. These people often benefit from referrals to Parents Anonymous or to local child abuse "hot lines," such as CALM.

Evidence of sexual molestation. Because sexual molestation also happens to young children, one must be alert when little children complain that they "hurt down there" or when genitals are inflamed or when underclothes or odors reveal the presence of pus or infection. Although venereal disease may seem an unthinkable condition in children so young, we cannot afford to blot this possibility from our minds entirely, because instances of this have also been reported (Sgroi, 1975). When venereal disease is present, it is almost always an indication of sexual abuse.

Some sexual attacks are perpetrated by strangers, and these are deeply upsetting to families who,

*From Mirandy, J. Preschool for abused children. In H. P. Martin (Ed.), *The abused child: A multidisciplinary approach to developmental issues and treatment.* Cambridge, Mass.: Ballinger Publishing Co., Copyright 1976. Reprinted with permission.

nevertheless, often prefer not to report them rather than risk notoriety for the child and endless rehashing of the event with authorities. Of course, if such attacks go unreported, the attacker is immune from arrest, but this can be a difficult and touchy situation to deal with. Actually, such an attack is likely to be more extraordinarily upsetting to the parent than to the child until the child picks up his parent's anxiety about it (Walters, 1975). Referral for psychological help for both parent and child is strongly recommended.

As preventive measures, all children should be taught not to take *anything* (typically candy) from any stranger and never to get in a car with such a person, even if he knows the child's name. Many police departments recommend that storekeepers be discouraged from giving candy to children because this may encourage the child to think taking candy from people he doesn't know is sometimes all right. Parents should be urged to explain to these well-meaning people why they should discontinue this practice.

Despite folklore to the contrary, however, the vast majority of sexual molestations are perpetrated *not* by strangers but by members of the child's family or by people known to the family (Brant and Tisza, 1977). One survey indicates that this is true for 72% of all reported cases (DeFrancis, 1969). Teachers need to be aware of this fact, because it means they should be wary of discussing the possibility of such abuse with the parent. Incredible as it may seem, it is not totally safe to assume that a close member of the family is not the molester. Once again, the teacher must be cautioned to seek the services of experts and follow their advice.

Helping the child's family: coping with the teacher's feelings. Even when the teacher has taken the expert's advice, has handled the referral successfully, and the family is receiving help, she must still deal with her feelings about the child and the parent or parents if she believes it is important to retain the child in nursery school. The relief to parents that such respite provides, as well as the protection and education of the child it affords, means that continuing at nursery school is usually *very* important.

Here we are confronted with a paradox. The teacher is more than likely experiencing feelings of revulsion and outrage over what the parents have done, and her impulse may be to judge and punish them. Yet experts tell us that what the parents need, among many other things, is understanding and acceptance—something they were woefully short on in their own childhoods (Davoren, 1974; Helfer and Kempe, 1974). This is particularly true because a characteristic of abusers is that many of them are social isolates (Steele, 1977). The question is, how can the teacher possibly behave in a nurturing fashion with people she regards with aversion?

One thing that may help the teacher master her feelings, or at least control them, is to understand the dynamics of child abuse as far as they are understood at the present time. In no other situation is the importance of caring and being cared for more clearly demonstrated than in the study of this kind of crisis, for many specialists in this field trace the reason for abuse back to early, unsatisfying emotional life experiences of the abusing parent when she or he was not cared for enough (Davoren, 1974; Helfer and Kempe, 1974). Steele (1977), for example, states that without exception the parents he has had in treatment felt they had been victims of very high parental expectations combined with a disregard of their true needs as children—a real absence of caring. In essence, the parent, then, transmits the same unreasonable expectations and severe responses they learned from their first family to their own children. These high expectations combined with a belief in the efficacy of violent punishment and poor impulse control may be reflected in such obvious ways as beating a child or burning him with a cigarette when he cannot stop crying or wetting himself. Or it may be evident in more subtle ways when the parent, seeking the affection he has never had, demands ''love'' and ''caring'' from his child by being dependent on him to an unreasonable, unrealistic extent. A mother of my acquaintance, for example, thought it wonderful that her 4-year-old son would get up, feed himself, and then bring her breakfast in bed.

This same dependent behavior is also character-istic of these adults when dealing with other grown-ups. Elizabeth Davoren (1974, 1975) points out that dependency demands are a noteworthy part of the particularly difficult relationship between social workers and such clients and that these demands must be accepted by the worker to an unusual degree if successful treatment is to occur. It is important for the teacher to be cognizant of this trait, too, in order that she be more tolerant of this emotionally needy behavior than she might otherwise be.

The reader should understand that there is more involved in generating an abusive situation than the basic structure outlined above. For example, Kempe and Helfer (1972) point out that there has to be a precipitating circumstance that tips the scale into violence. It may be alcohol, or a mother's being at home all day with a colicky baby, or anything else that arouses feelings of helpless frustration.

Surely, anyone who has ever cared for a baby agrees that there are times when young children can be persistently and tenaciously irritating; but several researchers have pointed out that some children appear to especially elicit abuse, whereas others in the same family do not (Freidrich and Boriskin, 1976; Lewis and Rosenblum, 1974; Martin, 1976; Parke and Collmer, 1975). The question of why this should be the case has not yet been resolved, but at this point we should recognize that parent-child interaction is a two-way street and that some children do appear to have an active role in abusive situations. Then, too, there is a whole additional point of view about abuse that emphasizes sociological causes related to environmental stress, such as unemployment and poverty (Gil, 1971; Parke and Collmer, 1975).

The basic generalization that can be safely drawn at this point seems to be that the causes of child abuse are rooted in a complex mixture of personality traits of parents and children combined with various malign environmental influences. Gelles' chart on the causes of child abuse illustrates some of the interactions that increase the probability that abuse may take place.

It may also help the teacher moderate her reac-

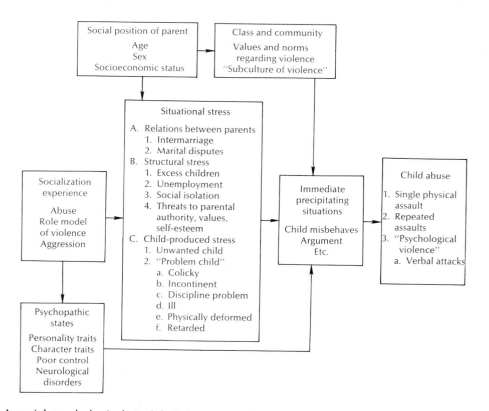

A social psychological model of the causes of child abuse.

From Gelles, R. J. Child abuse as psychopathology: A sociological critique and reformation. *American Journal of Orthopsychiatry*, 1973, *43*(4), 619. Copyright © 1973 the American Ortho-psychiatric Association, Inc. Reproduced by permission.

tion to the parents if she realizes that only 10% of these people are estimated to suffer from serious psychotic disorders (Steele, 1975). It is more realistic to think of the majority of child abusers as people who are often deeply ashamed of their behavior, who have been unable to control it, and who are the products of their own childhoods and environments as perhaps their parents were before them. The statement that ''abusive parents care much for their children but do not care well'' about sums it up.

Finally, the teacher will benefit by doing some thinking about the reasons why she, herself, is so angry over what these parents have done. Certainly, part of the reaction stems from the ugly painfulness of seeing a child suffer and from the teacher's commitment to helping children, but it seems to me that there is more to the anger than that. Perhaps some of the reaction comes also because, more than most people, nursery school teachers have had to learn to control their own angry impulses toward children. Any nursery school teacher who is honest with herself must admit that there have been times when she, too, has felt rage toward a child surge within her. Her anger toward the abusive parent may turn to compassion if she realizes that the difference between herself and them at that instant is that she was able to stop in time!

Helping the child while his family is in treatment. As Harold Martin (1976) so correctly points out, most of the material having to do with the treatment of child abuse deals with the treatment of the adults or amelioration of the family's environment, but the child needs help, too—help that must go beyond the simple level of physical rescue. In addition to whatever may be prescribed in the way of special therapies, nursery school is frequently recommended, and Dr. Martin and his associates place considerable faith in what can be accomplished in that environment to help the child. The points he makes as being desirable ones in caring for abused children are those generally stressed throughout *The Whole Child* as being important in the care of all children.

In particular, it is important with such youngsters to emphasize the building of trust and warmth between them and their teachers; steadiness and consistency are invaluable elements of such trust building. The enhancement of self-esteem is also important to stress, and since developmental delays of various kinds appear to be characteristic of these children, a careful analysis of these deficits should be made and attention paid to remediating them when this can be done without undue pressure. (Both Martin (1976) and Mirandy (1976) comment particularly on apparent deficits in perceptual-motor development skills and expressive language ability.)

Above all, every effort should be made to retain the child in school; to maintain consistent, regular contact with the other people who are working with the family; and to be as patient and caring with both the child and his family as possible.

SUMMARY

Practically all young children experience some form of crisis during their preschool years, and there are many things parents and nursery school teachers can do to help them come through these experiences in good condition and perhaps with added strengths. The teacher should encourage parents to *include* rather than exclude the child at such times; she should try not to overreact to the problem or violate the family's privacy, and to offer herself as a resource of information when the family needs such assistance.

The teacher can help the child and his family by facing the reality of the crisis with him, making certain he does not blame himself for situations he has not caused, keeping his life at school steady and calm, providing play opportunities for him that help him work through and understand his feelings, and helping him anticipate what will happen next.

A discussion of various specific crises that are of particular concern to children conclude the chapter. Problems related to sending the child to nursery school, the arrival of a new baby, and hospitalization of either the child or one of his parents are

308 WORKING WITH SPECIAL SITUATIONS

some of these important crises. Additional ones discussed specifically include problems related to divorce, death, and child abuse and molestation. Information and recommendations are provided to help teachers and families cope with each of these situations.

QUESTIONS

1. One of the youngsters at your school has been scratching his head a lot and, upon inspection, you discover that he has lice. How would you handle this minor but important crisis with the child and his family?
2. The rat at your nursery school has been getting fatter and fatter, and it is obvious he has a tumor. The veterinarian pronounces it inoperable—what to do? How would you approach this matter with the children?
3. Keep a list for a month noting all the crises that happen to children and staff during this time—how many were there? How were they handled?
4. Are there some crises children should *not* know about? What might these be, and how would you protect the children from them?
5. Can you recall being jealous of a brother or sister? What did it feel like? Would you handle it as your parents did if you had a child in a similar situation?
6. In the community in which you live, what is the recommended procedure for getting help for parents who abuse their children? Is there more than one agency available? What role does the police department play in such cases?
7. *Problem:* A child comes to school acting listless and looking pale and washed out. At nap time, when he undresses, you find he has several bruises on his chest and around his arms, and he complains that his neck hurts. There has been a previous occasion where he arrived with a bump on his head and a black eye, which his mother said were due to his falling down a flight of steps. Under these circumstances, do you think it wisest to approach the parent with your concern, or are there other alternative solutions that should be explored? If the parent, in your judgment, should not be approached, what agencies in your own community would be the most appropriate and effective ones to contact?

REFERENCES FOR FURTHER READING

Separation

Provence, S., Naylor, A., and Patterson, J. *The challenge of daycare.* New Haven: Yale University Press, 1977. Chapter 5 of *The Challenge of Daycare* deals with separation in some detail. It discusses adjustment for child and parents and has some practical suggestions about ways to lessen stress. The discussion centers on children 2 years old and younger.
NOTE: See also the Bernstein bibliography, 1976, listed under *Death.*

Overviews on the Subject of Dealing with Crises

Kliman, G. *Psychological emergencies of childhood.* New York: Grune & Stratton, Inc., 1968. A sensitive analysis written from a psychoanalytic point of view that focuses in particular on illness, death, and divorce, it also touches on moving and on entering school.

Ramos, S. *Teaching your child to cope with crisis.* New York: David McKay Co., Inc., 1975. *Teaching Your Child to Cope with Crisis* is written primarily for parents and cites the advice of many authorities for dealing with an assortment of crises. The advice is sound as far as it goes; however, the book would be strengthened if additional resources for information were included, or even if the books written by the authorities quoted in the text were identified more clearly.

Stein, M., Beyer, E., and Ronald, D. Beyond benevolence—the mental health role of the preschool teacher. *Young Children,* 1975, *30*(5), 358-372. This rare article documents a 4-year attempt to increase the mental health role of the nursery school teacher. It gives examples of teachers dealing with various crises, including death, illness, and divorce, and it contains sensible recommendations and interesting examples.

Warren, R. M. *Caring: Supporting children's growth.* Washington, D.C.: National Association for the Education of Young Children, 1977. The section on "Helping Young Children Handle Harsh Realities" is brief but offers some pithy advice, including the need to face "dreadful facts" and to help the child separate adult from child business; also included is a nice list of relevant books for children.

Books for Children Dealing With Various Crises

Braun, S. J., and Lasher, M. G. *Are you ready to mainstream? Helping preschoolers with learning and behavior problems.* Columbus, Ohio: Charles E. Merrill Publishing Co., 1978. This book is also cited in the Chapter 19, "Working with Exceptional Children," but it should be noted here because it contains such an excellent bibliography of children's books for ages 3 to 6 on special problems, such as death, divorce, handicaps, and illness.

Hospitalization

Haller, J. A. (Ed.), Talbert, J. L., and Dombro, R. H., (Asst. Eds.). *The hospitalized child and his family.* Baltimore: The Johns Hopkins University Press, 1967. An excellent book written for professionals in the field of medicine but of interest to all because of its humane approach, it covers preparation for surgery, play in the hospital, the return home, and much more.

Plank, E. N. *Working with children in hospitals.* Cleveland: The Press of Case Western Reserve University, 1962. This book remains one of the best, most sensitive discussions of how children feel when hospitalized and how staff and parents can help them adjust to the experience.

Hospitalization: Books for Children

Altshuler, A. *Books that help children deal with a hospital experience.* Rockville, Md.: Public Health Service, Health Services Administration, U.S. Dept. of Health, Education, and Welfare, 1974. HSA 74-5402. This is an excellent bibliography that lists books according to the age for which they are appropriate, rates them for quality, and gives short synopses of plots.

Divorce: Information for Teachers

Grollman, E. A. (Ed.). *Explaining divorce to children*. Boston: Beacon Press, 1969. This is an overview that includes articles by a number of authors on various aspects of divorce as it pertains to children.

Kelly, J. B., and Wallerstein, J. S. Brief interactions with children of divorcing families. *American Journal of Orthopsychiatry,* January 1977, *47*(1), 23-39. A rare discussion that focuses on the effect of divorce on preschool children as studied in a mental health clinic, this article presents research data as well as some practical recommendations.

Divorce: Information for Parents

Adams, M. *Single blessedness: Observations on the single status in a married society*. New York: Basic Books, Inc., Publishers, 1976. Without being defensive in tone, this is a sound book that makes a good case for remaining single. It is particularly valuable for women to read who are panicky following a divorce, feeling that unless they marry again, life is not worth living; highly recommended.

Atkins, E., and Rubin, E. *Part-time father: A guide for the divorced father*. New York: Vanguard Press, Inc., 1976. This is a good self-help book that faces up honestly to the stresses of divorce as well as offering practical suggestions about ways for fathers to continue sound relationships with their children.

Mindey, C. *The divorced mother: A guide to readjustment*. New York: McGraw-Hill Book Co., 1969. Written by a divorced mother, this book *does* talk about children but also offers a host of practical suggestions about all aspects of life as a divorced person. It is particularly helpful for the newly divorced woman or for the woman considering divorce.

NOTE: Parents should also be alerted to the possibility of joining groups such as Parents Without Partners or We Care.

Moving

Cohen, M. D. (Ed.). *When children move from school to school*. Washington, D.C.: Association for Childhood Education International, 1972. A rare publication that deals with school adjustment and family adjustment problems associated with moving, it also has a brief section on migrant children.

Death: Information for Teachers

Bernstein, J. E. *Helping children cope with death and separation: Resources for teachers*. Urbana, Ill.: Publications Office/ICBD, College of Education, University of Illinois, 1976. This bibliography is a treasury of resources of children's books, adult movies, and annotated references on research.

Bernstein, J. E. Helping young children cope with death. In L. G. Katz (Ed.). *Current topics in early childhood education* (Vol. 1). Norwood, N.J.: Ablex Publishing Corp., 1977. Bernstein's chapter presents the best recent overview of what is known and thought about death and its relationship to young children; well done and quite comprehensive for such a short chapter.

Grollman, E. A. *Explaining death to children*. Boston: Beacon Press, 1967. *Explaining Death to Children* has two chapters filled with information focussed on the younger child and his concerns; slightly dated, but still useful.

Kübler-Ross, E. *On death and dying*. New York: Macmillan Publishing Co., Inc., 1969. This classic book traces the emotional attitudes of dying persons through five stages: denial and isolation, anger, bargaining, depression, and acceptance.

Death: Information for Parents

Wolf, A. V. M. *Helping your child understand death*. New York: The Child Study Press, 1973. In my opinion this slender book remains *the* resource to offer parents. It is written in question-and-answer form and is matter-of-fact and sensible; should be in the library of every nursery school.

Child Abuse: Information for the Teacher

Costa, J. J., and Nelson, G. K. *Child abuse and neglect: Legislation, reporting and prevention*. Lexington, Mass.: D. C. Heath & Co., 1978. The greatest strengths of this book are its state-by-state survey of reporting requirements and lists of programs and agencies to contact for help—even including telephone numbers!

Halperin, M. *Helping maltreated children: School and community resources*. St. Louis: The C. V. Mosby Co., 1979. This rare book is the only one in the field that focusses on the role of the school with the abused child and his family. The tone of *Helping the Maltreated Child* is balanced and moderate, and the advice is practical though geared mainly to working with older children in public school situations.

Helfer, R. E., and Kempe, C. H. *The battered child* (2nd ed.). Chicago: University of Chicago Press, 1974. *The Battered Child,* a classic textbook on this subject, has now been updated to include current information. It is an invaluable resource. Teachers who need more information relating to abusing parents will benefit by reading Elizabeth Davoren's chapter, ''The Role of the Social Worker,'' and, personally, I found the chapter on forensic medicine, ''The Pathology of Child Abuse,'' fascinating, though grisly.

Kempe, C. H., and Helfer, R. E. *Helping the battered child and his family*. Philadelphia: J. B. Lippincott Co., 1972. This is another useful book by the same authors, covering the community as well as the family.

Kline, D. F. *Child abuse and neglect: A primer for school personnel*. Reston, Va.: Council on Exceptional Children, 1977. Although written primarily for teachers of older children, this pamphlet contains considerable general information that also applies to preschoolers.

Martin, H. P. *The abused child: A multidisciplinary approach to developmental issues and treatment*. Cambridge, Mass.: Ballinger Publishing Co., 1976. Of all the materials included in this reference list on abuse, this book is likely to be of the greatest interest and help to nursery school teachers, since it focuses on how to help the child. Nursery school teachers will feel very comfortable with Dr. Martin's prescriptions and point of view.

National Center on Child Abuse and Neglect. *Child abuse and neglect: The problem and its management*. (Vol 1: *An overview of the problem* and Vol. 2: *The roles and responsibilities of professionals*). Washington, D.C.: U.S. Dept. of Health, Education, and Welfare, OHD, OCD, Children's Bureau, National Center on Child Abuse and Neglect, 1975 (a) and (b).

OHD 75-30073 and OHD 75-30074. These meaty pamphlets present an excellent overview of this problem and what is known about it at the present time.

National Center on Child Abuse and Neglect. *How to plan and carry out a successful public awareness program on child abuse and neglect.* Washington, D.C.: National Center on Child Abuse and Neglect, Children's Bureau, OCD, OHD, U.S. Dept. of Health, Education, and Welfare, 1977. OHD 77-30089. The teacher who is truly concerned about child abuse in her community may wish to take part in community-wide education about it. This unusual reference has information on strategies for doing this successfully. It lists a few films, as well as available TV spots, examples of advertising, and so forth.

National Committee for Prevention of Child Abuse. *The national directory of child abuse services and information.* Chicago: The Committee, 111 East Wacker Drive, Chicago, Ill. 60601, 1974. This Directory includes names, addresses, telephone numbers, and contact persons for each agency.

National Institutes of Mental Health. *Child abuse and neglect programs: Practice and theory.* Rockville, Md.: U.S. Dept. of Health, Education, and Welfare, Public Health Service, National Institutes of Mental Health, 1977. ADM 77-344. For those interested in current treatment programs, this publication is highly recommended. The second part has a solid review of research that is worthwhile.

Steele, B. F. *Working with abusive parents from a psychiatric point of view.* Washington, D.C.: U.S. Dept. of Health, Education, and Welfare, OHD, OCD, National Center on Child Abuse and Neglect, 1977. OHD 77-30070. This pamphlet is another of the series listed above from the National Center on Child Abuse at Denver, a government-supported research center that is doing significant work in the area of child abuse; very helpful.

For the Advanced Student

The American Journal of Orthopsychiatry. 49 Sheridan Ave., Albany, N.Y. 12210. Teachers who are interested in preventive psychiatry will find this journal a worthwhile publication to subscribe to.

American Humane Association, Children's Division. *Fifth National Symposium.* Denver: The Association, 1976. The Humane Association has long been concerned about cruelty to children and offers many pamphlets on this subject. This particular volume of the Symposium has some interesting material on how social workers should prepare themselves for testifying in court. The same advice applies, I presume, to nursery school teachers.

Bowlby, J. *Attachment and loss* (Vol. 1: Attachment). New York: Basic Books, Inc. Publishers, 1969. *Attachment and loss* (Vol. 2: Separation). New York: Basic Books, Inc., Publishers, 1973. These are important references contributed by a man who pioneered studies of separation and young children. His work about young children in hospitals is particularly eloquent, as are the films he and James Robertson made on this subject.

Burlingham, D., and Freud, A. Young children in wartime: Traumatic effects of separation from parents. In Y. Brack-

bill and G. G. Thompson (Eds.), *Behavior in infancy and early childhood.* New York: The Free Press, 1967. This is an interesting and well-known account of how the authors worked with a group of displaced English children during World War II and how the children endured separation from their mothers during the crisis of wartime.

Coles, R. *Children of crisis: A study of courage and fear.* New York: Dell Publishing Co., Inc., 1967. This thorough, sensitive study by a psychiatrist on the effect of integration on the people of the South presents both sides of the integration question fairly and fully.

Coles, R. *Uprooted children: The early life of migrant farm workers.* Pittsburgh: University of Pittsburgh Press, 1970. Here is an account of the lives of migrant children who face the continuing crises of moving and poverty throughout their childhoods.

Furman, E. *A child's parent dies: Studies in childhood bereavement.* New Haven: Yale University Press, 1974. This intensive study of bereavement contains many case histories as well as general discussion. It is a valuable reference that approaches the subject of loss from a psychoanalytic perspective. Chapter 9 contains an extensive review of the literature.

Herzog, E., and Sudia, C. E. Children in fatherless homes. In B. E. Caldwell and H. N. Ricciuti (Eds.), *Review of child development research* (Vol. 3). Chicago: University of Chicago Press, 1973. An invaluable reference, this is an excellent, thorough, thoughtful review of research that concludes that results are still inconclusive!

Kliman, G. W. Analyst in the nursery: Experimental application of child analytic techniques in a therapeutic nursery: The Cornerstone method. In *The psychoanalytic study of the child* (Vol. 30). New Haven: Yale University Press, 1975. This is a description of how a therapist worked right within the nursery school to provide interpretations and assistance to children exposed to crisis situations. It focusses on a description of the treatment of a 4½-year-old girl, who, among other difficulties, experiences the death of a parent.

McDermott, J. F., and Harrison, S. I. (Eds.). *Psychiatric treatment of the child.* New York: Jason Aronson, Inc., 1977. This book is highly recommended for those readers who would like to read more in depth about various methods of psychiatric treatment, since it discusses therapy from many points of view; a sound basic reference.

Moustakas, C. *Psychotherapy with children.* New York: Ballantine Books, Inc., 1959. For those teachers who would like a deeper understanding of how play therapy can be used to help children, this book (and Virginia Axline's book on the same subject) will be useful. It contains theoretical discussions, comments on case histories, and many examples of therapeutic dialogue.

Parke, R. D., and Collmer, C. W. Child abuse: An interdisciplinary analysis. In E. M. Hetherington (Ed.), *Review of child development research* (Vol. 5). Chicago: The University of Chicago Press, 1975. This is a clearly written, comprehensive overview of research on child abuse that stresses psychiatric, sociological, and social-situational approaches, as well as describing a variety of treatment approaches.

Petrillo, M., and Sanger, S. *Emotional care of hospitalized children: An environmental approach.* Philadelphia: J. B. Lippincott Co., 1972. This book presents a comprehensive analysis of how to deal with children undergoing treatment in hospitals. It is addressed primarily to medical personnel but could be read with benefit to everyone.

Rice, E. P., Ekdahl, M. C., and Miller, L. *Children of mentally ill parents: Problems in child care.* New York: Behavioral Publications, Inc., 1971. The emotional reaction of children when their parents are hospitalized in mental institutions is often severe. This book recounts a study of such youngsters and also contains a comparative study of children whose parents were hospitalized for tuberculosis.

Steele, B. F. *Working with abusive parents from a psychiatric point of view.* Washington, D.C.: U.S. Dept. of Health, Education, and Welfare. OHD, OCD, Children's Bureau, National Center on Child Abuse and Neglect, 1977. DHEW Pub. no. OHD 77-30070. Teachers who desire to deepen their understanding of abusive parents will find Dr. Steele's pamphlet helpful. It discusses the personality structure often associated with being an abusive parent and then briefly describes modes of treatment.

Photo by Jason Lo'Cicero

19 □ Working with exceptional children

A handicapped child reacts to pity and solicitude either by withdrawing into himself or by just giving up the struggle for independence. The child needs support, warmth, interest, concern, appreciation of his achievements, and respect for his personality. Feeling for the child must be combined with knowledge of the child.*

Although all children have special educational needs at one point or another in their lives, some children require specialized attention more consistently. This group includes a wide assortment of youngsters ranging from those who are physically handicapped to those who are emotionally disturbed or who are experiencing intellectual development that lags behind or is markedly ahead of their peers. In short, the category of exceptionality covers children who deviate in at least one respect far enough from the typical that they are noticeable in the group because of this deviation.

The first part of this chapter is intended to increase the ability of the nursery school teacher to spot children who may have special problems and to develop her sensitivity and skills in bringing this problem to the attention of the parents and in carrying out a successful referral to a specialist. In the second portion of the chapter some basic educational recommendations are given for including exceptional children in the ordinary nursery school. An extensive bibliography is provided at the end of the chapter.

---

*From Schattner, R. *An early childhood curriculum for multiply handicapped children* (p. 36). New York: copyright © 1971, Intext Press.

THE NURSERY SCHOOL TEACHER AS A SCREENING AGENT

One of the most important services the nursery school teacher can provide is screening the children in her care for physical, emotional, and mental behavior that may indicate a serious underlying difficulty (Hayden and Edgar, 1977). It is a mistaken notion that such difficulties are always first noticed in the physician's office. Doctors see children for brief periods of time often under conditions that are quite stressful to the child. In addition, they can be hampered by mothers who either raise questions about symptoms that are insignificant or who resist being told anything about their youngsters that may be upsetting. When physicians are caught in this kind of situation, it is only to be expected that occasional difficulties slip past without notice. These comments are not intended to imply that a highly trained medical specialist knows less than the nursery school teacher does; rather, it means that the teacher should keep her eyes open because she has the advantage of seeing the child in a natural setting for extended periods of time, and she has seen many youngsters of similar age and background. Thus it is possible that she may become aware of difficulties that should be drawn to the attention of the physician or psychologist.

The sooner such potential handicaps are identified, the sooner they may be ameliorated and further formation of undesirable habit patterns and emotional reactions reduced (Caldwell, 1973). Sometimes early diagnosis means that a condition can be cleared up entirely (as when a child's hearing is restored following a tonsillectomy-adenoidectomy), and sometimes the effect of the condition can only be mitigated (as is often the case with mentally retarded youngsters); but *nothing* can be done until the child is identified as needing assistance and a referral has been successfully carried out. These are points at which the nursery school teacher's help is crucial.

Some physical conditions and symptoms of which the teacher should be aware

Speech and hearing problems. Various speech difficulties and symptoms of possible hearing impairment have already been reviewed in the chapter on language, so it will only be noted here that speech and hearing problems are among the physical disorders that occur most frequently in childhood. Speech difficulties are likely to be noticed, but hearing loss may be overlooked as a possible cause of misbehavior, inattention, or lack of responsiveness. However, once hearing loss is suspected, it is a relatively simple matter to refer the child to an otolaryngologist for examination. Since such losses may be due to infection, they can and should be treated promptly.

Difficulties of vision. Another physical disability that may pass unnoticed but that occurs frequently is an inability to see clearly. The incidence of visual defects may run as high as one in four or five children of elementary school age (Dalton, 1943). This means that in a nursery school group of fifteen children there may be three or four youngsters who have some kind of difficulty with their eyes.

The presence of the following symptoms* should alert the teacher to the possibility that the child needs to have his eyes examined.

---

*From Kirk, S. A. *Educating exceptional children* (2nd ed.). Boston: Houghton Mifflin Co., 1972. P. 295.

1. Strabismus (crossed eyes); nystagmus (involuntary, rapid movement of the eyeball)
2. How the child uses his eyes; tilting his head, holding objects close to his eyes, rubbing his eyes, squinting, displaying sensitivity to bright lights and rolling his eyes
3. Inattention to visual objects or visual tasks such as looking at pictures or reading
4. Awkwardness in games requiring eye-hand coordination
5. Avoidance of tasks that require close eye work
6. Affinity to tasks that require distance vision
7. Any complaints about inability to see
8. Lack of normal curiosity in regard to visually appealing objects

In addition to such physical symptoms, physiological ones include reddened or crusty eyelids, watery eyes, or eyes that are discharging (Gearheart and Weishahn, 1976).

One defect of vision in particular requires treatment during early childhood, since later attempts at correction are not so effective (Rosenthal, 1975). This is *amblyopia,* sometimes called *lazy eye,* a condition in which one eye is weaker than the other because of a muscle imbalance (Harley, 1973). Common signs of this condition include squinting with one eye or tilting the head to one side in order to see better. Since early treatment of this condition is important, if there is any possible way to incorporate visual screening tests into the nursery school program it should be done. Sometimes local ophthalmological or optometric societies will sponsor this service; sometimes a public health nurse can be prevailed upon, or an interested civic group will employ a trained nurse to visit the nursery schools and conduct such tests.

Screening is best done at school rather than at a central clinic because coverage of children attending the school is likely to be more complete and the environment in which testing takes place is familiar to the children, so they will be more at ease. Giving the children practice before the actual examination day in holding the "E" according to instructions will facilitate testing and help save the examiner's sanity. Central clinics should also be offered as a service to children who do not attend nursery school.

Following identification of a possible problem by means of the screening test, the youngster should be referred to an ophthalmologist for diagnosis and follow-up.

Hyperactivity. The term ''hyperactive'' tends to be abused by some parents and teachers who use it to describe every active, vigorous child (Grinspoon and Singer, 1973). For this reason, it is helpful to apply the following criteria developed by Paul Wender, a psychiatrist who specializes in this condition, when trying to determine whether a child should be referred for medical evaluation and possible treatment (1973).

The following behavior* characterizes this condition in young children; additional learning problems may arise during the elementary school years.

1. Restlessness—the child appears to be a bundle of energy. The mother may come to feel that she can't take her eyes off him for a minute without his climbing on the refrigerator or running into the street. At nursery school, the child may be incessantly in motion except that he seems able to settle down when given one-to-one attention.
2. The child is easily distracted and has a short attention span. In nursery school he may rush from activity to activity and then seem at a loss for what to do. He may do as the teacher asks but forget quickly and revert to his former behavior.
3. The child demands attention insatiably—monopolizes conversations, teases, badgers, repeats annoying activities. May be emotionally unresponsive or undemonstrative.
4. Shows a weaker than average ability to control his impulses. Hard for him to wait, he may become upset rapidly, has many temper tantrums, acts on the spur of the moment—often with poor judgment. Parents may complain that the child is incontinent.
5. About half of these children exhibit difficulties in the coordination of fine muscle activities such as using scissors, coloring and so forth, or with problems of balance.

*From *The hyperactive child: A handbook for parents* by Paul H. Wender, M.D. © 1973 by Paul H. Wender. Used by permission of Crown Publishers, Inc.

6. The child may have various kinds of interpersonal problems including resistance to social demands from parents and teachers, excessive independence, and a troublesome tendency to dominate the children he plays with, which makes him unlikable.
7. He may have various emotional problems including swings of mood, becoming excessively excited over pleasant activities, sometimes appearing to be insensitive to pain, demonstrating a low tolerance to frustration and overreaction to it when frustrated, low self-esteem.
8. Some of these children have real difficulty tolerating change.

Of course, most young children exhibit these kinds of behaviors from time to time. What sets the truly hyperactive child apart is the intensity and consistency of the behavior. Most youngsters seem to outgrow it as they reach adolescence, but the years of stress and the unhappy side effects of this condition have usually taken a painful toll by then. Dr. Wender suggests that the most adequate referral is one made to a child psychiatrist or a pediatrician conversant with behavior problems, since medication can be a factor in successful management of this condition. A child psychologist or social worker can also make a helpful contribution, but they are unable to prescribe medication should that prove necessary.

Convulsive seizures. Another condition that responds well to medication is epilepsy. Indeed, *grand mal* attacks, in which the individual loses consciousness, are now rarely witnessed in nursery schools. Unless a major convulsive seizure occurs for the first time at school, the teacher usually need not worry about referring such children, since it is almost certain that they are already under treatment by their physician. She should, however, report seizures to the family. If an attack occurs at school, the Epilepsy Foundation of America recommends that the following procedure be carried out.

1. Remain calm. Students will assume the same emotional reaction as their teacher. The seizure itself is painless to the child.
2. Do not try to restrain the child. Nothing can be done

to stop a seizure once it has begun. It must run its course.

3. Clear the area around the student so that he does not injure himself on hard objects. Try not to interfere with his movements in any way.
4. Do not force anything between his teeth. If his mouth is already open, a soft object like a handkerchief may be placed between his side teeth.
5. It generally is not necessary to call a doctor unless the attack is immediately followed by another major seizure or if the seizure lasts more than 10 minutes.
6. When the seizure is over, let the child rest if he needs to.

The teacher will also need to explain to the other children, who may be either curious or distressed, what happened. The explanation should be simple and matter of fact to make it as easy as possible for the child to return to the group with little comment.

The teacher needs to be more alert to the much milder form of convulsion, *petit mal,* because this lighter seizure sometimes escapes the notice of the family, to whom it may seem to be a case of daydreaming or inattention.

According to Robb (1965) these attacks are short (only a few seconds), and the child may indicate their presence only by a blank stare and immobility but does not fall to the ground. A second type of petit mal seizure is characterized by the eyes blinking or deviating, the head turning a little, lip smacking, and stereotyped movements of the hands. It is worthwhile to identify this behavior and refer the child for treatment to a pediatrician or neurologist because the probability of successful control by means of medication is high: Robb estimates that probably 75% to 80% of all patients afflicted with convulsive seizures experience good control when given medication.

Excessive awkwardness. The teacher should also notice children who are exceptionally clumsy. These are youngsters who, even though allowance has been made for their youthful age, are much more poorly coordinated than their peers. They may fall over their feet, run into things, knock things over, have trouble with climbing and balancing (and are often very apprehensive about engaging in these ac-

tivities), run consistently on their toes, or be unable to accomplish ordinary fine muscle tasks. This kind of behavior should not be "laughed off." Instead, it should be drawn to the attention of the parent and referral to the pediatrician suggested. There are numerous causes for such symptoms, and many are amenable to treatment but only if they are identified (Arnheim and Sinclair, 1979).

Other physical problems. In general, the teacher should watch for pronounced changes in the physical appearance of the child and, in particular, should take notice of children who are excessively pale or who convey a general air of exhaustion or lassitude. These conditions often develop so gradually that parents are unaware of the change. It is especially important to watch a child with care during the week or two after he has returned from a serious illness, such as measles, scarlet fever, or meningitis, since occasional potentially serious problems develop following such infections.

Signs of emotional disturbance that indicate a referral is needed

Deciding when referral for emotional disturbance is warranted and when it is unnecessary can be a difficult problem, because symptoms of emotional upset are common during early childhood (Buckle and Lebovici, 1960). One study, for example, found that the average child of nursery school age manifested between four and six "behavior" problems and that they seemed to appear and disappear over a period of time (Macfarlane, 1943). A good nursery school environment can accomplish wonders with children who are emotionally upset, and many physicians routinely refer children who are having emotional difficulties to nursery school because they have witnessed many happy results from such referrals.

There may come a time, however, when the staff begins to question whether the nursery school environment, no matter how therapeutic, can offer sufficient help to a particular youngster. Perhaps after a reasonable period for adjustment and learning, he persists in "blowing his stack" over relatively inconsequential matters, or perhaps he insists on spending most of each morning hidden within the housekeeping corner or even crouched beneath a table. These behaviors, to name only two of a much wider list of possibilities, should arouse feelings of concern in the staff, since they are examples of behavior that (1) is too extreme, (2) happens too often, and (3) persists too long. When these criteria describe a child's behavior, it is time for the staff to admit their limitations of time and training and to encourage the family to seek the advice of a qualified psychologist or psychiatrist.

The teacher should also apply a fourth criterion when considering the necessity of a referral: whether the number of symptoms manifested by the child at any one period is excessive. We have seen that signs of upset are common and often disappear either spontaneously or as a result of adequate handling by parents and teachers. Occasionally, though, a child will exhibit a number of reactions at the same time. He may begin to wet his bed again, be unable to fall asleep easily, insist on always having his blanket with him, cry a great deal, and refuse to play. If such habits are so numerous and so intense that they interfere with the child's enjoyment of life and are a burden to him and his family, the possibility of a referral should be explored.

Early infantile autism: a special case. Another psychological condition is seen occasionally in nursery schools, particularly in less sophisticated areas where medical and psychological advice is not readily available. A family may enroll a youngster who can generally be described in the following terms: he pays scant attention to other children or adults and seems emotionally distant and uninvolved; it is difficult or impossible to get him to look the person who is speaking to him in the eye; he may become very distressed when asked to change from one activity to another (for example, he may fly into a panic when asked to stop swinging and go inside for snack); his speech may be minimal or nonexistent; he may repeat phrases in a meaningless way; and he may show a marked interest in things that spin or twirl, such as a tricycle wheel, which he may sit by and spin absorbedly, or a

spoon, which he will twirl with great skill (Kanner, 1944; Rutter, 1966; Shaw and Lucas, 1970; Wing, 1976). When several of these symptoms occur together, the youngster may be suffering from infantile autism. This condition is rare, but my experience indicates that the nursery school teacher will come across such children from time to time. Treatment is difficult, and *these youngsters need highly professional help as soon as they can get it.* Therefore, the family should be urged to seek help from a child psychiatrist promptly.

Problems related to mental ability

Children with developmental lags. All nursery school teachers need to know enough about developmental sequences and the ages at which behavioral milestones can be anticipated that they can tell when a child is developing normally or when he is lagging markedly behind his peers or is quite advanced for his age. Lists of developmental standards have been included in many chapters in this book, not with the intention of urging developmental conformity, but in the hope that they will help the teacher be tolerant of behaviors characteristic of various ages and also alert to children who are developing so far out of phase that they require special help.

Many nursery school teachers do not recognize retardation when they see it. Being unaware of retardation can be an advantage in a way, since it means that a child is not stuck with a stereotyped reaction to his condition or burdened with an undesirable label. On the other hand, it may also mean that an undiagnosed, slow-learning 4-year-old who is actually operating at a 2½-year-old level may be expected to sit with the other 4-year-olds for long stories he does not comprehend or may be criticized and disciplined for refusing to share equipment when actually he is behaving in a way typical of his developmental but not chronological age. An adequate diagnosis would enable the teacher to match her expectations to the child's real level of ability.

Behavior that should be cause for concern includes a widespread pattern of delayed development that is a year or more behind the typical in physical, social, and intellectual areas. Such lags are usually accompanied by speech that is obviously immature for the child's chronological age.

Causes of slow development are numerous, ranging from chromosomal disorders to pseudoretardation induced by an insufficiently stimulating environment, and it is often impossible even for specialists to determine why the child is developing slowly (Bakwin and Bakwin, 1974; Kessler, 1966).

The simplicity and adaptability of the nursery school curriculum mean that many mildly or moderately retarded children can fit comfortably into the nursery school environment. Some, of course, require more special educational services. Since truly retarded children do not outgrow their condition or ultimately catch up with their more fortunate peers, it is necessary for teachers and parents to come to a realistic understanding of what can be expected of them. Knowledgeable, humane specialists can provide many helpful suggestions about how to maximize learning for these youngsters.

Pseudoretarded children. Although heredity appears to control the range of intelligence of each individual, environment has been shown also to have an effect on how well individuals develop (Lichtenberg and Norton, 1970), and there is general agreement that cognitive development can be depressed by the adverse environmental circumstances often associated with poverty. However, the extent of this pseudoretardation and the ability of education to remedy it are still the subject of debate.

Since the middle 1960s, infant and preschool education has been characterized by the development of many programs intended to overcome retardation due to environmental insult. Some results of these attempts have been disappointing (Cicerelli, Evans, and Schiller, 1969), but some programs have reported heartening successes in achieving this goal (Day and Parker, 1977; Evans, 1971; Heber, Garber, Harrington, Hoffman, and Falender, 1972; Lazar and others, 1977; Weber, 1970).

CHARACTERISTICS OF PSEUDORETARDED CHILDREN. Children who come from the lower socioeconomic class have many characteristics and needs that are common to all children, but many of them also have some characteristics that reduce the likelihood of their succeeding in a middle-class school. Teachers who wish to work with them need to take these characteristics into account when planning educational programs in order to help the children develop maximally.

Many of the children will have poorer health than middle-class children do, since they receive little medical care after they stop attending well-baby clinics around the age of 2 years. Poor diet (both prenatally and postnatally) also contributes to less than optimum conditions for fostering growth (Sunderlin and Wills, 1969; Thomas, 1972). Many poor children are behind in their ability to use standard English, although they may be fluent in a dialect such as black English or another language such as Spanish (Golden, Bridger, and Martare, 1974); and some lack verbal ability in any language. Children from families of the poor characteristically score lower on verbal tests than middle-class children (Bruner, 1970; Deutsch, 1971; L'Abate and Curtis, 1975). They may lack experiences that are common among middle-class children. (For example, in my own community we found that many of the children had never been to the beach or to a supermarket, even though they lived within walking distance of both.) These youngsters often appear more action oriented than given to reflective thought. When confronted with standard measures of intelligence, such as the Stanford-Binet or the Peabody Picture Vocabulary Test, they usually score, for many reasons, below the average performance of their middle-class peers (Loehlin, Lindsey, and Spuhler, 1975; Reese and Lipsitt, 1970).

Unfortunately, these kinds of reports may cause the teacher to overlook the positive strengths of such children, strengths that middle-class children may not possess. For example, children from poor families may be able to cope with various human failings, make money stretch, or get along with intrusive adults from welfare or law enforcement agencies with an aplomb that a middle-class child could not manage. There can also be a self-reliance, sense of humor, and a kind of wise cynicism expressed even by 4-year-olds, which may make a sentimental teacher's heart ache, but which should also arouse her admiration if she realizes how effective such attitudes are as coping mechanisms.

Unfortunately, most of the literature on working with children from the lower socioeconomic class makes it sound difficult and possibly frightening to the beginning teacher, but there are cogent reasons why many teachers who become involved in a Head Start or day-care program vow never to return to teaching middle-class children. This decision may partly be due to ego-gratification related to noblesse oblige, but some of it is also due to the pleasure of seeing children flourish and go on to a better school experience as a result of their years in preschool care.

It takes considerable energy, perseverance, and skill to help young "disadvantaged" children supplement their home educations with material that will enable them to fit into the middle-class school. A number of successful programs have demonstrated that this can be done (Gordon, 1969; Gray and Klaus, 1970; Heber, Garber, Harrington, Hoffman, and Falender, 1972; Levenstein, 1971; Weikart and Lambie, 1968), and it behooves the teacher who works with such youngsters to acquaint herself with a variety of these programs, select a model that fits her own tastes and predilections, make a consistent plan based on the model, and carry it out with determination.

Intellectually gifted children. Although the child who is slow to learn and the child who is pseudo-retarded have been receiving increased attention and service in the past few years, intellectually gifted preschoolers have been virtually ignored—unless the child is so precocious that he is singled out as a piece of curiosa. Why such promising children should be overlooked is difficult to say. Surely they deserve the interest and support of their teachers. Perhaps they are overlooked because many of them fit smoothly into the nursery school curriculum (although it may present insufficient challenges for them), or perhaps most preschool teachers are uncertain about what kinds of behavior indicate outstanding mental ability and thus fail to identify the children.

A child with exceptional mental ability usually exhibits a general pattern of advanced skills; his language is more elaborate and extended than that of other children of the same age, and his vocabulary is likely to be large; his attention span may be longer if his interest is aroused; he grasps ideas easily; he probably possesses an exceptional amount of general information, which is characterized not only by more variety but also by greater detail. Gifted preschoolers like to pursue reasons for things and talk about cause-and-effect relationships. They are often almost insatiably interested in special subjects that appeal to them. Some of them already know how to read. Teachers who do not build their curriculum and increase its complexity sufficiently during the year may find that these children become increasingly restless and gradually get into difficulties because they have lost interest in what is happening at school.

The teacher can deal satisfactorily with this kind of exceptionality by modifying the curriculum so that it meets the needs of these youngsters through the addition of challenges. Some suggestions are offered later in the chapter for accomplishing this.

Summary

The nursery school teacher must be aware of many different symptoms and behaviors as she works with her group of children so that she can determine when a child needs special help. These symptoms range from signs of physical disabilities to indications of pronounced emotional upset and deviations in intellectual development.

The teacher who has learned to recognize these signs has achieved the first step in working with children who have special needs. The next step is understanding how to go about making a referral so the youngster can obtain whatever special help he requires.

REFERRING CHILDREN FOR SPECIAL HELP
Calling the difficulty to the parent's attention

Calling a parent's attention to a special problem requires delicacy and tact on the part of the teacher, since it is all too easy for the parents to feel that they are being attacked or criticized and that they have failed to be good parents. This is particularly true if the teacher must raise the issue of a pronounced behavior problem. However, the teacher can do several things to reduce the strength of this understandable defensive reaction.

If the teacher listens carefully while in general conversation with the parent, she may find that the parent herself is raising the problem very tentatively. For example, the mother may ask nervously, "How did she do today?" or comment, "He's just like his older brother. Doesn't he ever sit still?" Many a teacher responds to such questions by just as nervously reassuring the mother, saying brightly, "Oh, he did just fine!" (while thinking wryly to herself, "Just fine, that is, if you don't count biting Henry, destroying Emily's block tower, and refusing to come to story time.") Rather than being falsely reassuring, the teacher could use the opening the parent has provided by responding, "I'm glad you asked. He *is* having some difficulties at school. I'm beginning to think it's time to put our heads together and come up with some special ways to help him."

It takes time to bring about a referral. It is best to raise problems gradually with parents over a period of time because it takes a while for families to accustom themselves to the fact that their child may need special help. Even such an apparently simple thing as having an eye examination may loom as either a financial or emotional threat to particular families, and the teacher should not expect acceptance and compliance with her recommendation just because she has finally worked her courage up to the point of mentioning a difficulty.

The teacher should have the reasons why the child needs special help clearly in mind before raising the issue with the parent. This recommendation is not intended to mean that the teacher should confront the parent with a long, unhappy list of grievances against the child, but that she should be prepared to provide examples of the problem while explaining gently and clearly to the family the reason for her concern.

It is not the teacher's place to diagnose. A particular behavior can have many different causes. For example, failure to pay attention in story hour may be the consequence of a hearing loss, inappropriate reading material, borderline intelligence, fatigue, poor eyesight, or simply needing to go to the toilet. The teacher's role is to recognize that a difficulty exists, do all she can to mitigate it in the nursery school group, inform the parent, and suggest a referral to an expert professional person for diagnosis and treatment when necessary.

Therefore, when she confers with the parent, she should discuss the symptoms and express her concern but avoid giving the impression that she knows for certain what the real cause of the problem may be. Instead, she should ally herself with the parent in a joint quest to find the answer together.

Finding the appropriate referral source

The teacher needs to acquaint herself with referral sources available in her community, since it is both senseless and cruel to raise a problem with parents and have no suggestions about where they can go for help. Some communities publish a directory that lists such services, but the teacher will often find she must locate them by calling the public health nurse, asking friendly pediatricians, checking with local children's hospitals, county medical societies, and mental health clinics, and by generally keeping her ears open and getting to know people in her community who have contacts in these areas. If possible, it is always desirable to list three referral possibilities so that the family has the opportunity to select the one they feel suits them best.

Observing professional ethics

I have already pointed out that the teacher should not assume the role of diagnostician. However, she often possesses information that is of value to the specialist to whom the child is referred. It can be a temptation to pick up the telephone and call this person without pausing to ask the parent's permission, but this is against professional ethics. The teacher must obtain the parent's consent before she talks to the specialist. Some professional people even require that this permission be in writing before any information is exchanged. After permission is obtained, exchanges of information and suggestions from the specialist can be extraordinarily helpful and should be utilized whenever the opportunity presents itself.

Also, when dealing with a special case, the teacher may be tempted to discuss it with people who are not entitled to know about it, because it is so interesting and perhaps makes the teacher feel important. This gossiping is an unforgivable violation of the family's privacy, and the desire to do this must never be indulged in.

LIVING AND WORKING WITH EXCEPTIONAL CHILDREN IN THE NURSERY SCHOOL
Including exceptional children

There has been a dramatic change in funding policies for the education of handicapped children since the first edition of this book was released, because Congress passed Public Law 94-142 in 1975. PL 94-142 applies, at least in theory, to all handicapped individuals in the United States ranging from age 3 to 21, although there is a loophole in the law that states that "coverage of children in the 3-to-5 and 18-to-21 ranges *will not be required* in states whose school attendance laws do not include those age brackets" (Van Osdol and Shane, 1977, p. 41).

Nevertheless, it behooves teachers of children aged 3 to 5 to become familiar with this law, because it gives strong financial and verbal encouragement to including preschool handicapped youngsters in educational programs, and this makes it likely that more and more states will comply as time goes on. This is significant for nursery school teachers because there is a provision in the law that allows local agencies to place children in private schools (including nursery schools) if it appears to be in the best interests of the child to do so. Moreover, such placements will be funded by public monies.

The basic policies established by PL 94-142 as summarized by Van Osdol and Shane (1977) are included here in order to give the reader an idea of the scope of this legislative mandate. ("Handicapped"

is defined in the law as "mentally retarded, hard of hearing, deaf, speech impaired, visually handicapped, seriously emotionally disturbed, orthopedically impaired, or other health impaired children, or children with specific learning disabilities.")

A free public education will be made available to all handicapped children between the ages of 3 and 18 by no later than September of 1978 and all those between 3 and 21 by September of 1980. *Coverage of children in the 3-to-5 and 18-to-21 ranges will not be required in states whose school attendance laws do not include those age brackets.* Nevertheless, it is now national policy to begin the education of handicapped children by at least age 3 and to encourage this practice. PL 94-142 authorizes incentive grants of $300 over the regular allocation for each handicapped child between the ages of 3 and 5 who is afforded special education and related services.

For each handicapped child there will be an "individualized educational program"—a written statement jointly developed by a qualified school official, by the child's teacher and parents or guardian, and if possible by the child himself. This written statement will include an analysis of the child's present achievement level, a listing of both short-range and annual goals, an identification of specific services that will be provided toward meeting those goals and an indication of the extent to which the child will be able to participate in regular school programs, a notation of when these services will be provided and how long they will last, and a schedule for checking on the progress being achieved under the plan and for making any revisions in it that may seem called for.

Handicapped and nonhandicapped children will be educated together to the maximum extent appropriate, and the former will be placed in special classes or separate schools "only when the nature or severity of the handicap is such that education in regular classes," even if they are provided supplementary aids and services, "cannot be achieved satisfactorily."

Tests and other evaluation material used in placing handicapped children will be prepared and administered in such a way as not to be racially or culturally discriminatory, and they will be presented in the child's native tongue.

There will be an intensive and continuing effort to locate and identify youngsters who have handicaps, to evaluate their educational needs, and to determine whether those needs are being met.

In the overall effort to make sure education is available to all handicapped children, priority will be given first to those who are not receiving an education at all and second to the most severely handicapped within each disability who are receiving an inadequate education.

In school placement procedures and in fact in any decisions concerning a handicapped child's schooling, there will be prior consultation with the child's parents or guardian, and in general, no policies, programs, or procedures affecting the education of handicapped children covered by the law will be adopted without a public notice.

The rights and guarantees called for in the law will apply to handicapped children in private as well as public schools, and *youngsters in private schools will be provided special education at no cost to their parents* if the children were placed in these schools or referred to them by state or local education agency officials.

The states and localities will undertake comprehensive personnel development programs, including in-service training for regular as well as special education teachers and support personnel, and procedures will be launched for acquiring and disseminating information about promising educational practices and materials coming out of research and development efforts.

In implementing the law, special effort will be made to employ qualified *handicapped persons.*

The principles set forth a few years ago in federal legislation aimed at the elimination of architectural barriers to the physically handicapped will be applied to school construction and modification, with the commissioner authorized to make grants for these purposes.

The state education agency will have jurisdiction over all education programs for handicapped children offered within a given state, including those administered by a noneducation agency (a state hospital, for example, or the welfare department).

An advisory panel will be appointed by each governor to advise the state's education agency of unmet needs, comment publicly on such matters as proposed rules and regulations, and help the state develop and report relevant data. Membership of these panels will include handicapped individuals and parents and guardians of handicapped children.*

---

*From Van Osdol, W. R., and Shane, D. G. *An introduction to exceptional children* (2nd ed.). Dubuque, Iowa: William C. Brown Co., Publishers, 1977. Pp. 41-43. Used by permission.

Of course, some handicapped youngsters are best served in schools specially geared to their particular needs (Jordan, Hayden, Karnes, and Wood, 1977). However, it is evident from reading the above material that the trend will be to include handicapped children in regular schools (including nursery schools) whenever this is possible. This is often termed "mainstreaming" and has the advantages of keeping the child with his normal peers, helping normal and exceptional children become accustomed to and feel comfortable with each other, emphasizing the typical aspects of the youngster's abilities and personality rather than focussing on the atypical aspects, and providing the child with the benefits of a good nursery school experience (Klein, 1975). Another advantage is that, since the trend is to place the great majority of handicapped children into regular classrooms in elementary school (Kirk, 1972; Shaffer, 1973), nursery school placement can gradually prepare the child for this experience. Placement in nursery school also aids the child's family by providing some relief for the mother from constant care of the youngster, perhaps by helping her see how similar his behavior is in many respects to that of all children, and by helping her feel a part of the educational community.

Head Start has taken the lead in mainstreaming preschoolers by mandating that 10% of the children it serves shall fall into the handicapped category (Jordan, 1973; Klein, 1975). The government has also supported a variety of programs for handicapped children (called First Chance Programs) that are intended to "serve as demonstration models for public schools and for other agencies who need information on how to provide a variety of kinds of special help to handicapped children and their families" (De Weerd, 1977, p. 3).

Determining which children should be admitted

Long before the government took action, many nursery schools made it a point to welcome exceptional children into their groups (Moor, 1960; Northcott, 1970), and their inclusion usually works out quite satisfactorily. The individualized curriculum characteristic of nursery schools in this country makes it relatively easy for children with special needs to participate in activities appropriate to their abilities, although the school may be weak in meeting the special educational requirements of exceptional children.

It must also be admitted, however, that occasional exceptional children will not be able to fit into the nursery school environment; thus the staff needs to handle potential placements carefully in order to maximize the possibility of success and provide emotional protection for the family, the child, and themselves in case the placement is not successful.

It is important to make it clear to the family that the staff has great goodwill but also has certain limitations and will not be able to work miracles. Very few nursery school teachers have much training in working with exceptional children. In addition, it is likely that during the year they will not be able to devote a large amount of extra time to studying this subject. On the other hand, they do know a great deal about working with children in general and will bring to this particular child the benefit of these insights and practical, matter-of-fact treatment that emphasizes the normal rather than the exceptional.

The staff will have to come to terms with how much extra effort the child will require them to expend every day. It is one thing to accept a mentally retarded child in a flush of helpfulness and sympathy, but it may turn out to be quite another when his pants have to be changed three or four times a morning. Some emotionally disturbed children may also require an inordinate amount of time and attention. The difficulty is that the staff has obligations to all the children, and the time required to work with an exceptional child may eventually deprive the other youngsters of their due share of energy and concern.

Fortunately, the examples given above are the exception rather than the rule, but the possibility of overtaxing the staff must be taken into consideration. However, experience has taught me that most exceptional children can and should be gathered in.

Usually the amount of special care is considerable during the first few weeks but gradually declines as the child and staff make the adjustment.

It will be necessary for the staff to examine their feelings about why they wish to accept the child. It is all too easy to succumb to a rescue fantasy and decide that what the handicapped youngster really needs is plenty of love and he will be all right. This is, of course, untrue. Children, whether exceptional or ordinary, require a great many other talents from their teachers besides the ability to express affection, and teachers should not delude themselves that affection can overcome all problems. If they intend to work with the child effectively, they must plan on learning the best ways to help him.

Recommended admission procedures

Once these potential hazards have been thought through and a positive decision to accept the youngster has been reached, then the staff and family should embark on a trial period that is as flexible and open minded as possible.

Many seemingly insurmountable problems can be solved during the trial period if the staff and family are creatively minded. For example, a child who cannot negotiate a flight of stairs and who is too heavy to be lifted can come to nursery school if his father builds a ramp over the stairs, or a child who requires a good deal of extra physical care may be able to attend if she is accompanied in the beginning by her mother or, if the parent needs relief, by a companion who tends to the extra chores until the child becomes more self-sufficient (Jones, 1977; Safford, 1978).

There are several ways to ease entry pangs. The regular practice of asking the mother to stay with the child until he has made friends should be followed when welcoming handicapped children into the group. Research has shown that this policy is of special importance for young retarded children (Kessler, Gridth, and Smith, 1968).

A chat with the child's physician may also reassure the teacher and provide any special guidelines that may be necessary for handling the youngster. Children with heart conditions, for instance, occasionally require special treatment, but sometimes arrive with firm instructions to let the child alone so he can pace himself.

Sometimes it also helps to begin with a short day and gradually extend the time the child attends as his skills and toleration of the group increase. The shorter day means that he can go home while he is still experiencing success and has not been overwhelmed with fatigue. It may be easiest if the child arrives in the middle of the morning and leaves when the other children do, since this means he does not have to depart when everyone else is still having a good time.

Many disabilities will pass unnoticed by the other children in the group, but some will require explanation. The explanations need not be elaborate. They should avoid the condescension of pity and should stress matter-of-fact suggestions about how to get along with the child who is being asked about (Cleary, 1974, 1976). It may be necessary, for example, to help the children understand that a particular child uses her ears and hands in place of her eyes, since she cannot see, to coach them to stand in front of a child who is hard of hearing and catch his attention before speaking to him, or to explain that another youngster has to stay outside the sandbox because the grit gets in his braces.

GENERAL RECOMMENDATIONS FOR WORKING WITH EXCEPTIONAL CHILDREN
See through the exceptional to the typical in every child

It can be easy to become so caught up in the differences of an exceptional child that the teacher loses sight of the fact that he is largely like the other children in her group and should be treated as much like them as possible. Feeling sorry for a child weakens his character and ultimately does him a terrible disservice. Many exceptional children have too many allowances made for them out of pity, misguided good intentions, and inexperience—and sometimes, where parents are concerned, as a consequence of guilt. The outcome is that the child may

become a demanding and rather unpleasant person to have around. In other words, he becomes just plain spoiled.

Consistency, reasonable expectations, and sound policies are, if anything, *more important* to employ when dealing with handicapped children than when dealing with ordinary children. The teacher should feel comfortable about drawing on her common sense and considerable experience, but she should also be able to turn freely to experts for consultation when she feels puzzled and uncertain about how to proceed.

Try to steer a middle course, neither overprotecting nor overexpecting

The most common pitfall in working with an exceptional child is becoming so concerned for his safety and well-being that the child is stifled and deprived of the opportunity to be as normal as he might be were he not overprotected. In general, the teacher should proceed on the assumption that the child should be encouraged to participate in every activity, with modifications provided only when necessary to ensure success. Thus a child who is behind his peers in intellectual development should be expected to participate in story hour but may enjoy it most if he sits with the youngest group.

On the other hand, some parents and teachers set their expectations unreasonably high and are unwilling to make any exceptions for the child with a handicap. This causes unnecessary strain and even despair for the child. Teachers can be helpful here by pointing out what is reasonable to expect of 3- or 4-year-old children in general and helping the parent understand what a reasonable expectation would be for her particular youngster. It is often helpful with such families to note each step as the child attains it and discuss what the next stage of development will be so that the parent can see progress coming bit by bit. This may reduce the feeling of desperate driving toward a difficult distant goal.

Be realistic. It is important to see the child as he is and to avoid false promises and unrealistic reassurances when talking with parents or the child himself. Everyone yearns for an exceptional child to "make it," and sometimes this yearning leads to unwitting self-deceptions, which can do the family and child a disservice by delaying acceptance of the disability or by encouraging them to make inadequate future plans. I once watched as a blind preschooler said to her teacher, "I can tell by feeling things with my hands what they are like; but when I grow up, then I will be able to see the colors, too, won't I?" The teacher replied, with tears in her eyes, "Yes, my darling, then everything will be all right."

Acceptance of the child's limitations as well as capitalization on his strengths is the balance to strive for and to model for the family. Some children will in time overcome a disability entirely, but others will not be able to do this. Helping the parents and the child accept this fact, as well as accepting it oneself, is difficult to do but valuable.

Keep regular records of the child's development. Since progress with all children, including exceptional ones, occurs a little at a time, it is easy to feel discouraged from time to time and lose sight of how far the youngster has come. If the teacher keeps regular written records, however brief, a review of them will encourage her.

It is particularly important to keep records on an exceptional youngster so that they may be summarized and added to his medical record or given to his next teacher to acquaint her with his interests and progress. The records should cover whatever incidents seem particularly important to the child, indications of growth or slipping backward, special interests and tastes, and significant information contributed by the parents and physician.

Occasionally, the teacher may be asked to participate in an in-depth study of an emotionally disturbed youngster, and so she will want to make more detailed written observations to be used in discussion and consultation. Although time-consuming, this kind of study can be helpful and revealing. The reader can refer to references at the end of the chapter for models and suggestions about how to carry out such observations successfully.

GUIDELINES FOR WORKING WITH PHYSICALLY HANDICAPPED CHILDREN

Since physical disabilities range from blindness to cerebral palsy, it is, of course, impossible to discuss each condition in detail here. The references at the end of the chapter provide further information on particular problems.

In general, the suggestions already listed apply to these children. A physically handicapped youngster should be treated as typically as possible, and he should be neither overprotected nor underprotected. A conference with his physician or physical therapist can help the staff ascertain the degree of protection that is necessary.

The teacher who bears these guidelines in mind and who approaches each situation pragmatically will find it relatively simple to deal with children who have physical handicaps. Also, parents are often gold mines of practical advice about how to help the child effectively, and their information, combined with the fresh point of view provided by the nursery school staff, can usually solve problems if they arise.

Sickle cell anemia. * Sickle cell anemia is a serious inherited condition that occurs mainly among black people (Mordock, 1975). Because it confers immunity for certain types of malaria, possession of this condition has been a biological advantage for some African peoples, but in the United States where malaria is not prevalent, the advantages are far outweighed by the disadvantages.

This serious disorder is not infectious and cannot be "caught." It is incurable at present and causes much misery, but it can be treated. As in other anemias, the child may lack energy and tire easily. When people have this condition, their red blood cells become sickle-shaped rather than round (hence the name), and painful episodes occur when these red cells stiffen because of lack of oxygen and stack up in small blood vessels. The plugging up of

---

*This condition is specifically included for discussion because I have had so many teachers ask about it, and it is still difficult to locate information on it for teachers to use.

capillaries then deprives surrounding cellular tissues of oxygen. This is termed a vasoocclusive crisis, and it may occur in various parts of the body. Depending on where it happens, the individual may have severe abdominal pain or an enlarged spleen, or the brain, liver, kidneys, or lungs may be affected. Children under age 3 are particularly likely to experience swollen hands and feet. Young children suffering from this condition are often characterized by a barrel-shaped chest, enlarged, protruding abdomen, and thin arms and legs (Lin-Fu, 1972). Sometimes, for unknown reasons, production of red blood cells stops altogether (aplastic crisis). Symptoms of this include increased lethargy, rapid heart rate, weakness, fainting, and paleness of the lining of the eyelids (Leavitt, 1975). *(If this occurs at school, the family and the doctor should be notified immediately.)* Children who have been diagnosed as suffering from sickle cell anemia must be under regular care by their physician. The teacher can help by encouraging families to keep medical appointments and by carefully carrying out the doctor's recommendations at school. These may include prohibiting vigorous exercise, since lowered oxygen levels increase the likelihood of a vasoocclusive attack. Careful, early attention should also be paid to cold symptoms because these youngsters are very vulnerable to pneumonia and influenza (Desforges, 1978).

Because the condition is inherited, parents sometimes ask advice on whether they should have more children. This question is a ticklish one to answer and is best referred to their physician for discussion.

GUIDELINES FOR WORKING WITH EMOTIONALLY DISTURBED CHILDREN

Even though the teacher may not have a chronically disturbed youngster in her nursery school, it is certain she will have to deal with children who are at least temporarily upset from time to time. These upsets may be as minor as occasional emotional outbursts or as major as a child who weeps frantically when he comes to school, refuses to eat anything, and is unable to lose himself in play.

Adults often discount the effect of important family crises on young children, either assuming that the children do not understand or that they simply aren't aware of what is going on; but this is far from the real truth. Children are very sensitive to the emotional climate of the home; and although they may draw incorrect conclusions about the reasons for the unhappiness, they are almost always aware that something is going on and are likely to respond with a variety of coping mechanisms.

There are many causes of such disturbances, including hospitalization of the child or of a family member, desertion by one of the parents, a death in the family, divorce, the birth of a sibling, moving from one home to another, a mother going to work, a father losing his job, chronic alcoholism, or involvement with drugs (Varma, 1973). Even something as relatively innocuous as a long visit from a grandparent can be upsetting to the child if it becomes an occasion for disturbances in routine or for dissension.*

The teacher should watch for any pronounced change in the child's behavior, as well as for signs of withdrawal, inability to give or receive affection, reduced ability to play either by himself or with other children, reduced interest in conversation, aggressive acting out, marked preoccupations with a particular activity or topic, and extreme emotional responses, such as bursting into tears or temper tantrums. She should also notice the usual signs of tension commonly seen in young children who are upset: whining, bed-wetting, increased fretfulness and irritability, hair twisting, thumb sucking, stuttering, an increased dependence on security symbols such as blankets or toy animals, and so forth.

The teacher should realize that these behaviors are not reprehensible and that it is not desirable for her to concentrate her energy on removing them from the child's repertoire. They *are* signs that the child is suffering from some kind of stress either at home or nursery school and that this should be looked into and mitigated.

---

*For a more detailed discussion of handling specific crisis situations, the reader is referred to Chapter 18, "Tender Topics: Helping Children Master Emotional Crises."

Short-term techniques

First, a note of caution is in order. When a child who has been getting along well at nursery school suddenly falls apart, it is always best to consider whether the upset could be due to physical illness. Many an inexperienced teacher has spent a sleepless night over such a child only to have his mother call and report an illness the next morning.

Make a special point of offering tension-relieving activities to the youngster who is upset. The best of these is water play in a relaxed atmosphere where the child can have his clothing well protected or can change afterwards into something dry. Mud, dough, and soft clay can also be helpful, as are the sublimated activities listed in the chapter on aggression (Chapter 7).

Relax standards somewhat in order to take stress off the child. This does not mean that anything goes; it does mean that the teacher should ease the child's way through the day with only the more important demands enforced. In other words, she should take the pressure off where she can without creating additional insecurity by letting the child get away with murder.

Talk things over with the family and work with them to identify what may be generating the upset in the child. Discussing a child's emotional problems requires a delicate touch to avoid the impression that the teacher is prying into personal matters that are none of her business, but the insight gained from such discussions can provide valuable information that can enable the teacher to draw the child out and express in play or words what is troubling him. Increased understanding of the cause will help the teacher be more tolerant of the child's behavior. She may also be able to offer some helpful counseling resources for the family to explore or may sometimes offer help herself by listening and assisting the parents in clarifying alternative ways to solve the difficulty.

Help the child work through his feelings by furnishing opportunities to use dolls, puppets, and dramatic play to express his concern. For example, a child who has been through a term of hospitaliza-tion may delight in using a doctor's kit and administering shots to dolls or other children with spirited malevolence. When such play is combined with the teacher's perceptive comments that recognize how frightened and angry the child is, this activity can do a world of good.

Long-term techniques

There are a few fortunate communities that offer special nursery school experiences for children categorized as chronically disturbed. However, because such opportunities are still quite rare and because many disturbed children profit from inclusion in regular nursery school, it is desirable for nursery school teachers to offer this special service whenever they feel they can manage it. Apart from treating psychotic children, who usually require a specialized environment that allows more one-to-one contact combined with special expertise, there is nothing particularly mysterious about providing care for emotionally disturbed youngsters. What it really takes to make such a placement turn out successfully is common sense, patience, determination, faith in oneself, and faith that the child and his family will be able to change.

Treat the chronically disturbed child as much like the other children as possible, and utilize his strengths to bring him into the life of the group. In my school one youngster who was unable to talk with either children or adults loved using the large push broom and spent many hours sweeping sand off the tricycle track. The first words he ever used at school grew out of this participation when, after weeks of sweeping, he yelled at one of the children who had bumped into his broom, "You just stay outta my way or I'll pop you one!" Once the sound barrier was broken, this youngster became increasingly verbal and was able to move on to kindergarten with reasonable success.

Anticipate that progress will be uneven. Chronically disturbed children may move ahead in an encouraging way and then suddenly backslide. This should not be cause for despair. If he progressed once, he will do it again, and probably faster the second time. It is, of course, desirable to identify and ameliorate the reason for the regression if this can be discerned.

Draw on the advice of specialists and encourage the family to continue to do this. A disturbed child often comes to school because he has been referred by a specialist. A regular arrangement for calling and reporting progress to the expert, invitations to him or her to come and visit the school, and perhaps some written reports during the year should be part of the teacher's professional obligation when she agrees to enroll a chronically disturbed youngster. Needless to say, the specialists who make such referrals should be willing to discharge their responsibilities by guiding the teacher when she requires their help.

GUIDELINES FOR WORKING WITH MENTALLY RETARDED CHILDREN

Mental retardation is defined as "subaverage intellectual functioning which originates during the developmental period and is associated with impairment of adaptive behavior" (Heber, 1961). The severity of the condition varies widely: mildly or moderately retarded children are the best prospects for inclusion in nursery school. The mildly retarded child will probably fit so easily into a nursery school curriculum serving a heterogeneous age group that no special recommendations are necessary other than reminding the teacher to see the child in terms of his actual developmental level rather than his chronological age.

The moderately retarded child will also often fit comfortably into the heterogeneous nursery school, but many teachers find it helpful to have a clear understanding of the most worthwhile educational goals for these children and also to understand some simple principles for teaching them most effectively.

Basic learning goals for a moderately retarded preschool youngster should center on (1) helping him to be as independent as possible, which includes learning simple self-help skills as well as learning to help other people by doing simple tasks, (2) helping the child develop language skills, and (3) helping him learn to get along with other children in an acceptable way.

These goals are really no different from ones that are part of the regular nursery school curriculum. The only differences are that the retarded child will be farther behind other children of his age and that he will need a simpler manner of instruction. Children who learn slowly should not be confused with a lot of talk and shadings of meaning. *They need concrete examples, definite rules, and consistent reinforcement of desired behavior.* In general, the bywords with these children are: keep it concrete, keep it simple, keep it fun—and be patient.

Some specific suggestions may also help the teacher:

1. As much as possible, treat the child as you would treat all children in the group, but exercise common sense so that you expect neither too much nor too little.

2. Know the developmental steps so that you understand what he should learn next as he progresses.

3. Remember that retarded children learn best what they repeat frequently. Be prepared to go over a simple rule or task many times until the child has it firmly in mind. (This need for patient repetition is one of the things inexperienced teachers may find most irritating, particularly when the child has appeared to grasp the idea just the day before. Don't give up hope: if the teaching is simple and concrete enough, he will eventually learn.)

4. Pick out behavior to teach that the child can use all his life; that is, try to teach ways of behaving that will be appropriate for an older as well as a younger child to use. For example, don't let him run and kiss everyone he meets, since this will not be acceptable when he is just a little older. He has enough to do without having to unlearn old behavior.

5. Allow sufficient time for him to accomplish a selected task. Complex things take longer; simpler things takes less time.

6. Encourage the child to be persistent by keep-

ing tasks simple and satisfying. This will encourage him to finish what he starts.

7. Remember that independence is an important goal. Make sure the child is not being overprotected.

8. Teach one thing at a time. For instance, teach him to feed himself, then to use a napkin, then to pour his milk.

9. Don't rely on talking as the primary means of instruction. Show the child what you mean whenever possible.

10. Encourage the development of speech. Wait for at least some form of verbal reply whenever possible. Gently increase the demand for a ''quality'' response as his skills increase.

11. Remember that retarded children are just as sensitive to the emotional climate around them as ordinary children are. Therefore, never talk about a child in front of him. It is likely that he will at least pick up the feeling of what you are saying, and this may hurt his feelings badly.

12. Show the child you are pleased with him and that you like him.

13. After a fair trial at learning something new, if he cannot seem to learn it, drop the activity without recrimination. Try it again in a few months; he may be ready to learn it by then.

There is much to be said for the value of step-by-step, prescriptive teaching for retarded children in particular. This requires careful identification of the present level of the child's skills as well as knowledge of the appropriate next step. There are several programs available that outline these steps in detail (Johnson and Werner, 1975; Meyer Children's Rehabilitation Institute, 1974; Portage Project, 1976), and teachers who have developmentally delayed children in their group should refer to these materials frequently as well as obtain suggestions from the other specialists working with the youngster. This step-by-step approach is most successful if it is combined with the use of behavior modification techniques. The deliberate, systematic application of these principles, wherein behavior is either rewarded or not rewarded in a very definite way, is of proven value with retarded children.

TEACHING MENTALLY GIFTED PRESCHOOL CHILDREN

Although there have been many interesting investigations of intellectual giftedness, ranging from Terman (Terman, Baldwin, and Bronson, 1925) to Marland (1972), these have focussed on older children and adults, and the possibility of educating intellectually gifted preschool children has been largely ignored (Safford, 1978). Yet it is obvious that children of exceptional mental ability must be present in this portion of the population since they exist at an older age! (In 1973, Martinson estimated that 3% of the older school population is intellectually gifted.) However, when I raise the question of making special provision for such youngsters at the nursery school level, my students and teaching colleagues appear bewildered at this possibility.*

Perhaps this is because we have fought a battle against undue intellectual pressure in the nursery school for so long that we forget that gifted children thrive when provided with additional stimulation and that we may be cheating them when we deprive them of it. Of course, gifted children should not be treated as precocious little adults or worshipped because of their special talent, but they should be provided with stimulating things to learn, while at the same time keeping their social and emotional life as natural and easy as possible.

The provision of an enriched curriculum does not necessarily mean that the teacher must teach the child to read, although many gifted children already know how to read before they enter kindergarten (Martinson, 1961). I will never forget my surprise when one of the bright lights in my school wandered

---

*Giftedness, of course, is expressed in many different forms (Safford, 1978), such as in the self-expressive giftedness of creative artists or the physical giftedness of talented athletes. Because ways of fostering such aspects of the child's abilities have been covered in previous chapters, this discussion will be limited to the giftedness of the intellectually superior preschooler.

into my office, picked up a plain bound book from my desk and commented, ''Hmmmmm, this looks interesting—*All about Dinosaurs*. Can I borrow this?'' (I let him.)

What the teacher *can* do is to make sure such children have plenty of opportunities to pursue subjects that interest them in as much depth as they desire. It is important to avoid the trap of thinking to oneself, ''Oh, well, *they* wouldn't be able to do *that!*'' It is astonishing what gifted children can do if they are provided with encouragement and materials. For example, I once had two young students, a boy and a girl, who were interested in the weather. They went from this to an interest in temperature and how heat makes thermometers work. Of course, all the children were interested in this subject to an extent, but these two youngsters, who later proved to be gifted, were truly absorbed. Their investigations included breaking open a thermometer to discover what it was made of, collecting different kinds of thermometers to see if they all worked the same way and if they all measured the same kinds of things, and even working out a number scale with drawings to show the range of temperatures measured by different instruments.

Intellectually gifted preschool children often love discussion that focusses on ''What would happen if . . .'' or ''How could we . . .'' These questions require creative reasoning as well as transforming old information into new solutions. These children will also relish the more difficult activities suggested in the chapter on mental development, since these activities can be adjusted to their level of ability and thus sustain their interest. Perhaps a few examples of some specific ways of enriching curriculum for gifted preschool youngsters will best illustrate how to accomplish this.*

Investigate how things work, either finding out by close observation or by taking them apart and reassembling them. A music box, a vacuum cleaner and all its parts, a Christmas tree stand, a flashlight, an old bicycle, and so forth can be offered.

Build additional language skills. Make a time to read books to the child that are longer and have more detail in them than picture books do. After story time, have a special discussion with him. Encourage him to expound on the stories that were just read—were they true? Has he ever had a similar or opposite experience? What did he like or dislike about the story? What would he have done differently if it had been him? Encourage the child to do most of the talking—and try to introduce new vocabulary. Select several pictures from the picture file, and ask the child to link them together by telling you a story about them—or allow him to select the pictures.

Offer more complex materials or advanced information. A good example of this is the use of more difficult puzzles. Cube puzzles can be used to reproduce particular patterns, or jigsaw puzzles can be offered rather than only the framed wooden ones typical of nursery school. On a library trip take the child to the older children's section and help him find books on a particular subject he cares about.

Offer enriched curriculum in the area of science. Be prepared to allow for expanded scientific activities. For example, provide vinegar for testing for limestone in various materials such as tiles, building materials, and so forth. Or explore the concept of time. The child could learn to identify specific hours on the clock and take responsibility for telling the teacher when it is snack time. Talk about ways of keeping track of time—perhaps help him make a simple sundial with a stick, letting the child mark the spot where the shadow falls when it's group time or time to go home. See if that spot stays at the same place over several weeks. Encourage the child to seek out people who speak different languages to tell him the names of different times of day in their own tongue. Visit a clock

---

*My thanks to Nursery School majors from the classes of 1976, 1977, and 1978 at Santa Barbara City College for these suggestions.

shop and write down for him all the kinds of clocks he sees there.

Note that language activities are particularly dear to mentally gifted preschoolers. They enjoy more advanced stories than average children do and also can put their superior ability to work by concocting tales of their own that are almost invariably complex, detailed, and advanced in vocabulary. An interesting example of this is the book, *Barbara* (McCurdy, 1966), which begins with the writings of an intensely gifted 4-year-old and continues through her young adulthood. Discussion and conversation should be employed at every opportunity to allow these children to put their ideas into words and to test them out against the ideas of other people.

Above all, the use of instructional methods that foster problem solving and encourage development of creative ideas should be employed. How can everyday items be put to new uses? How can old problems be solved in new ways? Here, once again, the value of asking pertinent questions and providing rich opportunities for children to propose answers and test them out, to see if they are correct, must be emphasized. I suggest the reader refer to Chapter 14, ''Fostering Creativity in Thought,'' for suggestions on how to go about doing this.

CONCLUSION

The teacher who works with an exceptional preschool child must seek all the information she can on his particular condition if she really wants to be an effective teacher. This chapter can do no more than scratch the surface.

There are increasing numbers of courses in exceptionality being offered by schools of education, as in-service training, and by university extension units as the general trend toward including exceptional children in regular public school classes gains ground. In addition to these courses, books are also available, and many are listed in the references at the end of this chapter. Unfortunately, the education of very young exceptional children is still only sparsely covered in the literature, but the Head Start

mandate combined with PL 94-142 is gradually changing this situation for the better.

SUMMARY

The nursery school teacher has two primary responsibilities to exceptional children. First, she must serve as a screening agent and help identify possible problems, whether they are physical, emotional, or mental, that have escaped the attention of the physician. Following identification of a difficulty, the teacher should attempt to effect a referral to the appropriate specialist.

Second, she must do all she can to integrate children with special problems into her nursery school group. This requires careful assessment before admission and flexibility of adjustment following entrance to school. It is vital that she treat the exceptional child as typically as possible and encourage his independence without demanding skills that lie beyond his ability. Specific suggestions for working with physically handicapped, emotionally disturbed, mentally retarded, and intellectually gifted preschool children conclude the chapter.

QUESTIONS AND ACTIVITIES

1. *Problem:* After viewing the film *One of Them Is Brett,* which describes children who were malformed as a result of thalidomide poisoning of the mother during pregnancy, discuss how you could integrate a youngster without arms into your nursery school. Be sure to consider not only practical ways he could participate in activities, but also how you will explain the nature of his handicap to other children and parents. What would be the most constructive attitude to take in relation to this youngster?
2. Many people are confused about the difference between children who are termed mentally ill and those termed mentally retarded. Explain the similarities and differences between these conditions.
3. Do you feel that it is generally wise to suggest medication as a means of controlling hyperactivity in children? Why or why not?
4. This chapter makes a strong case for the early identification of potentially handicapping disorders. What are the real disadvantages of labeling children as being different? What are some ways to obtain help for such youngsters without stigmatizing them at the same time?
5. What do you feel accounts for the fact that very intelligent children are often overlooked at the preschool level? Might the provision of a special curriculum for them result in precocity and overintellectualization, thereby spoiling their childhood?

6. *Problem:* Your staff has carefully interviewed and evaluated a severely handicapped youngster whose family has requested admission to school and has reluctantly decided that he cannot be accepted. How could this decision be relayed most effectively and humanely to the family?

7. *Problem:* You have a 4½-year-old girl attending your school who is mentally retarded and functions at about the 2½-year-old level. She hangs around the housekeeping corner and the blocks a lot, but the children push her aside. One of them, in particular, makes a point of saying, ''She can't play here. Her nose is snotty, and she talks dumb!'' (There is more than a modicum of truth in this.) What to do?

8. *Problem:* You have a 4-year-old boy in your group who has a heart condition. In addition to looking somewhat lavender around the gills, he is not supposed to exert himself by climbing or other vigorous exercise, which, of course, he yearns to do. He is well liked by the other children, who invite him frequently to climb around and play with them. What to do?

REFERENCES FOR FURTHER READING

Overviews

Bowlby, A. H., and Gardner, L. *The young handicapped child: Educational guidance for the young cerebral palsied, deaf, blind and autistic child* (2nd ed.). Edinburgh: E. & S. Livingstone, 1969. This small book is filled with practical advice about living with and educating exceptional children; very helpful.

Cohen, S., Semmes, M., and Guralnick, M. J. Public Law 94-142 and the education of preschool handicapped children. *Exceptional Children,* 1979, *45*(4), 279-284. For an excellent assessment of how PL 94-142 is being applied in relation to young children, the reader is referred to this article; it is important to keep up to date on what is happening in your own state concerning this matter.

Dunn, L. M. (Ed.). *Exceptional children in the schools: Special education in transition* (2nd ed.). New York: Holt, Rinehart and Winston, Inc., 1973. This excellent collection is written by specialists in the fields of various kinds of exceptionality, ranging from mental retardation to physical disabilities.

Jordan, J. B., and Darley, R. F. *Not all little red wagons are red: The exceptional child's early years.* Reston: Va.: Council for Exceptional Children, 1973. In this indispensable reference from the Invisible College Conference on Early Childhood Education and the Exceptional Child, Jordan and Darley emphasize the importance of beginning education early, discuss training of parents and teachers, and include a valuable list of resources for day care and for working with young handicapped children.

Kirk, S. A. *Educating exceptional children* (2nd ed.). Boston: Houghton Mifflin Co., 1972. Kirk, a well-known authority in the field, discusses many kinds of exceptionality as well as general practices that are used to educate exceptional youngsters.

Kliman, G. *Psychological emergencies of childhood.* New York: Grune & Stratton, Inc., 1968. Based on studies of emotionally healthy children's reactions to crisis situations, the book recommends directness and honesty when dealing with life's catastrophes. It has a particularly extensive section on illness and death.

Physical Education and Recreation for the Handicapped: Information and Research Utilization Center. *Early intervention for handicapped children through programs of physical education and recreation.* Washington, D.C.: American Alliance for Health, Physical Education, and Recreation (1201 16th St., N.W., Washington, D.C., 20036), 1976. Don't be ''put off'' by the title. This inexpensive reference is a treasure trove of annotated bibliographies *all dealing with the preschool handicapped child* plus lots of other information that is presented succinctly.

Project Head Start. *Head Start, Mainstreaming Preschoolers Series.* Washington, D.C.: U.S. Dept. of Health, Education, and Welfare, OHD, OCD, 1978. The titles in this series include *Mainstreaming preschoolers: Children with emotional disturbances* (OHDS 78-31115), *Mainstreaming preschoolers: Children with health impairments* (OHDS 78-31111), *Mainstreaming preschoolers: Children with orthopedic handicaps* (OHDS 78-31114), *Mainstreaming preschoolers: Children with visual handicaps* (OHDS 78-31112), *Mainstreaming preschoolers: Children with hearing impairments* (OHDS 78-31116), *Mainstreaming preschoolers: Children with mental retardation* (OHDS 78-31110), *Mainstreaming preschoolers: Children with speech and language impairments* (OHDS 78-31113), and *Mainstreaming preschoolers: Children with learning disabilities* (OHDS-31117). These are all outstanding, very practically oriented resources developed primarily for Head Start groups but useful in any preschool classroom that includes youngsters with special needs. They may be ordered from the U.S. Government Printing Office at nominal cost.

Safford, P. L. *Teaching young children with special needs.* St. Louis: The C. V. Mosby Co., 1978. To the best of my knowledge, this is the only comprehensive textbook that focusses on the young handicapped child, and so it fills a very special need. It is useful, up to date, and highly recommended.

Spock, B., and Lerrigo, M. O. *Caring for your disabled child.* New York: Macmillan Publishing Co., Inc., 1965. This is a good book for parents and teachers to read, because it is filled with practical, frank information about child care and also anticipates problems the disabled child may encounter as he reaches adulthood; highly recommended.

Identification of Disorders

Furman, R. A., and Katan, A. K. *The therapeutic nursery school.* New York: International Universities Press, 1969. An account of a nursery school that was established primarily to study and relieve emotional problems in young children, this book is of particular interest to students concerned with the applications of psychoanalytic theory to early childhood education.

Granato, S., and Krone, E. 8—*Serving children with special needs.* Washington, D.C.: U.S. Dept. of Health, Education, and Welfare, OCD, 1972. In this practical, information-filled pamphlet, Granato and Krone discuss admission policies and working with parents, and give useful suggestions for working with several kinds of exceptional children. The pamphlet has an outstanding list of community resources, associations dealing with special problems, and addresses of special educational programs and funding sources. It also has a good annotated bibliography.

Hayden, A. H., and Edgar, E. B. Identification, screening and assessment. In J. B. Jordon, A. H. Hayden, M. B. Karnes, and M. M. Wood, (Eds.), *Early childhood education for exceptional children*. Reston, Va.: The Council for Exceptional Children, 1977. This chapter identifies various screening devices and includes a sample form appropriate for preschool use that could be used for identifying children with handicaps severe enough to require special services.

Jordon, J. B., Hayden, A. H., Karnes, M. B., and Wood, M. M. (Eds.). *Early childhood education for exceptional children*. Reston, Va.: The Council for Exceptional Children, 1977. The title of this book may mislead teachers who are searching for information on teaching children with particular disabilities, because the focus is broader than that. The book discusses such problems as screening, evaluation, and parent participation and concentrates on descriptions of the First Chance programs. An exceptionally good chapter on facilities is included.

Lindsay, A. *Art and the handicapped child*. New York: Van Nostrand Reinhold Co., 1972. Lindsay suggests many kinds of creative materials that can be used successfully with children who have special needs. Many of these could be refreshing variations to use with ordinary preschoolers also.

Michal-Smith, H. *The exceptional child in the normal nursery*. New York: Early Childhood Education Council of New York, 1966. This is the best general article on the pros and cons of admitting exceptional children to nursery school that has been written; it is forthright, clear, and sensible.

Murphy, L. B., and Leeper, E. M. *The vulnerable child*. Washington, D.C.: U.S. Dept. of Health, Education, and Welfare, OCD, 1970. Murphy and Leeper identify several kinds of vulnerabilities in general terms and discuss how to handle stress effectively. Simply written, this is a useful introduction to the subject.

Schattner, R. *An early childhood curriculum for multiply handicapped children*. New York: Intext Press, 1971. This is a rare book because it discusses the education of preschool-aged multiply handicapped children—a subject just beginning to receive the attention it deserves.

Walker, J. E., and Shea, T. M. *Behavior modification: A practical approach for educators*. St. Louis: The C. V. Mosby Co., 1976. Behavior modification is particularly useful with disturbed and retarded children, and Walker and Shea provide a clear-cut description of how to apply its principles.

Working with Parents of Handicapped Children

Bloch, J. Impaired children: Helping families through the critical period of first identification. *Children Today*, 1978, 7(6), 3-6. This article is a sensitive description of how a school that was established for the purposes of offering diagnostic as well as educational services to young children having exceptional problems begins to develop a therapeutic alliance with parents right from the start. This is valuable for all teachers to read because of the descriptions of parents' feelings as they face their child's difficulties.

Morrison, G. *Parent involvement in the home, school and community*. Columbus, Ohio: Charles E. Merrill Publishing Co., 1978. Chapter 7, "Parent Involvement with Handicapped Children," discusses PL 94-142 and its implications for parent involvement and also offers special suggestions for achieving close cooperation between these parents and the school.

Southwest Educational Development Laboratory. *Working with parents of handicapped children*. Reston, Va.: The Council for Exceptional Children, 1976. Although it focusses on counselling parents of handicapped children, this publication contains sound advice for working with all parents.

Overviews of Mental and Emotional Disorders

Bakwin, H., and Bakwin, R. M. *Behavior disorders in children* (5th ed.). Philadelphia: W. B. Saunders Co., 1974.

Kessler, J. W. *Psychopathology of childhood*. Englewood Cliffs, N.J.: Prentice-Hall, Inc., 1966.

Shaw, C. R., and Lucas, A. R. *The psychiatric disorders of childhood* (2nd ed.). New York: Appleton-Century-Crofts, 1970. The Bakwins', Kessler's, and Shaw's books all offer competent discussions of a great many kinds of exceptionality and overviews of treatment procedures.

Mental Retardation

Adams, M. *Mental retardation and its social dimensions*. New York: Columbia University Press, 1971. *Mental Retardation* focusses on the problems of families with retarded children. The teacher who anticipates counseling such families will find the chapters on casework and on the dependent client and his family enlightening.

Conner, F. P., and Talbot, M. E. *An experimental curriculum for young mentally retarded children*. New York: Teachers College Press, Columbia University, 1970. In their extraordinarily helpful book, Conner and Talbot list five levels of difficulty for each curriculum item, describe behavior that would reflect each level, and outline teaching procedures that can be used to develop the skill in question. The book also contains a narrative description of the 5-year project for preschool educable mentally retarded children as it was developed by Teachers College of Columbia University and the U.S. Office of Education. This book should be in the library of every teacher who is interested in the development of a sequential curriculum, whether or not she is working with retarded children.

Hunter, M., Schucman, H., and Friedlander, G. *The retarded child from birth to five: A multidisciplinary program for child and family*. New York: The John Day Co., Inc., 1972. This excellent overview of the kinds of services that should be available to assist the retarded child has a helpful emphasis on working with the entire family. It also contains recommendations and suggestions for working with children who have developmental lags.

Kirk, S. A., Karnes, M. B., and Kirk, W. D. *You and your retarded child: A manual for parents of retarded children* (2nd ed.). Palo Alto, Calif.: Pacific Books, Publishers, 1968. Simply written and full of useful information, this manual is particularly good because of the developmental standards that are provided in one of the chapters. It also has an unusual chapter on teaching the retarded child through play.

Meyer Children's Rehabilitation Institute. *Meyer Children's Rehabilitation Institute teaching program for young children: Handicapped children in Head Start series*. Reston, Va.: The Council for Exceptional Children, 1974. The Meyer Teaching Program provides developmental evaluation sheets for many areas of the child's self (physical, social, receptive and expressive language, and so forth) and then lists sequences of skills and suggests playful activities for teaching them.

Pseudoretardation

Granger, R. C., and Young, J. C. (Eds.). *Demythologizing the inner city child.* Washington, D. C.: National Association for the Education of Young Children, 1976. This book makes a good case for seeing children from different backgrounds as being diverse but not necessarily inferior.

Hellmuth, J. (Ed.). *Disadvantaged child: Head Start and early intervention* (Vol. 2). New York: Brunner/Mazel, Inc., 1968.

Hellmuth, J. (Ed.). *Disadvantaged child: Compensatory education, a national debate* (Vol. 3). New York: Brunner/Mazel, Inc., 1970. Volumes 2 and 3 are good places to begin a study of the disadvantaged child, because the articles cover many aspects of this problem.

The Gifted Learner

Barbe, W. B., and Renzulli, J. S. *Psychology and education of the gifted* (2nd ed.). New York: John Wiley & Sons, Inc., 1975. This standard text provides an excellent overall discussion on the subject of giftedness but does not have much to say about that trait in very young children.

DeNevi, D. The education of a genius: Analyzing major influences on the life of America's greatest architect. *Young Children,* 1968, *23*(4), 233-239. DeNevi gives a fascinating account of the influence of Froebelian early education on the development of Frank Lloyd Wright, relating his interest in architecture to early experiences with block play. Diagrams are included.

Grost, A. *Genius in residence.* Englewood Cliffs, N.J.: Prentice-Hall, Inc., 1970. This is a good book for the reader who is looking for a chatty, informal account of what it can be like to bring up an extremely intelligent child. Mrs. Grost describes her trials with the school system and how her family managed to accommodate to her son's needs and yet keep him as natural and unaffected as possible.

Martinson, R. Children with superior cognitive abilities. In L. M. Dunn (Ed.), *Exceptional children in the schools: Special education in transition.* New York: Holt, Rinehart and Winston, Inc., 1973. Martinson provides a competent, up-to-date review of issues and research in the field of giftedness.

Teaching Emotionally Disturbed Preschoolers

Braun, S. J., and Lasher, M. G. *Are you ready to mainstream? Helping preschoolers with learning and behavior problems.* Columbus, Ohio: Charles E. Merrill Publishing Co., 1978. This rare, excellent book actually focusses on disturbed children of the age nursery school teachers need to know about and discusses behavior problems we need help with. It provides comprehensive, practical advice on how to work with such youngsters; the best in the field.

Cohen, S. How to alleviate the first-year shock of teaching emotionally disturbed children. In M. S. Auleta (Ed.), *Foundations of early childhood education: Readings.* New York: Random House, Inc., 1969. Cohen presents an understanding discussion of what teachers of disturbed children need to realize to help them survive their first difficult months with disturbed children.

Kanner, L. Early infantile autism. *Journal of Pediatrics,* 1944,

25, 211-217. In this unassuming, classic paper, Kanner identifies the psychosis called early childhood autism.

Menninger Clinic Children's Division. *Disturbed children.* San Francisco: Jossey-Bass, Inc., Publishers, 1968. This book describes the process of outpatient diagnosis of disturbed children and shows how the abilities of different specialists can work together to provide a comprehensive diagnosis; interesting reading.

Shaffer, H. B. *Emotionally disturbed children.* Washington, D.C.: Educational Research Reports, 1973. Shaffer outlines the history of litigation concerned with the rights of emotionally disturbed children to education and briefly discusses other problems, including diagnosis and cost of care.

Wing, J. K. (Ed.). *Early childhood autism: Clinical, educational and social aspects* (2nd ed.). Maxwell House, Fairview Park, Elmsford, N.Y.: Pergamon Press, Inc., 1976. This is a balanced, sensible book about a puzzling condition.

Information about Specific Physical Disabilities

Bleck, E. E., and Nagel, D. A. *Physically handicapped children—a medical atlas for teachers.* New York: Grune & Stratton, Inc., 1975. This is an indispensable reference containing simple, clear descriptions and diagrams of physical disabilities, ranging from heart defects to muscular dystrophy and sickle cell anemia. Most chapters include what the teacher should do in the classroom to help children afflicted with these conditions.

Buchanan, R., and Mullins, J. B. Integration of a spina bifida child in a kindergarten for normal children. *Young Children,* 1968, *23*(6), 339-344. Buchanan and Mullins give an account of the successful inclusion of a severely handicapped youngster into a normal kindergarten.

Fraiberg, S. with the collaboration of L. Frailberg. *Insights from the blind.* New York: Basic Books, Inc., Publishers, 1977. Written from the point of view of a developmental psychologist, this fascinating book about young blind children discusses a long-term study of how they develop and what can be done to help them.

Gearheart, B. R. *Learning disabilities: Educational strategies* (2nd ed.). St. Louis: The C. V. Mosby Co., 1977. Although a learning disability does not commonly become evident until the child is in kindergarten or the later grades, knowledge of this subject is increasing, and it may be that earlier identification at the preschool level will result in increased effectiveness of treatment. Therefore, it is a subject early childhood teachers need to know more about, and this book reviews many approaches to educating the child with this problem.

Goodman, W. When you meet a blind person. In S. A. Kirk and F. E. Lord (Eds.), *Exceptional children: Educational resources and perspectives.* Boston: Houghton Mifflin Co., 1974. Goodman gives valuable advice about what to do and not to do when accompanying a blind person and stresses ways to encourage independence.

Halliday, C. *The visually impaired child: Growth, learning and development: Infancy to school age.* Louisville, Ky.: American Printing House for the Blind, 1971. Halliday gives an interesting factual description of general developmental patterns combined with comments and suggestions about how to help the blind child achieve these developmental steps.

Lowenfield, B. *The visually handicapped child in school.* New

York: The John Day Co., Inc., 1973. This wide-ranging book is filled with practical information about the management of blind children as they grow and develop. The history of the education of the blind and teacher preparation are also discussed.

Northcott, W. H. Candidate for integration: A hearing-impaired child in a regular nursery school. *Young Children,* 1970. *25*(6), 267-380. Northcott discusses placement of such children in the typical nursery school and briefly discusses ways to facilitate their learning once they have been admitted.

Robb, P. *Epilepsy: A review of basic and clinical research.* Washington, D.C.: U.S. Dept. of Health, Education, and Welfare, National Institute of Neurological Diseases and Blindness, 1965. This inexpensive government publication contains a gold mine of information about epilepsy, although it does not discuss handling this condition in the classroom.

Ross, D. M., and Ross, S. A. *Hyperactivity: Research, theory, action.* New York: John Wiley & Sons, Inc., 1976. This is a comprehensive, up-to-date review of what is presently known about hyperactivity, including treatment, educational intervention, prevention, and causes. Of special interest is the material on how the children themselves feel about having this condition. An extensive bibliography is included.

Weiner, J. M. (Ed.). *Psychopharmacology in childhood adolescence.* New York: Basic Books Inc., Publishers, 1977. Readers who are concerned about the overuse of drugs will find this book reassuring in its balanced assessment of the pros and cons of medication to control such behavior as childhood schizophrenia, minimal brain dysfunction, depression, and anxiety.

Wender, P. H. *The hyperactive child: A handbook for parents.* New York: Crown Publishers, Inc., 1973. Wender discusses possible causes, symptoms, and treatment of hyperactivity; highly recommended.

Using Observations for Child Study

Cohen, D. H., and Stern, V. S. *Observing and recording the behavior of young children.* New York: Teachers College Press, Columbia University, 1958. In this classic reference, Cohen and Stern suggest many different aspects of the child's behavior that may be observed and recorded to deepen the teacher's insight into the child's personality; still in print.

Rowan, B. *The children we see.* New York: Holt, Rinehart and Winston, Inc., 1973. Rowan approaches child study by means of observation and uses these observations to illustrate basic principles of child development. A good section on characteristics of children at different developmental levels, as well as many examples, is included.

Council for Exceptional Children

The reader may have noted that many of the references cited in this chapter are published by the Council for Exceptional Children. This invaluable organization also makes available for a moderate fee a great many bibliographies on various aspects of exceptionality, as well as providing facilities for computer searches. They may be contacted at 1920 Association Dr., Reston, Va. 22091, or use the toll-free number (800) 336-3728.

Referral and Information Resources

Ellingson, C., and Cass, J. *Directory of facilities for the learning-disabled and handicapped.* New York: Harper & Row, Publishers, 1972. This referral resource contains succinct information on the type of service offered by facilities throughout the United States, listed by state.

Glassman, L., and Erickson, D. *A selected guide to government agencies concerned with exceptional children.* Arlington, Va.: IMC/RMC Network, 1972. A broad spectrum of programs concerned with activities for the handicapped is listed; a good way to get an overview of government-sponsored centers and resources.

Mycue, E. S. *Young children with handicaps:* (Part 4: Resources: Directories, newsletters, bibliographies and general information: An abstract bibliography). Urbana, Ill.: University of Illinois and the Educational Resource Information Center Clearinghouse for Early Childhood Education, 1973. The title is self-explanatory.

PART EIGHT

What lies ahead?

Los Niños Head Start

20 □ Recent trends in early childhood education

The moral test of government is how it treats those who are in the dawn of life, the children; those who are in the twilight of life, the aged; and those who are in the shadows of life, the sick, the needy, and the handicapped.*

We live in the midst of change, and it is interesting to reflect, as this book draws to a close, on what trends we may be dealing with in the future because, after all, a beginning textbook is only that—a beginning. The teacher who has mastered the fundamentals must always look ahead to see what to turn to next. So it is important to pause and consider what trends are developing and to ask ourselves what concerns we will be facing in the coming years.

Of course, many of these issues have already been reviewed in this volume. Such things as cross-cultural education, child abuse, the development of a code of ethics, the role of cognitive development, and the inclusion of the exceptional child will continue to concern us in the coming decade just as building emotional health, fostering creativity, following sound routines, and building healthy bodies will remain eternally important. But we must also be aware of the shifts in emphasis and new trends that are now taking place.

CHILD ADVOCACY MOVEMENT

The White House Conference of 1970 (Beck, 1973; Ward, Akers, Hines, and Eggleston, 1971) re-

flected, once again, a concern for the rights of children, and this concern is continuing to gain momentum in the Child Advocacy movement (Gross and Gross, 1977). The only common denominator of this movement is a "generalized commitment to children's rights and to improving social provisions for children" (Kahn, Kammerman, and McGowan, 1973, p. 84). Two of the best-known, nationally based advocacy groups with a broad range of interests are the Children's Defense Fund* and The Children's Foundation.† Other groups are more specialized, and their concerns range from improving the quality of children's television‡ to providing input from minority groups into the decision-making process.§ Still other organizations are pressing for all schools to avail themselves of federal financing for nutrition programs† or to alleviate child abuse.‖

In addition to these groups, there are the professional organizations such as The National Association for the Education of Young Children, the

339

Day Care and Child Development Council of America, The Association for Childhood Education International, and the Child Welfare League, who have had an interest in the well-being of children for many years. (For addresses of these organizations, see Appendix B.)

Besides continuing to act individually in accordance with their special areas of concern, many of these advocacy groups are also forming ''networks'' —coalitions that seek, by combining powers, to bring even stronger force and expertise to bear for the benefit of children (Jones, 1978). A good example of such an umbrella organization is the Coalition for Children and Youth.* Many of these networks are also forming on a more informal basis at the local and state level, and a heartening aspect of this movement is the intention of these groups to be, as they put it, ''in on the takeoffs instead of the crash landings'' (that is, to stress prevention and the enactment of effective legislation rather than eternally trying to clean up results after a disaster).

The recognition that children have rights that must be protected has required advocates to learn a great deal more about the legislative process and also to develop means of keeping abreast of legislation. The time is past when parents and teachers of young children can afford to remain ignorant of what is happening in Washington or in various state capitols across the nation. Fortunately, many organizations are now including this information in their publications. For example, *Young Children,* which is the official publication of the National Association for the Education of Young Children, regularly carries a ''Washington Update'' column.

At present it appears that the most vital issue on the legislative front is not only the provision of additional child care and early education opportunities but also the implementation and maintenance of standards that will help assure that the care provided is nurturing and generative rather than merely custodial (Auerbach, 1978; Governor's Advisory Com-

mittee on Child Development Programs, 1978; Morgan, 1977). *It is a terrible mistake to assume that any child care is better than no child care or to assume that once mediocre legislation has been passed, it can be easily modified to produce quality programs.* Young children are too vulnerable and precious to be subjected to crowded, underequipped environments staffed by ignorant, though well-meaning, caretakers. But this may come about unless parents and teachers take time to understand legislative matters, become acquainted with their elected representatives, and help these people understand the importance of adequate legislation and licensing. (See the references at the end of the chapter for further information on this subject.)

Still another concern closely related to legislation is the possibility that services to young children will be reduced because of tightening federal and state budgets (Spodek and Walberg, 1977; Steiner, 1976). If this should happen, the results could be quite serious for children and their families. It is necessary, therefore, to keep a close watch on lawmaking bodies and to make opinions known to them when such measures are raised for discussion in the legislature. Lawmakers do listen to their constituents, but constituents must speak up in order to be heard.

INCREASED NEED FOR SERVICES TO YOUNG CHILDREN

The years between 1965 and 1975 witnessed a marked increase in the number of young children participating in preschool programs, moving from 14% in 1967 to 32% in 1975 (Bureau of the Census, 1978). However, since that time, the Census Bureau reports that the enrollment of 3- and 4-year-olds has not increased appreciably and remains at 32% for 1977 (1978). (It is interesting to note, however, that the enrollment has held steady despite the fact that during the same period, enrollment in kindergarten declined by 8% for the first time in 30 years.)

Although additional Head Start funding may boost preschool enrollment somewhat in the coming years, there remains a tremendous discrepancy be-

*Coalition for Children and Youth, 815 15th St., N.W., Suite 600, Washington, D.C. 20005

tween the need for quality child care services and the provision of such facilities. For example, the Senate Finance Committee (1974) reported that, even when the capacity of public and private day-care centers and family day-care homes was combined, there were only 1,021,212 child care spaces available. Compare this with the estimate by the National Council of Organizations for Children and Youth (1976) that there are 6.5 million children under age 6 whose mothers work outside the home and 14 million more children between the ages of 6 and 14 years whose mothers also work. Moreover, the need is likely to become even more acute as more women enter the labor force and as more single-parent families require child care services. The number of women working outside the home has already jumped from 35% in 1965 to 49% in 1976 (U.S. Dept. of Labor, 1977), and in 1975 more than one in every seven children under age 3 were living in a single-parent family; 50% of the single mothers with children under age 3 were working, nearly 77% of them full-time (ERIC/ECE Newsletter, 1977).

If adequate care is to be provided for these children, it is highly probable that some form of institutional financial support, perhaps combined with a sliding scale of parent fees, will have to be provided. Such support could be obtained from union dues (Steinfels, 1973), industry (Stein, 1973), or government support at federal, state, or local levels (Auerbach, 1973; Commission on Child Care and Development Services, 1978; Education Commission of the States, 1971).

The children of migrant workers are desperately in need of child care service. At best, the preschool services for children of migrant workers range from specially constructed day-care centers open during the harvest season to mobile units that follow the workers as they move from crop to crop (Sunderlin, Osborn, and Cohen, 1971). At worst, service is nonexistent, and very young children spend long hours alone in shacks or locked in cars at the edge of the fields. Sad to say, conditions have not substantially improved for these workers since the first edition of

The Whole Child. A recent report illustrating the continuing plight of migrant children states that ". . . of an estimated 30,000 to 32,000 *preschool* migrant children in California, 2,000 receive child care services under the Office of Child Development at any one time, with 5,000 served during the May-October growing season. . . . Seven of 35 migrant camps offer infant care. . . . In a recent survey, *all* 6 month to 25 month old migrant children who were studied were anemic" (On the Capitol Doorstep, 1978, p. 3). This report is about California, which has one of the more advanced programs for migrant workers and their families. The problem of the migrant worker is widespread (only Alaska, Hawaii, and Rhode Island report no use of migrant labor), and the needs for better housing, health, and employment standards go far beyond provision of preschool care, although child care is most certainly an important area to consider (Dunbar and Kravitz, 1976; Hintz, 1976).

Statistics on migrant services make depressing reading. Over and over the states are able to list the number of children served (which ranges from 30 in Arkansas to 4,489 in Texas) but just as consistently list as "unknown" the number of children not served (Education Commission of the States, 1972). Of course, as child advocates are quick to point out, as long as the number of migrant children who require care remains "unknown," it is impossible to determine how much service is needed.

Infant care is being investigated as another area of possible service to children. As a result of early, shocking studies on the effect of institutionalization on infant development (Bowlby, 1951; Spitz, 1945), day-care personnel in the United States did all they could to further the well-being of very young children and infants by keeping them in the home. More recent research appears to indicate that merely spending time away from the mother's care is not the damaging factor. Rather, it is the possible lack of environmental stimulation and lack of personal, individualized care often characteristic of under-staffed, ill-informed institutional settings that lie at the heart of marasmic decline (Casler, 1968).

With these newer findings in mind, the possibility of providing infant care outside the home is once again being investigated (Caldwell and others, 1970; Frank Porter Graham Child Development Center, no date; Garber and Heber, 1973; Honig, no date; Kagan, Kearsley, and Zelazo, 1977; Keister, 1970). These meticulously supervised, carefully controlled studies report promising findings, and there is no denying that there is a very real need for such infant care among women who find they must work outside the home when their children are very young.

However, we must never forget that the younger the child is, the more vulnerable he is to environmental insult and the less able he is to protect himself from malign conditions or from overstimulation (Bromwich, 1977). We cannot depend on the possibility that parents will always be good judges of child care or infant care situations. I hear frequent tales of parents in my own community who simply call and enroll their youngsters in nursery schools without asking anything beyond the price and who express surprise when invited to visit. Inspection and licensing regulations do not necessarily ensure good care. Some states do not license nursery schools at all (Grotberg, Chapman, and Lazar, 1971), and even in those where licensing is in effect, quality of care provided varies widely (Keyserling, 1972). If these circumstances are true of preschool care, is it not likely that they would also be true of infant care? Yet poor infant care may have even more serious consequences for development than poor preschool care does. *For this reason infant care should still be regarded with caution and championed as a cause only if strong safeguards are built into the program and knowledgeable people are on hand to provide continuing supervision, guidance, and encouragement for the staff.*

INCREASED FLEXIBILITY AND VARIETY IN TYPES OF SERVICE AND INSTRUCTION

New patterns of service, such as franchised child care (Bank of America, 1969, 1970; Brown, 1971), education by means of television (Ball and Bogatz, 1972; Ratliff and Ratliff, 1972; Sprigle, 1971),

and evening and overnight care, are also being investigated to meet changing needs.

Of particular interest to students is the increasing trend toward offering child care on campuses — a movement that extends from the university (Cargill, 1977; Ravenscroft, 1973) to the junior college level. For example, a survey revealed that 46 of 98 community colleges in California already offer some form of child care on their campuses (Hendrick, 1974). Although considerable notoriety and radical political activity have attended the formation of some campus child care facilities (Simmons and Chayes, 1973), it is not true that the child care movement is necessarily the pawn of a few radical students. Offering child care is a popular cause with most students, and good services for children can come about as a result of this enthusiasm if early childhood personnel on campus are willing to take the risk of making friends with sponsors of these movements and helping them learn about what quality child care entails.

Still another innovative pattern of service is the move toward educating children in the home itself (Day Care and Child Development Council of America, 1975; Gordon, 1969; Gray and Klaus, 1970; Prescott, 1978; Schaefer, 1970; Weikart and Lambie, 1968). An interesting variation of this idea is the Home Start program under the auspices of Head Start. In this program, neighborhood mothers receive training and financial support and welcome small groups of youngsters into their homes for learning activities (O'Keefe, 1973).

Many home tutoring programs are based on the idea of a weekly visitor who brings materials for the children to use but who also focusses on drawing the mother in so that she gradually adds to her personal repertoire ideas and activities that enhance her youngster's growth. For example, when the mother herself understands how important it is to develop language competence in young children and also understands in simple, practical ways how she can foster this ability in her children, a positive, continuing influence has been built into her children's lives. The long-term benefits of this approach to the family are obvious.

INCREASED FLEXIBILITY IN APPROACHES TO TEACHER TRAINING

Accompanying increased demands for flexibility in patterns of care and instruction has come an interest in new patterns of teacher training. Junior colleges are offering training in the first two years of undergraduate work, which equips many people with sound training in early childhood education so that they qualify for jobs as teachers and aides in a wide variety of nursery school programs.

Television consortia are springing up that seek to offer high quality educational programs to be viewed at home and taken for unit credit at various colleges. Packaged programs of taped lectures and discussions are now more readily available, and films appear to be more numerous.

On a national level the concept of the Child Development Associate is gaining ground as an alternative way of educating teachers (Spencer and Carroll, 1977). A Child Development Associate would qualify for her degree by demonstrating actual competence with young children instead of by taking a specified number of college level courses. I believe that this approach has great merit, providing that various competencies prove to be measurable and the process of identifying them can be achieved without requiring an unreasonable amount of time or money. If the approach is successful, awarding credentials based on competence should result in an increased variety of educational options for students, combined with higher quality interaction between children and the staff who serve them—both highly desirable outcomes.

INCREASED RECOGNITION OF THE IMPORTANCE OF PARENTING

Along with the increasing interest in home visiting and home education goes an acknowledgment of the enduring importance of parental influence (Bronfenbrenner, 1976; *Children Today,* 1978; Gordon, 1969; Lally and Honig, 1977; Schaefer, 1972; White, 1973), and there is new hope that parenting education may turn out to be an effective means of preventing child abuse (Education Commission of the States, 1976). In addition, there is an increasing concern about effective ways to link home and school more closely and to educate parents (Gordon and Breivogel, 1976, Miller and Wilmshurst, 1975). Many schools now try to narrow the gap by asking parents to be resource people, to participate with the children during the day, or to serve in decision-making capacities on policy-making boards (Knitzer, 1972). Some teachers are also becoming more attuned to the contributions families make to educating their young children and are more appreciative of these contributions.

Parent education is taking many new forms, ranging from courses on parenting and family life offered at the high school level (Lazar and Chapman, 1972) to intensive tutoring of mothers of infants (Heber, Garber, Harrington, Hoffman, and Falender, 1972). In addition, the old standby parent cooperatives that have played a valuable role in educating families for many years continue to operate effectively and to gain in popularity (Taylor, 1968), since many of the new campus child care centers operate on parent cooperative principles. Finally, the staff of many nursery schools and daycare centers also work hard to provide stimulating, helpful parent meetings intended to broaden the parents' knowledge of child behavior and help them gain skills in living with their youngsters.

TREND TOWARD A BETTER SENSE OF PROPORTION

We have already seen that school doors are being opened for parents and that increased recognition of the importance of their influence in the life of the child is developing. The work of Christopher Jencks (1972) also reminds us that education is at best only a partial influence on the family and society and that many avenues must be explored and economic policies modified if the cycle of poverty is to be broken. On the other hand, while acknowledging that there are limits to what can fairly be expected of early education, we should also remember to take heart from the Lazar study (Lazar, Hubbell, Murray, Rosche, and Royce, 1977), which demonstrates convincingly that there can be substantial long-term benefits for children who have attended preschool programs of various kinds.*

We must also bear in mind that the education of the adolescent is both valuable and important (McCurdy, 1974; Rohwer, 1971); some research even indicates that apparent deficits that occur at younger ages may be made up at later stages of development (Kagan and Klein, 1972; Kagan, Klein, Haith, and Morrison, 1973).

Although these findings may at first glance seem threatening to early childhood teachers who have fought so long for a modicum of recognition, it is only sensible to acknowledge that the entire future of the child's life does not rest solely on the two or at the most three years he is in an early childhood program. Such findings need not be taken to imply that early childhood education does not have an important contribution to make in fostering the well-being of young children and their families—it does. But such reports as those mentioned above help us maintain a sense of proportion as well as retain a feeling of responsibility for bringing about all the good things we can for the children in our care.

RECOGNITION OF THE NEED FOR BETTER RESEARCH

Research has been cited throughout this book wherever possible to help substantiate opinions of what constitutes sound educational practice with young children. The citations have not been as numerous as one might wish, nor do they offer the comfort of replication. Moreover, the studies have often been characterized by small sample size and, in some of the earlier studies, by naive design.

The needs in this area are clear. Many fields remain to be explored (Almy, 1973; Datta, 1973; Grotberg, Chapman, and Lazar, 1971; LaCrosse, Lee, Litman, Ogilvie, Stodlosky, and White, 1970), and the need is particularly great for replicated studies using carefully randomized samples of adequate size. Longitudinal studies are still in very short supply, and we continue to explore areas that can be easily counted and measured and to ignore more

difficult but possibly more significant and relevant areas, such as play, which cannot be quantified so easily. We also need to know a great deal more about children who are functioning well and what benign circumstances in their lives have made this possible. Finally, there is a need for systematic exploration of topics so that we will not have to depend on hunt-and-peck results that must be fitted into the larger pattern of needed knowledge like pieces of a jigsaw puzzle.

Yet, with all these failings, we seem on firmer ground today with research than we were in the past. More areas are being investigated, and designs and statistical methods are increasing in sophistication and rigor. We must remain careful, however, that we employ these techniques to investigate things that really matter.

TWO GUIDELINES TO REMEMBER

With so much to do and so many problems to solve, the reader may well wonder if there are any general principles to keep in mind that will help in making decisions for the future. There are at least two that are helpful to remember.

First, there will be a continuing need for teachers to remain open to new ideas and continued growth. We must beware of becoming trapped in congealing philosophy, Lilian Katz (1974) said it well: "We must proceed—having enough skepticism to keep on learning, but with enough confidence to keep on acting." If I could leave students with only one thought about this, it would be, "Do not forget to question, but do not allow doubt to paralyze your ability to act."

The second guideline to remember is, "When in doubt about the value of a decision, put the child's welfare first." In the press of other concerns, whether it be legislation, teacher training, or the search for a "perfect" educational model, there is a real risk that in the struggle we will lose sight of the most important person of all—that small, vulnerable individual filled with fascinating complexities and bewildering contradictions whom we have named "the preschool child."

It is, after all, this child's well-being that we

---

*See Chapter 1 for a discussion of these findings.

Photo by Patrick Huglin

must put ahead of every other concern in early childhood education. And when policies are made or compromises suggested, then we must unhesitatingly apply the yardstick of what will be of maximum benefit to him as we make decisions that affect his future.

QUESTIONS

1. By the time you read this chapter on trends, even newer ones will be arising. What additional ones are you aware of that have developed in the field of early childhood education?
2. Are there any activities in your local community that reflect the Child Advocacy movement? Share with the class how these gained impetus and whether the advocacy activities appear to be producing positive changes in the lives of children.
3. Some people feel that the growth of day-care and other early childhood programs is a threat to the home life of the child and will contribute to the destruction of family life by weakening bonds between its members. Explain why you do or do not agree with this point of view.
4. Many women now champion the cause of infant care outside the home as one of women's fundamental rights. If you were asked to be on a panel to discuss the desirability of infant care for very young children, what position would you take? Be sure to state your reasons for your point of view.
5. *Problem:* You have two young children of your own and, like many other students, you need child care badly in order to continue your education. The licensing restrictions for child care are clearly defined and enforced in your state and require such things as a fenced yard, a toilet for every 7 children, 35 square feet of indoor and 75 square feet of outdoor space for every child, and some units of early childhood education for the teachers. You are desperately interested in starting a day-care center, but these restrictions obviously increase the cost and difficulty of beginning it. Under these circumstances, do you feel it would be all right for the center to "just begin" and go underground? What might the alternatives be to doing this?

REFERENCES FOR FURTHER READING

Child Advocacy

Berlin, I. N. (Ed.). *Advocacy for child mental health*. New York: Brunner/Mazel, Inc., 1975. This book contains a wide-ranging collection of articles from the diverse fields of law, psychiatry, pediatrics, education, and social work all by authors who served on the Joint Commission on the Mental Health of Children. The chapters analyze the basic needs of children and offer many suggestions of what can be done to meet these needs if only we will take effective action.

Coalition for Children and Youth, *1977-78 Directory for child advocates: Congress and federal agencies*. Washington, D.C.: The Coalition, 1978. This is a useful reference for advocates operating on the national level. (Another good source for federal and state directories of legislators is the League of Women Voters.)

Education Commission of the States. *The children's needs assessment handbook*. Denver: The Commission, 1976 (b).

Perhaps the reader is wondering how to find out and effectively document what is needed for children in a particular state or community. This booklet explains how to conduct a needs survey and provides three examples as well.

Gross, B., and Gross, R. *The children's rights movement: Overcoming the oppression of young people*. Garden City, N.Y.: Doubleday & Co., Inc., 1977. *The Children's Rights Movement* is, essentially, a collection of articles, some very well known, some less so, about how children are and have been oppressed in our society. It also contains some additional articles about what can be done, and there is a helpful list of Child Advocacy groups at the end of the book.

Katz, S. *The youngest minority: Lawyers in defense of children*. Chicago: American Bar Association, 1974. Still another collection of articles, this one deals with the legal aspects of advocacy, including problems of custody, adoption, rights of the retarded, and much more. It is important to realize that most truly effective advocacy depends on the law to get results.

Steiner, G. Y. *The children's cause*. Washington, D.C.: The Brookings Institution, 1976. Written before the latest wave of advocacy developed, most of this book deals with the author's analysis of "the failing cause" and slowing impetus for the development of child care services. However, his challenge to advocates to set clear priorities and build effective coalitions is excellent advice that is still needed.

Legislation

Children's Defense Fund. *National legislative agenda for children*. Washington, D.C.: Children's Defense Fund, PO Box 19085, Washington, D.C. 20006, 1978. This agenda focusses on children without homes, child health, child care and family support services, and education. It states facts and purposes short- and long-term legislative goals.

Education Commission of the States. *The children's political checklist: Education Commission of the States, Carnegie Council on Children, and The Coalition for Children and Youth* (Report 103). Denver, Colorado: The Commission, 1977. *The Children's Political Checklist* asks relevant questions in several areas of social welfare, provides examples of problems, and leaves the readers to draw their own conclusions and determine their own thrust toward advocacy. As the Commission puts it, "What you do about what you find is up to you."

Licensing

Education Commission of the States. *Early childhood programs: A state survey 1974-75* (Report 65). Denver: The Commission, Early Childhood Project, 1975. This valuable reference lists the amount of money each state invested in preschool and kindergarten programs during that year, and also lists educational requirements for day-care, prekindergarten, and kindergarten personnel for each state.

Morgan, G. G. Regulation of early childhood programs. In D. N. McFadden (Ed.), *Planning for action*. Washington, D.C.: NAEYC, 1972, Morgan provides a thoughtful and comprehensive discussion of the problems and issues concerning licensing at all levels, from the local fire marshal up through the federal government; an indispensable, authoritative reference.

United States Department of Health, Education, and Welfare. *Guides for day care licensing*. Washington, D.C.: The Department, Office of Child Development, 1973. These are the latest set of recommendations for day-care standards published by the federal government.

Day Care

Allen, S. B., Edelman, M. W., Hansen, O., and others. *Perspectives on child care*. Washington, D.C.: National Association for the Education of Young Children, 1972. The authors emphasize the need for adequate care and discuss this problem in relation to legislation and finances.

Education Commission of the States, Task Force on Early Childhood Education. *Early childhood development: Alternatives for program implementation in the states*. Denver: The Commission, 1971. This gold mine of material includes summaries of alternative ways to educate young children, estimates of operating costs, suggestions for different ways to include early childhood education in state budgets, lists of teacher certification requirements, and state funding efforts.

Robinson, H. B., and others. *Early child care in the United States of America*. New York: Gordon and Breach, Science Publishers, Inc., 1974. This book discusses child care from the point of view of national policy; clearly done.

Roby, P. *Child care—who cares? Foreign and domestic infant and early childhood development policies*. New York: Basic Books, Inc., Publishers, 1973. In this collection of articles about day care, Roby considers many aspects of the problem, including the need for service, child care trends in the United States, and child care abroad; *excellent*.

Migrant Education

Education Commission of the States, Task Force on Early Childhood Education. *Early childhood programs for migrants: Alternatives for the states*. Denver: The Commission, 1972. In this fact-filled, interesting publication from the Task Force, state and federal funding for migrant preschoolers is discussed, and a survey of child care service currently available is presented.

Hirshen, S., and Ouye, J. *The infant care center: A case study in design*. 2150 Dwight Way, Berkeley, Calif.: Sanford Hirshen and Partners, Architects, 1973. This pamphlet is one of the few relatively new things in print about migrant services. It describes functional centers built to serve the infants of migrant families in California. What the architects have to say about their approach to designing such centers makes sense for everyone.

Sunderlin, S., Osborn, K., and Cohen, M. D. *Migrant children: Their education*. Washington, D.C.: Association for Childhood Education International, 1971. The authors discuss appropriate curriculum and describe several programs now in operation for migrant children; interesting and readable.

Infant Care

Bromwich, R. Stimulation in the first year of life? A perspective on infant development. *Young Children,* 1977, *32*(2), 71-82.

Dittman, L. L. *The infants we care for*. Washington, D.C.: National Association for the Education of Young Children, 1973. This is a useful reference with which to begin the study of in-

fant care, either in terms of home visits or of setting up a center for care away from home. Helpful bibliographies are included at the end of each chapter.

Honig, A. S. *Infant development problems in intervention*. Washington, D.C.: Day Care and Child Development Council of America, Inc., no date. These three references provide a nice "feel" for the kinds of important problems that deserve special, careful consideration when planning care for infants and toddlers.

Current Status of the Family

Children Today. The family (entire issue). 1978, *7*(2), 1-49. The changing role of the family in the United States is a huge topic —and too big to be referenced here in detail. However, for a good, current, quick overview, the reader would do well to peruse this entire issue of *Children Today*.

Parent Involvement

Black Child Development Institute. From a black perspective: Optimum conditions for minority involvement in quality child development programming. In Roby, P. *Child care—who cares? Foreign and domestic infant and early childhood development policies*. New York: Basic Books, Inc., Publishers, 1973. A good set of recommendations is given for specific ways to help black families gain strength and representation in early childhood programs. The suggestions also apply very well to families from other minority groups.

Davies, D. *Schools where parents make a difference*. Boston: Institute for Responsive Education, 1976. This is a fascinating, readable series of articles describing various schools where parents have achieved a vigorous "say" in what happens. It includes descriptions of how this was accomplished by Mexican-American and Indian parents as well as by other groups. It makes exciting reading; the last chapter is full of sensible, general observations on how to bring about change.

Gordon, I. J., and Breivogel, W. F. *Building effective home-school relationships*. Boston: Allyn & Bacon, Inc., 1976. This book talks about parent involvement from the home tutoring point of view. It is quite practical and based on extensive experience with this approach.

Steinfels, M. O'B. *Who's minding the children? The history and politics of day care in America*. New York: Simon & Schuster, Inc., 1973. Chapter 6, "What Is It Like to Use Day Care?" contains a frank description of how one group of parents involved themselves actively with day-care staff. It should be read by all teachers to help them see their program from the vantage point of parents, who are often afraid to speak up directly.

Research

Hymes, J. L., Jr. *Early childhood education: The year in review. A look at 1976. A look at 1977*. Box A-1, Carmel, Calif.: Hacienda Press, 1977 and 1978. For those readers who wish to be kept up to date on what has just happened, these unique pamphlets are highly recommended because they cover a comprehensive range of national and regional trends and events.

Scott, M., and Grimmett, S. (Eds.). *Current issues in child development*. Washington, D.C.: National Association for the Education of Young Children, 1977. Some highly respected researchers in the field of early childhood and infant development have written chapters for this little book that single out subjects of current investigatory interest.

Stone, L. J., Smith, H. T., and Murphy, L. B. *The competent infant: Research and commentary*. New York: Basic Books, Inc., Publishers, 1973. A *thick* book packed with the most important research papers of the decade having to do with infants. *The Competent Infant* is a *must* for anyone interested in the field of infant education.

Statistical Resources

The following references are suggested as sources of useful current information for those in the field of early childhood education.

Bureau of the Census. *Population characteristics: School enroll-ment—social and economic characteristics of students: October, 1977* (Advance Report). Washington, D.C.: U.S. Dept. of Commerce, Bureau of the Census, U.S. Govt. Printing Office, 1978.

National Council of Organizations for Children and Youth. *America's children 1976: A bicentennial assessment*. Washington, D.C.: The Council, 1976.

United States Department of Health, Education, and Welfare. *Statistical highlights from the National Child Care Consumer Study*. Washington, D.C.: The OHD, OCD, Head Start Bureau, 1976. DHEW publication number OHD 76-31096.

United States Senate Finance Committee. *Child care: Data and materials*. Washington, D.C.: U.S. Govt. Printing Office, 1974. Stock no. 5270-02549.

□References*

Adams, M. *Mental retardation and its social dimensions*. New York: Teachers College Press, Columbia University, 1971.

Adams, M. *Single blessedness: Observations on the single status in a married society*. New York: Basic Books, Inc. Publishers, 1976.

Alexander, A. M. *The money world of your preschooler*. East Lansing, Mich.: Cooperative Extension Science, Michigan State University, 1967.

Allen, K., Hart, B., Buell, J. S., Harris, F. R., and Wolf, M. M. Effects of social reinforcement on isolate behavior of a nursery school child. *Child Development*, 1964, *35*(2), 511-518.

Allen, Lady of Hurtwood. *Planning for play*. Cambridge, Mass.: The M.I.T. Press, 1968.

Allen, Lady of Hurtwood, Flekkoy, M. S., Sigsgaard, J., and Skard, A. G. *Space for play: The youngest children*. Copenhagen: World Organization for Early Childhood Education, 1964.

Allen, S. B., Edelman, M. W., Hansen, O., and others. *Perspectives on child care*. Washington, D.C.: NAEYC, 1972.

Almy, M. Spontaneous play: An avenue for intellectual development. *Young Children*, 1967, *22*, 265-277.

Almy, M. *Early childhood play: Selected readings related to cognition and motivation*. New York: Simon & Schuster, Inc., 1968.

Almy, M. *Early childhood research: Second thoughts and next steps*. Urbana, Ill.: ERIC/ECE, University of Illinois, 1973.

Almy, M., Chittenden, E., and Miller, P. *Young children's thinking*. New York: Teachers College Press, Columbia University, 1966.

Altshuler, A. *Books that help children deal with a hospital experience*. Rockville, Md.: Public Health Service, Health Services Administration, U.S. Dept. of HEW, 1974. HSA 74-5402.

American Alliance for Health, Physical Education, and Recreation. *Choosing and using phonograph records for physical education, recreation and related activities*. Washington, D.C.: AAHPER, 1977.

American Humane Association, Children's Division. *Fifth annual symposium on child abuse*. Denver: The Association, 1976.

American National Red Cross. *Standard first aid and personal safety*. Garden City, N.Y.: Doubleday & Co., Inc., 1973.

Anderson, P. S. *Story telling with the flannel board: Book one*. Minneapolis: T. S. Denison & Co., Inc., 1963.

Anderson, R. B., St. Pierre, R. G., Proper, E. C., and Stebbins, L. B. Pardon us, but what was that question again? A response to the critiques of the Follow Through evaluation. *Harvard Educational Review*, 1978, *48*(2), 161-170.

Andry, A. C., and Scheep, S. *How babies are made*. New York: Time-Life Books, 1968.

Arasteh, A. R., and Arasteh, J. D. *Creativity in human development: An interpretive and annotated bibliography*. New York: Schenkman Publishing Co., Inc., 1976.

Arenas, S. Bilingual/bicultural programs for preschool children. *Children Today*, 1978, *7*(4), 2-6.

Arieti, S. *Creativity: The magic synthesis*. New York: Basic Books, Inc., Publishers, 1976.

Arnheim, D. D., and Pestolesi, R. A. *Elementary physical education: A developmental approach* (2nd ed.). St. Louis: The C. V. Mosby Co., 1978.

Arnheim, D. D., and Sinclair, W. A. *The clumsy child: A program of motor therapy* (2nd ed.). St. Louis: The C. V. Mosby Co., 1979.

Arnstein, H. S. *Your growing child and sex: A parent's guide to the sexual development, education, attitudes and behavior of the child—from infancy through adolescence*. New York: The Bobbs-Merrill Co. Inc., 1967.

Asher, S. R., Oden, S. L., and Gottman, J. M. Children's friendships in school settings. In L. G. Katz (Ed.), *Current topics in early childhood education* (Vol. 1). Norwood, N.J.: Ablex Publishing Corp., 1977.

Ashton, P. T. Cross-cultural Piagetian research: An experimental perspective. *Harvard Educational Review*, 1975, *45*(4), 475-506.

Ashton-Warner, S. *Teacher*. New York: Bantam Books, Inc., 1965.

Association for Childhood Education International, *Bibliography: Books for children*. Washington, D.C.: ACEI, 1977.

Atkins, R., and Rubin, E. *Part-time father: A guide for the divorced father*. New York: Vanguard Press, Inc., 1976.

Auerbach, S. Federally sponsored daycare. In P. Roby (Ed.), *Childcare—who cares? Foreign and domestic infant and early childhood development policies*. New York: Basic Books, Inc., Publishers, 1973.

Austin Association for the Education of Young Children. *Ideas for administrators: The idea box*. Washington, D.C.: NAEYC, 1973.

Axline, V. *Dibs: In search of self*. Boston: Houghton Mifflin Co., 1964.

---

*For full names and addresses of abbreviated organizations, refer to Appendix B.

Axline, V. *Play therapy* (Rev. ed.). New York: Ballantine Books, Inc., 1969.

Ayers, A. J. *Sensory integration and learning disorders.* Los Angeles: Western Psychological Services, 1973.

Bach, G. R., and Goldberg, H. G. *Creative aggression.* Garden City, N.Y.: Doubleday & Co., Inc., 1974.

Baer, J. *How to be an assertive (not aggressive) woman in life, in love, and on the job.* New York: Rawson Associates Publishers, Inc., 1976.

Baker, K. R. *Let's play outdoors.* Washington, D.C.: NAEYC, 1966.

Bakwin, H., and Bakwin, R. M. *Behavior disorders in children* (5th ed.). Philadelphia: W. B. Saunders Co., 1974.

Ball, S., and Bogatz, G. A. *Research on Sesame Street: Some implications for compensatory education.* Princeton, N.J.: Educational Testing Service, 1972.

Bambara, T. C. Black English. In Black Child Development Institute, *Curriculum approaches from a Black perspective.* Washington, D.C.: The Institute, 1973.

Bandura, A. *Aggression: A social learning analysis.* Englewood Cliffs, N.J.: Prentice-Hall, Inc., 1973.

Bandura, A. *Social learning theory.* Englewood Cliffs, N.J.: Prentice-Hall, Inc., 1977.

Bandura, A., Grusec, J. E., and Menlove, F. L. Vicarious extinction of avoidance behavior. *Journal of Personality and Social Psychology,* 1967, *5,* 16-23.

Bandura, A., and Huston, A. C. Identification as a process of incidental learning. *Journal of Abnormal Social Psychology,* 1961, *63,* 311-318.

Bandura, A., and Menlove, F. L. Factors determining vicarious extinction of avoidance behavior through symbolic modeling. *Journal of Personality and Social Psychology,* 1968, *8,* 99-108.

Bandura, A., and Walters, R. H. Aggression. In H. W. Stevenson (Ed.), *Child Psychology* (62nd Yearbook of the National Society for the Study of Education). Chicago: University of Chicago Press, 1963.

Bank of America. Day nurseries for preschoolers. *Small Business Reporter,* 1969, *8,* 10.

Bank of America. Franchising. *Small Business Reporter,* 1970, *9,* 9.

Bank Street College. *Early childhood discovery materials.* New York: Macmillan Publishing Co., Inc., 1968.

Banks, J. A. *Teaching strategies for ethnic studies.* Boston: Allyn & Bacon, Inc., 1975.

Barbe, W. B., and Renzulli, J. S. *Psychology and education of the gifted* (2nd ed.). New York: John Wiley & Sons, Inc., 1975.

Barsch, R. H. *Achieving perceptual-motor efficiency* (Vol. 1). Seattle: Special Child Publications, 1967.

Bartlett, E. J. Selecting preschool language programs. In C. B. Cazden (Ed.), *Language in early childhood education.* Washington, D.C.: NAEYC, 1972.

Bauer, C. F. *Handbook for storytellers.* Chicago: American Library Association, 1977.

Baumrind, D. Child care practices anteceding three patterns of preschool behavior. *Genetic Psychological Monographs,* 1967, *75,* 43-88.

Baumrind, D. Socialization and instrumental competence in young children. In W. W. Hartup, *The young child: Reviews of research* (Vol. 2). Washington, D.C.: NAEYC, 1972.

Bayless, K. M., and Ramsey, M. E. *Music: A way of life for the young child.* St. Louis: The C. V. Mosby Co., 1978.

Beard, R. *An outline of Piaget's developmental psychology for students and teachers.* New York: The New American Library Inc., 1972.

Beck, R. The White House Conferences on Children: An historical perspective. *Harvard Educational Review,* 1973, *43*(4), 653-668.

Becker, W. Teaching reading and language to the disadvantaged—what we have learned from field research. *Harvard Educational Review,* 1977, *47*(4), 518-543.

Beiswenger, H. Luria's model of the verbal control of behavior. *Merrill-Palmer Quarterly,* 1968, *14*(4), 267-284.

Bender, J. Have you ever thought of a prop box? In K. R. Baker (Ed.), *Ideas that work with young children.* Washington, D.C.: NAEYC, 1972.

Bengtsson, A. (Ed.). *Adventure playgrounds.* New York: Praeger Publishers, Inc., 1972.

Bereiter, C. *Academic preschool, Champaign, Illinois.* Washington, D.C.: U.S. Govt. Printing Office, 1969.

Bereiter, C., and Englemann, S. *Teaching disadvantaged children in the preschool.* Englewood Cliffs, N.J.: Prentice-Hall, Inc., 1966.

Bergmann, T., and Freud, A. *Children in the hospital.* New York: International Universities Press, 1965.

Berk, L. E. How well do classroom practices reflect teacher goals? *Young Children,* 1976, *32*(1), 64-81.

Berkowitz, L. Control of aggression. In B. M. Caldwell and H. N. Ricciuti (Eds.), *Review of Child Development Research* (Vol. 3). Chicago: University of Chicago Press, 1973.

Berlin, I. N. (Ed.). *Advocacy for child mental health.* New York: Brunner/Mazel, Inc., 1975.

Berman, L. M. Curriculum leadership: That all may feel, value, and grow. In L. M. Berman and J. A. Roderick (Eds.), *Feeling, valuing, and the art of growing: Insights into the affective.* Washington, D.C.: Association for Supervision and Curriculum Development, 1977.

Berman, L. M., and Roderick, J. A. (Eds.). *Feeling, valuing and the art of growing: Insights into the affective.* Washington, D.C.: Association for Supervision and Curriculum Development, 1977.

Bernstein, B. Language and social class. *British Journal of Sociology,* 1960, *11,* 271-276.

Bernstein, J. *Helping children cope with death and separation: Resources for teachers.* Urbana, Ill.: Publications Office/Institute for Child Behavior and Development, College of Education, University of Illinois, 1976.

Bernstein, J. E. Helping young children cope with death. In L. G. Katz (Ed.), *Current topics in early childhood education* (Vol. 1). Norwood, N.J.: Ablex Publishing Corp., 1977.

Bernstein, S. *Alternatives to violence: Alienated youths and riots, race, and poverty.* New York: Association Press, 1967.

Beuf, A. Doctor, lawyer, household drudge. *Journal of Communications,* 1974, *24,* 142-145.

Beuf, A. H. *Red children in white America.* Philadelphia: University of Pennsylvania Press, 1977.

Beyer, E. *Teaching young children.* New York: The Bobbs-Merrill Co., Inc., 1968.

Birch, H. G., and Gussow, J. D. *Disadvantaged children: Health, nutrition and school failure.* New York: Harcourt Brace Jovanovich, Inc., 1970.

Bissell, J. S. The cognitive effects of preschool programs for disadvantaged children. In J. L. Frost (Ed.), *Revisiting early childhood education: Readings.* New York: Holt, Rinehart and Winston, Inc., 1973.

Black Child Development Institute. From a black perspective: Optimum conditions for minority involvement in quality child development programming. In P. Roby, *Child care—who cares? Foreign and domestic infant and early childhood development policies.* New York: Basic Books, Inc., Publishers, 1973.

Blank, M., and Solomon, F. A. A tutorial language program to develop abstract thinking in socially disadvantaged preschool children. *Child Development,* 1968, *39*(1), 379-390.

Blank, M., and Solomon, F. A. How shall the disadvantaged child be taught? *Child Development.* 1969, *40*(1) 48-61.

Bleck, E. E., and Nagel, D. A. *Physically handicapped children—a medical atlas for teachers.* New York: Grune & Stratton, Inc., 1975.

Bloch, J. Impaired children: Helping families through the critical period of first identification. *Children Today,* 1978, *7*(6), 3-6.

Block, J., and Martin, B. Predicting the behavior of children under frustration. *Journal of Abnormal Social Psychology,* 1955, *51,* 281-285.

Block, S. D. *Me and I'm great: Physical education for children three through eight.* Minneapolis: Burgess Publishing Co., 1977.

Bloom, B. S. *Stability and change in human characteristics.* New York: John Wiley & Sons, Inc., 1964.

Bloom, L. Language development review. In F. D. Horowitz (Ed.), and E. M. Hetherington, S. Scarr-Salapatek, and G. M. Siegel (Assoc. Eds.), *Review of child development research* (Vol. 4). Chicago: University of Chicago Press, 1975.

Bloome, E. *The water we drink.* Garden City, N.Y.: Doubleday & Co., Inc., 1971.

Borke, H. Interpersonal perception of young children: Egocentrism or empathy? *Developmental Psychology,* 1971, *5*(2), 263-269.

Bos, B. *Please don't move the muffin tins: A hands-off guide to art for the young child.* Carmichael, Calif.: The burton gallery, 1978.

Bowlby, A. H., and Gardner, L. *The young handicapped child: Educational guidance for the young cerebral palsied, deaf, blind and autistic child* (2nd ed.). Edinburgh: E. and S. Livingstone, 1969.

Bowlby, J. Maternal care and mental health. *World Health Organization Monographs* (No. 2). Geneva: WHO, 1951.

Bowlby, J. *Attachment and loss* (Vol. 1: Attachment). New York: Basic Books, Inc., Publishers, 1969.

Bowlby, J. *Attachment and loss* (Vol. 2: Separation). New York: Basic Books, Inc., Publishers, 1973.

Bowser, P., and Eckstein, J. *A pinch of soul: Fast and fancy soul cookery for today's hostess.* New York: Avon Books, 1970.

Braine, M. D. S. The ontogeny of English phrase structure: The first phrase. *Language,* 1963, *39,* 1-13.

Brant, R. S. T., and Tisza, V. B. The sexually misused child. *American Journal of Orthopsychiatry,* 1977, *47*(1), 80-90.

Braun, S. J., and Lasher, M. B. *Are you ready to mainstream? Helping preschoolers with learning and behavior problems.* Columbus, Ohio: Charles E. Merrill Publishing Co., 1978.

Brearley, M., and Hitchfield, E. *A guide to reading Piaget.* New York: Schocken Books Inc., 1966.

Briggs, D. C. *Your child's self-esteem: The key to his life.* Garden City, N.Y.: Doubleday & Co., Inc., 1970.

Brittain, W. L. *Creativity, art and the young child.* New York: Macmillan Publishing Co., Inc., 1979.

Bromberg, S. L. A beginning teacher works with parents. In K. R. Baker (Ed.), *Ideas that work with young children.* Washington, D.C.: NAEYC, 1972.

Bromwich, R. Stimulation in the first year of life? A perspective on infant development. *Young Children,* 1977, *32*(2), 71-82.

Bronfenbrenner, U. In H. Chauncey (Ed.), *Soviet preschool education* (Vol. 2: Teacher's commentary). New York: Holt, Rinehart and Winston, Inc., 1969.

Bronfenbrenner, U. Is early intervention effective? Facts and principles of early intervention: A summary. In A. M. Clarke and A. D. B. Clarke (Eds.), *Early experience: Myth and evidence.* New York: The Free Press, 1976.

Brown, B. *Long-term gains from early intervention: An overview of current research.* Paper presented at the meeting of the American Association for the Advancement of Science, Denver, February 1977. Washington, D.C.: U.S. Dept. of HEW, OCD, 1977.

Brown, D. G. *Behavior modification in child and school mental health: An annotated bibliography on applications with parents and teachers.* Rockville, Md.: National Institutes of Mental Health, 1971.

Brown, H. *Legislative statement of Harold Brown on investigation of franchising, with attachments.* Washington, D.C.: Child Welfare League, 1971.

Brown, M., and Plihal, J. *Evaluation materials for use in teaching child development.* Minneapolis: Burgess Publishing Co., 1966.

Brown, R. *A first language: The early stages.* Cambridge, Mass.: Harvard University Press, 1973.

Brown, R., and Bellugi, U. Three processes in the child's acquisition of syntax. *Harvard Educational Review,* 1964, *34,* 133-151.

Bruck, M., and Tucker, G. R. Social class differences in the acquisition of school language. *Merrill-Palmer Quarterly,* 1974, *20*(3), 205-220.

Bruner, J. S. The course of cognitive growth. *American Psychologist,* 1964, *19,* 1-15.

Bruner, J. S. On the conservation of liquids. In J. S. Bruner, R. R. Olver, P. M. Greenfield, and others. *Studies in Cognitive Growth.* New York: John Wiley & Sons, Inc., 1966.

Bruner, J. S. *Poverty and childhood.* Detroit: Merrill-Palmer Institute, 1970.

Bruner, J. S. Nature and uses of immaturity. In K. Connolly and J. S. Bruner (Eds.), *The growth of competence.* New York: Academic Press, Inc., 1974.

Bruner, J. S. The ontogenesis of speech acts. *Journal of Child Language,* 1975, *2,* 1-19.

Bruner, J. S. Learning the mother tongue. *Human Nature,* 1978, *1*(9), 42-49.

Bruner, J. S., Jolly, A., and Sylva, K. (Eds.). *Play: Its role in development and evolution.* New York: Basic Books, Inc., Publishers, 1976.

Bryan, J. H. Children's reaction to helpers: Their money isn't where their mouths are. In J. Macaulay and L. Berkowitz (Eds.), *Altruism and helping behavior.* New York: Academic Press, Inc., 1970.

Bryan, J. H. Children's cooperation and helping behaviors. In E. M. Hetherington (Ed.), *Review of child development research* (Vol. 5). Chicago: University of Chicago Press, 1975.

Buchanan, R., and Mullins, J. B. Integration of a spina bifida child in a kindergarten for normal children. *Young Children,* 1968, *23*(6), 339-344.

Buckle, D., and Lebovici, S. *Child guidance centers.* Geneva: World Health Organization, 1960.

Budke, W. E., Bettis, G. E., and Beasley, G. F. *Career education practice.* Columbus, Ohio: ERIC Clearinghouse on Vocational and Technical Education, The Ohio State University, 1972.

Bureau of the Census. *Population characteristics: School enrollment—social and economic characteristics of students: October, 1977* (Advance report). Washington, D.C.: U.S. Dept. of Commerce, Bureau of the Census, U.S. Govt. Printing Office, 1978.

Burlingham, D., and Freud, A. Young children in wartime: Traumatic effects of separation from parents. In Y. Brackbill and G. G. Thompson (Eds.), *Behavior in infancy and early childhood.* New York: The Free Press, 1967.

Butler, A. L., Gotts, E. E., and Quisenberry, N. L. *Play as development.* Columbus, Ohio: Charles E. Merrill Publishing Co., 1978.

Buttolph, E. G. *Music without the piano.* New York: Early Childhood Education Council of New York, 1968.

Caffey, J. The parent-infant traumatic stress syndrome: (Caffey-Kempe Syndrome), (Battered Child Syndrome). *American Journal of Roentgenology, Radium Therapy and Nuclear Medicine,* 1972, *114,* 218-229.

Caldwell, B. M. What is the optimal learning environment for the young child? *American Journal of Orthopsychiatry,* 1967, *37*(1), 8-21.

Caldwell, B. M. The importance of beginning early. In J. B. Jorden and R. F. Dailey (Eds.), *Not all little red wagons are red.* Arlington, Va.: CEC, 1973.

Caldwell, B. M. Aggression and hostility in young children. *Young Children,* 1977, *32*(2), 4-13.

Caldwell, B. M., and others. Infant day care and attachment. *American Journal of Orthopsychiatry,* 1970, *40,* 397-412.

Cancer Care, Inc., and the National Cancer Foundation. *Listen to the children.* New York: Cancer Care, Inc., and the National Cancer Foundation, 1977.

Cargill, G. H. Child care on campus. *Young Children,* 1977, *32*(2), 20-23.

Carmichael, V. *Science experiences for young children.* Los Angeles: Southern California Association for the Education of Young Children, 1969.

Carson, R. *The sense of wonder.* New York: Harper & Row, Publishers, 1956.

Carter, J. L. *Language stimulation program, Auburn, Alabama.* Washington, D.C.: U.S. Govt. Printing Office, 1969. OE 37058.

Casler, L. Perceptual deprivation in institutional settings. In G. Newton and S. Levine (Eds.), *Early experiences and behavior.* Springfield, Ill.: Charles C Thomas, Publisher, 1968.

Castillo, M. S., and Cruz, J., Jr. Special competencies for teachers of preschool Chicano children: Rationale, content, and assessment processes. *Young Children,* September 1974, *30*(6), 341-347.

Cazden, C. Subcultural differences in child language: An interdisciplinary review. *Merrill-Palmer Quarterly,* 1966, *12,* 3.

Cazden, C. Children's questions: Their forms, functions and roles in education. *Young Children,* 1970, *25*(4), 202-220.

Cazden, C. B. *Language in early childhood education.* Washington, D.C.: NAEYC, 1972. (a)

Cazden, C. B. *Child language and education.* New York: Holt, Rinehart and Winston, Inc., 1972. (b)

Charles, C. M. *Teacher's petit Piaget.* Belmont, Calif.: Fearon Publishers, 1974.

Cherry, C. *Creative movement for the developing child: A nursery school handbook for non-musicians* (Rev. ed.). Belmont, Calif.: Fearon Publishers, 1971.

Cherry, C. *Creative art for the developing child: A teacher's handbook for early childhood education.* Belmont, Calif.: Fearon Publishers, 1972.

Cherry, C. *Creative play for the developing child: Early lifehood education through play.* Belmont, Calif.: Fearon Publishers, 1976.

Children Today. Child abuse. 1975, *4*(3).

Children Today. The family. 1978, 7(2), 1-49.

Children's Defense Fund. *National legislative agenda for children.* Washington, D.C.: Children's Defense Fund, 1978.

Children's Foundation. *Feed kids. It's the law.* Washington, D.C.: The Children's Foundation, various dates.

Christy, K. *Multi-cultural resource book for teachers of young children.* La Habra, Calif.: The Impact Co., 1974.

Chukovsky, K. *From two to five.* Translated by M. Morton. Berkeley: University of California Press, 1968.

Cicerelli, V. G., Evans, J. W., and Schiller, J. S. *The impact of Head Start on children's cognitive and affective development* (Preliminary Report). Washington, D.C.: Office of Economic Opportunity, 1969. PB 184 328 and 329.

Clark, A. N. *Journey to the people.* New York: The Viking Press, Inc., 1969.

Clark, C., and Rush, S. *How to get along with black people: A handbook for white folks *and some black folks, too.* New York: The Third Press, 1972.

Clark, E. V. What's in a word? On the child's acquisition of semantics in his first language. In T. E. Moore (Ed.), *Cognitive development and the acquisition of language.* New York: Academic Press, Inc., 1973.

Clark, K. B. *Prejudice and your child* (2nd ed.). Boston: Beacon Press, 1963.

Cleary, M. E. *Please know me as I am: A guide to helping children understand the child with special needs.* Sudbury, Mass.: Jerry Cleary Co., 1974.

Cleary, M. E. Helping children understand the child with special needs. *Children Today,* 1976, *5*(4), 6-10.

Coalition for Children and Youth. *1977-78 Directory for child advocates: Congress and federal agencies.* Washington, D.C.: National Council of Organizations for Children and Youth, 1978.

Cochran, N. A., Wilkinson, L. C., and Furlow, J. J. *Learning on the move: An activity guide for pre-school parents and teachers.* Dubuque, Iowa: Kendall/Hunt Publishing Co., 1975.

Cohen, D. H., and Stern, V. S. *Observing and recording the behavior of young children.* New York: Teachers College Press, Columbia University, 1958.

Cohen, M. D. (Ed.). *When children move from school to school.* Washington, D.C.: ACEI, 1972.

Cohen, M. D. (Ed.). *Growing free: Ways to help children overcome sex-role stereotypes.* Washington, D.C.: ACEI, 1976.

Cohen, M. D., and Hadley, S. (Eds.). *Selecting educational equipment and materials for home and school.* Washington, D.C.: ACEI, 1976.

Cohen, S. How to alleviate the first-year shock of teaching emotionally disturbed children. In M. S. Auleta (Ed.), *Foundations of early childhood education: Readings.* New York: Random House, Inc., 1969.

Cohen, S., Semmes, M., and Guralnick, M. J. Public Law 94-142 and the education of preschool handicapped children. *Exceptional Children,* 1979, *45*(4), 279-284.

Cole, M., and Bruner, J. S. Preliminaries to a theory of cultural differences. In I. J. Gordon (Ed.), *Early childhood education: The seventy-first yearbook of the National Society for the Study of Education* (Part 2). Chicago: University of Chicago Press, 1972.

Coles, R. *Children of crisis: A study of courage and fear.* New York: Dell Publishing Co., Inc., 1967.

Coles, R. *Uprooted children: The early life of migrant farm workers.* Pittsburgh: University of Pittsburgh Press, 1970.

Collison, G. O. Concept formation in a second language: A study of Ghanian school children. *Harvard Educational Review,* 1974, *44*(3), 441-457.

Combs, A. W. *Perceiving behaving becoming: A new focus for education* (Yearbook 1962). Washington, D.C.: Association for Supervision and Curriculum Development, National Education Association, 1962.

Commission on Child Care and Development Services. *Tentative recommendations* (Working paper). Sacramento: 1978.

Congressional Budget Office. Background paper. *Childcare and preschool: Options for federal support.* Washington, D.C.: Congress of the U.S., 1978.

Conner, F. P., and Talbot, M. E. *An experimental curriculum for young mentally retarded children.* New York: Teachers College Press, Columbia University, 1970.

Consortium on Developmental Continuity: Education Commission of the States. *The persistence of preschool effects: A long-term follow-up of fourteen infant and preschool experiments* (Final report). Washington, D.C.: Administration for Children, Youth, and Families, U.S. Dept. of HEW, OHDS, 1977. Stock no. 017-000-00202-3.

Cooper, T. T., and Ratner, M. *Many hands cooking: An international cookbook for girls and boys.* New York: Thomas Y. Crowell Co., 1974.

Coopersmith, S. *The antecedents of self-esteem.* San Francisco: W. H. Freeman and Co., Publishers, 1967.

Coopersmith, S. Building self-esteem in the classroom. In S. Coopersmith (Ed.), *Developing motivation in young children.* San Francisco: Albion Publishing Co., 1975.

Corrado, J., and Reed, J. *Play—with a difference.* New York: The Play Schools Association, 1970.

Costa, J. J., and Nelson, G. K. *Child abuse and neglect: Legislation, reporting and prevention.* Lexington, Mass.: D. C. Heath & Co., 1978.

Cox, F. N., and Campbell, D. Young children in a new situation, with and without their mothers. *Child Development,* 1968, *39,* 123-131.

Crandall, J. M. *Early to learn.* New York: Dodd, Mead & Co., 1974.

Cratty, B. J. *Perceptual and motor development in infants and children.* New York: Macmillan Publishing Co., Inc., 1970. (a)

Cratty, B. J.: *Some educational implications of movement.* Seattle: Special Child Publications, 1970. (b)

Cratty, B. J. *Intelligence in action: Physical activities for enhancing intellectual abilities.* Englewood Cliffs, N.J.: Prentice-Hall, Inc., 1973.

Cratty, B. J., and Martin, M. M. *Perceptual-motor efficiency in children: The measurement and improvement of movement attributes.* Philadelphia: Lea & Febiger, 1969.

Croft, D. *Recipes for busy little hands.* Palo Alto, Calif.: Croft, 1967.

Croft, D. *Be honest with yourself: A self-evaluation handbook for early childhood education teachers.* Belmont, Calif.: Wadsworth Publishing Co., Inc., 1976.

Cross-Cultural Family Center. *A multi-cultural curriculum for today's young children: An outgrowth of a cross-cultural nursery school.* San Francisco: The Center, 1969.

Cuffaro, H. K. Reevaluating basic premises: Curricula free of sexism. *Young Children,* 1975, *31*(6), 469-478.

Curry, N. E., and Arnaud, S. (Eds.). *Play: The child strives toward self-realization.* Washington, D.C.: NAEYC, 1971.

Dalton, M. M. A visual survey of 5,000 school children. *Journal of Educational Research,* 1943, *37,* 81-94.

Damon, W. *The social world of the child.* San Francisco: Jossey-Bass, Inc., Publishers, 1977.

Datta, L. *New directions for early childhood development programs: Some findings from research.* Urbana, Ill.: ERIC/ECE, 1973.

Davies, D. *Schools where parents make a difference.* Boston: Institute for Responsive Education, 1976.

Davis, C. M. Results of the self selection of diets by young children. *Canadian Medical Association Journal,* 1939, *4,* 257-261.

Davis, O. L., and Slobadian, J. J. Teacher behavior toward boys and girls during first grade reading instruction. *American Educational Research Journal,* 1967, *4,* 261-269.

Darvoren, E. The role of the social worker. In R. E. Helfer and C. H. Kempe, *The battered child* (2nd ed.). Chicago: University of Chicago Press, 1974.

Davoren, E. Working with abusive parents: A social worker's view. *Children Today,* 1975, *4*(3), 38-43.

Dawe, H. C. An analysis of two hundred quarrels of preschool children. *Child Development,* 1934, *5,* 139-157.

Day, M. S., and Parker, R. K. (Eds.). *The preschool in action* (2nd ed.). Boston: Allyn & Bacon, Inc., 1977.

Day Care and Child Development Council of America. *Multi-ethnic reading and audio-visual material for young children: Annotated bibliography.* Washington, D.C.: DCCDCA, 1972. Pub. no. 101.

Day Care and Child Development Council of America. *Principles of home visiting*. Washington, D.C.: DCCDCA, 1975.

DeBono, E. *The dog exercising machine*. New York: Simon & Schuster, Inc., 1970. (a)

DeBono, E. *Lateral thinking: Creativity step by step*. New York: Harper & Row, Publishers, 1970. (b)

DeFrancis, V. *Protecting the child victim of sex crimes committed by adults*. Denver: Children's Division, American Humane Association, 1969.

de Grazia, S. *Of time, work, and leisure*. New York: The Twentieth Century Fund, 1962.

DeNevi, D. The education of a genius: Analyzing major influences on the life of America's greatest architect. *Young Children*, 1968, *23*(4), 233-239.

Dennis, W. Causes of retardation among institutional children: Iran. *Journal of Genetic Psychology*, 1960, *96*, 47-59.

Desforges, J. F. Sickle cell anemia. In S. S. Gellis and B. M. Kagan (Eds.), *Current pediatric therapy* (8th ed.). Philadelphia: W. B. Saunders Co., 1978.

Despert, J. L. *The inner voices of children*. New York: Simon & Schuster, Inc., 1975.

Deutsch, M. The role of social class in language development and cognition. In E. M. Bower (Ed.), *Orthopsychiatry and education*. Detroit: Wayne State University Press, 1971.

Deutsch, M., Katz, I., and Jensen, A. R. *Social class, race, and psychological development*. New York: Holt, Rinehart and Winston, 1968.

D'Evelyn, K. E. *Individual parent-teacher conferences*. New York: Teachers College Press, Columbia University, 1963.

D'Evelyn, K. E. *Developing mentally healthy children*. Washington, D.C.: American Association of Elementary-Kindergarten-Nursery Educators, 1970.

DeVilliers, J. G., and DeVilliers, P. A. *Language acquisition*. Cambridge, Mass.: Harvard University Press, 1978.

DeWeerd, J. Introduction. In J. B. Jordan, A. H. Hayden, M. B. Karnes, and M. M. Wood. *Early childhood education for exceptional children: A handbook of ideas and exemplary practices*. Washington, D.C.: CEC, 1977.

DiLeo, J. H. *Young children and their drawings*. New York: Brunner/Mazel, Inc., 1970.

DiLorenzo, L. T., and Salter, R. An evaluative study of pre-kindergarten programs for educationally disadvantaged children: Followup and replication. *Exceptional Children*, 1968, *35*(2), 111-121.

Dimondstein, G. *Children dance in the classroom*. New York: Macmillan Publishing Co., Inc., 1971.

Dinkmeyer, D. C. *Child development: The emerging self*. Englewood Cliffs, N.J.: Prentice-Hall, Inc., 1965.

Dittman, L. L. *The infants we care for*. Washington, D.C.: NAEYC, 1973.

Duckworth, E. The having of wonderful ideas. In M. Schwebel and J. Raph (Eds.), *Piaget in the classroom*. New York: Basic Books, Inc., Publishers, 1973.

Duer, J. L., and Parke, R. D. The effects of inconsistent punishment on aggression in children. *Developmental Psychology*, 1970, *2*, 403-411.

Dunbar, T., and Kravitz, L. *Hard traveling: Migrant farm workers in America*. Cambridge, Mass.: Ballinger Publishing Co., 1976.

Dunn, L. M. (Ed.). *Exceptional children in the schools: Special education in transition* (2nd ed.). New York: Holt, Rinehart and Winston, Inc., 1973.

Dworkin, A. G. Stereotypes and self-images held by native born and foreign born Mexican-Americans. *Sociology and Social Research*, 1965, *49*, 214-224.

Ebbick, F. N. Learning through play in other cultures. *Childhood Education*, 1971, *48*, 2.

Ebel, R. L. Behavioral objectives: A close look. *Phi Delta Kappan*, November 1970, pp. 171-173.

Edmonds, M. H. New directions in theories of language acquisition. *Harvard Educational Review*, 1976, *46*(2), 175-195.

Education Commission of the States: Task Force on Early Childhood Education. *Early childhood development: Alternatives for program implementation in the states*. Denver: The Commission, 1971.

Education Commission of the States: Task Force on Early Childhood Education. *Early childhood programs for migrants: Alternatives for the states*. Denver: The Commission, 1972.

Education Commission of the States: Task Force on Early Childhood Education. *Early Childhood programs: A state survey: 1974-75*. Denver: The Commission, 1975.

Education Commission of the States. *Education for parenthood: A primary prevention strategy for child abuse and neglect*. Denver: The Commission, 1976. (a)

Education Commission of the States. *The children's needs assessment handbook*. Denver: The Commission, 1976. (b)

Education Commission of the States. *The children's political check list: Education Commission of the States, Carnegie Council on Children, and The Coalition for Children and Youth* (Report 103). Denver: The Commission, 1977. (a)

Education Commission of the States. *Teacher education—an active participant in solving the problem of child abuse and neglect*. Denver: The Commission, 1977. (b)

Educational Facilities Laboratories. *Found: Spaces and equipment for children's centers: A report from Educational Facilities Laboratories, 1972*. New York: Educational Facilities Laboratories, 1972.

El'Konin, D. B. Some results of the study of the psychological development of preschool-age children. In M. Cole and I. Maltzman (Eds.), *A handbook of contemporary Soviet psychology*. New York: Basic Books, Inc., Publishers, 1969.

Ellingson, C., and Cass, J. *Directory of facilities for the learning-disabled and handicapped*. New York: Harper & Row, Publishers, 1972.

Elliot, O., and King, J. A. *Psychological Reports*, 1960, *6*, 391.

Ellison, G. *Play structures: Questions to discuss, designs to consider, directions for construction*. Pasadena: Pacific Oaks College and Children's School, 1974.

Engel, R. C. *Language motivating experiences for young children*. Van Nuys, Calif.: DFA Publishers, 1968.

Epilepsy Foundation of America. *What everyone should know about epilepsy*. Washington, D.C.: Epilepsy Foundation of America, no date.

ERIC/ECE. *Bilingual education for children: An abstract bibliography*. Urbana, Ill.: ERIC Clearinghouse on Early Childhood Education, University of Illinois, 1975.

ERIC/ECE. *Cerebral dominance and its psychological and educational implications: An ERIC abstract bibliography*. Urbana, Ill.: ERIC/ECE, University of Illinois, 1978.

ERIC/ECE Newsletter. Children and public policy. *ERIC/ECE Newsletter*, 1977, *10*(4), 1.

Erikson, E. H. *Childhood and society*. New York, W. W. Norton & Co., Inc., 1950.

Erikson, E. H. *Young man Luther*. New York: W. W. Norton & Co., Inc., 1958.

Erikson, E. H. Identity and the life cycle. *Psychological Issues*, 1959, *1*(1, Monograph 1).

Erikson, E. H. *Childhood and society* (2nd ed.). New York: W. W. Norton & Co., Inc., 1963.

Erikson, E. H. A healthy personality for every child. In R. H. Anderson and H. G. Shane (Eds.), *As the twig is bent: Readings in early childhood education*. Boston: Houghton Mifflin Co., 1971.

Eron, L. D., Walder, L. O., and Lefkowitz, M. M. *Learning of aggression in children*. Boston: Little, Brown and Co., 1971.

Estvan, F. J. The social perception of nursery school children. *Elementary School Journal*, 1966, *66*, 7.

Estvan, F. J. Teaching the very young: Procedures for developing inquiry skills. In R. H. Anderson and H. G. Shane (Eds.), *As the twig is bent: Readings in early childhood education*. Boston: Houghton Mifflin Co., 1971.

Evans, E. *Contemporary influences in early childhood education*. New York: Holt, Rinehart and Winston, Inc., 1971.

Evans, E. K. *The beginning of life: How babies are born*. New York: Crowell-Collier Press, 1972.

Evers, W. L., and Schwarz, J. C. Modifying social withdrawal in pre-schoolers: the effects of filmed modeling and teacher praise. *Journal of Abnormal Child Psychology*, 1973, *1*, 248-256.

Fein, G., and Clarke-Stewart, A. *Daycare in context*. New York: John Wiley & Sons, Inc., 1973.

Feitelson, D., and Ross, G. The neglected factor: Play. *Human Development*, 1973, *16*, 202-223.

Feldman, B. N. *Jobs/careers serving children and youth*. Los Angeles: Till Press, 1978.

Feldman, R. Teaching self-control and self-expression via play. In S. Coopersmith, (Ed.), *Developing motivation in young children*. San Francisco: Albion Publishing Co., 1975.

Ferreira, N. J. *The mother-child cookbook*. Menlo Park, Calif.: Pacific Coast Publishers, 1967.

Feshbach, N., and Feshbach, S. Children's aggression. In W. W. Hartup (Ed.), *The young child: Reviews of research* (Vol. 2). Washington, D.C.: NAEYC, 1972.

Fishman, J. A. Bilingual education: A perspective. *IRCD Bulletin*, 1977, *12*(2), 1-11.

Flavell, J. H. *The developmental psychology of Jean Piaget*. Princeton, N.J.: D. Van Nostrand Co., 1963.

Flavell, J. H. Role-taking and communication skills in children. *Young Children*, 1966, *21*, 164-177.

Flavell, J. H. The development of inferences about others. In T. Mischell (Ed.), *Understanding other persons*. London: Blackwell, 1973.

Flavell, J. H., Botkin, P. T., Fry, C. L., Wright, J. W., and Jarvis, P. E. *The development of role-taking and communication skills in children*. New York: John Wiley & Sons, Inc., 1968.

Fleming. G. A. (Ed.). *Children's dance*. Washington, D.C.: AAHPER, 1973.

Fleming, J. W. Perceptual-motor programs. In R. N. Singer (Ed.), *The psychomotor domain: Movement behaviors*. Philadelphia: Lea & Febiger, 1972.

Forbes, J. *The education of the culturally different: A multicultural approach*. Washington, D.C.: U.S. Govt. Printing Office, 1968.

Formanek, R., and Gurian, A. *Charting intellectual development: A practical guide to Piagetian tasks*. Springfield, Ill.: Charles C Thomas, Publisher, 1976.

Forrester, F. *Preschool program, Fresno, California*. Washington, D.C.: U.S. Govt. Printing Office, 1969. OE 37034.

Foster, C. J. *Developing responsibility in children*. Chicago: Science Research Associates Inc., 1953.

Fowler, W. On the value of both play and structure in early education. *Young Children*, 1971, *27*(1), 24-36.

Fraiberg, S., with the collaboration of L. Fraiberg. *Insights from the blind*. New York: Basic Books, Inc., Publishers, 1977.

Frank, L. K. Play is valid. *Childhood Education*, 1968, *44*, 433-440.

Frank, L. K. Tactile communication. In C. B. Kopp (Ed.), *Readings in early development: For occupational and physical therapy students*. Springfield, Ill.: Charles C Thomas, Publisher, 1971.

Frank Porter Graham Child Development Center. *Perspectives: A progress report on child care*. Chapel Hill, N.C.: University of North Carolina, no date.

Frank, T., and Gordetsky, S. Child-focused mental health consultation in settings for young children. *Young Children*, 1976, *31*(5), 339-344.

Franklin, M. B., and Biber, B. Psychological perspectives and early childhood education: Some relations between theory and practice. In L. G. Katz (Ed.), *Current topics in early childhood education* (Vol. 1). Norwood, N.J.: Ablex Publishing Corp., 1977.

Freidrich, W. N., and Boriskin, J. A. The role of the child in abuse: A review of the literature. *American Journal of Orthopsychiatry*, 1976, *46*(4), 580-590.

Friedberg, M. P. *Playgrounds for city children*. Washington, D.C.: ACEI, 1969.

Fromm, E. Selfishness and self-love. *Psychiatry*, 1939, *2*, 507-523.

Frostig, M. *Movement education: Theory and practice*. Chicago: Follett Publishing Co., 1970.

Furman, E. *A child's parent dies: Studies in childhood bereavement*. New Haven: Yale University Press, 1974.

Furman, R. A. Experiences in nursery school consultations. In K. R. Baker (Ed.), *Ideas that work with young children*. Washington, D.C.: NAEYC, 1972.

Furman, R. A., and Katan, A. K. *The therapeutic nursery school*. New York: International Universities Press, 1969.

Gagné, R. Contributions of learning to human development. *Psychological Review*, 1968, *73*(3), 177-185.

Garber, H., and Heber, R. *The Milwaukee Project: Early intervention as a technique to prevent mental retardation*. Storrs, Conn.: National Leadership Institute, Teacher Education/Early Childhood, University of Connecticut, 1973.

Garvey, C. *Play* (Developing child series). Cambridge, Mass.: Harvard University Press, 1977.

Gaylin, W. *Caring*. New York: Alfred A. Knopf, Inc., 1976.

Gearheart, B. R. *Learning disabilities: Educational strategies* (2nd ed.). St. Louis: The C. V. Mosby Co., 1977.

Gearheart, B. R., and Weishahn, M. W. *The handicapped child in the regular classroom.* St. Louis: The C. V. Mosby Co., 1976.

Gelles, R. J. Child abuse as psychopathology: A sociological critique and reformulation. *American Journal of Orthopsychiatry,* 1973, *43*(4), 611-621.

Gesell, A., Halverson, H. M., Thompson, H., and Ilg, F. *The first five years of life: A guide to the study of the preschool child.* New York: Harper & Row, Publishers, 1940.

Getman, G. The visuomotor complex in the acquisition of learning skills. In J. Hellmuth (Ed.), *Learning disorders.* Seattle: Special Child Publications, 1965.

Getzels, J. W., and Jackson, P. W. *Creativity and intelligence.* New York: John Wiley & Sons, Inc., 1962.

Gil, D. A sociocultural perspective on physical child abuse. *Child Welfare,* 1971, *50,* 389-395.

Ginott, H. *Teacher and child.* New York: Macmillan Publishing Co., Inc., 1972.

Glasscote, R., and Fishman, M. E. *Mental health programs for preschool children: A field study.* Washington, D.C.: American Psychiatric Association and the National Association for Mental Health, 1974.

Glassman, L., and Erickson, D. *A selected guide to government agencies concerned with exceptional children.* Arlington, Va.: IMC/RMC Network, 1972.

Glazer, T. *Eye winker tom tinker chin chopper: Fifty musical fingerplays.* Garden City, N.Y.: Doubleday & Co., Inc., 1973.

Glockner, M., Shapira, H., and Spencer, M. Hurrah for H$_2$O. *ERIC/ECE Newsletter,* 1976, *10*(2), 1-3.

Goertzel, V., and Goertzel, M. G. *Cradles of eminence.* Boston: Little, Brown and Co., 1962.

Glueck, S., and Glueck, E. *Unraveling juvenile delinquency.* Cambridge, Mass.: Harvard University Press, 1950.

Goldberg, S., and Lewis, M. Play behavior in the year-old infant: Early sex differences. *Child Development,* 1969, *40,* 21-31.

Golden, M., Bridger, W. H., and Martare, A. Social class differences in the ability of young children to use verbal information to facilitate learning. *American Journal of Orthopsychiatry,* 1974, *44*(1), 86-91.

Gonzalez-Mena, J. English as a second language for preschool children. *Young Children,* 1976, *32*(1), 14-19.

Goodman, W. When you meet a blind person. In S. A. Kirk and F. E. Lord (Eds.), *Exceptional children: Educational resources and perspectives.* Boston: Houghton Mifflin Co., 1974.

Gordon, E. W. Compensatory education: Evaluation in perspective. *IRCD Bulletin,* 1970, *6*(5).

Gordon, I. J. *Parent involvement in compensatory education.* Urbana, Ill.: ERIC/ECE, no date.

Gordon, I. J. *Early child stimulation through parent education.* Gainesville, Fla.: Institute for Development of Human Resources, 1969. (a)

Gordon, I. J. Stimulation via parent education. *Children,* 1969, *16,* 57-59. (b)

Gordon, I. J., and associates. *Reaching the child through parent education: The Florida approach.* Jacksonville, Fla.: Institute for Development of Human Resources, 1969.

Gordon, I. J., and Breivogel, W. F. *Building effective home-school relationships.* Boston: Allyn & Bacon, Inc., 1976.

Gordon, T. *P. E. T. in action: Inside P. E. T. families: New problems, insights and solutions in Parent Effectiveness Training,* New York: Peter H. Wyden Publisher, 1976.

Gotkin, L. G. The telephone call: The direct line from teacher to family. In K. R. Baker (Ed.), *Ideas that work with young children.* Washington, D.C.: NAEYC, 1972.

Governor's Advisory Committee on Child Development Programs. *Child care licensing and regulations: A report by the Governor's Advisory Committee on Child Development Programs.* Sacramento: The Committee, 1978.

Gowan, J. C. *Development of the creative individual.* San Diego: Robert R. Knapp, Publisher, 1972.

Graham, A. *Foxtails, ferns and fish scales: A handbook of art and nature projects.* New York: Four Winds Press, 1976.

Granato, S., and Krone, E. *8: Serving children with special needs.* Washington, D.C.: U.S. Dept. of HEW, Office of Child Development, 1972.

Granger, R. C., and Young, J. C. (Eds.). *Demythologizing the inner city child.* Washington, D.C.: NAEYC, 1976.

Grant, L. *What do I need? How much will it cost?* 1971. (Available from Lou Grant, 1880 Craven's Lane, Carpinteria, Calif.)

Gray, S. W., and Klaus, R. A. The early training project and its general rationale. In R. C. Hess and R. M. Bear (Eds.), *Early education.* Chicago: Aldine Publishing Co., 1968.

Gray, S. W., and Klaus, R. A. The early training project: A seventh year report. *Child Development,* 1970, *41,* 909-924.

Grayson, M. *Let's do fingerplays.* Washington, D.C.: Robert B. Luce, Inc., 1962.

Green, E. H. Group play and quarreling among preschool children. *Child Development,* 1933, *4,* 302-307.

Greenberg, M. The male early childhood teacher: An appraisal. *Young Children,* 1977, *32,* 34-38.

Greenberg, P. *The Devil has slippery shoes: A biased biography of the Child Development Group of Mississippi.* New York: Macmillan Publishing Co., Inc., 1970.

Greenberg, P. J. Competition in children: An experimental study. *American Journal of Psychology,* 1932, *44,* 221-249.

Greenfield, P., Smith, J., and Laufer, B. Communication—the beginnings of language (unpublished working draft), Harvard University, 1972. Cited in M. Edmonds, New directions in theories of language acquisition. *Harvard Educational Review,* 1976, *46*(2), 175-197.

Greif, E. B. Peer interactions in preschool children. In R. A. Webb (Ed.), *Social development in childhood: Day-care programs and research.* Baltimore: The Johns Hopkins University Press, 1977.

Griffin, L. *Multi-ethnic books for young children: Annotated bibliography for parents and teachers.* Washington, D.C.: NAEYC, no date.

Grinspoon, L., and Singer, S. L. Amphetamines in the treatment of hyperkinetic children. *Harvard Educational Review,* 1973, *43*(4), 515-555.

Grollman, E. A. *Explaining death to children.* Boston: Beacon Press, 1967.

Grollman, E. A. (Ed.). *Explaining divorce to children.* Boston: Beacon Press, 1969.

Gross, B., and Gross, R. *The children's rights movement: Overcoming the oppression of young people.* Garden City, N.Y.: Doubleday & Co., Inc., 1977.

Grost, A. *Genius in residence.* Englewood Cliffs, N.J.: Prentice-Hall, Inc., 1970.

Grotberg, E., Chapman, J. E., and Lazar, J. B. *A review of the present status and future needs in day care research.* Washington, D.C.: Education Resources Division, Capitol Publications, 1971.

Gruber, H. E., and Vonèche, J. J. (Eds.). *The essential Piaget.* London: Routledge and Kegan Paul, Ltd., 1977.

Gruenberg, S. M. *The wonderful story of how you were born.* Garden City, N.Y.: Doubleday & Co., Inc., 1970.

Guilford, J. P. A system of psychomotor abilities. *American Journal of Psychology,* 1958, *71,* 146-147.

Guilford, J. P. *The nature of human intelligence.* New York: McGraw-Hill Book Co., 1967.

Guilford, J. P., and Hoepfner, R. *The analysis of intelligence.* New York: McGraw-Hill Book Co., 1971.

Guinagh, B. J., and Gordon, I. J. *School performance as a function of early stimulation* (Final report). Gainesville, Fla.: Institute for Development of Human Resources, University of Florida, 1976. Grant no. NIH-HEW-OCD-90-C-638.

Gussow, J. D. Bodies, brains and poverty: Poor children and the schools. *ERIC/IRCD Bulletin,* 1970, *6*(3), 1-20.

Guttridge, M. V. A study of motor achievements of young children. *Archives of Psychology,* 1939, *244,* 1-178.

Hagman, E. P. The companionships of preschool children. *University of Iowa Studies of Child Welfare,* 1933, *7*(4).

Haller, J. A. Preparing a child for his operation. In J. A. Haller (Ed.), *The hospitalized child and his family.* Baltimore: The Johns Hopkins University Press, 1967.

Haller, J. A. (Ed.), Talbert, J. L., and Dombro, R. H. (Asst. Eds.). *The hospitalized child and his family.* Baltimore: The Johns Hopkins University Press, 1967.

Halliday, C. *The visually impaired child: Growth, learning and development: Infancy to school age.* Louisville, Ky.: American Printing House for the Blind, 1971.

Halliday, M. A. K. Learning how to mean. In E. H. Lenneberg and E. Lenneberg (Eds.), *Foundations of language development: A multidisciplinary approach* (Vol. 1). New York: Academic Press, Inc., 1975.

Halperin, M. *Helping maltreated children: School and community resources.* St. Louis: The C. V. Mosby Co., 1979.

Hamilton, M. L., and Stewart, D. M. Peer models and language acquisition. *Merrill-Palmer Quarterly,* 1977, *23*(1), 45-55.

Harlan, J. D. *Science experiences for the early childhood years.* Columbus, Ohio: Charles E. Merrill Publishing Co., 1976.

Harley, R. K. Children with visual disabilities. In L. M. Dunn (Ed.), *Exceptional children in the schools: Special education in transition* (2nd ed.). New York: Holt, Rinehart and Winston, Inc., 1973.

Hartley, R. E. Play, the essential ingredient. *Childhood Education,* November 1971, as quoted in P. M. Markun, Play: Children's business: And a guide to play materials. Washington, D.C.: ACEI, 1974.

Hartley, R. E., Frank, L. K., and Goldenson, R. M. *Understanding children's play.* New York: Columbia University Press, 1952.

Hartup, W. W. Peer relationships: Developmental implications and interaction in same- and mixed-age situations. *Young Children,* 1977, *32*(3), 4-13.

Hartup, W. W., and Coates, B. Imitation of a peer as a function of reinforcement from the peer group and rewardingness of the model. *Child Development,* 1967, *38,* 1003-1016.

Hawkridge, D., Chalupsky, A., and Roberts, A. *A study of selected exemplary programs for the education of disadvantaged children.* Palo Alto, Calif.: American Institutes for Research in the Behavioral Sciences, 1968.

Hayden, A. H., and Edgar, E. B. Identification, screening and assessment. In J. B. Jordan, A. H. Hayden, M. B. Karnes, and M. M. Wood, (Eds.). *Early childhood education for exceptional children.* Reston, Va.: CEC. 1977.

Head Start Bureau. *Nutrition education for young children.* Washington, D.C.: HSB, ACYF, OCD, U.S. Dept. of HEW, 1976. OHDS 76-31015.

Heber, R. Modification in the manual on terminology and classification in mental retardation. *American Journal of Mental Deficiency,* 1961, *46,* 499-501.

Heber, R., Garber, H., Harrington, S., Hoffman, C., and Falender, C. *Rehabilitation of families at risk for mental retardation—progress report.* Madison, Wis.: Rehabilitation Research and Training Center in Mental Retardation, University of Wisconsin, 1972.

Hegeler, S. *Peter and Caroline: A child asks about childbirth and sex.* New York: Abelard-Schuman Ltd., 1957. (Translated from the Danish.)

Heinicke, C., and Westheimer, I. J. *Brief separations.* New York: International Universities Press, 1965.

Helfer, R. E., and Kempe, C. H. *The battered child* (2nd ed.). Chicago: University of Chicago Press, 1974.

Hellmuth, J. (Ed.). *Disadvantaged child: Head Start and early intervention* (Vol. 2). New York: Brunner/Mazel, Inc., 1968.

Hellmuth, J. (Ed.). *Disadvantaged child: Compensatory education, a national debate* (Vol. 3). New York: Brunner/Mazel, Inc., 1970.

Henderson, R. W., and Bergan, J. R. *The cultural context of childhood.* Columbus, Ohio: Charles E. Merrill Publishing Co., 1976.

Hendrick, J. B. Aggression: What to do about it. *Young Children,* 1968, *23*(5), 298-305.

Hendrick, J. B. What mothers need. *Young Children,* 1970, *25,* 109-114.

Hendrick, J. B. *The cognitive development of the economically disadvantaged Mexican-American and Anglo-American four-year-old: Teaching the concepts of grouping, ordering, perceiving common connections, and matching by means of semantic and figural materials.* Doctoral dissertation, University of California at Santa Barbara, 1973.

Hendrick, J. B. *An analysis and summary of a survey of child care needs and child care services available on California community college campuses as of March, 1974.* Santa Barbara: Santa Barbara City College, 1974.

Hendrick, J. B. *Total learning for the whole child: Holistic curriculum for children ages 2 to 5.* St. Louis: The C. V. Mosby Co. 1980.

Hendricks, G., and Wills, R. *The centering book: Awareness activities for children, parents and teachers.* Englewood Cliffs, N.J.: Prentice-Hall, Inc., 1975.

Herron, R. E., and Sutton-Smith, B. *Child's play.* New York: John Wiley & Sons, Inc., 1971.

Herzog, E., and Sudia, C. E. Children in fatherless homes. In B. E. Caldwell and H. N. Ricciuti (Eds.), *Review of child development research* (Vol. 3). Chicago: University of Chicago Press, 1973.

Hess, E. H. As quoted in L. Uhr and J. G. Miller (Eds.), *Drugs and behavior.* New York: John Wiley & Sons, Inc., 1960.

Hetherington, E. M., and Deur, J. L. The effects of father-absence on child development. *Young Children,* March 1971, 233-248.

Hetherington, E. M., and McIntyre, C. W. Developmental psychology. *Annual Review of Psychology,* 1975, *26,* 97-136.

Hewes, J. J. *Build your own playground: A sourcebook of play sculptures, designs and concepts from the work of Jay Beckwith.* Boston: Houghton Mifflin Co., 1974.

Hildebrand, V. *Introduction to early childhood education* (2nd ed.). New York: Macmillan Publishing Co., Inc., 1976.

Hilgard, E. R., and Bower, G. H. *Theories of learning* (3rd ed.). New York: Appleton-Century-Crofts, 1966.

Hill, C. A. A review of the language deficit position: Some sociolinguistic and psycholinguistic perspectives. *IRCD Bulletin,* 1977, *12*(4), 1-15.

Hill, D. M. *Mud, sand and water.* Washington, D.C.: NAEYC, 1977.

Hill, R. B. *The strengths of black families.* New York: Emerson Hall Publishers, Inc., 1971.

Hintz, J. *Seven families: A 2 year in-depth study of incomes and job experiences of 7 Ohio migrant farm worker families: 1974-76.* Tiffin, Ohio: Heidelberg College, 1976.

Hirsch, E. S. *Transition periods: Stumbling blocks of education.* New York: Early Childhood Education Council of New York City, 1972.

Hirsch, E. S. (Ed.). *The block book.* Washington, D.C.: NAEYC, 1974.

Hirshen, S., and Ouye, J. *The infant care center: A case study in design.* 2150 Dwight Way, Berkeley, Calif.: Sanford Hirshen and Partners, Architects, 1973.

Hodgden, L., Koetter, J., LaForse, B., McCord, S., and Schramm, D. *School before six: A diagnostic approach* (Vols. 1 and 2). St. Louis: Central Midwestern Regional Educational Laboratory, 1974.

Hodges, B. W. *How babies are born: The story of birth for children.* New York: Essandess Special Editions, 1967.

Hodges, W. L. The worth of the Follow Through experience. *Harvard Educational Review,* 1978, *48*(2), 186-192.

Hodges, W. L., McCandless, B. R., Spicker, H. H., and Craig, I. S. *Diagnostic teaching for preschool children.* Arlington, Va.: CEC, 1971.

Hoffman, M. L. Moral development. In P. H. Mussen (Ed.), *Carmichael's manual of child psychology* (Vol. 2) (3rd ed.). New York: John Wiley & Sons, Inc., 1970.

Hogan, P. *Playgrounds for free: The utilization of used and surplus materials in playground construction.* Cambridge, Mass.: The MIT Press, 1974.

Holling, H. C. *Paddle to the sea.* Boston: Houghton Mifflin Co., no date.

Holmes, M., and Kagle, A. Bowen Center, Chicago, Illinois. In National Institute of Mental Health, *Child abuse and neglect programs: Practice and theory.* Rockville, Md.: U.S. Dept. of HEW, NIMH, 1977. ADM 77-344.

Holt, B.-G., *Science with young children.* Washington, D.C.: NAEYC, 1977.

Holt, J. *How children fail.* New York: Dell Publishing Co., Inc., 1964.

Honig, A. S. *Infant development problems in intervention.* Washington, D.C.: DCCDCA, no date.

Hoppe, R. A., Milton, G. A., and Simmel, E. C. *Early experiences and the process of socialization.* New York: Academic Press, Inc., 1970.

Horowitz, F. D. Social reinforcement effect on child behavior. In W. W. Hartup and N. L. Smothergill (Eds.), *The young child: Reviews of research* (Vol. 1). Washington, D.C.: NAEYC, 1967.

Horowitz, F. D., and Paden, L. Y. The effectiveness of environmental intervention programs. In B. M. Caldwell and H. N. Ricciuti (Eds.), *Review of child development research* (Vol. 3). Chicago: University of Chicago Press, 1973.

House, E. R., Glass, G. V., McLean, L. D., and Walker, D. F. No simple answer: Critique of the Follow Through evaluation. *Harvard Educational Review,* 1978, *48*(2), 128-160.

Hovey, E. *Ethnicity and early education.* Urbana, Ill.: ERIC/ECE, University of Illinois, 1975.

Howard, N. K. *Sex differences and sex role development in young children: An abstract bibliography.* Urbana, Ill.: College of Education, University of Illinois, 1975.

Howe, P. S. *Basic nutrition in health and disease* (5th ed.). Philadelphia: W. B. Saunders Co., 1971.

Hughes, M. M., and Sanchez, G. I. *Learning a new language.* Washington, D.C.: ACEI, 1957.

Hunt, J. McV. *Intelligence and experience.* New York: Ronald Press, 1961.

Hunter, I. I., and Judson, M. *Simple folk instruments to make and play.* New York: Simon & Schuster, Inc., 1977.

Hunter, M., Schucman, H., and Friedlander, G. *The retarded child from birth to five: A multidisciplinary program for child and family.* New York: The John Day Co., Inc., 1972.

Huston-Stein, A., Freidrich-Cofer, L., and Susman, E. J. The relation of classroom structure to social behavior, imaginative play and self-regulation of economically disadvantaged children. *Child Development,* 1977, *48,* 908-916.

Hutt, C. Sex differences in human development. In P. B. Neubauer (Ed.), *The process of child development.* New York: Jason Aronson, Inc., 1976.

Hymes, J. L. *Teaching the child under six* (2nd ed.). Columbus, Ohio: Charles E. Merrill Publishing Co., 1974.

Hymes, J. L. *Early childhood education: An introduction to the profession* (2nd ed.). Washington, D.C.: NAEYC, 1975.

Hymes, J. L., Jr. *Early childhood education: The year in review. A look at 1976. A look at 1977.* Carmel, Calif.: Hacienda Press, 1977 and 1978.

Ingalls, A. J., and Salerno, M. C. *Maternal and child health nursing* (4th ed.). St. Louis: The C. V. Mosby Co., 1979.

Inhelder, B. *Recent trends in Genevan research.* Paper presented at Temple University, Philadelphia, Fall, 1968.

Inui, L., and Odo, F. *Asian American experience: Syllabus reader.* Long Beach, Calif.: Asian Studies Dept., California State University at Long Beach, 1974.

Ireland, R. R. The care and education of preschool non-whites in the Republic of South Africa. In B. C. Mills (Ed.), *Understanding the young child and his curriculum*. New York: Macmillan Publishing Co., Inc., 1972.

Irwin, D. M., and Moore, S. G. The young child's understanding of social justice. *Developmental Psychology, 1971, 5*(3), 406-410.

Irwin, O. C. Infant speech: Effect of systematic reading of stories. *Journal of Speech and Hearing Research, 1960, 3*, 187-190.

Jackson, N. W., Robinson, H. B., and Dale, P. S. *Cognitive development in young children*. Washington, D.C.: National Institute of Education, U.S. Dept. of HEW, 1976.

Jackson, P. W., and Wolfson, B. J. Varieties of constraint in a nursery school. *Young Children, 1968, 23*(6), 358-368.

Jacobson, E. *Progressive relaxation*. Chicago: University of Chicago Press, 1938.

Jacobson, E. *You must relax* (5th ed.). New York: McGraw-Hill Book Co., 1976.

Jencks, C. *Inequality: A reassessment of the effect of family and schooling in America*. New York: Basic Books, Inc., Publishers, 1972.

Jersild, A. *When teachers face themselves*. New York: Teacher's College Press, Columbia University, 1955.

John, V. P., and Horner, V. M. *Early childhood bilingual education*. New York: Modern Language Association of America, 1971.

Johnson, H. M. *The art of block building*. New York: Bank Street College of Education, 1933.

Johnson, V. M., and Werner, R. A. *A step-by-step learning guide for retarded infants and children*. Syracuse: Syracuse University Press, 1975.

Joint Commission on Mental Health of Children. *Crisis in child mental health: Challenge for the 1970's*. New York: Harper & Row, Publishers, 1970.

Joint Commission on the Mental Health of Children. *Mental health: From infancy through adolescence: Reports of Task Forces I, II and III and the Committees on Education and Religion*. New York: Harper & Row, Publishers, 1973.

Jones, M. Physical facilities and environments. In J. B. Jordan, A. H. Hayden, M. B. Karnes, and M. M. Wood (Eds.), *Early childhood education for exceptional children*. Reston, Va.: CEC, 1977.

Jones, P. Viewpoint: Coalitions: Is the price right? *Young Children, 1978, 33*(2), 11-12.

Jordan, J. B. OCD urges special education's support for new Head Start services to handicapped children. *Exceptional Children, 1973, 40*, 1.

Jordan, J. B., and Darley, R. F. *Not all little red wagons are red: The exceptional child's early years*. Reston, Va.: CEC, 1973.

Jordan, J. B., Hayden, A. H., Karnes, M. B., and Wood, M. M. (Eds.), *Early childhood education for exceptional children*. Reston, Va.: CEC, 1977.

Kagan, J., Kearsley, R. B., and Zelazo, P. R. The effects of infant day care on psychological development. *Evaluation Quarterly, 1977, 1*(1), 109-142.

Kagan, J., and Klein, R. E. *Cross-cultural perspectives on early development*. Paper presented to the American Association for Advancement of Science, Washington, D.C., 1972.

Kagan, J., Klein, R. E., Haith, M. M., and Morrison, F. J. Memory and meaning in two cultures. *Child Development, 1973, 44*(1), 221-223.

Kahn, A. J., Kamerman, S. B., and McGowan, B. G. *Child advocacy: Report of a national baseline study*. Washington, D.C.: U.S. Dept. of HEW, OCD, Children's Bureau, 1973.

Kamii, C. A sketch of the Piaget-derived preschool curriculum developed by the Ypsilanti Early Education Program. In S. J. Braun and E. P. Edwards, *History and theory of early childhood education*. Worthington, Ohio: Charles A. Jones Publishing Co., 1972.

Kamii, C. Pedagogical principles derived from Piaget's theory: Relevance for educational practice. In M. Schwebel and J. J. Raph (Eds.), *Piaget in the classroom*. New York: Basic Books, Inc., Publishers, 1973.

Kamii, C. One intelligence indivisible. *Young Children, 1975, 30*(4), 228-238.

Kamii, C. Getting it together from my point of view. Keynote address presented at the California Association for the Education of Young Children Conference, Sacramento, March 1976.

Kamii, C., and DeVries, R. *Piaget, children and number*. Washington, D.C.: NAEYC, 1976.

Kanner, L. Early infantile autism. *Journal of Pediatrics, 1944, 25*, 211-217.

Karnes, M. B. *Helping young children develop language skills* (2nd ed.). Reston, Va.: CEC, 1973. (a)

Karnes, M. B. Evaluation and implications of research with young handicapped and low-income children. In J. C. Stanley (Ed.), *Compensatory education for children, ages 2 to 8*. Baltimore: The Johns Hopkins University Press, 1973. (b)

Karnes, M. B., and Strong, P. S. *Nurturing creative talent in early childhood*. Urbana, Ill.: Publications Office, Institute of Child Behavior and Development, 1978. (a)

Karnes, M. B., and Strong, P. S. *Nurturing leadership talent in early childhood*. Urbana, Ill.: Publications Office, Institute of Child Behavior and Development, 1978. (b)

Karnes, M. B., Teska, J. A., and Hodgins, A. S. The effects of four programs of classroom intervention on the intellectual and language development of four-year-old disadvantaged children. *American Journal of Orthopsychiatry, 1970, 40*(1), 58-76.

Kastenbaum, R. The child's understanding of death: How does it develop? In E. A. Grollman (Ed.), *Explaining death to children*. Boston: Beacon Press, 1967.

Katz, L. G. Children and teachers in two types of Head Start classes. *Young Children, 1969, 24*(6), 342-349.

Katz, L. G. Condition with caution. *Young Children, 1972, 27*(5).

Katz, L. G. Closing address. California Association for the Education of Young Children, San Diego, March 1974.

Katz, L. G. *Ethical issues in working with young children*. Urbana, Ill.: ERIC/ECE, University of Illinois, 1977.

Katz, L. G. Needed: A code of ethics for teachers and caregivers. *Bulletin of the Northern California Association for the Education of Young Children, 1978, 11*(3) 7. (a)

Katz, L. G., and Ward, E. H. *Ethical behavior in early childhood education*. Washington, D.C.: NAEYC, 1978. (b)

Katz, S. *The youngest minority: Lawyers in defense of children*. Chicago: American Bar Association, 1974.

Keats, E. J. *Whistle for Willie*. New York, The Viking Press, Inc., 1964.

Keister, M. E. *A demonstration project: Group care of infants and toddlers* (Final Report submitted to the Children's Bureau). Greensboro, N.C.: University of North Carolina, 1970.

Kellogg, R. *Analyzing children's art.* Palo Alto, Calif.: National Press Books, 1969.

Kelly, J. B., and Wallerstein, J. S. Brief interactions with children of divorcing families. *American Journal of Orthopsychiatry, 47*(1), 23-39.

Kempe, C. H. The battered child syndrome. *Journal of the American Medical Association,* 1962, *181*(17), 17-24.

Kempe, C. H., and Helfer, R. E. *Helping the battered child and his family.* Philadelphia: J. B. Lippincott Co., 1972.

Kent, J. Toward a workable definition of mental injury. *Proceedings of the First National Conference on Child Abuse and Neglect.* Washington, D.C.: U.S. Dept. of HEW, 1977. OHD 77-30094.

Kephart, N. C. *The slow learner in the classroom.* Columbus, Ohio: Charles E. Merrill Publishing Co., 1960.

Kessen, W. *The child.* New York: John Wiley & Sons, Inc., 1965.

Kessler, J. W. *Psychopathology of childhood.* Englewood Cliffs, N.J.: Prentice-Hall, Inc., 1966.

Kessler, J. W., Gridth, A., and Smith, E. *Separation reactions in young mildly retarded children.* Paper presented at the Annual Convention of the American Orthopsychiatric Association, Boston, 1968.

Keyserling, M. D. The magnitude of day care needed. In S. V. Allen, M. W. Edelman, O. Hansen, and others, *Perspectives on child care.* Washington, D.C.: NAEYC, 1972.

Kirchner, E. P., and Vondracek, S. I. *What do you want to be when you grow up? Vocational choice in children aged three to six.* Paper presented at the Society for Research in Child Development, Philadelphia, March 1973.

Kirk, S. A. *Educating exceptional children* (2nd ed.). Boston: Houghton Mifflin Co., 1972.

Kirk, S. A., Karnes, M. B., and Kirk, W. D. *You and your retarded child: A manual for parents of retarded children* (2nd ed.). Palo Alto, Calif.: Pacific Books, Publishers, 1968.

Kirkhart, R., and Kirkhart, E. The bruised self: Mending in the early years. In K. Yamamoto, *The child and his image: Self-concept in the early years.* Boston: Houghton Mifflin Co., 1972.

Klein, J. Planned variation in Head Start programs. *Children,* 1971, *18*(1), 8-12.

Klein, J. W. Mainstreaming the preschooler. *Young Children,* 1975, *30*(5), 317-326.

Kliman, G. *Psychological emergencies of childhood.* New York: Grune & Stratton, Inc., 1968.

Kliman, G. W. Analyst in the nursery: Experimental application of child analytic techniques in a therapeutic nursery: The Cornerstone Method. In *The psychoanalytic study of the child* (Vol. 30). New Haven: Yale University Press, 1975.

Kline, D. F. *Child abuse and neglect: A primer for school personnel.* Reston, Va.: CEC, 1977.

Knitzer, J. Parental involvement: The elixir of change. In D. N. McFadden, *Planning for action.* Washington, D.C.: NAEYC, 1972.

Kohlberg, L. Stage and sequence: The cognitive-developmental approach to socialization. In D. A. Goslin (Ed.), *Handbook of socialization and research.* Chicago: Rand McNally & Co., 1969.

Kohlberg, L. The development of children's orientations toward a moral order: Sequence in the development of moral thought. In P. B. Neubauer (Ed.), *The process of child development.* New York: Jason Aronson, Inc., 1976.

Kohlberg, L., and Turiel, E. Moral development and moral education. In G. L. Lesser (Ed.), *Psychology and educational practice.* Glenview, Ill.: Scott, Foresman and Co., 1971.

Koocher, G. P. Talking with children about death. *American Journal of Orthopsychiatry,* 1974, *44*(3), 404-411.

Korner, A. Sex differences in newborns. In E. K. Oremland and J. D. Oremland, *The sexual and gender development of young children: The role of the educator.* Cambridge, Mass.: Ballinger Publishing Co., 1977.

Kraft, I., Fuschillo, J., and Herzog, E. *Prelude to school: An evaluation of an inner-city preschool program.* Washington, D.C.: U.S. Govt. Printing Office, 1968.

Kramer, R. B. *Changes in moral judgment response pattern during late adolescence and young adulthood.* Unpublished doctoral dissertation, University of Chicago, 1968.

Krasner, W. *Children's play and social speech: An NIMH program report.* Rockville, Md.: Public Health Service, National Institute of Mental Health, Alcohol, Drug Abuse and Mental Health Administration, 1975. Stock no. 017-024-00593-2.

Krebs, D., and Rosenwald, A. Moral reasoning and moral behavior in conventional adults. *Merrill-Palmer Quarterly,* 1977, *23*(2), 77-87.

Kritchevsky, S., Prescott, E., and Walling, L. *Physical space: Planning environments for young children.* Washington, D.C.: NAEYC, 1969.

Kübler-Ross, E. *On death and dying.* New York: Macmillan Publishing Co., Inc., 1969.

Laban, R. *The mastery of movement* (2nd ed.). London: Macdonald & Evans, Ltd., 1960.

L'Abate, L., and Curtis, L. T. *Teaching the exceptional child.* Philadelphia: W. B. Saunders Co., 1975.

Labov, W. The logic of nonstandard English. In F. Williams (Ed.), *Language and poverty.* Chicago: Markham Publishing Co., 1970.

LaCrosse, E. R., Lee, P. C., Litman, F., Olgilvie, D. M., Stodlosky, S. S., and White, B. L. The first six years of life: A report on current research and educational practice. *Genetic Psychology Monographs,* 1970, *82,* 161-266.

LaFontaine, H., Persky, B., and Golubchick, L. H. *Bilingual education.* Wayne, N.J.: Avery Publishing Group Inc., 1978.

Lally, J. R., and Honig, A. S. The family development research program. In M. Day and R. Parker (Eds.), *The preschool in action* (2nd ed.). New York: Allyn and Bacon, 1977.

Landek, B. *Songs to grow on: A collection of American folksongs for children.* New York: William Sloane Associates, 1950.

Lambert, W. E., and Klineberg, O. The development of children's views of foreign peoples. In M. D. Cohen (Ed.), *Learning to live as neighbors.* Washington, D.C.: ACEI, 1972.

Landis, J. T. The trauma of children when parents divorce. *Marriage and Family Living,* 1960, *22.*

Landreth, C., and Johnson, B. C. Young children's responses to a picture inset test designed to reveal reactions to persons of different skin color. *Child Development,* 1953, *24,* 63-80.

Lane, M., Elzey, F. F., and Lewis, M. *Nurseries in cross-cultural education: Final report.* Washington, D.C.: National Institutes of Mental Health, 1971.

Latimer, B. I. (Ed.). *Starting out right: Choosing books about black people for young children, pre-school through third grade.* Wisconsin Department of Public Instruction, 1972. Reprinted Washington, D.C.: DCCDCA, 1972.

Lavatelli, C. S. *Early childhood curriculum: A Piaget program.* Boston: American Science and Engineering, 1970. (a)

Lavatelli, C. S. *Piaget's theory applied to an early childhood curriculum.* Boston: American Science and Engineering, Inc., 1970. (b)

Lazar, J. B., and Chapman, J. E. *A review of the present status and research needs of programs to develop parenting skills.* OCD Grant no. CB-107, April, 1972.

Lazar, I., Hubbell, V. R., Murray, H., Rosche, M., and Royce, J. *Summary report: The persistence of preschool effects: A long-term follow-up of fourteen infant and preschool experiments.* Washington, D.C.: ACYF, OHDS, HEW, 1977. OHDS 78-30129.

Leavitt, T. J. Sickle cell disease. In E. E. Bleck and D. A. Nagel (Eds.), *Physically handicapped children—a medical atlas for teachers.* New York: Grune & Stratton, Inc., 1975.

Lee, P. C., and Gropper, N. B. Sex role, culture and educational practice. *Harvard Educational Review,* 1974, *44,* 369-410.

Lee, P. C., and Wolinsky, A. L. Male teachers of young children: A preliminary study. *Young Children,* 1973, *28*(6), 342-352.

Lee, P. R., Ornstein, R. E., Galin, D., Deikman, A., and Tart, C. T. *Symposium on consciousness.* Presented at the annual meeting of the American Association for the Advancement of Science, February 1974. New York: The Viking Press, Inc., 1976.

Leifer, A. D., and Lesser, G. S. *The development of career awareness in young children: NIE papers on education and work* (No. 1). Washington, D.C.: U.S. Dept. of HEW, National Institute of Education, 1976.

Lenski, L. *The little fire engine.* New York: Henry Z. Walck, Inc., 1946.

Lenski, L. *Cowboy Small.* New York: Henry Z. Walck, Inc., 1967.

Leonhard, B. Keynote address. Paper presented at the TAEYC Workshop, Santa Barbara, Calif., September 1963.

Levenstein, P. *Verbal interaction project: Aiding cognitive growth in disadvantaged preschoolers through the mother-child home program.* Washington, D.C.: Children's Bureau, U.S. Dept. of HEW, 1971.

Lewis, M., and Rosenblum, L. A. *The effect of the infant on its caretaker.* New York: John Wiley & Sons, Inc., 1974.

Lewis, M. M. *Language, thought and personality.* New York: Basic Books Inc., Publishers, 1963.

Lichtenberg, P., and Norton, D. G. *Cognitive and mental development in the first five years of life: A review of recent research.* Rockville, Md.: National Institutes of Mental Health, 1970.

Lieberman, J. N. Playfulness and divergent thinking ability: An investigation of their relationship at the kindergarten level. In M. Almy (Ed.), *Early childhood play: Selected readings related to cognition and motivation.* New York: Simon & Schuster, Inc., 1968.

Lindsay, Z. *Art and the handicapped child.* New York: Van Nostrand Reinhold Co., 1972.

Lin-Fu, J. *Sickle cell anemia: A medical review.* Rockville, Md.: U.S. Dept. of HEW, Public Health Service, 1972. Reprinted in 1978. HSA 78-5123.

Loehlin, J. C., Lindsey, G., and Spuhler, J. N. *Race differences in intelligence.* San Francisco: W. H. Freeman and Co. Publishers, 1975.

Lombard, A., and Stern, C. Effect of verbalization on young children's learning of a manipulative skill. *Young Children,* 1970, *25*(5), 282-288.

Looff, D. H. *Appalachia's children: The challenge of mental health.* Lexington, Ky.: University Press of Kentucky, 1971.

Lorenz, K. *On aggression.* Translated by M. K. Wilson. New York: Harcourt Brace Jovanovich, Inc., 1966.

Lowenfeld, B. *The visually handicapped child in school.* New York: The John Day Co., Inc., 1973.

Lystad, M. H. *Social aspects of alienation: An annotated bibliography.* Chevy Chase, Md.: National Institutes of Mental Health, 1969.

Maccoby, E. E. (Ed.). *The development of sex differences.* Stanford: Stanford University Press, 1966.

Maccoby, E. E., and Jacklin, C. N. *The psychology of sex differences.* Stanford: Stanford University Press, 1974.

Maccoby, E. E., and Zellner, M. *Experiments in primary education: Aspects of Project Follow-Through.* New York: Harcourt Brace Jovanovitch, Inc. 1970.

Macfarlane, J. W. Study of personality development. In R. G. Barker, J. S. Kounin, and H. F. Wright (Eds.), *Child behavior and development.* New York: McGraw-Hill Book Co., 1943.

Mackey, W. F., and Andersson, T. (Eds.). *Bilingualism in early childhood.* Rowley, Mass.: Newbury House, Publishers, 1977.

Macnamara, J. *Bilingualism in primary education: A study of Irish experience.* Edinburgh: Edinburgh University Press, 1966.

Mann, A. J. *A review of Head Start research since 1969 and an annotated bibliography.* Washington, D.C.: ACYF, OHDS, U.S. Dept. of HEW, 1977. OHDS 77-31102.

Margolin, E. Conservation of self expression and aesthetic sensitivity in young children. *Young Children,* 1968, *23,* 155-160.

Margolin, E. *Sociocultural elements in early childhood education.* New York: Macmillan Publishing Co., Inc., 1974.

Markun, P. M. *Parenting.* Washington, D.C.: ACEI, 1973.

Marland, S. P. (Submitter). *Education of the gifted and talented.* Washington, D.C.: U.S. Office of Education, 1972.

Martin, H. P. *The abused child: A multidisciplinary approach to developmental issues and treatment.* Cambridge, Mass.: Ballinger Publishing Co., 1976.

Martinson, R. A. *Educational programs for gifted pupils.* Sacramento: California State Department of Education, 1961.

Martinson, R. A. Children with superior cognitive abilities. In

L. M. Dunn (Ed.), *Exceptional children in the schools: Special education in transition*. New York: Holt, Rinehart and Winston, Inc., 1973.

Martorella, P. H. Selected early childhood affective learning programs: An analysis of theories, structure and consistency. *Young Children,* 1975, *30*(4), 289-301.

Marzollo, J., and Lloyd, J. *Learning through play*. New York: Harper & Row, Publishers, 1972.

Maslow, A. *Eupsychian management*. Homewood, Ill.: Dorsey Press, 1965.

Matterson, E. M. *Play and playthings for the preschool child*. Baltimore: Penguin Books, Inc., 1965.

Maudry, M., and Nekula, M. Social relations between children of the same age during the first 2 years of life. *Journal of Genetic Psychology,* 1939, *54,* 193-215.

May, R. *The courage to create*. New York: W. W. Norton & Co., Inc., 1975.

Maynard, F. *Guiding your child to a more creative life*. Garden City, N.Y.: Doubleday & Co., Inc., 1973.

McAfee, O., Haines, E. W., and Young, B. B. *Cooking and eating with children: A way to learn*. Washington, D.C.: ACEI, 1974.

McCandless, B. R., and Evans, E. D. *Children and youth: Psychosocial development*. Hinsdale, Ill.: Dryden Press, 1973.

McCarthy, D. Language development in children. In L. Carmichael (Ed.), *Manual of child psychology* (2nd ed.). New York: John Wiley & Sons, Inc., 1954.

McCord, W., McCord, J., and Howard, A. Familial correlates of aggression in non-delinquent male children. *Journal of Abnormal Social Psychology,* 1961, *62,* 79-93.

McCurdy, H. G. (Ed.). *Barbara: The unconscious autobiography of a child genius*. Chapel Hill, N.C.: The University of North Carolina Press, 1966.

McCurdy, J. Research puts new emphasis on teen-age education. *Los Angeles Times,* February 17 1974, Part 2, pp. 1; 6.

McDermott, J. F., and Harrison, S. I. (Eds.). *Psychiatric treatment of the child*. New York: Jason Aronson, Inc., 1977.

McGraw, M. B. Later development of children specially trained during infancy: Johnny and Jimmy at school age. In R. N. Singer (Ed.), *Readings in motor learning*. Philadelphia; Lea & Febiger, 1972.

McNeill, E., Allen, J., and Schmidt, V. *Cultural awareness for young children at the Learning Tree*. Dallas: The Learning Tree, 1975.

Meeker, M. N. *The Structure of Intellect: Its interpretation and uses*. Columbus, Ohio: Charles E. Merrill Publishing Co., 1969.

Meeker, M. N., Sexton, K., and Richardson, M. O. *SOI abilities workbook*. Los Angeles: Loyola-Marymount University, 1970.

Menninger Clinic Children's Division. *Disturbed children*. San Francisco: Jossey-Bass, Inc., Publishers, 1969.

Menyuk, P. Syntactic structures in the language of children. *Child Development,* 1963, *34,* 407-422.

Merrill, M. D. Psychomotor taxonomies, classifications and instructional theory. In R. N. Singer (Ed.), *The psychomotor domain: Movement behaviors*. Philadelphia: Lea & Febiger, 1972.

Meyer Children's Rehabilitation Institute. *Meyer Children's Rehabilitation Institute teaching program for young children:* *Handicapped children in Head Start series*. Reston, Va.: CEC, 1974.

Michal-Smith, H. *The exceptional child in the normal nursery*. New York: Early Childhood Education Council of New York, 1966.

Midlarsky, E., and Bryan, J. H. Training charity in children. *Journal of Personality and Social Psychology,* 1967, *5,* 405-415.

Miel, A., and Kiester, E. *The shortchanged children of suburbia*. New York: Institute of Human Relations Press, The American Jewish Committee, 1967.

Millar, S. *The psychology of play*. Baltimore: Penguin Books Inc., 1968.

Miller, B. L., and Wilmshurst, A. L. *Parents and volunteers in the classroom: A handbook for teachers*. San Francisco: R and E Research Associates, 1975.

Miller, L. B., and Dyer, J. L. Four preschool programs: Their dimensions and effects. *Monographs of the Society for Research in Child Development,* 1975, *40*(5-6, Serial No. 162).

Mindey, C. *The divorced mother: A guide to readjustment*. New York: McGraw-Hill Book Co., 1969.

Mirandy, J. Preschool for abused children. In H. P. Martin (Ed.), *The abused child: A multidisciplinary approach to developmental issues and treatment*. Cambridge, Mass.: Ballinger Publishing Co., 1976.

Mischel, W., and Grusec, J. Determinants of the rehearsal and transmission of neutral and aversive behaviors. *Journal of Personality and Social Psychology,* 1966, *3,* 197-205.

Mitchell, E. The learning of sex roles through toys and books. *Young Children,* 1973, *26*(4), 226-231.

Moffitt, M. W. *Woodworking for children*. New York: Early Childhood Council of New York, no date.

Moffitt, M. W., and Omwake, E. *The intellectual content of play*. New York: New York State Association for the Education of Young Children, no date.

Monaghan, A. C. Children's contracts: Some preliminary findings. Unpublished term paper, Harvard Graduate School of Education, 1971. Cited in C. B. Cazden, Paradoxes of language structure. In K. Connolly and J. Bruner (Eds.), *The growth of competence*. New York: Academic Press, Inc., 1974.

Monahan, R. *Free and inexpensive materials for preschool and early childhood* (2nd ed.). Belmont, Calif.: Fearon Publishers, 1977.

Montagu, A. *Touching: The human significance of the skin*. New York: Columbia University Press, 1971.

Montessori, M. *The discovery of the child*. Translated by M. J. Costelloe. Notre Dame, Ind.: Fides Publishers, 1967.

Montgomery, P., and Richter, E. *Sensorimotor integration for developmentally disabled children: A handbook*. Los Angeles: Western Psychological Services, 1977.

Moor, P. What teachers are saying—about the young blind child. *The Journal of Nursery Education,* 1960, *15,* 2.

Moore, O. K., and Anderson, A. R. The Responsive Environments Project. In R. C. Hess and R. M. Bear (Eds.), *Early education*. Chicago: Aldine Publishing Co., 1968.

Moore, S. G. Considerateness and helpfulness in young children. *Young Children,* 1977, *32*(4), 73-76.

Mordock, J. B. *The other children: An introduction to exceptionality*. New York: Harper & Row, Publishers, 1975.

Morgan, G. G. Regulation of early childhood programs. In D. N. McFadden (Ed.), *Planning for action*. Washington, D.C.: NAEYC, 1972.

Morgan, G. G. The trouble with licensing. *Early Childhood Project Newsletter: Education Commission of the States,* 1977, *35,* 3-6.

Morland, J. K. Racial acceptance and preference of nursery school children in a southern city. In A. R. Brown, *Prejudice in children*. Springfield, Ill.: Charles C Thomas, Publisher, 1972.

Morrison, G. *Parent involvement in the home, school, and community*. Columbus, Ohio: Charles E. Merrill Publishing Co., 1978.

Moskovitz, S. Behavioral objectives: New ways to fail children? *Young Children,* 1973, *28*(4), 232-235.

Moskovitz, S. *Cross cultural early education and day care: A bibliography*. Urbana, Ill.: ERIC/ECE, University of Illinois, 1975.

Moss, H. Sex, age, and state as determinants of mother-infant interaction. *Merrill-Palmer Quarterly,* 1967, *13*(1), 19-36.

Moustakas, C. E. *Psychotherapy with children*. New York: Ballantine Books, Inc., 1959.

Moustakas, C. E. *The authentic teacher: Sensitivity and awareness in the classroom*. Cambridge, Mass.: Howard A. Doyle, 1966.

Murphy, L. B. *Vulnerability, coping and growth*. New Haven: Yale University Press, 1976.

Murphy, L. B., and Leeper, E. M. *Away from bedlam*. Washington, D.C.: U.S. Dept. of HEW, 1970. (a)

Murphy, L. B., and Leeper, E. M. *More than a teacher*. Washington, D.C.: U.S. Dept. of HEW, 1970. (b)

Murphy, L. B., and Leeper, E. M. *The vulnerable child*. Washington, D.C.: U.S. Dept. of HEW, 1970. (c)

Murphy, L. B., and Leeper, E. M. *From "I" to "we."* Washington, D.C.: U.S. Dept. of HEW, 1974. OCD 74-1033.

Murray, F. B. Acquisition of conservation through social interaction. *Developmental Psychology,* 1972, *6,* 1-6.

Mussen, P. H., Conger, J. J., and Kagan, J. *Child development and personality* (3rd ed.). New York: Harper & Row, Publishers, 1969.

Mussen, P. H., Conger, J. J., and Kagan, J. *Child development and personality* (4th ed.). New York: Harper & Row, Publishers, 1974.

Mussen, P. H., and Parker, A. Mother nurturance and girls' incidental imitative learning. *Journal of Personality and Social Psychology,* 1965, *2,* 94-97.

Mycue, E. S. *Young children with handicaps:* (Part 4: Resources: Directories, newsletters, bibliographies, and general information: An abstract bibliography). Urbana, Ill.: ERIC/ECE, University of Illinois, 1973.

Nagi, S. Child abuse and neglect problems: A national overview. *Children Today,* 1975, *4*(3), 13-17.

Nagy, M. H. The child's view of death. In H. Feifel (Ed.), *The meaning of death*. New York: Macmillan Publishing Co., Inc., 1959.

National Center on Child Abuse and Neglect. *Child abuse and neglect: The problem and its management* (Vol. 1: An overview of the problem). Washington, D.C.: U.S. Dept. of HEW, OHD, OCD, Children's Bureau, The Center, 1975. OHD 75-30073. (a)

National Center on Child Abuse and Neglect. *Child abuse and neglect: The problem and its management* (Vol. 2: The roles and responsibilities of professionals). Washington, D.C.: U.S. Dept. of HEW, OHD, OCD, Children's Bureau, The Center, 1975. OHD 75-30074. (b)

National Center on Child Abuse and Neglect. *How to plan and carry out a successful public awareness program on child abuse and neglect*. Washington, D.C.: U.S. Dept. of HEW, OHD, OCD, Children's Bureau, The Center, 1977. OHD 77-30089.

National Committee for Prevention of Child Abuse. *The national directory of child abuse services and information*. Chicago: The Committee, 111 East Wacker Drive, Chicago, Ill. 60601, 1974.

National Council of Organizations for Children and Youth. *America's children 1976: A bicentennial assessment*. Washington, D.C.: The Council, 1976.

National Institute of Neurological Diseases and Stroke. *Learning to talk: Speech, hearing and language problems in the pre-school child*. Washington, D.C.: U.S. Dept. of HEW, Public Health Service, National Institute of Health, 1969.

National Institutes of Mental Health. *Child abuse and neglect programs: Practice and theory*. Rockville, Md.: U.S. Dept. of HEW, Public Health Service, The Institutes, 1977. ADM 77-344.

Nedler, S., and Sebera, P. Intervention strategies for Spanish-speaking children. *Child Development,* 1971, *42,* 259-267.

Neff, W. S. *Work and human behavior*. New York: Atherton Press, 1968.

Neill, A. S. *Summerhill*. New York: Hart Publishing Co., Inc., 1960.

Neill, C. A. The child and his family after hospitalization. In J. A. Haller (Ed.), *The hospitalized child and his family*. Baltimore: The Johns Hopkins University Press, 1967.

Neisser, E. *Your child's sense of responsibility*. New York: Public Affairs Pamphlets, 1956, Pamphlet No. 254.

Nelson, W. E., Vaughan, B. C. III, and McKay, R. J. *Textbook of pediatrics* (9th ed.). Philadelphia: W. B. Saunders, Co., 1969.

Neuman, D. Sciencing for young children. In K. R. Baker (Ed.), *Ideas that work with young children*. Washington, D.C.: NAEYC: 1972.

Nicolaysen, M. Dominion in children's play: Its meaning and management. In K. R. Baker (Ed.), *Ideas that work with young children*. Washington, D.C.: NAEYC, 1972.

Northcott, W. H. Candidate for integration: A hearing-impaired child in a regular nursery school. *Young Children,* 1970, *25*(6), 367-380.

Nye, I. F. Child adjustment in broken and in unhappy unbroken homes. *Marriage and Family Living,* 1957, *19,* 356-361.

O'Connor, R. D. Relative efficacy of modeling, shaping, and the combined procedures for modification of social withdrawal. *Journal of Abnormal Psychology,* 1972, *79,* 327-334.

Office of Economic Opportunity. *Project Head Start: Equipment and supplies—9. Guidelines for administrators and teachers in child development centers*. Washington, D.C.: Office of Economic Opportunity, no date.

O'Keefe, R. A. Home Start: Partnership with parents. *Children Today,* 1973, 1, 12-16.

On the Capitol Doorstep. Children in the camps. *On the Capitol Doorstep*, 1978, *8*(8), 3.

Orata, P. T. The Iloilo experiment in education through the vernacular. In *The use of vernacular languages in education. Monographs on Fundamental Education* (Vol. 8). Paris: UNESCO, 1953.

Ornstein, R. *The psychology of consciousness* (2nd ed.). New York: Harcourt Brace Jovanovich, Inc., 1977.

Ornstein, R. The split and whole brain. *Human Nature*, 1978, *1*(5), 76-83.

Orpet, R. E., and Meyers, C. E. Six Structure-of-Intellect hypotheses in six-year-old children. *Journal of Educational Psychology*, 1966, *57*, 341-346.

Otis, N. B., and McCandless, B. R. Responses to repeated frustrations of young children differentiated according to need area. *Journal of Abnormal Social Psychology*, 1955, *50*, 349-353.

Parke, R. D. (Ed.). *Recent trends in social learning theory*. New York: Academic Press, Inc., 1972. (a)

Parke, R. D. Some effects of punishment on children's behavior. In W. W. Hartup (Ed.), *The young child: Reviews of research* (Vol. 2). Washington, D.C.: NAEYC, 1972. (b)

Parke, R. D., and Collmer, C. W. Child abuse: An interdisciplinary analysis. In E. M. Hetherington (Ed.), *Review of child development research*, (Vol. 5). Chicago: University of Chicago Press, 1975.

Parke, R. D., and Duer, J. L. Schedule of punishment and inhibition of aggression. *Developmental Psychology*, 1972, *7*, 266-269.

Parten, M. B. Social participation among preschool children. *Journal of Abnormal and Social Psychology*, 1932, *27*, 243-269.

Parten, M. B. Social play among preschool children. *Journal of Abnormal and Social Psychology*, 1933, *28*, 136-147.

Pasamanick, J. *Talk about: An early childhood language development resource* (Books 1 and 2). Great Neck, N.Y.: Center for Media Development, 1976.

Patterson, C. Insights about persons: Psychological foundations of humanistic and affective education. In L. M. Berman and J. A. Roderick (Eds.), *Feeling, valuing, and the art of growing: Insights into the affective*. Washington, D.C.: ASCD, 1977.

Patterson, G. R., Littman, R. A., and Bricker, W. Assertive behavior in children: A step toward a theory of aggression. *Monographs of the Society for Research in Child Development*, 1967, *32*(5), 1-43.

Paulsen, M. G. The law and abused children. In R. E. Helfer and C. H. Kempe (Eds.), *The battered child* (2nd ed.). Chicago: University of Chicago Press, 1974.

Pavloff, G., and Wilson, G. *Adult involvement in child development for staff and parents*. Atlanta: Humanics Associates, 1972.

Pedersen, E., Faucher, T. A., with Eaton, W. W. A new perspective on the effects of first-grade teachers on children's subsequent adult status. *Harvard Educational Review*, 1978, *48*(1), 1-31.

Petersham, M., and Petersham, M. *The circus baby*. New York: Macmillan Publishing Co., Inc., 1950.

Petrillo, M., and Sanger, S. *Emotional care of hospitalized children: An environmental approach*. Philadelphia: J. B. Lippincott Co., 1972.

Petty, W. T., and Starkey, R. J. Oral language and personal and social development. In W. T. Petty (Ed.), *Research in oral language*. Champaign, Ill.: National Council of Teachers of English, 1967.

Physical Education and Recreation for the Handicapped: Information and Research Utilization Center. *Early intervention for handicapped children through programs of physical education and recreation*. Washington, D.C.: AAHPER, 1976.

Piaget, J. *The language and thought of the child*. New York: Harcourt Brace Jovanovich, Inc., 1926.

Piaget, J. *The child's conception of physical causality*. London: Routledge and Kegan Paul, Ltd., 1930.

Piaget, J. *The moral judgement of the child*. London: Routledge and Kegan Paul, Ltd., 1932.

Piaget, J. *The moral judgment of the child*. Translated by M. Gabain. New York: The Free Press, 1965. (Originally published 1932.)

Piaget, J. *The psychology of intelligence*. London: Routledge and Kegan Paul, Ltd., 1950.

Piaget, J. *Play, dreams and imitation in childhood*. Translated by C. Gattegno and F. M. Hodgson. New York: W. W. Norton & Co., Inc., 1962.

Piaget, J. *The origins of intelligence in children*. New York: W. W. Norton & Co., 1963.

Piaget, J. *The child's conception of number*. New York: W. W. Norton & Co., 1965.

Piaget, J., and Inhelder, B. *The child's conception of space*. New York: W. W. Norton & Co., 1967.

Piaget, J., and Inhelder, B. *The psychology of the child*. Translated by H. Weaver. New York: Basic Books Inc., Publishers, 1969.

Piper, M. R. *Sunset Mexican cook book*. Menlo Park, Calif.: Lane Magazine & Book Co., 1969.

Pitcher, E. G. Explaining divorce to young children. In E. A. Grollman (Ed.), *Explaining divorce to children*. Boston: Beacon Press, 1969.

Pitcher, E. G., Lasher, M. G., Feinburg, S. G., and Braun, L. A. *Helping young children learn* (3rd ed.). Columbus, Ohio: Charles E. Merrill Publishing Co., 1979.

Pitcher, E. G., and Prelinger, E. *Children tell stories: An analysis of fantasy*. New York: International Universities Press, 1963.

Plank, E. N. *Working with children in hospitals*. Cleveland: The Press of Case Western Reserve University, 1962.

Plank, E. N. Young children and death. *Young Children*, 1968, *23*(6), 331-336.

Polansky, N. A., Hally, C., and Polansky, N. F. *Profile of neglect: A survey of the state of knowledge of child neglect*. Washington, D.C.: U.S. Dept. of HEW, Social and Rehabilitation Service, 1976. SRS 76-23037.

Portage Project. *Portage guide to early education*. Portage, Wis.: The Portage Project, 1976.

Porter, J. D. R. *Black child, white child: The development of racial attitudes*. Garden City, N.Y.: Doubleday & Co., Inc., 1970.

Prescott, E. Is day care as good as home care? *Young Children*, 1978, *33*(2), 13-19.

Project Head Start. *Head Start, Mainstreaming Preschoolers Series*. Washington, D.C.: U.S. Dept. of HEW, OHD, OCD, 1978. The titles in this series include *Mainstreaming preschoolers: Children with emotional disturbances* (OHDS 78-

31115), *Mainstreaming preschoolers: Children with health impairments* (OHDS 78-31111), *Mainstreaming preschoolers: Children with orthopedic handicaps* (OHDS 78-31114), *Mainstreaming preschoolers: Children with visual handicaps* (OHDS 78-31112), *Mainstreaming preschoolers: Children with hearing impairments* (OHDS 78-31116), *Mainstreaming preschoolers: Children with mental retardation* (OHDS 78-31110), *Mainstreaming preschoolers: Children with speech and language impairments* (OHDS 78-31113), and *Mainstreaming preschoolers: Children with learning disabilities* (OHDS-31117).

Provence, S., Naylor, A., and Patterson, J. *The challenge of daycare.* New Haven: Yale University Press, 1977.

Publications Office/ERIC. *Bilingual education for children: An abstract bibliography.* Urbana, Ill.: ERIC/ECE, University of Illinois, 1975.

Ramos, S. *Teaching your child to cope with crisis.* New York: David McKay Co., Inc., 1975.

Ratliff, A. R., and Ratliff, R. G. Sesame Street: Magic or malevolence? *Young Children,* 1972, *27*(4), 199-204.

Rausher, S. R., and Young, T. (Eds.) *Sexism: Teachers and young children.* New York: Early Childhood Education Council of New York City, 1974.

Ravenscroft, P. Daycare on campus. *Day Care and Early Education,* 1973, *1*(2), 22-25.

Read, K. *Let's play outdoors.* Washington, D.C.: NAEYC, 1969.

Read, K. *The nursery school: Human relationships and learning* (6th ed.). Philadelphia: W. B. Saunders Co., 1976.

Read, M. S. The biological bases: Malnutrition and behavioral development. In I. J. Gordon (Ed.), *Early childhood education: The seventy-first yearbook of the National Society for the Study of Education* (Part 2). Chicago: University of Chicago Press, 1972.

Redl, F. *When we deal with children.* New York: The Free Press, 1966.

Redl, F., and Wattenberg, W. W. *Mental hygiene in teaching* (2nd ed.). New York: Harcourt Brace Jovanovich, Inc., 1959.

Redl, F., and Wineman, D. *Children who hate.* New York: The Free Press, 1951.

Redl, F., and Wineman, D. *Controls from within.* New York: The Free Press, 1952.

Reese, H. W., and Lipsitt, L. P. *Experimental child psychology.* New York: Academic Press, Inc., 1970.

Reif, T. F., and Stollak, G. E. *Sensitivity to young children: Training and its effects.* East Lansing: Michigan State University Press, 1972.

Resnick, R., and Hergenroeder, E. Children and the emergency room. *Children Today,* 1975, *4*(5), 5-9.

Rest, J. R. Developmental psychology as a guide to values education: A review of Kohlbergian programs. *Review of Educational Research,* 1974, *44*(2), 241-259.

Rey, H. A. *Curious George.* Boston: Houghton Mifflin Co., 1941.

Rice, E. P., Ekdahl, M. C., and Miller, L. *Children of mentally ill parents: Problems in child care.* New York: Behavioral Publications, Inc., 1971.

Riley, J. E. The self-concept and sex-role behavior of third and fourth grade boys. *Dissertation Abstracts,* 1966, *27,* 680.

Risley, T. R., and Baer, D. M. Operant behavior modification: The deliberate development of behavior. In B. M. Caldwell and H. N. Ricciuti (Eds.), *Review of Child Development Research* (Vol. 3). Chicago: University of Chicago Press, 1973.

Robb, M. D., Mushier, C. L., Bogard, D. A., and Blann, M. E. (Eds.). *Foundations and practices in perceptual motor learning—a quest for understanding.* Washington, D.C.: American Association for Health, Physical Education, and Recreation, 1971.

Robb, P. *Epilepsy: A review of basic and clinical research.* Washington, D.C.: U.S. Dept. of HEW, National Institute of Neurological Diseases and Blindness, 1965.

Robertson, S. M. *Rosegarden and labyrinth: A study in art education.* London: Routledge and Kegan Paul, Ltd., 1963.

Robinson, H. B. and others. *Early child care in the United States of America.* New York: Gordon and Breach, Science Publishers, Inc., 1974.

Roby, P. *Child care—who cares? Foreign and domestic infant and early childhood development policies.* New York: Basic Books, Inc., Publishers, 1973.

Roedell, W. C., Slaby, R. G., and Robinson, H. B. *Social development in young children: A report for teachers.* Washington, D.C.: National Institute of Education, U.S. Dept. of HEW, 1976.

Rogers, C. R. *On becoming a person.* Boston: Houghton Mifflin Co., 1961.

Rogers, C. R. *On personal power: Inner strength and its revolutionary impact.* New York: Delacorte Press, 1977.

Rogers, C. R.,. and Dymond, R. F. *Psychotherapy and personality change.* Chicago: University of Chicago Press, 1954.

Rohrer, G. K. Racial and ethnic identification and preference in young children. *Young Children,* 1977, *32*(2), 24-33.

Rohwer, W. D. Prime time for education: Early childhood or adolescence? *Harvard Educational Review,* 1971, *41*(3), 316-341.

Rosecrans, C. J. Play—the language of children. *Mental Hygiene,* 1968, *52,* 367-373.

Rosenberg, M. *Society and the adolescent self image.* Princeton, N.J.: Princeton University Press, 1965.

Rosenfeld, S. *A drop of water.* Irvington-on-Hudson, N.Y.: Harvey House, Inc., Publishers, 1970.

Rosenhan, D. Prosocial behavior of children. In W. W. Hartup. *The young child: Reviews of research* (Vol. 2). Washington, D.C.: NAEYC, 1972.

Rosenthal, A. R. Visual disorders. In E. E. Bleck and D. A. Nagel (Eds.), *Physically handicapped children—a medical atlas for teachers.* New York: Grune & Stratton, Inc., 1975.

Rosenthal, R., and Jacobson, L. *Pygmalion in the classroom: Teacher expectation and pupils' intellectual development.* New York: Holt, Rinehart and Winston, 1968.

Ross, D. M., and Ross, S. A. *Hyperactivity: Research, theory, action.* New York: John Wiley & Sons, Inc., 1976.

Rowan, B. *The children we see.* New York: Holt, Rinehart and Winston, Inc., 1973.

Rubin, K. H. The play behaviors of young children. *Young Children.* 1977, *32*(6), 16-24.

Rutherford, E., and Mussen, P. Generosity in nursery school boys. *Child Development,* 1968, *39,* 755-765.

Rutter, M. Behavioral and cognitive characteristics of a series of psychotic children. In J. K. Wing (Ed.), *Early childhood autism: Clinical, educational, and social aspects.* Maxwell

House, Fairview Park, Elmsford, N.Y.: Pergamon Press, Inc., 1966.

Saario, T., Jacklin, C. N., and Tittle, C. K. Sex role stereotyping in the public schools. *Harvard Educational Review,* 1973, *43*(3), 386-416.

Safford, P. L. *Teaching young children with special needs.* St. Louis: The C. V. Mosby Co., 1978.

Sagan, C. *The dragons of Eden: Speculations on the evolution of human intelligence.* New York: Random House, Inc., 1977.

Sahler, O. J. Z. (Ed.). *The child and death.* St. Louis: The C. V. Mosby Co., 1978.

Samuels, S. *Enhancing self-concept in early childhood: Theory and practice.* New York: Human Sciences Press, 1977.

Sander, E. When are speech sounds learned? *Journal of Speech and Hearing Disorders,* 1972, *37,* 1.

Satir, V. *People making.* Palo Alto, Calif.: Science & Behavior Books, Inc., 1975.

Schachter, F. F., Kirshner, K., Klips, B., Friedricks, M., and Sanders, K. Everyday preschool interpersonal speech usage: Methodological, developmental, and sociolinguistic studies. *Monographs for Research in Child Development,* 1974, *39*(3, Serial No. 156).

Schaefer, C. (Ed.). *The therapeutic use of children's play.* New York: Jason Aronson, Inc., 1976.

Schaefer, E. S. Need for early and continuing education. In V. Danenberg (Ed.). *Education of the infant and young child.* New York: Academic Press, Inc., 1970.

Schaefer, E. S. Parents as educators: Evidence for cross-sectional, longitudinal and intervention research. *Young Children,* 1972, *27*(4), 227-239.

Schattner, R. *An early childhood curriculum for multiply handicapped children.* New York: The John Day Co., Inc., 1971.

Scheffield, M., and Bewley, S. *Where do babies come from?* New York: Alfred A. Knopf, Inc., 1972.

Schima, M., and Bolian, P. *The magic of life.* Englewood Cliffs, N.J.: Prentice-Hall, Inc., 1970.

Schmidt, V. E., and McNeill, E. *Cultural awareness: A resource bibliography.* Washington, D.C.: NAEYC, 1978.

Schulman, E. D. *Intervention in human services* (2nd ed.). St. Louis: The C. V. Mosby Co., 1978.

Schwartz, J. C., and Wynn, R. The effects of mother presence and previsits on children's emotional reaction to starting nursery school. *Child Development,* 1971, *42,* 871-881.

Scott, M. *Some parameters of teacher effectiveness as assessed by an ecological approach.* Nashville: DARCEE Papers and Reports, George Peabody College, 1969.

Scott, M., and Grimmett, S. (Eds.). *Current issues in child development.* Washington, D.C.: NAEYC, 1977.

Scrimshaw, N. S. Early malnutrition and central nervous system function. *Merrill-Palmer Quarterly,* 1969, *15*(4), 375-388.

Sears, R. R. Relations of early socialization experience to self-concepts and gender role in middle childhood. *Child Development,* 1970, *41,* 267-289.

Sears, R. R., Maccoby, E., and Levin, H. *Patterns of child rearing.* New York: Harper & Row, Publishers, 1957.

Seeger, R. C. *American folk songs for children.* Garden City, N.Y.: Doubleday & Co., Inc., 1948.

Seligman, M. E. P. *Helplessness: On depression, development and death.* San Francisco: W. H. Freeman and Co. Publishers, 1975.

Selye, H. *The stress of life.* New York: McGraw-Hill Book Co., 1956.

Sgroi, S. M. Sexual molestation of children: The last frontier in child abuse. *Children Today,* 1975, *4*(3), 18-21; 44.

Shaffer, H. B. *Emotionally disturbed children.* Washington, D.C.: Editorial Research Reports, 1973.

Sharp, E. *Thinking is child's play.* New York: E. P. Dutton & Co., Inc., 1969.

Shaw, C. R., and Lucas, A. R. *The psychiatric disorders of childhood* (2nd ed.). New York: Appleton-Century-Crofts, 1970.

Sheehy, G. *Passages: Predictable crises of adult life.* New York: Bantam Books, Inc., 1976.

Sherman, J. A., and Bushell, D. Behavior modification as an educational technique. In F. D. Horowitz (Ed.), *Review of child development research* (Vol. 4). Chicago: University of Chicago Press, 1975.

Shneour, E. *The malnourished mind.* Garden City, N.Y.: Doubleday & Co., Inc., 1974.

Shriner, T. H. Economically deprived: Aspects of language skills. In L. E. Travis (Ed.), *Handbook of speech pathology and audiology.* New York: Appleton-Century-Crofts, 1971.

Siegel, L. S. Development of the concept of seriation. *Developmental Psychology.* 1972, *6,* 135-137.

Sigel, I. E. The Piagetian system and the world of education. In D. Elkind and J. H. Flavell (Eds.), *Studies in cognitive development.* New York: Oxford University Press, Inc., 1969.

Sigel, I. E., and Hooper, F. H. (Eds.). *Logical thinking in children: Research based on Piaget's theory.* New York: Holt, Rinehart and Winston, Inc., 1968.

Sigel, I. E., and McBane, B. Cognitive competence and level of symbolization among five-year-old children. In J. Hellmuth (Ed.), *The disadvantaged child.* Seattle: Special Child Publications, 1967.

Sigel, I. E., Starr, R., Secrist, A., Jackson, J. P., and Hill, E. Social and emotional development of young children. In J. L. Frost (Ed.), *Revisiting early childhood education: Readings.* Holt, Rinehart and Winston, Inc., 1973.

Simmons, A. S., and Chayes, A. H. University day care. In P. Roby (Ed.), *Day care—who cares? Foreign and domestic infant and early childhood development policies.* New York: Basic Books, Inc., Publishers, 1973.

Sinclair, C. B. *Movement of the young child: Ages two to six.* Columbus, Ohio: Charles E. Merrill Publishing Co., 1973.

Sinclair, H. Sensorimotor action patterns as a condition for the acquisition of syntax. In R. Huxley and E. Ingram (Eds.), *Language acquisition: Models and methods.* New York: Academic Press, Inc., 1971.

Sitkei, E. G., and Meyers, C. E. Comparative Structure of Intellect in middle- and lower-class four-year-olds of two ethnic groups. *Developmental Psychology,* 1969, *1,* 592-604.

Smart, M. S., and Smart, R. C. *Child development and relationships* (2nd ed.). New York: Macmillan Publishing Co., Inc., 1972.

Smedslund, J. Les origines sociales de la centration. In F. Bresson and M. de Montmalin (Eds.), *Psychologie et épistemologie génetiques.* Paris: Dunod, 1966.

Smilansky, S. *The effects of sociodramatic play on disadvantaged children.* New York: John Wiley & Sons, Inc., 1968.

Smith, H. Standard or nonstandard: Is there an answer? *Elementary English,* February 1973, 225-234. (a)

Smith, H. Black English: Considerations and approaches. *The English Journal,* February 1973, 311-318. (b)

Smith, J. A. *Setting conditions for creative teaching in the elementary school.* Boston: Allyn & Bacon, Inc., 1966.

Smith, M. J. *When I say no, I feel guilty.* New York: Bantam Books, Inc., 1975.

Snapper, K. J., and Ohms, J. S. *The status of children, 1977.* Washington, D.C.: U.S. Dept. of HEW, OCD, ACYF, 1977. ACYF 78-30133.

Snyder, A. *Dauntless women.* Washington, D.C.: ACEI, 1972.

Snyder, M. How desirable conscience can grow in the years three to five. *Chicago Theological Register,* 1977, *67*(2), 1-15.

Solomon, P., Kubjansky, P. E., Leiderman, P. H., Mendelson, J. H., Trumbull, R., and Wexler, D. *Sensory deprivation.* Cambridge, Mass.: Harvard University Press, 1965.

Southwest Educational Development Laboratory. *Working with parents of handicapped children.* Reston, Va: CEC, 1976.

Spanish Dame Bilingual Bicultural Project. *The daily curriculum guide: A preschool program for the Spanish-speaking child.* Austin, Tex.: Dissemination and Assessment Center for Bilingual Education, 1975.

Sparling, J. J., and Sparling, M. C. How to talk to a scribbler. *Young Children,* 1973, *28*(6), 333-341.

Spencer, M., and Carroll, E. C. *CDA. Child Development Associate instructional materials* (Books 1 to 8). Austin, Tex.: Texas Dept. of Community Affairs, Early Childhood Development Division, 1977.

Spinetta, J. J., and Rigler, D. The child abusing parent: A psychlogical review. *Psychological Bulletin,* 1972, *77,* 296-304.

Spitz, R. A. Hospitalism: An inquiry into the genesis of psychiatric conditions in early childhood. *The psycholanalytic study of the child* (Vol. 1). New York: International Universities Press, 1945.

Spock, B., and Lerrigo, M. O. *Caring for your disabled child.* New York: Macmillan Publishing Co., Inc., 1965.

Spodek, B. From the president. *Young Children,* 1977, *32*(4), 2-3. (a)

Spodek, B. *Teaching practices: Reexamining assumptions.* Washington, D.C.: NAEYC, 1977. (b)

Spodek, B. What constitutes worthwhile educational experiences for young children? In B. Spodek (Ed.), *Teaching practices: Reexamining assumptions.* Washington, D.C.: NAEYC, 1977. (c)

Spodek, B., Andrews, P., Lee, M., Riley, J., and White, D. *A black curriculum for early childhood education: Teaching units* (Rev. ed.). Urbana, Ill.: University of Illinois, 1976.

Spodek, B., and Walberg, H. J. *Early childhood education: Issues and insights.* Berkeley, Calif.: McCutchan Publishing Corp., 1977.

Sprigle, H. A. Can poverty children live on "Sesame Street"? *Young Children,* 1971, *26*(4), 202-218.

Sprung, B. *Non-sexist education for young children: A practical guide.* New York: Citation Press, 1975.

Stakelon, A. E. *Early childhood newsletters: A selected guide.* Urbana, Ill.: ERIC/ECE, University of Illinois, 1974.

Stangl, M. J. *Finger painting is fun.* Camarillo, Calif.: Educational Techniques, Inc., 1975.

Stebbins, L. B., St. Pierre, R. G., Proper, E. C., Anderson, R. B., and Cerva, T. R. *Education as experimentation: A planned variation model* (Vol. 4-A: An evaluation of Follow Through). Cambridge, Mass.: Abt Associates, Inc., 1977.

Stecher, M. B., and McElheny, H. *Joy and learning through music and movement improvisation.* New York: Macmillan Publishing Co., Inc., 1972.

Steele, B. F. *Working with abusive parents from a psychiatric point of view.* Washington, D.C.: U.S. Dept. of HEW, OHD, OCD, National Center on Child Abuse and Neglect, 1977. OHD 77-30070.

Stein, M., Beyer, E., and Ronald, D. Beyond benevolence—the mental health role of the preschool teacher. *Young Children,* 1975, *30*(5), 358-372.

Stein, S. The company cares for children. In P. Roby (Ed.), *Child care—who cares? Foreign and domestic infant and early childhood development policies.* New York: Basic Books, Inc., Publishers, 1973.

Steiner, G. Y. *The children's cause.* Washington, D.C.: The Brookings Institution, 1976.

Steinfels, M. O'B. *Who's minding the children? The history and politics of day care in America.* New York: Simon & Schuster, Inc., 1973.

Stent, M. D., Hazard, W. R., and Rivlin, H. N. *Cultural pluralism in education: Mandate for change.* New York: Appleton-Century-Crofts, 1973.

Stevens, J. H., and King, E. W. *Administering early childhood education programs.* Boston: Little, Brown and Co., 1976.

Stevenson, H. W., and Stevenson, N. G. Social interaction in an interracial nursery school. *Genetic Psychology Monographs,* 1960, *61* 41-75.

Stone, J. C., and DeNevi, D. P. (Eds.). *Teaching multicultural populations: Five heritages.* New York: Van Nostrand Reinhold Co., 1971.

Stone, J. W. G. *A guide to discipline* (Rev. ed.). Washington, D.C.: NAEYC, 1978.

Stone, L. J., Smith, H. T., and Murphy, L. B. *The competent infant: Research and commentary.* New York: Basic Books Inc., Publishers, 1973.

Stott, L. H., and Ball, R. S. Consistency and change in ascendance-submission in the social interaction of children. *Child Development,* 1957, *28,* 259-272.

Stott, L. H. *The longitudinal study of individual development.* Detroit: Merrill-Palmer School, 1955.

Stott, L. H., and Ball, R. S. Infant and preschool mental tests: Review and evaluation. *Monographs of the Society for Research in Child Development,* 1965, *30*(3, Serial No. 101).

Strain, F. B. *New patterns in sex teaching.* New York: Appleton-Century-Crofts, 1940.

Sunderlin, S., Osborn, K., and Cohen, M. D. *Migrant children: Their education.* Washington, D.C.: ACEI, 1971.

Sunderlin, S., and Wills, B. (Eds.). *Nutrition and intellectual growth in children.* Washington, D.C.: ACEI, 1969.

Sutton-Smith, B. A syntax for play and games. In R. E. Herron and B. Sutton-Smith, *Child's play.* New York: John Wiley & Sons, Inc., 1971.

Sutton-Smith, B. *Child psychology.* New York: Appleton-Century-Crofts, 1973.

Sutton-Smith, B., and Rosenberg, B. G. Sixty years of historical change in the game preferences of American children. *Journal of American Folklore,* 1961, *74,* 17-46.

Sweeney, R. T. (Ed.). *Selected readings in movement education.* Reading, Mass.: Addison-Wesley Publishing Co., Inc., 1970.

Tarnay, E. D. *What does the nursery school teacher teach?* Washington, D.C.: NAEYC, 1965.

Taylor, D. G., Sheatsley, P. B., and Greeley, A. M. Attitudes toward racial integration. *Scientific American,* 1978, *238*(6), 42-49.

Taylor, K. W. *Parent cooperative nursery schools.* New York: Teachers College Press, Columbia University, 1968.

Teitelbaum, H. T., and Hiller, R. J. Bilingual education: The legal mandate. *Harvard Educational Review,* 1977, *47*(2), 138-170.

Terman, L. M., Baldwin, B. T., and Bronson, E. *Mental and physical traits of a thousand gifted children: Genetic studies of genius* (Vol. 1). Stanford: Stanford University Press, 1925.

Thomas, S. B. *Malnutrition, cognitive development and learning.* Urbana, Ill.: ERIC/ECE, University of Illinois, 1972.

Thomas, S. B. *Concerns about gifted children: A paper and abstract bibliography.* Urbana, Ill.: ERIC/ECE, University of Illinois, 1974.

Thompson, G. G. The social and emotional development of preschool children under 2 types of educational program. *Psychological Monographs,* 1944, *56*(1-29, No. 5).

Thoreau, H. D. *Walden, or life in the woods.* Mount Vernon, N.Y.: Peter Pauper Press, no date.

Tillotson, J. A brief theory of movement education. In R. T. Sweeney (Ed.), *Selected readings in movement education.* Reading, Mass.: Addison-Wesley Publishing Co., Inc., 1970.

Torrance, E. P. *Guiding creative talent.* Englewood Cliffs, N.J.: Prentice-Hall, Inc., 1962.

Torrance, E. P. *Creativity.* Belmont, Calif.: Fearon Publishers, 1969.

Torrance, E. P. Freedom to manipulate objects and question-asking performance of six-year-olds. *Young Children,* 1970, *26*(2), 93-97. (a)

Torrance, E. P. Seven guides to creativity. In R. T. Sweeney (Ed.), *Selected readings in movement education.* Reading, Mass.: Addison-Wesley Publishing Co., Inc., 1970. (b)

Travis, L. E. *Handbook of speech pathology and audiology.* New York: Appleton-Century-Crofts, 1971.

Tresselt, A. *Rain drop, splash.* New York: Lothrop, Lee & Shepard Co., 1969.

Truax, C. B., and Tatum, C. D. An extension from the effective psychotherapeutic model to constructive personality change in preschool children. *Childhood Education.* 1966, *42,* 456-462.

Turiel, E. Stage transition in moral development. In R. Travers (Ed.), *Second handbook on research in teaching.* Chicago: Rand McNally & Co., 1973.

United States Commission on Civil Rights. *Teachers and students: Differences in teacher interaction with Mexican American and Anglo students* (Report 5: Mexican American education study). Washington, D.C.: The Commission, 1973.

United States Commission on Civil Rights. *Toward quality education for Mexican Americans* (Report 6: Mexican American education study). Washington, D.C.: The Commission, 1974.

United States Department of Agriculture. *Food buying guide for child care centers.* Washington, D.C.: U.S. Govt. Printing Office, 1974. FNS-108.

United States Department of Health, Education, and Welfare. *U.S. immunization survey: 1972.* Washington, D.C.: Center for Disease Control, Public Health Service, U.S. Dept. of HEW, 1973. (a)

United States Department of Health, Education, and Welfare. *Quantity recipes for child care centers.* Washington, D.C.: U.S. Govt. Printing Office, 1973. S/N 0124-00170. (b)

United States Department of Health, Education, and Welfare. *Guides for day care licensing.* Washington, D.C.: The Department, Office of Child Development, 1973. (c)

United States Department of Health, Education, and Welfare. *Child abuse and neglect: The problem and its management* (Vol. 1: An overview of the problem). Washington, D.C.: U.S. Dept. of HEW, OHD, OCD, Children's Bureau, National Center on Child Abuse and Neglect, 1975. OHD 75-30073. (a)

United States Department of Health, Education, and Welfare. *Child abuse and neglect: The problem and its management* (Vol. 2: The roles and responsibilities of professionals). Washington, D.C.: U.S. Dept. of HEW, OHD, OCD, Children's Bureau, National Center on Child Abuse and Neglect, 1975. OHD 75-30074. (b)

United States Department of Health, Education, and Welfare. *Child abuse and neglect: The problem and its management* (Vol. 3: The community team: An approach to case management and prevention). Washington, D.C.: U.S. Dept. of HEW, OHD, OCD, Children's Bureau, National Center on Child Abuse and Neglect, 1975. OHD 75-30075. (c)

United States Department of Health, Education, and Welfare. *Tips on the care and adjustment of Vietnamese and other Asian children in the United States.* Washington, D.C.: U.S. Dept. of HEW, OHD, OCD, Children's Bureau, 1975. OHD 75-72. (d)

United States Department of Health, Education, and Welfare. *Malnutrition, learning and behavior.* Bethesda, Md.: U.S. Dept. of HEW, 1976. (a)

United States Department of Health, Education, and Welfare. *Statistical highlights from the National Child Care Consumer Study.* Washington, D.C.: U.S. Dept. of HEW, OHD, OCD, Head Start Bureau, 1976. OHD 76-31096. (b)

United States Department of Health, Education, and Welfare. *Nutrition: Better eating for a head start.* Washington, D.C.: U.S. Dept. of HEW, 1976. (c)

United States Department of Labor. *Working mothers and their children.* Washington, D.C.: Women's Bureau, Employment Standards Administration, U.S. Dept. of Labor, 1977.

United States Public Health Service. Gonorrhea: The latest word. *Emergency Medicine,* 1975, *7*(2), 132-138.

United States Senate Finance Committee. *Child care: Data and materials.* Washington, D.C.: U.S. Govt. Printing Office, 1974, Stock No. 5270-02549.

Utzinger, R. C. *Some European nursery schools and playgrounds.* New York: Educational Facilities Laboratory and the Architectural Research Laboratory of the University of Michigan, 1970.

Valentine, C. W. *The normal child and his abnormalities* (3rd ed.). Baltimore: Penguin Books Inc., 1956.

Van Osdol, W. R., and Shane, D. G. *An introduction to exceptional children* (2nd ed.). Dubuque, Iowa: William C. Brown Co., Publishers, 1977.

Van Riper, C. *Speech correction: Principles and methods* (6th ed.). Englewood Cliffs, N.J.: Prentice-Hall, Inc., 1978.

Varma, V. P. *Stresses in children.* New York: Crane, Russak & Co., 1973.

Vaughn, G. *Mummy, I don't feel well: A pictorial guide to common childhood illnesses.* London: Berkeley Graphics, 1970.

Veatch, D. M. Choice with responsibility. *Young Children,* 1977, *32*(4), 22-25.

Vukelich, C., McCarty, C., and Nanis, C. Sex bias in children's books. In M. D. Cohen (Ed.), *Growing free: Ways to help children overcome sex-role stereotypes.* Washington, D.C.: ACEI, 1976.

Walker, J. E., and Shea, T. M. *Behavior modification: A practical approach for educators.* St. Louis: The C. V. Mosby Co., 1976.

Wallach, M. A., and Kogan, N. *Modes of thinking in young children: A study of the creativity-intelligence distinction.* New York: Holt, Rinehart and Winston, 1965.

Wallerstein, J., and Kelly, J. The effects of parental divorce: Experiences of the preschool child. *Journal of the American Academy of Child Psychiatry,* 1976, *14*(4) 600-616.

Walsh, A. M. *Self-concepts of bright boys with learning difficulties.* New York: Teachers College Press, Columbia University, 1956.

Walters, D. R. *Physical and sexual abuse of children: Causes and treatment.* Bloomington, Ind.: Indiana University Press, 1975.

Ward, E. H. A code of ethics: The hallmark of a profession. In L. G. Katz and E. H. Ward. *Ethical behavior in early childhood education.* Washington, D.C.: NAEYC, 1978.

Ward, E. H., Akers, M., Hines, R. P., and Eggleston, P. The 1970 White House Conference on Children—Reports by NAEYC official delegates. *Young Children,* 1971, *26*(4), 194-201.

Ward, W. C. Creativity in young children. *Child Development,* 1968, *39,* 737-754.

Warren, R. M. *Caring: Supporting children's growth.* Washington, D.C.: NAEYC, 1977.

Watson, J. D. *The double helix: Being a personal account of the discovery of the structure of DNA.* New York: Atheneum Publishers, 1968.

Weber, E. *Early childhood education: Perspectives on change.* Worthington, Ohio: Charles A. Jones Publishing Co., 1970.

Weikart, D. P. (Ed.). *Preschool intervention: A preliminary report of the Perry Preschool Project.* Ann Arbor: University of Michigan Press, 1967.

Weikart, D. P. *Relationship of curriculum, teaching, and learning in preschool education.* Ypsilanti, Mich.: High/Scope Educational Research Foundation, 1971.

Weikart, D. P. Paper presented at the CAEYC Legislative Symposium, Sacramento, Calif., February 1978.

Weikart, D. P., Bond, J. T., and McNeil, J. T. The Ypsilanti Perry Preschool Project: Preschool years and longitudinal results through fourth grade. *Monographs of the High/Scope Educational Research Foundation,* 1978, (No. 3).

Weikart, D. P., and Lambie, D. Z. Preschool intervention through a home teaching program. In J. Hellmuth (Ed.), *The disadvantaged child* (Vol. 2). New York: Brunner/Mazel, Inc., 1968.

Weikart, D., and Lambie, D. Early enrichment in infants. In V. Denenberg (Ed.), *Education of the infant and young child.* New York: Academic Press, Inc., 1970.

Weikart, D., Rogers, L., Adcock, C., and McClelland, D. *The cognitively oriented curriculum: A framework for preschool teachers.* Washington, D.C.: NAEYC, 1971.

Weiner, J. M. (Ed.). *Psychopharmacology in childhood and adolescence.* New York: Basic Books, Inc., Publishers, 1977.

Weiss, C. E., and Lillywhite, H. S. *Communicative disorders: A handbook for prevention and early intervention.* St. Louis: The C. V. Mosby Co., 1976.

Wellman, B. L. Motor achievement of preschool children. *Childhood Education,* 1937, *13,* 311-316.

Wender, P. H. *The hyperactive child: A handbook for parents.* New York: Crown Publishers, Inc., 1973.

Werner, N. E., and Evans, I. M. Perception of prejudice in Mexican-American preschool children. In N. N. Wagner and M. J. Haug. *Chicanos: Social and psychological perspectives.* St. Louis: The C. V. Mosby Co., 1971.

Weston, G. The pathology of child abuse. In R. E. Helfer and C. H. Kempe (Eds.), *The battered child* (2nd ed.). Chicago: University of Chicago Press, 1974.

White, B. L. Informal education during the first months of life. In R. D. Hess and R. M. Bear (Eds.), *Early education.* Chicago: Aldine Publishing Co., 1968.

White, B. L. *Human infants: Experience and psychological development.* Englewood Cliffs, N.J.: Prentice-Hall, Inc., 1971.

White, B. L. Address presented at the Conference of the California Association for the Education of Young Children, Los Angeles, February 1973.

White, R. W. Motivation reconsidered: The concept of competence. In M. Almy (Ed.), *Early childhood play: Selected readings related to cognition and motivation.* New York: Simon & Schuster, Inc., 1968.

White, R. W. *The enterprise of living: Growth and organization in personality.* New York: Holt, Rinehart and Winston, Inc., 1972.

Wickstrom, R. L. *Fundamental motor patterns* (2nd ed.). Philadelphia: Lea & Febiger, 1977.

Wilder, A., Sendak, M., and Engvick, W. *Lullabies and nightsongs.* New York: Harper & Row, Publishers, 1965.

Williams, F., Hopper, R., and Natalico, D. S. *The sounds of children.* Englewood Cliffs, N.J.: Prentice-Hall, Inc., 1977.

Williams, S. R. *Essentials of nutrition and diet therapy* (2nd ed.). St. Louis: The C. V. Mosby Co., 1978.

Wilson, J. A. R., Robeck, M. C., and Michael, W. B. *Psychological foundations of learning and teaching.* New York: McGraw-Hill Book Co., 1969.

Wing, L. (Ed.) *Early childhood autism: Clinical, educational and social aspects* (2nd ed.). Maxwell House, Fairview Park, Elmsford, N.Y.: Pergamon Press, Inc., 1976.

Wisler, C. E., Burns, G. P., and Iwamoto, D. Follow Through redux: A response to the critique by House, Glass, McLean, and Walker. *Harvard Educational Review,* 1978, *48*(2), 171-185.

Wittes, G., and Radin, N. *Ypsilanti home and school handbooks: Helping your child to learn: The learning through play approach.* San Rafael, Calif.: Dimensions Publishing Co., 1969. (a)

Wittes, G., and Radin, N. *Ypsilanti home and school handbooks:*

Helping your child to learn: The nurturance approach. San Rafael, Calif.: Dimensions Publishing Co., 1969. (b)

Wittes, G., and Radin, N. *Ypsilanti home and school handbooks: Helping your child to learn: The reinforcement approach.* San Rafael, Calif.: Dimensions Publishing Co., 1969. (c)

Wolf, A. V. M. *Helping your child understand death.* New York: The Child Study Press, 1973.

Wolfenstein, M. Loss, rage and repetition. *Psychoanalytic study of the child* (Vol. 24). New York: International Universities Press, 1969.

Wolfgang, C. H. *Helping aggressive and passive preschoolers through play.* Columbus, Ohio: Charles E. Merrill Publishing Co., 1977.

Wylie, R. *The self-concept.* Lincoln, Neb.: University of Nebraska Press, 1961.

Yardley, A. *Structure in early learning.* New York: Citation Press, 1974.

Yarrow, L. J. The effect of antecedent frustration on projective play. *Psychological Monographs,* 1948, *62*(6).

Yarrow, L. J. Separation from parents during early childhood. In M. L. Hoffman and L. W. Hoffman (Eds.), *Review of child development research* (Vol. 1). New York: Russell Sage Foundation, 1964.

Yarrow, M. R., Scott, P. M., and Waxler, C. Z. Learning concern for others. *Developmental Psychology,* 1973, *8,* 240-260.

Young, L. L., and Cooper, D. H. Some factors associated with popularity. *Journal of Educational Psychology,* 1944, *35,* 513-535.

Youniss, J. Another perspective on social cognition. In A. Pick (Ed.), *Minnesota Symposia on Child Psychology* (Vol. 9). Minneapolis: University of Minnesota Press, 1975.

Young Children. The development of the Child Development Associate (CDA) Program. *Young Children,* 1973, *28*(3), 139-145.

Young Children. An NAEYC code of professional ethics (proposed). *Young Children,* 1978, *33*(5), 41.

Zimbardo, P. G. *Shyness.* Menlo Park, Calif.: Addison-Wesley Publishing Co., Inc., 1977.

Zimmerman, B. J., and Bergan, J. K. Intellectual operations in teacher question asking behavior. *Merrill-Palmer Quarterly,* 1971, *17*(1), 19-26.

Zion, G. *Dear garbage man.* New York: Harper & Row, Publishers, 1957.

Zirkel, P. A. Self-concept and the disadvantage of ethnic group membership and mixture. *Review of Educational Research,* 1971, *41*(3), 211-226.

Appendices

A □ An initial code of ethics for early childhood educators*

Preamble

As an educator of young children in their years of greatest vulnerability, I, to the best of intent and ability, shall devote myself to the following commitments and act to support them.

For the child

I shall accord the respect due each child as a human being from birth on.

I shall recognize the unique potentials to be fulfilled within each child.

I shall provide access to differing opinions and views inherent in every person, subject, or thing encountered as the child grows.

I shall recognize the child's right to ask questions about the unknowns that exist in the present so the answers (which may be within the child's capacity to discover) may be forthcoming eventually.

I shall protect and extend the child's physical well-being, emotional stability, mental capacities, and social acceptability.

For the parents and family members

I shall accord each child's parents and family members respect for the responsibilities they carry.

By no deliberate action on my part will the child be held accountable for the incidental meeting of his

or her parents and the attendant lodging of the child's destiny with relatives and siblings.

Recognizing the continuing nature of familial strength as support for the growing child, I shall maintain objectivity with regard to what I perceive as family weaknesses.

Maintaining family value systems and pride in cultural-ethnic choices or variations will supersede any attempts I might inadvertently or otherwise make to impose my values.

Because advocacy on behalf of children always requires that someone cares about or is strongly motivated by a sense of fairness and intervenes on behalf of children in relation to those services and institutions that impinge on their lives, I shall support family strength.

For myself and the early childhood profession

Admitting my biases is the first evidence of my willingness to become a conscious professional.

Knowing my capacity to continue to learn throughout life, I shall vigorously pursue knowledge about contemporary developments in early education by informal and formal means.

My role with young children demands an awareness of new knowledge that emerges from varied disciplines and the responsibility to use such knowledge.

Recognizing the limitation I bring to knowing intimately the ethical-cultural value systems of the multicultural American way of life, I shall actively seek the understanding and acceptance of the chosen

*Reprinted, by permission, from Ward, E. A code of ethics: The hallmark of a profession. In L. G. Katz and E. H. Ward, *Ethical behavior in early childhood education,* pp. 20-21. Copyright © 1978, National Association for the Education of Young Children, 1834 Connecticut Avenue, N.W., Washington, D.C. 20009.

ways of others to assist them educationally in meeting each child's needs for his or her unknown future impact on society.

Working with other adults and parents to maximize my strengths and theirs, both personally and professionally, I shall provide a model to demonstrate to young children how adults can create an improved way of living and learning through planned cooperation.

The encouragement of language development with young children will never exceed the boundaries of propriety or violate the confidence and trust of a child or that child's family.

I shall share my professional skills, information, and talents to enhance early education for young children wherever they are.

I shall cooperate with other persons and organizations to promote programs for children and families that improve their opportunities to utilize and enhance their uniqueness and strength.

I shall ensure that individually different styles of learning are meshed compatibly with individually different styles of teaching to help all people grow and learn well—this applies to adults learning to be teachers as well as to children.

B □ Educational organizations, newsletters, and journals associated with early childhood

Educational organizations

ACEI
Association for Childhood Education International
3615 Wisconsin Ave., N.W.
Washington, D.C. 20016

AAHPER
American Alliance for Health, Physical Education, and Recreation
1201 Sixteenth St., N.W.
Washington, D.C. 20036

American Montessori Society
175 Fifth Ave.
New York, N.Y. 10010

Children's Defense Fund
PO Box 19085
Washington, D.C. 20006
Toll-free number: (800) 424-9602

Children's Foundation
1028 Connecticut Ave., N.W.
Suite 1112
Washington, D.C. 20036

Coalition for Children and Youth
815 15th St., N.W.
Suite 600
Washington, D.C. 20005

CEC
Council for Exceptional Children
1920 Association Dr.
Reston, Va. 22091

CWLA
Child Welfare League of America
67 Irving Place
New York, N.Y. 10010

DCCDCA
Day Care and Child Development Council of America, Inc.
622 14th St., N.W.
Washington, D.C. 20005

Early Childhood Education Council of New York City
196 Bleeker St.
New York, N.Y. 10012

Education Commission of the States
300 Lincoln Tower
1860 Lincoln St.
Denver, Colo. 80295

ERIC/ECE
Educational Resource Information Center/Early Childhood Education
805 West Pennsylvania Ave.
Urbana, Ill. 61801

NAEYC
National Association for the Education of Young Children
1834 Connecticut Ave., N.W.
Washington, D.C. 20009

U.S. Dept. of HEW
United States Department of Health, Education, and Welfare
Administration for Children, Youth, and Families
Office of Human Development
Washington, D.C. 20201

Newsletters

For a more complete list of references the reader is referred to Stakelon, A. E. *Early childhood newsletters: A selected guide.* Urbana, Ill.: ERIC/ECE, University of Illinois, 1974.

The Black Child Advocate
Black Child Development Institute
1028 Connecticut Ave., N.W.
Suite 514
Washington, D.C. 20036

ERIC/ECE Newsletter
805 West Pennsylvania Ave.
Urbana, Ill. 61801

Report on Preschool Education
Capitol Publications, Inc.
2430 Pennsylvania Ave., N.W.
Suite G-12
Washington, D.C. 20037

Today's Child
Roosevelt, N.J. 08555

Journals

American Journal of Orthopsychiatry
49 Sheridan Ave.,
Albany, N.Y. 12210

Childhood Education
ACEI
3615 Wisconsin Ave., N.W.
Washington, D.C. 20016

Children Today
U.S. Dept. of HEW
Administration for Children, Youth, and Families
Superintendent of Documents
U.S. Govt. Printing Office
Washington, D.C. 20402

Child Development
Society for Research in Child Development
University of Chicago Press
5801 Ellis Ave.
Chicago, Ill. 60637

Day Care and Early Education
Behavioral Publications
72 Fifth Ave.
New York, N.Y. 10011

Developmental Psychology
American Psychological Association
1200 Seventeenth St., N.W.
Washington, D.C. 20036

Harvard Educational Review
Longfellow Hall
13 Appian Way
Cambridge, Mass. 02138

Human Nature
Harcourt Brace Jovanovich, Inc.
757 Third Ave.
P.O. Box 10702
Des Moines, Iowa 50340

Merrill-Palmer Quarterly of Behavior and Development
Merrill-Palmer Institute
71 East Ferry Ave.
Detroit, Mich. 48202

Young Children
NAEYC
1834 Connecticut Ave., N.W.
Washington, D.C. 20009

C ☐ Communicable childhood diseases*

Infectious agent and general description	Importance	Mode of transmission	Communicable period
Bacillary dysentery (shigellosis)			
Shigella dysenteriae and *Shigella paradysenteriae* Acute inflammation of colon	Extremely widespread in areas with poor sanitary facilities and hygiene practices Disease often severe in infancy but often mild after age 3 yr.	Direct or indirect contact with feces of infected patients or carriers Contaminated food, water, and flies play important role	As long as patients or carriers harbor organisms (as determined by stool or rectal swab cultures) Healthy carriers common; they should not become food handlers In areas where sanitary treatment of sewage is not routine, stools should be disinfected
Chicken pox (varicella)			
Virus capable of causing varicella or herpes zoster Mild, chiefly cutaneous infectious disease Varicella—response to primary infection Herpes zoster-reactivation (in debilitated persons or persons receiving immunosuppressive therapy)	Very common, highly contagious, usually mild disease Complications other than secondary infection from scratching rare; however, encephalitis possible Overwhelming severe infection seen in children receiving immunosuppressive therapy CAUTION: Contact!	Direct or indirect contact with secretions from mouth or moist skin lesions of varicella or herpes zoster	Approximately 24 hr. before rash appears until 7 days after its onset; dried crusts not contagious

*From Ingalls, A. J., and Salerno, M. C. *Maternal and child health nursing* (4th ed.). St. Louis: The C. V. Mosby Co., 1979.

376

Incubation period	Symptoms	Treatment and nursing care	Prevention
1-7 days (usually 3-4 days)	Mild to severe diarrhea; in severe cases blood, mucus, and pus may be seen in stool Abdominal pain, fever, and prostration may be present	Treatment depends on severity of infection Ampicillin drug of choice; chloramphenicol; tetracycline (used after age 8 yr.); furazolidone Paregoric and bismuth may help control diarrhea Keep patient warm; oral fluids may be restricted; intravenous therapy may be necessary to prevent dehydration	Attack appears to confer limited immunity No preventive known other than improved individual and community hygiene
10-21 days (usually 14 days)	Slight fever; malaise; rapidly progressing papulovesiculopustular skin eruption in all stages of development, first appearing on trunk and scalp	Keep fingernails short and clean to minimize secondary infections caused by scratching Calamine lotion, oral antihistaminics reduce pruritus	None; immune after one attack Immune serum globulin (ISG) or hyperimmune zoster globulin for the corticosteroid-treated child or others at increased risk

Continued.

Communicable childhood diseases—cont'd

Infectious agent and general description	Importance	Mode of transmission	Communicable period
Diphtheria			
Corynebacterium diphtheriae (Klebs-Löffler bacillus)	Rarely seen because of routine childhood immunization, more comprehensive public health regulations, and enforcement of milk standards and carrier control	Direct or indirect contact with secretions from respiratory tract or skin lesions of patient or carrier	As long as virulent organisms are present in discharges and lesions
Severe, acute infectious disease of upper respiratory tract and perhaps skin	5%-10% mortality		Isolation until satisfactory nose and throat cultures obtained; contacts may be isolated
Toxins produced may affect nervous system and heart	Serious complications include neuritis, paralysis, and myocarditis		
German measles (rubella, 3-day measles)			
Virus	Very common, frequently occurring in epidemic form	Usually direct contact with secretions from mouth and nose	From 1 wk. before rash appears until approximately 5 days after its onset
Acute infectious disease characterized chiefly by rose-colored macular rash and lymph node enlargement	Complications rare for victim but may cause deformities of fetus if contracted by pregnant woman during first trimester	May be acquired in utero	
Herpes zoster shingles			
Virus	Overwhelming severe infection seen in children receiving immunosuppressive therapy	Direct or indirect contact with secretions from mouth or moist skin lesions	Approximately 24 hr before rash appears until 7 days after its onset
Same virus causes both chicken pox (varicella) and herpes zoster	CAUTION: Contact!	Zoster less contagious, but susceptible children exposed to zoster lesions may develop chicken pox	
Measles (rubeola, or 2-week, or red measles)			
Virus	Very common highly infectious disease frequently occurring in epidemic form	Direct or contact with secretions from nose and throat, perhaps airborne	From time of "cold symptoms" until about 5 days after rash appears
Acute infection characterized by moderately high fever, inflammation of mucous membranes of respiratory tract, and macular rash	Possible serious complications include pneumonia, otitis media, conjunctivitis, and encephalitis	May be acquired in utero	

Incubation period	Symptoms	Treatment and nursing care	Prevention
2-6 days	Depend on type and part of upper respiratory area inflamed Formation of fibrinous false membrane, which may or may not be visible in throat or nose Nausea, possible muscle paralysis, and heart complications	Administration of analgesics, antitoxin, erythromycin (preferred), and penicillin Absolute bed rest; gentle throat irrigations; bland, soft diet; humidification Possible need for tracheotomy Watch for muscle weakness	Immunity after one attack, but person may be immune without history of disease Immunity determined by Schick test Routine primary schedule—DTP booster injection on exposure
14-21 days (usually 18 days)	Rose-colored macular rash occurring first on face, then on all body parts; enlargement and tenderness of lymph nodes; mild fever	Supportive nursing care with good personal hygiene	Rubella vaccine Immune after one attack
10-21 days (usually 14 days)	Zoster lesions confined to skin over sensory nerves and preceded by local pain, itching, and burning Meningismus associated with cranial nerve involvement	Cut fingernails to prevent scratching Analgesics, sedation, thiamine; prednisone in severe cases; wet compresses to lesions	Usually immune after first attack Rarely, second attack seen in some individuals
About 10 days	Catarrhal symptoms, like a common cold; conjunctivitis; photophobia Fever followed by macular, blotchy rash involving entire body Koplik's spots (eruption on mucous membrane of mouth) diagnostic	Antibiotics (to prevent complications) Aspirin and tepid sponge baths for severe cases; various soothing lotions Boric acid eye irrigations; protection from bright lights—eyeshade Observation for onset of pneumonia or ear infection	Live measles vaccine, immune serum globulin (ISG) lessens disease Usually immune after first attack

Continued.

Communicable childhood diseases—cont'd

Infectious agent and general description	Importance	Mode of transmission	Communicable period
Meningococcal meningitis (cerebrospinal fever)			
Neisseria meningitidis (N. intracellularis) Meningococcus Serious, acute disease caused by bacteria that invade bloodstream and eventually meninges, causing fever and central nervous system inflammation	Occurs fairly often where concentrations of people are found (army bases, schools) because of healthy carriers Very severe or relatively mild Mortality depends on early diagnosis and treatment Complications include hydrocephalus, arthritis, blindness, deafness, impairment of intellect, and cerebral palsy	Direct contact with patient or carrier by droplet spread Organism may be found in urine	As long as meningococci are found in nose and mouth Usually not infectious after 24 hr. of appropriate therapy
Mononucleosis, infectious (glandular fever)			
Virus? Mildly contagious disease characterized by increase in monocyte-type white cell in blood, lymph node enlargement, fever, and fatigue Heterophil agglutinin studies positive fairly late in course of disease Isolation not recommended*	Typically, disease of teenagers or young adults Trauma may rarely cause ruptured spleen; hepatitis in 8%-10% of cases May involve prolonged convalescence	Probably droplets from nose and throat, saliva, or intimate contact	Not known Probably only during acute stage
Mumps (infectious parotitis)			
Virus Acute infectious disease causing inflammation of salivary glands and, at times, testes and ovaries	Possible serious consequences for male after puberty, when an attack is more severe; sterility can be complication Meningitis or encephalitis occur infrequently Mild pancreatitis may be encountered	Direct or indirect contact with patient by droplet spread	From several days before apparent infection until swelling disappears

*Report of the Committee on Infectious Diseases, ed. 16, Evanston, Ill., 1970, American Academy of Pediatrics.

Incubation period	Symptoms	Treatment and nursing care	Prevention
1-7 days (usually 4 days)	Sudden onset of fever, chills, headache, and vomiting (convulsions fairly common in children) Cutaneous petechial hemorrhages; stiffness of neck; opisthotonus; joint pain; possibly delirium; convulsions	Spinal tap and culture needed to confirm diagnosis Temperature control; penicillin G, ampicillin, analgesics, and sedatives Watch for clinical signs of increasing intracranial pressure or meningeal irritation and eye and ear involvement Maintain dim, quiet atmosphere; turn gently; watch for constipation and urinary retention; attention to fluid balance	Extent of immunity after attack unknown Sulfonamides have been used prophylactically during epidemics
Unknown (probably 2-6 wk.)	Sore throat, malaise, depression, enlarged spleen, liver, and lymph nodes Possible jaundice with liver damage	Symptomatic, no specific therapy known Bed rest, high carbohydrate, protein intake Possible use of corticosteroids with severe throat involvement and airway obstruction	No immunization available
14-21 days (usually 18 days)	Tender swelling chiefly of parotid glands in front of and below ear Headache; moderate fever; pain on swallowing	Bed rest; bland, soft diet; analgesics; warm or cold applications to swollen glands Watch for tenderness of testes —scrotal support may be necessary Observe for abdominal pain and signs of complications	Mumps vaccine Usually immune after first attack Immune serum globulin (ISG) may help those exposed to have milder cases of avoid symptoms

Continued.

Communicable childhood diseases—cont'd

Infectious agent and general description	Importance	Mode of transmission	Communicable period

Poliomyelitis (infantile paralysis)

Virus Acute infectious disease, may occur in many forms and degrees of severity Attacks primarily gastrointestinal and nervous systems; may cause muscular paralysis	New cases uncommon since vaccine When paralysis takes place, many complications may occur involving respiratory, musculoskeletal, urinary, and digestive systems	Direct or indirect contact with pharyngeal secretions and feces of infected persons (many infected persons have no symptoms)	Communicable for indefinite period before onset of symptoms Usually isolated for 7 days after onset or until fever subsides Virus may persist in stool for weeks; local sewage facilities should be evaluated Careful personal hygiene needed

Rabies (hydrophobia)

Virus Only one nonfatal case reported, acute infectious encephalitis, causing convulsions and muscle paralysis	Exceedingly dangerous Household pets may acquire rabies through bite of rabid wild animals All dogs should be immunized periodically; cats may also be carriers, but impractical to insist on immunization	Bite of rabid animals or entry of infected saliva through previous break in skin or mucous membrane	During clinical course of disease plus 3-5 days before appearance of symptoms

Smallpox (variola)

Virus Highly contagious infection involving constitutional symptoms—fever and characteristic scarring rash; may occur in severe or mild forms	There should be no cases of smallpox in United States; preventive vaccine has been known and available over 100 yr., but not everyone maintains protection, every year cases occur Mortality 20%-50% Complications include secondary infection, bronchitis, and bronchopneumonia	Direct or indirect contact with secretions from skin lesions or mouth; airborne for short distances	From first appearance of illness until all crusts disappear

Incubation period	Symptoms	Treatment and nursing care	Prevention

7-12 days?	Variable; may include diarrhea, constipation, emesis, painful stiff neck, rigid back, tender skeletal muscles, and respiratory distress
	Cranial nerve involvement
	Three main types
	1. Inapparent infection,
	2. Nonparalytic, and
	3. Paralytic
	   a. Spinal, affecting skeletal muscles and diaphragm
	   b. Bulbar, affecting swallowing, facial muscles, and respiration,
	   c. Mixed
		No specific treatment known
		Supportive treatment depends on patient needs; bed rest, hot packs to relieve muscle spasms, observation for respiratory or bulbar involvement
		Possible tracheotomy and respiratory support; observation for constipation and urinary retention
		Gentle positioning; physical and occupational therapy
			Routine primary schedule and boosters; OPV (Sabin-oral) optimum immunization schedule; IPV (Salk-injections) primary schedule plus repeated biennial booster doses

Usually 2-6 wk.	Mental depression, headaches, restlessness, and fever Progresses to painful spasms of throat muscles, especially when attempting to drink Delirium, convulsions, and coma	No effective treatment known Supportive nursing care to help prevent convulsions; analgesics; death usually occurs in about 7 days	Vaccination of dogs; 10-day confinement of any dog who has bitten human Laboratory investigation of brain of dog that dies during this period; if rabies is diagnosed, person bitten must receive rabies vaccine
10-14 days (usually 12 days)	Sudden onset of high fever with flulike symptoms; rash appears in 3-4 days, involving normally exposed parts of body, face, arms, and upper chest Rash progresses to deeply seated pustules, all at about same stage of development, leaving typical scars Photophobia	No specific treatment Antibiotics used to avoid secondary infection Procedures to relieve fever and itching Possible blood transfusions Shield eyes from light; special oral hygiene; encourage nutritious fluids; attention to fluid balance Deodorizing procedures for patient and room	Routine primary immunization smallpox vaccination Booster at school age and every 10 yr. Permanent immunity usually follows first attack

Continued.

Communicable childhood diseases—cont'd

Infectious agent and general description	Importance	Mode of transmission	Communicable period
Staphylococcal infections			
Coagulase-positive staphylococci (*Micrococcus pyogenes,* var., *aureus*) pus-producing coccus Descriptions variable	Found almost everywhere; causes many hospital infections; does not respond well to usual antibiotic therapy; extremely difficult to control; anyone may be carrier at intervals Complications include skin lesions, pneumonia, wound infections, arthritis, osteomyelitis, meningitis, and food poisoning	Depends on body area infected Asymptomatic nasal carriers common May be airborne Direct or indirect contact with infected secretions	As long as lesions drain or carrier state persists
Streptococcal infections			
Strains of hemolytic streptococci Diseases include septic sore throat, scarlet fever (scarlatina), erysipelas, impetigo, puerperal fever	Interrelated group of infections; septic sore throat probably most common Early complications include otitis media May cause serious complications not contagious in themselves—nephritis and rheumatic fever, with possible arthritis and carditis	In septic sore throat and scarlet fever, direct or indirect contact with nasopharyngeal secretions from infected patient; probably airborne In erysipelas, impetigo, and puerperal fever, direct or indirect contact with discharges from skin or reproductive tract	Variable Carrier state possible
Tetanus (lockjaw)			
Bacillus *Clostridium tetani* Acute infectious disease attacking chiefly nervous system Wounds deprived of good oxygen supply especially vulnerable	Always considered in event of burns, automobile accidents, or puncture wounds Mortality rate of about 35%	Entrance of spores into wounds through contaminated soil Person-to-person transmission unlikely unless discharges from infected wound contaminate open lesion	Infectious, but only potentially communicable if draining wound present

Incubation period	Symptoms	Treatment and nursing care	Prevention
Variable; 1-2 days to several weeks	Depend on area infected Fever and characteristic signs of inflammation typical	Antibiotics according to drug sensitivity pattern of organism; methicillin, oxacillin Topical antibiotics: bacitracin, neomycin, polymyxin	No immunization generally available and effective Good hygiene and aseptic technique best preventive
2-5 days	Depend on manifestations Septic sore throat, severe pharyngitis and fever Scarlet fever, pharyngitis, fever, and fine reddish rash and strawberry tongue Erysipelas, tender, red skin lesions and fever often recurrent Puerperal fever	Depends on manifestation Penicillin for at least 10 days	No artificial immunization available Penicillin prophylaxis may be used with special groups Good asepsis important
3-21 days (usually 8 days)	Irritability, rigidity, painful muscle spasms, and inability to open mouth Exhaustion and respiratory difficulty	Antitoxin and sedation plus muscle relaxant Quiet, dim room Possible suction and tracheotomy Observation of fluid balance; watch for constipation and respiratory distress; protect from self-injury during convulsions	Routine primary immunization booster at school age and Td every 10 yr.

Continued.

Communicable childhood diseases—cont'd

Infectious agent and general description	Importance	Mode of transmission	Communicable period
Tuberculosis			
Myobacterium tuberculosis (tubercle bacillus) Typically chronic infection that may affect many body organs Human type most often causes pulmonary infection Bovine type causes much of tuberculosis affecting areas outside lungs areas outside lungs	Serious world health problem, particularly in economically deprived areas Infants and young children very susceptible Pulmonary complications, hemoptysis, spontaneous pneumothorax, or spread to other organs with varied symptoms; possible orthopedic problems	Direct or indirect contact with infected patients; body excretions or droplet spread (depending on type) Respiratory tuberculosis often airborne; bovine type may result from drinking milk from infected cows (now rare in U.S.)	As long as organism is discharged in sputum or other body excretions Communicability may be reduced by medication, therapy, and teaching cough control and asepsis to patients Body often walls off a primary infection, controlling spread and preventing active disease
Typhoid fever (enteric fever)			
Salmonella typhosa, a bacillus (many types have been identified) Relatively severe febrile systemic infection with symptoms involving lymphoid tissues, intestine, and spleen, which may be accompanied by complete prostration and delirium Condition has prolonged course and convalescence	Always of potential public health importance when community hygiene breaks down Carrier states may persist Complications include intestinal hemorrhage and perforation, thrombosis, cardiac failure, and cholecystitis	Direct or indirect contact with urine and feces of infected patients and carriers Food and water supplies may be infected by contaminated *flies* or unsuspected *carriers*; community sewage facilities should be evaluated; excreta may have to be disinfected before being added to local system	As long as typhoid organism appears in feces or urine 2%-5% of those affected become permanent carriers
Whooping cough (pertussis)			
Bordetella pertussis (pertussis bacillus) Acute infection of respiratory tract, characterized by paroxysmal cough ending in "whoop," often accompanied by vomiting	Severe disease in infants, may terminate fatally Complications include bronchopneumonia and convulsions, widespread hemorrhages, hernia, and possible activation of pulmonary tuberculosis	Direct or indirect contact with nasopharyngeal secretions of infected patients (droplet infection)	From 7 days after exposure to 3 wk. after onset of typical cough Greatest in catarrhal stage before onset of paroxysms

Incubation period	Symptoms	Treatment and nursing care	Prevention
From infection to primary lesion, 2-10 wk. Time of appearance of active symptoms variable	Active pulmonary tuberculosis: anorexia, weight loss, night sweats, afternoon fever, cough and dyspnea, fatigue, and hemoptysis; in children dyspnea and cough often absent Diagnosis based on symptoms and microscopic studies of sputum, gastric washings, and chest x-ray examination	Several drugs may prevent growth of organism, including streptomycin (STM), para-aminosalicylic acid (PAS), and isoniazid (INH) Nursing care includes provision for mental and physical rest; nutritious diet; observation for toxic drug reactions and increasing respiratory distress; provision for and instructions in personal hygiene; moral support	BCG vaccine to build up immunity in high-risk populations advised by some Early detection and control of known cases through periodic x-ray examination, possible skin tests, and close medical supervision
1-3 wk. (usually 2 wk.)	In children symptoms may be atypical, may at first resemble upper respiratory infection; intestinal tract becomes inflamed and even ulcerated; spleen enlarges; fever mounts; pulse relatively slow; rash, "rose spots" may be present	Chloramphenicol and supportive nursing care; liquid to bland, soft diet as tolerated; bed rest Watch for abdominal distention and hemorrhage; small enemas may be ordered; observation of fluid balance	Immunity usually acquired after one attack Triple vaccine against forms of paratyphoid as well as typhoid available
5-21 days (usually within 10 days)	Early symptoms resemble typical common cold Cough worsens and may become violent and paroxysmal Vomiting may be caused by coughing or nervous system irritation; cough may linger after convalescence	Diagnosis confirmed with bacterial studies of exposed cough plates and presence of leukocytosis Immune serum globulin; erythromycin antibiotic of choice; provision for rest and quiet; sedatives Light nutritious diet; judicious fluid intake to prevent dehydration; weight determinations Observation for onset of respiratory distress or other complications	Immunity produced after one attack Routine primary schedule plus boosters

D □ Ten quick ways to analyze children's books for racism and sexism*

Both in school and out, young children are exposed to racist and sexist attitudes. These attitudes—expressed over and over in books and in other media—gradually distort their perceptions until stereotypes and myths about minorities and women are accepted as reality. It is difficult for a librarian or teacher to convince children to question society's attitudes. But if a child can be shown how to detect racism and sexism in a book, the child can proceed to transfer the perception to wider areas. The following ten guidelines are offered as a starting point in evaluating children's books from this perspective.

1. Check the illustrations

• *Look for stereotypes.* A stereotype is an over-simplified generalization about a particular group, race, or sex, which usually carries derogatory implications. Some infamous (overt) stereotypes of Blacks are the happy-go-lucky watermelon-eating Sambo and the fat, eye-rolling "mammy"; of Chicanos, the sombrero-wearing peon or fiesta-loving, macho bandito; of Asian Americans, the inscrutable, slant-eyed "Oriental"; of Native Ameri-

cans, the naked savage or "primitive" craftsman and his squaw; of Puerto Ricans, the switchblade-toting teenage gang member; of women, the completely domesticated mother, the demure, doll-loving little girl, or the wicked stepmother. While you may not always find stereotypes in the blatant forms described, look for variations which in any way demean or ridicule characters because of their race or sex.

• *Look for tokenism.* If there are non-White characters in the illustrations, do they look just like Whites except for being tinted or colored in? Do all minority faces look stereotypically alike, or are they depicted as genuine individuals with distinctive features?

• *Who's doing what?* Do the illustrations depict minorities in subservient and passive roles or in leadership and action roles? Are males the active "doers" and females the inactive observers?

2. Check the story line

The Civil Rights Movement has led publishers to weed out many insulting passages, particularly from stories with Black themes, but the attitudes still find expression in less obvious ways. The following checklist suggests some of the subtle (covert) forms of bias to watch for.

• *Standard for success.* Does it take "White" behavior standards for a minority person to "get ahead"? Is "making it" in the dominant White society projected as the only ideal? To gain acceptance

*Reprinted with permission from the *Bulletin* of the Council on Interracial Books for Children, Inc., 1841 Broadway, New York, NY 10023. Copies are available from the Council at 10¢ each plus a self-addressed, stamped envelope. The Council also publishes the *Bulletin* (eight issues a year), which reviews new children's books for the human and antihuman messages they convey.

and approval, do non-White persons have to exhibit extraordinary qualities—excel in sports, get A's, etc.? In friendships between White and non-White children, is it the non-White who does most of the understanding and forgiving?

• *Resolution of problems.* How are problems presented, conceived, and resolved in the story? Are minority people considered to be "the problem"? Are the oppressions faced by minorities and women represented as causally related to an unjust society? Are the reasons for poverty and oppression explained, or are they accepted as inevitable? Does the story line encourage passive acceptance or active resistance? Is a particular problem that is faced by a minority person resolved through the benevolent intervention of a White person?

• *Role of women.* Are the achievements of girls and women based on their own initiative and intelligence, or are they due to their good looks or to their relationship with boys? Are sex roles incidental or critical to characterization and plot? Could the same story be told if the sex roles were reversed?

3. Look at the lifestyles

Are minority persons and their setting depicted in such a way that they contrast unfavorably with the unstated norm of White middle-class suburbia? If the minority group in question is depicted as "different," are negative value judgments implied? Are minorities depicted exclusively in ghettos, barrios, or migrant camps? If the illustrations and text attempt to depict another culture, do they go beyond oversimplifications and offer genuine insights into another lifestyle? Look for inaccuracy and inappropriateness in the depiction of other cultures. Watch for instances of the "quaint-natives-in-costume" syndrome (most noticeable in areas like costume and custom, but extending to behavior and personality traits as well).

4. Weigh the relationships between people

Do the Whites in the story possess the power, take the leadership, and make the important decisions? Do non-Whites and females function in essentially supporting roles?

How are family relationships depicted? In Black families, is the mother always dominant? In Hispanic families, are there always lots and lots of children? If the family is separated, are societal conditions—unemployment, poverty—cited among the reasons for the separation?

5. Note the heroes and heroines

For many years, books showed only "safe" minority heroes and heroines—those who avoided serious conflict with the White establishment of their time. Minority groups today are insisting on the right to define their own heroes and heroines based on their own concepts and struggles for justice.

When minority heroes and heroines do appear, are they admired for the same qualities that have made White heroes and heroines famous or because what they have done has benefitted White people? Ask this question: Whose interest is a particular figure really serving?

6. Consider the effects on a child's self-image

• *Are norms established that limit the child's aspirations and self-concepts?* What effect can it have on Black children to be continuously bombarded with images of the color white as the ultimate in beauty, cleanliness, virtue, etc., and the color black as evil, dirty, menacing, etc.? Does the book counteract or reinforce this positive association with the color white and negative association with black?

What happens to a girl's self-image when she reads that boys perform all of the brave and important deeds? What about a girl's self-esteem if she is not "fair" of skin and slim of body?

In a particular story, is there one or more persons with whom a minority child can readily identify to a positive and constructive end?

7. Consider the author's or illustrator's background

Analyze the biographical material on the jacket flap or the back of the book. If a story deals with a minority theme, what qualifies the author or illustrator to deal with the subject? If the author and illustrator are not members of the minority being written about, is there anything in their background that would specifically recommend them as the creators of this book?

Similarly, a book that deals with the feelings and insights of women should be more carefully examined if it is written by a man—unless the book's avowed purpose is to present a strictly male perspective.

8. Check out the author's perspective

No author can be wholly objective. All authors write out of a cultural as well as a personal context. Children's books in the past have traditionally come from authors who are White and who are members of the middle class, with one result being that a single ethnocentric perspective has dominated American children's literature. With the book in question, look carefully to determine whether the direction of the author's perspective substantially weakens or strengthens the value of his/her written book. Are omissions and distortions central to the overall character or ''message'' of the book?

9. Watch for loaded words

A word is loaded when it has insulting overtones. Examples of loaded adjectives (usually racist) are savage, primitive, conniving, lazy, superstitious, treacherous, wily, crafty, inscrutable, docile, and backward.

Look for sexist language and adjectives that exclude or ridicule women. Look for use of the male pronoun to refer to both males and females. While the generic use of the word ''man'' was accepted in the past, its use today is outmoded. The following examples show how sexist language can be avoided: ancestors instead of forefathers; chairperson instead of chairman; community instead of brotherhood; firefighters instead of firemen; manufactured instead of manmade; the human family instead of the family of man.

10. Look at the copyright date

Books on minority themes—usually hastily conceived—suddenly began appearing in the mid-1960s. There followed a growing number of ''minority experience'' books to meet the new market demand, but most of these were still written by White authors, edited by White editors, and published by White publishers. They therefore reflected a White point of view. Only very recently in the late 1960s and early 1970s has the children's book world begun to even remotely reflect the realities of a multiracial society. And it has just begun to reflect feminists' concerns.

The copyright dates, therefore, can be a clue as to how likely the book is to be overtly racist or sexist, although a recent copyright date, of course, is no guarantee of a book's relevance or sensitivity. The copyright date only means the year the book was published. It usually takes a minimum of one year—and often much more than that—from the time a manuscript is submitted to the publisher to the time it is actually printed and put on the market. This time lag meant very little in the past, but in a time of rapid change and changing consciousness, when children's book publishing is attempting to be ''relevant,'' it is becoming increasingly significant.

E □ A beginning list of free materials and resources*

Empty ribbon rolls	Gift wrapping section of department stores	Natural materials for collage	Seed pods, pebbles, leaves, and cones abound
Wood shavings	Building scrap piles, carpentry shops	Feathers	Bird refuge
Material remnants	Interior design stores, upholsterers, clothing manufacturers	Wood scraps	Carpenters and cabinet shops
		Burlap	Horse-boarding barns
Scraps of suede and leather	Leather good stores	Small cardboard boxes	Dime stores, hearing-aid stores, department and stationery stores
Boxes and pieces of styrofoam	Throwaways from drug stores, five and tens, radio and television shops	Ticker tape and newsprint rolls and ends	Local newspaper office
Computer paper used on one side, or cards	Almost anywhere computers are used	Wallpaper sample books	Wallpaper stores
Empty bolts from material	Textile stores	Art papers of various sizes and colors	Print shops
Large appliance boxes	Almost all appliance stores are delighted to get rid of these	5-gallon ice cream containers	Drive-ins and ice cream stores
		Rug scraps	Carpet stores and installers
Cardboard rolls	Textile stores	One- or two-day animal loans	Local pet shops

---

*Suggested by the Principles and Practices class, 1972, of Santa Barbara City College. See also Hodgen, Koetter, Laforse, McCord, and Schramm, 1970, for an additional helpful list.

F □ Activities to develop auditory discrimination*

Have the children put their heads down on the table. Display on a nearby shelf or table various instruments: xylophone, cymbals, tambourine, bells, and so forth. While they have their heads down, play one instrument. Children can take turns making the sounds for others to identify.

I was in the kitchen at the sink, and D. was standing at the kitchen gate. He was swinging the gate back and forth so that it would bang against the stopper. As it got louder and louder I was about to tell him to stop when I decided to use this situation for auditory discrimination. We were promptly joined by two other children. First we listened to how loud the gate could bang shut. Then I asked them if they could make it very quiet so that there wasn't any noise. We did these two opposites several times. Then we started very quietly and got louder and louder and louder. We tried this with our feet stamping on the floor and also clapping our hands. First we did it loud then quiet, then quiet and louder, and then as loud as we could.

Under the table I made different sounds and asked the children to identify them. I used a bell, sandpaper rubbed together, two blocks hit together, scissors opening and closing, and tearing paper. Then I asked one child to make his own sound and let the rest of the children guess what it was.

Using one sound, have the children shut their eyes while you move about the room, and ask the children to point to where you are. Then let the children be the sound makers.

Record on a tape recorder familiar sounds such as a car starting, water running, train, door shutting, refrigerator door opening or closing, or a toilet flushing (if you use this last one, do it at the end, as it tends to break up the group). Stop at each sound and have the children identify it. For older children play a series of sounds, and see how many they can remember.

I put several things in a box, one at a time, and had the children listen to the sounds: a tennis ball, tooth brush, piece of metal, and a comb. Then I put the box behind my back, put one of the objects in the box, brought it in front of me and rattled it. The children guessed what made the noise.

With my children we listened to the sounds around us when we were outside. We heard the leaves blowing, other children yelling, a car going by, and sand falling. It was fun and made the children really aware of the sounds around them.

I used a triangle with a wooden stick and a metal one. The children listened while I showed them the sticks; then I had them close their eyes and tell me which stick I had used.

Using a xylophone, strike a middle note, then play other notes and ask the children if the new note is higher or lower than the middle one. Also, for degree of loudness, strike the notes hard or lightly and ask the children if the sound is loud or soft.

Material. Cans with tops, small nails, rice, beans, salt.

I made up two cans of each material. I had all the cans on the table and went around and asked the children to pick one and shake it. Then I asked them

*Suggested by the Language and Cognitive Development classes, 1973, 1976, and 1978, of Santa Barbara City College.

to try and find one that sounded exactly the same. Then we opened the cans to see if the cans really did contain the same ingredient. The children enjoyed playing this and wanted to have many turns.

Material. Six bottles, same size; one spoon; water.

Take two bottles and put the same volume of water in them, then two other bottles with the same volume of water, and finally two more. I covered the bottles with contact paper so the children couldn't see how much water each bottle held. Taking turns, the children tried to pick out sounds that matched by hitting the bottle with the spoon. If we were in doubt that the tones matched, we poured the water out and measured it.

In a small group, have one child turn his back and then have the teacher or a selected child point to someone in the group who says something. The child with his back turned guesses who has spoken; then the speaker takes his turn guessing, and the former guesser picks the next speaker.

I let each child draw out an animal picture from the "secret" box, and then they listened to me while I made various animal noises. They brought me the picture when they heard the noise that belonged to their animal. For variety, we played a tape recording of the sounds and had each child wave his card in the air when he heard "his" sound.

An activity for 4-year-olds that fosters auditory discrimination is to take different flannel board pictures in which the words rhyme—for instance, cat/hat, mouse/house, rug/bug, and so on. Either put up a few at a time and ask children to pair the ones that rhyme, or have groups of three pictured words and ask the children to remove the one that doesn't rhyme.

For older fours, have children stand in a circle and close their eyes. One child moves around the outside of the circle several times and then stops behind one of the children, who guesses whether the child was hopping, jumping, tiptoeing, and so forth.

G □ Definitions of the parameters and categories of the Structure of Intellect*

Formal definitions of the parameters and their categories are given below. . . . Letter symbols applied to the various categories are also given here. Their use will be explained later.

Operations

Major kinds of intellectual activities or processes; things that the organism does in the processing of information, information being defined as "that which the organism discriminates."

Cognition (C). Immediate discovery, awareness, rediscovery, or recognition of information in its various forms; comprehension or understanding.

Memory (M). Fixation of newly gained information in storage. The operation of memory is to be distinguished from the memory store.

Divergent production (D). Generation of logical alternatives from given information, where the emphasis is upon variety, quantity, and relevance of output from the same source. Likely to involve transfer recall (instigated by new cues).

Convergent production (N). Generation of logical conclusions from given information, where emphasis is upon achieving unique or conventionally best outcomes. It is likely that the given (cue) information fully determines the outcome, as in mathematics and logic.

*From Guilford, J. P. *The analysis of intelligence.* New York: © 1971, McGraw-Hill Book Co. Pp. 20 and 21. Used with permission of McGraw-Hill Book Co.

Evaluation (E). Comparison of items of information in terms of variables and making judgments concerning criterion satisfaction (correctness, identity, consistency, etc.).

Contents

Broad, substantive, basic kinds of areas of information.

Figural (F). Pertaining to information in concrete form, as perceived or as recalled in the form of images. The term "figural" minimally implies figure-ground perceptual organization. Different sense modalities may be involved—visual, auditory, kinesthetic, and perhaps others.

Symbolic (S). Pertaining to information in the form of denotative signs having no significance in and of themselves, such as letters, numbers, musical notations, codes, and words (as ordered letter combinations).

Semantic (M). Pertaining to information in the form of conceptions or mental constructs to which words are often applied, hence most notable in verbal thinking and verbal communication, but not necessarily dependent upon words. Meaningful pictures also convey semantic information.

Behavioral (B). Pertaining to information, essentially nonfigural and nonverbal, involved in human interactions, where the attitudes, needs, desires, moods, intentions, perceptions, thoughts, etc. of others and of ourselves are involved.

Products

Basic forms that information takes in the organism's processing of it.

Units (U). Relatively segregated or circumscribed items or "chunks" of information having "thing" character. May be close to Gestalt's psychology's "figure on a ground."

Classes (C). Conceptions underlying sets of items of information grouped by virtue of their common properties.

Relations (R). Connections between items of information based upon variables or points of contact that apply to them. Relational connections are more definable than implicational connections.

Systems (S). Organized or structured aggregates of items of information; complexes of interrelated or interacting parts.

Transformation (T). Changes of various kinds (redefinitions, shifts, transitions, or modifications) in existing information.

Implications (I). Circumstantial connections between items of information, as by virtue of contiguity, or any condition that promotes "belongingness."

The SI code system

The code letters for the 15 SI categories and their use will now be explained. Each SI ability is often designated in terms of its special trigram, composed of a letter for each of its parameters—its operation, content, and product, in that order. For example, CMS is a shorthand expression for "cognition of semantic systems," and EFT is the label for "evaluation of figural transformations." Some letters happen to be used twice, but never for categories of the same parameter—for example, MMR means "memory for semantic relations," and NSS means "convergent production of symbolic systems." Keeping in mind the order of the three parameters in a trigram should help the reader avoid confusions. The code system is summarized here for convenient reference:

Operation	*Content*	*Product*
C—cognition	F—figural	U—unit
M—memory	S—symbolic	C—class
D—divergent production	M—semantic	R—relation
N—convergent production	B—behavioral	S—system
E—evaluation		T—transformation
		I—implication

☐ Author index

☐ **Subject index**

Relaxation, tension releasers for, 61, 62
Relaxation activities, 62, 107, 185
Repetition
  mentally retarded child and, 328
  in play, 193-195
  in speech, 243
Representation, development and, 166, 258
Research
  language development programs and, 238
  trends in, 344
Resources; *see also* Activities; Equipment; Materials
  for cross-cultural education, 143-145
  free, 391
  in language development programs, 237-238
Respect
  for child, 24-25
  of rights of others, 129
  self-esteem and, 114; *see also* Self-esteem
Resting times, 44-45
Retardation, mental, 317-319, 329-331
  developmental lag and, 317-319
Retention, demonstration and, 240
Reversibility, concept of, 192, 207
Rewards
  for behavior, 90, 95; *see also* Reinforcement
  and satisfaction, work and, 161-162
Rhythm, temporal awareness and, 61
Rhythm instruments, 186-187
Rights
  of children, 340
    to refuse self-expressive materials, 172-173
    to reject work experiences, 161
  cross-cultural education and, 150
  to fail, 216
  teaching social skills and, 129
Rivalry, 129; *see also* Competition
Role models, 123, 124, 129, 134-136
Role playing
  play and, 192, 194, 203-205
  social skills and, 126
  work and, 156-158
Rote learning, 213-214
Routines, 33-47
  arrival and departure in, 34-35
  eating in, 35-42
    basic principles in, 38-41
    nutrition in, 35-40
    special problems in, 41-42
  emotional health and, 72
  learning goals and, 34
  nap times and, 44-45
  refusal to follow, 34
  toileting and, 42-44
  transitions into, 34

Rules
  aggression and, 105
  deviations from, 105
  discipline and, 91
  emotionally disturbed children and, 327
  equal application of, 129
  explanations of, 114

S

Safety, 51-52
  student teacher and, 26
Sameness, concept of, 260, 267-268
Sand and mud, 201-203
Scheduling of basic experiences, 10, 14-15; *see also* Routines
Schools; *see* Nursery schools
Scientific method in experiments, 268-270
Screening
  exceptional children and, 313-319
  for visual difficulties, 314
Seeing
  difficulties in, 314
  as sensory experience, 56-58
Seizures, 315-316
Self-actualization, 155
Self-assertiveness; *see also* Aggression
  development and, 102-103
  toilet training and, 70
Self-concept; *see* Self-esteem
Self-control; *see* Self-discipline and self-control
Self-discipline and self-control, 85-97; *see also* Aggression; Discipline
  bad environment for, 89-90
  basic goals in, 85-89
  child's feeling of self-worth and, 85-87
  comments on favorable behavior and, 95
  crises and, 92-95
  ego strength and, 86-87
  helping children behave in acceptable ways in, 89-95, 103, 104-105
  learning steps in, 94-95
  prevention of discipline situations in, 90-92
  toilet training and, 70
Self-esteem, 111-117
  creativity and, 115, 166
  discipline and, 86-87
  enhancement of, 27, 113-116
  expressive materials and, 115, 166
  nonsexist education and, 115
  pleasure of accomplishment and, 114-116, 156
  reduction of, 112-113
  relation of work to, 158
  self-concept and, 111
  sources of, 112
Self-expressive materials, 163-189
  beauty and, 174